D0146211

CHINA, THE UNITED NATIONS, AND WORLD ORDER

Written under the auspices of the
Center of International Studies,
Princeton University

A list of other Center publications
appears at the back of the book.

China,
the United Nations,
and World Order

SAMUEL S. KIM

PRINCETON UNIVERSITY PRESS
PRINCETON, NEW JERSEY

Copyright © 1979 by Princeton University Press
Published by Princeton University Press, Princeton, New Jersey
In the United Kingdom: Princeton University Press, Guildford, Surrey

ALL RIGHTS RESERVED

Library of Congress Cataloging in Publication Data will be
found on the last printed page of this book

This book has been composed in Linotype Caledonia

Clothbound editions of Princeton University Press books
are printed on acid-free paper, and binding materials are
chosen for strength and durability.

Printed in the United States of America
by Princeton University Press, Princeton, New Jersey

For
SONYA
Who deserves to grow up in a better world

LIBRARY
ALMA COLLEGE
ALMA, MICHIGAN

CONTENTS

PART III. CONCLUSION:
CHINA AND WORLD ORDER

TABLES

FIGURES

LIST OF FIGURES

ACKNOWLEDGMENTS

A study of this nature and magnitude owes a great deal to the contributions of a number of individuals and institutions. My intellectual evolution has been helped by the works of several scholars. I was fortunate enough to be a graduate student of the late Quincy Wright—he planted seeds of an interdisciplinary approach in my study of international relations. The work of Johan Galtung has often served as a stimulant in redefining conceptual, methodological, and substantive issues in my teaching and research. Richard A. Falk's prolific writings, coupled with his untiring campaign in the domain of global reform, provided an example of concerned scholarship—this study, too, shies away from the irrelevance of a value-neutral approach to world politics.

Without field interviews this study would have lost a vital primary source for delineating behavioral dimensions of Chinese global policy. I am therefore most grateful to the 110 interviewees listed in the Interview Schedule. It may not be inappropriate to single out those individuals who have been of particular help. For working out the logistics of scheduling interviews in a relatively short notice and span of time, my special thanks are due to Louise McNutt, UN and regional affairs advisor, US Department of State; John E. Fobes, deputy director-general of UNESCO; Fernand J. Tomiche, director, Division of Public Information, WHO; Emily Zay, Office of Public Information, ICAO; Roy Jackson, deputy director-general of FAO; and Chusei Yamada, minister, Permanent Mission of Japan to the United Nations.

A number of international civil servants have been particularly generous with their time and knowledge, not only in granting me interviews but also in responding promptly to my subsequent inquiries and requests for additional documents. I extend my special thanks to the following individuals: Jean Gazarian, director of General Assembly Affairs, the UN Secretariat; Philip R. Thomford, senior liaison officer of FAO; Donald B. Hall, chief, Conference and General Services, ICAO; Richard H. Foote, director of Technical Co-operation Department, WMO; Daniel W. Caulfield, senior legal liaison officer, Division for Conference Affairs and External Relations, UNCTAD; and Jacques Lemoine, advisor for International Organization Affairs, ILO.

The staff personnel of the following libraries have been most patient and helpful in my search for source materials: the Social Science Reference Center (UN Documents Collection) of the Firestone Library and the Gest Oriental Library at Princeton University; the Dag Hammarskjöld Library at UN Headquarters in New York; the IMCO library in London; the UNESCO library in Paris; the FAO library in Rome; and the ICAO library in Montreal. My deep appreciation goes to the following individuals: Zaida Dillon of the Social Science Reference Center; Maureen Donovan of the Gest Oriental Library; Tahany El-Erian Wahab of the Dag Hammarskjöld Library; and Nicolae St. Dumitrescu, director, Library and Documentation Systems Division, FAO.

A special senior faculty research grant from Monmouth College and a research grant from the Center of International Studies, Princeton University, made it possible for me to take a year's research leave (1976-77) for uninterrupted concentration to complete the study. I also acknowledge with gratitude a faculty creativity grant from Monmouth College for 1977-78 for the preparation of the manuscript in its final form. In addition, my home institution, especially its Dean of the Faculty, Robert S. Rouse, has been most accommodating to the claim on my time made by this study over the protracted period of its preparation.

Most of the research and writing for this book developed in the stimulating environment of the Center of International Studies, Princeton University, where I worked as a visiting fellow in 1976-78. I am greatly indebted to the Center, especially its director, Cyril E. Black, for both moral and financial support. He has shown a great personal interest in my project from its skeletal inception and has made my stay at the Center most pleasant and productive by liberally extending the facilities and resources at his disposal. The Center's research atmosphere was most congenial to my particular project.

Indeed, under Professor Black's leadership, the Center's multifaceted research enterprise has flourished in recent years. The Center has already developed the most prominent world-order studies of its kind in the country, sponsoring publications of numerous projects including *World Politics* and World Order Studies Occasional Papers. Chapter 2 of this book is a revised version of the paper originally published as the Center's World Order Studies Occasional Paper No. 5 and is reproduced here with its kind permission. In addition, the Center's World Order Studies Colloquia, skillfully planned and executed by Fouad Ajami and Richard A. Falk, and John Parker Compton Fellows in World Order Studies have all proved to be a constant source of challenging dialogue in the clarification of my own thinking on world-order issues.

In the course of revising the manuscript for publication, I have benefited from the critical reading and helpful comments of a number of individual friends and colleagues at various universities throughout the country. An early draft was read in its entirety by James C. Hsiung,

James Patrick Sewell, and Allen S. Whiting. Parts of the manuscript have been read critically and commented on by Hungdah Chiu (Chapter 3), Leon Gordenker (Chapter 3), Jeffrey Hart (Chapters 5-6), Thomas Ilgen (Chapters 5-6), John Kringen (Chapter 4), Suzanne Ogden (Chapters 3 and 8), Lynn T. White, III (Chapter 2), and Kim Woodard (Chapters 3-4).

It was indeed a great pleasure to work with Princeton University Press in the production of this book. Sanford G. Thatcher, Social Science Editor, was invaluable in providing wise and friendly counsel and guiding this manuscript through the various stages of its Odyssey to completion. Jennifer Sparks gave unstintingly of her enthusiasm, imagination, and editorial talents to make the book more readable.

To all the above-mentioned individuals and institutions, I most gratefully acknowledge my indebtedness. Needless to say, none of them should be held accountable in any way for whatever errors and defects that may still persist or for any particular views and interpretations reflected in the book.

S. S. K.
Elberon, New Jersey
January 1978

ABBREVIATIONS

ACABQ	Advisory Committee on Administrative and Budgetary Questions
ACD	Arms Control and Disarmament
AJIL	*American Journal of International Law*
A/PV . . .	Provisional verbatim records of the General Assembly
CAAC	Civil Aviation Administration of China
CBW	Chemical and Biological Warfare
CCP	Chinese Communist Party
CFYC	*Cheng-fa yen-chiu* [Research on Politics and Law]
CQ	*China Quarterly*
DPRK	Democratic People's Republic of Korea
ECOSOC	Economic and Social Council
ECOSOR	*Official Records* of the Economic and Social Council
EEC	European Economic Community
EPTA	Expanded Programme of Technical Assistance
FAO	Food and Agricultural Organizations of the United Nations
GAOR	*Official Records* of the General Assembly
GARP	Global Atmospheric Research Programme, WMO
GATT	General Agreement on Tariffs and Trade
GGP	Gross Global Product
HC	*Hung-ch'i* [Red Flag]
IAEA	International Atomic Energy Agency
IBRD	International Bank for Reconstruction and Development
ICAO	International Civil Aviation Organization
ICJ	International Court of Justice
I.C.J. Reports	*ICJ: Reports of Judgments, Advisory Opinions and Orders* (annual)
ICSU	International Council of Scientific Unions
IDA	International Development Association
IDB	Industrial Development Board, UNIDO
IFAD	International Fund for Agricultural Development
IFC	International Finance Corporation
IGOs	Inter-Governmental Organizations
ILO	International Labour Organization
IMCO	Inter-Governmental Maritime Consultative Organization
IMF	International Monetary Fund
IMO	International Meteorological Organization
IO	*International Organization*
IPFs	Indicative Planning Figures, UNDP
ITU	International Telecommunication Union

IWSM-HF	*Ch'ing-tai ch'ou-pan i-wu shih-mo* [The complete account of the management of barbarian affairs under the Ch'ing dynasty], the Hsien-feng period, 1851-61
IWSM-TC	Ditto, the T'ung-chih period, 1862-74
IWSM-TK	Ditto, the Tao-kuang period, 1836-50
JMJP	*Jen-min jih-pao* [People's Daily]
KTTH	*Kung-tso t'ung-hsün* [The Work Bulletin]
LDCs	Less Developed Countries
LOS	Law of the Sea
NCNA	New China News Agency
NGOs	Non-Governmental Organizations
NIEO	New International Economic Order
NPT	Non-Proliferation Treaty
NYT	*New York Times*
ONUC	United Nations Operation in the Congo
PLA	People's Liberation Army
PLO	Palestinian Liberation Organization
PR	*Peking Review*
PRC	People's Republic of China
—/PV . . .	Verbatim records of meetings [procès-verbaux]
ROC	Republic of China
ROK	Republic of Korea
SCCS	*Shih-chieh chih-shih* [World Knowledge]
SCMP	*Survey of China Mainland Press*
SCOR	*Official Records* of the Security Council
SPRCP	*Survey of People's Republic of China Press*
S/PV . . .	Provisional verbatim records of the Security Council
—/SR . . .	Summary records of meetings
SW, I-IV	*Selected Works of Mao Tse-tung*, Vols. I-IV (1961, 1965)
TDB	Trade and Development Board, UNCTAD
UNCTAD	United Nations Conference on Trade and Development
UNCURK	United Nations Commission for the Unification and Rehabilitation of Korea
UNDOF	United Nations Disengagement Observer Force
UNDP	United Nations Development Programme
UNEF I	United Nations Emergency Force (1956-1967)
UNEF II	United Nations Emergency Force (1973-)
UNEP	United Nations Environment Programme
UNESCO	United Nations Educational, Scientific and Cultural Organization
UNFICYP	United Nations Peace-keeping Force in Cyprus
UNIDO	United Nations Industrial Development Organization
UNIPOM	United Nations India-Pakistan Observation Mission
UNMOGIP	United Nations Military Observer Group for India and Pakistan

UNOGIL	United Nations Observer Group in Lebanon
UNTEA	United Nations Temporary Executive Authority
UNTSO	United Nations Truce Supervision Organization in Palestine
UNYOM	United Nations Observer Mission in Yemen
UPU	Universal Postal Union
Wan-sui (1967)	*Mao Tse-tung ssu-hsiang wan-sui* [Long Live Mao Tse-tung's Thought], (1967)
Wan-sui (1969)	*Mao Tse-tung ssu-hsiang wan-sui* [Long Live Mao Tse-tung's Thought], (1969)
WFC	World Food Council
WHO	World Health Organization
WIPO	World Intellectual Property Organization
WMO	World Meteorological Organization
WOMP	World Order Models Project
WWW	World Weather Watch, WMO

Transliteration of Chinese into English throughout this book follows the Wade-Giles romanization system, unless convention is otherwise. The date sequence for UN documentary references and resolutions conforms to UN practice.

CHINA, THE UNITED NATIONS, AND WORLD ORDER

INTRODUCTION

With all the conceptual challenges, methodological hazards, and presumptuous claims it entails, this study purports to be "pioneering" in two senses. First, it ventures into the *terra incognita* of Chinese foreign policy.[1] Despite the availability of a large amount of new empirical and behavioral data,[2] Chinese participation in the United Nations system has received no major scholarly treatment. This is indeed a curious phenomenon. During the preentry period (1950-71), there was no shortage of scholarly and semischolarly studies on the subject of Communist China and the United Nations, but these were based necessarily on hypothetical conjectures.[3] Specialists in the field bewailed the lack of empirical and behavioral data needed for a systematic and empirical study of Chinese foreign policy. Now, as of mid-1977, China has participated in the United Nations, the specialized agencies, and UN-sponsored global conferences for nearly six years, generating a substantial quantity of policy or debate statements on a variety of global issues (verbal behavior), as well as empirical data on its voting behavior, consultative (behind-the-scenes) behavior, administrative behavior, and financial and budgetary behavior. Yet all of these activities and data have generated only a few essays and articles.[4] As far as the literature of Chinese foreign policy is concerned, China still remains outside the heuristic framework of the global political system.

Second, this study attempts to make a disciplined macro-inquiry into Chinese global politics by wedding Chinese foreign policy to world-order studies. The principal objective here is to examine China's conceptualization of world order as manifested behaviorally in the United Nations, the specialized agencies, and some of UN-sponsored global

[1] Unless otherwise specified, the term "China" or "Chinese" throughout this study refers to the People's Republic of China (PRC). This conforms to UN practice.

[2] See Table 3.2 in Chapter 3 to get a sense of magnitude of the available UN documents. The number of pages written and distributed by UN Headquarters in 1971 reached almost 558 million. In addition, the UN offices in Geneva produced in 1971 an additional 234,000,000 pages. Approximately one-seventh of the UN budget for 1971 was spent on paperwork.

[3] See note 3 in Chapter 3.

[4] The sum total of works on the PRC's participation in the United Nations published between 1972 and 1976 includes the following: Richard E. Bissell, "A Note on the Chinese View of United Nations Finances," *AJIL* 69 (July 1975), 628-33; William R. Feeney, "The Participation of the PRC in the United Nations," in Gene T. Hsiao, ed., *Sino-American Détente and Its Policy Implications* (New York: Praeger, 1974), pp. 104-34; John G. Stoessinger, "China and the United Nations," in *ibid.*, pp. 97-103; Samuel S. Kim, "The People's Republic of China in the United Nations: A Preliminary Analysis," *World Politics* 26 (April 1974), 299-330.

conferences. By adopting such a systemic and globalist framework, I hope to shed some light on the emerging pattern and strategy of Chinese global policy and on the role China is playing in the creation of a new and just world order. Specifically, this study defines and elaborates China's position on key global issues and problems in the context of UN multilateral diplomacy; it describes, explains, and, at times, projects Chinese global politics; and it assesses the impact of Chinese participation on the working of the various organs of the United Nations system, on the one hand, and the impact of the United Nations system on the development of China's own conceptualization of world order, on the other.

Why not simply study China's UN policy for what it is rather than mixing and complicating it with world-order studies? This is a valid methodological question. As a student whose teaching and research interests have been divided between Chinese foreign policy and world-order studies, I am increasingly concerned over the widening gaps between China specialists and analysts of world politics in general and between Chinese foreign policy specialists and world-order specialists in particular.[5] The tendency of China specialists to overspecialize—which may very well be a corollary of many years of intensive language study—and the tendency of international relations specialists to dwell increasingly on methodology have set the two fields on divergent paths. In the process, China has become too esoteric for most students of international relations, while international relations itself has become too "scientific" or "quantitative" for most China specialists. In addition, too many students in both fields—but especially the former—have been subject to the dominant bias in the social sciences against work that explicitly employs a normative framework as a way of defining problems to be researched.

Instead, this study accepts the avowed and explicitly normative perspective of the World Order Models Project (WOMP), a cross-cultural, transnational and global research enterprise committed to the realization of four central values: (1) the minimization of collective

---

[5] In a personal communication to me dated June 2, 1975, Allen S. Whiting of the University of Michigan, in his capacity as chairman of the Steering Group on Chinese Foreign Relations of the Joint Committee on Contemporary China, Social Science Research Council, expressed a "growing concern over the lack of development in this field [Chinese foreign policy] as well as over the continuing gap between China specialists and analysts of world politics." Subsequently, the Joint Committee on Contemporary China of SSRC/ALCS sponsored a three-day workshop on Chinese foreign policy in mid-August 1976 at the University of Michigan, where some twenty-two scholars addressed themselves to this problem. Chapter 4 of this study is a revised, expanded, and updated version of a paper originally presented at the workshop. See also Allen S. Whiting, "Chinese Foreign Policy: A Workshop Report," *Items* 31 (March/June 1977), 1-3.

violence; (2) the maximization of social and economic well-being; (3) the realization of fundamental human rights and conditions of political justice; and (4) the maintenance of ecological balance and harmony.[6] A value-free research, even if the still youthful state of scientism in our two fields permitted it, would be neither desirable nor relevant. In fact, it might even be dangerously deceptive, since the claim to be value-free could easily become a functional smoke screen behind which status quo values could flourish.

Thus, this study is predicated on the desirability of pursuing a greater use of "policy science" in both fields. The field of world-order studies is a policy science *par excellence*, since it strives toward the realization of values, while at the same time attempting to retain methodological rigor and integrity.[7] Yet one would search in vain through the pages of *Alternatives, Bulletin of Peace Proposals, China Quarterly, Foreign Affairs, International Organization, Journal of Conflict Resolution, Journal of Peace Research*, and *World Politics* for articles that attempted to bring Chinese foreign policy into world-order studies or vice versa.[8]

My special concern, and the modest contribution I hope to make through this study, is to bridge this particular gap. My personal moral

[6] WOMP is sponsored by the Institute for World Order (formerly World Law Fund), the publisher of *Alternatives* (A Journal of World Policy), and has already produced the following series of books appearing under the umbrella title *Preferred Worlds for the 1990s*: Rajini Kothari, *Footsteps into the Future* (New York: Free Press, 1974); Saul H. Mendlovitz, ed., *On the Creation of a Just World Order* (New York: Free Press, 1975); Richard A. Falk, *A Study of Future Worlds* (New York: Free Press, 1975); Ali A. Mazrui, *A World Federation of Cultures* (New York: Free Press, 1976); Gustavo Lagos and Horacio H. Godoy, *Revolution of Being* (New York: Free Press, 1977); and Johan Galtung, *The True Worlds* (New York: Free Press, 1978).

[7] Peace research or world-order studies as a form of policy science in which an explicit set of values is merged with a scientifically rigorous methodology is more easily postulated than accomplished. But the works of Johan Galtung in the pages of the *Journal of Peace Research* and other publication media demonstrate its feasibility. A good sample of Galtung's works has often been collected and published in the following: *Peace: Research, Education, Action*, Vol. I (Copenhagen: Christian Ejlers, 1975); *Methodology and Ideology: Essays in Methodology*, Vol. I (Copenhagen: Christian Ejlers, 1977). Vol. II, entitled *Peace, War and Defense*, Vol. III, entitled, *Peace and Social Structure*, Vol. IV, entitled *Peace and World Structure*, and Vol. V, entitled, *Peace Problems: Some Case Studies*, are all scheduled for future publication.

[8] A few exceptions include the following: Paul T. K. Lin, "Development Guided by Values: Comments on China's Road and Its Implications," in Mendlovitz, *On the Creation of a Just World Order*, pp. 259-96; Andres D. Onate, "Conflict Interactions of the PRC, 1950-70," *Journal of Conflict Resolution* 18 (December 1974), 578-94; and Benjamin I. Schwartz, "The Maoist Image of World Order," *Journal of International Affairs* 21 (1967), 92-102. On the other hand, Allen S. Whiting's works provide a fine example of judicious integration of Chinese foreign policy with international relations. See note 20 below and note 63 in Chapter 2.

and intellectual commitment is to finding a meeting ground between the relative "idealism" of world-order specialists and the relative "parochialism" of China specialists, and, by adopting a normative and globalist paradigm, interpret more fully and accurately China's global or UN policy and its impact upon the evolving world order.[9] Current world-order challenges, in the final analysis, are profoundly moral and political.

The underlying assumption of the normative and globalist approach is that the traditional concept of national interest or security is rapidly losing whatever utility it may have had in the past. Its costs, whether judged in political, economic, or moral terms, have become increasingly high. Moreover, it cannot cope effectively with the fundamentals of human misery in our times. Competitive balance-of-power politics or any contemporary variation on it—whether bipolar, tripolar, pentagonal, or multipolar—invites conflict and confrontation. At best, it is an investment in waste, distracting our resources from the pressing business of the nuclear-ecological age.[10] The gap between the requirements of our threatened ecosystem and the realities of power politics among nations is, therefore, a critical obstacle to the creation of a new and just world order.

The sooner this challenge is met, however, the more likely it is that violent change or traumatic catastrophe can be obviated. The United Nations system is a microcosm of man's hopes and despairs in the nuclear-ecological age. On the one hand, it is an institutionalized expression of faith in the moral and intellectual capacity of men and nations to cosurvive, coexist, and cooperate in the face of the clear and continuing danger of violent conflict among nations possessing vast and unprecedented destructive power. While it offers no guarantee that all or any of the planetary crises are soluble, it does provide a framework for the joint exploration of all avenues to a more just world order. Practically all the recent global conferences on environment, food supply, population growth, the status of women, human settlements, water supply, the law of the sea, and desertification are UN-sponsored.

On the other hand, the United Nations reflects, and often exacer-

[9] Throughout this study, I use the terms "Chinese global policy" and "Chinese UN policy" interchangeably. Conceptually, it is possible to separate one from the other, but such a separation makes little sense in behavioral terms. Practically all the global problems and issues confront China in one forum or another of the United Nations system, eliciting China's response in word and/or deed. China's nonresponse is also a form of "response," from which we can draw certain inferences. This study is organized in such a way as to maximize the areas of overlap between China's UN policy and global policy.

[10] See my elaboration of this theme, "Pax Atomica à la Kissinger," Bulletin of Peace Proposals 7 (1976), 181-85.

6

bates, petty nationalistic jealousies and rivalries. The image of impotence and irrelevance generated in the process then serves as an excuse or rationale for abuse or nonuse of the Organization which, in turn, by weakening its functional effectiveness or usefulness as an instrument of world order, becomes a self-fulfilling prophecy. Each fulfillment acts as a gravitational pull for Member States to return to Realpolitik. Viewed in this dualistic light, the United Nations provides a useful heuristic framework for systemic inquiry into China's image and strategy of world order. Chinese behavior on the global stage not only sheds light on the key global issues but also provides a firm basis for a comparative analysis of Chinese global politics with those of the other major actors.

However, we should note some caveats at the outset. The objective and thorough study of Chinese politics has been beset by some serious methodological and interpretative problems.[11] First, there were numerous gaps and discontinuities in both the coverage and the sources of the PRC's foreign policy.[12] Second, the party-controlled press,[13] the multiple controls over resident foreign observers,[14] and the weak or concealed statistical network have raised the problem not so much of the scarcity but of the diversity and unreliability of the available sources. Third, an excessive use of Aesopian language—fraught with literary and historical allusions and metaphors—in political and policy communications inside China have posed an additional language problem. Fourth, a discrepancy between policy pronouncement and policy performance has presented a constant temptation to the researcher to accept the former at face value and ignore the latter. Finally, until recently, the fluid and uncertain configurations and realignments in the power structure have made it difficult to identify any one authoritative voice in policy making, and therefore to make any predictions about Chinese politics.

Fortunately, the study of Chinese global policy as expressed in the

[11] For a perceptive essay on source and methodological problems in the study of contemporary China, see Michel Oksenberg, "Sources and Methodological Problems in the Study of Contemporary China," in A. Doak Barnett, ed., *Chinese Communist Politics in Action* (Seattle and London: University of Washington Press, 1969), pp. 577-606.

[12] This is the most serious problem in the study of the Chinese theory and practice of international legal order. For an elaboration of the problem, see Chapter 8.

[13] Red Guard publications during the peak of the Cultural Revolution when the party lost its control represent a temporary exception, but the point still remains valid.

[14] The PRC's "expulsion"—the refusal to renew the visa "due to obvious reasons"—of the Canadian resident journalist Ross H. Monro of the *Globe and Mail* in November 1977 adds another twist to this problem. See *NYT*, November 26, 1977, p. 7.

institutional framework of the United Nations system is not handicapped by the above-mentioned problems. Since her entry into the United Nations on October 25, 1971, the PRC has generated a sufficient amount of independent empirical referents. It may be useful here to typologize the sources that the PRC's participation in the United Nations system has produced. First, all the PRC delegates are given numerous opportunities to speak out on global issues in the committees, organs, commissions, plenaries, conferences, and the specialized agencies of the system. It is now possible to measure the volume, frequency, and distribution of the PRC's policy statements on different issues in different institutional contexts. Altogether, the PRC's statements as recorded in the UN documents constitute a rich repertory from which to draw a composite of how various issues fit into the hierarchy of values in the Chinese image of world order.

More importantly, we now have the PRC's voting record on a multitude of global issues in the General Assembly and the Security Council for a period of over half a decade, and, to a limited degree, in other organs of the United Nations system.[15] All studies of Chinese global policy during the preentry period, whether approached from the vantage point of the United Nations or from that of China, were largely hypothetical speculations based almost exclusively on Peking's rhetorical pronouncements. No empirical analysis was possible, since there existed no revealed patterns of behavior that could be distilled from participation in international organizations.

Chinese participation in the United Nations system and the data it has generated for over five years now provide a firm basis for a disciplined empirical inquiry into the institutional and behavioral dimensions of Chinese global strategy. It is now possible to approach the much debated question of discrepancy between words and deeds systematically and empirically. As if also to challenge the adequacy of scholarship in the West on Chinese foreign policy, Ch'iao Kuan-hua, head of the Chinese delegation to the 26th Session of the General Assembly, declared in the plenary of the General Assembly on November 26, 1971: "A simple but important principle of Marxism is that one must judge a person not merely by his words but [also] by his deeds."[16]

Finally, personal interviews with the delegates of other participating Member States and international civil servants who have had firsthand

[15] Because of the trend from voting to consensus, it is not possible to make a voting analysis of any Member State in many organs and agencies of the United Nations system. Even in the Security Council and the General Assembly, this trend is pronounced. However, controversial issues have been pressed to a roll-call or recorded vote in both organs. For details, see Chapters 3 and 4.

[16] GAOR, 26th Sess., 1996th plenary meeting (26 November 1971), para. 136.

contact or working relationships with the Chinese delegates in a variety of UN organs and conferences can generate additional primary source materials. The value of such materials for descriptive analysis of Chinese behind-the-scenes consultative behavior is indisputable, since the published UN documents record only the verbal and voting behavior of the participating Member States. In an increasing number of UN organs, including the Security Council, where more and more decisions grow out of behind-the-scenes consensual and consultative practices, the testimonial accounts of the participating delegates provide a unique source of information that is not otherwise available.[17]

Apart from its wide-ranging implications for the creation of a just world order, then, Chinese participation in the United Nations system has already generated *new* source materials for the students of Chinese foreign policy. In the empirical part of the book (Part II) this study makes extensive use of the three types of source materials discussed above. In the period November 1976-May 1977, I conducted 110 field interviews in the United Nations (New York), Washington, D.C., Montreal, London, Paris, Geneva, Berne, and Rome in my pursuit of "live" sources. These interviews have been extremely valuable in my analysis of the theory and practice of Chinese global policy; they have also enabled me to correct numerous errors I would otherwise have made in my descriptive analysis. As far as the behavioral aspect of Chinese global policy is concerned, the documentary materials are not only inadequate but can often be misleading, revealing trivial or uninteresting aspects while concealing vital ones.

The normative and globalist framework of this study raises some difficult conceptual, methodological, and organizational problems. Nonetheless, in order to maintain a modicum of methodological rigor, to reduce my personal biases, and to make the finished work as complete and undistorted a picture of Chinese global policy as possible, I have taken care, whenever and wherever feasible, to sort and order the data in such a way as to keep them in line with the general requirements of a scientific model: description, explanation, and prediction.[18]

[17] However, the major problem with this source material is that it is difficult, expensive (travel costs), and time consuming to obtain interviews with national UN delegates and international civil servants. Those who make themselves available for interviews are not always the most ideal source of information on a particular problem. Nonetheless, the availability of the interview materials now makes it possible to carry the behavioral analysis of Chinese global strategy a step farther by adding the dimension of consultative diplomacy. The author was both tenacious and fortunate in getting most of the interviews he had wanted. Two notable exceptions include Secretary-General Kurt Waldheim and former Ambassador Huang Hua. See interview schedule.

[18] Two works in the literature of international relations are particularly helpful on this methodological question. See J. David Singer, "The Level-of-Analysis Problem in International Relations," in Klaus Knorr and Sidney Verba, eds., *The*

However, by choice and necessity, this study is more heavily oriented toward descriptive than predictive analysis, while explanatory analysis falls in between.

DESCRIBING CHINESE GLOBAL POLICY

It is axiomatic in any field of scholarly inquiry that we must first describe before we can hope to explain, much less to predict. This basic methodological principle has not always been followed in the study of Chinese foreign policy, partly because of the lack of empirical rigor among many China specialists and partly because of the paucity of data, given the diplomatic isolation of the PRC from the world community in the 1950s and 1960s. Except in case studies focusing on a specifically delimited subject or a bilateral relationship, the literature of Chinese foreign policy is fraught with grandiose explanations and generalizations made in an empirical and behavioral vacuum. I have attempted to correct this problem by making a more extensive descriptive analysis of many issues than may sometimes seem necessary or justified from the standpoint of one of the two fields: world-order studies and international relations respectively.[19]

The steps I have taken in my descriptive analysis may be briefly summarized here. First, I have sought China's own description of her global or UN policy by recourse to the following sources: speeches and statements by the Chinese delegates as recorded in the UN documents; official policy or editorial pronouncements as published in such PRC publications as *Jen-min jih-pao* (People's Daily), the New China News Agency (NCNA), and *Peking Review*. Second, I have sought descriptions of Chinese global policy by other participants, using the following sources: speeches and statements by delegates, whether friendly, adversary, or neutral, as recorded in the UN documents and as obtained through my own field interviews. Finally, I have consulted nongovernmental descriptions of the PRC's global policy in news media of international repute as well as my "live" sources, international civil servants. Discrepancies in the above sources have been resolved

---

International System: Theoretical Essays (Princeton, N.J.: Princeton University Press, 1961), pp. 77-92; and David O. Wilkinson, *Comparative Foreign Relations: Framework and Methods* (Belmont, Calif.: Dickenson, 1969).

[19] To acquaint students of Chinese foreign policy who are not too familiar with the workings of UN bodies, I have also included some background materials in each chapter in Part II so as to place Chinese behavior in proper historical and institutional contexts. The student of international organization should skip these background materials and move on directly to the substantive part of each relevant chapter.

by examining the PRC's actual behavior as revealed through her voting and consultative behavior.

Explaining Chinese Global Policy

Why is the PRC's global policy what it is? What main factors or influences lie behind the making and execution of it? The causal questions worth raising and pondering through a balanced analysis of the PRC's words and deeds are numerous. Can China's global policy be explained by her "national interests"? If so, what are they and how are they defined and manifested? Can it be explained in terms of China's doctrines and ideologies? If so, what is the main doctrinal or ideological thrust of the PRC? How is it translated into a global policy? In what sense does China's global or UN policy enhance her values? Can it be explained in terms of past and emerging international systems? If so, what is China's perception of the past international system? How is it different from her perception of the emerging international system? Can it be explained as an *ad hoc* or opportunistic response to the policy and behavior of other national actors? Or is it a result of the compromise between China's own principled stand and the pressures and requirements of the constituent units of the global political system? I do not pretend that this study provides firm and satisfactory answers to all these questions, but I have been conscious of these explanatory questions and hypotheses in my analysis.

Predicting Chinese Global Policy

What are the future prospects and directions of Chinese global policy? The study of Chinese foreign policy cannot be regarded as being very scientific at this stage of development. It cannot *predict* the development of general classes of political phenomena, let alone the rise or fall of specific or individual classes of political events and personalities. However, the modest aim here is not to attempt to predict what will happen—no one, for example, predicted or even attempted to predict the development of the Sino-Soviet rift, the coming of the Cultural Revolution, the rise and fall of Teng Hsiao-p'ing and Wang Hung-wen (and rise again of the former), and the meteoric rise of Hua Kuo-feng —but rather to *project* future trends and alternative policy options regarding selected issues on the basis of past and present events.

This latter approach belongs to a species of forecasting known as extrapolation, an intellectual exercise of linking the past, the present, and the future by projecting future trend curves based on, and extrap-

11

olated from, our knowledge of important and recurring patterns, regularities, and relationships of the social process in the past.[20] The tables and figures in this study are provided to highlight not only the salient features of the past and present policy but also to provide an empirical basis for extrapolative forecasting of China's future policy options. Still, it should be noted at the outset that forecasting China's future policy is not one of the principal objectives; hence, it represents a weak link in the present study.

The scope is limited both spatially and temporally. Spatially, it is limited to the United Nations system. Even within this scope, it must be pointed out that this is not a study of the United Nations or China in the United Nations as such but rather a study of Chinese global policy using the United Nations system as a heuristic framework. Hence, no attempt is made to cover Chinese participation in every organ, committee, or specialized agency. In spite of the importance that China attaches to decolonization, for example, no mention is made in this study of Chinese participation in the Trusteeship Council, as the work of this organ has now diminished to the point that there remained in 1976 only one trust territory—the US-administered trust territory of the Pacific Islands, which was designated as a strategic area.[21] Therefore, Chinese views on decolonization can be more meaningfully examined in the context of the General Assembly in general, and in the Special Committee on the Situation with Regard to the Implementation of the Declaration on the Granting of Independence to Colonial Countries and Peoples (the Committee of 24) in particular.

Temporally, the scope is limited to the period of Chinese participation in the United Nations from 1971 to the end of 1976. However, Part I relies extensively on the materials of the preentry period to establish a conceptual framework that is largely historical and normative. The thread that ties together the first two chapters in Part I—and one that I have also employed as a useful analytical device here and there

[20] A recent book by two prominent China specialists has broken a new path in this direction by forecasting various options and alternatives of China's foreign and economy policy in the next ten to fifteen years under different sets of assumptions and conditions. See Allen S. Whiting and Robert F. Dernberger, *China's Future: Foreign Policy and Economic Development in the Post-Mao Era* (New York: McGraw-Hill, 1977).

[21] Even though the Economic and Social Council and the Trusteeship Council represents two of the six principal organs of the United Nations, they operate under the Assembly's authority. "In practice," observed Stephen G. Xydis, "the Assembly has exercised to the full its supervisory authority over those two principal UN organs so that they have come to resemble permanent subsidiary organs of the Assembly." See Stephen G. Xydis, "The General Assembly," in James Barros, ed., *The United Nations: Past, Present, and Future* (New York: Free Press, 1972), p. 73.

throughout the book—is the concept of image (or perception theory). When I have departed from the established limit of 1971-76, however, it has been in order to bring certain analyses more up to date. Hence, the reader will find some references to materials dating from the first half of 1977.[22]

I have deliberately chosen "image" as a useful conceptual tool because of my belief that human or national behavior cannot be understood, let alone judged, without first knowing the actor's image of himself and of the outside world. "If men define situations as real, they are real in their consequences."[23] This famous statement made in 1928 by W. I. Thomas, the dean of American sociologists, has now become "a theorem basic to the social sciences."[24]

Image as a conceptual or analytical tool has now become familiar in the literature of international relations.[25] For purposes of analysis in this study, image is defined as an epistemological paradigm that functions in three separate but closely interrelated ways: (1) it serves as the structure of the lens through which we view the outside world or reality, and also as a filter through which the message from the outside world is processed—that is, accepted or rejected with or without modification; (2) it serves as a scale of valuation whereby we interpret

[22] The writing of this book was completed by the end of August 1977, and I have resisted the temptation of *ad hoc* and piecemeal updating of many parts in the light of subsequent developments both in China and the United Nations. The reader should keep this cutoff date in mind in reading some parts of the study which may have been outdated by developments since the latter half of 1977.

[23] W. I. Thomas, *The Child in America* (New York: Knopf, 1928), p. 572.

[24] Robert K. Merton, *Social Theory and Social Structure: Toward the Codification of Theory and Research* (Glencoe, Ill.: Free Press, 1949), p. 179.

[25] For a pioneering essay urging a greater use of perception theory in the study of Chinese foreign policy, see Robert Boardman, "Perception Theory and the Study of Chinese Foreign Policy," in Roger Dial, ed., *Advancing and Contending Approaches to the Study of Chinese Foreign Policy* (Halifax, Canada: Centre for Foreign Policy Studies, Dalhousie University, 1974), pp. 321-52. For a sample of works in the international relations literature that employs the concept of image, see the following: Kenneth E. Boulding, "National Images and International Systems," in James N. Rosenau, ed., *International Politics and Foreign Policy: A Reader in Research and Theory* (rev. ed., New York: Free Press, 1969), pp. 422-31; "The Learning and Reality-Testing Process in the International System," *Journal of International Affairs* 21 (1967), 1-15; Urie Bronfenbrenner, "The Mirror Image in Soviet-American Relations: A Social Psychologist's Report," *Journal of Social Issues* 17 (1961), 45-56; Hebert C. Kelman, ed., *International Behavior: A Social-Psychological Analysis* (New York: Holt, Rinehart and Winston, 1966); Ole R. Holsti, "The Belief System and National Images: A Case Study," *Journal of Conflict Resolution* 6 (1962), 244-52, "Cognitive Dynamics and Images of the Enemy," *Journal of International Affairs* 21 (1967), 16-39; and Robert Jervis, *The Logic of Images in International Relations* (Princeton, N.J.: Princeton University Press, 1970), and *Perception and Misperception in International Politics* (Princeton, N.J.: Princeton University Press, 1976).

the meaning of the message received; and (3) it serves to prescribe the proper line of action to be followed, based on (1) and (2).[26] In short, it performs cognitive, evaluative, and prescriptive functions.

National behavior is a mirror of its image. Every nation has a self-image. Every nation has an image of its friends and foes. Every nation has an image of the outside world or the international system—often called the "definition of the situation." Every nation has an image of how world affairs should be managed and what issues should take precedence. To understand and explain why a nation behaves the way it often does, therefore, we need to take a close look at that nation's image of itself and of the world—or, more simply, that nation's world view, *Weltanschauung* (or *shih-chieh kuan* or *yü-chou kuan*, in Chinese).

China, too, has her own world view. Chapter 1 shows the extent to which the traditional Chinese image of world order influenced China's response to the Western challenge in modern times. Chapter 2 discusses Mao's conceptual preoccupation with a world outlook and its implications for the PRC's image of world order. The conceptual framework established in Part I is also useful in dealing with the perennial change-continuity theme (diachronic analysis) in the study of Chinese foreign policy.

Part II is the empirical section, focusing specifically on Chinese behavior in the global political system. The institutional contexts selected for this behavioral analysis include the General Assembly, the Security Council, and such development organs or agencies as ECOSOC, UNCTAD, UNIDO, and UNDP. In addition, a cross-sample of four specialized agencies—UNESCO, FAO, ICAO, and WMO—has been selected to highlight the Chinese theory and practice of functionalism. Two chapters (5 and 6) are devoted to a New International Economic Order (NIEO), to stress its integral role in the establishment of a new world order and the particular interest and active participation of the PRC in that process. Part III strives toward a general overview of the most salient characteristics of Chinese global strategy within the framework of the WOMP values, in order to draw the necessary conclusions and implications about the reciprocal interaction between China and a new world order.

Given the difficulty, complexity, and novelty of pursuing this transdisciplinary study, as well as of wedding Chinese foreign policy to world-order studies under the two requirements (normative and scien-

---

[26] It is also possible that image may function in a totally self-sufficient manner, losing contact with reality. Such a state of communication patterns in which messages from within the self dominate over messages from the outside world is called autism.

tific), I have avoided following any single, straight, methodological path. It should be obvious from the above discussion that I have been somewhat arbitrary in my choice and use of conceptual and methodological tools in the present study. This may irritate the pure methodologists, to be sure, but the systemic scope of the subject matter, coupled with the novelty of wedding the two divergent fields, warns of the danger of any straitjacket empiricism. I hope only that this study may make a small contribution to the WOMP efforts to lay foundations for disciplined inquiry into the normative issues of world order.

PART I. CONCEPTUAL FRAMEWORK:
THE CHINESE IMAGE OF WORLD ORDER

· 1 ·

THE TRADITIONAL CHINESE
IMAGE OF WORLD ORDER

The image of world order in traditional China[1] seems to bear out the sociological maxim that men—and nations—react not to the objective reality of the world but to their image of that reality. In theory, if not always in practice, the traditional Chinese image remained tenaciously resistant to change. It was the Chinese officials' perception of what the world was like, not what it was actually like, that determined their response to international situations, and provided a comprehensive and unifying frame of reference for the conceptualization and execution of external ("barbarian") policy throughout most of Chinese history. The strength and persistence of this perception were most dramatically revealed during the first half of the nineteenth century, when China was faced with a continuing threat from the dynamic and expansionistic West.

THE CHINESE SELF-IMAGE

What is so striking about the Chinese image of world order is the extent to which it was colored by the assumptions, values, and beliefs of the Confucian moral order. Indeed, the traditional Chinese image of world order was no more than a corollary of the Chinese image of internal order, and thus really an extended projection of her self-image. Hence, the chief concern of China's traditional foreign policy centered upon the ways and means of making diplomatic practice conform to that idealized self-image. Even when the empire was weak and lacked the power to translate her image of world order into a political reality, China persisted in acting out her self-image in international relations. At times, the desire to preserve the purity of self-image led to a distor-

---

[1] By "traditional China" I am referring to the China of the pre-Republican period. However, a caveat is in order. Any generalization I make about the *traditional* Chinese image of world order should be viewed within the context of the slow historical change that began to take place after the Opium War. That is, the salient features of the traditional Chinese image of world order followed a classical development in the Ming and Ch'ing dynasties down to the Opium War, but were subjected to an imperialistic onslaught in the latter part of the nineteenth century. For the portion of this chapter centering on the transitional period (1842-58), I have tapped liberally the materials used in my article, "The Transitional Period of Chinese Diplomacy with the West: An Assessment," *The Ohio University Review* 12 (1970), 51-65.

tion of the official record so as to square deviant practice with idealized theory.[2]

The essence of the traditional Chinese world order was Sinocentric cosmology. China perceived herself to be the center of human civilization—hence the name Middle Kingdom (*Chung-kuo*)—and the Chinese emperor, the Son of Heaven (*t'ien-tzu*), had *de jure*, if not always *de facto*, the right to reign and rule over all human affairs. Although pre-Confucian in origin, the notion of a universal state ruled by a universal king developed and culminated in the state orthodoxy of the Confucian order. The Son of Heaven ruled by virtue (*te*) in order to promote and preserve universal harmony and order among all things and all men. Thus, the Chinese world order logically led to an ordinance of *Pax Sinica*, which all non-Chinese states and peoples had to accept if they were to enter into any relations with China. The history of China's relations with her Asian neighbors lent some credence to such a claim. As a result, the claim was transformed into a creed, and the dividing line between the Chinese image of what the world order *ought* to be like and the changing practical reality virtually disappeared from the Chinese world view.

To the extent that *Pax Sinica* was claimed as a function of China's cultural superiority and moral virtue, the Chinese image of world order may have been more ethical than political. Such a view needs to be qualified, however, when we examine its ideological components. Clearly, the value of harmony (*ho*) stands out as a salient feature in the Chinese images of domestic and world order. *The Doctrine of the Mean*, a Confucian canonical text that guided the socialization process of traditional China for centuries, idealizes harmony in the following terms:

> While there are no stirrings of pleasure, anger, sorrow, or joy, the mind may be said to be in the state of EQUILIBRIUM. When those feelings have been stirred, and they act in their due degree, there ensues what may be called the state of HARMONY. This EQUILIBRIUM is the great root *from which grow all the human actings in the world*, and this HARMONY is the universal path *which they all should pursue*.
>
> Let the states of equilibrium and harmony exist in perfection, and a happy order will prevail throughout heaven and earth, and all things will be nourished and flourish.[3]

[2] A classical example is the case of Lord Macartney in 1793, who was entered in the Chinese record as having performed the kowtow before the Ch'ien-lung Emperor. In fact, Lord Macartney refused to perform that ritual. Nor did George III send tributary gifts to the Chia-ch'ing Emperor in 1804, contrary to a Chinese documentary assertion.

[3] Capitalizations and italics in the original. James Legge, *The Chinese Classics*, Vol. I (London: Trubner, 1861), pp. 248-49.

Note here that harmony is romanticized not only as the proper norm in human relations but also in the relationship between man and nature. Whatever aesthetic appeal such an idealization of harmony may possess, it also served as a political and social doctrine designed to perpetuate the conservative status quo. The written Chinese language, which is rich in evocative symbolism, was used extensively in schools, civil service examinations, and the Court as the conveyer of harmony as a supreme value. Indeed, the symbols of harmony became all-pervasive "in innumerable era names, place names, personal names, street, palace, temple, and studio names throughout Chinese history."[4]

However, the sociopolitical status quo to be preserved in the Chinese world order through a universal symbolization of harmony was hierarchical and antiegalitarian, based on sex, kinship, age, and social function. The Confucian orthodoxy laid heavy stress on the doctrine of superordination-subordination in the Five Relationships—ruler and subject, husband and wife, father and son, elder brother and younger brother, and friend and friend—as well as in the distinction between the superior men who work with their brains and the inferior men who labor with their muscles. The Confucian social stratification also ranked the classes hierarchically in the order of scholar-official, farmer, artisan, and merchant. Harmony in such a sociopolitical context really aimed at replacing individual originality and creativity with individual subordination and submissiveness. Moreover, the hierarchical social order at home provided an absolute criterion for conceptualizing China's relations with non-Chinese states.

Sinocentrism, in all its pretense of paternalistic benevolence and cultural chauvinism, was an outgrowth of centuries of Chinese contacts with surrounding peoples in the Sinic (East Asian) world order. The notion of the Middle Kingdom originated in the Chou dynasty, when "China" was a group of feudal states around the Yellow River, surrounded by the "barbarian" tribes at the four quarters of the kingdom—*jung* on the west, *i* on the east, *ti* on the north, and *man* on the south. Chinese historical scholarship records a glorification of Chinese civilization at a time when other contemporary states such as Korea, Vietnam, and Japan were all cast under the powerful shadow of Chinese culture. Thus, the absence of any rival civilization became a potent factor in the development of the Chinese image of world order.

True, the Chinese were aware of the existence of *Pax Romana*, but it seems to have had little direct impact on their own world view. Limited contacts with west Asia and the Byzantine world during the T'ang dynasty (618-906) merely confirmed the rightness of the Sino-

---

[4] Arthur F. Wright, "Struggle v. Harmony: Symbols of Competing Values in Modern China," *World Politics* 6 (October 1953), 34.

centric image. Even the Buddhist invasion, the most serious foreign challenge to Chinese culture until modern times, failed to modify Chinese perceptions. The Indian world view as expressed in Buddhism was devoid of political imperative. While Buddhism exerted a substantial and lasting influence on art and religious thought in traditional China, it had little political impact on Chinese cosmology. On the contrary, the anti-Buddhist campaign was marked by "a most vehement and absolutist reassertion of the Chinese image of world order."[5]

In a remarkable way, even the alien conquerors—the Yüan or Mongol (1279-1367) and the Ch'ing or Manchu (1644-1911)—contributed to reinforcing the Sinocentric world order.[6] They seized political power through military conquest and ruled from the top down, without altering the ideological continuity of Confucianism or the Chinese image of world order. The relatively short tenure of Mongol rule may have been a result of inadequate Sinicization of the Mongols.[7] As if determined to avoid the fate of the Mongols, the Manchus, the most thoroughly Sinicized of all the alien dynasties, became staunch champions of the Chinese cultural heritage. By the mid-nineteenth century, the triumph of Chinese civilization over the Manchu was nearly complete, with the abolition of Manchu even as a secondary official language. The Manchus themselves no longer knew their mother tongue. An imperial edict of January 1862 acknowledged this *fait accompli* by exempting Manchu candidates in the civil service examinations from translating Chinese classics into Manchu.[8] "If the government of the Ch'ing had faults," observed the reformer K'ang Yu-wei, "they were the ancient faults of the Han, T'ang, Sung, and Ming—'It was not a special Manchu system'."[9]

In addition, natural geographical barriers exerted some influence in the evolution of the Chinese image of world order. China is guarded on the west by almost endless deserts, on the southwest by the Hima-

[5] Benjamin I. Schwartz, "The Chinese Perception of World Order, Past and Present," in John K. Fairbank, ed., *The Chinese World Order: Traditional China's Foreign Relations* (Cambridge, Mass.: Harvard University Press, 1968), p. 280.

[6] For the tradition of "synarchy" (joint Sino-foreign administration) in Chinese history, see John K. Fairbank, "Synarchy Under the Treaties," in John K. Fairbank, ed., *Chinese Thought and Institutions* (Chicago: University of Chicago Press, 1957), pp. 204-31.

[7] See C. P. Fitzgerald, *The Chinese View of Their Place in the World* (London: Oxford University Press, 1967), p. 25; and John K. Fairbank, "A Preliminary Framework," in *idem, The Chinese World Order*, p. 15.

[8] An English translation of this edict is printed in *The North China Herald*, March 1, 1862.

[9] Quoted in Mary C. Wright, *The Last Stand of Chinese Conservatism: The T'ung-Chih Restoration, 1862-1874* (Stanford, Calif.: Stanford University Press, 1962), p. 53.

laya Mountains, and on the east by vast oceans. Admired but often attacked by the "barbarians" of the semiarid plateau lands on the north and west, and cut off from the other centers of civilization by oceans, deserts, and mountains, China gradually developed a unique sense of her place under heaven. The geopolitical dimension of the Chinese world order has been analyzed by some scholars in terms of a model of hierarchical concentric zonation. "For centuries upon centuries," one scholar has written, "the perceived political spatial system remained Sinocentric, zonal, roughly concentric, without formal boundaries, characterized by a distance-intensity relationship between power and territorial control, almost exclusively Asia-oriented, and separated from the rest of the world by indifference or ignorance. Nowhere in those centuries of China's history for which the model appears to apply did China perceive of herself as a state of states, a neighbor among neighbors, a member of a family of nations."[10]

In short, the Sinic world order was a concentric extension of the hierarchical principle which prevailed in the domestic social structure of the Middle Kingdom. It was a system of "interstate" relations unto itself with its own rules of the game. It was not a system of international relations in the modern European sense, whose stability was maintained by the balance of power among more or less equal member states. It was instead a system of hierarchical harmony enforced by the preponderance of power and virtue anchored in China.

THE TRIBUTE SYSTEM

What have been the practical or operational consequences of the Sinocentric image of world order? Although there is no comparable Chinese term, "tribute system" has been used by Western Sinologists to designate the sum total of complex, practical, and institutional expressions of the Chinese world order. International diplomacy or international relations, as we understand the terms today, were alien to the letter and spirit of the tribute system. Such principles as national independence, national sovereignty, and national equality, upon which modern international law is built, were meaningless for the Chinese; in fact, they were repugnant to their sense of a universal state and civilization. The boundaries in the Chinese world order were strictly cultural, separating the civilized from the barbarian. Likewise, the dividing line between power and virtue—that is, between "might" and

[10] Norton Ginsberg, "On the Chinese Perception of a World Order," in Tang Tsou, ed., *China in Crisis*, Vol. II, *China's Policies in Asia and America's Alternatives* (Chicago: University of Chicago Press, 1968), p. 80. John Fairbank also uses the zonation model in his analysis of the traditional Chinese world order. See Fairbank, "A Preliminary Framework," pp. 1-19.

"right"—was never drawn. In fact, one could argue that in traditional China "right" defined "might," not the other way around, and that national power was viewed as the reflection of national virtue.[11]

Viewed in this light, China was neither a state nor a nation but a civilization ruled by the Son of Heaven. The idea of nationality or nationalism as yet had had no impact. For example, when Charles Eliot, the British superintendent of trade in China, urged the viceroy of Canton on the eve of the outbreak of the Opium War (1839-42) to settle the differences between the two nations peacefully, the viceroy was quite puzzled by the term, "two nations," for he took them to mean England and the United States.[12] Even the concept of barbarians was devoid of any racial or nationalistic imperative, as it merely conveyed to the native-born that the people so designated stood outside the pale of Chinese cultural and linguistic refinement. In addition, we find in traditional China a conspicuous absence of any institution corresponding to a Ministry of Foreign Affairs in the West. The Book of Rites ordained in fact that "the officials of the Empire shall have no intercourse with foreigners."[13]

Until the mid-nineteenth century, when Chinese world order was subjected to a massive onslaught by the Western powers, all types of external intercourse were supposed to take place within the established norms and precedents of the tribute system. Formal intercourse was bilateral merely in the sense of involving the two parties at a time, not in the contemporary sense of a mutual exchange of ambassadors or of political and economic activities flowing more or less equally in both directions. The Son of Heaven was the tribute receiver who was firmly anchored in the Forbidden City, while all other states were tribute bearers whose envoys had to follow the specifically designated routes to and from Peking in the course of their tributary journey. Curiously, the 1818 Collected Statutes of the Ch'ing Dynasty (*Ta-Ch'ing hui-tien*) categorized Tibet, Corea (Korea), Liu Ch'iu (Ryū-kyū), Cambodia, Siam, Sulu, Holland, Burma, Portugal, Italy, and England as tributary states, while Russia, Japan, Sweden, and France were listed merely as states having only commercial relations with China.[14]

[11] See Mark Mancall, "The Persistence of Tradition in Chinese Foreign Policy," *The Annals of the American Academy of Political and Social Science* 349 (September 1963), 18.

[12] Immanuel C. Y. Hsü, *China's Entrance into the Family of Nations: The Diplomatic Phase 1858-1880* (Cambridge, Mass.: Harvard University Press, 1960), p. 13.

[13] Cited in Werner Levi, *Modern China's Foreign Policy* (Minneapolis, Minn.: University of Minnesota Press, 1953), p. 4.

[14] *Ta-Ch'ing hui-tien* [Collected Statutes of the Ch'ing Dynasty] (Peking: 1818), 31:1a-3a; 52:23b-24b; 52:30b.

The regulations governing tributary missions were spelled out in the Collected Statutes in specific terms for each tributary state. They included such matters as the frequency and size of tributary missions, the designated points of entry and departure as well as the routes to be traveled in China by each mission, the appointment of Chinese envoys to deliver imperial edicts to the rulers of tributary states, and the ritual requirements to be performed at the Court.[15] In purely economic terms, the tribute system made little sense to China; in fact, it represented a financial burden since all expenditures incurred during the tributary envoy's sojourn in China were paid by the Chinese government. Yet to the extent that the tribute system served as an institutionalized expression of the Chinese image of world order, economic considerations had to be subordinated to cultural symbolism.

It should also be noted that the source of Chinese authority over tributary states was not always military, as there were periods when China had to accept the military supremacy of the surrounding barbarians, and the cycle of alternating Chinese military superiority and inferiority became a recurring feature in Chinese history. Yet the Sinocentric image of world order was seldom compromised, because it was seldom challenged in any fundamental way. As noted earlier, the Ch'ing dynasty was the last example of alien rule of China within the realm of the Chinese image of world order.

The tribute system worked relatively well for centuries, reaching its height of classical refinement in the Ming (1368-1664) and Ch'ing dynasties. Its longevity may have been due to its ability to foster mutually complementary interests on the part of the tribute receiver and the tribute bearer. For the Chinese, the system proved to be politically and culturally useful as it served as a first step in bringing the barbarians into the edifying influence of Chinese civilization. The smug assumption that the barbarians could not help but be transformed (*lai-hua*) by the awe-inspiring virtue of Chinese civilization was once expressed by Mencius: "I have heard of men using *the doctrines* of our great land to change barbarians, but I have never yet heard of any being changed by barbarians."[16] The tribute system also served as an acceptable vehicle for regulating commercial relations with other states. Finally, it was an ever-present symbol exemplifying and legitimizing the Sinocentric world order.

The interests and motives of the tributary states were more complex

---

[15] For a more detailed listing of the regulations, see Masataka Banno, *China and the West 1858-1861: The Origins of the Tsungli Yamen* (Cambridge, Mass.: Harvard University Press, 1964), pp. 3-4.

[16] James Legge, *The Four Books: Confucian Analects, the Great Learning, The Doctrine of the Mean, and The Works of Mencius* (New York: Paragon Book Reprint Corp., 1966), p. 633. Emphasis in original.

and less subject to neat generalizations. For many, the system had a commercial value. It was accepted as an unavoidable price to pay for the privilege of trade, and the China trade was sufficiently lucrative to justify suffering whatever humiliation might be entailed in the ritual requirements, especially the performance of the kowtow—three kneelings and nine prostrations (*san-kuei chiu-k'ou-li*)—symbolizing acceptance of the Chinese world order. In such a case, "the tributary system really worked in reverse, the submission of the barbarians being actually bought and paid for by the trade conceded to them by China."[17]

For others, however, the tribute system proved to be useful in establishing and maintaining their own political legitimacy at home. Korea, which has served as a model tributary state longer than any other, is a case in point. The Sino-Korean tributary relationship was more political than economic. The Confucianized ruling classes in Korea found the tribute system not only congenial ideologically—as expressed in the Korean term *mohwa-sasang* (ideology in the emulation of things Chinese)—but also useful politically in legitimating and perpetuating their own status and power by suppressing any popular or nationalistic movement.[18] In short, the Korean ruling classes saw the tribute system as providing in effect a Chinese political and ideological blessing, while interfering little in domestic affairs.[19]

In the face of the Russian challenge, however, the tribute system demonstrated a capacity for adjustment to the power reality. Between 1728 and 1858, the tribute system really worked by avoidance as far as the Sino-Russian relationship was concerned. A special system of communications between court officials of secondary or tertiary rank in both St. Petersburg and Peking was set up to bypass the sensitive question of the czar's having to address the Son of Heaven as a superior, while Russian trade caravans to Peking "could be entered in official Manchu court records as tribute caravans, if necessary."[20] Thus, the Chinese image of world order was preserved intact, while the Russians were allowed to pursue their commercial activities in China without direct participation in the tribute system. As these diverse examples show, so long as both parties viewed their respective interests

[17] John K. Fairbank and S. Y. Teng, "On the Ch'ing Tributary System," *The Harvard Journal of Asiatic Studies* 6 (1941-42), 141.

[18] For my elaboration of this point, see Samuel S. Kim, "The Developmental Problems of Korean Nationalism," in Se-jin Kim and Chang-hyun Cho, eds., *Korea: A Nation Divided* (Silver Spring, Md.: Research Institute on Korean Affairs, 1976), pp. 10-37.

[19] For a detailed analysis of Sino-Korean tributary relations, see Hae-jong Chun, "Sino-Korean Tributary Relations in the Ch'ing Period," in Fairbank, *The Chinese World Order*, pp. 90-111.

[20] Mancall, "The Persistence of Tradition," p. 21.

as complementary—or at least mutually acceptable—the tribute system could continue to work.

THE CHINESE RESPONSE TO THE WEST

The initial Chinese response toward Western traders (largely Portuguese adventurers) in the early part of the sixteenth century was not unfriendly. The Chinese were, in fact, kindly disposed toward the Portuguese at the start and welcomed them at Canton in 1517. It is unfortunate, however, that this first critical contact with the West was made with adventurous traders who went on to ravage the shores of China with piracy, plunder, and rapine, as revealed in the following Chinese description of the first encounter between the Portuguese and the Chinese: "They [the Portuguese] went about reconnoitring, and made themselves familiar with our roads and streets; they stole or bought little children in order to cook and eat them. Recently the king of Malacca reported in a memorandum that they had taken his land away from him and killed [many men] in enmity. The harm they caused by their killing plundering was without parallel."[21]

To be sure, this is an exaggerated picture, but the Portuguese adventurers had undeniably succeeded in reviving the dormant Chinese image of outlandish barbarian traders. Once Chinese imagination was quickened, a predictable cognitive process took place: the image of Western traders acquired through this contact with the Portuguese became their image of all European traders. Consequently, the Chinese attitude toward the Western trader rigidified: "They [Western] barbarians are beasts, and not to be ruled on the same principles as subjects of China. Were any one to attempt to control them by the great maxims of reason, it would lead to nothing but confusion. The ancient kings [of China] well understood this, and accordingly ruled barbarians by misrule; therefore to rule barbarians by misrule is the best and true way to govern them."[22]

This image was soon translated into a policy of restricting the maritime (Western) trade and traders to the remote port of Canton, and the Ch'ing Court proceeded with affairs of state as usual, refusing to deal with the newcomers directly. The presence of Western Jesuit missionaries at Peking—who, incidentally, were referred to as "men of the Western Ocean" (*Hsi-yang jen*), not barbarians—did not influence the Sinocentric image. Nor did they increase the Chinese knowledge of the West, as the missionaries merely performed useful

[21] Cited in Wolfgang Franke, *China and the West*, trans. R. A. Wilson (New York: Harper Torchbooks, 1967), p. 29.
[22] Quoted in Chester Holcombe, *The Real Chinese Question* (New York: Dodd, Mead, 1900), p. 224.

technical and scientific work for the Court in the time-honored tradition of alien service within the realm of Chinese civilization. However, the arrival in 1793 of a British diplomatic mission, headed by Lord Macartney, in the pursuit of diplomatic representation and free trade, was the harbinger of an approaching confrontation between two diametrically opposed self-images. Just as the Europeans were barbarians in the Chinese view because they did not embrace Chinese civilization or language, so were the Chinese heathens in European eyes because they did not accept Christianity.

The response of the Ch'ing Court to the challenge posed by the Macartney Mission shows the persistence of the Sinocentric image of world order in the early phase of Sino-Western confrontation. The logic of Lord Macartney's request for diplomatic representation at Peking completely escaped Emperor Ch'ien Lung (1736-95). That the Chinese image of world order was no more than an outward projection of a self-image is also revealed in a most illuminating way in the emperor's condescending edict to King George III and deserves quotation at length:

> You, O King, are so inclined toward our civilization that you have sent a special envoy across the seas to bring to our Court your memorial of congratulations on the occasion of my birthday and to present your native products as an expression of your thoughtfulness. . . .
>
> As to the request made in your memorial, O King, to send one of your nationals to stay at the Celestial Court to take care of your country's trade with China, this is not in harmony with the state system of our dynasty and will definitely not be permitted. Traditionally people of the European nations who wished to render some service under the Celestial Court have been permitted to come to the capital. But after their arrival they are obliged to wear Chinese court costumes, are placed in a certain residence, and are never allowed to return to their own countries. This is the established rule of the Celestial Dynasty with which presumably you, O King, are familiar. Now you, O King, wish to send one of your nationals to live in the capital, but he is not like the Europeans, who come to Peking as Chinese employees, live there and never return home again, nor can he be allowed to go and come and maintain any correspondence. This is indeed a useless undertaking.
>
> . . . As a matter of fact, the virtue and prestige of the Celestial Dynasty having spread far and wide, the kings of the myriad nations come by land and sea with all sorts of precious things. Consequently there is nothing we lack, as your principal envoy and

others have themselves observed. We have never set much store on strange or ingenious objects, nor do we need any more of your country's manufactures. . . .[23]

The stage was set for confrontation as an increasing number of Westerners began to arrive in China in the wake of the Macartney Mission. Inevitably, the two separate "worlds," with two distinct claims of superiority based on two different culture systems, collided head-on. Each had developed within its orbit an acceptable standard for private and public action. Each wanted to apply its own world view in entering into relations with the other because each believed its own culture infinitely superior. "Are we not," asked a veteran China missionary from Great Britain, "much superior to them [the Chinese]? Are we not more manly, more intelligent, more skillful, more human, more civilized, nay, are we not more estimable in every way? Yes, according to our way of thinking. No, *emphatically* no, according to theirs. And it would be nearly as difficult for us to alter our opinion on the subject as it is for them to alter theirs."[24] There was, in short, no meeting of minds between the West and China, and therein lay the root of the conflict. For the conflict between the two diametrically opposed images of world order was bound to be expressed in a conflict of diplomatic action. It only needed an opportune moment and a plausible excuse for the stronger party to impose its standard and will upon the weaker one.

The institutional arrangement of the Sino-Western relationship prior to the Opium War (1839-42) was the so-called Canton Co-hong System. It was a latter-day version of the tribute system as applied to the maritime traders of the West. According to this arrangement, the Western powers participating in Canton trade were classified as tributary states under the jurisdiction of the reception department of the Board of Rites (*Li-pu*). They were socially, commercially, and culturally isolated within the area of the thirteen factories at Canton and they were denied any direct communication with the Ch'ing Court. They could communicate with the provincial authorities only through the mediation of Hong merchants who were privileged to handle foreign trade, and even this only in the form of a petition symbolizing their inferior status.

The management of Western traders under the Canton Co-hong System became increasingly difficult, however. First, because of its

[23] Ssu-yü Teng and John K. Fairbank, *China's Response to the West: A Documentary Survey 1839-1923* (New York: Atheneum, 1963), p. 19.
[24] A letter of Griffith John to the London Missionary Society, *c.* 1869, in R. Wardlaw Thompson, ed., *Griffith John, The Story of Fifty Years in China* (New York: A. C. Armstrong and Son, 1906), p. 254.

distant bases and the mobility of European traders, maritime trade was less subject to Chinese control than the land trade carried on by the tributary states of Asia. Second, its volume and value increased rapidly, inviting more and more participation by Chinese merchants. Finally, Western traders challenged not only the operational aspects but also the philosophical premises of the tribute system.

Yet trade and tribute were always interconnected in the traditional Chinese image of world order, requiring a constant symmetrical balance between the two. That is, the barbarian desire for trade was balanced by the Chinese desire to control relations with other states within the framework of the Chinese world order. In Chinese official thinking, international trade was seldom considered as a means of national enrichment. This point of view still prevailed on the eve of the first Anglo-Chinese war. The Western barbarians could not get along a single day without Chinese tea and rhubarb, Commissioner Lin Tse-hsü bluntly advised Queen Victoria in 1839, whereas foreign articles entering China "can only be used as toys."[25]

It is against this background that we should view the Opium War. For the Chinese, the issue was simple enough: the opium traffic was morally unjustifiable, legally indefensible, and economically detrimental because of the drain of specie. For the British, however, the opium issue was an incident growing out of the institutional anomaly of the Canton Co-hong System. Since the system was commercially restrictive, administratively frustrating, and diplomatically humiliating for them, the only logical solution was to eliminate it. Viewed in this light, Commissioner Lin's drastic policy in suppressing the opium traffic gave the British a pretext to restructure their relations with China through a military showdown.

From the Tribute System to the Treaty System

The defeat suffered by China in the Opium War ushered in a new era of Sino-Western relations. The age-old tribute system was dealt a heavy blow, and a new treaty system was inaugurated by four "peace treaties" signed between China and the Western powers. Taken together, these treaties established a general framework for commercial and diplomatic relations between China and the West. The more important treaty provisions merit special attention. First, maritime trade was liberalized and expanded by abolishing the monopoly of the Co-hong merchants and opening four additional treaty ports as means of communication between the Chinese authorities and the Western

[25] For Commissioner Lin Tse-hsü's advice to Queen Victoria, see Teng and Fairbank, *China's Response to the West*, pp. 24-28.

traders. As a result, indirect communication gave way to direct communication to be carried out on an equal footing.[26] In addition, the Ch'ing government improvised an institutional arrangement known as the Canton Viceroy System or the Imperial Commissioner System to cope with postwar foreign relations. Under this system, the governor-general of Kwangtung and Kwangsi provinces, residing in Canton, was supposed to conduct foreign affairs, with the title of imperial commissioner.

However, the time-tested tribute system was abolished only in theory. Its theoretical replacement by the treaty system was not accompanied by any discernible change in the Chinese image of world order. The ensuing Sino-Western conflicts in the interwar period of the 1840s and 1850s, which were eventually resolved by the Arrow War of 1856-1858 and the allied military expedition to Peking in 1860, dramatized the Chinese response to the Western challenge; the period also highlighted the traditional Chinese image of world order on trial. Peace treaties signed under the pressure of *force majeure* in the wake of the Opium War seldom lived up to their promise in practice. While Ch'ing officials were absorbed in reviving and embellishing ancient Chinese strategies toward the barbarians in a desperate attempt to rescue the tribute system, the Western treaty powers became more determined than ever to open up the Middle Kingdom.

The crushing defeat of China in her first military confrontation with the West failed to modify the Sinocentric image of outlandish barbarians. On the contrary, the British resort to force reaffirmed it. The confidential diplomatic documents, *Ch'ing-tai ch'ou-pan i-wu shih-mo* (The Complete Account of the Management of Barbarian Affairs under the Ch'ing Dynasty)[27]—often shortened to *I-wu shih-mo*—give a clear picture of the Ch'ing official mentality. The use of the derogatory terminology "barbarians" or "barbarian affairs"—even the colloquial word "foreign devil" (*fan-kuei*)—became commonplace in intrabureaucratic communications. The Western traders were called "barbarian merchants," while the Western consuls and ministers were referred to as "barbarian chieftains."[28] Similarly, Chinese officialdom

[26] See Article XI of the British Treaty of Nanking, Article XXX of the American Treaty of Wanghia, and Article XXXIII of the French Treaty of Whampoa, in William F. Mayers, ed., *Treaties between the Empire of China and Foreign Powers* (Shanghai: Kelley and Walsh, 1906).

[27] *Ch'ing-tai ch'ou-pan i-wu shih-mo* (Peiping: Palace Museum, 1930). Photolithograph of the original compilation. 80 *chüan* for the later Tao-kuang period, 1836-50 (hereafter cited as *IWSM-TK*), 80 *chüan* for the Hsien-feng period, 1851-61 (hereafter cited as *IWSM-HF*), and 100 *chüan* for the T'ung-chih period, 1862-74 (hereafter cited as *IWSM-TC*). As these documents were not originally meant to be published, their value is indisputable for the study of the traditional Chinese image of world order.

[28] For a clarification of terminological practice along this line, see a statement

31

was scornful of the use of the imperial pronoun *chen* for the president of the United States.[29] As late as 1858, the Grand Secretariat in its official edict referred to Imperial Commissioner Yeh Ming-ch'en at Canton as "Imperial Commissioner in charge of barbarian affairs" (*Ch' in-ch'ai ta-ch'en pan-li i-wu*).[30] This type of traditional terminological practice continued until 1861.

At the root of the Ch'ing officials' thinking lay a tenacious refusal to meet the Western challenge except in traditional terms, because "the laws of the Heavenly Court, being firmly established, cannot suffer any slightest change."[31] The benevolence of the emperor toward both Chinese and foreigners is stressed repeatedly, for he "rules by soothing those who obey and chastises those who rebel."[32] In granting readily the American demand for a most-favored-nation treatment in the wake of the British Treaty of Nanking, the Chinese also revived the old concept of *lai-hua*, holding as they did that an equal and benevolent treatment of barbarians would "encourage them with admiration and gratitude and further strengthen their desire in turning toward [our] civilization."[33] Behind the facade of such a benevolent posture lay a genuine apprehension that exposure of the populace to the Westerners and their ideas might pollute China's ideological purity and thus undermine the Confucian social order.[34] The contemptuous characterization of the Westerners as barbarians thus served as a weapon to arouse hostile sentiments of the populace against Western influence in China.[35]

Confucian culture added a human dimension to the conduct of Ch'ing diplomacy. The long and detailed descriptions of the characters and personalities of Western diplomats in the *I-wu shih-mo*[36] stem from the Confucian concept of viewing all forms of social relations as highly interpersonal affairs. As applied to diplomacy, it was assumed that a correct understandnig of the characters of individual diplomats was the basis for formulating diplomatic strategy. Ch'ing officials

---

made by Ho Kuei-ch'ing, governor of Liang-chiang in 1858 in *IWSM-HF*, 31:18a, 9-18b, 2.

[29] *Ibid.*, 13:16b, 7.

[30] *Ibid.*, 17:4b, 9.

[31] *IWSM-TK*, 63:30a, 4.

[32] *Ibid.*, 24:36b, 8.

[33] *Ibid.*, 72:34b, 2-3.

[34] For elaboration of this thesis, see Masataka Banno, "Gaikō kōshō ni okeru Shinmatsu kanjin no kōdō yōshiki—1854-nen no jōyaku kaisei kōshō o chūshin to suru ichikōsatu" [Behavior of Mandarins as Diplomats in the late Ch'ing Period—With Special Reference to the Treaty Revision Negotiations of 1854], *Kokusaihō Gaikō Zasshi* [The Journal of International Law and Diplomacy] 48 (October 1949), Part I, 39-40.

[35] See *IWSM-HF*, 22:39b, 3-8.

[36] For a sample of these characterizations of Western diplomats, see *IWSM-HF*, 9:39b; 69:30a; 71:11a-b; *IWSM-TK*, 23:33b.

thought that they had to understand and satisfy individual Western diplomats in order to satisfy the nations that they represented. Conversely, the Ch'ing officials themselves became more easily influenced by the personalities of the Western diplomats involved than by the views they put forth. Hence what the officials were willing to concede to someone whom they found personally attractive could be emphatically denied to another who had failed to make a favorable impression.[37]

Inevitably, the Ch'ing officials' intellectual energies were taken up not with formulation of a long-term policy but with efforts to define the characters of the new barbarians in order to set up suitable temporizing schemes. To their surprise, however, they discovered that the character of the Western barbarians was by no means uniform: the English and French were unreasonable and uncontrollable; the Russians and Americans were amiable but too eager to seek profit.[38] This introduced some confusion into Ch'ing diplomacy. What followed was not a new strategy but an alternating zigzag from one traditional barbarian strategy, *chi-mi* (an appeasement policy of getting the barbarians under control through concessions) to another, *I-i chih-i* (using barbarians to control barbarians, the divide-and-rule strategy of Western diplomatic practice).[39] The assumption implicit in such an approach was that there was no essential difference between the traditional land barbarians and the new "sea barbarians"; hence the time-tested strategies were thought to be adequate to cope with the new challenge.

In addition, the Ch'ing philosophy of external affairs placed special stress upon the personal accountability of individual diplomats. Each diplomat who was supposedly a barbarian specialist was held responsible for the consequences of his diplomacy. As a result, the practice · developed of personally rewarding or punishing individual barbarian specialists in terms of their success or failure in diplomatic negotiations. It is instructive to note in this connection that few barbarian

---

[37] I have developed this theme elsewhere. See Samuel S. Kim, "The Influence of Personality in Sino-Western Relations," *Asian Profile* 3 (June 1975), 265-81. In a different time framework, Wolfgang Franke argues the same point. See Franke, *China and the West*, pp. 53-54.

[38] *IWSM-HF*, 8:21a; 21:38a.

[39] For the strategy of *chi-mi*, see John K. Fairbank, *Trade and Diplomacy on the China Coast: The Opening of the Treaty Ports, 1842-1854* (Cambridge, Mass.: Harvard University Press, 1954), Vol. I, p. 94. For the strategy of *I-i chih-i*, see *IWSM-HF*, 19:2a, 20:7b; *IWSM-TK*, 24:37a. The PRC historian Hu Sheng argues that what the Ch'ing officials did during the transitional period was to suppress the people, on the one hand, and to appease the foreigners, on the other. See Hu Sheng, *Ti-kuo chu-i yü chung-kuo cheng-chih* [Imperialism and Chinese Politics] (Peking: Jen-min ch'u-pan she, 1952), p. 10.

specialists fared well during the transitional period: Lin Tse-hsü was banished to Ili; Ch'i-ying was executed; Ch'i-shan was cashiered in disgrace; and Yeh Ming-ch'en was captured and shipped to Calcutta by the British. Such practices lasted until the 1860s, when such provincial leaders as Tseng Kuo-fan and Li Hung-chang became too powerful to be easily controlled by the Court.

The mechanism of personal accountability, while serving as a system of centralized control, in effect deprived the provincial authorities of diplomatic initiative and maneuverability. Since their standing was entirely at the mercy of the Peking Court, they became more sensitive to the caprices of the Court than to the objective demands of a given situation.[40] They would frequently memorialize to the throne what they believed the emperor wanted to hear rather than what he needed to hear, confiding their true feelings only in their most trusted friends.

The Canton Viceroy System thus contained an element of self-defeat. The imperial commissioner and other provincial officials charged with foreign affairs were denied the freedom of action that they needed in order to carry out their task effectively. The inevitable result was that the imperial commissioner operated not as a representative of the central government but as a mediator between two contending forces, the Peking Court and the Western treaty powers. Caught between reactionary orders from the Court and radical demands from the Western merchants and envoys, provincial officials evaded the main problem by presenting to the throne stereotyped memorials with such banal statements as "It is hard to estimate the foreign situations."[41]

At the same time, they made ingenious efforts to avoid any contact with Western envoys. (Yeh Ming-ch'en, the imperial commissioner at Canton (1848-58), for example, refused to meet with the American representatives, Humphrey Marshall in 1852, Robert M. McLane in 1856, and William B. Reed in 1857, and British representative Sir John Bowring in 1854, either on the pretext that his time was completely occupied in military operations or that there was no appropriate place to meet them.) If such ruses failed, they would either pigeonhole communications or procrastinate on the issues brought to their attention. Indeed, what infuriated Western envoys was not so much definite repudiation as indefinite procrastination on a host of issues that they felt required immediate settlement. Some viceroys even used "officers inferior to themselves, at times down to personal servants, in negotiating with foreign diplomats."[42]

[40] Banno, "Gaikō kōshō ni okeru Shinmatsu kanjin no kōdō yōshiki," p. 65.
[41] *Ibid.*, p. 52.
[42] Levi, *Modern China's Foreign Policy*, pp. 6-7.

These conditions became not only the source of contradictory policy for China but also the excuse for arbitrary use of force on the part of the Western powers. Denied any intercourse with the central government and subjected to all manner of delaying and derogatory devices by the provincial authorities, the Western powers lost no time in using gunboats at the orders of consular officers to remedy their grievances in the treaty ports. Thus, diplomacy gave way to force because, as one contemporary observer noted, "too often irregularities committed, now by the foreigners, now by the natives, caused troubles which were not referred to Peking until the use of force had made diplomatic action almost impossible."[43] Such was the genesis of the so-called gunboat diplomacy that characterized Western policy in China during much of this transitional period.

However, the conviction gradually grew among Westerners that the source of all troubles was in the anomalous mode of conducting diplomatic affairs at the periphery rather than at the center of the Ch'ing government, and that direct contact and communication with the Peking Court must be established as a prerequisite to normal relations.[44] Demand for such direct contact, whether for the enhancement of trade or for diplomatic prestige, soon became universal among contemporary foreign consuls, merchants, and journalists as well as diplomatic representatives. It was natural that these groups should be so united, for all of them had been subjected to what they regarded as humiliating treatment by the provincial authorities. The opening of Peking, the Forbidden City, to permanent diplomatic representation was seen to be "the sovereign cure for all the ills of which we [the Westerners] had to complain."[45] Yet direct contact was what the Court most feared and therefore was most determined to resist.

It is against this background that we should view two incidents in 1856—the hauling down of the British flag on a lorcha (a small craft with a Chinese hull and a foreign rig), the *Arrow*, and the murder of Père Chapdelaine, a French Catholic missionary, in Kwangsi province —which touched off the Arrow War. It would be shortsighted, however, to explain this second Anglo-Chinese war, in which France also joined, in terms of the two incidents alone, for they were surface symptoms, not underlying causes, of the war. It might be argued that

[43] Raphael Pumpelly, "Western Policy in China," *The North American Review* 106 (April 1868), 598.

[44] See Lord Elgin's dispatch of July 12, 1858, to Lord Malmesbury in Great Britain, *Parliamentary Papers* (Blue Books, hereafter cited as *BPP*), 1859, Vol. XXXIII [2571], *Correspondence relative to the Earl of Elgin's Special Missions to China and Japan, 1857-1859*, 346.

[45] [Baron] A. B. Freeman-Mitford, *The Attaché at Peking* (London: Macmillan, 1900), p. xliv.

the war had actually been brewing since the conclusion of the First Treaty Settlement in the early 1840s, following the Opium War. Each passing year added combustible elements to tense relations until the situation reached a breaking point in 1857.

China suffered once again a humiliating defeat. Superior military forces subdued Ch'ing resistance and the city of Canton was occupied by the joint Anglo-French expeditionary forces. A series of peace treaties signed at Tientsin with Great Britain, France, Russia, and the United States constituted the Second Treaty Settlement.[46] The signing of the Tientsin treaties, however, opened a Pandora's box for the traditional Chinese image of world order. Most obnoxious of all was the opening of the Forbidden City to permanent residence by foreign diplomatic representatives.

The intensity of Ch'ing opposition to the issue of diplomatic representation can be seen in the abortive scheme known as the Secret Plan.[47] Its main purpose was to repudiate or at least to revise the four most offensive clauses in the British Tientsin Treaty concerning permanent diplomatic residence in Peking (Articles II, III, IV, and V), the opening of the Great River to trade (Article X), travel into the interior (Article IX), and indemnification for military expenses and occupation of Canton until the amount had been paid in full (a separate article). In return, China would exempt the English barbarians from all customs duties. This plan shows clearly the somewhat peculiar Chinese concept of national interest that prevailed in the mid-nineteenth century even in the face of foreign encroachment. Concessions that became burning nationalistic issues in the twentieth century— such as extraterritoriality, tariff restrictions, and the most-favored-nation treatment—were granted readily, while such ceremonial matters as diplomatic accreditation or audience without the kowtow were jealously guarded. Although the Secret Plan was never officially submitted to the British, the Ch'ing plea was so strong that London decided to shelve the right to permanent diplomatic representation in Peking for the time being.[48]

A compromise on the resident minister issue as well as on other important matters might still have been possible had not another unfortunate incident occurred on June 25, 1859, when the ratification of the Tientsin Treaties was to be exchanged. The Ch'ing Court executed

[46] For the texts of these treaties, see Mayers, ed., *Treaties*, pp. 7-21, 59-75, 84-95, 100-111.

[47] The whole episode of the Secret Plan was not known until 1930 when the *I-wu shih-mo* was discovered. For details of the Plan, see *IWSM-HF*, 30-31.

[48] See *BPP*, 1859, Vol. XXXIII [2571], 411-12, 484-85. See also *IWSM-HF*, 31:49-51; 32:1-4, 15-16; 36:12-14.

36

with a self-confidence born of ignorance the bold stratagem of ambushing the allied envoys who were approaching the capital to complete the exchange of treaty ratification. In the surprise attack and ensuing hostilities at Taku, the allied forces suffered a setback and retreated in defeat. The Court, still dominated by the war party, rejoiced over the victory, without realizing that this had set the stage for a joint Anglo-French expedition to Peking.

Thus, what could have been a peaceful diplomatic procession was eventually transformed into a joint military expedition to Peking in 1860.[49] The reinforced Anglo-French troops launched an all-out military campaign, shooting their way to the capital, burning the Summer Palace (Yüan-ming-yüan), forcing the emperor to flee to Jehol, and securing confirmation of all their previous demands and others as well with the ratification of the Tientsin Treaties and the signing of the Peking Conventions in the fall of 1860. The last fortress of the Chinese world order thus crumbled at the point of Western bayonets.

The closing of the year 1860 marked a significant turning point in traditional Chinese diplomacy. The conclusion of the Tientsin Treaties and the Peking Conventions represented, in effect, a whimpering cry of the tribute system vis-à-vis the Western powers. In spite of the First Treaty Settlement and of sufficient military power to enforce it on the part of the West, Ch'ing officials of the transitional period continued to wage a desperate and doomed struggle to deal with the West in the framework of the Sinic system of international relations.

In the end, however, China paid a heavy price for this evasion of reality: a series of major concessions had to be made, each one followed by another more demanding and detrimental to her traditional image. The net effect of all the concessions extracted by the treaty powers amounted to an "unequal treaty system," which China was unable to change until 1943. It is ironic, then, that China's struggle to preserve her hierarchical system of world order as expressed in the tribute system should have ended with her acceptance of the unequal treaty system imposed by the West. China's response to the West should not be viewed within the framework of the international system. The Sino-Western confrontation was no less than a system-to-system conflict between two diametrically opposed images of world order. The Second Treaty Settlement represented the absorption of the Sinic system of international relations into the Eurocentric system of international relations.

---

[49] The standard work on the Anglo-French expedition still remains that of Henri Cordier, *L'expédition de Chine de 1860: histoire diplomatique, notes et documents* (Paris: F. Alcan, 1906).

THE DEMISE OF THE TRADITIONAL CHINESE WORLD ORDER

The formal acceptance by China of direct diplomatic intercourse with the Western powers in 1860 marks the end of the long journey China was forced to take, departing at first with resistance and finally with great reluctance from the tribute system. This continued vestigially until 1894 with Korea, but was really destroyed beyond repair in 1860 as far as Sino-Western relations were concerned. In the face of the imminent establishment of permanent diplomatic representation by the Western treaty powers, Prince Kung and his colleagues (Kuei-liang and Wen-hsiang) sent an epoch-making memorial to the throne on January 13, 1861, proposing the establishment of "an office for the general management of the affairs of all nations" (*tsung-li ko-kuo shih-wu ya-men*).[50] On January 20, 1861, the emperor issued an edict approving the establishment in the capital of "an office for the general management of the trade affairs of all nations" (*tsung-li ko-kuo t'ung-shang shih-wu ya-men*)—commonly shortened to the Tsungli Yamen or the Yamen.[51] The insertion of the word "*t'ung-shang*" (trade) in the name of the new institution shows the persistence of the Sinocentric image of world order, however. Thus, the establishment of the Tsungli Yamen represents a first halting step in China's entry into the family of nations. The replacement of the Tsungli Yamen by a full-fledged Ministry of Foreign Affairs (Wai-wu Pu) did not come about until 1901, when it was required by the Boxer Protocol.

Faced with the twin dangers of the internal disorder created by the Taiping Rebellion (1850-64) and the external menace posed by the West, a recurrence of the traditional *bête noire* (*nei-luan wai-huan*) of dynastic survival, China began a concerted campaign to put her own house in order under the so-called self-strengthening (*tzu-ch'iang*) movement in the early 1860s.[52] Protected for the time being by the Co-operative Policy of the Western treaty powers under the sympathetic and enlightened leadership of Anson Burlingame, the first American resident minister (1861-67), and Sir Frederick Bruce, the first British resident minister,[53] the Ch'ing Court was encouraged to initiate a series of self-strengthening reform measures at her own pace and on her own terms. As a result, some important reforms were adopted in

---

[50] *IWSM-HF*, 71:19-20.　　　　[51] *Ibid.*, 72:1-3.

[52] However, Prince Kung took the position that the internal disorder created by the Taiping rebels posed a greater evil than the foreign menace. Accordingly, he memorialized to the throne that the suppression of the Taiping rebellion should take top priority. See *IWSM-HF*, 71:18.

[53] For the inauguration of the Co-operative Policy and the roles played by Burlingame and Bruce, see my "Burlingame and the Inauguration of the Co-operative Policy," *Modern Asian Studies* 5 (October 1971), 337-54.

diplomatic, fiscal, educational, and military fields with the help of an increasing number of Western experts.[54]

By means of a curious cooperative interplay between the Sinicized "barbarians"—Robert Hart and Anson Burlingame, to cite two outstanding examples—and the Westernized members of the Tsungli Yamen, China began to discuss sending diplomatic missions abroad in the mid-1860s. The elements of change and continuity in the traditional Chinese image of world order are reflected in this groping preparation for diplomatic representation abroad. The Confucian preoccupation with proper conduct (li) surfaces once again in the debate about the character of the diplomat to be sent abroad. Feng Kuei-fen, a prominent scholar of Soochow, who was responsible for the celebrated term tzu-ch'iang (self-strengthening), advocated in the early 1860s the study of Western languages so as to do away with the service of the "Canton-style linguists," who were boorish in nature, shallow in knowledge, and mean in moral principles.[55] In the secret correspondence between the Tsungli Yamen and the leading officials of China in 1867 on major foreign policy issues, we sense an even greater apprehension about the possible disgrace that might result from sending men of dubious character as envoys abroad.[56]

The consensus in this grand secret debate on foreign policy in the 1860s was that men of experience, integrity, scholarship, and courage should be sent abroad, if and when occasion arose. Li Han-chang, governor of Kiangsi, who was concurrently acting as governor-general of Hupeh and Hunan, added to those qualifications the knowledge of foreign languages and the ability to carry on debate effectively.[57] Tso Tsung-t'ang, governor-general of Fukien and Chekiang, who was one of the first proponents of a modern Chinese navy, cautioned against the Cantonese, who, in spite of their knowledge of Western language and customs, were too "unsteady, deceptive and quarrelsome" for diplomatic service.[58] In requesting the appointment of Anson Burlingame to head China's first diplomatic mission abroad—better known as the Burlingame Mission—Prince Kung candidly admitted that there existed no native who could act in such a capacity. Burlingame possessed, he asserted, a combination of experience, knowledge, eloquence, and personal virtues, all of which uniquely fitted him to represent China in the West.[59]

[54] For a comprehensive treatment of this theme, see Wright, *The Last Stand of Chinese Conservatism, passim.*
[55] Teng and Fairbank, *China's Response to the West*, p. 51.
[56] See *IWSM-TC*, 50:32a-32b; 51:21a-21b; 52:19b-20a, 26b-27a, 32b-33b.
[57] *Ibid.*, 52:32b-33b.   [58] *Ibid.*, 51:21a-21b.
[59] *Ibid.*, 51:27a.

The appointment of an American barbarian to head the first Chinese diplomatic mission abroad highlights the existence, at one and the same time, both change and continuity in the Chinese image of world order. It also shows the extent to which personal or human factors dominated the thought and action of Ch'ing officials in their conduct of foreign affairs. Confucian ideology assumed that human nature was basically good and malleable, including barbarian nature. This aspect of traditional Chinese thought was not fully comprehended by many foreigners in China, but for a few, like Burlingame, Robert Hart, and General Frederick Ward (an American who organized, trained, and commanded the famous Chinese brigade known as the "Ever Victorious Army" against the Taiping forces), it provided an opportunity to exert extraordinary personal influence in Ch'ing politics.[60] Whether the Burlingame Mission merely represented a replay of the traditional Chinese strategy of using barbarians to control barbarians or was, in

[60] For Burlingame's extraordinary personal influence on the Tsungli Yamen, see my "America's First Minister to China: Anson Burlingame and the Tsungli Yamen," *The Maryland Historian* 3 (Fall 1972), 87-104. Robert Hart served nearly a half century as head of the Chinese Maritime Customs Administration and was undoubtedly one of the most influential Western figures in nineteenth-century Ch'ing politics. In his letter to Hart informing the latter of his appointment, Prince stated: "Your prudence, tact, and experience are known to all, both Chinese and foreign, and it will behoove you to be still more careful and diligent, so as to justify your present appointment." Prince Kung to Hart as enclosure 3 in Bruce to Russell, No. 25, Peking, November 27, 1863, *BPP*, 1864 [3271], p. 36. For the unprecedented honors the Ch'ing government posthumously bestowed upon General Ward when he died in September 1862 in the course of his service for the Ch'ing "Ever Victorious Army," see the *North China Herald*, January 3, 1863; March 15, 1877. See also Burlingame to Seward, No. 27, Peking, October 27, 1862, National Archives, Diplomatic Despatches, China, XX.

In a dispatch dated May 19, 1870, the American Minister Frederick F. Low describes the Ch'ing reaction to the sudden death of Anson Burlingame at St. Petersburg in the following terms: "It is a matter of sincere gratification to know that the difficult duties entrusted to Mr. Burlingame had been performed to the entire satisfaction of the Emperor and his advisers; and that his services are acknowledged in a manner evincing great respect, gratitude, and liberality. In this connection I would observe that the honorary title of the first rank, conferred by the Emperor places the name of Mr. Burlingame on a par with those of the four members of the Privy Council, and is one grade higher than that bestowed upon presidents of the Boards and members of the Foreign Office [the Tsungli Yamen]. It is the highest rank possible to be given any one, either living or dead, outside of the royal family.

A posthumous title conferred directly by the emperor is considered by the Chinese the highest mark of respect that can be shown to the memory of a deceased public officer, as the decree granting it becomes a part of the official records of the Empire, which will perpetuate the name and fame of the deceased longer than statues or monuments." Low to Fish, No. 6, Peking, May 19, 1870, National Archives, Diplomatic Despatches, China, XXVIII.

The PRC historian Hu Sheng singles out Burlingame, Bruce, Hart, and Alcock (Bruce's successor) as having exerted considerable influence on Ch'ing politics. See *Ti-kuo chu-i yü chung-kuo cheng-chih*, pp. 41-42, 45-46.

fact, a genuine and major departure from the traditional Chinese world is now hard to determine, because the mission ended abruptly with Burlingame's sudden death in the spring of 1870 at St. Petersburg. It was not until 1877 that Chinese diplomatic missions really began to function abroad.

In the end, however, the self-strengthening movement failed because the requirements for an effective response to Western encroachment ran counter to the requirements of preserving the Confucian internal order.[61] The ideological disruption created by Western imperialism required a revolutionary response, but the self-strengthening reformers were no more than "realistic" conservatives who wanted to borrow Western science and technology, especially "strong warships and efficient guns," to preserve the Confucian order. All the successive reform measures in economic, administrative, and constitutional matters during the last quarter of the nineteenth century also failed because what China needed was a transformation not only in institutions but, more importantly, in ideology. Such an ideological transformation did not come about until China was thoroughly humiliated by an Asian neighbor in the Sino-Japanese War of 1894-95. The vestigial influence of the traditional Chinese image of world order was finally shattered beyond recall. And, around the turn of the century, a group of revolutionaries began to emerge that would lead the way to national salvation.

The extent to which the traditional Chinese view of world order was subjected to the onslaught of the West from the Opium War down to the Treaty of Versailles is reflected in the unequal treaty system. Sun Yat-sen characterized China under the unequal treaty system as a "hypo-colony," which is a grade worse than a semicolony because of the multiple control and exploitation exercised by the imperial powers.[62] Although China's territorial losses are difficult to pinpoint, given the concentric and cultural zonation of the traditional Chinese world, the perceptions of Chinese nationalists on both sides of the ideological polarization are revealing. Sun Yat-sen, Chiang Kai-shek, and Mao Tse-tung all advanced rather expansive irredentist claims.[63] It is even

[61] This is the main thesis of Mary Wright's book, *The Last Stand of Chinese Conservatism*.

[62] Sun Yat-sen, *San Min Chu I: The Three Principles of the People*, trans. Frank W. Price (Shanghai: Commercial Press, 1932), p. 39.

[63] Sun Yat-sen's list of lost Chinese territories includes the following: Port Arthur, Dairen, Kowloon, Korea, Taiwan, the Pescadores, Burma, Annam, Ryūkyū Islands, Siam, Borneo, the Sulu Archipelago, Java, Ceylon, Nepal, Bhutan, the Amur and Ussuri river basins; the areas north of the Ili, Khokand, Amur rivers. Sun Yat-sen then declares: "In its age of greatest power the territory of the Chinese Empire was very large, extending northward to the north of the Amur, southward to the south of the Himalayas, eastward to the China Sea, westward to the T'sung Lin." Likewise, Chiang Kai-shek wrote: "The memory of the

41

FIGURE 1.1. A PRC Image of China's Territorial Losses.

KEY TO FIGURE 1.1.

Territory	Recipient	Year
Assam [North-East Frontier]	England	1826
The Great Northeast [Left Bank of Amur River]	Russia	1858
The Great Northeast [Maritime Province]	Russia	1860
The Great Northwest [Tashkent Area]	Russia	1864
Bhutan (Went to England after "independence" in 1865)	England	1865
Liu-ch'iu Archipelago [Ryukyu Islands]	Japan	1879
Annam [Vietnam, Laos, and Cambodia]	France	1885
Burma	England	1886
Sikkim	England	1889
Malaya	England	1895
Taiwan and P'eng-hu Archipelago [Pescadores]	Japan	1895
Korea (Became "independent" in 1895 and annexed by Japan in 1910)	Japan	1895
Pamirs [Ladakh Area] (Secretly divided between England and Russia in 1896)	England and Russia	1896
Nepal (Went to England after "independence" in 1898)	England	1898
Thailand (Declared "independent" under joint Anglo-French control in 1904)	England and France	1904
Andaman Archipelago [Andaman Islands]	England	no date
Sulu Archipelago	England	no date
Region where the British committed aggression	England?	no date
Sakhalin (Divided between Russia and Japan)	Russia and Japan	no date

more instructive for our purposes to examine the perception of the Chinese communists concerning the lost territories since they captured power in 1949. Figure 1.1, which was published in Peking in 1954, was perhaps designed merely to convey the PRC's sense of historical grievance vis-à-vis the imperialist West and Japan. Nonetheless, it does tend to give some credence to the Soviet accusation that the PRC made expansionistic and irredentist claims in Asia. The annotations in the nineteen boxes on the map are translated and arranged in chronological order opposite Figure 1.1. It is particularly worth noting that the map categorized such Asian states as Korea, Nepal, Sikkim, Bhutan, Burma, Malaya, Thailand, Indochina, Sulu Archipelago, and Ryūkyū islands under the rubric of *"Chinese* territories taken by imperialism [imperialists]" during the "old democratic revolutionary period (1840-1919)," while leaving out Hong Kong and Macao.[64]

LEGACIES OF THE TRADITIONAL CHINESE WORLD ORDER

The foregoing analysis, even though dealing largely with the nineteenth century, when a succession of historic confrontations between Confucian China and the imperial West took place, provides a basis for outlining a few conceptual and operational legacies of the traditional Chinese world order. First of all, it was Sinocentric in scope and

---

disastrous loss of Ryūkyū [Liuch'iu Islands], Hong Kong, Formosa, the Pescadores, Indo-China, Burma, and Korea was still fresh, while the final calamity of the partitioning of the whole country was impending."

However, Mao Tse-tung's irredentist claims appear to be less sweeping. In an interview with Edgar Snow on July 16, 1936, Mao stated: "It is the immediate task of China to regain all our lost territories, not merely to defend our sovereignty below the Great Wall. This means that Manchuria must be regained. We do not, however, include Korea, formerly a Chinese colony, but when we have re-established the independence of the lost territories of China, and if the Koreans wish to break away from the chains of Japanese imperialism, we will extend them our enthusiastic help in their struggle for independence. The same applies for Formosa. As for Inner Mongolia, which is populated by both Chinese and Mongolians, we will struggle to drive Japan from there and help Inner Mongolia to establish an autonomous State." In a text entitled *The Chinese Revolution and the Chinese Communist Party*, written in the winter of 1939, Mao presents a long list of exploitations of China by the imperialist powers but seems deliberately vague on his irredentist claims, as seen in this statement: "After defeating China in war, they [the imperialist powers] not only occupied many neighbouring countries formerly under her protection, but seized or 'leased' parts of her territory. For instance, Japan occupied Taiwan and the Penghu Islands and 'leased' Kwangchowwan. In addition to annexing territory, they exacted huge indemnities. Thus heavy blows were struck at China's huge feudal empire." For the citations above, see respectively the following: Sun Yat-sen, *San Min Chu I*, pp. 33-35, 35; Chiang Kai-shek, *China's Destiny* (New York: Roy Publishers, 1947), p. 58; Edgar Snow, *Red Star Over China* (New York: Grove Press, 1961; originally published in 1938), p. 96; *SW*, II, p. 311.
[64] Emphasis added.

44

orientation. As elaborated earlier, China's self-image reproduced itself on a concentrically larger scale as China's image of a world order. There was no link between domestic and foreign policy in traditional China, since there was no foreign policy in the contemporary sense of the term. The management of external affairs was handled for centuries by the Board of Rites. The Tsungli Yamen, while functioning as a centralized office of foreign affairs, was nonetheless a suborgan of the Grand Council. Its members were composed of officials who had their principal posts elsewhere in the government. Thus, domestic and foreign affairs in Ch'ing politics were coterminous both conceptually and institutionally.

The traditional Chinese world order suffered from a chronic gap between policy pronouncement and policy performance. This phenomenon may be explained by the fact that the Chinese image of world order was richer in cultural symbolism than in political dynamics. It was more passive than active, more defensive than imperialist, and more rhetorical than real. On the whole, the Chinese image lacked a dynamic and aggressive imperative to expand and impose its will upon recalcitrant non-Chinese states. There was no concerted drive, for example, to bring Japan back into the tributary relationship. However, if any non-Chinese states wanted to enter into the orbit of *Pax Sinica*, the entry had to be made by means of the time-honored tributary framework. But here again practice did not always correspond to theory, as exemplified by Sino-Russian relations during the period 1728-1858. Even such a loyal tributary state as Korea was left alone as far as her domestic politics was concerned. When the imperialistic powers began to destroy the external bases of the Chinese world order by colonizing Asian tributary states in the last quarter of the nineteenth century, the Tsungli Yamen's response was one of avoidance and nonentanglement.

Thus, the legitimacy of the Sinocentric world order rested more on moral virtue than military power. The concept of a universal state ruled by the Son of Heaven with a cosmic virtue (the heavenly mandate) was devoid of any racial or nationalistic imperative. However, power cannot be separated from ideology in Ch'ing politics. The Manchus as alien conquerors were ever mindful of the fate of Mongol rule and were determined to rule China by Chinese virtues. In short, power and ideology were blended in the Manchu championship of the Chinese cultural heritage. Defense of that heritage made it easy for the Ch'ing Court to suppress racialist-nationalist sentiments by inculcating the virtue of harmony and obedience in the political socialization process.

The suppression of Chinese nationalism in Ch'ing politics was a critical factor in the failure of China's response to the Western challenge. An excessive reliance on harmony as the regulatory norm of the social process poorly equipped Ch'ing officials to play their role in international politics, which became more and more dominated by the ideology of Social Darwinism. The concept of the balance of power or alliance was also alien to the vocabulary of Ch'ing officials, since there never had been an ally of equal status or strength in the Sinic system of international relations. The hierarchical image of their world view made the Ch'ing officials incapable of conceptualizing foreign relations in egalitarian terms. When the strategy of avoidance and procrastination did not work, they revived the old barbarian strategies of *chi-mi* and *i-i chih-i*. However, an application of these strategies to territorially ambitious Russia, in order to play her off against the imperialistic pressures of the other treaty powers, proved to be disastrous. China lost some 600,000 square miles of territory to Russia in the process (see Figure 1.1) without any appreciable gains. Her struggle to contain the Western powers within the hierarchical framework of the Sinic international system boomeranged; when she finally entered the family of nations, it was as an inferior member.

It is clear that the traditional Chinese world order left no room for egalitarianism in international relations. While the Chinese image of world order cannot be construed as containing either a crusading or a colonial doctrine, it represented a formidable barrier against the thought of external policy in terms of mutually beneficial interactions between or among equal sovereign states. The burden of adjustment always fell on the tributary states. This also explains China's unresponsiveness to the Western challenge. It was not until eighty-four years after the Macartney Mission and sixteen years after the establishment of permanent diplomatic missions in Peking by the treaty powers that China could reciprocate by sending her own diplomatic missions abroad.

As of yore, China expected the Western powers to make whatever adjustments were necessary to fit their relations into the hierarchical image of the Chinese world order. In the ensuing confrontation between the two world views, Chinese culture was no match for Western arms. To a large extent, then, the traditional Chinese world order was undone by its own past success. The dead weight of the past crippled the initiative and flexibility of the Ch'ing bureaucracy to readjust the traditional mode of handling barbarian affairs in the face of Western encroachment. Instead, the worship of the past became almost a national opium. The repeated failures of Ch'ing officials to adjust their image of world order to rapidly changing international reality, their theory of the tribute system to changing practice, and their Confucian values to modernization were largely cultural and historical in origin. This inward-looking self-sufficiency in political thought made Ch'ing officials contemptuous of Western ideas, if not Western arms, and correspondingly ignorant of the West. To depart from the ideological continuity of tradition was viewed not as a necessity for survival but an ultimate betrayal of *raison d'état.*

Thus, China's unresponsiveness to the West was deeply rooted in the Confucian tradition. Owing to their excessive reliance on ritual, harmony, and hierarchy in the social process, the Chinese were poorly prepared to cope with conflicts generated from within or without. Their regard for harmony as a supreme value taught the bureaucracy the art of harmonizing divergent social and political pressures. This may have been successful in times of peace and prosperity but it proved totally inadequate in times of crisis. The pursuit of harmony also inculcated the habit of submissiveness and passivity into Chinese social and political life. More often than not the bureaucrats allowed crises to occur and then avoided them when they did occur. A similar bureaucratic style characterized Ch'ing diplomacy during the critical transitional period, when the Ch'ing barbarian specialists practiced the art of avoidance and *ad hoc* temporizing in the face of accelerating imperialistic pressures from the treaty powers.

At long last Chinese nationalism was born in the wreckage of the traditional Chinese world order. Ironically, the stimulus for this birth came from the encroachment of European imperialism on the tributary states in the Sinocentric world order. It was imperial Japan who acted as a catalytic agent for the birth of modern Chinese nationalism. By the turn of the century the cumulative impact of the unequal treaty system, coupled with the rise of expansionistic Japan, had discredited the Sinocentric world order beyond redemption. A new generation of young nationalists jettisoned from their world view the traditional image of China's unique place under heaven as they began to chart a new course toward national respect, freedom, and equality in the family of nations.[65]

Clearly the atmosphere in which they grew up was one of humiliation, charging them with a vivid sense of nationalistic outrage and grievance. As they watched their nation sliced up like a melon in imperialist rivalry, they learned the lesson of power in world politics —and that China could not be respected without power. They became equally convinced that Western learning—not just science and technology but also ideas and institutions—was essential if China were to be made powerful enough to compete with Western nations on an equal footing, or even beat them at their own game. Indeed, this is an

[65] This is one of the major themes in Sun Yat-sen's *San Min Chu I.*

47

important legacy of the disintegration of the traditional Chinese world order. However, given the repeated failures of all previous reformers to synthesize Western ideas successfully with Chinese values, the critical question as to whether the new nationalists can accomplish this task of synthesis remains to be explored.

· 2 ·

THE MAOIST IMAGE OF
WORLD ORDER

The laws of war, like the laws governing all other things,
are reflections in our minds of objective realities; everything
outside of the mind is objective reality.

Mao Tse-tung, December 1936

One recurring theme in Mao's theoretical writings is the notion that
human behavior is a reflection of human thought, and that human
thought is in turn a reflection of material reality. In Mao's funnel of
causality, action is the subjective transformed into the objective. Likewise, China's behavior in the global community can be viewed as a
reflection of her image of the self and of the world. This image represents an integrated systemization of both substance and method. Sub-
stantively, it is a conscious systemization of values and norms to which
the ideology aspires; it also serves as an intellectual assumption about
the international order. Methodologically, it is a manner of thinking;
it provides an epistemological paradigm that performs cognitive, evaluative, and prescriptive functions for decision makers, helping them to
define the state of the world, to *evaluate* the meaning of the world so
defined, and to *prescribe* a correct line of action.

Indeed, the notion that correct behavior is a manifestation (*piao-
hsien*) of correct thought is postulated in practically all important
theoretical writings in the People's Republic of China. An analytical
device with which to probe the inner logic and rationality of Chinese
global policy is thus afforded by what Chinese publicists have interchangeably referred to as *shih-chieh kuan* or *yü-chou kuan* (literally
"world view" or "cosmic view," but both terms are officially translated
as "world outlook").

Available evidence suggests that it was Mao who played the definitive role at the critical turning points in the history of the PRC's
foreign policy. Even Mao's retreat to the "second line of command"
in the day-to-day operation of domestic policy making during the period 1959-65 helped to increase his involvement in the redefinition of
China's place in the world, in the face of deepening Sino-Soviet conflict. In the eyes of the Chinese people, Mao remained the revered
and charismatic, if not always loved, leader who was perceived of

being capable of shaping their destiny in the world. Nor can it be doubted that Mao retained control of the superstructure of Chinese society during his political reign.[1] This personal origin of China's recent view of the world makes it justifiable to focus our discussion on Mao himself as a conceptual background for the study of Chinese behavior in the global community. In short, this chapter is based on the methodological premise that Chinese foreign policy behavior is a reflection of the thought of Mao Tse-tung, at least at the official or policy pronouncement level.

What, then, is Mao's image of world order? Does it have a coherent and well-defined structure? What kinds of values and norms does it embody? What manner of thinking or methodology does it adopt? Is it rigid and dogmatic? Or is it flexible, adaptable, and dynamic? Is it consistent, rational, and predictable, or the opposite? Before we can deal with these and related questions, a few words about source materials are in order.

Although all documents published in the PRC may be regarded as reflections of Mao's thought, some reflect it more clearly than others. For the period before the establishment of the PRC in 1949, the four volumes of the *Selected Works of Mao Tse-tung* (1926-49) and the accounts of personal interviews by Edgar Snow and Anna Louise Strong are indispensable.[2] The delay in the publication of Mao's writings after 1949 caused a critical gap in the material available for a well-rounded picture of Mao's world outlook during the first two decades of the PRC's international life. However, this gap was narrowed considerably in the summer of 1973, when there became available to major research libraries in the West a two-volume collection of Mao's speeches and writings entitled *Mao Tse-tung ssu-hsiang wan-sui* (Long Live Mao Tse-tung's Thought), produced by photo-offset in Taiwan.[3] The two volumes total 995 pages in Chinese, covering ap-

[1] For various roles that Mao played in the policy-making process during the period 1949-68, see Michel Oksenberg, "Policy Making Under Mao, 1949-68: An Overview," in John M. Lindbeck, ed., *China: Management of a Revolutionary Society* (Seattle, Wash.: University of Washington Press, 1971), pp. 79-115.

[2] *Selected Works of Mao Tse-tung* (hereafter cited as *SW*), 4 vols. (Peking: Foreign Languages Press, 1961, 1965); also available in Chinese in one-vol. ed., *Mao Tse-tung hsüan-chi* (Peking: Jen-min ch'u-pan she, 1969, 1406 pp.); Edgar Snow, *Red Star Over China* (New York: Grove Press, 1961, originally published in 1938), "Chinese Communists and World Affairs: An Interview with Mao Tse-tung," *Amerasia* 1 (August 1937), 263-69; Anna Louise Strong, "A World's Eye View from a Yenan Cave," *Amerasia* 11 (April 1947), 122-26, and "The Thought of Mao Tse-tung," *Amerasia* 11 (June 1947), 161-74.

[3] *Mao Tse-tung ssu-hsiang wan-sui* [Long Live Mao Tse-tung's Thought] (n.p., 1967, 280 pp., hereafter cited as *Wan-sui* (1967)), and *Mao Tse-tung ssu-hsiang wan-sui* [Long Live Mao Tse-tung's Thought] (n.p., August 1969, 716-plus pp., hereafter cited as *Wan-sui* (1969)). For discussion of the authenticity of these

proximately 70 percent of the four volumes of the *Selected Works* (1,406 pages in Chinese). The *Wan-sui* documents reveal with clarity the basic logic and consistency of Mao's world outlook and the extent to which it has dominated the foreign-policy thinking of the Chinese Communist Party (CCP) for nearly four decades. Altogether, the *Selected Works* and the *Wan-sui* volumes now provide an adequate documentary basis for analyzing the Maoist image of world order.

MAO'S EPISTEMOLOGY

The picture that emerges from the available writings of Mao Tse-tung is one of a restless and vigorous mind in continuous dialectical struggle with a rapidly changing world. Indeed, it is difficult to codify the thought of Mao Tse-tung as a fixed set of dogmas because "Mao's creation of thought is a continuing process without any foreseeable conclusion."[4] *Chieh-fang chün-pao* (Liberation Army Daily) characterized the thought of Mao Tse-tung as the "microscope and telescope" of the Chinese revolutionary cause.[5] The *Wan-sui* volumes also reflect a vivid image of Mao as a "native philosopher,"[6] tirelessly struggling to teach the Chinese a correct method of thinking and learning. Of the four titles given to him during the Cultural Revolution (Great Teacher, Great Leader, Great Supreme Commander, and Great Helmsman), Mao confided to Edgar Snow in December 1970 that he wished to be remembered by only one of the four—that of Teacher.[7] It is therefore important we begin with Mao's epistemology.

Of all the writings of Mao Tse-tung, three essays—"On Practice" (July 1937), "On Contradiction" (August 1937), and "On the Correct Handling of Contradictions Among the People" (February 1957)—are generally regarded as the most theoretical, if not the most original, works.[8] It is instructive to note in this connection that the secret docu-

---

documents, see Stuart Schram, "Mao Tse-tung: A Self-Portrait," *CQ*, No. 57 (January/March 1974), 156-65.

[4] Franz Schurmann, *Ideology and Organization in Communist China* (2nd ed.: Berkeley, Calif.: University of California Press, 1968), p. 29.

[5] *Chieh-fang chün-pao*, editorial, June 6, 1968.

[6] Mao made this self-characterization in his "Speech on Philosophical Problems" (August 18, 1964), and in another speech delivered at Hangchow (December 21, 1965). See *Wan-sui* (1969), pp. 558, 628.

[7] Edgar Snow, "A Conversation with Mao Tse-tung," *Life* (April 30, 1971), 46.

[8] It is beyond the purview of this study to establish the dates and originality of these essays. However, there is little doubt that Mao truly believed in the views and ideas expressed in them, judging from the consistency and frequency with which he advocated them. For discussion of the issue of originality, see Arthur A. Cohen, *The Communism of Mao Tse-tung* (Chicago: University of

ments of the People's Liberation Army (PLA), *Kung-tso t'ung-hsün* (The Work Bulletin), stress the primacy of Mao's works, while urging that the classical writings of Marx, Engels, Lenin, and Stalin should be studied on a selective basis only, concentrating on such key points as might be useful to China. The main texts for learning philosophy, the *Kung-tso t'ung-hsün* further declares, are "On Practice," "On Contradiction," and the "Sixty Articles on Work Method."[9] Mao himself told Snow that he regarded "On Practice" as a more important essay than "On Contradiction."[10] "On Practice" stands out as the most elaborate exposition of Mao's epistemology. As late as mid-1971, it still provided the official "guiding principle for knowing and changing the world."[11]

A few salient characteristics of Mao the philosopher need to be spelled out. First, he was a practical thinker. He had no use for pure or abstract knowledge; in fact, he did not believe that any knowledge could be developed apart from man's "social practice." Epistemology detached from practice made no sense to him. Second, Mao's conceptualizing process on both domestic and foreign policy questions was permeated with dialectical reasoning. Whether in this he was influenced by the Chinese *yin-yang* or Hegelian dialectics cannot be easily distinguished. Third, despite what his detractors say, Mao had a resilient, open mind, constantly seeking to steer clear of the danger of "dogmatism" on the one hand and "empiricism" on the other. Fourth, even in his Yenan cave Mao seldom lost sight of the larger realities of the international situation, constantly defining and redefining China's interests in terms of her principal friends and foes in the international system. In part, Mao's broad vision was due to his wide-ranging interest in, and knowledge about, world affairs, and in part to his conceptual propensity to look at any situation in its totality and then examine the relations between the components.[12] Finally, Mao was a value-

---

Chicago Press, 1964), pp. 7-28; and H. Arthur Steiner, " 'On the Record' with Mao and His Regime," *Journal of Asian Studies* 17 (February 1958), 215-23.

[9] *KTTH*, No. 8 (February 6, 1961), 12.

[10] Edgar Snow, "Interview with Mao," The *New Republic* (February 27, 1965), 14.

[11] See "Guiding Principle for Knowing and Changing the World—A Study of 'On Practice'," *PR*, No. 25 (June 18, 1971), 6-10.

[12] For elaboration of Mao's wide-ranging interest in, and knowledge about, world affairs, see the following: Jerome Ch'en, ed., *Mao: Great Lives Observed* (Englewood Cliffs, N.J.: Prentice-Hall, 1969), p. 128; John Gittings, *The World and China, 1922-1972* (New York: Harper & Row, 1974), pp. 64-65; Oksenberg, "Policy Making Under Mao," p. 87; Edgar Snow, *Red China Today* (New York: Vintage Books, 1971), p. 177, and *Red Star Over China*, pp. 76-77; and Strong, "A World's Eye View from a Yenan Cave," p. 123. Throughout the *Wan-sui* volumes, Mao admits his ignorance about a number of subjects (foreign languages, natural science and engineering, industry and commerce, etc.); but never of international affairs. In fact, he became a student of world affairs by reading

oriented thinker. All of his theoretical writings were linked in one way or another to revolutionary causes or values.

At the core of Mao's epistemology lies the notion that there have been two concepts concerning the law of development of the universe, the metaphysical and the dialectical. These constitute two clashing world outlooks. In Mao's epistemological vocabulary, the three terms "world outlook," "way of thinking," and "conception concerning the law of development of the universe" are used interchangeably in a methodological sense.

For a long period in both Chinese and European history, Mao argued, the metaphysical, or idealistic, world outlook played a dominant role in human thought. But the metaphysical outlook is seriously flawed for two main reasons. First, it has too static a conception of social change. Second, it ascribes the motive force of change to factors external to society. Mao rejected the cliché that history repeats itself. He attacked the metaphysical thinkers for contending that "a thing can only keep on repeating itself as the same kind of thing and cannot change into anything different."[13] This kind of static metaphysical thinking was exemplified, Mao argued, in the traditional Chinese saying, "Heaven changeth not, likewise, the Tao changeth not."[14]

In contrast, the Marxist or dialectical world outlook sees the fundamental cause of social development as internal: the primary cause of change lies in the internal contradictions of nature. External causes are the condition of change, while internal causes are the basis of change. The dialectical world outlook is not an end, but merely a methodological instrument for resolving contradictions in the course of social and historical development. As Mao put it, "This dialectical world outlook *teaches us primarily how to observe and analyze* the movement of opposites in different things and, on the basis of such analysis, to indicate the methods for resolving contradictions."[15]

How does man form and develop his knowledge of the world? Mao argued that knowledge is inseparably linked to practice. Man's social practice is not only the sole determinant of knowledge, but also the only criterion of the truth of his knowledge of the world. Mao defined man's social practice in a broad generic way to include not only productive activities—the most important—but also "many other forms— class struggle, political life, scientific and artistic pursuits; in short, as

every day two volumes of *Ts'an-k'ao hsiao-hsi* [Reference Material], a daily bulletin of translated foreign news circulated to cadres throughout China. See Stuart Schram, *Chairman Mao Talks to the People: Talks and Letters: 1956-1971* (New York: Pantheon Books, 1974), p. 298. On the latter point—Mao's conceptual propensity—see SW, I, pp. 121, 163, 179, 184, and *Wan-sui* (1969), p. 446.

[13] SW, I, p. 312.   [14] *Ibid.*, p. 313.

[15] *Ibid.*, p. 315; emphasis added.

a social being, man participates in all spheres of the practical life of society."[16] Viewed in this light, the limitations of man's knowledge are reflections of the limitations of his social practice.

Several limitations of man's social practice operate as obstacles in his learning process. First, the thinking of every man in a class-based society is inescapably stamped with the brand of his class. Second, his knowledge is limited by the character and scale of his productive activities; for example, it was not possible for a member of a feudal society to raise his consciousness to the point of acquiring a proletarian world outlook. Third, a man's limitation in direct experience works as a constraint because the dialectical-materialist theory of knowledge holds that knowledge begins with experience and that "all *genuine* knowledge originates in direct experience."[17] Finally, man's thinking lags behind reality, adding another obstacle to the learning process.

Within this general framework, Mao spelled out an incremental (step-by-step) and progressive (lower-to-higher) process in man's acquisition and development of knowledge. The schematic representation in Figure 2.1 gives an overview of Mao's three-step epistemologi-

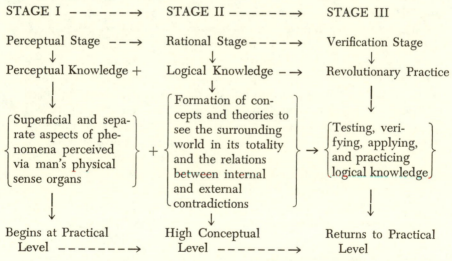

FIGURE 2.1. Mao's Epistemological Model.

cal model, although we should keep in mind that he did not make a clear distinction between the descriptive and prescriptive uses of his model.

That Mao is a practical (utilitarian) theorist is made clear in the above model. Knowledge begins with practice and returns—or must

[16] *Ibid.*, p. 296.   [17] *Ibid.*, p. 300; emphasis added.

return?—to practice. The progression from the stage of sense perception to the rational stage of theory formation involves "an integrated process of cognition"; the process entails not only a quantitative change but also a qualitative difference.

Theory cannot be formed without practice, to be sure, but to have practice without theory is to commit the historical error of "empiricism," as evidenced in the indiscriminate antiforeign struggles of the Taiping and Boxer Rebellions. The progressive integration of empirical perception and logical reasoning "holds true for a minor process of cognition (for instance, knowing a single thing, or society, or a revolution)."[18] But "Marxism emphasizes the importance of theory precisely and only because it can guide action."[19] Rational knowledge "must be redirected to the practice of changing the world, must be applied anew in the practice of production, in the practice of revolutionary class struggle and revolutionary national struggle, and in the practice of scientific experiment."[20] In this way, man's knowledge can be further developed. It can also be tested and verified in practical revolutionary situations.

No revolution can succeed if the knowledge of the revolutionaries lags behind the rapidly changing situation. Marxism-Leninism "has in no way exhausted truth but ceaselessly opens up roads to the knowledge of truth in the course of practice."[21] Mao prescribed the fulfillment of the following tasks on the part of revolutionary people: "to change the objective world and, at the same time, their own subjective world—to change their cognitive ability and change the relations between the subjective and the objective world."[22] Apparently, there is no end to this "epistemological struggle" in Mao's thinking, since the epoch of world communism will not be reached until "all mankind *voluntarily and consciously* changes itself and the world."[23]

CONTRADICTION, DIALECTICS, AND STRUGGLE

The central idea in the thought of Mao Tse-tung is the law of contradiction. The concept has been given sweeping characterizations in Mao's writings at different times: "the basic law of materialist dialectics," "the fundamental law of the universe," "the fundamental law of nature and of society," and "the fundamental law of thought."[24] If any-

---

[18] *Ibid.*, p. 304.　　[19] *Ibid.* See also *Wan-sui* (1969), p. 219.
[20] SW, I, p. 304.　　[21] *Ibid.*, pp. 307-308.　　[22] *Ibid.*, p. 308.
[23] *Ibid*; emphasis added. For repetition of this point, see also "Guiding Principle for Knowing and Changing the World," p. 10.
[24] See SW, I, p. 311; Mao Tse-tung, *On the Correct Handling of Contradictions Among the People* (Peking: Foreign Languages Press, 1966, originally published in 1957), p. 13; Jerome Ch'en, ed., *Mao Papers* (New York: Oxford University Press, 1970), p. 29; *Wan-sui* (1969), p. 629.

thing sums up Mao's philosophy of life (*jen-sheng kuan*), it is that contradiction is inherent in life itself, and that without it there can be no life, society, or world. Every contradiction represents an objective reality in Mao's world outlook.

The law of contradiction is inseparably linked to the theory of dialectical materialism, for it is only through the dialectical method that one can properly understand and analyze contradictions. To resolve contradiction, however, is to engage in a protracted struggle, because as the motive force of the development of all things in nature, contradictions rise, resolve, and rise again in a seemingly endless wavelike motion. In sum, contradictions as the substance of human life, dialectics as the analytical method of understanding contradictions, and struggle as the necessary process of resolving contradictions, all mingle and interact in the dynamic kaleidoscope of Mao's world outlook.

Mao's apocalyptic historical vision sees the world as engaged in a deadly conflict between the two major opposing forces. "The proletariat seeks to transform the world according to its own world outlook," Mao declared in 1957, "so does the bourgeoisie."[25] Hence, the question of correctly assessing China's principal foes and friends is of the first importance. All previous revolutionary struggles in Chinese history were aborted, according to Mao, because of the conceptual failure to distinguish real friends from real enemies. The law of contradiction is supposed to rectify this historical error by accurately identifying the major forces at work in terms of the principal and nonprincipal contradictions.

What appears to be an inconsistent zigzag pattern of turns and twists in Chinese foreign policy is not necessarily a blind pursuit of "national interest" dictated by expediency (as some believe), but a manifest element of realism and flexibility inherent in the analysis of contradictions. The law of contradiction provides Chinese decision makers with an ever-changing and ever-expanding set of tactical accommodations. Although contradiction and struggle are universal and absolute, surviving even in the socialist countries, Mao warns of the danger of indiscriminate analysis and application. In theory, Maoist analysis of contradictions is supposed to be capable of characterizing the nature of contradictions, typologizing their categories, and prescribing correct methods for their resolution.

In Mao's terms, all contradictions are qualitatively different in nature and category. This theory becomes fuzzy with Mao's insistence that there is a sort of "contradiction" within each contradiction. Specifically, Mao argued that each contradiction has dualistic aspects: cooperative (interdependent) and conflictive; universal and particular;

---

[25] *On the Correct Handling*, p. 37. See also *Wan-sui* (1969), p. 677.

and principal and nonprincipal (secondary). What is the positive criterion for characterizing a contradiction along these dimensions? Apparently there is none, for Mao insisted that "what is correct invariably develops in the course of struggle with what is wrong."[26] The situation is never static, because "the principal and the non-principal aspects of a contradiction transform themselves into each other and the nature of the things changes accordingly."[27] Such an analysis provides the Chinese leadership with a continuing challenge to assess China's principal enemies and friends accurately in the international system. In short, the analysis of contradictions injects an element of realism and flexibility into Chinese foreign policy.

In the relationship between the various contradictions, one and only one is supposed to be the principal contradiction that necessarily determines the development of the others. It is apparent, then, that the crucial task of leadership is first to identify and then to concentrate on the resolution of the principal contradiction in each given period or situation. The remaining problems (secondary contradictions) can easily be solved as they are subordinated to the resolution of the principal contradiction. The clear lesson of the *Wan-sui* documents, as far as foreign policy is concerned, is Mao's growing concern about and preoccupation with the rising contradictions in the Soviet Union and their implications for Sino-Soviet relations.

The method of resolving contradictions is contingent upon the particular characteristics of each contradiction. In antagonistic contradictions, the interests of the actors are fundamentally opposed; hence, they can be resolved only through armed struggle (revolution or war) in which one actor inevitably wins. However, coercive means can sometimes be deferred because the antagonistic contradiction in question is not the principal one at the moment. In nonantagonistic contradictions, the interests of the actors are basically the same; hence, they are solved by noncoercive methods of criticism and self-criticism. The criterion for distinguishing antagonistic from nonantagonistic contradictions is simple enough: contradictions between "ourselves and the enemy" are antagonistic; those between friends or among the people themselves are nonantagonistic. Antagonistic contradictions are absolute and protracted, whereas nonantagonistic contradictions are relative, mobile, temporary, and conditional.[28]

What are the practical and operational consequences of the law of contradiction in the Maoist image of world order? Mao made a fundamental break from the traditional Chinese image of world order by substituting the value of struggle for the Confucian value of

---

[26] *On the Correct Handling*, p. 37.   [27] SW, I, p. 333.
[28] *Ibid.*, p. 344; and *On the Correct Handling*, pp. 1-2.

harmony. Indeed, for him struggle was *sine qua non*, because without it no contradiction could be resolved. Struggle is not only desirable because it accelerates progress (social change), but also inevitable because the world, in the vision of Mao, is characterized by disequilibrium—that is, an uneven development and distribution of contradiction.[29]

Viewed in this light, Peking's behavior on the international scene can be perceived as an adjustment of struggles whose weights must shift from time to time, from place to place, and from actor to actor. Conflict, competition, coexistence, and cooperation are all forms of struggle. In short, struggle is the way of political life. This concept throws a drastically different light on Peking's crisis perception and behavior. In contrast to the common understanding of crisis as a situation that presents a *high threat* with a *short response time*, and *surprise* to the decision makers,[30] the Chinese perceive international crises as *recurrent and protracted* phenomena, generated by *economic factors* and related to the *domestic* crises of political actors.[31] In other words, military conflict situations in international relations are not generally regarded as crises in the modern Chinese view of world order. Thus, the Chinese term *wei-chi* (crisis) does not appear in Chinese documents relating to the Sino-American confrontation over Quemoy in 1958, the Sino-Indian border conflict in 1962, or the Gulf of Tonkin incident in 1964.[32]

THE MAOIST IMAGE OF HUMAN NATURE, WAR, AND REVOLUTION

Practically all the significant theories of war and peace in the literature of Western political thought have been postulated either implicitly or explicitly on certain images of human nature. To cite one recent example, the "struggle for power" model has been advanced by the so-called realists in terms of *animus dominandi*, the notion that individuals or nations act like beasts of prey, driven by an insatiable lust

[29] "We must oppose the theory of even development or the theory of equilibrium," Mao declared in 1937. In his "Sixty Articles on Work Methods" (1958) Mao states that "Disequilibrium is normal and absolute, whereas equilibrium is temporary and relative." See SW, I, p. 336, and Ch'en, *Mao Papers*, p. 66.

[30] See Charles F. Hermann, "Threat, Time, and Surprise: A Simulation of International Crisis," in Charles F. Hermann, ed., *International Crises: Insights from Behavioral Research* (New York: Free Press, 1972), pp. 187-211.

[31] John A. Kringen and Steven Chan, "Chinese Crisis Perception and Behavior: A Summary of Findings" (Paper delivered at the meeting of the Joint Committee on Contemporary China, Workshop on Chinese Foreign Policy, Ann Arbor, Michigan, August 12-14, 1976), p. 3.

[32] *Ibid.*, p. 28.

for power.[33] Can we also attribute such a Hobbesian image of human nature to Mao's model of struggle? The answer is clearly no. Mao's image of human nature was more Rousseau-like than Hobbesian, for he believed that conflicts (or contradictions) were inherent in the social process itself rather than in the biological or psychic make-up of man.

Mao's repeated stress on the importance of remolding one's world outlook as a necessary condition for changing the objective world stemmed from his belief in the principle of the malleability of human nature. The human mind is like clay in a potter's hand. As Mao put it: "The concept of man lacks content; it lacks the specificity of male and female, adult and child, Chinese and foreign, revolutionary and counter-revolutionary. The only thing left is the vague features differentiating man from beast."[34] Mao also believed in "man's *inherent unlimited* capacity for knowledge,"[35] although he may fall short of fulfilling this capacity in social practice. In a recent article put out by the Writing Group of Liaoning Provincial Committee of the CCP, this view has been reaffirmed. Attacking Liu Shao-ch'i for his alleged view that man's intelligence was endowed by nature, the group declared:

. . . it [Mao's instruction] shows that man's knowledge (ability and capability belong to the category of knowledge) is not inborn but is acquired after birth by summing up the experience in social practice. In different historical periods, large numbers of outstanding revolutionary persons, without exception, came forward in the storm of revolutionary practice. Describing capability and ability as transcending practice and as something endowed by nature is nothing but self-glorification and fabrication by the arrogant idealists, and such capability and ability are non-existent in social life.[36]

However, the conceptual logic and consistency of the Maoist theory of human nature are considerably compromised by the ideological need to maintain vigilance against the corrupting influence of bourgeois literature and art. Since the Cultural Revolution, the writers of the PRC have advanced a fuzzy and undifferentiated equation of the theory of human nature (*jen-sheng lun*) and the *bourgeois* theory of human nature (*tzu-ch'an chieh-chi jen-sheng lun*). It is not clear what is meant by the bourgeois theory of human nature, as even

---

[33] See Arnold Wolfers, *Discord and Collaboration* (Baltimore, Md.: Johns Hopkins University Press, 1962), pp. 83-84; and Hans J. Morgenthau, *Politics Among Nations* (4th ed., New York: Knopf, 1967), p. 4.

[34] Quoted in Donald J. Munro, "The Malleability of Man in Chinese Marxism," *CQ*, No. 48 (October/December 1971), 617.

[35] *SW*, I, p. 317; emphasis added.

[36] "Guiding Principle for Knowing and Changing the World," p. 7.

Beethoven—particularly in his Ninth Symphony—was attacked for "spreading bourgeois humanitarian ideas."[37] What is clear is the concern that any theory of human nature has practical utility for revolutionary practice. Any theory of human nature that fails to make a clear class distinction is asserted to be detrimental because it deprives people of their revolutionary vigilance in the face of pervasive bourgeois attacks and ultimately leads to capitulation to the bourgeoisie.[38]

Thus, man's capacity for infinite malleability or unlimited knowledge does not work spontaneously in the transformation of the proletarian world outlook. "In class society," Mao argued, "there is only human nature of a class character; there is no human nature that transcends classes."[39] This is where the necessity for ideological struggle comes in. And this struggle is also a protracted one. "As long as one makes revolution all his life, one needs to remould his world outlook throughout his life[,] for it is a long-term task."[40] There is a contradiction between man's good and malleable nature and evil social (bourgeois) forces. It takes nothing less than a determined and continuous ideological struggle to prevent man from falling prey to the corrupting influence of the bourgeois world outlook.

Although there was always a half-hearted attempt to reconcile determinism with voluntarism, the classical Marxism by and large viewed the historical process as being determined by the interplay of forces and not by the will of man. Indeed, one of Marx's most famous statements is that man's social existence determines his consciousness, not, as had been previously assumed, that man's consciousness determines his existence. In the process of Sinicizing Marxism, however, Mao to all practical purposes gave primacy to voluntarism. The overwhelming lesson of the Chinese Communist Revolution, as Mao saw it, was the triumph of the human will over innumerable obstacles—or the strategic triumph of "millet plus rifles" over "Chiang Kai-shek's aeroplanes plus tanks." It was from this revolutionary romanticism that Mao drew his main inspiration in his search for the answer to a multitude of domestic and foreign problems.[41]

[37] Beethoven has been "restored" in the post-Mao era, however. On March 26, 1977, China marked the 150th anniversary of Beethoven's death by lifting a ban on his music. The Central Symphony Orchestra played the third and fourth movements of Beethoven's Fifth Symphony before a capacity audience and received an enthusiastic reception. The concert was later shown on television. See *NYT*, March 27, 1977, p. 5.

[38] For further elaboration of this point, see "Penetrate Deeply into the Critique of the Bourgeois Theory of Human Nature," *HC*, No. 4 (1974), 57-63.

[39] Quoted in *ibid.*, p. 58.

[40] "Guiding Principle for Knowing and Changing the World," p. 10.

[41] Mao's revolutionary romanticism, according to one psycho-historian, "*is the hero's quest for doing more than the possible, risking and even courting death*

As a practical philosopher, Mao was always conscious of the practical implications of his theorizing. That is also the case with his theory of human nature. In a country with an agricultural economy which is unevenly endowed with the factors of production, it makes practical sense to exalt the power of the human will as the motive force of social development. In his speech before the Enlarged Session of the Military Affairs Committee and the External Affairs Conference, on September 11, 1959, Mao exhorted the cadres to the effect that *"all things* can be successfully achieved, if you are resolute, *if you only have the will."*[42] To prove his point, he went on to cite the recent completion of the Great Ceremonial Hall at the T'ien An Men as a testimonial to human strength (*jen ti li-liang*). It was completed in only ten months, Mao proudly reminded his audience, by 12,000 workers who had worked three shifts a day without material rewards, defying the credulity of Soviet experts, who had argued at first that it could not be done.[43]

In Mao's world outlook, it is the conquering human spirit more than anything else that acts as the prime motive force of successful revolution. It is also the conquering human spirit that translates the impossible into the realm of the possible. Indeed, Mao recalls Max Weber's paragon of a leader and hero: "Certainly all historical experience confirms the truth—that man would not have attained the possible unless time and again he had reached out for the impossible. But to do that a man must be a leader, and not only a leader but a hero as well, in a very sober sense of the word."[44]

It may not be an exaggeration to say that Mao spent more time in fighting the enemy within—the pessimistic thinking among the cadres—than in fighting the enemy without. Both the *Selected Works* and the *Wan-sui* documents are permeated with Mao's "protracted struggle" against the recurrence of pessimism within the ranks and his effort to generate anew a spirit of strategic optimism. The most revealing and moving example is the speech entitled "The Foolish Old Man Who Removed the Mountains," which he delivered on June 11, 1945, at the Seventh National Congress of the CCP. After retelling the ancient Chinese fable in which God is finally moved by the dogged

---

in order to alter the meaning of both life and death, 'storming heaven' and challenging the claims of existing deities, political as well as theological, in order to replace them with the claims of revolutionary immortality." Robert Jay Lifton, *Revolutionary Immortality: Mao Tse-tung and the Chinese Cultural Revolution* (New York: Vintage Books, 1968), p. 82; emphasis in original.

[42] *Wan-sui* (1967), p. 100; emphasis added.   [43] *Ibid.*

[44] H. H. Gerth and C. Wright Mills, eds., *From Max Weber: Essays in Sociology* (New York: Oxford University Press, 1958), p. 128.

determination of the Old Man in carrying the mountains away, Mao declared: "Today, two big mountains lie like a dead weight on the Chinese people. One is imperialism, the other is feudalism. The Chinese Communist Party has long made up its mind to dig them up. We must persevere and work unceasingly, and we, too, will touch God's heart. Our God is none other than the masses of the Chinese people. If they stand up and dig together with us, why can't these two mountains be cleared away?"[45]

Willing may not change reality, but it was a crucial element in Mao's thinking. If the Great Leap Forward was Mao's attempt to substitute human will power for technology, the Cultural Revolution was Mao's answer "to the reactionary bourgeois dictum: 'You can't change human nature.'"[46] The two models for popular emulation during the Cultural Revolution—the Tachai production brigade in agriculture in Shansi and the Tach'ing oilfield industry in Heilungkiang, both of which stressed ideological rewards for hard work—were publicized as Maoist examples of a conquering spirit over extremely adverse material conditions.

Mao had, however, some moments of doubt about the omnipotence of the human will. He confessed to Snow in 1965 that "events did not move in accordance with the individual human will."[47] But a poor and underdeveloped economic system such as China's can hardly afford to offer the material rewards of meritocracy without undermining the distributive justice of social egalitarianism. Mao was profoundly contemptuous of traditional elitism in Chinese society and was determined to stop its revival. Thus, the reality of the Chinese economy and the egalitarian norm of Mao led to a reliance on moral virtues and ideological incentives in Chinese mobilization politics. In sum, Mao's optimistic image of human nature was in accord with the developmental values of the Chinese Revolution.

Mao's revolutionary optimism was not a confident blueprint for overseas aggression or adventurism. It was a prime mover for the strategy of protracted conflict, the notion that struggle to resolve antagonistic contradictions was necessarily and inevitably a protracted and arduous process, fraught with many temporary setbacks and defeats. The principle was originally enunciated by Mao in the 1930s to combat the Left adventurists in times of victory and the Right defeatists in times of setback in the revolutionary struggle, thus providing a correct party line to be adopted vis-à-vis the enemy. In "A Single Spark

[45] SW, III, p. 322.
[46] China Policy Study Group, London, *The Broadsheet* 5 (March 1968), 4.
[47] Snow, "Interview with Mao," p. 23.

Can Start a Prairie Fire," Mao addressed himself to the pessimists: "Marxists are not fortune-tellers. They should, and indeed can, only indicate the general direction of future developments and changes; they should not and cannot fix the day and the hour in a mechanistic way."[48] However, it was not until mid-1938, when Mao delivered a series of lectures at Yenan entitled "On Protracted War," that the principle was fully refined.

Central to the principle of protracted conflict is the well-known Maoist axiom that the enemy must be despised strategically but respected tactically. This bold strategic principle was designed, first, to assess realistically the relative ratio of forces between a revolutionary challenger and the defender of the status quo and then, to devise short-term tactics and long-term strategies for reversing the original imbalance between the two opposing forces. The process of moving from the original position of inferiority to one of parity and eventually to one of superiority is long and tortuous. It becomes imperative for the followers of Mao's protracted war to weaken the enemy through a step-by-step process, waging only such battles as will ensure victory, and avoiding all unnecessary risks and adventures. In this way, the principle also works to sustain a revolutionary *élan* during the seemingly endless struggle against a militarily superior enemy.

In foreign policy, the principle of protracted conflict is supposed to work toward a progressive bridging of the gap between China's ambitious objectives and her meager means. In a word, it is the strategy of transforming weakness into strength. Mao first translated the principle of protracted conflict into the "paper tiger" thesis in his famous interview with Anna Louise Strong immediately after the end of World War II. Mao used the term paper tiger in a strategic sense. This point becomes clear in a statement he made at a meeting of the Political Bureau of the Central Committee of the CCP on December 1, 1958: "Imperialism and all reactionaries, looked at in essence, from a long-term point of view, from a strategic point of view, must be seen for what they are—paper tigers. On this we should build our strategic thinking. On the other hand, they are also living tigers, iron tigers, real tigers which can eat people. On this we should build our tactical thinking."[49]

Mao's conceptualization of war is amenable to divergent interpretations. At the dialectical level, Mao made no distinction between war and peace as they constitute the unity of opposites, transforming themselves into each other. At the experiential level, Mao held a romantic

[48] SW, I, p. 127.
[49] Cited in full as the editors' note in SW, IV, pp. 98-99.

view of war as the supreme test of man's courage and will. The weight of the past impinged on his thinking as he reached back to his own revolutionary experience as a guide for evaluating new problems.

At the operational level after 1949, however, Mao was subjected to cross-pressures. Certainly, the Korean War proved to be anything but an exalting experience, and one whose repetition had to be avoided if possible in the future. Social and economic development at home required a long and stable period of peace. Yet Mao was also preoccupied with the paralyzing psychological impact that any excessive "peace posturing" might have upon the fighting will of the people. At the same time, he feared that China's pacifist posture and ideological disarmament might stimulate more aggressive behavior on the part of the imperialist enemy. Such cross-pressures may explain the gap between his militant verbal behavior and prudent, defense-oriented policy. It seems safe to generalize that Mao, the ruler in the post-revolutionary period, became progressively less sanguine about war than Mao the revolutionary hero of the 1930s and 1940s.

There is always a methodological hazard of making too much of Mao's writings on war, since they were mostly formulated in the 1930s in the course of waging the day-to-day struggle against imperialist Japan. With this caveat in mind, however, a few salient characteristics of Mao's image of war need to be mentioned. Mao accepted the axiom that war is the continuation of politics, but he insisted that it is a means of resolving contradictions between classes, nations, and states. He typologized all wars throughout history into just and unjust wars (*cheng-yi ti chan-cheng* and *fei-cheng-yi ti chan-cheng*), a distinction based on that between predator and prey. Mao refuted "liberalism" for its stand on "unprincipled peace." To oppose war with war was the only way to eliminate it. The era of perpetual peace for mankind would come—there would be no more wars—when human society advanced to the point where classes and states were eliminated. China's anti-Japanese war was seen as sacred and just; its aim was both transnational peace and perpetual peace. The weapons-decide-everything approach was a mechanical approach to war. Weapons were an important, but not the decisive, factor; it was people, not material things, that were decisive.[50]

Mao's writings on war after 1949 were fragmentary. There is nothing comparable to his three major essays on war—"Problems of Strategy in China's Revolutionary War" (December 1936), "Problems of Strategy in Guerrilla War Against Japan" (May 1938), and "On Protracted War" (May 1938)—which make up the bulk of Mao's

[50] See *SW*, I, pp. 170-71, 180, 182-83, 190-91, 339; *SW*, II, pp. 31, 148-53, 265, 354.

Selected Military Writings.[51] Nonetheless, Chinese polemics in the course of the deepening Sino-Soviet conflict provide a glimpse into Mao's conceptualization of war and peace in contemporary international relations.

First, Mao adhered tenaciously to the belief that it is man who decides the fate of mankind. The revolution in weapons technology has not changed the basic laws of historical development as Mao understood them. His disenchantment with the Soviet Union went back to Stalin—to a lesser degree, even to Lenin—whose lack of confidence in the "mass line" led him to overemphasize technology while ignoring the superstructure, on the one hand, and an attempt to prevent the successful completion of the Chinese Revolution, on the other.[52]

Second, Mao refused to accept the liberal-pacifist assumption that war and peace can be generalized into two independent categories in the system of world dominance. In its most acute form, violence expresses itself in war, to be sure, but it expresses itself in other forms as well. War and peace as abstract concepts did not concern Mao. What concerned him most was the question of *who* is using violence against *whom*, in what sociopolitical context, for what purposes. To use peace research parlance, Mao was more concerned with structural than with physical violence. In *Long Live Leninism*, which is generally believed to be the work of Mao although published (on April 16, 1960) under the auspices of the editorial department of *Hung-ch'i* (Red Flag), the juxtaposition and interchangeability of physical violence (war) and structural violence (social injustice) in capitalist countries are described in the following terms:

> In capitalist countries, bourgeois war is the continuation of the bourgeois policies of ordinary times, while bourgeois peace is the continuation of bourgeois wartime policy. The bourgeoisie are always switching back and forth between the two forms, war and peace, to carry on their rule over the people and their external struggle. In what they call peace time, the imperialists rely on armed force to deal with the oppressed classes and nations by such forms of violence as arrest, imprisonment, sentencing to hard labour,

[51] An English translation of Mao's military writings under this title was published by the Foreign Languages Press in Peking in 1963.

[52] Mao's criticism of Stalin will be more fully discussed later in this chapter. His criticism of Lenin focuses specifically on Lenin's statement: "The more backward the country, the more difficult the transition from capitalism to socialism." This is an incorrect view, Mao argued, because what is most important is the superstructure. Given the prevalence of the bourgeois world outlook in the developed capitalist countries, he argued, the superstructure there is too strong to permit revolutionary movements to seize power. However, such is not the case in the weakest link of imperialism—the underdeveloped part of the world. See *Wan-sui* (1969), pp. 333-34.

massacre and so forth, while at the same time, they also carry on preparations for using the most acute form of violence—war—to suppress the revolution of the people at home, to carry out plunder abroad, to overwhelm foreign competitors and to stamp out revolutions in other countries. Or, peace at home may exist side by side with war abroad.[53]

Third, Mao attributed the source of modern wars to the imperialist system itself. In his view, given the inherent class character of violence, wars of one kind or another would persist so long as the imperialist system and its exploiting classes continued to exist. The socialist system, on the other hand, "determines that we [the Chinese] do not need war, absolutely would not start a war, and absolutely must not, should not, and could not encroach one inch on the territory of a neighbouring country."[54] This kind of dialectical reasoning makes Mao's analysis of war and peace rather simple: there are only two kinds of wars—just and unjust—as there are only two kinds of violence —counter-revolutionary and revolutionary. Whether a war will break out or not is determined by the imperialist predator.

Finally, any relaxation of vigilance on the part of the prey only increases the danger of the imperialists launching an aggressive war. Given the predatory nature of imperialism, world peace can only be won by struggle (though the form of struggle remains flexible), and not by bending to the nuclear blackmail of the imperialists. One form of struggle to maintain "world peace"—that is, to deter the imperialists from launching an aggressive war—is to beat them at their own game of nuclear brinkmanship, because imperialists always bully the fainthearted but fear the firm. Mao's preoccupation with the question of *who appears to be more afraid of whom* and his deliberate and measured provocation of the 1958 Quemoy-Matsu crisis should be regarded as a form of his deterrent strategy.[55] In short, Mao believed that peace depends not so much on the objective reality of material and military strength as on the posture of ideological and psychological confidence and strength that the revolutionary forces project to the imperialists.

At the operational level, Mao's thinking on war had a defensive

[53] Reprinted in John Gittings, *Survey of the Sino-Soviet Dispute: A Commentary and Extracts from the Recent Polemics 1963-1967* (New York: Oxford University Press, 1968), pp. 338-39.

[54] *Ibid.*, p. 340.

[55] See *On the Correct Handling*, p. 48; *Wan-sui* (1969), pp. 83, 103, 216, 231-32, 239-41, 254, 267; Snow, "Interview with Mao," p. 22. For an analysis of Mao's strategy during the Quemoy crisis based on the *Wan-sui* documents, see Allen S. Whiting, "New Light on Mao: Quemoy 1958: Mao's Miscalculations," *CQ*, No. 62 (June 1975), 263-70.

orientation. Defense-oriented tactics and strategies are the *leitmotif* of the *Kung-tso t'ung-hsün*. Chinese military thinking, as reflected in these secret PLA documents (1961), is almost exclusively preoccupied with defensive measures needed to cope with a possible surprise attack from the United States. While Peking has publicly disparaged the destructive impact of nuclear weapons by reiterating the theme of the superiority of men over weapons—the atomic bomb is a paper tiger—these documents reveal a more sober assessment of the impact of nuclear attack by admitting that such an attack could destroy the industrial centers and economic potential of China. However, the imprint of Maoist strategic thinking is also evident in the assertion that nuclear weapons cannot be the *final* arbiter of war against a country such as China, with her vast territory and population; the final resolution of war still rests on man. What is really to be dreaded is not powerful weapons but political corruption, deviation from the mass line, ideological disarmament, and loss of the will to fight. In contrast to Peking's public braggadocio, the *Kung-tso t'ung-hsün* shows some realistic assessments—coupled with ideological pep talk—of China's military capabilities and vulnerabilities in comparison with those of the enemy, and of the possibility of local conflicts escalating to a higher, even nuclear, level of violence.[56]

In a similar vein, the *Wan-sui* documents reveal a dialectical interplay between Mao's prudential appeal for peace and his periodic resort to militant rhetoric to boost the fighting morale of the people. In his summing-up speech of October 11, 1955, delivered at the Sixth Plenum of the Seventh Central Committee, Mao strongly urged cadres in the Ministry of Foreign Affairs, the international liaison departments, and the armed forces to exert their best efforts to ensure peace, because China badly needed a period of peaceful reconstruction to achieve the goals of the first Five-Year Plan.[57] In 1958, however, Mao's thought took a new turn. On the one hand, he insisted that defense expenditure in peacetime had to be small, while reiterating, on the other, that China must be prepared for war because of the continuing danger of a world conflict launched by the imperialists.[58] He also admitted that the decision to go it alone in China's development—the policy of self-reliance (*tzu-li keng-sheng*)—was made in 1958.[59]

[56] See Yeh Chien-ying's speech at the Military Affairs Committee Conference on Training in *KTTH*, No. 10 (February 20, 1961), 1-9; No. 3 (January 7, 1961), 6; No. 7 (February 1, 1961), 9; No. 29 (August 1, 1961), 5-11. See also Mao's speech of December 19, 1958, delivered at the 6th Plenum of the 8th Central Committee in *Wan-sui* (1969), pp. 259-69, especially his tenth point (pp. 266-68).

[57] *Ibid.*, p. 15. [58] *Ibid.*, pp. 163, 208.

[59] Mao made this point in his speech of January 30, 1962, at an Enlarged

Crying wolf, going it alone, appealing for a prudent peace, and propagandizing for fighting morale—these were the competing themes in Mao's thought. How did he attempt to reconcile them? On the one hand, Mao pledged again and again to his audience at home and abroad that China would never start a war. He reassured General Montgomery of Great Britain in 1960 that China as a true socialist nation would not invade other countries in a hundred or even ten thousand years.[60] "Only if the United States attacked China, would the Chinese fight," Mao told Snow in 1965, when the United States was already fully engaged in the Vietnam War.[61] In his speech at the First Plenum of the Ninth Central Committee of the CCP on April 28, 1969, he again issued a clear-cut affirmation:

> Others may come and attack us but we shall not fight outside our borders. We do not fight outside our borders. I say we will not be provoked. Even if you invite us to come out, we will not come out, but if you should come and attack us we will deal with you. It depends on whether you attack on a small scale or a large scale. . . . They [the enemies] would be easy to fight, since they would fall into the people's encirclement. As for things like aeroplanes, tanks and armoured cars, everywhere experience proves that they can be dealt with.[62]

That this is more than mere rhetoric is shown in the historical record of the PRC's use of force. Although more than half of the American public, according to a Gallup Poll of September 1971, regarded China to be the greatest threat to world peace, scholarly studies generally agree that the Chinese use of force has been of a limited and defensive character, and that China poses no major threat to the stability

Central Work Conference. See *Wan-sui* (1969), p. 416. Likewise, *Jen-min jih-pao* published in mid-1967 a statement Mao allegedly made in June 1958 to the effect that China could complete the development of atomic and nuclear bombs in ten years. However, on December 25, 1976, the New China News Agency made public Mao's report (dated April 25, 1956) to an enlarged meeting of the Politburo, in which he is reported to have said among other things: "If we are not to be bullied in the present-day world, we cannot do without the bomb." See *JMJP*, June 18, 1967, p. 1; and *NYT*, December 26, 1976, p. 14.

[60] *Wan-sui* (1969), p. 412.

[61] Snow, "Interview with Mao," p. 22. This assertion is corroborated by the fact that Lo Jui-ch'ing, then Chief of Staff, who advocated direct Chinese intervention on behalf of North Vietnam, was purged following the 1965 strategic debate. See Harold C. Hinton, "China and Vietnam," in William Richardson, ed., *China Today* (Maryknoll, N.Y.: Maryknoll Publications, 1969), pp. 117-44; and Donald Zagoria, "The Strategic Debate in Peking," in Tang Tsou, ed., *China in Crisis* (Chicago: University of Chicago Press, 1968), Vol. II, pp. 237-68.

[62] See Schram, *Chairman Mao Talks to the People*, pp. 285-86.

of the international system in the foreseeable future.[63] The detonation of the atomic bomb in 1964 and subsequent acquisition of both medium- and intermediate-range nuclear delivery capability have not affected China's defensive posture, as evidenced in the repeated unilateral "no-first-use" pledge. Nor is there any evidence that suggests China's nuclear status made her more aggressive or warlike.

However, it must be noted that Mao was always hypersensitive to the psychological effects that fear of war might have on the people's revolutionary morale; he believed that this fear stemmed from the twin errors of overestimating the enemy's strength and the destructive potential of war. He also believed that imperialists are always eager to exacerbate such a fear through nuclear bluff and blackmail. His well-publicized optimistic assessment of mankind's ability to survive a nuclear war *à la* Herman Kahn provided his Soviet opponents with ammunition to attack him as a highly dangerous nuclear madman. However, Mao's strategic optimism about nuclear war served as a deterrent device to counter imperialist nuclear blackmail on the one hand, and as a propaganda device to bring about a psycho-ideological mobilization of the Chinese masses on the other.[64]

At the First Plenum of the Ninth Central Committee in 1969 Mao declared likewise that "the most important thing is to be psychologically prepared. To be psychologically prepared means that we must be *spiritually* prepared to fight."[65] Viewed in this light, the "spiritual-atom-bomb" dictum, a variation on the men-over-weapons theme, serves several domestic and foreign purposes: it bolsters internal morale; it legitimizes the axiom that politics take the command; it emphasizes China's strength (manpower); it underplays the enemy's strength (weapons); and it signals to the enemy that China is always prepared to fight.

Indeed, there is little in the PRC's policy pronouncements and policy performance in the 1950s and 1960s that suggests the desirabil-

[63] James C. Hsiung, *Law and Policy in China's Foreign Relations: A Study of Attitudes and Practice* (New York: Columbia University Press, 1972); Neville Maxwell, *India's China War* (New York: Anchor Books, 1972); Allen S. Whiting, *China Crosses the Yalu: The Decision to Enter the Korean War* (New York: Macmillan, 1960); *The Chinese Calculus of Deterrence: India and Indochina* (Ann Arbor, Michigan: University of Michigan Press, 1975). For an excellent short essay summarizing the findings of recent scholarly studies, as well as of his own on the subject, see Allen S. Whiting, "The Use of Force in Foreign Policy by the People's Republic of China," *Annals of the American Academy of Political and Social Science* 402 (July 1972), 55-66.

[64] For Mao's optimistic assessment of the possibility of survival after a nuclear war, see the following: Gittings, *The World and China*, pp. 147-48, 218, 230-32; SW, IV, pp. 22, 99-100; Snow, "Interview with Mao," pp. 19, 21.

[65] Schram, *Chairman Mao Talks to the People*, p. 285; emphasis added.

ity of a nuclear war, or for that matter even the right to initiate a war by invoking a just cause.[66] Although Mao admitted the possibility of a surprise nuclear attack initiated by some madman, the *raison d'être* of imperialism, for him, was to exploit, not to destroy people. Hence, avoidance of nuclear war is inherent in the very logic of imperialism —a point which, he believed, the Soviet Union had failed to understand. Contrary to the impression that the Soviet Union has propagandistically generated in its dispute with China,[67] Peking has consistently underplayed the danger of such a global holocaust during its preentry period.

The major difference between the two Communist powers has centered really on the desirability and inevitability of local revolutionary wars. According to the Chinese, the Soviet leaders, by uncritically accepting and advocating the policy of peaceful coexistence, have blurred the crucial distinction between revolutionary and global (interstate) wars. The former are desirable and inevitable, while the latter can be, and should be, avoided. Moreover, the Chinese insisted that local wars—revolutionary and anticolonial—would not necessarily escalate into a larger or atomic war, as the postwar history of all local wars shows. China has indeed advocated and practiced the policy of peaceful coexistence with countries having different social and political systems (see Appendix A), but has insisted that this principle cannot be extended to the exploitative relationship between oppressed peoples and their oppressors.

Chinese ideological polemics embodied the assumption that the basic Marxist laws of historical development remained unchanged by the revolution in weapons technology. The Chinese refused to admit any conflict between the policy of peaceful coexistence and the policy of supporting revolutionary war. "While persevering in peaceful coexistence with countries having different social systems," China

[66] See Hsiung, *Law and Policy in China's Foreign Relations*, pp. 293-96.

[67] A statement by the Soviet Government issued on August 21, 1963 charged: "Every communist-Leninist will feel disgust at an attitude to thermonuclear war such as this: 'Never mind if a half of mankind perishes, if 300 million Chinese die, for on the other hand imperialism will be wiped from the face of the Earth and those who survive will rapidly create on the ruins of imperialism a new civilization that will be a thousand times higher.' And it is precisely such an attitude to thermonuclear war that has been present on more than one occasion in the pronouncements of highly-placed Chinese representatives. Even if the Chinese makes, not two, but one hundred and two statements that it is dying to achieve the prohibition and destruction of nuclear weapons and that its only concern is the interests of the peoples, it will not be able to wash off the shame of gambling on the death of hundreds of millions of people, including Chinese people, in a thermonuclear war." The Soviet text is reprinted in William E. Griffith, *The Sino-Soviet Rift* (Cambridge, Mass.: M.I.T. Press, 1964), pp. 354-70.

responded to the Open Letter of the Central Committee of the Communist Party of the Soviet Union (CPSU) in December 1963, "we unswervingly perform our proletarian international duty. We actively support the national liberation movements of Asia, Africa and Latin America."[68]

Yet the Chinese concept of support has been largely moral and ideological. *Long Live Leninism* explicitly states that China has "always held that revolution is each nation's own affair" and that "revolution can neither be exported nor imported."[69] Likewise, Lin Piao's "Long Live the Victory of People's War," though characterized as a Chinese *Mein Kampf* by some, reiterated the theme of self-reliance: "The liberation of the masses is accomplished by the masses themselves—this is a basic principle of Marxism-Leninism. Revolution or people's war in any country is the business of the masses in that country and should be carried out primarily by their own efforts; *there is no other way.*"[70] Mao told Snow in 1965 that "China gave support to revolutionary movements but not by sending troops." "Of course," he went on, "whenever a liberation struggle existed, China would *publish statements and call demonstrations to support it.* It was precisely that which vexed the imperialists."[71]

That China's unrestrained proselytizing for wars of national liberation was largely a device of ideological model projection as well as of moral and psychological mobilization of revolutionaries abroad has been borne out by its practice. By any definition, Hong Kong and Macao are remnants of Western imperialism in China. It is also a widely shared belief that no nation would prevent Peking from "liberating" them. In fact, Nikita Khrushchev reminded the world during the

[68] *Peaceful Coexistence—Two Diametrically Opposed Policies* (Peking: Foreign Languages Press, 1963), p. 16.
[69] Gittings, *Survey of the Sino-Soviet Dispute*, p. 342.
[70] *PR*, No. 36 (September 3, 1965), 19; emphasis added. This is consistent with Mao's private remarks to a PLO delegation in March 1965. See *Wan-sui* (1969), pp. 614-15.
[71] Snow, "Interview with Mao," p. 22; emphasis added. In a secret speech delivered on May 20, 1975 at the auditorium of the Political Department of the Tientsin Garrison Command, according to Taiwan sources, Ch'iao Kuan-hua in his capacity as foreign minister also repeated the Maoist line on this question: "As long as we have not sent troops to invade other countries and have not sent agents, as the Soviet revisionists have, to wield batons and stand on the heads of fraternal parties, there will be no question of whether the revolution is being 'exported'." See "Ch'iao Kuan-hua 'Kuan-yü tang-ch'ien shih-chieh hsing-shih chi Chung-kung tui-wai cheng-ts'e ti chiang-hua'" ["Ch'iao Kuan-hua's 'Speech on the Current World Situation and China's Foreign Policy'"], *Fei-ch'ing yüeh-pao* [Chinese Communist Affairs Monthly] 18 (October 1975), 84-93; trans. in *Chinese Law and Government* (hereafter cited as "Ch'iao Kuan-hua's Secret Speech") 9 (Spring-Summer 1976), 33.

Cuban missile crisis that Peking failed to practice what it advocated for others, using Hong Kong and Macao as examples.[72] The American Communist Party followed suit by asking: "Why this double-standard approach?"[73] The Chinese reaction, as expressed in an editorial of *Jen-min jih-pao* on March 8, 1963, is revealing: "With regard to the outstanding issues, which are a legacy from the past, we have *always* held that, when conditions are ripe, they should be settled *peacefully through negotiations* and that, pending a settlement, the *status quo* should be maintained. Within this category are the questions of Hong Kong, Kowloon, and Macao and the questions of all those boundaries which have not been formally delimited in each case by the parties concerned."[74]

Apart from its militant rhetoric, China has been relatively consistent in both theory and practice on wars of national liberation. The doctrinal pronouncement on the desirability and inevitability of revolutionary wars has been projected as a model for others to emulate, not as a blueprint for Chinese global strategy. None of China's actual use of force across her national boundaries since 1949 falls within the category of support for wars of national liberation.[75] As if to validate the theme of self-reliance, China has taken a rather dim view of Castro's strategy of exporting revolution.[76] In 1965, according to a well-documented study, China *endorsed* only 23 out of a possible 120 revolutionary and armed struggles in Asia, Africa, and Latin America.[77] Although Africa was singled out in 1961 as "the center of the struggle against colonialism,"[78] China's African policy between 1949 and 1970 has been "pragmatic, evolutionary, and non-disruptive."[79] Peking's support of revolutionary movements around the world has been largely confined to model projection through sustained ideological propaganda.

[72] Excerpts from Khrushchev's speech are reprinted in Dennis J. Doolin, *Territorial Claims in the Sino-Soviet Conflict: Documents and Analysis* (Stanford, Calif.: The Hoover Institution on War, Revolution, and Peace, 1965), pp. 27-28.

[73] *Ibid.*, p. 29.

[74] English trans., *ibid.*, pp. 29-31; emphasis added.

[75] Hsiung, *Law and Policy in China's Foreign Relations*, pp. 293-96; Thomas W. Robinson, "Peking's Revolutionary Strategy in the Developing World: The Failures of Success" (Santa Monica, Calif.: RAND corporation, P-4169, August 1969), p. 12.

[76] See Ernest Halperin, "Peking and Latin American Countries," *CQ*, No. 29 (July/September 1967), 111-54.

[77] Peter Van Ness, *Revolution and Chinese Foreign Policy: Peking's Support for Wars of National Liberation* (Berkeley, Calif.: University of California Press, 1971), p. 82. See also Jay Taylor, *China and Southeast Asia: Peking's Relations with Revolutionary Movements* (New York: Praeger, 1974).

[78] *KTTH*, No. 17 (April 25, 1961), 22.

[79] Main conclusion of Bruce D. Larkin, *China and Africa 1949-1970* (Berkeley, Calif.: University of California Press, 1973), p. 210.

Mao's Changing Image of Contradictions in the International System

It may be useful to specify the salient characteristics of Mao's analytical process. First, he has always shown a tendency to view both domestic and international realities largely through the prism of China's own revolutionary experience. The weight of the past that impinged on his thinking was not of a Golden Age long since gone but of revolutionary China, giving rise to the so-called Yenan complex.[80] Second, Mao's primary concern was always the fate of China rather than any abstract notion of international order. Third, Mao's strategic optimism manifested itself repeatedly in his analysis of the international system. His optimistic assessment was made less in terms of China's own strengths than in terms of the enemy's endemic weaknesses, which transform themselves into China's strengths through an inexorable historical process. Finally, Mao's preoccupation with the great powers led him to develop rather sharply delineated views of the United States and the Soviet Union, but his view of the developing nations remained fuzzy and undifferentiated.[81] His progressive disenchantment with the Soviet Union was a decisive factor in his changing definition of the international system as a whole.

Mao's dialectical analysis of the international system followed the law of the unity of opposites by first identifying and typologizing the system's major actors into enemies and friends, and then formulating appropriate tactics and strategies. The two-camp view of the world was a logical corollary of his dialectics. Mao resisted the idea of struggling against too many enemies at one time by stressing the strategic necessity of clearly distinguishing the principal contradiction (the enemy) from the secondary ones. Clearly, Mao assigned to himself the crucial role of the leadership—namely, determination of the principal contradiction. However, the Manichaean element in Mao's image of world order made it difficult, at least in theory, to accommodate non-aligned actors floating and flirting between the socialist camp and the imperialist camp, holding diametrically opposed world views. How did Mao's dialectics work out in practice in his analysis of the changing international situation?

The task of determining the principal contradiction during the Sino-Japanese War (1937-45) was simple enough. The contradiction be-

[80] See Mao's second talk with his nephew (Mao Yüan-hsin) on February 18, 1966, in *Wan-sui* (1969), p. 631.

[81] In his interview with M. M. Ali of Zanzibar on June 18, 1964, Mao candidly admitted that he was not very familiar with the situation in Africa. See *Wan-sui* (1969), p. 509.

tween China and imperialism in general had suddenly been transformed into "the particularly salient and sharp contradiction between China and Japanese imperialism."[82] The contradictions between China and "certain other imperialist powers" had been reduced to a secondary status; hence, the aim of the united front, Mao argued, was resistance to the principal contradiction—Japanese imperialism—rather than simultaneous opposition to all the imperialist powers. Simultaneously, China's internal contradictions had also been relegated to a subordinate place.[83] In short, the status of both internal and external contradictions had been changed by an aggressive act of Japanese imperialism. Yet Mao argued un-Sinocentrically that the center of gravity in world politics still lay in Europe, not in Asia.[84]

Defying the pessimistic prophets and doubters at home and abroad in the aftermath of World War II, Mao declared in 1946 that the international situation was "extremely favourable."[85] The paper-tiger thesis, which he had just expounded in his interviews with Anna Louise Strong, was counter-propaganda against what he believed to be an exaggerated fear of American imperialism and of the outbreak of a new world war. Mao's analysis of the international situation at this time minimized the dangers of Soviet-American war because, as Mao explained to Strong, the United States had to attack the American people first and then subjugate a vast zone—"which includes many capitalist, colonial and semi-colonial countries in Europe, Asia and Africa"[86]—before an attack on the Soviet Union was possible. The conceptual and strategic logic of this argument is not clear. Nonetheless, obviously referring to this statement, Mao maintained in 1958 and 1964 that he had first formulated the theory of the intermediate zone in 1946.[87]

This retroactive assertion should not be taken too seriously. The actual term "intermediate zone" (*chung-chien ti-tai*) was not used by Mao until his speech to the Supreme Soviet in Moscow on November 6, 1957.[88] Nor was there any follow-up on his casual reference to a vast zone separating the United States and the Soviet Union. It may in fact be argued that in 1946 there existed no intermediate zone in the political sense in which the term came to be used in the 1960s. The postwar decolonization process was still in its embryonic stage and the cold war just getting underway. Under the circumstances it is doubt-

[82] SW, I, p. 263.
[83] See SW, I, pp. 153, 263-64, 277-78; SW, II, pp. 313-14.
[84] Gittings, *The World and China*, p. 59.
[85] SW, IV, p. 117.   [86] *Ibid.*, p. 99.
[87] See *Wan-sui* (1969), pp. 256, 514-15.
[88] The text of Mao's speech is reprinted in *1958 Jen-min shou-ts'e* [1958 People's Handbook] (Tientsin: Ta-kung pao she, 1958), pp. 294-96.

ful that Mao, the practical thinker who was fully preoccupied with the civil war at the time, would theorize on the geopolitical implications of the intermediate zone. His main concern in 1946 was to explain matters "to those comrades in the Party [most probably also referring to Stalin] who are gloomy about the future of the struggle owing to their inadequate understanding of the favourable situation at home and abroad."[89]

Whatever misgivings Mao may have had about Stalin—or whatever hopes he may have cherished about American neutrality in the civil war—were all put aside by mid-1949, as Mao's two-camp view of the world began to assert itself. In his "On the People's Democratic Dictatorship" (June 30, 1949), Mao left no doubt as to what constituted the principal contradiction in the postwar international system. All Chinese, without exception, Mao declared, "must lean either to the side of imperialism or to the side of socialism. Sitting on the fence will not do, *nor is there a third road.*"[90]

In practice, however, the two-camp theory was subject to progressive modifications in the 1950s, as the PRC began to cultivate diplomatic relations with the nonaligned countries, as shown in Appendix A. The Five Principles of Peaceful Coexistence, which were first enunciated in the Sino-Indian Trade Agreement in Tibet on April 29, 1954, soon became the codified principles for the PRC's official relations with other states. The PRC also viewed the 1954 Geneva Conference on Indochina as "another great victory for the principle of peaceful negotiation and peaceful coexistence," which "demonstrated to the whole world that the use of force to settle international disputes is fruitless, and that the age of settling international disputes by negotiation is here to stay."[91]

In the wake of the Bandung Conference, neutralism began to emerge as a positive force rather than as the immoral act that US Secretary of State John Foster Dulles made it out to be. Such posturing on the part of China as yet presented no problem in Sino-Soviet relations. The two-camp theory received an official burial by Khrushchev in February 1956 as a foreign policy offshoot of the de-Stalinization campaign.[92] Likewise, Premier Chou En-lai declared in his address to the Third Session of the First National People's Congress on June 28,

[89] SW, IV, p. 117.   [90] *Ibid.*, p. 415; emphasis added.

[91] "Peaceful Negotiations Score Another Victory," *JMJP*, editorial, July 22, 1954, p. 1

[92] See N. S. Khrushchev, "The Central Committee Report," Leo Gruliow, ed., *Current Soviet Policies II: The Documentary Record of the 20th Party Congress and Its Aftermath* (New York: Praeger, 1957), p. 33. For a comprehensive analysis of Soviet posture toward the Third World, see Thomas Ferry Thornton, ed., *The Third World in Soviet Perspective* (Princeton, N.J.: Princeton University Press, 1964).

1956, "the Asian and African countries are playing an increasingly important role in international affairs."[93]

"Unlike the Russians," Franz Schurmann has perceptively observed, "the Chinese like to let their theories grow slowly and naturally, like plants responding to the environment."[94] This comment is pertinent to the Chinese development of the theory of the intermediate zone, for the theory grew slowly and naturally as a byproduct of Mao's changing perception of the international environment, dominated by the two superpowers. If Chou En-lai's star performance at the Bandung Conference generated a sense of diplomatic euphoria and of the possibility of exploiting the nonaligned countries as an instrument of Chinese foreign policy, the situation in Eastern Europe in 1956 was a major problem that required the careful attention and analysis of the chairman. In the wake of the Hungarian uprising, Mao saw a need to launch a major propaganda campaign to expound China's principled stand. His argument suggested that the "lean-to-one-side" policy was still valid, and that what happened to Hungary would not happen to China because the lean-to-one-side policy was based—or had to be based—upon the principle of Sino-Soviet equality.[95] As if to validate this line of reasoning, Mao declared that "the Soviet Union *and* China are the *principal* components of the socialist camp."[96]

In his speech of November 6, 1957, at the Moscow Conference, Mao made his first explicit public reference to the intermediate zone. American imperialism, he argued, "interferes in the internal affairs of all nations, particularly in the various nations of the intermediate zone situated between the American and socialist camps."[97] In 1958, Mao's explicit statements on the intermediate zone became more and more frequent as he drove home his central point. The national liberation movements in the intermediate zone had now become a new ally for the socialist camp because they constituted a protective buffer. To use Mao's own phrase, they were "the rear areas of imperialism" (*ti-kuo chu-i ti hou-fang*),[98] absorbing the imperialist aggressive thrust.

As China found herself increasingly at odds with both superpowers in the early 1960s, Mao's theory of contradictions began to show some doctrinal conflict over the relative importance of the various parts of the world. This is evident in the absence of public assurance as to

---

[93] "On Present International Situation, China's Foreign Policy, and the Liberation of Taiwan: An Address by Premier and Foreign Minister Chou En-lai to the Third Session of the First National People's Congress, June 28, 1956," *People's China*, No. 14 (July 16, 1956), Supplement, p. 3; emphasis added.

[94] Franz Schurmann, *The Logic of World Power* (New York: Pantheon Books, 1974), p. 355.

[95] *Wan-sui* (1969), p. 64.　　　　　　　　　[96] *Ibid.*, pp. 62-63; emphasis added.

[97] *1958 Jen-min shou-ts'e*, p. 295.

[98] *Wan-sui* (1969), p. 198. See also *Wan-sui* (1969), pp. 137, 239.

what now constituted the principal contradiction in the international system. Instead, Mao's analysis began to grope slowly in the direction of an expanded version of the theory of the intermediate zone. As late as January 1961, he was still explaining to the cadres the necessity of uniting with the Soviet Union, with fraternal socialist parties, and with the eighty-seven national parties, no matter what accusations they might make against China.[99] But in his "7,000 Cadres" speech a year later, Mao stated that the peoples of the whole world (an expanded intermediate zone) would now have to struggle against imperialism. Mao left little doubt in the minds of his audience that the Soviet revisionists had already gone astray beyond redemption, although this view was not explicitly stated in public until after the open split. At the same time Mao, the perennial optimist, invoked the revolutionary saga of the past to fight off a fresh outbreak of pessimism among his colleagues.[100]

Mao's analysis of the international situation took another major step in his speech at the Tenth Plenum of the Eighth Central Committee on September 24, 1962. He singled out three major forces in the international system—imperialism, nationalism, and revisionism—and declared somewhat parenthetically that the contradiction between the peoples of the entire world and imperialism was now the principal (*chu-yao*) one.[101] However, such a redefinition of the principal contradiction was not made in public until 1965. On the eve of the open Sino-Soviet break in July 1963, following the signing of the Test Ban Treaty, official Chinese analyses of the contemporary world situation listed the four *major* contradictions: between the socialist and imperialist camps; between the proletariat and the bourgeoisie in capitalist countries; between the oppressed nations and imperialism; and among the imperialist countries themselves. In addition, it was asserted that the various types of contradictions in the contemporary world were concentrated in the vast areas of Asia, Africa, and Latin America.[102] Thus, Mao's thinking was revealed to be in a state of flux, enumerating too many contradictions without making any clear distinction between the principal and secondary ones.

Perhaps responding to internal dissension within NATO as well as to

[99] Speech at the Ninth Plenum of the Eighth Central Committee of the CCP, January 18, 1961, *Wan-sui* (1967), p. 262.

[100] See Mao's "7,000 Cadres" speech, delivered at an Enlarged Central Work Conference, January 30, 1962, *Wan-sui* (1969), pp. 399-423; see also *ibid.*, pp. 316-19.

[101] *Ibid.*, p. 433.

[102] "A Proposal Concerning the General Line of the International Communist Movement: The Letter of the Central Committee of the Communist Party of China in Reply to the Letter of the Central Committee of the Communist Party of the Soviet Union of March 30, 1963," *PR*, No. 25 (June 21, 1963), 7, 9.

the deepening Sino-Soviet conflict, Mao began to move in the direction of establishing the broadest antiimperialist (anti-American) united front. Against this background, his further refinement of the theory of the intermediate zone began to appear in 1964. In an interview with a visiting French parliamentary delegation in January 1964, Mao is reported to have defined the Third World in the following manner: "France, . . . Germany, Italy, England provided that she ceases being an American broker, Japan *and ourselves* [China]—there is the Third World."[103] However, this version of Mao's refinement of the theory of the intermediate zone is at variance with the official statement of the theory as published in the January 21, 1964, editorial of *Jen-min jih-pao*, as well as with Mao's own exposition in interviews with M. M. Ali of Zanzibar (June 18, 1964) and a visiting Japanese socialist delegation (July 10, 1964) as recorded in the *Wan-sui* documents.

With minor variations, the revised theory of the intermediate zone in the *Jen-min jih-pao* editorial and Mao's interviews with the Zanzibari and Japanese delegations typologized the international system into four main categories: two camps and two intermediate zones between the two camps. Specifically, the revised theory stated that there were two intermediate zones. Asia, Africa, and Latin America constituted the first, while the capitalist world—Western Europe, North America (Canada), Oceania (Australia and New Zealand), and Japan—made up the second.[104] Curiously, however, neither Mao nor the official *Jen-min jih-pao* editorial mentioned to which camp or zone China itself belonged, reflecting the ambivalence and tentativeness of Mao's analysis of the changing international situation.

Furthermore, the official media of the PRC began to pronounce in 1964 that Asia, Africa, and Latin America—Peking studiously avoided using the term Third World (*ti-san shih-chieh*) at this time—represented the countryside of the world, while Europe and North America were its cities.[105] This rural-urban typology of the world was more fully refined and elaborated by Lin Piao in his 1965 essay on "People's War." Taking a bird's-eye view of the forces of the historical process and emphasizing that Mao's theory of the encirclement of the cities from rural revolutionary base areas was "of outstanding and universal practical importance for the present revolutionary struggles of all the oppressed nations and peoples," Lin Piao declared flatly: "In the final analysis, the whole cause of world revolution hinges on the revolutionary struggles of the Asian, African and Latin American peoples,

---

[103] *L'Humanité* (Paris), February 21, 1964, p. 3; emphasis added.
[104] See *JMJP*, editorial, January 21, 1964, p. 1; *Wan-sui* (1969), pp. 515, 535.
[105] *PR*, No. 13 (March 27, 1964), 17.

who make up the overwhelming majority of the world's population."[106] It should be noted here that Lin Piao's rural-urban zoning of the globe contrasts sharply with Mao's four-zone typology of the international system.

During the first half of the 1960s, Peking's public pronouncements carefully avoided any positive identification of the principal contradiction in the world. However, this ambivalence began to change in 1965. In May 1965, P'eng Chen declared in a major policy speech in Djakarta, Indonesia, that the contradiction between the oppressed nations of Asia, Africa, and Latin America on the one hand, and imperialism headed by the United States on the other, had now become the principal contradiction.[107] Lin Piao's essay on "People's War" a few months later reaffirmed this view, except for a minor change of phrasing from "the oppressed nations" to "the revolutionary peoples."[108] Yet Mao, responding to a specific question from Snow in his interview of January 9, 1965, confessed that he had not reached an opinion as to what constituted the principal contradiction in the contemporary world.[109]

Because of the disruptive spillovers of revolutionary turmoil during the Cultural Revolution, Chinese foreign policy was in limbo between 1966 and 1968. However, the transition from revolutionary chaos to pragmatic reconstruction started in late 1968 and culminated at the First Plenum of the Ninth Party Congress (April 1969), ushering in a new era in Chinese foreign policy. Lin Piao's report to the Congress quoted Mao's latest assessment of the international situation as follows: "With regard to the question of world war, there are but two possibilities: One is that the war will give rise to revolution and the other is that revolution will prevent the war." This new assessment followed a new analysis of contradictions, which listed four major contradictions in the world: (1) the contradiction between the oppressed nations on the one hand, and imperialism *and social imperialism* on the other; (2) the contradiction between the proletariat and the bourgeoisie in the capitalist *and revisionist countries*; (3) the contradiction between imperialist *and social-imperialist countries* and among the imperialist countries; and (4) the contradiction between socialist countries on the one hand, and imperialism *and social imperialism*, on

[106] "Long Live the Victory of People's War," PR, No. 36 (September 3, 1965), 24.

[107] P'eng Chen, "Speech at the Aliarcham Academy of Social Sciences in Indonesia," PR, No. 24 (June 11, 1965), 11. See also SCCS, No. 11 (June 10, 1965), 2-4.

[108] PR, No. 36 (September 3, 1965), 25-26.

[109] Snow, "Interview with Mao," p. 18.

the other.[110] There is no clear evidence that this analysis of multiple contradictions has been changed or revised during the first half of the 1970s.[111]

The Chinese ambivalence and difficulty in singling out the principal contradiction reflect the constant state of flux that attended the "agonizing reappraisal" of the international system. The structural change from bipolarity to multipolarity, coupled with the deepening Sino-Soviet conflict, led Mao to try out different variations on the theme of multiple zones. By 1972 the theory of the intermediate zone was revised once again, as the Chinese typologized the international system into four major zones: (1) the superpower zone, consisting of US imperialism and Soviet social-imperialism; (2) the socialist zone, made up of the socialist countries; (3) the first intermediate zone, representing the Asian, African, and Latin American countries; and (4) the second intermediate zone, comprising "certain major capitalist countries in the East and the West," except for the two superpowers.[112] Because of the superpowers' hegemonic contention and collusion in both intermediate zones, Peking declared publicly that it was now desirable and possible to link the two intermediate zones in order to form the broadest united front. Yet in a confidential document of the PLA, issued in early 1973, Soviet social-imperialism was depicted as "more crazy, adventurist, and deceptive" than American imperialism; hence "our [China's] *most important enemy*."[113]

What appears to be the final refinement of the theme of multiple zones emerged as a model of three worlds in Mao's interview with the leader of a Third World country in February 1974. Mao is reported to have said: "In my view, the United States and the Soviet Union form the first world. Japan, Europe and Canada, the middle section, belong to the second world. We are the third world. . . . The third world has a huge population. With the exception of Japan, Asia belongs to the third world. The whole Africa belongs to the third world, and Latin America too."[114] In a major policy speech before the plenary of

[110] *PR*, Special Issue (April 28, 1969), 26; emphasis added.

[111] See "A Powerful Weapon to Unite the People and Defeat the Enemy," *HC*, No. 9 (1971), 10-17; Chou En-lai's "Report on the Work of the Government," delivered on January 13, 1975 at the 1st Session of the Fourth National People's Congress of the PRC, *PR*, No. 4 (January 24, 1975), 21-25.

[112] See Shih Chün, "On Comprehending Some History of the National Liberation Movement—Fourth Talk on Studying Some World History," *HC*, No. 11 (1972), 71-72; and Hua Chih-hai, "Study Some Geography," *ibid.*, p. 75.

[113] The Propaganda Division of the Political Department of the Kunming Military Region, "Hsing-shih chiao-yü ts'an-k'ao ts'ai-liao" [Reference materials concerning education on situation], Nos. 41-43 (March 30, 1973), trans. and printed in *Issues and Studies* (Taipei) 10 (June 1974), 94-108; reprinted in *Chinese Law and Government* 8 (Spring 1975), 30-60; quote from *ibid.*, p. 39; emphasis added.

[114] Cited in the editorial department of *Jen-min jih-pao*, "Chairman Mao's

the 6th Special Session of the United Nations General Assembly on April 10, 1974, Teng Hsiao-p'ing officially proclaimed to the world audience this new strategic principle. After noting the demise of the socialist camp and the disintegration of the Western imperialist bloc, Teng declared: "Judging from the changes in international relations, the world today actually consists of three parts, or three worlds, that are both interconnected and in contradiction to one another. The United States and the Soviet Union make up the First World. The developing countries in Asia, Africa, Latin America and other regions make up the Third World. The developed countries between the two make up the Second World."[115]

It should be noted further that in a major policy speech before the 31st Session of the General Assembly, Ch'iao Kuan-hua, chairman of the Chinese delegation, declared in tribute to the Helmsman who had just passed away that the three-worlds typology was indeed Mao's "great strategic concept."[116] The Chinese press in 1977 was saturated with articles extolling Chairman's Mao's theory of the three worlds (*Mao chu-hsi san-ke shih-chieh li-lun*), and in the most elaborate and comprehensive foreign policy posture statement issued in recent years, the editorial department of *Jen-min jih-pao* devoted its entire issue (six pages) of November 1, 1977, to an article, entitled "Chairman Mao's Theory of the Differentiation of the Three Worlds Is a Major Contribution to Marxism-Leninism."[117] Thus, the theory of the three worlds has now been canonized as the strategic principle to guide Chinese global policy in the post-Mao era.

To sum up, then, China's definition of her place in the world has undergone a protracted struggle. The 1950s saw a dialogue between

---

Theory of the Differentiation of the Three Worlds Is a Major Contribution to Marxism-Leninism," *PR*, No. 45 (November 4, 1977), 11. The leader of a Third World country referred to above is most likely to be Dr. K. D. Kaunda, president of the Republic of Zambia, who had "a cordial and friendly conversation" with Mao on the afternoon of February 22, 1974. See "Chairman Mao Meets President and Madame Kaunda," *PR*, No. 9 (March 1, 1974), 3.

[115] *PR*, No. 16 (April 19, 1974), 6. It should be noted that Premier Chou En-lai's "Report to the Tenth National Congress of the CCP," delivered on August 24, 1973, had already laid the ground for the three-worlds typology. Specifically, Chou stated: "The just struggles of the Third World *as well as* of the people of Europe, North America and Oceania support and encourage each other. Countries want independence, nations want liberation, and the people want revolution—this has become an irresistible historical trend." *PR*, Nos. 35-36 (September 7, 1973), 22; emphasis added.

[116] *PR*, No. 42 (October 15, 1976), 13.

[117] See *JMJP*, November 1, 1977, pp. 1-6; English trans. in *PR*, No. 45 (November 4, 1977), 10-41, followed by a series of reference commentaries on the article in *ibid.*, pp. 41-43; No. 46 (November 11, 1977), 25-27, 29; No. 47 (November 18, 1977), 25-27; and No. 48 (November 25, 1977), 27-28, 30.

the two-camp theory and the theory of the intermediate zone. In the 1960s China was in a state of conceptual and normative confusion as she searched and groped for her place in the rapidly changing international system. The identity crisis of the 1960s was evident in her attempts to define and redefine the theory of the intermediate zone. Finally, however, China made peace with herself as a member of the Third World, which is now characterized as "a great motive force in pushing forward the wheel of history."

POPULISM, EGALITARIANISM, AND NATIONALISM

In order to understand the values and norms embodied in the Maoist image of world order, we need to mention the close link between domestic and international aspects in Mao's world view. Mao always connected social development at home with the antiimperialist struggle abroad. No doubt such a conceptual link was due to the material-dialectical world outlook that was supposed to be applicable to the analysis of the part (Chinese reality) and the whole (international reality). However, it was also due to Mao's cultural and nationalistic assumptions about the importance of China in any scheme of world order.

Repeatedly, Mao argued that there was no point in discussing international problems without discussing internal problems, because "China is an important part of the international situation."[118] Just as his epistemological process progressed from the immediate to the larger environment, so the analytical process in Mao's world outlook moved from the domestic to the international scene. Likewise, the values and norms that guided domestic politics were transferred to international politics. In the methodological sense, then, the Maoist image of world order worked the same way as the traditional Chinese image of world order. That is, if the traditional Chinese image of world order was an extension of the Confucian moral order, so was the Maoist image of world order an extension of revolutionary order and justice at home.

China's self-projection as the populist champion struggling against

[118] For illustrative purposes, only two examples from the *Wan-sui* documents will be cited here. Under the section subtitled, "The Domestic Situation" in his first speech at the 2nd Session of the 8th CCP Congress on May 8, 1958, Mao's opening declaration reads: "China is an important part of the international situation. When we discuss the international situation, we have to discuss China." In his "Spring Festival Speech" of February 13, 1964, Mao declared: "We have discussed international problems at this forum today. However, domestic problems are fundamental. If we don't handle domestic problems well, there is no point in talking about external affairs." See *Wan-sui* (1969), pp. 198, 457.

the injustices and inequities of a system of world dominance represents more than routine proselytizing rhetoric. Indeed, populism as epitomized in the slogan "Serve the people" (*wei jen-min fu-wu*) permeated Mao's private and public thought and behavior to such an extent that it must be regarded as the supreme value in his world outlook. Unlike Lenin, who was distrustful of unguided popular impulses (*What Is To Be Done?*), Mao believed that the masses of the people were the creative forces of history, and that therefore they should be constantly urged to shape their own destiny by liberating themselves from the pernicious influence of the "slave mentality." It was this brand of populism that led to a major campaign against the doctrines of Confucius and Mencius "which propagate despising of labor and the laboring people."[119] It was also this brand of populism that led Mao to attack Lin Piao's theory of "super-genius" in history.[120]

Just as Mao's theory was always close to practice, so was his value of populism close to the *rural* reality of Chinese society. Mao Sinicized Marxism by reversing the traditional Marxist assumption about the moral and revolutionary superiority of the urban proletariat over the peasant. Mao's excessive peasant populism brought about chaos from time to time, to be sure, but it must also be recognized that it was his unshakable confidence in the enthusiasm and creative upsurge of the Chinese peasantry that served as the foundation of self-reliance. Mao recognized the countryside as the source and strength of the national revolution as early as 1927 in his "Report on an Investigation of the Peasant Movement in Hunan"; in the 1950s and 1960s he portrayed the peasantry as the main source of wisdom, virtue, and discipline in the pursuit of a new moral order in China.

Mao's peasant populism manifested itself in a variety of ways in his trenchant criticism of Stalin. Essentially, Mao's basic criticism of Stalin centered on the latter's lack of trust in the people. In his view, this lack of trust caused Stalin's failure to adopt a "mass line" in both domestic and foreign policy. In turn, this lack of a mass line led Stalin to take a dim view of the prospects of the Maoist revolution in China, and to try to stop it.[121] In the opening paragraph of his comments on Stalin's *Economic Problems of Socialism in the Soviet Union*, Mao presents the following criticism of the Russian leader: "he [Stalin] says nothing about the superstructure"; "he sees things, but not people"; and "*his fundamental mistake (chi-pen ts'o-wu) is his lack of faith in the peasant.*"[122]

[119] *JMJP*, February 7, 1974, p. 3.
[120] See Schram, *Chairman Mao Talks to the People*, pp. 293-94, 297, 299, 350n.
[121] *Wan-sui* (1969), pp. 164, 432, 552.
[122] *Wan-sui* (1967), p. 156; emphasis added.

Mao sarcastically characterized Stalin's approach as "cadres decide everything" and "technology decides everything." If this is so, Mao asked, what about the masses?[123] He was also disturbed by Stalin's lack of dialectics. Stalin's propensity to execute people instead of engaging in the dialectical method of criticism and self-criticism to resolve non-antagonistic contradictions is explained in terms of his deficiency in dialectics. When Khrushchev's de-Stalinization campaign began in 1956, Mao admitted that he was happy and apprehensive at the same time: it was necessary to emancipate thought from Stalinism, but it was also dialectically wrong to demolish him at one blow.[124] On the evidence of the *Wan-sui* volumes, it is now possible to trace the Sino-Soviet conflict back to Stalin. And the underlying cause of the conflict appears to lie less in the clash of national interests (which has become the fashionable argument among China specialists) than in the clash of world outlooks—Mao's value-oriented world view moving on a collision course with Stalin's power-oriented one.

Mao's concepts of the paper tiger and the superiority of men over weapons represent a transformation of peasant populism into strategic thinking. For Mao, the masses constitute an important factor in the equation of national power. "The Chinese peasant is even better," Mao proudly boasted, "than the English-American worker."[125] It is not just the size of the population but the percentage of the population taking the mass line that must be taken into account in assessing a "position of strength." About 95 percent of the Chinese population, Mao argued, stand on the side of the popular masses; this, according to Mao's logic, adds another element—just cause—to the equation of national power. He extended this kind of populist reasoning to the international sphere by asserting that between 90 and 95 percent of mankind do not have anti-Chinese sentiments. On the so-called anti-Chinese question, Mao reassured the cadres, China need not fear because only about 10 percent of the world population would continue to engage in anti-Chinese activities over a prolonged period of time.[126] In the end, the just cause always prevails; to change the metaphor, where there is a just cause, there is a triumph.

In contrast to the traditional Chinese image of world order, Mao's world outlook reflected his vigorous and unceasing quest for an egalitarian society. Egalitarianism is not a value in and of itself, Mao admitted in his interview with André Malraux in 1965, but "it is important because it is natural to those who have not lost contact with

---

[123] *Wan-sui* (1969), p. 204.   [124] *Ibid.*, p. 163.
[125] *Ibid.*, p. 27.
[126] "On the Anti-Chinese Question," *Wan-sui* (1969), pp. 316-19.

the masses."[127] He then revealed his egalitarian vision in the following passage:

Humanity left to its own devices does not necessarily reestablish capitalism (which is why you are perhaps right in saying they [the Russians] will not revert to private ownership of the means of production), but it does reestablish inequality. The forces tending toward the creation of new classes are powerful. We have just suppressed military titles and badges of rank; every "cadre" becomes a worker again at least one day a week; whole trainloads of city dwellers go off to work in the people's communes. Khrushchev seemed to think that a revolution is done when a communist party has seized power—as if it were merely a question of national liberation.[128]

Mao conceptualized egalitarianism as an operational principle of unification between the masses and elites. The parasitic elitism in traditional China was sustained and legitimized by the twin pillars of superordination-subordination in the social process and the superiority of mental over manual labor in the cultural process. Any disturbance of this conservative status quo was minimized by the universal inculcation of the value of harmony. It was against this tenacious cultural and historical tradition that Mao showed an uncompromising will to push forward his struggle for an egalitarian society. Whether it was the "red versus expert" debate or the *hsia-fang* (downward transfer) movement, the central objective was to unify leadership with broad mass participation, thus fighting off "the forces tending toward the creation of new classes." This was Mao's way of dealing with the rise of national parasitic elites.

[127] André Malraux, *Anti-Memoirs*, trans. Terence Kilmartin (New York: Holt, Rinehart and Winston, 1968), p. 373. Mao's populist ethos was codified in The Three Main Rules of Discipline and The Eight Points for Attention. These rules were drawn up by Mao himself for the Chinese Workers' and Peasants' Red Army during the Agrarian Revolutionary War, but later became the codified principles of conduct for the PLA. The standard version of these rules as issued by the General Headquarters of the PLA in October 1947 is as follows: The Three Main Rules of Discipline: (1) Obey orders in all your actions; (2) Do not take a single needle or piece of thread from the masses; and (3) Turn in everything captured. The Eight Points for Attention: (1) Speak politely; (2) Pay fairly for what you buy; (3) Return everything you borrow; (4) Pay for anything you damage; (5) Do not hit or swear at people; (6) Do not damage crops; (7) Do not take liberties with women; and (8) Do not ill-treat captives. As late as August and September 1971, during his provincial tour, Mao complained that some of these rules were not clearly remembered and urged that they be used again to "educate the army, educate the cadres, educate the masses, educate the Party members and the people." See Schram, *Chairman Mao Talks to the People*, p. 298; *PR* (September 3, 1965), 30n.

[128] Malraux, *Anti-Memoirs*, p. 373.

The *hsia-fang* movement was perhaps the most daring egalitarian campaign launched by any political leader in modern times. At the inception of the movement, Mao expressed his concern about the dangerous tendency creeping in among leadership personnel "not to share the sufferings of the masses but rather to be mindful of personal position and profit."[129] When it was launched in mid-1957, the movement embodied Mao's image of a good society. It proceeded on his assumption that man's world outlook had to be transformed *before* a societal transformation (a good society) could be brought about. It was a major ideological campaign to remold man's world outlook, with clearly defined values guiding the process. That populist egalitarianism served as a value guide in the campaign is seen from the targets: the estrangement of the city from the countryside; and the estrangement of the mental worker (cadres, bureaucrats, intellectuals, and military officers) from the manual worker. In order to overcome the widening gap between the center and the periphery in Chinese society, the party directive of May 14, 1957, stated that "in principle all communists, regardless of their position and seniority, should assume similar and equal work as ordinary labourers."[130]

The logic of the campaign is simple enough: it is only through the sharing of common sufferings and labors that the bondage between the masses and leadership can be formed and maintained. The movement did not attack expertise *per se*, but rather what may be characterized as an ideological misappropriation of talents and skills available for the collective good of the society. It was in this spirit that Mao condemned the following: extensive reliance on private secretaries, which was a sign of declining revolutionary vigor; the Ministry of Public

---

[129] Cited in Rensselaer W. Lee III, "The *Hsia Fang* System: Marxism and Modernisation," *CQ*, No. 28 (October/December 1966), 44. It may be noted in this connection that Mao's personal life-style exemplified his populist-egalitarian convictions. The posthumous testimonial presented on September 15, 1976, by Mao's bodyguards—members of the PLA's 8341 Unit—noted: "Esteemed and beloved great leader Chairman Mao, you lived in a plain and hard-working way and [were] unassuming and approachable. The house you lived in was old, but you declined all offers to have it repaired in the more than 20 years after liberation. Your shirts, blankets and shoes were worn thin from many years of use. We suggested many times that they be changed, but you would not allow it." This image of Mao as a frugal and self-sacrificing worker in his relentless quest for an egalitarian social order had already been described by Edgar Snow and Anna Louise Strong in the 1930s and 1940s. In the last interview he had with Mao before Snow died, the correspondent, observing Mao's vegetable garden, noted: "Perhaps he needs the output, since he is said to have taken a recent cut of 20% in his subsistence 'wages.'" See *NYT*, September 16, 1976, p. 10; Snow, *Red Star Over China*, pp. 74-76; Strong, "A World's Eye View from a Yenan Cave," p. 123; Snow, "A Conversation with Mao Tse-tung," p. 46.

[130] Cited in Lee, "The *Hsia Fang* System," p. 45.

Health, for diverting its scarce resources to narrow specialization in order to serve only 15 percent of the population; creeping corruption, arrogance, and complacency among party officials; and his own nephew (Mao Yüan-hsin), for spending too much time with the children of cadres and looking down on other people.[131] Mao's populism has also been translated into a code of behavior for Chinese aid personnel abroad, as reflected in the following statement: *"Abiding by Chairman Mao's teachings, Chinese aid personnel have travelled thousands of miles to help the people of other countries in their construction. . . . Defying hardships and fatigue, they persist in a style of hard work and simple living, and share weal and woe with the working people of other countries."*[132]

Despite the *hsia-fang* movement, Mao's apprehension about the regressive forces eroding the egalitarian social order became more and more pronounced in 1965. Around that time, as noted earlier, he uncharacteristically struck a note of pessimism in his talk with Snow about events not always bending themselves to human will. Again, Mao's worry centered on creeping embourgeoisement in the superstructure. To Mao, the "pragmatic" belief that a higher production of goods and services would automatically bring about egalitarian social well-being and justice—as implied in Teng Hsiao-p'ing's oft-quoted statement about cats being good, whether black or white, so long as they caught mice—was an illusion, as attested to by the rise of revisionism in the Soviet Union.

The Great Proletarian Cultural Revolution, notwithstanding all the turmoil and disruption it caused, was a necessary and desirable risk in Mao's hierarchy of values, because it attempted to deal with the problem of the superstructure in a fundamental way that had never been tried before: an ideological and structural transformation of the whole establishment in China. Mao admitted that such a cultural revolution to reassert a proletarian quest for social justice and equality, and once again "to touch the souls of the people,"[133] can be taken two or three times at most in the course of one century.[134]

There is little dispute that Mao has always remained a nationalist and that his Sinicization of Marxism was a synthesis of alien ideology and Chinese reality. How did his populist-egalitarian ethos translate itself into his brand of nationalism? Historical grievances influenced his thinking in a way that never permitted him to free himself from his

[131] *Wan-sui* (1969), pp. 465-71, 551, 615-16; Ch'en, *Mao Papers*, p. 72.

[132] "Wholeheartedly Serving the People of the World—Chinese Aid Personnel Abroad," *PR*, No. 11 (March 15, 1968), 32; emphasis in original.

[133] *JMJP*, September 5, 1966, p. 1.   [134] *Wan-sui* (1969), p. 677.

preoccupation with building a powerful nation in the family of nations. The assessment of Mao's leadership will no doubt continue for some time among China specialists around the world. Its most critical challenge was to fulfill this nationalistic ambition without undermining the principle of socioeconomic justice and equality at home. Here, Mao applied a special form of contradictions analysis. Just as the contradiction between "red" and "expert" was supposed to be resolved through a *unification* of the two, so Mao approached the question in terms of balancing and unifying, rather than of one subjugating the other, as in the antagonistic contradictions. In short, the two objectives were conceptualized as mutually complementary rather than conflicting. That this did not always work out in practice is seen in the zigzag course of the Chinese polity in the last two and a half decades.

Mao's dialectical mind did theoretically synthesize the two objectives. In order to generate a psychological mobilization of the masses for rapid national development, Mao repeatedly told the cadres and the people that China would not be respected by the rest of the world unless she became strong and powerful. To achieve this, however, China had to catch up with—and eventually surpass—England, France, West Germany, Japan, and even the United States in steel production. Such a big country with so many illiterates and so little steel production was understandably an object of international contempt, Mao reminded the cadres; but it was good to be despised, because it aroused the national determination of the Chinese masses to redouble their efforts to leap forward.[135]

Partly to convince the skeptics and partly to synthesize the national objective of rapid economic development and the social objective of maintaining egalitarian justice, Mao introduced the concept of "social justice" as a critical component in the equation of national power. Obviously reflecting the Maoist line of reasoning, *Jen-min jih-pao* declared:

> They [the skeptics at home and abroad] do not understand that the balance of forces cannot be decided simply by the quantity of iron and steel or other products. The basic question is—on which side is justice; to which side do the people give their support; what is the nature of the political strength; what is the nature of the system. History frequently shows that the weak defeats the strong and the unarmed defeats the fully-armed. . . . Though, for the time being, the output of some products is smaller on our side than in the imperialist countries, yet since we are on the side of socialism, the

[135] *Wan-sui* (1967), pp. 260-61; *Wan-sui* (1969), pp. 64, 209, 216-17, 267, 392.

socialist system plus a certain level of material strength gives us superiority in the entire balance of forces.[136]

Such an argument was also Mao's way of struggling against what he believed to be the most serious developmental obstacle: the psychological legacy of old superstitions, habits, thoughts, and behavioral patterns. In particular, Mao singled out as a mental disease the inferiority complex that Confucianism and imperialism had inculcated in the minds of the Chinese masses. While consistently praising Dr. Sun Yat-sen for his trail-blazing contribution to the national-democratic revolution, Mao contemptuously dismissed Chiang Kai-shek for having produced only 50,000 tons of steel in twenty years![137]

Yet, to a remarkable degree, Mao's nationalism was devoid of any racial and chauvinistic imperative. While clearly recognizing nationalism as a powerful force in social development, he constantly warned of the dangers of a revival of Han chauvinism. Mao saw no inherent or independent quality of good or bad in nationalism: its character was determined by the value or purpose for which it was being advocated. Nationalism, in Mao's cosmology, was like a double-edged sword: it could cut either way—positive or negative, constructive or destructive, unifying or divisive.

Contrary to journalistic and semischolarly suggestions advanced from time to time, there is no substantive evidence that Mao was trying to revive the old tribute system or that he was embellishing his role as a contemporary emperor in a red robe. Breaking away from China's long tradition of cultural self-glorification, Mao's world outlook worked on the assumption that China's development is part of the world's historical process. In his essay "In Memory of Norman Bethune," which was canonized as one of three articles constantly read during the Cultural Revolution, Mao wrote that "the spirit of absolute selflessness" with which Comrade Bethune served the people "is our internationalism, the internationalism with which we oppose both narrow nationalism and narrow patriotism."[138] He strongly emphasized the transnational ideology of Marxism in his "Instruction on Nationalities Problems" (1958) by citing three pertinent examples: Marx was a Jew; Stalin was of a minority nationality (Georgian); and Chiang Kai-shek was a Han Chinese.[139] If there was any doubt about Mao's attitude toward the tribute system, it was clearly dispelled when

---

[136] "Great Revolutionary Declaration," *JMJP*, editorial, November 25, 1957, p. 1; trans. in *People's China*, No. 24 (December 16, 1957), 6. For a similar line of reasoning, see also *KTTH*, No. 17 (April 25, 1961), 19-25.

[137] *Wan-sui* (1969), pp. 59-61, 71-72. [138] SW, II, p. 337.

[139] "Instruction on Nationalities Problems," *Current Background*, No. 891 (October 8, 1969), 30.

he compared the so-called Western unity under American atomic bombs to a modern tribute system. Under that type of unity, Mao declared, both big and small partners had to pay tribute and prostrate themselves as inferiors.[140]

As if to underscore one of the underlying causes of the Sino-Soviet dispute, Mao's attack against "big-nation chauvinism" (*ta-kuo sha-wen chu-i*) became more and more frequent after 1958.[141] China, he declared, must behave *properly*, steering carefully between the twin dangers of an inferiority complex and great power chauvinism. In September 1962 Mao singled out nationalism, imperialism, and revisionism as the three major forces shaping international politics. This was a conceptual turning point. Although the three-worlds theory developed rather slowly, the view of a world in which the struggle between the imperialist and the socialist camps represented the principal contradiction was now being replaced by one in which the main struggle was taking place between the forces of nationalism and revolution on the one side, and the forces of imperialism and social-imperialism on the other. The new image of world order was eventually codified in the party's and the state's constitutions; in both China proclaimed her opposition to great power chauvinism and pledged herself *never* to be a superpower.[142]

CHANGE AND CONTINUITY

The debate on the question as to whether tradition still persists in contemporary Chinese foreign policy has generally been polarized into two contending schools: (1) the "continuity" school, which asserts that the Chinese image of world order has not been altered in its fundamentals from the traditional one; and (2) the "complete break" school, which argues that the lines of continuity with traditional China have been broken. Let us now recapitulate the salient features of the traditional and Maoist images of world order in order to draw up a balance sheet on this issue.

On the side of continuity, we have noticed some conceptual and stylistic similarities between the traditional and the Maoist images of

[140] *Wan-sui* (1969), p. 245.

[141] For an example of an attack on great power chauvinism, see Mao's first speech delivered at the 2nd Session of the Eighth Party Congress on May 8, 1958, *Wan-sui* (1969), pp. 186-96.

[142] The Constitution of the Chinese Communist Party adopted by the Tenth National Party Congress on August 28, 1973, stipulates in Chap. I that the Communist Party of China "opposes great-power chauvinism." Likewise, the Constitution of the People's Congress of the People's Republic of China states in its preamble: "China will never be a superpower." See *PR*, Nos. 35-36 (September 7, 1973), 26, and No. 4 (January 24, 1975), 13.

world order. Both images have shown a strong and recurring tendency toward model projection. Just as the traditional Chinese image of world order was an outward projection of the Confucian moral order, so the Maoist image of world order is an outward projection of revolutionary China's self-image. In traditional and Communist China, the conceptual frameworks relevant to domestic and international politics are identical. Likewise, the conceptual tendency to define national power in terms of moral virtue has persisted in Mao's China, although the definition and content of these terms have differed rather sharply. If virtue was might in Confucian China, justice is might in Communist China.

This way of defining national power may in part explain the chronic gap between policy pronouncement and policy performance in both traditional and Communist China. Just as the practice of the tribute system often fell short of the theory, so the practice of Mao's support for revolutionary struggles abroad has fallen short of militant rhetoric. Both images of world order show a pronounced tendency to *declare* policy beyond their power and willingness to *fulfill*. The imbalance between policy and power is compensated for by excessive moralizing and ideologizing, as if purity of doctrine would somehow work toward the establishment of an equilibrium between the two.

The foregoing points give some credence to the continuity school, but they do not necessarily demonstrate the persistence of tradition in Mao's image of world order. Is it unique or endemic to China, for example, that her image of world order represents an outward extension of her self-image? Or is this a reflection of a generalized sociopsychological phenomenon, in which every nation's world view is a reflection of her self-image? I am inclined to accept the latter hypothesis rather than the former. It seems to be stretching "evidence" too far to assert that the above-mentioned conceptual and stylistic similarities are endemic to China, and that therefore they establish continuity between the traditional and Maoist images of world order. Given the ponderous size, weight, and dimension of China in both the traditional and the contemporary international systems, her image of world order, no matter what form it takes, may appear to the outsider to be larger than its true size, hence always Chinese and always unique.

While the traditional and Maoist images share the same conceptual tendency of projecting outward a model of domestic values, they differ in the values so projected. The cosmology on the basis of which Mao projected his image of world order is far removed from the cosmology of the traditional tribute system, because the history that influenced Mao's thinking most was *modern* history. The Maoist image

91

of world order has substituted a new value of struggle for the traditional value of harmony; a new value of populism for the traditional value of elitism; a new value of egalitarianism for the traditional values of status and hierarchy; and new values of national sovereignty, independence, and equality for the traditional value of tributary relations.

The hierarchical conception of world order has played a negative and traumatic role in the shaping of Mao's image of world order. While the hierarchical order of the tribute system invited national disaster, the hierarchical order of Western and Japanese imperialism brought national disgrace and humiliation. Mao's ferocious attack against great power chauvinism, coupled with the pledge that China would never be a superpower, represented his opposition to the imperialist (US) and social-imperialist (USSR) hierarchical conceptions of world order in the contemporary international system. Stripped to their essence, then, the differences outweigh the similarities between the traditional and the Maoist views. In cosmological terms, the Maoist image of world order is a break from the traditional image. To be sure, this break does not—and cannot—represent a total break with the whole gamut of habits of thought and behavior inherited from the past, but in terms of normative orientation, the two images are on divergent paths.

In the final analysis, the Maoist image of world order represents an underdog perspective from below, struggling to redefine the basic values and rules of the game in the international system, rather than a topdog perspective from above, preserving the existing status quo through the enforcement of "world law and order." The indiscriminate advocacy of the nonuse of force in international relations serves the preservation of superpower hegemonic conceptions of world order. By stressing the concepts of just and unjust war and of revolutionary and counter-revolutionary violence, the Maoist image shows that its values are oriented toward "world justice" rather than toward "world order." To put it differently, the Maoist image defines "world order" in terms of its own conception of justice rather than in terms of peace. Peace or order is an illusion that blinds our perception of the structural violence inherent in the asymmetrical distribution of social and economic goods and justice in the present system of world dominance. Peace will eventually come as a happy byproduct, Mao reasoned, when class antagonisms and exploitative relationships are eliminated.

Mao's is, in short, a radical-populist model of world order. Such an orientation is in part psychological and in part conceptual. Psychologically, Mao found it difficult to render support to the structures, values, and rules of the postwar international system in which China had been prevented from playing her legitimate role. Conceptually—and normatively, too—Mao believed it to be an overriding imperative that the old structures of the exploitative system give way to new ones if the populist needs of the global underdog were to be met. By refusing to join the superpower club and by casting China's fate with that of the Third World in the restructuring of global forces and institutions in the late 1960s and early 1970s, Mao laid down a new strategic principle for China. How long Mao's successors will keep it unrevised is a matter of global significance that transcends the interests of both China and world-order specialists. For the moment, however, we can turn to Part II to examine closely how Mao's image of world order has actually expressed itself behaviorally in the course of Chinese participation in the global political system in the 1970s.

PART II. EMPIRICAL ANALYSIS: BEHAVIORAL DIMENSIONS OF CHINESE GLOBAL POLICY

· 3 ·

GLOBAL POLITICS IN THE
GENERAL ASSEMBLY

> What the Soviet leadership is practising is certainly not socialism but, as Lenin put it, socialism in words, imperialism in deeds—that is, social-imperialism. . . . A simple but important principle of Marxism-Leninism is that one must judge a person not merely by his words but [also] by his deeds.
>
> Ch'iao Kuan-hua

> China is attempting to use this "third world" as a means to achieve its real aims, i.e. as a spring-board for immediately becoming a "super-super-Power."
>
> Yakov A. Malik

The above polemical exchange represents the opening salvos of the Sino-Soviet confrontation in the global international organization. It took place only ten days after the Chinese debut in the General Assembly, during a plenary debate on the Soviet proposal for a world disarmanent conference.[1] Chinese participation in the multitude of UN organs and specialized agencies since 1971, apart from its important implications for humanity's pursuit of an elusive world order with justice in the nuclear-ecological age, provides a firm empirical basis for a disciplined macro-inquiry into Chinese global politics. Of all the international organizations, however, the General Assembly is the most suitable—and the most accessible—arena for such an inquiry.

"The assembly was created," Woodrow Wilson once remarked about the League of Nations, "in order that anybody that purposed anything wrong should be subjected to the awkward circumstance that everybody could talk about it."[2] This description is hardly less applicable to the UN General Assembly today. If parliamentary diplomacy in plenary sessions generates voluminous verbal and voting records, private consultations behind the closed doors of numerous committees, subcommittees and subsidiary bodies keep in reserve a wealth of valuable information that can be tapped through field interviews.

---

[1] GAOR, 26th Sess., 1996th plenary meeting (26 November 1971), paras. 133, 136, 141.

[2] Quoted in Sydney B. Bailey, *The General Assembly of the United Nations: A Study of Procedure and Practice* (rev. ed., New York: Praeger, 1964), p. 8.

While lacking the power to "legislate" except on matters related to internal administrative and budgetary questions, the General Assembly has never suffered from a shortage of power and willingness to initiate, discuss, and recommend any number of solutions to deepening global problems and crises. The role and posture assumed by a Member State in this political process make a mirror image of its global strategy. In short, it is possible to compare words and deeds, parliamentary diplomacy and private consultative behavior, and the rhetoric and performance of any Member State through the combined use of documents and field interviews, and to draw up in the process a composite of the style and strategic thrust of that nation's global policy.

The General Assembly is especially well suited to the study of the development of Chinese global politics. The question of Chinese representation that plagued the United Nations system for over two decades was resolved by the changing political process in the General Assembly, while the other UN organs and the specialized agencies passively played second fiddle to the tune set by the Assembly's decision. It was the Assembly that determined both China's exclusion from and entry into the global community. There is also ample evidence that China sees the General Assembly as the most important arena, where "an irresistible historical trend" is taking shape. If the Third World is indeed the motive force in pushing the wheel of history toward a new world order, as China claims, the politics of the Assembly serves as a mirror image of such a historical process.

The General Assembly is particularly well suited for the pronouncement and performance of Chinese global politics. The decision-making process in the Assembly, especially its one-state-one-vote formula, is congenial to the Chinese normative advocacy that world affairs should be managed by all nations, large or small, on an equal footing. This advocacy of "participatory democracy" is most clearly reflected in China's stand on the question of Charter review. That the General Assembly is a central arena of struggle in the development of Chinese global strategy is also reflected in the extensive coverage it has received in the Chinese media—*Jen-min jih-pao* and New China News Agency releases, in particular—as well as in the fact that China's participation in the activities of the General Assembly is more active and more extensive than that in any organ or agency in the United Nations system. In short, Chinese participation in the General Assembly provides a logical point of departure for an overview of Chinese global politics. However, to place China's global politics in the Assembly during the last six years in a broader historical perspective, we need to review briefly the evolution of Chinese attitudes and policy toward the United Nations during the exclusion period.

The Transition from Exclusion to "Admission"

China's posture toward the United Nations during the preentry period may be characterized as one of "Love me or leave me, but don't leave me alone," passing through the stages of naive optimism, frustration, disenchantment, rebellion, disinterest, revived hope, and a sophisticated diplomatic campaign to gain her seat.[3] In contrast to a very negative attitude toward the League of Nations,[4] however, the PRC

[3] The literature on the PRC's attitude and posture toward the United Nations during the preentry period is uneven. For a representative sample of writings, see the following: Mervyn W. Adams, "Communist China and the United Nations: A Study of China's Developing Attitude Towards the UN Role in International Peace and Security" (M.A. Thesis, Columbia University, 1964); Lincoln P. Bloomfield, "China, the United States, and the United Nations," *IO* 20 (Autumn 1966), 653-76; Winberg Chai, "China and the United Nations: Problems of Representation and Alternatives," *Asian Survey* 10 (May 1970), 397-409; Hungdah Chiu, "The United Nations," in Shao-chuan Leng and Hungdah Chiu, eds., *Law in Chinese Foreign Policy: Communist China and Selected Problems of International Law* (Dobbs Ferry, N.Y.: Oceana, 1972), pp. 195-242; Hungdah Chiu and R. R. Edwards, "Communist China's Attitude Toward the United Nations: A Legal Analysis," *AJIL* 62 (January 1968), 20-58; Poeliu Dai, "Canada and the Two-China Formula at the United Nations," *Canadian Yearbook of International Law* 5 (1967), 217-28; R. R. Edwards, "The Attitude of the People's Republic of China Toward International Law and the United Nations," *Papers on China* 17 (December 1963), 235-71; A. M. Halpern, "China, the United Nations, and Beyond," *CQ*, No. 10 (April-June 1962), 72-77; Myres S. McDougal and Richard M. Goodman, "Chinese Participation in the United Nations," *AJIL* 60 (October 1966), 671-727; Mostafa Rejai, "Communist China and the United Nations," *Orbis* 9 (Fall 1966), 823-38; F. B. Schick, "The Question of China in the United Nations," *International and Comparative Law Quarterly* 12 (October 1963), 1232-50; Byron S. Weng, "Communist China's Changing Attitudes Toward the United Nations," *IO* 20 (Autumn 1966), 677-704, and *Peking's UN Policy: Continuity and Change* (New York: Praeger, 1972). The last entry by Weng still remains a standard work on the PRC's preentry policy toward the United Nations. For this section in the chapter dealing with China's evolving posture toward the United Nations during the preentry period, however, I have relied extensively on section I of my own article, "The People's Republic of China in the United Nations," pp. 303-305.

[4] The attitude of the Chinese Communists toward the League of Nations was very negative, as evidenced by a telegram of the Chinese Soviet Government (dated October 6, 1932) signed by Mao Tse-tung, Hsiang Ying, and Chang Kuo-t'ao: "The Provisional Central Government of the Chinese Soviet Republic long ago told the popular masses of the whole country that the League of Nations is a League of Robbers by which the various imperialisms are dismembering China. The principal task of the Lytton Commission of Enquiry sent to China by the League was to prepare the dismemberment of China and the repression of all the revolutionary movements that have raised the flag of the Chinese Soviets." Cited in Stuart R. Schram, *The Political Thought of Mao Tse-tung* (New York: Praeger, 1963), pp. 266-67. For additional references, see Jerome Alan Cohen and Hungdah Chiu, *People's China and International Law: A Documentary Study*, 2 vols. (Princeton, N.J.: Princeton University Press, 1974), pp. 91, 92, 94-95, 294-295, 328-29, 423, 728, 1116, 1287, 1289, 1300, 1356-1357, 1389-1390, 1415, 1417, 1424.

assumed a positive posture toward the United Nations from the beginning.

Commenting on the San Francisco Conference then in progress, for example, Mao Tse-tung declared on April 24, 1945: "The Chinese Communist Party fully agrees with the proposals of the Dumbarton Oaks conference and the decisions of the Crimea conference on the establishment of an organization to safeguard international peace and security after the war. It welcomes the United Nations Conference on International Organization in San Francisco. It has appointed its own representative on China's delegation to this conference in order to express the will of the Chinese people."[5] In its policy pronouncements in the 1950s the PRC's support of the principles of the UN Charter remained largely unchanged. Despite her exclusion from participation, the principles of the Charter were cited in numerous bilateral treaties that the PRC signed in the 1950s.[6]

However, the Indonesian withdrawal on January 7, 1965, triggered off a series of polemics against the United Nations. Indeed, Peking's bill of complaints was broad and sweeping: that blind faith in the United Nations must cease because the Organization was by no means sacred and inviolable; that by committing sins of commission and omission, the United Nations had become an adjunct of the US State Department; that the United Nations had become a channel for United States' economic and cultural penetration into Asian, African, and Latin American countries; and that the United Nations, in the final analysis, was a paper tiger.[7] "As a matter of fact," an editorial of *Jen-min jih-pao* fulminated, "the United Nations has degenerated into a dirty international political stock exchange in the grip of a few big powers; the sovereignty of other nations, particularly that of small ones, is often bought and sold there by them like shares."[8]

The PRC's polemics against the United Nations also cited new preconditions for joining the Organization. Whereas the expulsion of Chiang Kai-shek's representatives had been the only precondition before 1965,[9] Peking's demands now included, *inter alia*, the explusion

[5] SW, III, pp. 306-307.

[6] For numerous references to the principles of the UN Charter in the PRC's bilateral treaties in the 1950s and early 1960s, see Hsiung, *Law and Policy in China's Foreign Relations*, pp. 89-90.

[7] See the Chinese government's statement of January 10, 1965, in *JMJP*, January 10, 1965, p. 1; English trans. in *PR*, No. 3 (January 15, 1965). See also *JMJP*, editorial, January 10, 1965, p. 1; English trans. in *PR*, No. 3 (January 15, 1965), 7-9.

[8] *JMJP*, editorial, January 10, 1965, p. 1; English trans. in *PR*, No. 3 (January 15, 1965), 8-9.

[9] The PRC's last statement on the United Nations before Indonesia's withdrawal was contained in Premier Chou En-lai's report on the work of the government,

of "all imperialist countries," the admission of "all independent countries," the cancellation of the UN resolutions against the PRC and the Democratic People's Republic of Korea (DPRK), the adoption of a resolution condemning the United States as an aggressor, and a review and revision of the Charter.[10] The PRC then presented two sharply worded alternatives: "Either the organization rids itself of United States domination, corrects its mistakes and gets thoroughly reorganized, or a revolutionary United Nations will be set up to replace it."[11]

Having received little attention, let alone support, for her call for a reorganization and/or a replacement of the United Nations, the PRC's interest in the world organization declined rapidly during the next few years. In a comment on the disappointing results of the vote on the question of Chinese representation at the 22nd Session of the General Assembly (see Appendix B), the PRC declared on December 8, 1967: "Speaking frankly, the Chinese people are not at all interested in sitting in the United Nations, a body manipulated by the United States, a place for playing power politics, a stock exchange for the United States and the Soviet Union to strike political bargains, and an organ to serve the U.S. policies of aggression and war."[12] Shortly thereafter, PRC commentaries on the United Nations practically disappeared from the official media, as seen in Table 3.1.

It was no mere happenstance that the termination of China's Cultural Revolution should coincide with the beginning of a "new and revolutionary" foreign policy. Historically, a moderate and pragmatic foreign policy has generally followed political stability and lull on the domestic scene. However, the new foreign policy adopted by the PRC leadership represented much more than a restoration of a pre-

---

delivered at the 1st Session of the Third National People's Congress on December 21-22, 1964, which stated that "unless the United Nations expels the representative of the Chiang Kai-shek clique and restore China's legitimate rights in their entirety, we will have absolutely nothing to do with the United Nations." See *PR*, No. 1 (January 1, 1965), 19. In contrast, Lin Piao's celebrated programmatic essay, "Long Live the Victory of People's War!" published on September 3, 1965, failed to mention the United Nations. This shows the decisive impact of Indonesia's withdrawal on the evolution of the PRC's attitude.

[10] These new demands were spelled out by Foreign Minister Ch'en Yi in his press conference of September 29, 1965, in Peking. See *PR*, No. 41 (October 8, 1965), 11-12. That these new demands were presented to rationalize the PRC's lack of interest in the United Nations is indicated by Ch'en Yi's statement made at the same press conference: "During the U.S. war of aggression against Korea, the United Nations adopted a resolution naming China as an aggressor. How can China be expected to take part in an international organization which calls her an aggressor? Calling China an aggressor and then asking the aggressor to join would not the United Nations be slapping its own face?"

[11] *PR*, No. 42 (October 15, 1965), 11.

[12] *Ibid.*, No. 50 (December 8, 1967), 21.

TABLE 3.1. Articles on the United Nations System Appearing
in *Peking Review*, 1962-72

Year	No. of Articles	Year	No. of Articles
1962	0	1968	1
1963	7	1969	1
1964	8	1970	5
1965	29	1971 (before Oct. 25)	15
1966	7	1971 (after Oct. 25)	37
1967	5	1972	88

Source: PR, January 5, 1962-December 29, 1972.

Cultural Revolution status quo or simply a return of ambassadors to their diplomatic posts.[13] It demonstrated an extraordinary—almost unprecedented—degree of flexibility and moderation by extending the permissible limits of normalization toward former enemies such as the United States, Japan, and Yugoslavia. Under the impetus of this new policy, the PRC's attitude toward the United Nations also assumed a direct, conciliatory, and flexible posture. All the polemical indictments against the United Nations and the extraneous preconditions for participation disappeared. Instead, the PRC launched a new and sophisticated campaign to gain entrance to the family of nations.

Greatly buoyed up by the vote in the 1970 General Assembly session on the eighteen-nation draft resolution, the PRC leadership now incorporated the objective of winning a UN seat into its grand strategy of a new foreign policy. In orchestrating this strategy, Peking used several diplomatic techniques. First, the PRC quietly pursued a "banquet diplomacy," an ingenious technique of inviting prominent Western and Third-World statesmen or former statesmen to visit China—Prince Sihanouk of Cambodia, former Premier Maurice Couve de Murville of France, Emperor Haile Selassie of Ethiopia, and Premier Alfred Raoul of the Congo (Brazzaville), to cite a few notable examples. At lavish banquets in Peking, the hosts praised their guests' statesmanship and expressed China's deep gratitude and indebtedness for their support of China's legitimate rights in the United Nations.

Second, Peking resumed the people-to-people diplomacy of the Bandung period. This was an exercise in popular showmanship intended to beautify the PRC's tarnished image in the international community. In 1971 alone, some 290 delegations from eighty nations were invited to China, while the PRC herself sent out some 70 delegations

[13] The return of the PRC's ambassadors began in mid-May 1969, shortly after the end of the Ninth Party Congress.

to forty nations to carry out people-to-people or "ping-pong" diplomacy.[14]

Third, Peking launched a major drive to expand the scope of state-to-state relations. Between October 1970 and October 1971, the PRC established diplomatic relations with fourteen nations, resumed diplomatic relations with Burundi and Tunisia, and elevated diplomatic relations with the United Kingdom and the Netherlands to the ambassadorial level. (See Appendix A.) It seems that Peking's campaign to expand its state-to-state relationships was carefully orchestrated to reach its climax at the beginning of the 26th Session of the General Assembly.[15] This technique served to generate a sense of bandwagon movement in regard to the forthcoming vote on the China issue among the wavering Member States of the United Nations.

Fourth, in her official media the PRC gave unusual coverage to the question of Chinese representation on the eve of the 26th Session of the General Assembly. In the past, PRC commentaries on the United Nations had usually *followed* the returns of the Assembly vote on the China issue. This time, during the months immediately preceding the Assembly's discussion of the subject, fifteen articles dealing with the United Nations appeared in the authoritative *Peking Review*—compared with one in 1968, one in 1969, and five in 1970, as shown in Table 3.1. Thus, the PRC leadership gave evidence of the serious importance it attached to its UN seat.

Finally, the PRC's aid diplomacy was accelerated at an unprecedented rate in 1970 and 1971. The complete figures now show that the PRC's economic aid increased from $13 million in 1969 to $728 in 1970, in contrast to $394 million jointly extended by the Soviet Union and East European countries in the latter year. The 1970 aid extension by the PRC represents 64.9 percent of the total communist aid for the year; more significantly, it represents 71.1 percent of all PRC aid extended to noncommunist countries during the period 1954-69. Peking's aid pledges for 1971 dropped to $562 million; still, they represented a substantial commitment of resources by a developing country.[16]

[14] *Peking Review*, which for many years had hardly published any statistical and empirical data, compiled and proudly presented these figures for 1971 in an annual review of events of 1971. See *PR*, No. 1 (January 7, 1972), 21.

[15] Some American specialists argued that Peking's objective to gain its UN seat had top priority, ranking above the improvement of relations with the United States; Secretary-General U Thant commented on the complementary nature of Peking's strategy toward the United States and the United Nations in a statement issued on July 16, 1971: "It seems that the chances for a solution of the question of the representation of China at the next session of the General Assembly are brighter in the light of the announcements in the United States and Peking last night." See *UN Monthly Chronicle* 8 (August/September 1971), 68.

[16] CIA, *Communist Aid to the Less Developed Countries of the Free World, 1976*, ER 77-10296, August 1977, p. 7.

Moreover, Chinese aid was "the most concessionary program" of all communist aid to developing noncommunist countries.[17]

The most immediate impact of the Chinese entry was largely symbolic. On the one hand, China in the United Nations, particularly in the Security Council, has come to serve as a vivid reminder of the end of *Pax Americana* in the world organization.[18] True, the de-Americanization process actually started earlier following the membership explosion and the American retreat from the Article 19 showdown in the General Assembly in 1965. However, the process was not completed until October 25, 1971, when the Assembly, notwithstanding a total mobilization of American diplomatic capital to defeat the Albanian draft resolution,[19] crossed the Rubicon on the China question. The reaction of the American public was swiftly negative; the prestige of the United Nations dropped to an all-time low in a Gallup poll conducted in the week following the China vote.[20] Congressional reaction was vehement, too, and a number of representatives introduced resolutions reducing the US share of the UN regular budget to about 6 percent (ratio of US to world population).[21] In the Senate, Senator Barry Goldwater went further: "The time has come to recognize that the United Nations for the anti-American, antifreedom organization it has becomes [sic]. The time has come for us to cut off all financial help, withdraw as a member, and ask the United Nations to find a headquarters location outside of the United States that is more in keeping with the philosophy of the majority of voting members, some place like Moscow or Peking."[22]

Within the United Nations system as a whole, on the other hand,

[17] *Ibid.*, p. 5.

[18] For further discussion, see Chapter 4.

[19] It was reported that American UN Ambassador George Bush had "conferred" with 94 of the 126 UN delegations on the question of Chinese representation, thus establishing a "new quantitative track record" in the annals of UN multilateral diplomacy. Diplomatic sources also reported that even President Nixon was in direct contact with the presidents of Argentina, Senegal, and a number of other countries in the ten days prior to the vote in an effort to win their support for the American "two Chinas" plan. See *NYT*, August 30, 1971, p. 4, and October 30, 1971, p. 10.

[20] The poll was conducted between October 29 and November 1, 1971, in more than 300 localities throughout the United States. The results showed that 35 percent of the sample rated the United Nations as doing a good job, 43 percent a poor job and 22 percent had no opinion. That this trend has continued can be seen in another Gallup Poll conducted during the period November 21-24, 1975, when the "good job" rating dropped to 33 percent while the "poor job" rating rose to 51 percent. See "Gallup Says U.S. Public Rates U.N. Prestige at a Record Low," *NYT*, November 12, 1971, p. 17, and "Gallup Poll Reports a Decline in U.N.'s Prestige in the U.S.," *NYT*, December 28, 1975, p. 3.

[21] For discussion of congressional reactions, see (Rep.) Jonathan B. Bingham, "The US, China and the UN," *Foreign Service Journal* (February 1972), 18-20.

[22] *NYT*, October 27, 1971, p. 16.

there was general enthusiasm and euphoria—sentiments that were not obviously shared by the two superpowers—that this "admission" of one-fifth of the human race to the United Nations had made the world organization much more representative, more realistic, more interesting, and more able to deal with global problems. "I am convinced," declared one Third World representative on the eve of the Chinese entry, "that it [Chinese participation in the United Nations] is an element which, in today's world and the world of tomorrow, is essential to the human race, to the development of the universe, to its equilibrium, to its progress and to its peace."[23] Most representatives expressed similar sentiments in the course of the Security Council's 1599th meeting on November 23, 1971, when Ambassador Huang Hua made his debut.[24]

The Evolving Pattern of Chinese Participation

There has been no shortage of Cassandras warning of disruptive or disastrous consequences from the PRC's participation in the United Nations. "To seat such aggressors [as Communist China] in the United Nations," declared a House-Senate joint consensus resolution in the US Congress, "would be a compromise with principle which would mean moral bankruptcy for the United Nations and destroy every last vestige of its effectiveness as a force for world peace and security."[25] In a similar vein, a prominent scholar of international organization warned that Peking's entry would seriously disrupt the UN Secretariat, "whether from the need to create new positions or the displacement of the 50-odd present Chinese officials [international civil servants] that is sure to be demanded by Peking. Above all, the Chinese Communists sent to work in the UN will be charged with a mission reflecting the fanatical world view of their masters. The absorption of large numbers of indoctrinated Chinese Communists can only have a disruptive and stultifying effect on the Secretariat."[26] There was also the "Trojan Horse" warning that China would use her diplomatic privileges

---

[23] GAOR, 26th Sess., 1975th plenary meeting (22 October 1971), para. 80. On the occasion of the first anniversary of China's participation in the United Nations, the same representative expressed his gratification for having had his view vindicated in the space of a year. See SCOR, 27th Yr., 1675th meeting (21 November 1972), p. 6.

[24] SCOR, 26th Yr., 1599th meeting (23 November 1971).

[25] U.S. Congress, House, Committee on Foreign Affairs, *Expressions by the House of Representatives, the Senate, and the Committee on Foreign Affairs that the Chinese Communists are not entitled to and should not be recognized to represent China in the United Nations*, 84th Congress, 2nd Sess., p. 4. Numerous resolutions and riders expressing a strong Congressional opposition to the seating of the PRC in the United Nations are contained in this document.

[26] Bloomfield, "China, the United States, and the United Nations," p. 664.

and immunities as a shield in carrying out espionage activities, as the Soviet Union had sometimes tended to do in the past.[27]

To examine what many predicted or anticipated that Peking would do, and to appraise the style and substance of Chinese global politics, we may begin with the PRC delegation to the 26th Session of the General Assembly and the permanent UN mission established in New York City, for it was through them that the immediate and direct responsibility of Chinese multilateral diplomacy was exercised. Judging by the three criteria often used by the UN community in evaluating the significance, interest, and performance of a delegation—professional expertise, strategic access to the key policy makers at home, and size— the PRC's delegation to the 26th Session General Assembly, led by Ch'iao Kuan-hua (chairman of the delegation) and Huang Hua (vice-chairman and the permanent representative to the United Nations), was indeed a first-rate team.

The delegation constitutes an impressive list of "Who's Who" in the foreign policy establishment of the PRC. Both Ch'iao Kuan-hua and Huang Hua belonged to the coterie of Chou En-lai's closest advisors, whose diplomatic experience predates the establishment of the PRC in 1949. I have described elsewhere the kinds of qualifications and experience both men possessed at the time of their debut at the 26th General Assembly, and they need not be repeated.[28] However, it should be noted here that both men headed the Chinese delegation in the succeeding five sessions (27th-31st) of the General Assembly. Ch'iao Kuan-hua later advanced to become the foreign minister, only to fall from power suddenly after his return home from the 31st Session of the General Assembly because of his alleged involvement in the conspiracy by "the Gang of Four." That Ch'iao Kuan-hua's dismissal on December 2, 1976 is unrelated to any change in foreign policy or UN diplomacy is evidenced by Huang Hua's recall home to head the Foreign Ministry.[29]

---

[27] Note, for example, Bloomfield's assertion: "It should be assumed that Chinese Communists, although doubtless confined to the Headquarters district, will, like the Soviets, use any opportunity for espionage." *Ibid.* For equally pessimistic predictions about the disruptive impact of Chinese entry, see McDougal and Goodman, "Chinese Participation in the United Nations," *passim.*

[28] See my "The People's Republic of China in the United Nations," pp. 306-307. It may also be mentioned in this connection that Huang Hua was the only ambassador who was not called home for "rectification" during the heyday of the Cultural Revolution in 1967. As of 1974, Huang Hua and Huang Chen, the chief of the PRC's Liaison Office in Washington, D.C., were the only ambassadors who enjoyed full membership in the 10th Central Committee. For a table showing past and present ambassadors of China and their full and alternative membership in the Seventh, Eighth, Ninth, and Tenth Central Committees, see Donald W. Klein, "The Chinese Foreign Ministry" (Ph.D. Dissertation, Columbia University, 1974), pp. 122-24.

[29] See "Wai-chiao-pu tang-tsu kuan-yü Ch'iao Kuan-hua wen-t'i ti ch'ing-shih

The remaining representatives to the 26th Session of the General Assembly—Fu Hao, Ch'en Ch'u, and Hsiung Hsiang-hui—all came from the ranks of professional career diplomats with extensive experience abroad or in the Ministry of Foreign Affairs.[30] In April 1972 Fu Hao was elevated from his position as director of the General Office to a vice-ministership in the Ministry of Foreign Affairs; in September 1974, he received a new assignment as China's ambassador to Hanoi. It is of particular significance that China's first ambassadors to Mexico and Japan—Hsiung Hsiang-hui and Ch'en Ch'u, respectively—were recruited from this group. It is even more significant that Ch'en Ch'u, after a year's service at the United Nations as deputy permanent representative, and some five years in Tokyo (considered one of the major diplomatic posts in the PRC's diplomatic service), assumed his duties as China's permanent representative to the United Nations on May 10, 1977.[31]

Evidently, the importance the PRC leadership attached to participation in the General Assembly was reflected in the composition of, and a send-off reception for, its delegation. As one leading authority on the Chinese leadership put it: "It's about the best possible delegation they could send in terms of professionalism."[32] Although we witnessed numerous incidents involving Chinese diplomatic personnel caught in overzealous revolutionary demonstrations abroad during the peak of the Cultural Revolution, actual espionage cases implicating Chinese diplomats are unknown. In the more than 100 field interviews I have conducted with international civil servants and national UN representatives (see Interview Schedule), not a single reference was made that raised suspicion or doubt about "espionage" or "subversive" activities on the part of any Chinese UN delegates.

---

pao-kao" [Report and Request for Instructions Concerning the Problem of Ch'iao Kuan-hua Submitted by the Party Leadership Group of the Ministry of Foreign Affairs], *Chung-yang jih-pao* [Central Daily], January 19, 1977; trans. in *Chinese Law and Government* 10 (Spring 1977), 106-08. There is no indication in this report that Ch'iao's dismissal had anything to do with substantive foreign policy matters. Rather, the charges are vague and in the nature of Ch'iao and his wife, Chang Han-chih, having had close personal and social ties with Chiang Ch'ing. The Party Leadership Group of the Ministry of Foreign Affairs suggests in conclusion that "examination of Ch'iao Kuan-hua and Chang Han-chih be continued while holding them in isolation, and that no work be assigned to them until their problems are cleared."

[30] For background data of the Chinese delegates, see Donald W. Klein, "The Men and Institutions Behind China's Foreign Policy," in Roderick MacFarquhar, ed., *Sino-American Relations, 1949-71* (New York: Praeger, 1972), pp. 43-56; Donald W. Klein and Anne B. Clark, *Biographic Dictionary of Chinese Communism*, 2 vols. (Cambridge, Mass.: Harvard University Press, 1971); *Who's Who in Communist China*, 2 vols. (Hong Kong: Union Research Service, 1969-70).

[31] For Ch'en Ch'u's biographical sketch, see *NYT*, May 11, 1977, p. A4; and *United Nations Chronicle* 14 (June 1977), 61.

[32] Donald W. Klein, cited in *NYT*, November 3, 1971, pp. 1, 10.

For each regular session, a Member State is entitled to have, according to Rule 25, "not more than five representatives and five alternatives and as many advisers, technical advisers, experts and persons of similar status as may be required by the delegation." The size of the Chinese delegation has been comparatively large. For the 26th through the 31st Sessions of the General Assembly, the number of personnel was 39, 49, 40, 45, 43, and 40 respectively, placing the Chinese delegation in the second largest category just below the delegations of the two superpowers. While the top echelon of the Chinese delegation remained unchanged from the 26th through the 31st Sessions of the General Assembly, a great many lateral transfers and shufflings have occurred among the remaining three representatives and the five alternative representatives, as seen in Appendix C. Apparently the Chinese leadership believes that participation in the annual session of the General Assembly is a useful experience to be shared by as many diplomatic personnel as possible.

The immediate responsibility for perusing voluminous UN documents, for preparing the tactics of multilateral diplomacy, and for deciding the choice, level, and scope of participation in a myriad of meetings at UN Headquarters rests with the Chinese permanent mission in New York. Even after the annual session of the General Assembly has closed and its delegates all returned home (January-August), bilateral and multilateral diplomatic activities continue at UN Headquarters, with the meetings of *ad hoc* or special committees, subcommittees and other subsidiary organs of the General Assembly, not to mention the meetings of the Security Council and ECOSOC.[33] The magnitude of the job to be performed by the Chinese permanent mission in New York can be extrapolated from Table 3.2.

Yet the average number of diplomatic personnel in all the missions of the Member States, especially those of the new nations, tends to be small. A dozen "mini-states" restrict themselves to sending delegations to the annual session, "when the United Nations picks up the travel tab for one first-class ticket and four economy-class."[34] China has established the third largest permanent mission in New York. However, the

[33] According to one study based on field interviews, "Even when the Assembly is not in session 51 percent of the members of permanent missions go to United Nations Headquarters three or more times a week and 82 percent go twice a week." See Chadwick F. Alger, "Personal Contact in Intergovernmental Organizations," in Robert W. Gregg and Michael Barkun, eds., *The United Nations System and Its Functions: Selected Readings* (Princeton, N.J.: Van Nostrand, 1968), p. 109. For an excellent study of nonplenary organs, see Catherine S. Manno, "Problems and Trends in the Composition of Nonplenary UN Organs," in *ibid.*, pp. 368-83.

[34] Kathleen Teltsch, "Smaller Nations Find U.N. Membership Brings Benefits, Despite High Costs," *NYT*, October 5, 1976, p. 47.

TABLE 3.2. Level of Activities at UN Headquarters, 1971-72

	1971	1972
Meetings held	2,665	2,685
Interpreter Assignments	18,264	19,539
Meetings provided with:		
Verbatim records	379	311
Summary records	1,011	1,031
Pages of translation and revision (in all languages)	247,624	233,037
Pages of typing (in all languages)	508,298	533,822
Pages edited for inclusion in the official records	115,112	121,160
Page-units reproduced internally	557,768,550	518,837,445

Source: *Report of the Secretary-General on the Work of the Organization 16 June 1972-15 June 1973*, GAOR, 28th Sess., supp. No. 1 (A/9001), p. 110.

number of diplomatic personnel in the Chinese permanent mission has fluctuated, starting at 24 in January 1972 and reaching a peak of 46 in February 1973. It remained in the mid-40s in 1973 and 1974, dropped to 32 in 1975, and then rose slightly to 34 in August 1976. In comparison, the ranking of the largest permanent missions (as of January 1976) was as follows: 86 for the Soviet Union; 47 for the United States; 27 for France; 26 for Japan; 25 for the Federal Republic of Germany; and 20 for the United Kingdom. The average "small" Member State has 3 or 4, while such "medium-sized" member states as Algeria, Australia, Hungary, Italy, the Netherlands, and Poland have either 10 or 11.[35]

The Member States may have relatively large or small delegations or permanent missions for different reasons. Hence, the size of the delegation or the mission does not necessarily indicate the nature, type, level, or scope of its participation. This is especially the case with the PRC delegation and permanent mission, for their large size stands in sharp contrast with the low profile and apprentice-like posture the PRC's UN delegates have assumed in practically all the organs of the United Nations system. As if determined to undo the projected image of a reckless bull entering a china shop, the PRC leadership made a fundamental policy decision against any *unprepared* plunge into UN politics. In an interview with Moto Goto, managing editor of *Asahi*

[35] Data used here are taken from *Permanent Missions to the United Nations*, Nos. 229-240 (January 1972, May 1972, August 1972, February 1973, May 1973, September 1973, January 1974, August 1974, July 1975, January 1976, August 1976, and February 1977).

Shimbun (Japan) on October 28, 1971, Premier Chou En-lai candidly explained the Chinese approach: "We have not yet made adequate preparations. In connection with our attitude toward the United Nations, there is an old Chinese saying which goes, 'Be careful when facing a problem.' We do not have too much knowledge about the United Nations and are not too conversant with the new situation which has arisen in the United Nations. We must be very cautious. This does not mean, however, that we do not have self-confidence; it means that caution is required and that we must not be indiscreet and haphazard."[36]

Table 3.3 puts in a sharper focus the evolving pattern of Chinese participation in the work of the General Assembly. Of the seven Main Committees, China opted not to participate during her first year in the Second Committee (Economic and Financial), Fourth Committee (Trusteeship and Non-Self-Governing Territories), and Sixth Committee (Legal). Furthermore, participation in the Fifth Committee (Administrative and Budgetary) was limited to one appearance by Hsing Sung-yi on December 16, 1971, merely to acknowledge and accept his election as a member of the 13-member Advisory Committee on Administrative and Budgetary Questions (ACABQ). In fact, Hsing's seat was newly created to permit the PRC's participation in the work of ACABQ. China could not participate in the General Committee because her membership had already been determined before her debut on November 15, 1971. In general, China during the first year of her participation assumed the low-profile posture of a diligent apprentice who was preoccupied in learning a new trade, rather than the high-profile posture of a revolutionary challenger attempting to impose her own concept of how the United Nations should be operated.[37]

In his debut before the First Committee (which deals with political and security questions, including the regulation of armaments, and admission, suspension, and expulsion of UN members) on November 16, 1971, for example, Ambassador Ch'en Ch'u made the following opening statement: "As we begin to participate in the work of the UN there will be a period of learning for us, so that we may understand the actual workings of the UN. The representative of the PRC is ready

[36] *NYT*, November 9, 1971, p. 1. For excerpts from the official record of Moto Goto's interview, see *ibid.*, p. 16. John Stewart Service, who interviewed Chou En-lai on October 27, 1971, said to a reporter: "I have the impression that they [the Chinese] don't plan to cut any wide swathe. They probably will approach it all very modestly for the time being." *Ibid.*, October 29, 1971, p. 14.

[37] During the first week of his participation in the 26th Session of the General Assembly, Ch'iao Kuan-hua told the Assembly President, Adam Malik, that his delegation could not participate immediately in all the Assembly's activities because the Chinese delegation "was small and United Nations affairs were new to its members." See *NYT*, November 17, 1971, p. 14.

TABLE 3.3. The PRC's Participation in the General Assembly
as Measured by the Number of Statements and Speeches, 1971-76

Organ (Documentary Symbol)	1971[b] (26th Session)	1972 (27th Session)	1973 (28th Session)	1974 (29th Session)	1975 (30th Session)	1976 (31st Session)
General Committee (A/BUR/SR.–)	NP[c] (8)[d]	3 (7)	10 (11)	3 (6)	9 (3)	1 (2)
Plenary (A/PV.–)[a]	10 (98)	13 (85)	15 (91)	18 (94)	18 (94)	12 (107)
First Committee (A/C.1/PV.–)[a]	9 (56)	11 (63)	11 (65)	12 (59)	23 (64)	10 (58)
Special Political Committee (A/SPC/SR.–)[a]	2 (52)	4 (52)	7 (48)	5 (44)	8 (44)	2 (36)
Second Committee (A/C.2/SR.–)[a]	NP (81)	16 (67)	12 (72)	20 (68)	14 (60)	14 (69)
Third Committee (A/C.3/SR.–)[a]	3 (85)	12 (70)	7 (75)	13 (60)	12 (71)	4 (77)
Fourth Committee (A/C.4/SR.–)[a]	NP (55)	7 (52)	5 (53)	7 (54)	14 (58)	8 (49)
Fifth Committee (A/C.5/SR.–)[a]	1 (68)	16 (68)	21 (73)	8 (65)	8 (77)	6 (62)
Sixth Committee (A/C.6/SR.–)[a]	NP (63)	6 (86)	4 (66)	12 (62)	5 (61)	3 (70)

[a] Documentary symbol changes, beginning with the 31st Session.
[b] The 1971 figure for the number of meetings includes those that were held before the PRC's debut on November 15, 1971.
[c] Nonparticipation.
[d] The number in parentheses is the number of meetings held.
Source: These figures were taken and computed by the author from the summary and verbatim records of all the above listed organs from the first meeting in the 26th Session through the last meeting in the 31st Session.

to listen and to note the opinions and viewpoints of other delegations."[38] Likewise, Ambassador Fu Hao declared in his opening statement before the Special Political Committee (which shares the work of the First Committee), on the same day that he "hoped for the assistance and co-operation of its colleagues" because his delegation "was not yet familiar with the procedures in the UN."[39]

After having carefully observed behavior of the Chinese delegates during their first year, one UN envoy observed: "They have been like a

[38] UN Doc. A/C.1/PV.1829 (16 November 1971), pp. 1-2.
[39] UN Doc. A/SPC/SR.780 (16 November 1971), p. 161.

vacuum picking up information from other delegations and from the Secretariat."[40] This view has been confirmed in my own field interviews at UN Headquarters. It is of special interest and significance, however, that the PRC's UN delegates in the course of their apprenticeship have relied extensively on the knowledge and expertise of non-Communist Chinese international civil servants who had joined the UN Secretariat long before the PRC's entry in 1971. One high-ranking official described his own experience with the PRC delegates in the following manner: "They came to me often but never asked me 'improper questions,' for which I am very grateful. They asked me a lot of technical and procedural questions about the United Nations. They were thorough in their homework on the background of each issue that was being brought up. They went through every detail, every past resolution, every past proceeding, etc."[41]

While the cautious and low-profile posture continued with only a slight and subtle degree of change, the scope of Chinese participation expanded in the second year, marking the 27th Session as the beginning of China's full participation in the work of the General Assembly. As Table 3.3 shows, China's participation now extended to all seven Main Committees. In addition, China, following her election as a member, began to participate in the procedural committees (General Committee and Credentials Committee) and in one of the two standing committees (ACABQ and Committee on Contributions) in 1972 and the other standing committee in 1973. Taking into account some unavoidable fluctuation resulting from the intrusion of highly politicized issues or crises from time to time, the level of Chinese participation as measured by the number of statements and speeches in the plenary as well as in the procedural, main, and standing committee sessions has been stabilized at the level established in 1972.

The year 1972 also marked the beginning of Chinese participation in the Assembly's subsidiary, *ad hoc*, and related bodies with limited membership. The list of Chinese membership in these organs, as shown in Table 3.4, may appear to be impressive, but it is not. Of some sixty nonplenary subsidiary organs of the Assembly that were either in existence or functioning in 1973, for example, China was a member of only eleven. It is safe to assume that China would have had little difficulty in getting herself elected as a member of practically all these subsidiary organs, given her size, population, contribution (financial), status (a permanent member of the Security Council), and geograph-

---

[40] *NYT*, October 28, 1972, p. 2.

[41] Quotations without sources throughout the book are from the author's field interviews with delegates and international civil servants, whose comments were solicited with the assurance that there would be no direct attribution.

TABLE 3.4. The PRC's Membership (M) in the General Assembly Subsidiary (Nonplenary) Organs with Limited Membership, 1972-76

Organ	1972	1973	1974	1975	1976
General Committee	M	M	M	M	M
Credentials Committee	M	M	M	M	M
Advisory Committee on Administrative and Budgetary Questions	M[a]	M	M	M	M
Committee on Contributions		M	M	M	M
Ad Hoc Committee on the Indian Ocean	M	M		M	
Committee on the Peaceful Uses of the Sea-bed and the Ocean Floor Beyond the Limits of National Jurisdiction	M	M			
Special Committee on the Situation with Regard to the Implementation of the Declaration on the Granting of Independence to Colonial Countries and Peoples	M	M	M	M	M
UN Council for Namibia		M		M	
Trade and Development Board of UNCTAD	M[b]	M			
Industrial Development Board of UNIDO		M	M	M	
Governing Council of UNEP	M	M	M	M	M
Executive Committee of UNHCR	M	M			
Special Committee on the Financial Situation of the UN	M				
Consultative Panel on Public Information	M	M			
Committee on Applications for Review of Administrative Tribunal Judgments	M[c]	M	M	M	M
Committee on Relations with the Host Country	M	M	M		
Ad Hoc Committee on the Charter of the United Nations				M	
Special Committee on the Charter of the United Nations					M

[a] Composed of experts in their individual capacity.
[b] As of September 26, 1972.
[c] Composition based on membership in the General Committee.

ical and strategic location in the political process of the General Assembly. On many occasions, however, China made it known either directly or indirectly that "her delegation was not ready" to participate in the remaining subsidiary bodies.[42]

An overall review of China's participation in the work of the General Assembly from 1971 to 1976 reveals a discernible pattern of selective concentration and targeting. Her participation has been most extensive in the General Committee and least extensive in the Sixth Committee (Legal). The General Committee—composed of the President of the Assembly as chairman, the seventeen vice-presidents (China as a permanent member of the Security Council is automatically elected as a vice-president), and the chairmen of the seven Main Committees —organizes the work of the Assembly by first considering provisional agenda items submitted by Member States through the Secretary-General and then deciding what items to recommend or not to recommend for inclusion in the Assembly's provisional agenda for each annual session. The Committee also makes recommendations concerning the closing date of the session, the assignment of items to the plenary Assembly or to the main committees, the rewording of agenda items, and the regrouping or coupling of related items. In short, the first battle of the multiphased process of parliamentary diplomacy in the Assembly takes place in this committee.

Although China's participation in the General Committee has been more extensive than that in any other committee, she nevertheless employed the tactics of selective targeting in her approach to the procedural battle in the Committee. Of the more than 100 agenda items that were eventually adopted by the Assembly upon the recommendation of the Committee—92 in 1972, 101 in 1973, 110 in 1974, 126 in 1975, and 124 in 1976—for example, China took a public stand on less than a dozen items. She supported vigorously the inclusion of the following agenda items: "Creation of Favourable Conditions to Accelerate the Independent and Peaceful Reunification of Korea"; "Inclusion of Chinese among the Working Languages of the General Assembly and the Security Council"; "Illegal Occupation by Portuguese Military Forces of Certain Sectors of the Republic of Guinea-Bissau and Acts of Aggression Committed by Them Against the People of the Republic"; "Restoration of the Lawful Rights of the Royal Government of National Union of Cambodia in the United Nations"; and the Charter review question. With equal vigor, China opposed the inclusion of all the Soviet-sponsored items on disarmament and the non-

[42] The statement "We are not ready yet" has become a standard response to all the invitations or inquiries concerning possible Chinese participation in many limited-membership organs.

use of force, as well as the Bangladesh membership question (during the 27th Session), terrorism, and a US-sponsored item on the Korean question.[43]

In sum, then, China concentrated on what she considered to be important to her interests and/or principles during the first six years of her participation in the work of the General Assembly. Judging by the evolving pattern of participation, the issue ranking in the conceptualization and execution of the PRC's multilateral diplomacy in the political process of the Assembly is of the following order: political, economic, decolonization, and environmental issues rank high, while social, humanitarian, cultural, and legal questions attract the least attention. China's participation in the Sixth Committee, for example, has been nominal, as shown in Table 3.3. As will be discussed in detail in Chapter 8, Chinese comments in the Sixth Committee have been confined to such highly politicized legal issues as terrorism, the Charter review, and the definition of aggression.

BEHAVIORAL DIMENSIONS OF CHINESE MULTILATERAL DIPLOMACY

In order to exercise political leadership so as to influence both the process and the outcome of global politics in the General Assembly, a Member State must possess the power of persuasion. However, this power is an elusive diplomatic commodity that requires a proper mix of subjective and objective attributes of leadership and of positive and negative conditions. What sort of political influence, if any, has China exerted, or attempted to exert, in Assembly politics? How accurate is the accusation of Ambassador Malik that China is attempting to use the Third World as a springboard for immediately becoming a "super-super-Power"? How accurate is the often repeated assertion of the Chinese UN delegates that they always mean what they say? To answer these and related questions, we need to examine various behavioral dimensions—verbal, voting, consultative, administrative, and financial and budgetary—of Chinese participation in the political process of the General Assembly.

The institutional milieu of the General Assembly—particularly during the three months when the annual session is in progress—is congenial to the give-and-take of bilateral and multilateral political influence. Several thousand UN delegates representing well over 100 Member States—147 as of the 31st Session—participate in public and

[43] For complete record of Chinese participation in the General Committee during the period 1972-76, see UN Docs. A/BUR/SR.199 (20 September 1972)-A/BUR/31/SR.2 (4 October 1976).

115

private debate in the plenary, committee, and geographical-caucusing group sessions, while concurrently lobbying, log rolling, horse trading, and arm twisting in small or large groups is carried on backstage. Since the political process of the Assembly goes through different stages, from the submission of agenda items by Member States to the final plenary voting on resolutions, covering more than 100 items, a Member State is indeed faced with a bewildering range of choice in issues and forums. A choice a Member State makes depends largely on the subjective and objective, as well as the positive and negative influence it possesses in Assembly politics.

Verbal Behavior

Of all the organs of the General Assembly, the plenary's opening "General Debate" provides the best sounding board for the policy pronouncement of a Member State. While elaborate arguments on details of particular issues and on the drafting of resolutions transpire in the Main Committees, it is in the plenary that general policy pronouncements, rhetorical appeals, and theatrical posturings by the Member States are engaged in for the benefit of a variety of audiences inside and outside the Assembly Hall. Although there is no provision in the Rules of Procedure of the General Assembly for a General Debate, the 1963 Committee on Procedure described the General Debate as "a series of statements made by most Chairmen of delegations on world problems and the role of the United Nations, in the light of the annual report of the Secretary-General on the work of the Organization and reports of other United Nations organs."[44] Indeed, the General Debate has now become a widely used forum for the Member States to present their "state of the globe" reports.

China has proved to be no exception. Ch'iao Kuan-hua's major policy speech during the General Debate has customarily attracted a full audience in the Assembly Hall. It has been widely disseminated inside China as *Jen-min jih-pao* has invariably published the full text of the speech on the front page.[45] It has also become a conceptual map for Chinese delegates, as they state and restate their stand on a variety of global issues in various committees or subsidiary organs of the Assembly. It has, in short, become a Chinese "state of the globe" report: what is wrong with the state of the world and what can and should be done about it. Table 3.5 is a content analysis of the six major speeches delivered by Ch'iao Kuan-hua during the plenary's General

[44] GAOR, 18th Sess., Annexes, Agenda item 25, UN Doc. A/5423 (28 May 1963), para. 17.
[45] See *JMJP*, November 17, 1971, p. 1; October 5, 1972, p. 1; October 3, 1973, p. 1; October 3, 1974, p. 1; September 27, 1975, p. 1; and October 6, 1976, p. 1.

Debate from 1971 to 1976. The table gives a glimpse of the Chinese world view as expressed in the world community, for each speech invariably includes what may be characterized as a "trend-of-history" analysis.

A number of salient characteristics of the Chinese "state of the globe" report can be identified. First, it looks at the world with a selective focus. It says little or nothing on a wide range of "functional" issues or problems such as food, population, environment, human settlement, water, and human rights, although these can be subsumed under the generic rubric of a New International Economic Order. Second, it is highly loaded with general declaratory principles but lacks details on tactics or strategies. Third, it falls short of concrete and specific proposals for making the United Nations a more effective instrument in the pursuit of a new world order. Fourth, it treats the Soviet Union, in tone and substance, as the principal contradiction of the contemporary international system, as the discussion of practically every political issue from the Middle East to the Charter review contains anti-Soviet overtones. Finally, it is presented in the form of a militant revolutionary appeal for the underdog, struggling to reorder the political process in the world community so that all nations, large or small, can participate in the decision-making process on an equal footing.

Table 3.3, presented earlier in this chapter, gives a quantitative overview of Chinese verbal behavior in the plenary as well as in the Main Committees. It must be noted that the figure in each category in the table represents all the speeches and statements, including many short statements explaining votes or rebuttal argument. A consensus that emerges from field interviews with fellow delegates who have observed Chinese verbal behavior in the General Assembly is that Chinese participation is rather low and passive when measured by the frequency and length of speeches or statements. "They are popular at the United Nations," observed one delegate from the Second World, "because of their short speeches." This is indeed a revealing commentary on the verbal behavior of most Member States. Faced with a seemingly endless verbal marathon during the October 29, 1975, meeting of the First Committee, Huang Hua made a rare intervention against a Third World delegate: "Mr. Chairman, I think all of us have listened with great patience to Mr. Baroody's statement on his amendment. As we may recall, a moment ago the Chairman already announced that we have entered the stage of voting. . . . We hope that this hall should be used as a conference hall of the United Nations and not as anyone's house for chatting."[46]

[46] UN Doc. A/C.1/PV.2071 (29 October 1975), p. 161.

TABLE 3.5. Content Analysis of Chinese Major Policy Speeches (X) During the Plenary's General Debate, 1971-76

Themes or Subjects	1971 (26th Session)	1972 (27th Session)	1973 (28th Session)	1974 (29th Session)	1975 (30th Session)	1976 (31st Session)
The Two Chinas Question	X					
The Trend-of-History Analysis	X	X	X	X	X	X
The Korean Question	X	X	X	X	X	X
The Middle East Question	X	X	X	X	X	X
Colonialism in All Its Manifestations	X	X	X	X		X
China Is a Developing Nation	X	X				X
Struggle Against Maritime Hegemony	X	X	X	X		
Arms Control and Disarmament	X	X	X	X	X	X
Guiding Principles of Foreign Aid	X					
Opposition to Power Politics	X			X		
Opposition to Superpower Hegemony	X	X	X	X	X	X
International Egalitarianism and Democratization in the Management of UN and World Affairs	X	X	X		X	
The Five Principles of Peaceful Coexistence	X					
The Vietnam War	X	X			X	
Delusion of Détente		X		X		
Pacific Settlement of International Disputes		X	X			
The Bangladesh Question		X	X			

Topic						
Assassination and Hijacking		X				
The European Security Question		X	X			
Development	X	X				
SALT		X				
The Cause-of-War Analysis		X	X	X	X	X
African Questions		X	X	X	X	X
Accomplishment or Effectiveness of the United Nations		X	X			
The Charter Review Question		X			X	
History of Sino-Soviet Relations						
The Cambodian Question			X	X		
The Cyprus Question			X	X		
The Nuclear-Free Zones Question				X		X
A New International Economic Order					X	X
Struggle of the Second World					X	
Legacy of Mao Tse-tung						X

Sir Harold Nicholson once identified "truth, accuracy, calm, patience, good temper, modesty and loyalty" as the qualities of both an ideal diplomatist and an ideal diplomacy.[47] China's verbal behavior in the General Assembly provides a means of assessing the qualities of her UN diplomacy. A critical test in this connection is the one China has repeatedly urged should be used in judging both individual and national behavior—measuring words against deeds. To probe this question, I never failed to put forward the following question in my field interviews: "Do you see any credibility problem in Chinese UN diplomacy resulting from a discrepancy between what the Chinese say and what they do?" A preponderant majority of respondents answered in the negative. Not a single one responded in the positive, while a small minority said they could not answer the question because of limited or irrelevant experience. Some typical responses to the question are worth citing here:

They are very honest; I don't think they would deceive you. They are not difficult to deal with because they are very candid and straightforward.

They are very honest eschewing diplomatic double-talk. They are also very correct. Not a sense of protocol but a certain sense of dignity in their behavior.

I have the gut feeling that there is a high degree of consistency if you make an allowance for excessive rhetoric. What they say is often much more drastic than what they do. I do not recall any occasion when I was struck by any discrepancy between Chinese words and deeds—if there existed such a discrepancy, it must have been of a minor nature that I cannot now recall.

Even to the nonleading question, "What is the most unique feature of Chinese UN diplomacy?" one former UN ambassador who had extensive dealings with Huang Hua replied: "I always had the feeling that when Huang Hua gave me an assurance on any matter, it would be carried out. This is a matter of principle, even though the principle espoused may be a curious one to the outsider. In this sense, then, the Chinese are very consistent and principled." It has also been found through field interviews that China takes the same position in the behind-the-scenes consultative process as in public on most issues, tempered by the importance and environment of the situation.

While the verbal behavior of the Chinese enjoys a high degree of credibility because of its candor, honesty, and straightforwardness, the logic of their argument, the persuasiveness of their analysis, the

[47] *Diplomacy* (2nd ed., London: Oxford University Press, 1950), p. 126.

accuracy of their statements, the rigidity of their stand, and the obsession with the Soviet Union in their world view are often questioned by many thoughtful UN delegates. As will be elaborated throughout this study, the crusading posture of the Chinese vis-à-vis the Soviet Union represents a potential hazard not only to China's own diplomatic credibility but also to the endeavor of the United Nations to build a better world order with justice for all.

Voting Behavior

The General Assembly may vote by show of hands, by standing, or by mechanical means, but any single representative may also request a roll-call or a recorded vote. In the case of a recorded vote, the Assembly dispenses with the procedure of calling the names of the Member States, but the result of the voting is still inserted in the official record in the same manner as that of a roll-call vote. When a roll-call or a recorded vote is made, each delegation has the option of replying, "Yes," "No," or "Abstention." Thus, the Rules of Procedure do not recognize the fourth option, "Present but not participating in the vote."[48]

During the 18th Session of the General Assembly, however, the president of the Assembly (Carlos Sosa Rodríguez of Venezuela), after consultation with the chairmen of the Main Committees, proclaimed the following procedural guideline for nonparticipation: (1) a delegation wishing its nonparticipation in a vote to be recorded in the summary or verbatim record must make a statement to that effect, either before or after the vote; and (2) "nonparticipation" would be considered as absence as far as the actual counting of the votes is concerned.[49] In short, nonparticipation can in no way be considered in the counting of the vote, and in the absence of any specific request from the delegations, all nonparticipations in the vote are treated as absences in the record.

To a Member State such as China, which takes a special pride in matching her words with deeds, the roll-call vote in the plenary of the General Assembly presents a continuing challenge and opportunity. When all is said and done, it is the voting record by which a Member State judges, and is in turn judged by, others. A Member State that sponsored a draft resolution on an issue of particular interest or importance to itself is more likely to remember how others voted than what they said before or after the vote, given the fact that verbal align-

---

[48] Rule 87 of Rules of Procedure of the General Assembly. See *Rules of Procedure of the General Assembly* (embodying amendments and additions adopted by the General Assembly up to 31 December 1973), A/520/Rev.12 (1974), p. 19.
[49] GAOR, 18th Sess., 1255th plenary meeting (6 November 1963), para. 19.

ment does not necessarily agree with voting alignment in the political process of the General Assembly. The voting record of many "client" and "dependent" Member States also provides an accessible means of reappraisal on the part of the great powers, enabling them to invoke a system of sanctions; that is, rewards or punishment in the bilateral relationship commensurate with the "proper" voting behavior in the General Assembly.

Yet to vote "properly" either in terms of one's principles or one's interests is not an easy task. By the time draft resolutions reach the plenary for voting, they may have picked up in the preambular paragraphs too many principles—some of which may be mutually contradictory—to accommodate the pressures of divergent groups, or they may have embodied principles phrased in such ambiguous or diluted terms as to neither please nor offend anybody. The most crucial task for a delegation is to make a balanced overall judgment before it decides to vote in a particular way.

Furthermore, this task calls for a delicate adjustment of principles and interests. For these and related reasons, the delegates often work toward a compromise formula, in order to have a given draft resolution adopted without vote or by consensus or acclamation. To cite a few prominent recent examples, the resolutions approving the Definition of Aggression, the Declaration on the Establishment of a NIEO, and the Programme of Action on the Establishment of a NIEO were all adopted without vote.[50] More than 50 percent of the draft resolutions have been adopted without vote in recent years.[51] Still, it must be recalled that it takes a request by at least one Member State to set in motion a roll-call or recorded vote.

For a time series analysis of Chinese voting behavior, see Figure 3.1. It plots the evolving pattern of Chinese voting behavior in the plenary of the General Assembly during the period 1971-76. It shows that the Chinese voting record accorded with the UN consensus on about 65 percent of the recorded or roll-call votes, while the negative votes never exceeded 9.1 percent.[52] What is unique and striking about Chi-

[50] See General Assembly Resolution 3314 (XXIX) of 14 December 1974; General Assembly Resolution 3201 (S-VI) of 1 May 1974; and General Assembly Resolution 3202 (S-VI) of 1 May 1974.

[51] The ratio between the number of resolutions adopted and the number of recorded votes during the period 1972-76 is as follows: 146:82 for 1972; 150 : 74 for 1973; 158 : 55 for 1974; 179 : 78 for 1975; and 208 : 89 for 1976. It should be noted that some resolutions may have more than one recorded vote.

[52] Since most draft resolutions are first discussed and adopted in the Main Committees, it is a rare draft resolution that fails to be passed by the plenary. Hence, it is safe to equate draft resolutions reaching the final plenary stage with the UN consensus. Over 90 percent of draft resolutions reaching the plenary voting pass by an overwhelming majority.

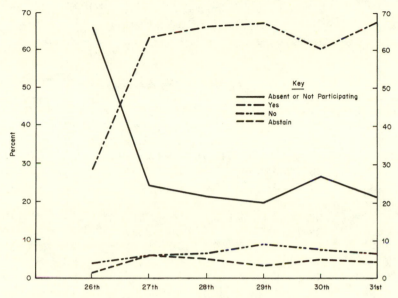

Key

——— Absent or Not Participating
—·—· Yes
—··— No
— — — Abstain

FIGURE 3.1. Evolving Pattern of Chinese Voting Behavior in the General Assembly (based on all the recorded or roll-call votes from November 15, 1971 to December 31, 1976).

nese voting behavior is the relatively high percentage of nonparticipation, coupled with the relatively low percentage of abstention. Table 3.6, which juxtaposes the Chinese voting record with those of the remaining four of the Big Five for a comparative analysis, verifies this point. That China assumed an apprentice-like posture during the first year of her participation is also borne out by Table 3.6, which shows that Chinese nonparticipation or absence was 66.2 percent of the roll-call or recorded votes.

The extensive use of the fourth option, "nonparticipation," in Chinese voting behavior represents an attempt to expand the scope of flexibility in Chinese multilateral diplomacy. Apparently, China does not object to consensual voting, for she has never challenged this method in the Assembly nor has she ever requested a roll-call or recorded vote. In the course of the November 16, 1971, plenary debate on the Soviet draft resolution for convening a world disarmament conference, Ch'iao Kuan-hua proposed that the Soviet draft resolution should not be put to the vote. "Our desire is," Ch'iao Kuan-hua argued, "that we should strive to enable the UN, on the principle of reaching a consensus through consultation, to make a new start on this question that is truly conducive to disarmament." "If the Soviet delegation insists on putting its draft resolution to a vote," Ch'iao Kuan-hua warned,

TABLE 3.6. Voting Record of the Big Five on the Resolutions
Adopted by the General Assembly, 1971-76[a]
(percentages in parentheses)

	In Favor	Against	Abstention	Absent or not partici- pating	Total
26th Sess.[b]					
PRC	21 (28.4)	3 (4.1)	1 (1.4)	49 (66.2)	74 (100)
USA	36 (48.6)	14 (18.9)	23 (31.1)	1 (1.4)	74 (100)
USSR	48 (64.9)	10 (13.5)	16 (21.6)	0	74 (100)
UK	33 (44.6)	14 (18.9)	25 (33.8)	2 (2.7)	74 (100)
FRANCE	32 (43.2)	10 (13.5)	31 (41.9)	1 (1.4)	74 (100)
27th Sess.					
PRC	52 (63.4)	5 (6.1)	5 (6.1)	20 (24.4)	82 (100)
USA	38 (46.3)	11 (13.4)	33 (40.2)	0	82 (100)
USSR	57 (69.5)	5 (6.1)	20 (24.4)	0	82 (100)
UK	40 (48.8)	10 (12.2)	31 (37.8)	1 (1.2)	82 (100)
FRANCE	42 (51.2)	9 (11.0)	30 (36.6)	1 (1.2)	82 (100)
28th Sess.					
PRC	49 (66.2)	5 (6.8)	4 (5.4)	16 (21.6)	74 (100)
USA	24 (32.4)	15 (20.3)	35 (47.3)	0	74 (100)
USSR	51 (68.9)	3 (4.1)	20 (27.0)	0	74 (100)
UK	25 (33.8)	12 (16.2)	36 (48.6)	1 (1.4)	74 (100)
FRANCE	26 (35.1)	9 (12.2)	37 (50.0)	2 (2.7)	74 (100)
29th Sess.					
PRC	37 (67.3)	5 (9.1)	2 (3.6)	11 (20.0)	55 (100)
USA	15 (27.3)	14 (25.5)	26 (47.3)	0	55 (100)
USSR	39 (70.9)	6 (10.9)	10 (18.2)	0	55 (100)
UK	21 (38.2)	5 (9.1)	29 (52.7)	0	55 (100)
FRANCE	17 (30.9)	6 (10.9)	32 (58.2)	0	55 (100)
30th Sess.					
PRC	47 (60.3)	6 (7.7)	4 (5.1)	21 (26.9)	78 (100)
USA	24 (30.8)	22 (28.2)	32 (41.0)	0	78 (100)
USSR	55 (70.5)	11 (14.1)	12 (15.4)	0	78 (100)
UK	31 (39.7)	13 (16.7)	33 (42.3)	1 (1.3)	78 (100)
FRANCE	30 (38.5)	7 (9.0)	40 (51.3)	1 (1.3)	78 (100)
31st Sess.					
PRC	60 (67.4)	6 (6.7)	4 (4.5)	19 (21.3)	89 (100)
USA	20 (22.5)	28 (31.5)	39 (43.8)	2 (2.2)	89 (100)
USSR	67 (75.3)	9 (10.1)	13 (14.6)	0	89 (100)
UK	29 (32.6)	13 (14.6)	42 (47.2)	5 (5.6)	89 (100)
FRANCE	27 (30.3)	11 (12.4)	49 (55.1)	2 (2.2)	89 (100)

[a] To draw a sharp picture of consensus and cleavage among the Big Five, all the resolutions adopted by acclamation or unanimously have been omitted from the table. The tabulation lists only those resolutions adopted by recorded votes.

[b] The tabulation for the 26th Session includes only those resolutions adopted after November 15, 1971, when the PRC delegation made its debut.

"the Chinese delegation cannot but declare with regret that China will not participate in the voting and will assume no obligation as to the result of the voting."[53] Thereafter, the Soviet draft resolution was adopted by acclamation.[54]

The Chinese delegates offered various explanations for the different types of votes. For the positive vote, explanatory statements are minimal. Still, the Chinese voted "yes" on some draft resolutions in spite of the following reservations: (1) that the preambular paragraphs refer to resolutions, decisions, conventions, and covenants that China has not supported;[55] (2) that a reference is made to IBRD and IMF, both of which have failed to implement the Assembly resolution on the question of Chinese representation;[56] (3) that there is reference to a convention that was ratified by the Chiang Kai-shek clique and therefore was null and void;[57] (4) that there is a failure to draw a line of distinction between the aggressor and the victim of aggression;[58] and (5) that China has reservations about the wording of operative paragraphs.[59] Nonetheless, China voted in the positive for draft resolutions covering such a wide range of subjects as apartheid, refugee relief, colonialism, racism, sea-bed control, natural disaster relief, aid to developing nations, human rights in occupied territories, Charter review, no first-use principle, nuclear-free zones, napalm and other incendiary weapons, UNCTAD, UNIDO, the UN University, special assistance to the least developed countries, and a New International Economic Order.

Even though there is no danger of her negative vote paralyzing the work of the Assembly or preventing the passage of a draft resolution as it would in the Security Council, China has been extremely cautious and sparing in the use of her negative vote. Table 3.6 highlights this point. Between November 15, 1971, and the end of 1976, China cast 30 negative votes in all the recorded votes of the General Assembly, compared with 104 by the United States, 67 by the United Kingdom, 52 by France, and 44 by the Soviet Union. This translates into an annual average percentage of 6.7 percent for China, 9.8 percent for the Soviet Union, 11.5 percent for France, 14.6 percent for the United

[53] GAOR, 26th Sess., 1996th plenary meeting (26 November 1971), para. 138.
[54] General Assembly Resolution 2833 (XXVI) of 16 December 1971.
[55] GAOR, 28th Sess., Third Committee, 2033rd meeting (20 November 1973), para. 15.
[56] GAOR, 27th Sess., Second Committee, 1513rd meeting (11 December 1972), para. 51; UN Doc. A/C.4/31/SR.25 (15 November 1976), p. 14.
[57] GAOR, 27th Sess., Third Committee, 1947th meeting (10 November 1972), para. 59.
[58] GAOR, 26th Sess., 2003rd plenary meeting (7 December 1971), para. 496.
[59] GAOR, 28th Sess., Fourth Committee, 2064th meeting (20 November 1973), para. 496.

Kingdom, and 23 percent for the United States. China resorted to the negative vote only on those issues that she felt vital to her national security interest. The 30 negative votes were concentrated on the question of arms control and disarmament (ACD), with the exception of Korea: the nonuse of force in international relations, suspension of nuclear tests, the nuclear nonproliferation treaty, the reduction of military budgets. Every item on the list has a superpower connection; every item on the list also has a security interest connection. Korea is related to US-sponsored draft resolutions, while the remainder are either Soviet-sponsored or Soviet-supported draft resolutions. The Soviet sponsorship of any ACD proposals automatically triggers a negative vote from China.

China abstained only twenty times during the six-year period under review here. This amounts to an annual average of about 4 percent on all the recorded votes, and is in sharp contrast to 49 percent for France, 44 percent for the United Kingdom, 42 percent for the United States, and 20 percent for the Soviet Union. This is one measure of the extent to which the South-North polarity has come to dominate the political process in the General Assembly and of the extent to which the great powers deviate from the UN consensus in the 1970s. There is no predictable pattern of China's abstention as far as issues are concerned, as she abstained on such a disparate array of matters as the Middle East, chemical and biological warfare, capital punishment, and the establishment of UN Human Rights Commissioner. However, China has offered the following explanations for her abstention: (1) the Chinese delegation would need more time to study the matter;[60] (2) the subject was still being studied by the relevant departments in China;[61] (3) the parties concerned had not reached an agreement on the proposed draft resolution;[62] (4) there was a failure to condemn imperialism in the resolution;[63] (5) the proposed resolution was addressed to IBRD, which had not yet implemented the Assembly resolution on the question of Chinese representation.[64]

As Table 3.6 shows, the fourth option, "present but not participating in the vote" is seldom exercised by four of the Big Five. The

[60] GAOR, 29th Sess., Third Committee, 2061st meeting (10 October 1974), para. 8; GAOR, 30th Sess., Third Committee, 2122nd meeting (6 October 1975), para. 30.
[61] GAOR, 28th Sess., Third Committee, 2043rd meeting (29 November 1973), para. 12.
[62] GAOR, 30th Sess., Third Committee, 2164th meeting (19 November 1975), para. 52.
[63] GAOR, 26th Sess., 2016th plenary meeting (13 December 1971), paras. 232-33.
[64] GAOR, 28th Sess., Second Committee, 1571st meeting (27 November 1973), para. 18.

verbatim record of the plenary does not make a distinction between absence and nonparticipation, as both are left out of the record, unless a Member State makes a specific request to have its nonparticipation in the vote recorded as such. However, given the Chinese reputation for diligence and good attendance, it seems safe to treat all the "blanks" in the voting record as nonparticipation rather than as absence. China has made extensive use of this peculiar option on a wide range of subjects, such as human rights in armed conflict, effects of atomic radiation, financing of UNEF and UNDOF, report of IAEA, Angolan membership, human rights in Chile, ICJ advisory opinion, chemical and biological warfare, and many social, cultural, and budgetary matters.

Nonparticipation has most often been explained in terms of China's dissatisfaction with or reservations regarding parts of draft resolutions. As such, it is a method of registering a partial objection to a given draft resolution. China has often opted for nonparticipation on many budgetary resolutions because they included expenditure items that she found objectionable.[65] Likewise, she resorted to nonparticipation because she objected to draft resolutions containing references to the bank group (IBRD, IMF, and IDA), or to a multilateral treaty or convention that was signed or ratified by the Chiang Kai-shek regime or contained certain points of view with which she could not agree.[66] Disagreement with the wording of a draft resolution has also invoked China's nonparticipation.[67] She has expressed, via nonparticipation, her disenchantment with the haste with which a draft resolution was prepared and pushed for passage.[68] During the early years of 1971-72, China sometimes resorted to nonparticipation for the following reasons: (1) unfamiliarity with UN procedure; (2) unfamiliarity with the subject matter; (3) lack of sufficient information; and (4) lack of instructions from the home government.[69]

[65] GAOR, 27th Sess., Fifth Committee, 1558th meeting (18 December 1973), para. 2; GAOR, 28th Sess., Fifth Committee, 1632nd meeting (18 December 1973), para. 45; UN Doc. A/C.5/31/SR.62 (22 December 1976), p. 6.

[66] See GAOR, 27th Sess., Second Committee, 1480th meeting (3 November 1972), para. 32; GAOR, 27th Sess., Second Committee, 1509th meeting (5 December 1972), para. 16; GAOR, 27th Sess., Second Committee, 1511th meeting (6 December 1972), para. 1; GAOR, 27th Sess., Second Committee, 1513th meeting (11 December 1972), para. 51; GAOR, 28th Sess., Second Committee, 1574th meeting (30 November 1973), para. 8; GAOR, 29th Sess., Second Committee, 1652nd meeting (10 December 1974), para. 17; GAOR, 27th Sess., Third Committee, 1964th meeting (29 November 1972), para. 54; GAOR, 27th Sess., First Committee, 1892nd meeting (15 November 1972), p. 12; GAOR, 27th Sess., Third Committee, 1957th meeting (22 November 1972), para. 24.

[67] GAOR, 27th Sess., 2113th plenary meeting (18 December 1972), paras. 69-70.

[68] GAOR, 27th Sess., Third Committee, 1974th meeting (8 December 1972), para. 48.

[69] GAOR, 27th Sess., Fourth Committee, 2015th meeting (6 December 1972),

Two additional points about the Chinese concept of nonparticipation in the vote need to be mentioned. When a draft resolution to cancel out the unpaid balance of China's assessment incurred before October 25, 1971, was put to a recorded vote on December 19, 1972,[70] China decided not to participate in the vote and made a specific request to have this reflected in the official record. Nonparticipation was thus used in this case to express China's own sense of propriety—that it would be improper for a disputed party to participate in the vote on a resolution designed to settle the dispute. On another occasion, Chinese delegate Wang Lien-sheng lodged a protest in the Fifth Committee against an erroneous press release which showed China as having voted against the revised budget estimates recommended by ACABQ when in fact China had opted for nonparticipation.[71] It is also worth noting that China explained on numerous occasions how she would have voted if the draft resolution under consideration were put to a vote, but she has never requested a roll-call or recorded vote to defy consensual voting.

Consultative Behavior

Both the structure and the process of the General Assembly have contributed greatly toward an institutionalization of multilateral conference diplomacy in modern times. However, diplomacy, whether bilateral or multilateral, cannot be conducted without actors talking with and consulting each other on matters of common concern or interest. The setting of the General Assembly is particularly congenial to a continuous flow of diplomatic consultations. First, the General Debate, in addition to providing a platform for "state of the globe" reports by the heads of delegations, generates "a great deal of informal activity: personal contacts, private meetings, casual discussions, exchanges of view, exploratory soundings; the carefully arranged chance meetings in corridors, elevators, lounges, or dining rooms; the cocktail parties, receptions, lunches, and dinners; even the breakfasts."[72] Former Secretary of State Dean Rusk is claimed to have conferred with fifty-four heads of government or foreign ministers during an eleven-day period in 1963.[73]

Second, the existence of permanent missions in New York makes it easy for informal consultations to be continued throughout the year. In spite of over 2,600 meetings held at UN Headquarters each year

---

para. 1; GAOR, 27th Sess., Fourth Committee, 2021st meeting (12 December 1972), para. 38; GAOR, 26th Sess., Special Political Committee, 780th meeting (16 November 1971), p. 162.

[70] See General Assembly Resolution 3049 C (XXVII) of 19 December 1972.
[71] UN Doc. A/C.5/31/SR.62 (22 December 1976), p. 10.
[72] Bailey, *The General Assembly*, pp. 70-71.   [73] *Ibid.*, p. 71.

(see Table 3.2), the consultative process involving preparations of meetings and negotiations of draft resolutions is carried out back-stage in private. Finally, a myriad of global issues and problems on the agenda, periodic elections for all kinds of posts in limited-membership organs, and the activities of various geographical groups and ideological coalitions all make the Assembly a quasi-parliamentary body in global politics. In short, much of UN politics centers on a continuing series of informal consultations between delegations, within groups of delegations, and between delegations and the Secretariat, on matters of mutual interest.

Because the milieu of the UN political process is congenial to diplomatic consultations, it is also congenial to diplomatic lobbying. The line between the two is often difficult to draw. What may be considered lobbying by some may be considered consultation by others. The difference is partly a matter of style and partly a matter of substance. Consultation pursued too aggressively or without a diplomatic sense of *savoir faire* may be perceived as lobbying, on the one hand, while lobbying pursued with skill and sophistication may be perceived as consultation, on the other. In terms of substance, issues of intense national or ideological interest—US interest in the China question in the 1950s and 1960s, for example—may be perceived as lobbying, whereas issues of global and institutional concern—the interest of the Nordic countries in UN peace-keeping, for example—may be perceived as consultation. There are many other factors that tend to separate one sort of issue from the other, to be sure, but in the final analysis it is largely a function of perception on the part of those who are being "lobbied" or "consulted."

In this context, which form does China practice? Without imposing my own concept of lobbying or consultation, I put the following question in my field interviews: "Do the Chinese engage in lobbying? If so, to what extent and on what issues?" Some respondents immediately declined to answer this question on the grounds that their particular experience fell beyond the purview of UN political and lobbying activities. This may be taken as a partial answer to the question. Among those who did respond, an overwhelming majority gave such negative answers as: "Not to my knowledge"; "If they do, they do it with subtlety and secrecy"; "I have a hunch they do with some Member States on a bilateral basis, but I have no direct or indirect evidence to prove it"; "No—I would say this is indeed one of the most striking characteristics of Chinese UN diplomacy"; "Yes, but only on a few issues involving Cambodia, Korea, and the Soviet Union." For what it is worth, the Chinese have generally conveyed the impression that they do not lobby in their UN diplomacy.

However, when the matter was pursued with a differently phrased question, "Do they [the Chinese] participate in the consultative process?" the universal response was in the positive, but with the following qualifications: "In a very passive way"; "Yes, but with modesty and caution"; "Like a diligent student listening, observing, and learning"; and "Yes, but they never assume the posture of leadership." Chinese consultative behavior tends to give some credence to the claim that China will never be a superpower. It must be noted that the Chinese define a superpower in *behavioral* terms. This point was sharply stated by Ch'iao Kuan-hua during the first Sino-Soviet confrontation in the plenary on November 26, 1971:

> It is entirely China's own business how the Chinese delegation should speak and act and what stand it should take here. There is no need whatsoever for the Soviet representative [Malik] to lecture us. The Soviet attitude toward the Chinese delegation is exactly the same as the crude behavior towards some Afro-Asian countries adopted by another super-Power not long ago. The Soviet representatives have probably become used to acting the patriarch within their small realm, and they consider that whatever they say others will have to obey. Otherwise they will label you anti-Soviet. Distinguished representatives of the Soviet Union, you are wrong. This is not anti-Sovietism; this is opposition to your attitude of great-Power chauvinism and your policies of social imperialism. We have long had experience with such behaviour of yours. The Chinese people do not buy such stuff of yours, and your baton no longer works. The days are gone when the super-Powers could dominate the world.[74]

The same sort of passive but generally supportive role characterizes Chinese participation in the consultative process of the geographical-caucusing groups in the General Assembly. There are now five unofficially recognized geographical-caucusing groups working with frequency and regularity in the political process of the Assembly: (1) the Asian; (2) the African; (3) the Latin American; (4) the East European (including the USSR); and (5) the West European and other states.[75] It should be noted here that the Republic of China

[74] GAOR, 26th Sess., 1996th plenary meeting (26 November 1971), para. 135.
[75] Note that the Afro-Asian Group of the 1950s and 1960s became defunct in 1970 and a much larger coalition of Asian, African, and Latin American countries —the Group of 77—emerged as a "geographical-ideological" coalition to play the dominant role in the North-South confrontation. As noted below, China is not a member of the Group of 77 (see also Appendix K) but plays the role of passive spectator who cheers and supports the South in the UN political process on economic and developmental issues.

(ROC), along with Israel and South Africa, was excluded from the group-caucusing process. Formal organizations of these groups have been kept to a minimum, with the emphasis being placed upon informal consultative politics. Interestingly enough, the PRC joined the Asian group, while declining to be a part of the Group of 77. Hence, participation in the consultative process of the former group provides a new means of analyzing Chinese behavior in the world organization.

Since there is no record of the caucusing process of the Asian group, the discussion below relies exclusively on soft data collected from my field interviews. There is a consensus among the participants that the Asian group is indeed a very amorphous and disparate collection of thirty-six UN Member States (as of December 31, 1976) representing a broad geographical sweep from East Asia to West Asia.[76] It is composed of countries with some curious "status inconsistency." Japan is an Asian and a developed country at the same time. China is the only Asian and developing country that enjoys the status of a permanent membership in the Security Council. The group not only mixes some Buddhist Asian states with Islamic Arab states but also such populous states as China, India, Indonesia, and Japan with such mini-states as Maldives, Fiji, and the United Arab Emirates. All the countries in the group except Japan, Mongolia, and China belong to the Group of 77 (see Appendix K). There is no fixed leadership in the group, as it varies with issues, personalities, and chairmen. The chairmanship rotates monthly in English alphabetical order, excluding some mini-states that do not maintain permanent missions in New York. And China declines chairmanship even under such a rotational system.

The Asian group meets on an average of two or three times a month, but its work is unevenly distributed throughout the year, with a heavy concentration of caucusing activities during the months of April and May and the last four months of the year, when the Assembly is in session. The primary *raison d'être* and the central concern of the Asian group have been and continue to be the advancement of Asian representation in the structure of power and influence in numerous organs

---

[76] The thirty-six Member States of the United Nations that make up the Asian Group are as follows: Afghanistan; Bahrain; Bangladesh; Bhutan; Burma; China; Cyprus; Democratic Kampuchea (Cambodia); Democratic Yemen; Fiji; India; Indonesia; Iran; Iraq; Japan; Jordan; Kuwait; Laos; Lebanon; Malaysia; Maldives; Mongolia; Nepal; Oman; Pakistan; Papua New Guinea; Philippines; Qatar; Samoa; Saudi Arabia; Singapore; Sri Lanka (Ceylon); Syria; Thailand; United Arab Emirates; and Yemen. Turkey is a quasi-member of the Asian group, because she participates in the consultative process of the Asian group but belongs to the West European and other states group for purposes of election. I have therefore excluded Turkey from the membership list.

of the United Nations system, evolving around the supervisory role of the General Assembly. Given its diversity and lack of cohesion, the group seldom approaches the question of a common strategy on global issues or bloc voting strategy. Its discussion of the issues, except on the principle of geographical distribution, tends to be a mere exchange of different viewpoints.

Because of the ponderous size of the group, detailed consultation takes place in a committee known as the "*Ad Hoc* Committee on Under-Representation of Asian States and Guides for Candidate Choice." This is an open-ended committee of the whole. Its work centers specifically on two issues: establishment of equitable criteria for candidate selections from the Member States of the group; and formulation of common tactics or strategies toward an advancement of a better Asian representation in the United Nations.

China has declined not only her turns at chairmanship through the rotational system, but also participation in the *Ad Hoc* Committee. Chinese participation in the caucusing process of the Asian group has been described by fellow participants in the following terms: "Very cautious, very discreet, and very correct"; "very passive and very perfunctory"; "influential without trying to be so"; "extremely careful not to overplay her role"; "very conscious and very successful in harmonizing her behavior with the unique status [one of the Big Five] that she enjoys in the group."

In short, China participates in a very modest and passive way, without attempting to exert any pressure or influence. She maintains a friendly and supportive posture toward all the Member States of the Asian group, with one striking exception: Mongolia. Apparently, China treats Mongolia as a proxy representative of the Soviet Union in the Asian group. The PRC's overt hostility toward Mongolia represents a curious replay of the ROC's behavior in the United Nations. It may be recalled here that the only veto the ROC cast during her tenure (1946-71) as a permanent member of the Security Council was against the Mongolian membership question on December 13, 1955.

China's participation in the consultative process of all the UN organs has been marked by a generalized pattern of behavior—a modest, cautious, passive, and generally supportive posture toward the Third World. Indeed, China's absolute respect for the sovereignty of other nations and dogged determination not to play the role of a dominating superpower seem to be the *leitmotif* of Chinese behavior in the UN political process. For example, the coalition of coastal states in the 5th Session of the Third United Nations Conference on the Law of the Sea has invited China to join its ranks, so as to provide its movement with the sponsorship of a major power that keeps its distance from the superpowers. Yet the Chinese have not responded to the call. There appears to be no prospect that they will avail themselves of the opportunity and challenge. Chinese consultative behavior tends generally to support the credibility of a self-defined role in the global community, which China has proclaimed in the following terms:

US imperialism is now calling China a "potential superpower," implying that China may also squeeze into the ranks of the superpowers some day. Thank you, American lords, but China will never accept this kind of compliment! China will never seek the so-called big-power position. We will forever stand side by side with all nations subjected to aggression, control, intervention or subversion by superpowers, we will forever stand side by side with all oppressed people and oppressed nations. The Chinese people will fight together with the people of the whole world to resolutely smash the doctrine of big-nation hegemony![77]

In line with the above role definition, the Chinese have pursued a rather unique diplomacy in the corridors of the United Nations, making a considerable impression on the delegates of the smaller Member States. Having learned that the representatives of the big powers never strolled into the delegates' lounge—the preserve of the delegates from the smaller states of Europe, Latin America, Africa, and Asia—for coffee or a chat, Huang Hua and his colleagues made it a point to mingle with the other delegates in the lounge. "This is where the 'third world' meets at the United Nations," one African diplomat observed, adding: "And the Chinese evidently got this point quickly. I don't remember seeing Mr. Bush or Mr. Malik just drifting in for a cup of tea or coffee. Of course, they are the representatives of the 'superpowers' and they must be too busy to mix with us little fellows."[78]

While China refuses to play an active role—let alone a leadership role—in any UN committee or group politics, she does engage in an active consultative diplomacy on a *bilateral* basis during the annual session of the General Assembly. In November 1971 alone, for example, the Chinese delegates to the General Assembly collectively or individually paid a visit to twenty-seven separate permanent missions in New York. Such "consultative visits" also extend to the Secretary-General and important elected officials of the General Assembly. Almost invariably Chinese consultative or delegation diplomacy takes the form of a visit by Ch'iao Kuan-hua and Huang Hua to permanent missions or UN headquarters. "When we need mutual consultation,"

[77] "Down With Big-Nation Hegemonism," *JMJP*, editorial, January 23, 1971, p. 1; trans. in *PR*, No. 5 (January 29, 1971), 7.
[78] *NYT*, November 21, 1971, p. 14.

observed one participant, "the Chinese usually come here for a talk, but never the other way around. When we go to the Chinese permanent mission, it is for social purposes only."

A curious feature emerges from the practice of Chinese consultative diplomacy. The Chinese delegates usually seek information, ask questions, and solicit advice in a manner of a novice student, but they are seldom helpful in providing information that other delegates seek of them. Hence, there is very little mutual exchange in the consultative process. Nor do the Chinese attempt to curry favor or seek influence in these consultative talks. Almost every one of the international civil servants I have interviewed has characterized the relationship between his department and the Chinese delegation or mission as "excellent." In further discussion of the matter, it soon became clear that such a characterization was based on the Chinese practice of seeking only information or advice in their consultative visits; they seldom present difficult or unreasonable demands. The UN bureaucrats, like all bureaucrats, enjoy predictable behavior, and the Chinese are popular because they prove to be simple and predictable in their relationship with the Secretariat.

The most prominent part of Chinese delegation diplomacy takes the form of banquets and receptions. The Chinese extend to UN Headquarters the "banquet diplomacy" they employ at home, as described earlier in the chapter. At a National Day reception given on October 2, 1972, for example, some 900 guests from 120 countries, plus Secretary-General Kurt Waldheim and other high officials of the Secretariat, were invited.[79] The Chinese delegation has also given large film receptions—usually at the United Nations Library Auditorium—for Chinese staff personnel in the Secretariat, for overseas Chinese in America, and for UN correspondents from the Member States. One of the most highly prized invitations in the UN community, however, is a banquet at the Chinese permanent mission. The mission has given numerous banquets for small and large groups of UN delegates from various categories of Member States. One European UN delegate who has attended similar banquets at various other missions described her experience this way:

> They [the Chinese] are much better, oddly enough, in social and diplomatic hospitality in the UN community than the Russians.

[79] For details on this reception, see "Chinese Delegation to UN General Assembly Gives National Day Reception in New York," NCNA-English, United Nations, October 3, 1972, in *SMCP*, No. 5237 (October 18, 1972), 107-08. It should be noted in this connection that there is a constant flow of visits to China by high-ranking officials of the UN Secretariat and of the secretariats of the specialized agencies. These visits are well reported by the New China News Agency.

The Russians have this awful and dreary party in their Mission hall with Lenin looking down at you. The Chinese, on the other hand, give lovely parties; they are not very selective in inviting guests, with a nice mixture of UN delegates. They are very relaxed hosts. In fact, the Chinese mission is the only communist mission to the UN that does such a party well. And they do not engage in proselytizing at these social gatherings.

The element that tends to dominate—and considerably complicate—the generalized pattern of Chinese consultative behavior is the super-power connection. The Sino-Soviet conflict goes so deep that it affects Chinese behavior in many UN organs and on many issues. It is most expressive in verbal duels in the public forum, but it also colors Chinese consultative behavior, adding a dangerous and unpredictable element to otherwise predictable behavior. The United Nations had already witnessed a strange bedfellowship in which the Chinese and Americans were voting on the same side on issues stemming from the Indo-Pakistani War, and which came in the wake of American opposition to the Albanian draft resolution on the Chinese representation question. Likewise, the Sino-American minuet on the Angolan membership question—to be elaborated upon in Chapter 4—stands out as a problem in the fairly consistent and credible Chinese UN diplomacy.

In fact, field interviews with reliable American sources have revealed a new dimension of Chinese consultative behavior of which all other respondents were totally unaware. Despite the trenchant attack on the two superpowers in all the public forums, China's most serious consultative diplomacy was conducted at the US permanent mission in New York on two highly politicized questions: world disarmament conference and Korea. The Chinese were so anxious to defeat the Soviet proposal to convene a world disarmament conference that Ambassador Huang Hua on his own initiative called on US Ambassador John Scali on two separate occasions to express his contempt for the Soviet proposal and to make sure that the United States would stand firm in her refusal to join such a conference. On each occasion, Scali assured Huang Hua that the United States had no intention of joining the conference; in effect, China and the United States saw eye to eye on this key issue.

Sino-American consultations on the Korean question in the United Nations add another complicating factor to our analysis because of the contrast between the PRC's rigid ideological stand in public and her flexible negotiating posture in private. In 1973, for example, there were a series of consultations between Huang Hua and John Scali at the US permanent mission to work out a formula that both the

United States and China could accept on the Korean question. After three or more meetings, both ambassadors agreed on a compromise formula to postpone the Korean issue until the following Assembly.[80] When the US representative raised doubts about the acceptability of the consensus formula to the North Koreans, who had already established themselves at the United Nations as observers, Huang Hua assured him that there would be no problem. "There was none of this business about interfering in or acting on behalf of another sovereign state." However, it was up to the Chinese to inform the North Koreans what the consensus formula was going to be. Within a week, the Chinese returned to the US mission, saying that they were having difficulties persuading the North Koreans. The United States expressed surprise, and the Chinese responded with an assurance that they would pursue the matter further with the North Koreans. Four or five more "bilateral-trilateral" consultations followed, after which the North Koreans finally agreed to go along with the consensus formula, but "it was not nearly as clear-cut a case as it appeared to be in the initial stage." In spite of difficulties in this complex trilateral consultative process, there was no suspicion in the minds of American negotiators that Huang Hua was dishonest or double-crossing. On the contrary, he gained American respect for his honesty and trustworthiness.

Administrative Behavior

The General Assembly makes internal and external as well as binding and recommendatory decisions. In general, General Assembly resolutions may be classified into four types: (1) internal decisions, which are legally binding on UN organs; (2) recommendatory decisions, compliance with which is nonmandatory; (3) scale of assessment decisions, which are legally binding on Member States; and (4) declaratory statements, which require no substantive action.[81] It is through internal decisions that the Assembly "organizes itself and guides and budgets the activities of its own subsidiary organs, the Secretariat, and other organs and agencies insofar as they come under its jurisdiction."[82] Internal decisions are also self-executing, because they

[80] At its 2181st plenary meeting on November 28, 1973, the General Assembly adopted without objection a consensus recommendation of the First Committee (A/9341), expressing "the general hope that the South and the North of Korea will be urged to continue their dialogue and widen their many-sided exchanges and co-operation in the above spirit so as to expedite the independent peaceful reunification of the country." Note that the consensus was too fragile to be put to a vote.

[81] Catherine S. Manno, "Majority Decisions and Minority Responses in the UN General Assembly," in Greggs and Barkun, *The United Nations System*, pp. 256-57.

[82] *Ibid.*, p. 257.

depend largely on the actions of organs subject to the jurisdiction of the Assembly.

Chinese behavior on administrative matters falls into one of the four types of decisions mentioned above. For illustrative purposes, our analysis here centers on Chinese policy toward the UN Secretariat. The widely expressed fear that the PRC's entry would pose an administrative and legal nightmare because of her expected demand to replace all Secretariat personnel under the Chinese quota was based on the fact that this was the prevalent practice among many Member States. While the UN Charter clearly stipulates that the staff of the Secretariat "shall not seek or receive instructions from any government or from any other authority external to the Organization,"[83] many Member States have developed the habit of regarding their nationals in the Secretariat as an auxiliary instrument of national policy and influence in the global community. The Soviet Union is widely regarded as a notorious, if not untypical, example of this approach to the Secretariat.[84] Hence, the PRC's entry generated an intense apprehension among the Chinese staff at the Secretariat, while the UN community itself was watching and weighing every step of the Chinese processional march into Turtle Bay.

At the time of the PRC's entry into the United Nations, the minimum-maximum desirable range for Chinese staff in Secretariat posts, subject to geographical distribution, was 57-78, as shown in the first column of Table 3.7. Of this range of the Chinese quota, 51 places were occupied (as of August 31, 1971) by those who carried ROC passports. The situation presented several possible options: (1) to demand an immediate and/or progressive replacement of the 51 places already occupied; (2) to leave the 51 Chinese personnel alone, waiting for their natural retirement or resignation, applying such direct or indirect pressure as necessary to expedite their withdrawal from the Chinese quota; (3) to leave the question of the existing staff in abeyance, while filling up rapidly the remainder of the Chinese quota with personnel directly from the mainland; and (4) to leave the "status

---

[83] Article 100(1) of the UN Charter.

[84] A prominent authority on the United Nations has written that the "[Soviet] demand that more Soviet nationals be employed is a reasonable one; the difficulty arises when it comes to implementation. By denying the whole conception of an international career service, by seeking to place its nationals in what it regards as key policy positions, by denying the possibility of free recruitment, by insisting that all appointments be made from persons proposed and approved by the government and by taking the position that its nationals refuse fixed-term career appointments, the Soviet Union makes the task of the Secretary-General in meeting its request for increased participation of its nationals extremely difficult, if not impossible." See Leland M. Goodrich, "Geographical Distribution of the Staff of the UN Secretariat," *IO* 16 (Summer 1962), 481.

TABLE 3.7. Chinese Staff in Secretariat Posts Subject to
Geographical Distribution, 1971-76

As of Rank	8/31/71	6/30/72	6/30/73	6/30/74	6/30/75	6/30/76
USG		1	1	1	1	1
ASG	1					
D-2	1		2	2	2	2
D-1	6	6	6	7	6	8 (2)[a]
P-5	11	8	10	11	11	8 (1)[a]
P-4	11	10	7	7	7	10 (1)[a]
P-3	6	6	8	9	8	8 (1)[a]
P-2	14	14	15	12	11	11 (7)[a]
P-1	1	1			1	6 (4)[a]
Total	51	46	49	49	47	54 (16)
Desirable Range	57-78	56-76	56-76	84-116	83-115	91-126

[a] Female staff.

Source: Adapted from the following: UN Docs. A/8831, p. 15; A/8483, p. 22;
A/9120, Annex, p. 9; A/9724, Annex, p. 9; A/10184, Annex, p. 9; and A/31/154,
Annex, p. 7.

quo ante entry" intact, with only minor adjustments to be made from
time to time with whatever available and qualified Chinese were
found at home and overseas.

Much to the surprise and delight of all parties concerned, the PRC
adopted a modest, conciliatory, and pragmatic posture toward the personnel question. Immediately upon his arrival in New York, Huang
Hua paid his "consultative visit" to Secretary-General U Thant, who
was then convalescing at a New York hospital. Huang Hua conveyed
to the Secretary-General an assurance coming directly from Premier
Chou En-lai to the effect that the Chinese staff in the Secretariat had
no cause to worry about the change in Chinese representation at the
United Nations and that they should continue their work according to
their conscience. "U Thant knew that I was very worried," recalled one
high-ranking Chinese international civil servant, "so he called me that
evening to assure me that my concern was unfounded; I in turn
conveyed this happy message to other Chinese staff personnel in the
Secretariat."

"Immediately upon his arrival," recalled another Chinese staff member, "Ch'iao Kuan-hua gave a very warm and friendly reception for
us [the Chinese staff members in the Secretariat]—let me remind you

that we never had such a reception when the ROC was representing China in the United Nations—and told us that this was indeed a long overdue reunion. Ch'iao Kuan-hua also told us that China has changed a lot in the last two decades and that we were welcome to come back and see the new China. 'We do not want to brainwash you,' he said, 'or we might be brainwashed by you.' It was a very professional meeting. We were very impressed, to say the least. I immediately seized the opportunity and went back to China for a visit." Variations on this note were expressed by all the Chinese international civil servants whom I have interviewed. "We are not communists, as you know, but have come to develop a deep appreciation for the PRC, for she has restored the Chinese sense of dignity, pride, and patriotism in the global community," observed another.

Table 3.7 explains in part the policy of the PRC toward the Chinese staff in the Secretariat. It must be noted in this connection that the Secretary-General is subject to continuing cross-pressures on recruitment policy from many quarters. To cite a recent example, US delegate Ersa Poston strongly criticized Secretary-General Waldheim's handling of Soviet and Third World pressure for jobs in the Secretariat. Speaking before the Fifth Committee (Administrative and Budgetary) in October 1976, Poston bluntly declared that the time was long overdue for the Secretary-General to act more forcefully on recruitment policy so as to change the negative image of the UN staff in the public mind.[85] The implication of Poston's criticism was quite obvious— that the Secretariat had been hiring too many incompetents in order to accommodate the demands of geographical distribution from Member States.

The PRC proved to be a notable exception in this respect. While the desirable range of the Chinese quota increased from 57-78 in 1971 to 91-126 in 1976 (see Table 3.7 and Appendix D), the number of Chinese staff subject to geographical distribution actually declined in 1972-75, and increased only slightly in 1976. This decline came about because of normal retirements and slow response on the part of the PRC to suggest new nominees. A high-ranking international civil servant in the Office of Personnel Service authoritatively noted: "Not one single Chinese staff member has left his post since 1971 because of pressure from the PRC. The PRC's only expressed concern is a good performance in post."

This situation has brought about a unique relationship between the Chinese mission and the Secretariat. Whereas many Member States often apply pressure on it to hire more of their national nominees, the Secretariat itself has been approaching the Chinese mission to

[85] UN Doc. A/C.5/31/SR.6 (11 October 1976), p. 3.

put up more candidates. When thus approached, the Chinese have almost invariably said that "they are not in a position to provide the United Nations with more qualified candidates because China is still a developing nation, suffering from the shortage of experts." Appendix E gives a quantitative overview of this matter.

During the five-year period from mid-1971 to mid-1976, there were 6 retirements and 9 new appointments, adjusting the total number of Chinese staff slightly upward from 51 to 54. As of June 30, 1976, there were 3,500 staff members in the inner Secretariat who belonged to the "Professional category and above" (that is, from P-1 to USG), 2,600 of whom were subject to geographical distribution. In sum, China, with 54 staff members in the Secretariat, had about 2 percent of the total staff members subject to geographical distribution; this placed her in the category of ten Member States whose representation in the Secretariat fell below the lower figure of their quota range—in the case of China, we might add, well below the lower figure of the quota range.[86] More than half of the Chinese quota range remains to be filled.

It is of some significance that only three of the nine new appointments involved PRC diplomats who came directly from China, the remainder being recruited from overseas Chinese.[87] Of the three, the appointment of T'ang Ming-chao as Under-Secretary-General for Political Affairs, Trusteeship, and Decolonization on April 5, 1972, is the most important and prominent one.[88] It may be recalled here that

[86] The ten Member States falling into the described category are: Byelorussian Soviet Socialist Republic, China, Czechoslovakia, German Democratic Republic, Germany (Federal Republic of), Japan, Mexico, Ukrainian Soviet Socialist Republic, Union of Soviet Socialist Republics, and Venezuela. It should be also noted that until 1962 the contribution factor was the only factor in establishing quotas. However, General Assembly Resolution 1852 (XVII) of 19 December 1962 changed the method of establishing each Member State's desirable range by two additional factors: the membership factor and the population factor. For details, see Report of the Secretary-General entitled "Personnel Questions: Composition of the Secretariat," UN Doc. A/31/154 (19 August 1976).

[87] The established recruitment policy for the Secretariat regarding Chinese staff members is as follows: (1) China has always been, and remains, one and indivisible; (2) Chinese nationals are nationals of the whole country whatever authorities issue their passports; (3) staff members of Chinese nationality who entered the Secretariat before October 25, 1971, had, as a matter of course, to give evidence of their nationality by producing a valid national passport recognized by the authorities of the Republic of China; (4) candidates of Chinese nationality who have sought appointment since October 25, 1971, are required to produce passports *recognized* by the PRC; and (5) once a staff member is appointed, his nationality does not affect his continued employment. I have put together this policy guideline based on my field interviews.

[88] T'ang Ming-chao served as editor of the *Overseas Chinese Daily* in New York City from 1945 to 1949, when he returned to China. His US-born daughter, T'ang Wen-sheng (also known as Nancy T'ang) served as an interpreter for the late Premier Chou En-lai.

T'ang Ming-chao made his appearance at the 26th Session of the General Assembly as a member of the Chinese delegation. When the news spread among the Chinese staff in the Secretariat that an offer of this post was being made to the PRC, there was a universally shared and expressed belief among them that China was entitled to a more important political post in the Secretariat. Yet the PRC accepted the offer without much ado by nominating T'ang Ming-chao. The two other PRC nominees who later joined the Secretariat are Chang Shu, deputy director in the Department of Political and Security Council Affairs, and Chao Ming-te, Special Assistant to the Under-Secretary General for Political Affairs, Trusteeship and Decolonization.

For obvious reasons, the staff members in posts with special language requirements are not subject to geographical distribution. As Appendix F shows, a most dramatic change has occurred in this category of Chinese staff in the Secretariat, as the number of Chinese interpreters and translators nearly doubled from 1971 to 1976. This increase came about gradually in the course of implementing General Assembly Resolution 3189 (XXVIII) of 18 December 1973, which made Chinese one of the working languages of the General Assembly. In the course of debate on this question in the Fifth Committee on October 29, 1973, Huang Hua explained how the Chinese delegation had adopted a gradual approach, allowing ample time for the Secretariat to prepare on this question. Huang Hua further explained:

> Once Chinese became a working language, the main difference compared with the existing situation would be the need to provide provisional verbatim and summary records in Chinese in good time. Therefore the additional workload would be limited. Nevertheless, in order to avoid too large an increase in expenditure resulting from the inclusion of Chinese among the working languages, his delegation, following the principle of economy, proposed that the increase in staff should be restricted to those who were absolutely necessary. At the same time, it agreed to the workload suggested in document A/C.5/1528 for the present stage.[89]

[89] GAOR, 28th Sess., Fifth Committee, 1586th meeting (29 October 1973), para. 5. It may be noted that Chinese, French, Russian, English, and Spanish became the official languages of the Organization when the Charter recognized in Article 111 the Chinese, French, Russian, English, and Spanish texts as being equally authentic. English and French were among the working languages from the beginning and the remaining three official languages have been made working languages in the following chronological order: Spanish by General Assembly Resolution 262 (III) of 11 December 1948; Russian by General Assembly Resolution 2479 (XXIII) of 21 December 1968; and Chinese by General Assembly Resolution 3189 (XXVIII) of 18 December 1973. In addition, General Assembly Resolution 3190 (XXVIII) of 18 December 1973 made Arabic both an official and a working language of the General Assembly and its Main Committees. It

The PRC's pragmatic approach is also shown in the fact that most of the new Chinese interpreters and translators have been recruited from overseas Chinese in New York, London, Geneva, Paris, and Hong Kong. However, in marked contrast to the warm and cordial posture shown toward the Chinese staff subject to geographical distribution in the Secretariat, the Chinese delegates to the 26th Session of the General Assembly expressed dissatisfaction with the performance of Chinese interpreters. This led Ch'en Ch'u to conduct a well-publicized "bull session" with seventeen Chinese interpreters in January 1972, in which he scolded them severely for their poor performance and told them to make a major improvement.[90] Since then, relations between the Chinese delegation and the interpreters have improved steadily, to their mutual satisfaction, and most of the Chinese staff members with special language requirements spend their biennial home furlough in China, not in Taiwan.[91]

On the whole, China has been rather passive and reticent in the Fifth Committee on many issues relating to the Secretariat. The most salient feature of Chinese behavior on administrative matters has been her general support for the underprivileged and her opposition to what she regards as an elitist approach. When a draft resolution for a 6 percent across-the-board salary increase for the Secretariat personnel came up for debate in the plenary, Chinese delegate Hsing Sung-yi argued that such an indiscriminate raise "would mean that the higher the salaries, the greater the increase, and the lower the salaries, the less the increase. This is indeed most unreasonable."[92] He argued unsuccessfully that the salaries of high-ranking officials of the level of Assistant Secretaries-General and above—which were "already very high"—should be frozen, while giving "an appropriate increase in salaries" for the low-ranking staff members.[93] When this argument fell on deaf ears, China abstained on the draft resolution.

should also be noted that the introduction of Chinese as a working language was gradual. As of mid-1975, for example, the summary records of General Assembly committees were not issued in Chinese because of the shortage of Chinese translators. In addition, the summary records of subsidiary bodies of the General Assembly were not issued in Chinese. For details, see Report of the Secretary-General, *Publications and Documentation of the United Nations*, UN Doc. A/C.5/1670 (27 June 1975).

[90] *NYT*, January 24, 1972, p. 2.

[91] The United Nations pays for travel expenses for the families of staff members of the Secretariat, but there is no *per diem* allowance. Home leave is granted once every two years.

[92] UN Doc. A/PV.2325 (18 December 1974), p. 51.

[93] *Ibid.* Likewise, Chinese delegate Wang Lien-sheng stated in the Fifth Committee of the General Assembly on December 17, 1974, that the Secretary-General's salary was already high; hence, it should not be raised for the time being. See GAOR, 29th Sess., Fifth Committee, 1697th meeting (17 December 1974), para. 41.

Given a choice between the need to economize and the need to remedy the disequilbrium in geographical distribution of UN personnel or units, China invariably sided with the Third World in favor of the latter. She argued in favor of the employment of women in senior and other professional positions by the secretariats of organizations in the United Nations system. Likewise, she supported the demand of the Third World that greater attention should be given in recruitment policy to candidates from developing countries, based on the principle of equitable geographical distribution. "The affairs of the United Nations should be managed by all Member States," argued Hsing Sung-yi in the Fifth Committee, "and not controlled by a small number of countries or one or two super-Powers. The current UN personnel regulations and the composition of the Secretariat fell far short of reflecting the will of the majority of Member States."[94] Such an argument was invariably put forth in support of demands or requests advanced by the Third World, not in terms of what China herself wanted from the Secretariat.

On the question of the reorganization of the top echelon of the Secretariat, China maintained that "functional necessity" should be the basis for introducing any reclassification, not personal considerations.[95] In a similar vein, the Secretariat has been criticized for being overstaffed, overbureaucratized, overconcentrated in location, extravagant (unreasonably high salaries for the top echelon officials), and inefficient (resulting from overlapping jurisdictions and functions between departments). The Chinese have also noted that there is an empire-building tendency in the Secretariat. Consistent with this critical posture, China supported the financial expenditure involved in establishing the UNEP secretariat at Nairobi, "since so far there had been an unwarranted overconcentration of United Nations bodies in the United States of America and Western European countries."[96]

Financial and Budgetary Behavior

Chinese behavior in regard to financial and budgetary questions raises a number of important issues and problems that can be analyzed constitutionally, administratively, functionally, and politically. The operational impact of China's refusal to pay her share of UN peace-keeping expenses will be assessed in Chapter 4, while the legal implications

[94] GAOR, 29th Sess., Fifth Committee, 1665th meeting (19 November 1974), para. 37; see also GAOR, 27th Sess., Fifth Committee, 1547th meeting (11 December 1972), para. 45.

[95] GAOR, 28th Sess., Fifth Committee, 1628th meeting (14 December 1973), para. 10.

[96] GAOR, 27th Sess., Fifth Committee, 1551st meeting (13 December 1972), para. 45; GAOR, 27th Sess., Second Committee, 1483rd meeting (6 November 1972), para. 15.

of her unilateral and selective withholding of support on certain items in the regular budget to which she objects will be explored in Chapter 8. Similarly, the nature and extent of Chinese contributions to the financing of the specialized agencies will be separately reviewed in Chapter 7. The present discussion is of a general political nature, revolving around budgetary politics in the General Assembly.

The financial and budgetary issues that come annually before the General Assembly through its Fifth Committee, ACABQ, and the Committee on Contributions, have several unique characteristics. First, they concern decisions that are purely internal. Second, the Charter in Article 17 gives the "power of the purse" to the General Assembly; hence, the Assembly has the power to make binding decisions on financial and budgetary issues. It is the Assembly that considers and approves the regular budget, that considers and approves the scale of assessment for each Member State. Third, the crucible of budgetary politics is the regular budget. Though it represents only a small portion of the total financial commitment of the United Nations system, the regular budget affects the political nerve center, while voluntary contributions impinge only on the periphery. Finally, budgetary politics tend to generate a mixture of constitutional, political, and ideological issues, an interplay of principles and interests, and a clash of conflicting conceptualizations of world order among Member States.

It is common knowledge by now that the United Nations was pushed to the precipice of a serious political, constitutional, and financial crisis in the 19th General Assembly. When a showdown on Article 19 was averted in 1965, the financial crisis, which had acted as the catalytic agent, was shelved, not solved. By the time of the PRC's entry, the financial crisis had reached another critical point; this led the Assembly to establish a Special Committee on the Financial Situation of the United Nations, with a mandate to study and submit suggestions and concrete proposals to the Assembly at its 27th Session.[97] By becoming elected as a member of this 15-member Special Committee, China was catapulted into UN budgetary politics.

Table 3.8 gives a grim financial picture of the United Nations during the first year of the PRC's participation. Several points are in order here. First, the crisis can be attributed to three major causes: (1) refusal by some Member States to contribute to certain regular budget items because they violate the Members' position of principle ($37.4 million); (2) the cost of UNEF I ($39.5 million); and (3) ONUC ($50

[97] On December 22, 1971, the General Assembly, on the proposal of the President, decided without objection to establish this committee. This took a form of "decision" rather than a resolution. The fifteen Member States elected to membership in this committee are: Brazil, Canada, China, France, Ghana, India, Japan, Kenya, Mexico, Nigeria, Norway, Poland, the Soviet Union, the United Kingdom, and the United States.

TABLE 3.8. Account of the Short-Term Deficit of the United Nations as of December 31, 1972 (estimated in million $)

Category	Deficit[a]
1. Regular budget and Working Capital Fund (Amounts withheld by Member States who, because of positions of principle, have not participated in the financing of certain regular budget items)	37.4
2. United Nations Emergency Force (UNEF) Conditional voluntary contributions received (repayable to governments)	0.6
Obligations incurred in excess of assessed contributions, voluntary contributions, and miscellaneous income	38.9
Less: Financed from the UN bonds	(8.1)
Financed from the UN Special Account	(3.9)
Net obligations incurred in excess of available funds	27.5
3. United Nations Operations in the Congo (ONUC) Conditional voluntary contributions received (repayable to governments)	1.6
Obligations incurred in excess of assessed contributions, voluntary contributions, and miscellaneous income available	48.4
Less: Financed from the UN bonds	(35.9)
Net obligations incurred in excess of available funds	14.1
4. *Less*: Voluntary contributions and pledges	(25.9)
5. Net Deficit	53.1

[a] Of the two deficit estimates in the report, this is the "A" deficit showing a lower estimate of "surplus accounts." The "B" deficit is $16.7 million higher in net deficit than the "A" deficit used in this table. Furthermore, this table excludes the unpaid assessed contribution due from China prior to October 25, 1971.

Source: Adapted from *Report of the Special Committee on the Financial Situation of the United Nations*, GAOR, 27th Sess., Supp. 29 (A/8729), pp. 9-10.

million). The net total deficit thus generated amounts to $126.9 million. Second, UN finances are chronically plagued by such factors as the lateness of many Member States in paying their assessed contribution; currency fluctuations—note two devaluations in the 1970s of the US dollar, the currency on which the UN budget is based; and inflationary pressures.

Finally, the UN bonds ($44 million), the UN Special Account ($3.9 million), and voluntary contributions and pledges ($25.9 million) have reduced the net total deficit by $73.8 million; this still leaves a net deficit of $53.1 million. The Chinese deficit, which is excluded from Table 3.8, posed a special financial and political problem for the United Nations.

The PRC would not have had to face a succession of international obligations if the ROC delegation had paid its dues. However, Nationalist China "has been the largest single debtor and has usually been responsible for over three-quarters of the total arrears."[98] This was in part attributable to the anomaly of her claim that she represented the whole of China. As a result, the ROC's assessment was based on the resources of the whole of China, while her capacity to pay was limited to the resources in Taiwan. The actual debts of the ROC delegation at the time of its expulsion exceeded $30 million: $18,207,518 for the UN regular budget and Working Capital Fund; $5,274,570 for the UNEF Special Account; and $6,687,207 for the ONUC *Ad Hoc* Account. In addition, the ROC left unpaid some $13.6 million for the specialized agencies. The amount of contributions due from China in respect of the regular budget and Working Capital Fund on January 1, 1972 would have exceeded the amount of the assessed contributions for the years 1970 and 1971 by $4,675,643.00; thus, the ROC was in imminent danger of losing her voting rights under Article 19 of the UN Charter.[99]

Faced with this desperate financial legacy, the PRC immediately took two unilateral actions. First, she refused to assume any of the financial obligations incurred by the "illegal and illegitimate" representative of China. She could not be held responsible for these debts, declared the PRC delegation, as "this is self-evident both from the *legal* point of view and from common knowledge."[100]

However, the PRC disappointed the curious legal community by refusing to elaborate on the issue. It should be noted in this connection that during her exclusion period the PRC advanced the widely held legal argument that China had always been and would continue to be a founding member of the United Nations; hence, the "important-question resolution" introduced by the United States in the 1960s to block her entry was a legal absurdity. In short, the PRC maintained that the China issue in the United Nations was a procedural question of credentials, rather than a substantive matter of admission, based largely on the doctrine of state continuity in international law. Apparently, the PRC makes a distinction between state continuity and

[98] John G. Stoessinger, "Financing the United Nations," *International Conciliation*, No. 535 (November 1961), 12. For elaboration on the ROC's financial performance in the United Nations system, see John G. Stoessinger, *Financing the United Nations System* (Washington, D.C.: The Brookings Institution, 1964).
[99] GAOR, 27th Sess., *Report of the Committee on Contributions*, Supp. 11 (A/8711), p. 8.
[100] GAOR, 27th Sess., 2116th plenary meeting (19 December 1972), para. 211; emphasis added. See also GAOR, 27th Sess., Fifth Committee, 1556th meeting (16 December 1972), para. 98.

representational discontinuity in deciding what obligations to assume or not to assume.

Second, as if to muddle the legal situation even more, the PRC paid rather promptly the assessed contributions due from China for 1971 (prorated from October 25, 1971) and 1972. The PRC made a payment of $3 million (and later another payment of $3,597,667) as partial payments of her 1972 contribution; this was followed up by two payments on May 16, 1972, in amounts of $400,000 and $1,013,486.13, which she stated were intended respectively as an advance to the Working Capital Fund and a contribution to the UN regular budget for 1971.[101] The PRC's refusal to participate in any of meetings of the 15-member Special Committee on the Financial Situation of the United Nations may also be accepted as evidence of her determination not to get entangled in any legal argument on the "self-evident" position of China on her short-term deficit.

In the meantime, the Special Committee held a series of meetings followed by informal negotiations and reached a general understanding among twelve of its fifteen members with respect to the content and financing of future regular budgets. The general understanding— in which Poland and the Soviet Union refused to join and China did not participate—was formulated as a "total package" with three major elements: (1) that the items of expenditures toward which certain Member States refused to pay for reasons of principles would no longer be included in the expenditure section of the regular budget but would instead be financed from miscellaneous income; (2) that the technical assistance programs for developing countries would be removed from the regular budget and would instead be financed from UNDP without any reduction in amount; and (3) that all Member States would undertake to pay in full, beginning with 1973, all amounts assessed for the regular budget and that the short-term deficit of the past would be settled once and for all.[102]

On the question of eliminating or financing the past deficit, with special focus on China's deficit, the Special Committee merely noted "general agreement" that the major part of the deficit could be eliminated only by voluntary contributions or by a cancellation of obligations. The Soviet Union quickly intervened with the argument that she had no intention of participating in paying-off the Chinese debt, and that "it would be entirely logical for the various States Members of the United Nations which had supported the 'illegal

---

[101] GAOR, 27th Sess., *Report of the Committee on Contributions*, Supp. 11 (A/8711), p. 8.

[102] GAOR, 27th Sess., *Report of the Special Committee on the Financial Situations of the United Nations*, Supp. 29 (A/8729), pp. 4-5.

presence of the Chiang Kai-shek regime' in the United Nations for so long to take it upon themselves to liquidate that debt."[103] The Special Committee threw this question back to the Assembly for solution.

Likewise, the Committee on Contributions, unwilling to offend the most prominent "new" Member State, advised in its 1972 report to the Assembly that the question of China's short-term deficit was beyond the purview of its reference. "Given the circumstances of the representation of China in the United Nations today, the legal and political problems involved, and the on-going discussions with the People's Republic of China," the Committee agreed, this question should be resolved by the General Assembly itself.[104] Although I have been unable to obtain as much information as I would like on the behind-the-scenes bilateral negotiations between the PRC and the Secretariat alluded to in the Committee report, Chapter 7 will give some specific examples of this kind of bilateral negotiation between the PRC and some specialized agencies in respect to the settlement of China's financial obligations.

It was against this background that the General Assembly, at the end of its 27th Session, decided to resolve the problem. The first major step was taken in the Fifth Committee, when a proposal sponsored by Mexico, Norway, Pakistan, the United Republic of Tanzania, Yugoslavia, and Zambia was adopted on December 16, 1972, by 47 votes to 8, with 20 abstentions. Three days later, the General Assembly adopted the same text in the form of a resolution, in effect deleting China's preentry dues from its assessment account.[105]

The Assembly instructed the Secretary-General to create a "special account" for China's preentry debts and to regard the amount "as a part of the short-term deficit of the Organization." In this way, the General Assembly decided to take a political short-cut to resolve the Chinese deficit problem, while inflating its own net short-term deficit. The voting alignments on this important resolution (92 in favor, 9 against, with 24 abstentions) are revealing: the United States joined the 92-majority made up of a curious mixture of Second and Third World countries; Brazil voted "no" with the solid Soviet bloc (Bulgaria, Byelorussia, Czechoslovakia, Hungary, Mongolia, Poland, Ukraine, and USSR); Albania, Gambia, Honduras, Jordan, Lesotho, and Maldives were absent; and China did not participate in the vote and requested that this fact be inserted in the official record.

Chinese behavior in this scale-of-assessments politics adds another

[103] *Ibid.*, p. 7.
[104] GAOR, 27th Sess., *Report of the Committee on Contributions*, Supp. 11 (A/8711), p. 8; emphasis added.
[105] General Assembly Resolution 3049 C (XXVII) of 19 December 1972.

strange chapter to the history of UN financing. While many Member States constantly appeal to the Committee on Contributions for reduction in their scale of assessments for various reasons, China made an unprecedented gesture in requesting that its assessment be increased, at the very time when the United States was engaged in a carrot-and-stick campaign to have its assessment reduced from 31.52 percent to 25.00 percent.

Hsing Sung-yi stated in the Fifth Committee on October 9, 1972, that his government had fulfilled its financial obligations to the United Nations to the best of its capacities. "It was true," he continued, "that the rate of assessment for China was lower than that for some other Member States [obviously alluding to the remaining permanent members of the Security Council], but that was because China was still a developing country with a relatively backward economy and a relatively low national income." Then came the surprise announcement: "Thanks to the development of its national economy, however, China intended to raise [unilaterally?] its rate of assessment gradually to 7 percent during the coming five years."[106]

However, the budgetary process in the General Assembly begins with its two standing committees—ACABQ and the Committee on Contributions—each of which is composed of experts in their individual capacities, serving for a three-year term. ACABQ is responsible for expert examination of the UN budget, while the Committee on Contributions advises the Assembly on the scale of assessments for Member States on a triennial basis. On November 9, 1972, the Assembly, following its action on ACABQ a year earlier, decided to enlarge the Committee on Contributions from twelve to thirteen members, with effect from January 1, 1973, in order to include a member from China. On December 4, 1972, the Assembly appointed Wang Wei-tsai, the nominee of China, as an expert member of the Committee on Contributions; thus, Chinese representation in both standing committees has been assured.

Wang Wei-tsai attended the 33rd Session of the Committee on Contributions held at UN Headquarters in May and September 1973. This was a particularly important session because the Committee had to review the existing scale of assessments and to recommend changes to the 28th General Assembly for the financial years 1974, 1975, and 1976. It was in this committee that the PRC, following up on Hsing Sung-yi's declaration of intention in the Fifth Committee, specifically requested to have her assessment raised to 5.5 percent for the next triennium. Faced with General Assembly Resolution 2961 B (XXVII), which had

[106] GAOR, 27th Sess., Fifth Committee, 1498th meeting (9 October 1972), para. 2.

established the 25 percent ceiling principle for any one Member State (but clearly applicable only to the United States), and numerous requests and appeals for reduction in assessment rates, the Committee was not in a mood to ponder the legal implications of China's request to revise its assessment upward. Legal or not, it promptly accepted China's request and embodied it in its recommendation to the Assembly. Table 3.9 places the financial implications of this unusual gesture in a comparative and historical framework for further analysis.

TABLE 3.9. Scale of Assessments for the Big Five, 1961, 1971-77
(percent of the total UN budget)

	1961	1971	1972	1973	1974	1975	1976	1977
CHINA	4.57	4.00	4.00	4.00	5.50	5.50	5.50	5.50
USA	32.02	31.52	31.52	31.52	25.00	25.00	25.00	25.00
USSR	14.97	14.18	14.18	14.18	12.97	12.97	12.97	11.33
UK	7.58	5.90	5.90	5.90	5.31	5.31	5.31	4.44
FRANCE	5.94	6.00	6.00	6.00	5.86	5.86	5.86	5.66
TOTAL	65.08	61.60	61.60	61.60	54.64	54.64	54.64	51.93

What was China really up to? A number of plausible but unproven explanations have been offered. It has been suggested that the "Chinese gift horse"—a variation on the old Trojan Horse theme?—contained a big catch: namely, it was intended to cover additional costs involved in providing Chinese-language facilities.[107] This is an unfair argument, based on a misleading equation of Chinese and Arabic, both of which were adopted as working languages of the General Assembly at its 28th Session. The Arab Member States agreed in advance that they would meet all the costs ensuing from this decision for the first three years (1974-76)[108] and the Chinese have advanced no such offer.

But there is no reason in UN law or practice why the Chinese *should* make any additional contributions. Chinese was recognized as one of the five official languages of the Organization by the Charter and, as such, should enjoy the same treatment as accorded the other official languages. There were no such additional costs to English- or French-

[107] Don Shannon, "Peking Offers to Raise UN Contribution—With a Catch," *Los Angeles Times*, October 10, 1972, p. 1, in Cohen and Chiu, *People's China and International Law*, Vol. II, pp. 1363-64.

[108] One of the preambular paragraphs of General Assembly Resolution 3190 (XXVIII) of 18 December 1973 reads: "*Noting with appreciation* the assurances of the Arab States Members of the United Nations to meet collectively the costs of implementing the present resolution during the first three years [1974-76]." Emphasis in original.

speaking Member States, nor were any additional costs assumed by Spanish- and Russian-speaking Member States when Spanish and Russian were made working languages in 1948 and 1968 respectively. It may also be noted in this connection that from January 1977 the costs of Arabic translation have been met from the UN regular budget. As a result, the Arabic translation services now cost more than $4 million annually (in 1977) while the total budget contributions of Arab-speaking Member States come to only $3.9 million. Even the "super-rich" Saudi Arabia contributes only one-fourth of 1 percent of the UN regular budget.[109]

Even if the costs of the Chinese translation services were indeed the motive behind the Chinese move, the additional income generated far exceeds the estimated cost of $1 million for 1974-75. Additional revenues for the United Nations—estimated here on the basis of regular and supplementary appropriations—resulting from the increase in the Chinese assessment rate amount to $9,188,250 for the biennium 1974-75 and to $11,758,993 for the biennium 1976-77. It may also be noted here that the summary records of the subsidiary bodies as well as of the Main Committees were not issued in Chinese as of mid-1975 because of the shortage of Chinese translators.[110] Hence, we need to seek explanations other than a Trojan Horse with a linguistic catch.

In a perceptive essay on this subject, Richard Bissell suggested three alternative explanations: (1) that the Chinese may have wanted to pay off the old ROC debts (over $40 million) through an indirect and installment plan; (2) that this may be the Chinese way of demonstrating their proper status in the global community; and (3) that the Chinese may have attached special importance to the figure of 5.5 percent in the context of Asian international politics, because this figure stood slightly above Japan's assessment rate of 5.4 percent.[111] Although difficult to substantiate, I would accept all of these explanations as persuasive and plausible, given the importance of representational symbols in Chinese global politics.

However, one additional explanation is suggested here. The Chinese have shown an extreme sensitivity—and reluctance—about providing the United Nations with any kind of statistical data. In order to deter-

[109] The 32nd Session of the General Assembly ended with a major dispute over budgetary matters. See *NYT*, December 21, 1977, p. A13, and December 22, 1977, p. A6.

[110] See Report of the Secretary-General, *Publications and Documentation of the United Nations*, UN Doc. A/C.5/1670 (27 June 1975); Advisory Committee on Administrative and Budgetary Questions, 28th Sess., *Sixth Report*, Supp. 8A, UN Doc. A/9008/Add.5 (1973).

[111] Bissell, "A Note on the Chinese View of United Nations Finances," pp. 631-32.

mine accurately China's capacity to pay, the Committee on Contributions would need detailed national income statistics. The Committee used averages of national income at market prices for the three years 1969-71, for example, in calculating the capacity to pay for the 1974-76 triennial scale of assessments for Member States.[112] In the case of Member States for which official statistics were not available, the Committee used methods of estimation and extrapolation following the example set by the Statistical Office of the United Nations in the compilation of data. A critical key question for the Committee in a hypothetical determination of China's assessment rate is whether to use its own estimate of the PRC's GNP alone or to use the estimates of the GNP of both the PRC and the ROC.

Certainly, this is the kind of problem that the PRC might wish to avoid getting into. By making a generous gesture at a time when the assessment rates of the other permanent members of the Security Council have been relatively and steadily declining (see Table 3.9), the PRC seems to have found a "strategic" solution with multiple aims: (1) to show a measure of China's sensitivity to the UN financial predicament without seemingly betraying her own principled stand, thus demonstrating China's ability to reconcile principles with interests; (2) to demonstrate that China has her own method of defining her proper role and status in the management of the internal (administrative and budgetary) questions, rather than having her role and status defined for her; and (3) to avoid potential hazards and embarrassments in having her capacity to pay determined by the Committee on Contributions in the face of her refusal to provide detailed statistical data.

The PRC's politicized approach to the UN budgetary process, while it has worked out to the practical convenience of all parties concerned in the case of her own assessment, is nonetheless fraught with some logical inconsistencies, administrative difficulties, and legal hazards. Clearly, the PRC conceptualizes the UN budget as an expression of what the United Nations ought to be doing. Repeatedly, Hsing Sung-yi argued in the Fifth Committee that the budget was not only a sum of the revenues and expenditures; it should also be a reflection of the implementation of the Charter; it is therefore incumbent on the Committee to examine each budget item to see whether it is in accord with the Charter principles and purposes. Likewise, in a periodic debate over supplementary appropriations requests, the PRC has taken

[112] The capacity-to-pay principle is the most important guide in determining a Member State's assessment. However, such other principles as ceiling, per capita ceiling, and floor are also taken into account in the final determination. See GAOR, 28th Sess., *Report of the Committee on Contributions*, Supp. 11 (A/9011), pp. 9-15.

the stand that such requests should be approved only if they are "for the safeguarding of international peace, the struggle against aggression and interference, the support of national liberation and the development of friendly relations and co-operation between the peoples of various countries."[113] On the other hand, the PRC was firmly opposed to the supplementary expenses "which constituted a violation of the purposes and principles of the Charter of the UN and an interference in other countries' internal affairs."[114]

Based on such a stand, the PRC has given firm and consistent support to all the "just and reasonable" demands of the Third World. Since the Sixth Special Session, another important element has been added to Peking's principled stand: support for the establishment of the New International Economic Order and the promotion of the economic development of the Third World.[115] Specifically, the PRC has argued for special considerations in the determination of the scale of assessments, especially for the least developed countries with the lowest capacity to pay and certain developing countries that have suffered losses in their national income as a result of natural disasters.[116] The PRC strongly supported appropriations for all the activities of the Committee of 24 on Decolonization, including additional expenditures for holding meetings of the Committee in three African countries.[117] In spite of her opposition to UNIDO's assistance to South Korea, South Vietnam (before the unification), Israel, and the Lon Nol regime, the PRC also voted for the budget estimates of UNIDO recommended by ACABQ.[118] In general, the PRC's support for existing and additional expenditures involved in meeting the demands and needs of the developing countries has been firm and consistent.

On the other hand, the PRC expressed a concern about the steady downward trend in the assessment rates of the two superpowers. In her view, the assessment process was moving away from the capacity-to-pay principle; it was therefore "entirely proper and justified for many developing countries to object to the unreasonable and unfair

[113] GAOR, 28th Sess., Fifth Committee, 1612th meeting (28 November 1973), para. 9.

[114] *Ibid*; see also GAOR, 27th Sess., Fifth Committee, 1532nd meeting (21 November 1972), para. 5.

[115] UN Doc. A/C.5/SR.1773 (19 December 1975), p. 12. The PRC's position on NIEO is more fully discussed in Chapters 5 and 6.

[116] See GAOR, 27th Sess., Fifth Committee, 1536th meeting (27 November 1972), para. 52; GAOR, 28th Sess., Fifth Committee, 1583rd meeting (25 October 1973), para. 39; UN Doc. A/C.5/31/SR.23 (4 November 1976), pp. 10-11.

[117] GAOR, 27th Sess., Fifth Committee, 1510th meeting (23 October 1972), para. 45; GAOR, 27th Sess., Fifth Committee, 1532nd meeting (21 November 1972), para. 5.

[118] GAOR, 27th Sess., Fifth Committee, 1513th meeting (26 October 1972), para. 51.

tendencies in the new scale of assessments" for the triennium 1977-79. Thus, the request of many representatives from the developing countries for a postponement of the new scale of assessment and a reformulation of the necessary criteria merited serious consideration.[119]

Yet, the PRC as a major contributor to the UN budget has joined the other great powers in assuming a posture of fiscal conservatism, expressing an alarmed concern about the accelerating rate of UN budget expenditure. In the Fifth Committee Hsing Sung-yi expressed his incredulity that UN expenditure had increased over 70 percent from 1971 to 1974 and that the budget estimates for the biennium 1976-77 represented an increase of 22.7 percent over the revised appropriations for the biennium 1974-75 or of 38.6 percent over the initial budget estimates. "Such a huge increase in budget expenditure and staff," Hsing Sung-yi maintained, to the delight of the US delegation, "was unreasonable and hampered efficiency."[120]

From this standpoint of fiscal conservatism, the Chinese argued repeatedly for the practice of economy and efficiency in the Secretariat. "The United Nations should economize in its expenditures," Hsing Sung-yi pleaded, "simplify its administration and reduce its personnel as far as possible, so that the existing manpower and material resources could be put to the fullest use."[121] Curiously, China has singled out the Department of Political Affairs, Trusteeship, and Decolonization (headed by T'ang Ming-chao) as "having done a great work in implementing decisions relating to decolonization," but maintains that much remains to be done. Therefore, China "could not accept any reduction in the budget or in the number of posts" in this department.[122]

Unfortunately, China also joined the rank of the withholders in the United Nations by refusing from the very beginning of her participation to contribute to certain items in the regular budget which, she claims, "do not conform to the spirit of the Charter."[123] The list of items in the regular budget targeted for withholding includes: (1) the UN Commission for the Unification and Rehabilitation of Korea (UNCURK);[124] (2) the offices of UN High Commissioner for Refugees

[119] UN Doc. A/C.5/31/SR.23 (4 November 1976), p. 11.
[120] UN Doc. A/C.5/SR.1773 (19 December 1975), pp. 12-13.
[121] *Ibid.*, p. 13; see also GAOR, 29th Sess., Fifth Committee, 1665th meeting (19 November 1974), para. 40.
[122] UN Doc. A/C.5/SR.1740 (18 November 1975), p. 7.
[123] GAOR, 27th Sess., Fifth Committee, 1506th meeting (18 October 1972), para. 39.
[124] GAOR, 27th Sess., Fifth Committee, 1510th meeting (23 October 1972), para. 45; GAOR, 28th Sess., Fifth Committee, 1630th meeting (17 December 1973), para. 41. At its 2181st plenary meeting on November 28, 1973, the

at Macao, New Delhi and Katmandu;[125] (3) the UN cemetery in Korea;[126] (4) the UN bond issues;[127] (5) the service of outside consultants;[128] and (6) the expenses to be incurred for a study of military budgets.[129] Thus, China follows the example of the Soviet Union and quite a few other Member States who, since 1963, have refused as a matter of principle to contribute to items (1), (3), and (4), above.

The actual amounts withheld from China's annual contribution are relatively small, as Table 3.10 shows. Hopefully, there is a discernible downward trend in the percentage of amounts withheld from her annual contribution to the regular budget: 6.8 percent for 1972; 4.9 percent for 1973; 3.8 percent for 1974; and 3.1 percent for 1975. In cumulative terms, China contributed $41,996,674 to the regular budget as of December 31, 1975, but her short-term deficit resulting from selective withholding on expenditure items to which she objected stood at $1,817,557. Although relatively small, such withholding is a violation of the international obligations that she has assumed by joining and participating in the decision-making process of the General Assembly.

More seriously, China has also refused to pay her contributions to UNEF II and UNDOF. Indeed, this represents the most salient contradiction of Chinese budgetary behavior in the United Nations. In the face of the threat that unilateral Congressional or executive action might follow if the Fifth Committee failed to adopt the American proposal for reduction in assessment to 25 percent, Hsing Sung-yi flatly —and rightly—declared: "China held that once the General Assembly had adopted the scale of assessments, it was incumbent upon every Member State to bear its share in accordance with the assessment."[130] However, after the establishment of UNEF II and UNDOF, the Chinese delegates have repeatedly stated their opposition to including the expenses of UNEF II and UNDOF *as a UN expenditure* in the form of nonparticipation in the vote.[131]

General Assembly dissolved UNCURK, thus eliminating one of the most objectionable expenditure items from the UN regular budget.

[125] GAOR, 27th Sess., Fifth Committee, 1511th meeting (24 October 1972), para. 52; GAOR, 28th Sess., Fifth Committee, 1581st meeting (23 October 1973), para. 41.

[126] GAOR, 27th Sess., Fifth Committee, 1514th meeting (27 October 1972), para. 51.

[127] *Ibid.* See also GAOR, 28th Sess., Fifth Committee, 1571st meeting (9 October 1973), para. 48; UN Doc. A/C.5/SR.1731 (10 November 1975), p. 2.

[128] GAOR, 29th Sess., Fifth Committee, 1681st meeting (4 December, 1974), para. 27.

[129] UN Doc. A/C.5/SR.1766 (15 December 1975), p. 27.

[130] GAOR, 27th Sess., Fifth Committee, 1536th meeting (27 November 1972), para. 50.

[131] See UN Doc. A/PV.2303 (29 November 1974), pp. 76-80; GAOR, 28th

TABLE 3.10. Chinese Payment Record on Assessed Contributions, 1970-75, ($)

Financial Year	Assessed %	Assessed Amount[c]	Paid Amount	Unpaid Balance	% Assessed Amount	Cumulative Unpaid Balance as of December 31
1970[a]	4.00	5,625,637	–	5,625,637	(100)	11,934,547
1971[a]	4.00	6,272,971	–	6,272,971	(100)	16,607,518
1971[b]	4.00	6,272,971	1,568,663	–		–
1972[b]	4.00	7,078,828	6,597,667	481,161	(6.8)	481,161
1973[b]	4.00	7,497,930	7,134,210	363,720	(4.9)	844,881
1974[b]	5.50	12,860,588	11,767,348	493,240	(3.8)	1,338,121[d]
1975[b]	5.50	15,408,222	14,928,786	479,436	(3.1)	1,817,557

[a] Applicable to the ROC.
[b] Applicable to the PRC.
[c] Less credits from estimated staff assessment income and adjustments of advance to Working Capital Fund.
[d] As of January 1, 1975, instead of December 31, 1974. The entries for 1974 are taken from miscellaneous sources because the United Nations did not publish its *Annual Financial Report and Accounts* for the 30th Session of the General Assembly in the process of making a transition to a biennial budget cycle. The discrepancies for 1974 are attributable to this gap in the documents.

Source: Financial Report and Accounts, GAOR, 26th Sess., Supp. 7 (A/8407); GAOR, 27th Sess., Supp. 7 (A/8707); GAOR, 28th Sess., Supp. 7 (A/9007); GAOR, 29th Sess., Supp. 7 (A/9607); and GAOR, 31st Sess., Supp. 7 (A/31/7).

Surely, the Assembly decision on appropriation is no less legally binding than its decision on assessment. The Assembly decided to appropriate the expenses of UNEF II and UNDOF and then to apportion them among all Member States on a special scale.[132] Yet, China acted as if her nonparticipation in the vote made the Assembly decisions not legally binding upon herself and hence canceled her obligation to pay. China thus defied the decision of the Assembly as well as her own declaration in the Fifth Committee on the question of UN financing. As of December 31, 1975, China's cumulative arrears to UNEF II-UNDOF account stood at $16,754,642.

Of course, there is no novelty in China's political approach, as a number of Member States, including the Soviet Union and France, refused to pay their share of expenses for peace-keeping operations in the Congo (ONUC) and the Middle East (UNEF I) even after the International Court of Justice handed down its opinion on July 20, 1962, advising by a 9:5 majority that the expenses of both UNEF I and ONUC could be regarded as expenses of the Organization within the meaning of Article 17 of the Charter. While the United States has yet to resort to unilateral withholding as far as the UN regular budget is concerned, she, too, has withheld assessed contributions from both ILO and UNESCO. The financial, operational, and legal implications of Chinese position on UN peace-keeping will be more fully explored in Chapter 4. China's participation in UN voluntary contributions and pledges has been spotty and selective. The details of contributions are spelled out in Appendix G, and reference to and analysis of various voluntary programs shown in the Appendix will be found throughout this study.

Viewed as a whole, UN financing has been helped more than hindered by the PRC's participation. Despite the legal hazards inherent

---

Sess., Fifth Committee, 1604th meeting (20 November 1973), paras. 60-66; GAOR, 28th Sess., Fifth Committee, 1609th meeting (23 November 1973), para. 14; GAOR, 29th Sess., Fifth Committee, 1654th meeting (31 October 1974), para. 16; GAOR, 29th Sess., Fifth Committee, 1674th meeting (27 November 1974), para. 48; UN Doc. A/PV.2389 (30 October 1975), p. 16; UN Doc. A/C.5/SR.1725 (4 November 1975), p. 3; UN Doc. A/C.5/SR.1752 (3 December 1975), p. 12; UN Doc. A/31/PV.41 (26 October 1976), p. 6; UN Doc. A/C.5/31/SR.14 (22 October 1976), p. 13.

[132] General Assembly Resolution 3101 (XXVIII) of 11 December 1973; General Assembly Resolution 3211 A (XXIX) of 31 October 1974; General Assembly Resolution 3211 B (XXIX) of 29 November 1974; General Assembly Resolution 3374 A (XXX) of 30 October 1975; General Assembly Resolution 3374 B (XXX) of 28 November 1975; General Assembly Resolution 3374 C (XXX) of 2 December 1975; General Assembly Resolution 31/5 A of 26 October 1976; General Assembly Resolution 31/5 B of 1 December 1976; General Assembly Resolution 31/5 C of 22 December 1976; General Assembly Resolution 31/5 D of 22 December 1976.

in subjective political interpretation of her financial obligations in the United Nations, the PRC has been—and is most likely to continue to be—a greater contributor to UN finances than the ROC, who, contrary to her publicized image, proved to be one of the worst defaulters in UN history. A few concluding points about Chinese financial and budgetary behavior and its impact on UN financing are in order. First, the PRC has established a reputation for sending her payment in good time, thus easing the chronic cash flow problem of the United Nations. Second, the PRC has refused to be a recipient of any UN assistance program, despite her status as a developing country. As a result, as will be elaborated in Chapters 6 and 7, a substantial amount of UN money, has been siphoned off to other developing countries. This amounts, in effect, to a contribution by self-denial. Third, the PRC's minimal participation in UN voluntary contributions has been in part a function of her status as a developing country and in part a function of her strong belief that the best development strategy is self-reliance. Finally, the PRC's withholding on the UN regular budget has constituted a rather small—and steadily declining—percentage of her annual payment to the United Nations.

Chinese Influence in the General Assembly

The foregoing analysis of Chinese behavior in its various dimensions provides a basis for assessing Chinese influence in Assembly politics. Table 3.11 is based on soft data collected from the author's field interviews. It should be emphasized that the sources of influence are inversely related to the objective hierarchies of physical size, population, economic and military capability, and financial contributions to the UN budget. In a word, a small or medium-sized power needs to possess a greater variety of the sources of influence than a great power. Likewise, the subjective source of desire and willingness to play a leadership role is less crucial in the case of the great powers, who can be influential even when they choose not to be. As Robert Keohane observed in his much acclaimed study of political influence in the Assembly, "Beyond the great powers, political influence in the Assembly is limited, temporary, and insecure."[133]

While Keohane's observation of the *positive* influence of the great powers in the Assembly political process certainly has become less valid in recent years than it was in the 1950s and early 1960s, the great powers still retain *negative* influence. They have the power to present convincing and credible threats of obstruction to the implementation of Assembly resolutions repugnant to their principles or interests, to

[133] Robert O. Keohane, "Political Influence in the General Assembly," in Greggs and Barkuns, *The United Nations System*, p. 38.

TABLE 3.11. Author's Rating of the PRC by Sources of Political Influence in the General Assembly

Typology of the Sources of Influence	Rating
1. Desire and willingness to assume a leadership role	Low
2. Size, population, and financial contribution	High
3. Economic and military capability	High[a]
4. Strategic location in the structure of power and influence in the Assembly (that is, chairmanship of important committees or subsidiary bodies)	Low
5. Sponsorship of draft resolutions	Low
6. Knowledge and expertise of UN politics and procedures	Low
7. Discretionary power of the chief representative in personal diplomacy (delegation of power from home government)	Low to Medium
8. Private contacts and friendship ties with other delegates	Low
9. Prestige and esteem of the representative stemming from his diplomatic diligence, finesse, and *savoir faire* (Huang Hua)	High
10. Symbolic and status prestige of the country in the Assembly	High
11. Congruence with the prevailing values and consensus of the Assembly	Medium to High
12. Tactical maneuverability stemming from an independent and nonaligned foreign policy	Medium
13. Tactical advantage stemming from lack of ideological rigidity	Low
14. Size and quality of delegation and permanent mission	High

[a] The PRC was rated third in "military strength" and seventh in "economic strength" in 1970. See US Arms Control and Disarmament Agency, *World Military Expenditures 1971*, Publication 65, July 1972, p. 50. See also Appendix L.

restrict the scope of UN activities or programs, to disrupt the fragile world order through unilateral military action around the world, to withhold financial contributions, or even to threaten to withdraw from the Organization.[134] In assessing Chinese influence, therefore, we need to keep in mind both positive and negative aspects of political influence.

China has shown no desire or willingness to assume a leadership role in the United Nations. Except in the Security Council, where the presidency rotates on a monthly basis, according to Rule 18 of Provisional

[134] *Ibid.*, p. 25.

Rules of the Security Council, obligating Huang Hua to serve as the president four times during the period 1971-76, the PRC has consciously and deliberately avoided occupying any leadership role. None of the PRC delegates has ever served as chairman of any committee or subsidiary body of the General Assembly. In the Asian group meeting, China declines chairmanship even by the rotational system. China's support for the Third World countries generally takes the form of a partisan spectator who cheers, moralizes, and votes when necessary, rather than an active, not to say leading, player in the game of global politics. While China has been candid, self-righteous, and often adopted a militant tone in pronouncing her principled stand in the public forum, she has shown backstage a high degree of caution and sensitivity to playing anything more than a supportive role for the Third World. China almost never sponsors a draft resolution on her own initiative, the most conspicuous exception being the draft resolution to adopt Chinese among the working languages of the General Assembly. Occasionally China allows herself to be a cosponsor of resolutions drafted by other developing countries. In curious contrast, it may be observed in this connection that the ROC during her turbulent tenure at the United Nations never sponsored a draft resolution "because of the negative effects such action would have on their prospects."[135]

Moreover, China seldom submits explanatory memoranda or documentary materials even in support of those views that she strongly supports. In terms of legislative politics, then, China has shown little interest or readiness to intervene in such a way as to have her own views incorporated in the end-products of the General Assembly organs.

Table 3.11 shows that the PRC rates "low" to "low to medium" on seven of the fourteen sources of political influence. In spite of this, however, the PRC's influence has been rather substantial in the Assembly, especially on those issues or questions that affect particular Chinese interests and principles. The Chinese debts have been put in abeyance by an overwhelming majority vote; Chinese was made a working language; UNCURK was dissolved in 1973; both ACABQ and the Committee on Contributions have been expanded in order to allow Chinese participation; and numerous chairmen of subsidiary bodies constantly solicit Chinese participation in their work. When China speaks in the General Assembly, almost everybody listens—this is indeed a far cry from the ostracism, indignity, discrimination, and humiliation suffered by the ROC delegation during its participation in the United Nations.

[135] *Ibid.*, p. 32.

The PRC's behavior in the General Assembly may well be recorded in the annals of UN history as a classic case of a major power commanding respect and influence without really trying. Besides being a major power, the PRC has enjoyed several additional and unique advantages in the political process of the Assembly, which more than compensate for the low rating on half of the sources of influence in Table 3.11.

First, she enjoys the symbolic advantage of being the most populous Member State, representing one-fifth of humanity. The old belief that the United Nations without China could not meaningfully deal with global problems has turned into a new belief that the United Nations with China in it has finally become universal, if nothing else. In short, there is now a widely shared belief in the UN community that China is doing the Organization a great service merely by being a member.

Second, she enjoys the psychological advantage of having been a "victimized" party in the family of nations, as she had been excluded from the Organization for over two decades. This predisposes most Member States—and the Secretariat, too—to be willing to take an extra step to compensate for the political and psychological injury that the United Nations is believed to have inflicted upon China.

Third, China enjoys the affiliational advantage of being at one and the same time a great power as a permanent member of the Security Council and a member of the Nuclear Club, and an underdog as a developing country.

Fourth, she enjoys the tactical advantage of being independent from group, bloc, or alliance politics. Most Member States quickly realized that China could not be taken for granted on any issue in UN global politics, and that China is an entity of her own with her own principled stand and her own particular security interests. This pattern of behavior deviates from that of many Member States, who are willing to follow an ideological or geographical-bloc voting line.

Finally, China enjoys the behavioral advantage of being a major power who assumes a modest and self-effacing role, a major power who shows an absolute respect for the sovereignty and independence of other Member States, irrespective of their size and status in the international system, and a major power who never bullies small powers. In addition, although China certainly has the negative power to disrupt the work of the Assembly, she has instead proven false the gloomy predictions of the Cassandras of the preentry period. One cannot deny that China has gained influence by *not* exercising her negative power in the political process of the General Assembly.

161

CHINESE GLOBAL POLICY: AN OVERVIEW

Chinese global policy as expressed in the political process of the General Assembly has been marked by a distinctive normative orientation, analytical method, strategic thrust, and issue selection. The most salient value in Chinese global policy is oriented toward a protracted diplomatic struggle to weaken the strong and the rich, and to strengthen the weak and the poor in the global community. At the level of policy pronouncement, this dominant value expresses itself as the united struggle of the small and medium powers—the Second and Third Worlds—against the two superpowers. At the level of policy performance, however, the social imperialist superpower has been targeted as being more insidious, more aggressive, more hegemonic, and more dangerous to genuine world peace than the capitalist superpower.

Indeed, it may not be an exaggeration to say that the Soviet Union has become an obsession in China's world view, distorting her analytical and perceptual focus, weakening her credibility as a true believer of international populism and egalitarianism, and distracting her effort to unite fully with the Third World in the formulation of tactics and strategies for the establishment of a New International Economic Order. It is also the Moscow connection that powerfully influences the Chinese definition of the state of the globe, pattern of participation in the organs of the General Assembly, and conceptualization of the proper role of the United Nations. China could have been even more popular in the UN community and thus more effective in the advancement of her principles and interests by moderating overkill on the Soviet Union. Malik's charge that the ghost of John Foster Dulles has returned to the United Nations in the form of Ch'iao Kuan-hua contains a certain element of truth.

The formulation of Chinese global policy has followed the method of deductive linkage, progressing from general principles to specific issues or program areas. Repeatedly, Chinese UN delegates have argued that particular world problems or issues should not be discussed in abstract terms or in isolation from the larger forces of historical trends. There could be, they say, no women's emancipation, much less women's participation in economic and social development, for example, as long as imperialism, colonialism, neocolonialism, and superpower hegemony prevail in the world.[136] Similarly, there could never be "human rights and equality, still less any guarantee of or respect for human rights, if the struggle for them was divorced from the

---

[136] GAOR, 29th Sess., Second Committee, 1641st meeting (2 December 1974), para. 12.

struggle against imperialism and hegemonism."[137] On the other hand, the root cause of poverty and backwardness among the developing nations is not overpopulation, but prolonged exploitation and plundering by imperialist predators. Other examples of a similarly deductive analysis abound.

Thus, the politics-take-the-command approach at home has been projected onto the UN parliamentary stage in the form of a deductive and antifunctional approach to global problems.[138] This easily explains the greater interest and participation of China in the plenary than in committees or subsidiary bodies, as the former is more congenial to the pronouncement of sweeping principles, while the latter tend to become absorbed in specifics and details. "China stands firm on principles," Ch'iao Kuan-hua declared during the General Debate of the 27th Session of the General Assembly, and "on matters of principle China will never retreat."[139] Such a preoccupation with matters of principle may also explain the untypically active—and influential—role China played in the drafting of the Stockholm Declaration, containing a set of "common principles to inspire and guide the peoples of the world in the preservation and enhancement of the human environment," at the United Nations Conference on the Human Environment, held in Stockholm from June 5 to June 16, 1972.[140]

The strategy of Chinese global policy has a distinctive geopolitical thrust, based on a sharply delineated perception of what is really happening in the major continents of the world. According to the Chinese geopolitical perception of the state of the globe, Europe is the most important focal point of the superpowers' contention for world hegemony. It is in such a perceptual context that China adopted a positive, conciliatory, and friendly posture toward the Second World. She even established diplomatic relations with EEC in 1975 (see Appendix A). Her relations with the West European Member States in the General Assembly were uniformly good. Even on those issues where China and West European countries disagreed sharply, Chinese polemics was generally muted.

Even though the General Assembly has seldom debated European

[137] GAOR, 29th Sess., Third Committee, 2085th meeting (8 November 1974), para. 43.

[138] Chapter 7 discusses more fully functionalism or the functional approach and China's stand on this particular approach to world order in the context of her behavior in the specialized agencies.

[139] *PR*, No. 41 (October 13, 1972), 6.

[140] For the active and influential role China played at the Stockholm Conference, see Louis B. Sohn, "The Stockholm Declaration on the Human Environment," *Harvard International Law Journal* 14 (Summer 1973), 423-515; and Markus Timmler, "Die Unwelt-Konferenz in Stockholm," *Aussenpolitik* 23 (October 1972), 618-28. See also Chapter 9 for further discussion.

problems in the 1970s, China has managed to project her strategic posture toward Europe in the course of the General Debate in the plenary (see Table 3.5) by targeting her attack on détente and "the so-called European security conference" as examples of "the power politics and hegemonism practised by the superpowers."[141] She has assumed a "conservative" posture toward NATO and left-wing political developments in Portugal. In spite of her trenchant attack on power politics, China's strategic posture toward Europe appears to be more Machiavellian or Gaullist than Marxist. Eastern Europe is depicted as a bridgehead in Soviet preparations for aggression against Western Europe, the strategic focal point of superpower contention for global hegemony. Based on such a geopolitical perception, the General Assembly has been used as a forum to further good bilateral relations with West European countries, on the one hand, and to expose the dangers of Soviet hegemonic expansionism, on the other.

In the Chinese geopolitical prism, the Middle East is an active arena, where the superpowers' contention for world hegemony is clearly and continuously manifested. Situated on the flank of Europe, the Middle East represents an important strategic link to Europe in hegemonic power politics, Huang Hua argued in the plenary, inasmuch as both superpowers admitted openly that whoever controlled the Middle East would be able to control Europe and then the rest of the world.[142] Yet, the anti-Soviet bias in the Chinese geopolitical perception, coupled with a pronounced tendency to carry argument to the extreme in public forum, has led China to a highly selective reading of the complex reality, and thus a one-sided analysis of Soviet strategy in the Middle East.

In the Chinese analysis, the Soviet Union is characterized as having surpassed the United States in bullying and blackmailing the Arab countries. "With honey on its lips and a dagger in its heart," the Chinese argue, the Soviet Union is stepping up its infiltration and expansion in the Middle East, taking advantage of the busy involvement of the United States in her own internal problems. The Soviet Union employs the old imperialist trick of divide and rule, sowing the seeds of discord in the Middle East. "The internal disputes and bloodshed incidents in Arab countries and certain temporary differences and discord among them," Chinese representative Lai Ya-li maintained in the plenary, "can all be traced to its [the Soviet Union's] sinister meddling."[143] At the same time, the Soviet Union is accused of helping Israel with "a steady flow of manpower" (Jewish emigration), of step-

[141] *PR*, No. 41 (October 13, 1972), 7; No. 40 (October 5, 1973), 12.
[142] UN Doc. A/PV.2394 (5 November 1975), pp. 18-20.
[143] *SPRCP*, No. 6233 (December 6, 1976), 50.

ping up her flirtation with Israel, and of expanding contacts and dialogue with Israel from nongovernmental to official levels so as to help Israeli Zionism extricate itself from its predicament.[144]

Following this line of reasoning, China has opposed the step-by-step solution put forward by the United States as "a standstill, indefinite procrastination and sustained stalemate." China has even more vigorously opposed the Soviet proposal of a Geneva Conference in order to reach a comprehensive solution as being "even more a demagogic step designed to pull the wool over the eyes of the public as a smokescreen for its own further meddling."[145] Nor has China favored UN involvement in the solution of the Middle East problem, a point that will be elaborated in Chapter 4. What China favors is self-solution by means of popular struggle. As Huang Hua put it in a plenary debate on the Middle East:

> History is made by the masses of the people. The future of the Middle East can only be determined by the great Palestinian and other Arab peoples and by their unity and struggle, but not by Israeli Zionism or the one or two super-Powers, nor by a piece of United Nations resolution. The victory of the October war and the application of the oil weapon constitute a brilliant example of the Arab and Palestinian people winning victory over the enemy through their close unity and co-ordinated endeavours. It eloquently proves that unity is strength and that victory can be won by persevering in struggle.[146]

The notion that the solution of the Middle East dilemma can be found only through the perseverance and unity of the Arab peoples was shattered by the fratricidal war in Lebanon. This war so embarrassed the pro-Arab Third World majority in the United Nations that they decided to do absolutely nothing about it in the 31st Session of General Assembly. Even Arab speakers played down the role of the PLO, which created an uproar in the 29th Session of the General Assembly when its leader, Yasir Arafat, made a chief-of-state appearance at the Assembly rostrum. In the face of this kind of Arab disunity, Ch'iao Kuan-hua's 1976 "state of the globe" report before the plenary had only one short paragraph on the Middle East. In a muted and almost despondent tone, Ch'iao stated: "We sincerely hope that the various political forces in Lebanon, together with the Arab states concerned and the Palestinian people, will set store by the national interests of Lebanon and the militant unity of the Arab countries and find a reasonable solution to their temporary differences through

[144] *Ibid.*   [145] *Ibid.*
[146] UN Doc. A/PV.2394 (5 November 1975), p. 22.

peaceful consultations free from superpower interference."[147] China has a *declaratory principle* on the Middle East, to be sure; but it is difficult to discern any coherent strategy or abiding interest in the Chinese approach to this troubled region that she wants to pursue with vigor.[148]

As another flank of Europe, Africa has also become, in the Chinese view, an integral part of the Soviet global strategy for world hegemony. While US influence has steadily declined owing to domestic constraints, the shadow of the Soviet military presence now hovers over every place of unrest in Africa. "Such a huge military force deployed off Africa's coasts and in its interior," a Chinese publicist argued, "is tantamount to a double-edged sword, with one edge directed at the other superpower to scramble for world domination and the other edge at the African countries and people, independent or on the way to independence, with a view to seizing, maintaining and expanding its colonial interests—political, military and economic privileges—in the region."[149] The Soviet and Cuban intervention in the Angolan civil war produced some strange Chinese behavior in the Security Council, which will be discussed in Chapter 4.

More recently, the invasion of Zaire by what the Chinese call "Soviet mercenaries" also affected world politics in such a way as to produce some strange bedfellows in Southern Africa, with China, France, Egypt, Belgium, West Germany, Morocco, and the United States defending and supporting the pro-Western conservative Mobutu regime, while the Soviet Union, Cuba, and Algeria gave their support to the revolutionary insurgents.

In the Chinese view, Soviet expansionism in Southern Africa is not a local or fortuitous event; it is a part of coordinated global strategy

[147] *PR*, No. 42 (October 15, 1976), 14.

[148] In his secret speech of May 20, 1975, referred to previously, Ch'iao Kuan-hua made a very revealing statement about the Middle East situation. Ch'iao's statement stands in such sharp contrast with Peking's public pronouncements in the United Nations that it deserves a lengthy quotation: "Since a Republic of Israel has already been established, it will not do to deny its existence. After all, it would not do to resettle the Palestinian refugees in their old home and, in the process, create a band of Jewish refugees. . . . As for Israel, from my personal point of view, it is better for it to be there than for it not to be there; [the best thing] is to keep it there but not recognize it. The matter could be put aside for awhile, and we could wait awhile and see what happens. There is no hurry, and we could talk about it at some later date. After all, the old revisionists insist on a test of bravado with the American imperialists, and this gives the big and small Arab kings in the area something to do with all their money and a place to spend their fortune. They do not love their countries, but love their own small courts; they do not love their people, but love their personal comforts. . . ." "Ch'iao Kuan-hua's Secret Speech," pp. 22-23.

[149] Jen Ku-p'ing, "Africa's Destiny Is in the Hands of Its Péople," *PR*, No. 20 (May 13, 1977), 19.

166

for world hegemony. It has been characterized as a "peripheral war" in the contention for Europe. The Kremlin's strategic aim is, it is argued, "to start on the underbelly of Africa, slice horizontally across the African continent, seize control of vital coastal sections, gradually squeeze out U.S. and other Western influence from Southern Africa and control that region's strategic resources and the important strategic passage-way from the Indian Ocean to Western Europe so as to cut the Western countries' vital supply line at any time, thereby getting a stranglehold on Western Europe."[150] While paying lip service to the Maoist axiom that Africa's destiny, too, is in the hands of the African people, China has taken a clear-cut stand in support of Western intervention in Zaire to oppose the alleged Soviet-supported invasion. Also, given a choice between opposing social imperialism and supporting a "war of national liberation," China has left little doubt as to which takes precedence in Chinese global strategy.

As for the continent of Asia, China's opposition to Soviet global strategy has expressed itself in several ways in the Assembly forum. First, China gave a strong support to Pakistan during the Indo-Pakistani War. India's invasion of East Pakistan (Bangladesh) was viewed as being largely aided and abetted by the Soviet Union, to further her expansionistic designs in the Asian subcontinent. Curiously enough, Ch'iao Kuan-hua explained before the plenary that the Soviet Union and her followers had "forced" China to resort to the veto in the Security Council by precipitously introducing the Bangladesh membership question before the relevant UN resolutions on the troop withdrawal and release of war prisoners by all those concerned were implemented.[151] There is an element of truth in this unusual public explanation of the first PRC veto, as she gave her full and unqualified support for Bangladesh's membership into the United Nations in June 1974.

Second, China voted with India on six related resolutions between 1971 and 1976 on the "Declaration of the Indian Ocean as a Zone of Peace," while the United States, the Soviet Union, the United Kingdom, and France abstained on all of them.[152] Third, China stated her unequivocal contempt for and opposition to the Soviet proposal for the "Asian collective security system." Finally, on other issues emanat-

[150] *Ibid.*, pp. 19-20.　　　　　　[151] *PR*, No. 41 (October 13, 1972), 6.

[152] General Assembly Resolution 2832 (XXVI) of 16 December 1971; General Assembly Resolution 2992 (XXVII) of 15 December 1972; General Assembly Resolution 3080 (XXVIII) of 6 December 1973; General Assembly Resolution 3259 (XXIX) of 9 December 1974; General Assembly Resolution 3468 (XXX) of 11 December 1975; General Assembly Resolution 31/88 (XXXI) of 14 December 1976. It may be noted here that the last three resolutions had to do with the implementation of the first three.

ing from Asia, such as the Korean question, the Cambodian representational issue, and Vietnam membership, however, the Soviet Union and China differed in supportive style, vigor, and tone, but agreed in substance by voting concurrently—and even joining together as cosponsors—on the related issues in the General Assembly.[153]

China's posture toward Latin America strikes the most positive and functional note in the development of Chinese global policy. Chinese Third World diplomacy toward Latin American countries has shown a desire to broaden state-to-state relationships (see Appendix A), coupled with pragmatic attempts to work together in areas of common interest. Sensing among the Latin American countries strong support for and apprehension about China's stand on the Treaty for the Prohibition of Nuclear Weapons in Latin America (Treaty of Tlatelolco), the then Foreign Minister Chi P'eng-fei issued an official statement on November 14, 1972, declaring: "China will never use or threaten to use nuclear weapons against non-nuclear Latin American countries and the Latin American nuclear weapon-free zone, nor will China test, manufacture, produce, stockpile, install or deploy nuclear weapons in these countries or in this zone, or send her means of transportation and delivery carrying nuclear weapons to traverse the territory, territorial sea or territorial air space of Latin American countries."[154]

Following up on this declaration, Hsiung Hsiang-hui, Chinese ambassador to Mexico, signed Additional Protocol II to the Treaty of

[153] At its 2191st meeting, the General Assembly adopted by a roll-call vote of 53:50:21 a motion to defer the Cambodian representation question. Both China and the Soviet Union voted against this motion. The Sino-Soviet rivalry to woo two Asian communist states—North Vietnam and North Korea—has expressed itself in the form of the communist giants converging as cosponsors of the following items: request for the inclusion of an item "Creation of Favourable Conditions to Accelerate the Independent and Peaceful Reunification of Korea" in the provisional agenda of the 27th Session; a draft resolution entitled "Creation of Favourable Conditions to Accelerate the Independent and Peaceful Reunification of Korea" during the 28th Session; request for the inclusion of an item "Withdrawal of All the Foreign Troops Stationed in South Korea Under the Flag of the United Nations" in the provisional agenda of the 29th Session; request for the inclusion of a supplementary item "Creation of Favourable Conditions for Converting the Armistice into a Durable Peace in Korea and Accelerating the Independent and Peaceful Reunification of Korea" in the agenda of the 30th Session; request for the inclusion of a supplementary item "Removal of the Danger of War and Maintenance and Consolidation of Peace in Korea and Acceleration of the Independent and Peaceful Reunification of Korea" in the agenda of the 31st Session; a draft resolution requesting the Security Council to reconsider favorably the applications of both the Democratic Republic of Vietnam and the Republic of South Vietnam for UN membership for the 30th Session; and a draft resolution recommending that the Security Council should reconsider the membership application of the Socialist Republic of Vietnam for the 31st Session. See UN Docs. A/8752/Add.7; A/9145; A/9703; A/10191; A/31/192; A/L.763; A/31/L.21.
[154] PR, No. 47 (November 24, 1972), 7.

Tlatelolco on August 21, 1973 in Mexico City.[155] On April 23, 1974, China ratified Additional Protocol II and the instrument of ratification was delivered to the government of Mexico, the depository country of the treaty, on June 11, 1974.[156] Thus, China joined the three other nuclear powers in signing and ratifying Additional Protocol II of the treaty, exposing the Soviet Union as the only nuclear power refusing to sign. Perhaps the motive of embarrassing the Soviet Union cannot be ruled out; still, this is a positive step that the PRC has taken on arms control and disarmament issue and one that substantially weakens her stated opposition to the Non-Proliferation Treaty (NPT). It also shows the positive influence the Third World countries can exert in the development of Chinese global policy.

To strengthen her support of Latin American countries further, China, in an apparent departure from her own Declaration Regarding Territorial Waters, issued on September 4, 1958, supported the struggle of many Latin American countries to stretch their territorial seas to 200 nautical miles. In fact, the Latin American countries have been characterized as the vanguard in the common struggle of the Third World against the maritime hegemony of the superpowers. It was in this vein that China vigorously—and successfully—endorsed the demand of most Latin American countries to hold the Third United Nations Conference on the Law of the Sea in Santiago, Chile (later changed to Caracas, Venezuela, after the right-wing military coup d'état) in 1974. Likewise, China praised and supported the contribution of the Latin American countries in the establishment of a New International Economic Order, especially Mexico's contribution to the adoption of the Charter of Economic Rights and Duties of States by the 29th Session of the General Assembly.[157] On the other hand, China refused to join the three Assembly resolutions on "Protection of Human Rights in Chile,"[158] as if not to offend the sensitivity of certain right-wing regimes in Latin America.

Chinese global policy has shown a well-structured hierarchy of issues, with the three Ds—disarmament, decolonization, and development—playing a dominant role. Other issues—social, cultural,

[155] UN Doc. A/9209 (9 October 1973), p. 2.

[156] China submitted a document describing this development and requested this to be circulated as an official document of the General Assembly so as to make it known to all Member States that she had implemented General Assembly Resolution 3079 (XXVIII) of 6 December 1973. See UN Doc. A/9718 (4 September 1974).

[157] General Assembly Resolution 3281 (XXIX) of 12 December 1974.

[158] General Assembly Resolution 3219 (XXIX) of 6 November 1974; General Assembly Resolution 3448 (XXX) of 9 December 1975; General Assembly Resolution 31/124 of 16 December 1976. China exercised the fourth option of non-participation in the vote on these resolutions.

humanitarian, and legal—are consigned to a secondary or minor role. Or they have been redefined in terms of the three Ds, following the Chinese deductive and antifunctional approach alluded to earlier in this chapter. That China has shown the highest sensitivity to and the most active concern about arms control and disarmament issues is hardly surprising, given their direct linkage to vital national security interests. Nor is it surprising that China, as a nuclear underdog, often takes a position reminiscent of the Soviet Union in the late 1940s and 1950s, or that her voting behavior in the General Assembly often coincides with that of her nuclear equal—France.

No single issue in the history of the General Assembly has been as perennially and universally popular, yet as ineffectually and unfruitfully dealt with as disarmament. There has been no shortage of calls in and out of the United Nations for a world disarmament conference. Even China joined the disarmament crusaders in 1964, following her first nuclear test, and again in November 1970, calling for a world conference to prohibit and destroy nuclear weapons.[159] However, two major factors have greatly complicated her position in the Assembly on the question of such a conference: the propaganda-inspired one-upmanship of the Soviet Union; and uncertainty about the conference's probable nature, scope, and participants.

Apparently sensing the imminent entry of the PRC into the United Nations, the Soviet Union seized the initiative in mid-1971 by calling for a disarmament conference of the five nuclear powers. On June 15, 1971, the Soviet Union delivered this invitation to the PRC. Interestingly, France accepted the call, while the United States and the United Kingdom kept their own counsel. One of the first—and rare—documents the PRC submitted to the United Nations was a government statement dated July 30, 1971, replying to the Soviet invitation. This statement became the guiding principle for Chinese elaboration on disarmament in the Assembly. The statement declared, *inter alia*:

> China develops nuclear weapons because it is compelled to do so under imperialist nuclear threats, and it does so entirely for the purpose of defence and for breaking the imperialist nuclear monopoly and finally eliminating nuclear weapons. China's nuclear weapons are still in the experimental stage, and *at present it is not yet a nuclear Power, nor will it ever be a "nuclear super-Power"* practising the policies of nuclear monopoly, nuclear threats and nuclear blackmail. At no time will China ever agree to participate in the so-called nuclear disarmament talks between the nuclear Powers behind the backs of the non-nuclear countries.[160]

[159] See "China Again Asks Nuclear Parley," *NYT*, November 2, 1970, p. 4.
[160] UN Doc. A/8536 (24 November 1971), p. 3; emphasis added.

China's position on arms control and disarmament (ACD) is fraught with numerous ambiguities and the contradictions inherent in her novel attempt to reconcile past principles with changing interests in the milieu of multilateral parliamentary diplomacy. The strange notion that China as of mid-1971 was not yet a nuclear power makes little sense, except when approached via the Chinese logic of defining a great power or nuclear power in purely motivational and behavioral terms. In other words, China is trying to say that nuclear weapons do not have an independent will or motive apart from that of the national actors who command them and that the intentions of China as a nuclear power are entirely defensive; hence, Chinese nuclear weapons work toward peace, while those of the superpowers work toward war.[161] It is not clear what functions, if any, the nuclear weapons of France and Britain would perform in this context.

Thus, China rejects the causal relationship between arms and war, or the philosophical premise behind the modern disarmament approach that men and nations fight because they have the means with which to fight. Instead, world peace requires a selective disarmament on the part of the predator, coupled with a selective armament on the part of the prey. As if to support this line of reasoning, China has repeatedly declared her no-first-use pledge, while serving notice to the other nuclear powers, especially the two superpowers, to do the same. From this follows the Chinese stand on the question of a world disarmament conference: that it should have a clear aim and the necessary preconditions. The aim should be the complete prohibition and thorough destruction of nuclear weapons, not the limited, partial, and selective SALT approach. The necessary preconditions are: (1) a no-first-use pledge by all nuclear countries, especially by the two nuclear superpowers; and (2) the withdrawal by the superpowers of all their armed forces, including nuclear-missile forces, from other countries.

By imposing such unrealistic preconditions, China shut herself out of any UN negotiations on a world disarmament conference. Yet, in the face of sustained "consultative pressure" from the Third World (especially from Argentina, Zambia, and Yugoslavia) in the 27th Session of the General Assembly, China cast a positive vote for the establishment of a 35-member Special Committee on the World Disarmament Conference, placing the United States in the position of the sole

---

[161] In his first major policy speech before the plenary, Ch'iao Kuan-hua declared: "The idea that all countries must adopt measures for disarmament without distinguishing between the aggressors and the victim of aggression, and between those who threaten others and those who are threatened can only lead the question of disarmament into a wrong path and benefit imperialism." GAOR, 26th Sess., 1995th plenary meeting (24 November 1971), para. 40.

recalcitrant abstainer. China stated during the consultative process that she "would not be prepared to participate" in the committee but would maintain contact with it. However, the president of the 27th Session of the General Assembly (Stanislaw Trepczynski of Poland) arbitrarily appointed China as a member of the Committee, inviting a furious reply from Huang Hua. "Evidently, such self-contradictory, crude and arbitrary practice," Huang Hua declared in his letter to the Secretary-General, "can only be construed as a submission and catering to the needs of a certain super-Power for executing a political fraud."[162] Fraud or not, the alleged Soviet connection has greatly rigidified the Chinese position.

On the whole, China argued against UN involvement in the preparation or study of ACD issues because "the lack of progress in disarmament is not due to the lack of appropriate international forums but due to the lack of the will for genuine disarmament on the part of the superpowers."[163] When the superpowers presented ACD proposals in the General Assembly, they were invariably characterized as frauds. Thus, China opposed such superpower-supported resolutions as a partial or comprehensive nuclear test ban, NPT, a convention on environmental warfare, and military budget reduction. On the question of chemical and biological warfare (CBW), China has taken a self-contradictory stand. On the one hand, she declared that she had always supported the complete prohibition and thorough destruction of CBW, citing her 1952 ratification of the 1925 Geneva Protocol as evidence. On the other hand, she opposed the US/USSR-sponsored convention on biological warfare as a tool of the two superpowers for peddling their disarmament fraud. Yet, China showed little hesitation in voting for the 1973 resolution on napalm and other incendiary weapons with the encouragement of the abstention of the solid Soviet bloc.

The most hopeful, if somewhat contradictory, note in the PRC's stand on ACD is her firm, positive, and unequivocal support for the establishment of the nuclear-free zones around the globe. In spite of its apparent inconsistency with her stated opposition to the NPT, which has been characterized as an unequal and unjust treaty "designed only to disarm the non-nuclear countries while maintaining the arms of the fully equipped nuclear countries,"[164] China's support for the denuclearization of Latin America, the Indian Ocean, the Middle East, Africa, and South Asia constitutes an important step in the direction of curbing the proliferation of nuclear weapons. China has distinguished herself on this issue as the only nuclear power voting

---

[162] UN Doc. A/9033 (10 January 1973), p. 4.
[163] UN Doc. A/C.1/31/PV.50 (2 December 1976), p. 6.
[164] UN Doc. A/C.1/PV.2095 (21 November 1975), p. 38.

consistently for all the resolutions relating to the establishment of nuclear-free zones in the above-mentioned regions.[165]

In contrast to her negative attitude toward the UN involvement in disarmament, China has adopted a "liberal and expansive" interpretation of the Charter on decolonization. Decolonization, China flatly declared, "was one of the primary tasks of the United Nations."[166] Given the dominant role the anticolonial forces have come to play in the Assembly politics, this posture is both logical and congruent with Chinese global policy. The 15th General Assembly in 1960 proved to be a milestone on decolonization. Joined by sixteen new African states and Cyprus, the Afro-Asian Group—now numbering forty-four out of a total membership of one hundred—pushed for the adoption of a Declaration on the Granting of Independence to Colonial Territories and Peoples. The Declaration, which was adopted on December 14, 1960 by a vote of 89-0, with 9 abstentions (Australia, Belgium, Dominican Republic, France, Portugal, Spain, Union of South Africa, United Kingdom, and United States), replaced the Charter, to all practical purposes, as the guiding principle of UN work on decolonization.[167]

To implement this Declaration, the Assembly subsequently established a Special Committee on the Situation with Regard to the Implementation of the Declaration on the Granting of Independence to Colonial Countries and Peoples, with seventeen members initially and later with twenty-four (hence, it was called the Committee of 24). Since 1963, the Committee has expanded its functions to such an extent as to overshadow completely the work of the Trusteeship Council. In addition, it has taken over the work of the 1947 Committee on Information (which was promptly dissolved), and has even acquired the unusual right to apprise the Security Council of any development in any territory that it deems as threatening international peace and security, an extraordinary power for a subsidiary organ of the Assembly to possess. It is not surprising that China showed interest in the Committee of 24 upon her entry into the United Nations and promptly got herself elected as a member. Her participation (since January 1972 to the present) in the Committee has been more extensive and con-

---

[165] UN Docs. A/C.1/PV.2007 (4 November 1974), p. 62; A/C.1/PV.2024 (20 November 1974), pp. 53-55; A/C.1/PV.2026 (21 November 1974), p. 27; A/C.1/PV.2084 (11 November 1975), pp. 23-25; A/C.1/PV.2095 (21 November 1975), p. 38.

[166] GAOR, 28th Sess., Fifth Committee, 1568th meeting (4 October 1973), para. 44; see also UN Doc. A/PV.2168 (16 November 1973), p. 31.

[167] General Assembly Resolution 1514 (XV) of 14 December 1960. According to one study on the legal significance and implications of re-citation of General Assembly resolutions, this Resolution 1514 is "the most cited resolution of the General Assembly." See Samuel A. Bleicher, "The Legal Significance of Re-citation of General Assembly Resolutions," AJIL 68 (July 1969), 470-75.

tinuous than that in any other subsidiary organs of the General Assembly.[168]

The PRC's policy on decolonization represents another example of the selective political interpretation of the Charter. During the exclusion period, the PRC publicists insisted time and again that the United Nations, in exercising its role in the maintenance of international peace and security, should not intervene in the internal affairs of states in violation of Article 2, paragraph 7, of the Charter. However, they also argued in support of UN interventions and sanctions in colonial and apartheid questions involving Portugal, Southern Rhodesia, and South Africa. The PRC's rationale for this apparent double standard was that acts in support of national liberation movements could not constitute "matters which are essentially within the domestic jurisdiction of any state."[169] On the contrary, such acts, argued one leading PRC authority on the Organization, run counter to the fundamental Charter principles of national self-determination and respect for human rights, and also endanger the peace and security of the world. Hence, both the General Assembly and the Security Council have the duty and the authority to deal with this question.[170]

Consistent with this preentry position China argued that the United Nations was indeed the proper authority to administer Namibia (South West Africa). Accordingly, South Africa's presence in that country was illegal, and she had no right whatsoever to enter into any discussion or negotiation on Namibia's political future with anyone.[171] With predictable vigor and regularity, China has also insisted that the United Nations should give greater support to the decolonization struggle of the people of Southern Africa by (1) strengthening and broadening its sanctions against Southern Rhodesia; (2) extending the sanctions to Portugal and South Africa—in fact, applying "total and effective sanctions" to the latter; and (3) condemning all violations of the relevant UN resolutions on sanctions against Southern Rhodesia.[172] Departing from her generally muted criticism of the Western powers in the United Nations, China declared:

[168] Between 1972 and 1976, the Committee held 225 meetings and Chinese delegates in the Committee made sixty-five speeches and statements. For details on China's participation in the Committee of 24, see the verbatim records of the Committee from January 21, 1972, to October 26, 1976, in UN Docs. A/AC.109/PV.833-A/AC.109/PV.1057.

[169] Article 2(7) of the UN Charter.

[170] Kuo Ch'ün, *Lien-ho-kuo* [The United Nations] (Peking: Shih-chieh chih-shih she, 1956), p. 15.

[171] See UN Doc. A/PV.2168 (16 November 1973), p. 31; GAOR, 29th Sess., Fourth Committee, 2103rd meeting (4 November 1974), para. 41.

[172] GAOR, 27th Sess., Special Political Committee, 819th meeting (20 October 1972), para. 30; GAOR, 27th Sess., Third Committee, 1919th meeting (11 Oc-

Regrettably, while some Western Powers professed a desire to defend the principles of the Charter and to strengthen the role of the United Nations, they were daily trampling on the Charter and deliberately violating the relevant resolutions. They extended political, diplomatic, economic and military assistance to the white racist regimes in southern Africa. . . . His delegation strongly condemned those countries which violated the General Assembly and the Security Council resolutions on sanctions, and demanded that those countries which gave political and economic support to the racist regimes in southern Africa should sever all contacts with them.[173]

Yet, she maintained a curious double standard in regard to the categorization of "colonial territories." The Committee of 24 has kept its own list of colonial territories covered by the 1960 Declaration in a continuing effort to pressure the administering authorities to expedite self-determination or independence for those colonies. Shortly after its participation in the Committee's work, however, the PRC delegation challenged the *inclusion* of Hong Kong and Macao on the Committee's list of colonial territories, declaring:

> As is known to all, the questions of Hong Kong and Macao belong in the category of questions resulting from the series of unequal treaties which the imperialists imposed on China. [They] . . . are part of Chinese territory. . . . The settlement of the questions of Hong Kong and Macao is entirely within China's sovereign right and does not at all fall under the ordinary category of "colonial territories." . . . The Chinese Government has consistently held that they should be settled in an appropriate way when conditions are ripe. The UN has no right to discuss these questions. . . .[174]

In the ensuing debate the Committee, despite opposition from several delegations, honored the PRC's request by removing Hong Kong and Macao from its list.[175] No one on the Committee has insisted, as in other cases, that the wishes of the local inhabitants be ascertained by plebiscite. In a monumental contradiction, however, Chinese rep-

---

tober 1972), para. 7; GAOR, 27th Sess., Fourth Committee, 1991st meeting (1 November 1972), para. 28; GAOR, 28th Sess., Special Political Committee, 867th meeting (19 October 1973), para. 46; GAOR, 29th Sess., Fourth Committee, 2095th meeting (22 October 1974), para. 41; GAOR, 29th Sess., Fourth Committee, 2111st meeting (14 November 1974), para. 15; GAOR, 30th Sess., Fourth Committee, 2159th meeting (3 November 1975), paras. 9-10; UN Doc. A/C.4/31/SR.34 (29 November 1976), p. 11.

[173] GAOR, 28th Sess., Third Committee, 1982nd meeting (1 October 1973), paras. 73-74.

[174] UN Doc. A/8723 (Part I), pp. 29-30.

[175] UN Doc. A/AC.109/PV.873 (6 June 1972), pp. 16-20.

resentative Chang Yung-kuan argued, during the Committee's debate on the Cuban request to include Puerto Rico in the list of colonial territories covered by the 1960 Declaration, that Puerto Rico "is actually a colony of the United States" and, as such, the Cuban request is "reasonable," deserving the support of the Chinese delegation.[176] Other examples of the PRC's ambiguous and contradictory posture toward Angola and Zaire abound and will be further elaborated upon in Chapter 4.

The last D in the trinity of important issues in Chinese global policy —development—is a long and complex subject, deserving a special and separate treatment in Chapters 5 and 6. Suffice it here to say that Chinese global policy on development evolved through the 6th and 7th Special Sessions of the General Assembly in 1974 and 1975. Since then, the New International Economic Order (NIEO) has been covered so far by the four Assembly resolutions on the Declaration on the Establishment of a New International Economic Order, a Programme of Action on the Establishment of a New International Economic Order, the Charter of Economic Rights and Duties of States, and an omnibus resolution on development and international economic cooperation.[177] It has practically replaced the Charter in the PRC's policy pronouncement and elaboration at such functional organs and agencies of the United Nations system as ECOSOC, UNDP, UNCTAD, UNIDO, and the specialized agencies. Likewise, *Jen-min jih-pao's* coverage of international economic issues evolves through the conceptual framework of NIEO. As already mentioned, the social, cultural, humanitarian, and legal issues play a rather minor part in Chinese global policy; nonetheless, these issues will also be examined throughout this book under various functional analyses.

It is beyond the purview of this synoptic chapter to make a critical appraisal of Chinese strategies of world order, or to evaluate whether the Chinese global policy as expressed in the General Assembly is congruent with Chinese functional behavior in the other organs and agencies of the United Nations system. This task is specifically reserved for the concluding chapter. However, a few general points about Chinese policy and behavior in the political process of the General Assembly may be in order here.

First and foremost, China's opposition to the issues and activities repugnant to her interests or principles has expressed itself in the form of nonparticipation. China has often exercised the fourth voting option

[176] UN Doc. A/AC.109/PV.883 (18 August 1972), p. 18.
[177] General Assembly Resolution 3201 (S-VI) of 1 May 1974; General Assembly Resolution 3202 (S-VI) of 1 May 1974; General Assembly Resolution 3281 (XXIX) of 12 December 1974; General Assembly Resolution 3362 (S-VII) of 16 September 1975.

of nonparticipation on a large number of resolutions to which she objects, rather than casting the negative vote. Second, China has expressed her opposition to such UN involvements as in the World Disarmament Conference and UN peace-keeping by opting not to participate, rather than undertaking the role of a Trojan Horse.

Third, and related to her form of opposition from without, China has assumed a cautious, modest, and self-effacing role in those organs or activities of the United Nations in which she participates. While the impact of the PRC on the planning and execution of the UN programs and activities has been minimal both in the negative and the positive sense, the symbolic capability—ideological, political, and behavioral—that she has projected in her novel multilateral diplomacy in the Assembly cannot be gainsaid. Finally, while China has maintained an ideological rigidity (integrity) at the level of policy pronouncement in such public forums as the plenary, at the level of policy performance, the pragmatic and compromising, if somewhat contradictory, posture she has adopted—thanks to continuing "consultative pressure" from the Third World—augurs well for the prospects of a world order with justice.

· 4 ·

CHINA AND THE SECURITY COUNCIL

It is obvious that much of the world press and the public has demanded a great deal from the Security Council on the fulfillment of the Charter promise to save "succeeding generations from the scourge of war." This may be a function of the promise of the United Nations in general and the Security Council in particular having been oversold during the early euphoric days of United Nations history.[1] It may also be due to popular oversimplification of the possibilities of the United Nations. In both theory and practice, the United Nations has adopted many paths and approaches to the pursuit of world order, as can be seen in the separate but shared—and mutually complementary—functions of the six principal organs.

Such a pluralism in function and approach enabled the United Nations to develop in its body organism several safety valves, so that the paralysis of a part, say, of the Security Council, would not automatically cause irreparable damage to the whole. In practice, the United Nations has adopted several distinct approaches to world order: (1) the peace-building approach, as embodied in the functional organs and activities; (2) the peace-making approach, as expressed in pacific settlement of disputes; and (3) the peace-keeping approach, which developed since UNEF I as a necessary and realistic alternative to the paralyzed Charter system of collective security (the peace-enforcing approach).[2]

It is perhaps inevitable that world attention should be so fixed on the Security Council, for the immediate task of maintaining international peace and security rests with this political organ of the United Nations. In addition, the prominent role assigned to, and played by, the Big Five in the handling of international crises and disputes makes the Security Council a heuristically useful device for evaluating the capacity of the Organization to maintain world order. All the passion and polemics expended on the question of Chinese representation during much of UN history can likewise be attributed to the generally pessimistic assessment of the impact of the PRC's participation on the decision-making process in the Council.

[1] See, for example, Robert E. Riggs, "Overselling the UN Charter—Fact and Myth," *IO* 14 (Spring 1960), 277-90.
[2] Inis L. Claude, Jr., "The Peace-keeping Role of the United Nations," in E. Berkeley Tompkins, ed., *The United Nations in Perspective* (Stanford, Calif.: Hoover Institution Press, 1972), p. 50.

While China was kept out of the United Nations, there was never a shortage of studies warning of the disastrous or disruptive consequences her "admission" would have upon the work of the Organization in general and of the Security Council in particular.[3] Chinese participation in some 384 meetings of the Security Council from November 23, 1971, to the end of 1976 (see Table 4.1) now provides an empirical basis for making a disciplined inquiry into the behavioral dimensions of the Chinese concept and strategy of world order, as expressed in the decision-making process of the Council. Specifically, this chapter focuses on interaction between the Security Council and China. To avoid the hazard of mixing cause and effect in such an analysis, however, we need to review at the outset the evolution of the substantive and constituent functions of the Security Council prior to the PRC debut on November 23, 1971.[4]

THE SECURITY COUNCIL BEFORE CHINA

From Colective Security to Consensual Peace-keeping

World politics in the first twenty-five years of the Security Council shattered many of the hopeful assumptions of the founders at the San Francisco Conference. There is a sense in which the Charter system, as originally conceived in 1945, was more an expression reactive to the trauma of the past than a visionary blueprint for a warless future. The Charter system reflected the conceptualization of the causes of war and the conditions of peace as it emerged from the ashes of World War II. The regulation of armaments, for example, was relegated to a secondary role, to be undertaken only after an effective system of collective security had been assured by the placing of the necessary armed forces at the disposal of the Council. There was also a clear presumption in the Charter system that the major threats to world order would come from well-defined cases of international ag-

---

[3] For expressions of varying degrees of apprehension, see Bloomfield, "China, the United States, and the United Nations," pp. 653-76; Leland M. Goodrich, "The UN Security Council," in Barros, The United Nations, pp. 16-63; McDougal and Goodman, "Chinese Participation in the United Nations," pp. 671-727; Oran R. Young, "The United Nations and the International System," in Leon Gordenker, ed., The United Nations in International Politics (Princeton, N.J.: Princeton University Press, 1971), pp. 10-59, and "Trends in International Peacekeeping," in Linda B. Miller, ed., Dynamics of World Politics (Englewood Cliffs, N.J.: Prentice-Hall, 1968), pp. 236-59.

[4] The Council's substantive functions are related to the handling of the substantive issues of its primary responsibility, namely, the maintenance of international peace and security. The constituent functions include such matters as membership, appointment of the Secretary-General, elections of judges of the ICJ, and establishment of its own rules of procedure and subsidiary organs.

gression, involving the use of overt military force across recognized international boundaries. Hence, the major "peace-loving" military powers—that is, the victorious Allied powers of World War II—had a special responsibility for keeping the peace. This line of reasoning was institutionalized in the voting procedures of both the Security Council and the General Assembly.

It should be noted that the Charter system, while endorsing a broad theoretical range of collective security, has in its practical application been circumscribed. Since it was widely assumed that the permanent members of the Council were to be the mainstays of UN military forces, the system of collective security in practice could not be organized without the unanimous support of the Big Five. Nor could it be invoked against aggression launched or supported by one of the Big Five, notwithstanding the theoretical assumption underlying the concept of collective security that an attack against one automatically becomes an attack against all. In short, the Charter system, as it applies to the permanent members of the Security Council, has a built-in contradiction between what should be done in theory and what can be done in the practice of collective security.

The inability of the Security Council to fulfill its intended role under Chapter VII of the Charter, coupled with the widely shared belief that the United Nations must exert a minimal demonstration of authority for maintaining peace if it were not to suffer the fate of its predecessor, brought about a groping search for a politically more feasible alternative to collective security. In responding to unanticipated problems of "brush-fire wars," the United Nations began to show some flexibility. Truce supervision and police forces were mobilized and dispatched to the Balkans, Kashmir, and Palestine. However, it was not until the establishment of the United Nations Emergency Force (UNEF I)[5] during the Suez Crisis of 1956 that a transition from collective security to what came to be known as "peace-keeping" took place.

Clearly, Secretary-General Dag Hammarskjöld was the prime mover in emancipating the United Nations from its preoccupation with collective security and in redirecting its concerns toward peace-keeping. His "summary report" to the General Assembly dated October 9, 1958, was an authoritative exposition of the basic principles and guidelines underlying the new approach.[6] Hence, peace-keeping has

[5] To avoid possible confusion between the two United Nations Emergency Forces established respectively in 1956 and 1973, the first is identified throughout this book as UNEF I, and the second as UNEF II.

[6] "United Nations Emergency Force: Summary Study of the Experience Derived from the Establishment and Operation of the Force," *Report of the Secretary-General*, UN Doc. A/3943 (9 October 1958), pp. 1-75.

also come to be known as the "Hammarskjöld approach" or "preventive diplomacy."[7] The Hammarskjöld approach provided a conceptual foundation upon which to build subsequent UN peace-keeping operations.

In both underlying assumptions and operational principles, peace-keeping differs sharply from collective security. Its operations may be of a military, paramilitary or nonmilitary character,[8] but its objective is not to frustrate or punish aggressors—the fixation of collective security—but to freeze local conflict by politically *impartial* and essentially *noncoercive* methods. Its operations are nonmandatory, requiring the consent of both the host and participating Member States. It should, as such, be characterized as "consensual peace-keeping." Consensual peace-keeping shifts its emphasis away from the use of the military forces of the great powers, as envisaged in the Charter system, to the use of the military and logistic resources of impartial and moderate middle Member States—Canada and the Nordic countries in particular—who have accepted the leadership of articulating and organizing world community interest. The immediate objective of peace-keeping is to contain and neutralize local violence without entangling UN operations in great power rivalry. Consensual peace-keeping resulted from a sobering reappraisal of the possibilities and limits of the United Nations in the contemporary international system.[9]

Even though Hammarskjöld characterized UNEF I as an operation under Chapter VI of the Charter, peace-keeping is a novel approach that cannot be subsumed either under the pacific settlement provisions of Chapter VI or under the enforcement provisions of Chapter VII.

[7] Hammarskjöld himself characterized his approach as "preventive diplomacy" in his *Introduction to the Report of the Secretary-General on the Work of the Organization 16 June 1959-15 June 1960.* See GAOR, 15th Sess., Supp. No. 1A (A/4390/Add.1), p. 4.

[8] UN peace-keeping operations generally fall into two broad categories: (1) observer operations such as UNTSO, UNMOGIP, UNOGIL, UNYOM; and (2) operations involving the deployment of military forces such as UNEF I, ONUC, UNTEA, and UNFICYP.

[9] Secretary-General U Thant put the point in this way: "The idea that conventional military methods—or, to put it bluntly, war—can be used by or on behalf of the United Nations to counter aggression and secure the peace, seems now to be rather impractical." Likewise, Secretary-General Kurt Waldheim observed: "The Organization has, for example, proved to be of limited value as an instrument of collective security. . . . The idea of maintaining peace and security in the world through a concert of great Powers . . . would seem to belong to the nineteenth rather than to the twentieth century . . . " See "United Nations Peace Force," an address to the Harvard Alumni Association (delivered in Cambridge, Mass., June 13, 1963) in Richard A. Falk and Saul H. Mendlovitz, eds., *The United Nations* (New York: World Law Fund, 1966), p. 527; and GAOR, 27th Sess., Supp. IA (A/8701/Add.1), pp. 1-2.

Its forces consist of "soldiers without enemies"[10] and are too modest in size for collective security operations, but larger than necessary for the requirements of pacific settlement. In practice, too, a consensus to establish and dispatch peace-keeping forces proved to be much easier to reach than a consensus to solve the underlying problem. That UN peace-keeping operations were more suitable as a conflict-freeze instrument than as a conflict-resolution method was recognized by the Council when it responded to the Cyprus crisis of 1964 by establishing a UN mediator to undertake a peaceful settlement and the United Nations Peace-keeping Force in Cyprus (UNFICYP) to contain the conflict and maintain law and order. Hence, the categorization of peace-keeping under an area entitled "Chapter VI½" seems proper.[11]

To be effective and durable, consensual peace-keeping has been dependent on several conditions. First, it could not be formed or sustained without fully accepting the United Nations as an agency for achieving neutralization of local violence. Second, the realization of consensus has been dependent on whether the permanent members of the Security Council, in particular the two superpowers, would meet, or at least acquiesce in, competing demands placed on their behavior. They were expected to place their shared community interest in arresting the globalization of local wars above their short-term political interest in exploiting local conflicts for cold war purposes. They were also expected to give moral, political, and even financial support to peace-keeping operations, but to refrain from interfering in the actual operation. In short, they were asked to give their consent without control, their blessing without participation in the execution of peace-keeping missions.

The difficulties of maintaining these operations in the absence of sustained joint support from the superpowers were clearly shown in the ONUC crisis. The Soviet Union permitted UNEF I to maintain a truce on the Israeli-Egyptian border for over a decade, limiting her objections to nonpayment of assessments. However, she began a vehement attack on ONUC in the fall of 1960 when its operation took on a political coloration that ran counter to her expectations. The clash of political views as to the purpose of ONUC soon politicized its operation to such a degree that the United Nations itself was brought to the brink of the most serious political and financial crisis in its history.[12]

[10] This phrase provides the title of one study on UN peace-keeping: Larry L. Fabian, *Soldiers Without Enemies* (Washington, D.C.: The Brookings Institution, 1971).

[11] *Building Peace*, Reports of the Commission to Study the Organization of Peace 1939-72 (Metuchen, N.J.: Scarecrow Press, 1973), Vol. II, p. 596.

[12] For a review of step-by-step development in this crisis, see Meg Greenfield,

The grand debate generated by the ONUC crisis taught the United Nations a lesson on the outer limits of peace-keeping. It also marked a conceptual turning point in setting in motion new patterns and trends in this area. It soon became clear that consensus on peace-keeping as an ideal concept was a far cry from consensus on the authorization process. Specifically, the questions that began to plague the United Nations centered on the respective roles of the Security Council, the General Assembly, and the Secretary-General, as well as on the proper method of financing past and future operations. The Special Committee on Peace-keeping Operations, which was established by the Assembly in February 1965 to undertake a comprehensive review of this whole question in all its aspects, has been laboring on these and related questions, but its failure thus far to codify well-defined guidelines should not obscure some new developments and directions in UN peace-keeping in the 1960s and 1970s.

Both superpowers realized the advantage of cooperation in the Security Council over confrontation in the General Assembly on peace-keeping. As a result, the Council resumed its active role as the United Nations' principal organ for authorizing peace-keeping operations, beginning with the establishment of UNFICYP by the Council in 1964. The Council has also come to exercise a tighter control over peace-keeping than it did on UNEF I and ONUC. This has meant a more precise and restricted delegation of power to the Secretary-General, reducing the scope of his legal mandates and discretionary authority. The Council's initial authorization of UNFICYP for three months and periodic extensions highlight the point. The Council is thus taking an *ad hoc* approach in establishing and maintaining a consensus rather than the sweeping ONUC approach, which had proved to be destructive of its consensual foundation.

The upswing in Council supervision of peace-keeping activities reflects the tacit agreement of the two superpowers that they should have a greater hand in any future operation, signifying in a sense a return to the original concept of the Charter system. The fundamental shifts in the international system from bipolar to multipolar cleavages, coupled with a change in international conflict from an East-West to a North-South direction, have also brought a kind of "conservatism" on the part of the two superpowers, causing them to act as co-champions of an international status quo. That is, the two superpowers, faced with an increasing challenge from a new genera-

"The Lost Session at the U.N.," *The Reporter* 32 (May 6, 1965), 14-20. For a more comprehensive analysis of the financial crisis and its implications, see Stoessinger, *Financing the United Nations System*, passim, and *The United Nations and the Superpowers* (3rd ed., New York: Random House, 1973), chap. 6.

tion of UN membership, have come to develop an area of shared concern in UN politics.

Since the financial crisis of 1965, the superpowers have accepted *de facto* that no Member State should be forced to pay for any peacekeeping operation that it could not fully support. By placing UNFICYP under the category of voluntary contributions, the Council has in fact taken a first step to legitimizing this tacit understanding. The resolution adopted in 1967 by the Assembly's Special Political Committee on the Work of the Special Committee on Peace-keeping Questions states that the permanent members assume responsibility for 70 percent of the costs in any year, provided that states not supporting the operations are not bound to pay and that no one state needs to pay more than 50 percent of the annual costs.[13]

This brief review of the development of the Security Council from 1946 to 1971 on matters related to peace and security affords several conclusions. First, contrary to popular belief, a series of crises involving peace-keeping operations may have strengthened the Organization. Each of the three principal political organs has learned how to interpret the Charter flexibly and adapt itself to the changing demands and requirements of each crisis situation. On the one hand, the Soviet Union found that she was unable to halt the ONUC operation by the troika formula or by the refusal to pay. On the other hand, the United States also realized the limitations of her financial weapon when she abandoned her attempt to influence the future of peacekeeping by withholding her pledge to the Special Fund in 1964, and when she gave up the showdown on Article 19 in 1965. Even on the troublesome question of financing peace-keeping operations, the United Nations has adopted a wide variety of methods—regular assessments, voluntary contributions, special assessments, or some combination of all three. To a degree, peace-keeping has acquired its own life. The cliché that the United Nations is what its Member States make it has proved to be only a half-truth.

Second, the Security Council can enjoy its dominant role in peacekeeping only so long as it can muster a consensus or at least the acquiescence of the great powers. In order to cultivate such a consensual basis, the Council may have to come forward from time to time with a delicate combination of peace-keeping arrangements which would meet the requirements of a given crisis, on the one hand, and the acceptability test of the permanent members, on the other.

[13] UN Doc. A/6603 (15 December 1966). As it turned out, these operations were being paid for by the special UN bonds and voluntary contributions. For the financial legacy of the expenses incurred for UNEF I and ONUC and its continuing impact on the UN financial situation, see Table 3.8 in Chapter 3.

Failing this, the Council may again lose its control over peace-keeping to the Assembly. Given such competing requirements, peace-keeping is most likely to remain as an *ad hoc* expedient responding to different crisis situations in unpredictable ways.[14]

Finally, despite the continuing difficulties of the Special Committee in codifying authorization and implementaton guidelines, the necessity of some UN peace-keeping has been recognized by most Member States. Given the tenacity of conflict in several problem areas of the world and the wide acceptance of UN peace-keeping as a realistic alternative to collective security, the real danger is not that peace-keeping will soon go out of business but that it will perpetuate itself, distracting UN concern from the underlying causes of conflict throughout the world.

The Evolution of the Decision-Making Process

The basic rules and procedures governing the decision-making process in the Security Council on the eve of China's entry were still provisional.[15] There were only nine minor amendments to the Provisional Rules of Procedure prior to the Chinese entry. The Council has resisted any attempt to formalize the provisional rules. The International Court of Justice has also discouraged any attempt by the General Assembly to question the validity of any of the Council resolutions by advising in the *Competence of the General Assembly* case that "nowhere has the General Assembly received the power to change, to the point of reversing, the meaning of a vote of the Security Council."[16]

However, the Provisional Rules of Procedure do not reveal the Council's decision-making process. In practice, members of the Council have come to exercise one of five options: to vote yes; to vote no; to abstain; to decline to participate in the vote (nonparticipation); and to be absent when the vote is taken. There appears to be no distinction between decisions made by vote and those without vote, or between decisions adopted by a majority vote and those by unanimity,

[14] UN peace-keeping has become part and parcel of the bargaining process, involving the whole gamut of issues. This fact introduces an element of uncertainty as to the specific course of UN response in a given crisis. One scholar has observed in this connection that "not every security issue had to be settled so as to satisfy each major nation or bloc because compensating advantages could be and were provided by the UN in other issue areas sometimes of greater importance to many nations." Ernst B. Haas, "Collective Security and the Future of the International System," in Richard A. Falk and Cyril E. Black, eds., *The Future of the International Legal Order*, Vol. I: *Trends and Patterns* (Princeton, N.J.: Princeton University Press, 1969), pp. 295-96.

[15] For a comprehensive description and analysis of the decision-making process in the Security Council, see Sydney D. Bailey, *The Procedure of the UN Security Council* (London: Clarendon Press, 1975).

[16] *I.C.J. Reports 1950*, p. 10.

since any decision of the Council enjoys the same legal effect under the Charter.[17] As a matter of common practice, the Council has also routinely disposed of a wide range of questions without taking a vote.[18]

Despite the somewhat expansive stand taken by the sponsoring governments and France at San Francisco on the veto, especially on the double veto,[19] the practice of the Council prior to China's entry shows a progressive limitation of the scope and the applicability of the veto. The requirement of "an absolute majority of votes" in the elections of judges of the International Court of Justice[20] was early accepted as meaning an absolute majority of the members of the Council, not an absolute majority of those members participating in the vote, with no distinction between the permanent and nonpermanent members.[21] The use of the double veto receded as a potential weapon, as its use was confined to the early years 1946-48.

In addition, the consistent practice of the Council has been *not* to treat abstention by a permanent member as tantamount to a veto.[22]

[17] F. T. Chai, *Consultation and Consensus in the Security Council* (New York: United Nations Institute for Training and Research, 1971), p. 40. However, Leo Gross makes a distinction between resolutions that are legally *valid* and those that are legally valid but not necessarily *binding*. See "Voting in the Security Council: Abstention in the Post-1965 Amendment Phase and Its Impact on Article 25 of the Charter," *AJIL* 62 (April 1968), 315-34.

[18] Sydney D. Bailey, *Voting in the Security Council* (Bloomington, Ind.: Indiana University Press, 1969), p. 75.

[19] A "Statement by the Delegations of the Four Sponsoring Governments on the Voting Procedure in the Security Council," issued on June 8, 1945, declared: ". . . it will be unlikely that there will arise in the future any matters of great importance on which a decision will have to be made as to whether a procedural vote would apply. Should, however, such a matter arise, the decision regarding the preliminary question as to whether or not such a matter is procedural must be taken by a vote of seven members of the Security Council, including the concurring votes of the permanent members." This statement provides an authoritative definition of the double veto. See *Documents of the United Nations Conference on International Organization, San Francisco, 1945*, Vol. XI: Commission III (New York: United Nations Information Organizations, 1945), p. 714.

[20] Article 10 of Statute of the ICJ.

[21] SCOR, 1st Year, 1st series, 9th meeting (6 February 1946), p. 134; Supp. No. 1, p. 81, A25 (31 January 1946), para. 7.

[22] The practice seems to run counter to some evidence that the sponsoring governments at the San Francisco Conference took the view that abstention by a permanent member would have the same effect as a negative vote and thus be incompatible with the requirement of Article 27(3) of the Charter. The statement issued by the delegations of the sponsoring governments and France reads in part, for example: "In view of the primary responsibilities of the permanent members, they could not be expected, in the present condition of the world, to assume the obligation to act in so serious a matter as the maintenance of international peace and security in consequence of a decision in which they had not concurred. Therefore, if a majority voting in the Security Council is to be made possible, the only practicable method is to provide, in respect of non-procedural decisions, for unanimity of the permanent members plus the concurring votes of at least two

This practice, according to a comprehensive study of the subject published by the Legal Counsel of the United Nations, "has been acquiesced in by other Members of the Organization, and can now be considered a firm part of the constitutional law of the United Nations."[23] During the period 1946-66, for example, permanent members voluntarily abstained "at least 264 times in connection with the vote on part or the whole of various non-procedural decisions of the Council which were declared to be adopted" with the following distribution: 14 times for Nationalist China; 67 for France; 146 for the Soviet Union; 20 for the United Kingdom; and 17 for the United States.[24]

The records of the Council suggest that the permanent members have resorted to "voluntary abstention"[25] on nonprocedural questions for a variety of reasons. But voluntary abstention has been most frequently used as an escape clause to make a point of distinction between opposition and obstruction. An abstaining permanent member may be opposed to a draft resolution either because it is too weak or too strong in part or in whole, but not so strongly opposed as to prevent the Council from acting. At times the Western powers have resorted to a kind of "collective abstention" on draft resolutions, obviating the onerous exercise of their veto power. The Soviet Union characterized such a device as "the hidden veto" or "the indirect veto."[26]

Unlike voluntary abstention, absence and nonparticipation in the vote by a permanent member have been relatively rare. In the Korean case of 1950, the majority of Council members accepted the Soviet

---

of the non-permanent members." See *Documents of the United Nations Conference on International Organization, San Francisco, 1945*, Vol. XI: Commission III (New York: United Nations Information Organizations, 1945), p. 713.

[23] Constantine A. Starvropoulos, "The Practice of Voluntary Abstentions by Permanent Members of the Security Council under Article 27, Paragraph 3, of the Charter of the United Nations," *AJIL* 61 (July 1967), 752.

[24] *Ibid.*, pp. 743-44.

[25] Theoretically, we should distinguish between "voluntary abstention" and "obligatory abstention." The latter is stipulated in Article 27(3) of the Charter as an exception in fulfilling the voting requirement on nonprocedural matters: "provided that, in decisions under Chapter VI, and under paragraph 3 of Article 52, a party to a dispute *shall* abstain from voting." Emphasis added. This distinction has been blurred considerably in practice, as abstaining members have seldom attempted to categorize their abstentions as falling under a voluntary or obligatory typology. At least in two cases, nonparticipation was used in place of obligatory abstention. In the 1947 *Corfu Channel* case, the United Kingdom as a party to the dispute opted for nonparticipation on a draft resolution which would recommend that the United Kingdom and Albania refer the dispute to the ICJ. In the Eichmann case of 1960, Argentina as a party to the dispute again resorted to nonparticipation rather than obligatory abstention. For Argentina's explanation, see note 32 below.

[26] SCOR, 4th Yr., 428th meeting (21 June 1949), p. 16; UN Doc. S/PV.1340 (16 December 1966), pp. 112-15.

absence as an abstention rather than a veto *in absentia*. Despite the Soviet objection, the practice of the Council has been to treat absence as identical to abstention, as no fewer than nine resolutions had been adopted in the absence of a permanent member during the period 1946-67.[27] It has been rarer still for a permanent member to decline to participate in the vote, even though that, too, was treated as abstention for purposes of Article 27(3) of the Charter.[28] Of the 244 resolutions adopted by the Council during the period 1946-67, only 3 registered nonparticipation by permanent members.[29]

The Security Council found it unnecessary to follow the practice of the General Assembly, which had established a recognized procedure for nonparticipation, as discussed in Chapter 3. Nonparticipation, though seldom used, has been justified on the following grounds: failure to receive necessary instructions from home government;[30] challenge to the manner in which a given issue is handled or disagreement with the validity of the Council proceedings;[31] and reasons of tact and propriety.[32] It should be noted in this connection

[27] Bailey, *Voting in the Security Council*, p. 71.

[28] Rosalyn Higgins, "The Place of International Law in the Settlement of Disputes by the Security Council," *AJIL* 64 (January 1970), 2.

[29] The three cases referred to are as follows: the United Kingdom in the Corfu Channel case (S/RES/22); France in the 1961 Tunisian case (S/RES/164); and Nationalist China in the Mongolian membership question (S/RES/166).

[30] Both India and Egypt resorted to nonparticipation in the Korean case of 1950 on this ground. See SCOR, 5th Yr., 474th meeting (27 June 1950), pp. 14-16, and 530th meeting (30 November 1950), pp. 12, 20-25.

[31] See SCOR, 3rd Yr., 353rd meeting (19 August 1948), pp. 23-24; 354th meeting (19 August 1948), p. 37; 5th Yr., 462nd meeting (17 January 1950), pp. 7-9; 501st meeting (12 September 1950), pp. 13, 27-28; 507th meeting (29 September 1950), p. 8; 15th Yr., 868th meeting (23 June 1960), paras. 51-52; 16th Yr., 962nd meeting (22 July 1961), paras. 55-58; 971st meeting (25 October 1961), paras. 36, 70; 17th Yr., 998th meeting (23 March 1962), paras. 157-58.

Perhaps the most revealing explanation of nonparticipation was given by the representative of Yugoslavia on January 17, 1950, during the Council debate on the regulation and reduction of armaments questions. He opted for nonparticipation, challenging the propriety of Council proceedings on such important questions as disarmament in the face of the following: absence of both the Soviet Union and "China"; the presidency of the representative of the ROC, whose credentials had been challenged; and the fact that the delegation of the ROC no longer represented China. See SCOR, 5th Yr., 462nd meeting (17 January 1950), pp. 7-9.

[32] This seems to be a diplomatic euphemism for obligatory abstention for Council members who are parties to disputes. During the debate preceding voting in the Eichmann case, for example, the representative of Argentina explained his intention to not participate in the vote as follows: "Article 27, paragraph 3, of the Charter states that 'a party to a dispute shall abstain from voting.' My delegation does not wish to enter into a legal or procedural analysis of the application of that wording to the case we are considering, but for *reasons of tact*, which I am sure the Council will understand, my delegation requests the President and, through him, the Council for permission not to take part in the vote." SCOR,

that the representative of Nationalist China opted for nonparticipation in the vote on the Mongolian membership question on October 25, 1961—notwithstanding his strong opposition—in deference to the appeals of African friends that his veto would jeopardize Mauritania's admission into the United Nations by inviting a Soviet veto.[33]

The veto is undoubtedly the most widely known, if not the most accurately assessed, feature of the decision-making process in the Council. Table 4.1 provides the veto record in a chronological-comparative framework and affords an empirical basis for a brief analysis here. The Charter conception that collective security could neither be invoked against a great power nor even be organized without the great powers acting in concert, soon gave way to the competitive use of the veto as an instrument of cold war diplomacy in the Security Council. The disproportionate use of the veto by one superpower is misleading in several ways. First, the United States enjoyed the "hidden veto" resulting from her political advantage.[34] Second, the Soviet Union was placed in a position where her delegation was forced to repeat the veto on the same membership question throughout the first decade. With the package deal over the membership question in 1955, the Soviet use of veto began to drop rather sharply. Finally, a moderation in cold war politics, coupled with a gradual recognition on the part of the Soviet Union that the veto was becoming less effective and more harmful for her UN policy, began to be felt in the Council's decision-making process.

The disruptive impact of the veto on the Council's decision-making process has been greatly overstated. The American public has developed the habit of equating the veto with Soviet policy. The membership question is rather unique because it does not permit the possibility of compromise in the form of amendments. A membership application had to be either accepted or rejected as it stood. However, on many other questions the veto can be overcome. Of the 109 vetoes cast by the Soviet Union during the period 1946-72, according to one study, three-fourths have been made less effective in one way or another,

---

15th Yr., 868th meeting (23 June 1960), p. 10; emphasis added. The United Kingdom resorted to nonparticipation in the Indo-Pakistani question before the Council on December 23, 1952, obviously as a party to the dispute. See SCOR, 7th Yr., 611th meeting (23 December 1952), p. 25.

[33] SCOR, 16th Yr., 971st meeting (25 October 1961), pp. 8, 13.

[34] The representative of the Soviet Union put the matter in the following terms in a Council meeting: "I think that all or almost all of us here . . . know quite well that, given the existence in the Security Council of a firm majority prepared at all times to defend and support certain views of the Western Powers, there is no need for the representatives of those powers to cast a negative vote." SCOR, 16th Yr., 960th meeting (7 July 1961), para. 61.

Table 4.1. Select Data on Security Council Performance, 1946-76

Year	No. of Meetings	No. of Resolutions	No. of Consensual Resolutions	No. of Vetoes Cast by the Big Five					
				ROC	USA	USSR	UK	FRANCE	TOTAL
1946	88	15				9		1	10
1947	137	22				13		1	14
1948	171	29				7			7
1949	62	12				14			14
1950	72	11				4			4
1951	39	7							
1952	42	2				8			8
1953	43	5				1			1
1954	32	2	1			4			4
1955	23	5	2	1		17			18
1956	50	11	1			2	2	2	6
1957	49	5				3			3
1958	36	5	1			5			5
1959	5	1							
1960	71	28	1			5			5
1961	68	10				7			7
1962	38	7				1			1
1963	59	8	1			1	1		2
1964	104	14	4			2			2
1965	81	20	8						
1966	70	13	3			1			1
1967	46	12	10						

Year				PRC	USA	USSR	UK	FRANCE	TOTAL
1968	76	18	10			1			1
1969	64	13	3						
1970	38	16	5		1		2		3
1971[a]	34	10	2						
Subtotal					1	105	5	4	116
1971[b]	25	6	3			3	1		4
1972	60	17	6	2	1	1	4		8
1973	77	20	5		3		1		4
1974	52	22	16		1	1	1	1	4
1975	57	18	11		6		1	1	8
1976	113	18	7		6		1	2	9
Subtotal				2	17	5	9	4	37

[a] Ends with the 1598th meeting on October 20, 1971.

[b] Begins with the 1599th meeting on November 23, 1971, when Huang Hua and Ch'en Ch'u made their first appearance in the Security Council.

Source: Data presented in this table were adapted from the official records of the Security Council (SCOR). The performance data in the last few years were adapted from the provisional verbatim records (S/PV.) of the Security Council.

and 23 percent of the vetoed issues, including peace-keeping operations, were circumvented directly by compensatory UN action.[35]

The Charter and evolving custom have made matters of international peace and security an area of shared concern for both the Security Council and the General Assembly. The International Court of Justice advised in the *Certain Expenses* case that the responsibility conferred on the Security Council was primary, not exclusive.[36] In addition, one of the consensuses that emerged from the 1965 grand debate on UN peace-keeping was that the functions and powers of the Council and the Assembly had to be treated as mutually complementary. To the extent that the Council is unable or unwilling to discharge its primary responsibility, the Assembly may offer itself as an alternative forum. The establishment of UNEF I by the Assembly, following the French and British vetoes in the Council, has come to serve as a potent reminder that the veto on peace-keeping can easily translate itself into an involuntary delegation of power to the Assembly by inviting an invocation of the Uniting for Peace procedure.

As the data in Table 4.1 show, the veto as the *bête noire* of the Council's decision-making process largely vanished in the 1960s. Instead, private consultative practice and consensual decision making became the new means of operation.[37] Even though the records of the Council sometimes use the terms "consensus" and "unanimity" interchangeably, they are not necessarily identical. Consensus as part of the decision-making process shows the following characteristics: (1) prior private consultations among all members; (2) approximation of a general agreement; (3) finalization in the form of either a consensual presidential statement or a draft resolution with or without vote, eschewing public debate; (4) a tacit understanding that no public reference should be made to behind-the-scenes consultations.[38] Hence, a unanimous decision as a product of public debate is not subsumed under consensual decision.

Indeed, this is a new phenomenon in the Council proceedings, as all the consensual decisions of the early years were of a procedural or routine nature, requiring little or no prior consultation. Of the 185 resolutions adopted by the Council between 1946 and 1963, for example, only seven (3.8 percent) were consensual resolutions. In con-

---

[35] For a detailed analysis of the Soviet veto, see Stoessinger, *The United Nations and the Superpowers*, pp. 6-13.

[36] *I.C.J. Reports 1962*, p. 163.

[37] For detailed analysis of consensual decision making in the Security Council, see Chai, *Consultation and Consensus, passim* and Richard Hiscocks, *The Security Council* (New York: Free Press, 1973), chap. 4.

[38] Chai, *Consultation and Consensus*, p. 41 and Hiscocks, *The Security Council*, p. 106.

trast, 39 percent of the 122 resolutions adopted by the Council between 1964 and 1971 were consensual resolutions, as shown in Table 4.1.

The inauguration of consultative and consensual practices in the Council in the 1960s marks a transition from the era of cold war confrontation to a new era of negotiation. Détente in superpower relations, which in a sense is an expression of combat fatigue, undoubtedly helped the transition by moderating the style and substance of UN policy on the part of both superpowers. Experience has taught many Member States that international conflicts are not as amenable to the process of parliamentary diplomacy as they are to private consultation and compromise. The consensual decision-making process, Secretary-General Kurt Waldheim stated in his 1975 annual report on the work of the Organization, "has allowed the Council to work effectively on many crucial, complicated questions and to lay down guidelines for the settlement of highly complex political problems."[39] The presence of permanent missions to the United Nations in New York has also transformed the Council into a congenial rendezvous for quiet and informal consultative practices.

Finally, it may be asked: How has the 1965 constitutional change in the structure of the Council influenced the decision-making process? Since February 1966, when the Council first met under amended Articles 23 and 27 of the Charter, the nonpermanent members, who had nearly doubled their voting strength, could theoretically do the following: take control of procedural matters; exercise, when united, a kind of collective hidden veto over nonprocedural questions either by voting negatively or by abstaining; and adopt a resolution without the affirmative vote of any permanent member when no veto was cast. Although none of these possible theoretical threats materialized, the fact remains that there is now a new sword of Damocles hanging over the Council chamber. The enlargement of membership, as pointed out by the Japanese president in February 1966, has indeed made the Council directly and proportionately representative of all regions of the world for the first time in UN history.

Several salient points in the evolution of the Council's decision-making process prior to the PRC's entry need to be recapitulated. First, the Provisional Rules of Procedure remained provisional. Clearly, the Council has jealously guarded its Charter right (Article 30) to make its own rules of procedure by resisting any attempt at formalization. Second, the scope of veto applicability has been progressively limited

[39] *Introduction to the Report of the Secretary-General on the Work of the Organization* (August 1975), GAOR, 30th Sess., Supp. No. 1A (A/10001/Add.1), p. 2.

through custom and usage. In addition, the effectiveness of the veto in paralyzing the work of the Council, especially on UN peace-keeping activities, has been considerably lessened by the blurring of the line between the Council's primary responsibility and the Assembly's residual responsibility on matters relating to international peace and security.

Third, the Council has been more democratic and more representative with the amendments to Article 23 and 27. However, the theoretical possibility of the tyranny of the majority on the part of the non-permanent members has not materialized, owing in part to the progressive development and use of consultative and consensual practices in the decision-making process, eschewing parliamentary majoritarianism. It may also be noted that the Council is so organized as to be able to function at all times. In spite of its limited membership, it acts on behalf of all Member States; it has the constitutional authority (Articles 25 and 49) to make binding decisions on all Member States and, to some extent, even on non-Members (Article 2 (6)).

The Security Council After China

On November 23, 1971, China became, at one and the same time, both a participant and a decision maker in the Security Council, from which she had been excluded for over two decades. What kind of behavior could the Council expect from a major power whose seat had been preempted by an exiled rival political regime, and which had been treated as a pariah and even branded as an "aggressor" by the United Nations? Moreover, all of Peking's policy and ideological pronouncements about the international system, the United Nations, and world order contributed little to the prospects of a positive impact resulting from China's participation in the Security Council. The immense weight of past grievances, the rhetorical opposition to all peace-keeping operations, the routine reassertion of national sovereignty, the conceptualization of global problems in terms of immutable struggle between the superpowers and the Third World, and the characterization of the contemporary era as one of "great disorder under Heaven," —all of these easily conjured up the image of a fanatical revolutionary challenger entering the organization for world peace. In short, the nature of both China's ideology and experience made many students of international organizations skeptical of the outcome.

Given its limited size and membership, coupled with its continuing and critical management of international crises, the Security Council is more susceptible than the General Assembly to the positive or negative impact of a new member entering its decision-making bailiwick.

Hence, the key question raised in the global community on the eve of the PRC's entry into the Council in November 1971 centered more on the ominous functional word "impact" than on the diplomatic word "influence." Could prudent realism and ideological purity, both of which influenced the making and execution of Chinese foreign policy in varying degrees and different phases, be somehow reconciled in such a way as to make them all work for China, without disrupting the work of the Security Council in the process? In what way could China be distinguished from the other major powers who also participated in the Council's work? To what extent would the development of consensual decision making be helped or hindered by the presence of China in the Council? What about the Council's role in peace-keeping operations? These were only a few of the questions that were being asked.

Impact on Image and Prestige

The most immediate impact of the Chinese entry was largely symbolic. On the one hand, the presence of China in the United Nations, particularly in the Security Council, served as a vivid reminder that the days of the Americanized or Westernized Council were gone. There is a sense in which the Security Council was "remade" overnight to resemble more closely the original image of the Charter. Perhaps it was in this vein that most representatives in the Security Council expressed warm sentiments of welcome in the course of the 1599th meeting on November 23, 1971, when Ambassador Huang Hua made his debut.[40]

Both the image and the prestige of the Security Council have been substantially enhanced as a result of China's participation. In part, the image enhancement was a function of perceptions on the part of most Member States, since the Council can be no more or less important than the Member States perceive it to be. Clearly, the presence of China solved the legitimacy problem which had plagued the Council since 1950. There is now a widely shared belief—and this point was stressed time and time again by Huang Hua's diplomatic colleagues in the Security Council in the course of my field interviews—that the United Nations has finally achieved the status of being the truly universal organization it was intended to be and that the representation and power in the Council now approximate the political and geographical realities of the contemporary international system more closely than before.

[40] SCOR, 26th Yr., 1599th meeting (23 November 1971). See also "Chinese Permanent Representative, Deputy Representative Attend UN Security Council Meeting," NCNA-English, United Nations (November 23, 1971), in *SCMP*, No. 5028 (December 7, 1971), 51-52.

The enhanced prestige of the Security Council is also a result of the manner in which the PRC entered and behaved in the Security Council. As if determined to undo the prophesied image of a reckless bull, China adopted a low-profile and apprentice-like posture as her diplomatic style in the Security Council, as she did in the General Assembly. Recalling the behavior of the PRC representatives in the Council during the early months of their participation, one UN delegate from the Second World observed: "They [Huang Hua and Ch'en Ch'u] sat back and said little on the subjects with which they were not yet familiar or for which they lacked experts. And they took a rather low-profile and modest approach, which is not the usual approach for newcomers at the Security Council. The Chinese behavior in the Council impressed a lot of people." The PRC, in short, scored a major victory in her symbolic diplomacy in the Security Council.

When one looks at her overall performance in the period 1971-76, China appears to have behaved admirably toward an organization in whose establishment and development she was allowed to play no part. Instead of defying or ignoring the rules of the game in the Security Council, she has attempted to master them in the pursuit of her principles and/or interests. The PRC's representatives have already established a reputation in the UN community as a first-rate professional team, "winning friends and influencing delegations to a degree observers here find astonishing."[41] They have the reputation of being well prepared and well mannered. They behave more like a workhorse than a showhorse, constantly asking incisive and relevant questions behind the scenes, but keeping a rather low profile in public except on Soviet-supported issues. In politely and routinely declining to answer questions about the way his delegation works and lives, Huang Hua says, "We are not interested in publicity."[42] Huang Hua has been circumspect in confining his activities to the UN community, declining all offers of speaking engagements and all scholarly and journalistic requests for interviews.[43] Unlike the Soviet delegation, the PRC delegation has not sponsored any proposals that were mainly propaganda inspired. And, again unlike the Soviet delegation, Huang Hua or his deputy has been extremely brief and to the point in Council debate.

In assessing China's impact on the Security Council, we need to

[41] David Winder, "China's UN 'New Boys' Win Friends," *Christian Science Monitor*, September 21, 1971, p. 9.

[42] Kathleen Teltsch, "Chinese at U.N. Emerging from Isolation," *NYT*, November 6, 1975, p. 43.

[43] I do not know of any journalist or scholar who has managed to get an interview with Huang Hua. My own request for one was politely but firmly declined on the pretext that "our Mission is very busy and has a limited staff."

focus on the reputation of its chief representative, Huang Hua. After all, the first and foremost responsibility of Huang Hua has indeed been to represent China before the Council. He has been not only the ears and mouth of his government but also the personified image of China as far as his colleagues are concerned. What prestige, if any, did he bring to his job? What manner of a man or diplomat is he? What kind of role has he played? Was he perceived as having large discretionary powers or as being merely a puppet on the diplomatic stage?

The impressive list of diplomatic qualifications and experience that Huang Hua brought to his challenging role as the PRC's first permanent representative to the Security Council does not need to be repeated here. Suffice it to say that he was one of the most experienced and cosmopolitan diplomats in the PRC's foreign service establishment. It is worth noting two additional points in this connection: (1) he was the only ambassador who escaped recall home for "rectification" during the Cultural Revolution; and (2) he was one of the two ambassadors—the other being Huang Chen, the chief of the PRC's Liaison Office in Washington, D.C.—who was elected to full membership of the Central Committee by the 10th Congress of the CCP in August 1973.

Conscious of Huang Hua's unique place in the PRC's foreign service establishment, Ambassador Kulaga of Poland in his capacity as the president of the Security Council made a presidential consensus statement on November 23, 1971, in welcoming Huang Hua's debut: "I am convinced that all the members of the Security Council are gratified, as I am, that the People's Republic of China has chosen so distinguished a personality."[44]

Based on the general consensus that emerges from my field interviews with those who have worked closely with him both in public meetings and private consultations, a composite picture of Huang Hua the man and the diplomat can be drawn. Apparently, he is a man of considerable charm and intelligence. He has in addition established a reputation as a man of great fortitude, capable of sitting at a conference table for hours, chain-smoking but otherwise motionless. He proved to be a formidable match for his Soviet counterpart, not only showing no visible external reaction in the face of a heavy barrage of Soviet salvos aimed in his direction, but also achieving something that has eluded many Western diplomats—making Ambassador Malik lose his diplomatic composure in public.

In addition, Huang Hua emerges as a person capable of objectivity and of adapting to new situations. He is highly admired as a gracious

[44] SCOR, 26th Yr., 1599th meeting (23 November 1971), para. 3.

host; the parties given by him and his wife, Ho Li-liang, who also served as a PRC delegate in the Sixth Committee of the General Assembly, have been described as the most popular and eagerly attended in the UN community. Huang Hua speaks English, and has proved himself equally at ease with diplomats from the Third World as with those from the West. As noted in Chapter 3, Huang Hua has established a reputation as someone whose words can be accepted at face value. One European UN envoy noted "a sense of dignity in his behavior, for he would often counsel his colleagues in the Council not to rush into something." "Let us proceed in a more dignified manner," he would plead.

During his five-year tenure at the Security Council, Huang Hua served four times—September 1972, December 1973, February 1975, and April 1976—as the Council's president. Huang Hua's handling of this sensitive job is generally characterized as having been very competent and fair. One colleague of his saw in it "the virtuosity worthy of a veteran of international organizations."[45] Ambassador Louis de Guiringaud of France, who later (like Huang Hua) became his country's foreign minister, described his performance in the following terms:

> It is a specific pleasure to congratulate Ambassador Huang Hua for the constant effectiveness and the courteous authority with which, in the course of last month, he presided over the Security Council. The prestige with which he carried out his work and the eminent place in which he stands in our eyes do not have to be mentioned. Inflexible on matters of principle, but open to discussion, Ambassador Huang Hua made known the views of his country—sometimes rigorous but always logical and dictated by national interests—concisely and in measured tones that only stressed the weight of his arguments. In this arena, as in the world scene, China speaks and it is listened to.[46]

However, the opinions and perceptions among Huang Hua's diplomatic colleagues diverge on the question of the discretionary power he enjoyed during his tenure as China's representative to the Security Council. One UN envoy observed: "Apparently, the Ministry of Foreign Affairs has a very high degree of trust and confidence in his performance at the United Nations. He gave the impression of being solid and confident in the discretionary exercise of power. His discretionary power was fairly strong. If one judges from his behavior in

---

[45] SCOR, 27th Yr., 1675th meeting (21 November 1972), para. 60.
[46] UN Doc. S/PV.1761 (17 January 1974), p. 36.

the Council, he was autonomous on most issues. This contrasts sharply with the Soviet representative, who is constantly on the phone to Moscow." Yet, another UN envoy offers a contrary opinion: "I had the impression that he had no discretionary power; he had to be on the phone talking with Peking—sometimes a few minutes before voting." Still another UN envoy noted: "You had four or five on the top echelon in the PRC mission who moved rather freely and the rest acted much like programmed robots."

The symbolic and political significance of the PRC's participation in the work of the Security Council lies not so much in what she did than in what she did not do. The old conflict between the claim for political legitimacy and the claim for political stability, which characterized much of the debate on the Chinese representation question during the preentry period, has been resolved. Paradoxically, China has also helped her old nemesis, the United States. As one former American ambassador to the United Nations put it, "China has helped us greatly, because we don't have to expend our diplomatic capital on the China issue any longer in the United Nations." China has made the Council more universal, more representative, and more relevant without adding a measure of political ineffectiveness. That is, China through her low-keyed and self-effacing behavior has enhanced both political legitimacy and political stability at one and the same time. Herein lies the most significant impact of the PRC on the Council's image and prestige.

Conscious of the symbolic importance of Chinese participation, the Council followed the General Assembly on January 17, 1974, in adopting without a vote a resolution making Chinese one of its working languages.[47] "We are convinced," observed Huang Hua following the adoption of the consensual resolution, "that this action of the Security Council has terminated the abnormal state of affairs that existed in the UN for a prolonged period. This action is entirely logical and in accord with the spirit of the UN Charter."[48]

More dramatically, almost every organ or meeting of the UN system expressed its condolences and sympathy to China in regard to four major events in 1976: the death of Chou En-lai in January; the earthquake at Tangshan in July; the death of Chu Teh in July; and the death of Mao Tse-tung in September. Tributes to the memory of both Chou En-lai and Chu Teh were made in the Security Council.

However, the Security Council accorded Mao Tse-tung a quite exceptional tribute, devoting all but twenty minutes of the September

[47] Security Council Resolution 345 (1974).
[48] UN Doc. S/PV.1761 (17 January 1974), p. 58.

10, 1976, meeting (on the Vietnam membership question) to speeches in his memory,[49] while the United Nations flag flew at half-mast outside the building. The General Assembly was not yet in session at the time of Mao's death but the 5th Session of the Third United Nations Conference on the Law of the Sea meeting in New York (August 2-September 17, 1976) devoted its 73rd and 74th plenary meetings to paying tribute to Mao Tse-tung.[50]

In short, both China and the Council benefited from a mutual enhancement of image and prestige. Both in symbolic and representational terms, there seems little doubt that Chinese participation had a positive impact on the image and prestige of the Security Council. Equally, there can be no doubt that the Security Council enhanced the prestige of China in the family of nations.

Impact on the Decision-Making Process

Functional paralysis in the Council's decision-making process resulting from Chinese overkill with the veto has failed to materialize, despite the ominous scenario projected by many analysts. Tables 4.1, 4.2, 4.3 and Appendix H offer some pertinent data that can be used here to assess the impact of Chinese participation. The activities of the Council, as measured by the number of meetings held, show no effect. Of course, as a procedural matter, the number or frequency of the Council's meetings is not subject to the veto; it is a direct function of the number of issues successfully brought to the attention of the Council.

In spite of her fiscal conservatism on administrative matters, China gave firm support to the demand of the Organization of African Unity (OAU) to hold Council meetings in an African capital so as to give special attention to African questions.[51] For the first time in its history, the Council held its meetings in Addis Ababa, away from Headquarters, from January 28 to February 4, 1972, at an estimated cost of $144,-000, devoting itself to "Consideration of questions relating to Africa with which the Security Council is currently seized and the implementation of the Council's relevant resolutions." Likewise, China

[49] See UN Docs. S/PV.1870 (12 January 1976); S/PV.1945 (28 July 1976); S/PV.1955 (10 September 1976). Some 1,700 people from more than 120 countries called on the PRC mission to the United Nations in New York City to express their condolences following the news of Mao Tse-tung's death. The visitors included Secretary-General Kurt Waldheim and senior staff members of the UN Secretariat.

[50] See Third United Nations Conference on the Law of the Sea, *Official Records*, Vol. VI (1977), pp. 9-20. At its first plenary meeting of September 21, 1976, the General Assembly also paid its tribute to Mao Tse-tung. See UN Doc. A/31/PV.1 (21 September 1976).

[51] UN Docs. S/PV.1624 (11 January 1972), p. 6; S/PV.1626 (19 January 1972) p. 3.

supported unequivocally the proposal of Panama to hold Council meetings in Panama City to consider "measures for the strengthening of international peace and security and the promotion of international co-operation in Latin America, in accordance with the provisions and principles of the Charter and the resolutions relating to the right of self-determination of peoples and strict respect for the sovereignty and independence of States."[52] The Council meetings in Panama City, from March 15 to March 21, 1973, incurred an estimated cost of $92,000.

To assess the functional effectiveness of the Council's decision-making process, however, we need to look at the volume and frequency of the resolutions adopted. For comparative purposes, let us choose from Table 4.1 two four-year periods (1967-70 and 1972-75) and see if they reveal any impact of Chinese participation. The ROC period produced a total of 59 resolutions—28 of which were consensual—thus averaging 14.7 resolutions per annum and 7 consensual resolutions per annum. In contrast, the PRC period produced a total of 77 resolutions—38 of which were consensual—averaging 19 resolutions per annum and 9.5 consensual resolutions per annum. This translates into the following percentage increases from the ROC to the PRC periods: a 30.5 percent increase in all resolutions and a 35.7 percent increase in consensual resolutions, whether measured by the total or by the annual rate.

The veto records of the Big Five shed additional light on the impact of Chinese participation on the process of decision making in the Council. During the period November 23, 1971-December 31, 1976, 37 vetoes on 29 different nonprocedural questions were cast; in contrast, only 4 vetoes were cast in a comparable ROC period (1967-71), showing a substantial increase in the use of the veto since the PRC's entry. But contrary to what might be inferred, the veto record of the PRC is the "best" among the Big Five, as shown by the following distribution of the vetoes cast during the period by the five permanent members: 17 by the United States; 9 by the United Kingdom; 5 by the Soviet Union; 4 by France; and 2 by the PRC. Table 4.2 provides a typology of the 37 vetoes by subject matter and permanent members. To the extent that the Council's decision-making process was slowed down or hampered during the first five years of Chinese participation, the cause cannot be attributed to the PRC.

What can we make out of the Chinese theory and practice of the veto? China seldom attempted *officially* to clarify or rationalize her defense of the veto *per se* prior to her entry into the United Nations. But the fact that Chinese support of the principles of the Charter

[52] UN Doc. S/PV.1684 (16 January 1973), p. 8.

TABLE 4.2. Veto Record of the Security Council Since the PRC's Entry (November 23, 1971-December 31, 1976)

Veto No.	Date	Meeting No.	Item (Documentary Reference)	Permanent Member(s) Casting Negative Vote
1	12/4/71	1606	India v. Pakistan (S/10416)	USSR
2	12/5/71	1607	Ditto (S/10423)	USSR
3	12/13/71	1613	Ditto (S/10446/Rev.1)	USSR
4	12/30/71	1623	S. Rhodesia (S/10489)	UK
5	2/4/72	1639	Ditto (S/10606)	UK
6	8/25/72	1660	Bangladesh membership (S/10771)	PRC
7	9/10/72	1662	The Middle East Question (S/10786)[a]	PRC, USSR
8	9/10/72	1662	Ditto (S/10784)	USA
9	9/29/72	1666	S. Rhodesia (S/10805/Rev.1)	UK
10	9/29/72	1666	Ditto (oper. para. 1)[a]	UK
11	9/29/72	1666	Ditto (oper. para. 5)[a]	UK
12	3/21/73	1704	The Panama Canal Question (S/10931/Rev.1)	USA
13	5/22/73	1716	S. Rhodesia (S/10928)	USA, UK
14	7/26/73	1735	The Middle East Question (S/10974)	USA
15	7/31/74	1788	Cyprus (S/11400)	USSR
16	10/30/74	1808	S. African Expulsion (S/11543)	USA, UK, FRANCE
17	6/6/75	1829	Namibia (S/11713)	USA, UK, FRANCE

18	8/11/75	S. Vietnam Membership (S/11795)	USA
19	8/11/75	N. Vietnam Membership (S/11796)	USA
20	9/30/75	S. Vietnam Membership (S/11832)	USA
21	9/30/75	N. Vietnam Membership (S/11833)	USA
22	12/8/75	Palestinian Question (S/11898)	USA
23	1/26/76	Ditto (S/11940)	USA
24	2/6/76	The Comoros Membership Question (S/11967)	FRANCE
25	3/25/76	The Middle East Question (S/12022)	USA
26	6/23/76	The Angolan Membership Question (S/12110)	USA
27	6/29/76	Palestinian Question (S/12119)	USA
28	10/19/76	Namibia (S/12211)	USA, UK, FRANCE
29	11/15/76	The Vietnam Membership Question (S/12226)	USA

ª Veto cast on an operative paragraph or an amendment to a draft resolution; the remainder represent vetoes on draft resolutions.
Source: Adapted from UN Docs. S/PV. 1599 (23 November 1971)-S/PV. 1982 (22 December 1976).

remained firm and largely unaffected from 1945 to 1964 and that the veto was staunchly defended in all Chinese writings on the United Nations and international law should be accepted as *prima facie* evidence of Chinese support of Article 27(3) of the Charter. Kuo Ch'ün, a leading PRC authority on the United Nations in the 1950s, argued that China (then the ROC) along with the United States, the Soviet Union, and the United Kingdom, supported the power of the veto at the founding conference at San Francisco; yet, the United States, departing from its 1945 stand, made a series of pernicious attempts to destroy the unanimity principle from 1946 to 1955.[53] Kuo Ch'ün defended the PRC's strong support of the veto by asserting that the principle of unanimity protected not only the interests of big powers but also those of all other states, especially in preventing the latter from being dragged into participating in the United Nations' "aggressive activities" (peace-keeping operations).[54]

In a similar vein, Ch'en T'i-ch'iang, perhaps the most prominent PRC authority on international law in the 1950s, declared that "the Charter itself is beyond criticism" and then characterized the veto as "the political foundation of the UN Charter" and "the most fundamental canon for safeguarding world peace."[55] "This is why the United States has been racking its brains to destroy this principle," Ch'en T'i-ch'iang continued.[56] "If there is any difference between 1955 and 1945 because of the atomic bomb, it is that the principle of unanimity among the Big Powers is much more important in 1955 than in 1945."[57] Despite such strong and passionate support of the veto, Chinese writers accepted the generally recognized practice that an abstention, as distinguished from an absence, of a permanent member does not amount to a veto.[58]

If the conceptualization of the veto as a protective device against peace-keeping activities were still true, China would have vetoed all the Council resolutions establishing UN peace-keeping operations, instead of opting for nonparticipation (see Appendix H). This highlights a conflict in her UN diplomacy between her principles and interests, and nonparticipation, as will be elaborated later in the chapter, is a device to resolve the conflict.

Less than a month after the start of her participation in the Security

---

[53] Kuo Ch'ün, *Lien-ho-kuo*, pp. 6, 101-07.

[54] *Ibid.*, p. 101.

[55] "Uphold the United Nations Charter, Says Jurist," NCNA-English, Peking (December 2, 1955), in *SCMP*, No. 1183 (December 7, 1955), 6-7.

[56] *Ibid.*, p. 7. On the same point, see also Kuo Ch'ün, *Lien-ho-kuo*, pp. 101-07.

[57] "Uphold the United Nations Charter, Says Jurist," p. 7, n. 55.

[58] Ting Liu, "The Question of Admission of New Members to the United Nations," *CFYC*, No. 1 (February 1956), 33.

Council, China was faced with the decision on the selection of Secretary-General U Thant's successor, in which a veto by any of the Big Five could have presented an insurmountable barrier. However, Rule 48 of the Provisional Rules of Procedure stipulates: "Any recommendation to the General Assembly regarding the appointment of the Secretary-General shall be discussed and decided at a private meeting." Hence, there is no documentary basis for analyzing Chinese voting behavior in the three private meetings the Council held on December 17, 20, and 21, 1971.[59] The only available reference to voting issued by the Council in the form of a *communiqué* is that "having received a number of nominations for the post of Secretary-General, the Council voted by secret ballots on those nominations. As a result of the balloting, the Security Council proceeded to adopt unanimously the following resolution."[60] The resolution referred to was adopted unanimously, recommending Kurt Waldheim be appointed Secretary-General of the United Nations.[61]

Based on field interviews, however, I have constructed a composite description of Chinese voting behavior. Apparently, China voted against Waldheim in the first two ballots. In the second ballot, he received nine positive votes and two negative votes from the United Kingdom and China. When it soon became apparent that the United Kingdom was switching her vote to the majority and that China stood alone as the obstacle, Huang Hua immediately withdrew his negative vote to clear the path for the unanimous recommendation of Kurt Waldheim as the next Secretary-General.[62]

Five years later, when the Council was faced with another decision on the same question, China counseled other members of the Council not to rush, while keeping her own voting intention to herself. Apparently, the 1976 Council decision was easier and simpler than in 1971, as it took just one private meeting to dispose of the matter, with a unanimous recommendation for Waldheim's reappointment for an-

---

[59] Rule 51 of the Provisional Rules of Procedure states: "The Security Council may decide that for a private meeting the record shall be made in a single copy alone. This record shall be kept by the Secretary-General. The representatives of the States which have participated in the meeting shall, within a period of ten days, inform the Secretary-General of any corrections they wish to have made in this record." *Provisional Rules of Procedure of the Security Council* (January 1974, S/96/Rev.6), p. 9.

[60] UN Doc. S/PV.1620 (21 December 1971), p. 1.

[61] Security Council Resolution 306 (1971).

[62] It should be noted here that Table 4.1, Table 4.2, and Figure 4.1 in this chapter exclude the votes in private meetings. Likewise, all the quantitative references to the veto in the chapter do not include the negative votes cast by any permanent members in private meetings on the question of selecting the Secretary-General since the balloting is secret and no authoritative breakdown of the votes for the candidates, which were taken separately on each ballot, is possible.

other five-year term.[63] China is believed to have cast her first ballot for Luis Echeverria Alvarez of Mexico, as a symbolic gesture to show her preference for a Third World leader who had served as the main architect of the Charter of Economic Rights and Duties of States. In the second ballot, taken a few minutes later, China joined the 14-member majority (Panama abstained) to pave the way for the unanimous adoption of Security Council Resolution 400 (1976).[64]

Chinese behavior in the Council's decision-making process on the appointment of the Secretary-General reveals several characteristics worth noting. First, China has made no attempt to emulate the Soviet troika plan of 1960 or any variations of it. Second, she showed herself flexible and willing to compromise by changing her vote from negative to positive for the candidate of the majority preference in both 1971 and 1976, even though Kurt Waldheim was not her first choice. More revealingly, she decided not to exercise her favorite voting option of nonparticipation. Finally, China kept her voting intention secret in both cases until the very end. She has thus demonstrated that she follows an independent course of action rather than joining the bandwagon or bloc voting, and that her support can never be taken for granted.

We need now to look at the two vetoes cast by China. On August 25, 1972, China cast her first veto on the Bangladesh membership question, after her own draft resolution (S/10768 and Corr.1) to postpone the issue had failed earlier by a vote of 3:3:9. This was a solo veto that decisively killed Bangladesh's membership in the United Nations for the time being, as the draft resolution failed by a vote of 11:1:3. Fully conscious of his own attack on the abuses of the veto by the big

[63] The official *communiqué* of the 1978th meeting of the Security Council held in private on December 7, 1976, reads in part: "As a result of the voting on the candidates by secret ballot, the Security Council *unanimously* adopted the following resolution." The resolution herein referred to is Resolution 400 (1976), which recommends to the General Assembly that Mr. Kurt Waldheim be appointed Secretary-General of the United Nations for a second term of office from January 1, 1977, to December 31, 1981. It should be noted in this connection that each of the permanent members receives a marked ballot so as to make a clear distinction between the ballots returned from permanent and nonpermanent members in the secret balloting. See UN Doc. S/PV.1978 (7 December 1976), p. 1.

[64] The scenario projected by many UN delegates as to how the Chinese would behave in private on the question of the Secretary-General proved to be remarkably accurate. A few days before the actual balloting in the private Council meeting, David Anable, the *Christian Science Monitor* UN correspondent, after having interviewed UN delegates, wrote: "Delegates who have been trying to read the hints and winks emanating from the otherwise austere Chinese mission see a different way out: The Chinese may veto Mr. Waldheim once or twice, simply to ensure that the 'third world candidate' (Mr. Echeverria) has a chance to be considered. Thereafter they will let Mr. Waldheim through." See David Anable, "UN Security Council Faces Secretary-General Decision," *Christian Science Monitor*, December 3, 1976, p. 38.

powers, especially in reference to the three Soviet vetoes (veto nos. 1-3 in Table 4.2), Huang Hua declared defensively: "Since it took part in the work of the United Nations, the Chinese delegation has always been very serious and cautious on the use of veto."[65] To justify his own use of the veto on this occasion, Huang Hua went on to make a lengthy and somewhat labored legal argument, with repeated references to the 1949 Geneva Convention, Security Council Resolution 307 (1971), General Assembly Resolution 2793 (XXVI), and Article 4 of the Charter.[66] Even *Jen-min jih-pao* editorialized, declaring: "It is China's duty, as a member of the United Nations and a permanent member of the Security Council, to uphold principle and justice in the United Nations."[67]

Sensing the mounting pressure of the majority opinion in the United Nations in favor of the admission of Bangladesh, Huang Hua considerably softened the position of his government by indicating that the repatriation of 90,000 Pakistani prisoners of war held in India could pave the way for Bangladesh's admission into the United Nations. When the Bangladesh membership question came up again in June 1974, China supported it without any qualifications or reservations, declaring that all the relevant resolutions had now been fulfilled. In short, the impact of the PRC's first veto was to *delay* Bangladesh's admission.

In spite of the elaborate, and often persuasive, legal argument in justification of her first veto,[68] this was in effect a proxy veto cast on behalf of an ally. On the one hand, Pakistan placed in question China's credibility as her friend. On the other hand, the Soviet Union and India forced an immediate showdown, challenging China's

[65] *PR*, No. 35 (September 1, 1972), 9.

[66] Specifically, Huang Hua cited Article 118 of the 1949 Geneva Convention, which stipulates: "Prisoners of war shall be released and repatriated without delay after the cessation of active hostilities." The Security Council resolution referred to was adopted on December 21, 1971, by a vote of 13:0:2 (Poland and the USSR voting against), and demanded, *inter alia*, that a durable cease-fire and cessation of all hostilities in all areas of conflict be observed between India and Pakistan. The General Assembly resolution Huang Hua cited was adopted by a vote of 104:11:10, and called, *inter alia*, upon India and Pakistan to take all measures for an immediate cease-fire and withdrawal of their armed forces to their respective territories. For numerous speeches Huang Hua made in the United Nations and elaborate legal arguments advanced by China, see *PR*, No. 33 (August 18, 1972), pp. 12-13; No. 35 (September 1, 1972), 5-9; No. 40 (October 6, 1972), 29; and No. 49 (December 8, 1972), 9-12.

[67] *JMJP*, editorial, August 28, 1972, p. 1.

[68] It is doubtful whether China would have resorted to the legal argument if the military situation had developed in favor of Pakistan. Be that as it may, she had a legally strong case. For a legal analysis of the Bangladesh problem that would have greatly strengthened the Chinese position, see Michael Berkowitz, "Bangladesh," *Harvard International Law Journal* 14 (Summer 1973), 563-73.

credibility as a self-styled supporter of the Third World. As will be seen later, the escape route between Scylla and Charybdis in such a predicament is nonparticipation. However, it took a little while for China to discover this.

On September 10, 1972, China cast her second veto on an amendment to a three-Power draft resolution (S/10784) on the Middle East question. The amendment, which was defeated by a vote of 9:6:0, since two of the six negative votes were cast by China and the Soviet Union as permanent members, would have changed the phrase "the parties" in the operative paragraph of the three-Power draft resolution to "all parties." As it turned out, the draft resolution was vetoed by the United States (veto no. 8 in Table 4.2). Given the absence of any post mortem explanation or justification, it is possible that the Chinese may not regard such a negative vote on an amendment to a draft resolution as tantamount to a veto. At any rate, the impact of the Chinese veto was substantially diluted by three facts: (1) it was a non-solo veto; (2) it was on an amendment, not a draft resolution; and (3) the original draft resolution itself was vetoed by another permanent member.

If there was ever merit in the Chinese defense of the veto as a protective shield to prevent imperialist big powers from dragging small states into "aggressive activities" (peace-keeping operations), such a use of the veto is no longer possible, given the greater number of nonpermanent members and the noncoercive and nonmandatory nature of peace-keeping operations. Does this mean that the veto has lost its *raison d'être* for the Chinese? As the utility of the veto as a legal shield to protect the sovereignty and interests of the small nations reaches the point of diminishing returns in the Security Council,[69] the veto has become an ideological burden, increasingly challenging the

[69] No important political issue can be successfully placed on the agenda of the Security Council in the 1970s—note, for example, the membership question of the two Koreas—without the support of the Third World countries. Once an item is placed on the Council's agenda, however, a conflict usually develops between the Third World countries who press for quick or decisive sanction measures, on the one hand, and the western powers wanting to stop short at enforcement actions under Chapter VII of the Charter, on the other.

Viewed in this light, the veto as a supportive instrument of the great powers for the Third World countries has lost much of its utility. The Fifth Conference of Heads of States or Governments of Non-Aligned Countries, held in Colombo, Sri Lanka, from August 16 to August 19, 1976, passed a resolution on the use of the veto, which declared, *inter alia*: "2. Considers that the hegemony of the Big Powers within the Security Council and their use of the veto have diminished the prestige of the United Nations and the importance of its resolution vis-a-vis the international community. 3. Calls upon all United Nations Member States to direct all their efforts toward the reconsideration of the United Nations Charter, particularly as regards the right of veto, enjoyed by the permanent members of the Security Council." Reprinted in *Alternatives* 3 (December 1977), 294.

legitimacy and credibility of the Chinese claim of belonging to the Third World. Is it possible for a nation which has *constitutionally* pledged herself never to be a superpower, to possess, let alone to exercise, what is universally regarded as the privilege of the great powers in the world organization? Is it possible to reconcile Chinese advocacy of "participatory democracy" in UN affairs with Chinese use, however limited, of the veto?

In order to minimize the ambiguities and contradictions inherent in her possession of the veto, China has adopted several tactical postures. First, she has frequently attacked the *abuse* of the veto power by "certain superpowers." During the Council debate on December 15, 1971, Huang Hua stated, for example:

> This is the first time that the Chinese delegation takes part in the work of the United Nations. The Soviet representative has three times flagrantly abused the veto power in disregard of all consequences with the obvious aim of marking time so as to shield India in its occupation of East Pakistan. We are deeply shocked by such things, which we did not expect when we first took part in the work of the United Nations. This cannot but make people think: How can a superpower defy the opinion of well over a hundred countries and behave so arrogantly and truculently?[70]

Second, China has already begun exercising great caution in her own use of the veto by making a distinction between opposition based on her "principled stand" and obstruction of the majority will. As Appendix H shows, of the 101 resolutions adopted by the Council between November 24, 1971 and December 22, 1976, no less than 39 (38.6 percent) of the total registered abstention and nonparticipation. In fact, the PRC's use of nonparticipation in the vote is so extensive that one UN envoy has characterized it as follows: "I would go so far as to say that China has 'invented' nonparticipation. Now it is becoming a common practice not only in the Council but also in the Assembly. Clearly, this is a major Chinese contribution to the voting procedures of the UN organs. In the beginning, people were laughing about this but now more and more people have come to accept this as another form of expression in the voting process."

Table 4.3 places China's voting record in a comparative framework. During the period under review, China exercised nonparticipation 46 times on 158 nonprocedural questions, compared to none for the United States and the United Kingdom, one each for the Soviet Union and France. Figure 4.1, which plots the evolving pattern of Chinese voting behavior in the Council during the same period, reveals the

[70] *PR*, No. 52 (December 24, 1971), 11.

TABLE 4.3. Voting Record of the Big Five on All Nonprocedural
Questions from November 23, 1971 to the end of 1976
(percentages in parentheses)

	In favor	Against	Abstaining	Not Partici- pating	Total
PRC	97 (61.4)	8 (5.1)	7 (4.4)	46 (29.1)	158 (100)
USA	109 (68.9)	17 (10.8)	32 (20.3)	0	158 (100)
USSR	133 (84.2)	9 (5.7)	15 (9.5)	1 (0.6)	158 (100)
UK	119 (75.3)	10 (6.3)	29 (18.4)	0	158 (100)
FRANCE	126 (79.7)	4 (2.5)	27 (17.1)	1 (0.6)	158 (100)

Source: Based on UN Docs. S/PV. 1599 (23 November 1971)-S/PV. 1982
(22 December 1976).

trend that, while China is most likely to continue to exercise extreme
caution in the use of the veto, she is not likely to make a positive
contribution to about 35 percent of the resolutions the Council adopts.
It may also be noted that abstention has virtually disappeared from
Chinese voting behavior since mid-1974.

Nonparticipation as practiced by China in the Security Council is
a dialectical exercise to resolve, or at least to attempt to resolve, the

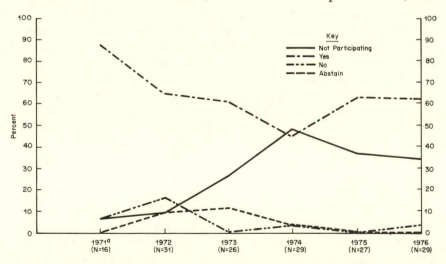

ᵃThe 1971 computation begins with the 1599th meeting (November 23, 1971) when the PRC delegation made its
first appearance in the Security Council.

FIGURE 4.1. Evolving Pattern of Chinese Voting Behavior in the Security
Council (based on all nonprocedural questions, including those resolutions
adopted by consensus or without a vote from November 23, 1971 to December 31, 1976).

contradictions inherent in the policy of pursuing both ideological and pragmatic interests at one and the same time. Like the "superpower contention and/or collusion" argument, nonparticipation can be justified for a variety of issues to a variety of audiences. It is thus perceived as maximizing the flexibility of the Chinese position in the Council with little "financial cost" or political responsibility. The Chinese could argue that they *opposed* all peace-keeping operations consistent with their past "principled stand" by not voting for the authorizing resolutions. Or they could argue that they *supported* peace-keeping operations by not vetoing the authorizing resolutions. For the Soviet Union, however, Chinese nonparticipation "shows the cowardice and unprincipledness [*sic*]."[71]

China's dialectical reasoning is also present in the stand she has taken on the Charter review question. Fully conscious of the fact that the remaining four permanent members of the Security Council were all united in their opposition to the issue of the Charter review and/or revision and therefore that there was little practical possibility of abolishing the veto, China posed as the only permanent member going on record in support of the "just and legitimate" demands of the small and medium-sized powers for Charter review. It should be noted here that China did not initiate the Charter review question, but simply responded to the egalitarian demands of the Third World nations; moreover, Chinese support took the ambiguous form of giving "serious consideration" to all views regarding the revision of the Charter, including the question of limiting or abolishing veto power in the Council.[72]

While the decision-making process in the Council has progressed with little obstruction from China, it must be recognized that consultative and consensual practices face the danger of being disrupted by Sino-Soviet rivalry in the United Nations. Whether the consensual process can be helped is contingent not only on the substance but also on the manner of consultation. Soviet-American cooperation in the form of joint sponsorship of a draft resolution is a sure invitation for confrontation in Council proceedings. When the Soviet Union and the United States worked out hurriedly and secretly two joint draft resolutions (S/11036 and S/11039) and presented them as a *fait accompli* during the 1973 Middle East War, for example, an ugly and disorderly situation ensued. In the debate on the first Soviet-American draft resolution on October 21, 1973, Huang Hua attacked, declaring: "This time, these two super-Powers have hurriedly introduced a draft resolu-

[71] UN Doc. S/PV.1748 (23 October 1973), p. 53.
[72] *Report of the Ad Hoc Committee on the Charter of the United Nations*, GAOR, 30th Sess., Supp. No. 33 (A/10033), pp. 10-11. The PRC's position on the Charter review question is further elaborated on in Chapter 7.

tion of their concoction to the Security Council and asked for its immediate adoption *allowing of no full consultation between the States members of the Security Council* and preventing them from seeking instructions from their respective Governments. This practice of *imposing* one's views on the Security Council is most unreasonable and is one we cannot agree to."[73]

Two days later when the Council resumed its debate on the second Soviet-American draft resolution, Ch'iao Kuan-hua, who participated in the proceedings as head of the Chinese delegation, swiftly responded in the following manner, defying a call for a point of order: "The Chinese delegation firmly opposes such a malicious practice of using the United Nations Security Council as a tool to be juggled with by the two super-Powers at will. In our opinion, this also shows utter disrespect for the other States members of the Security Council. The Chinese delegation cannot tolerate such a practice. *We have something to say.* We believe that the other States members of the Security Council also have something to say from the bottom of their hearts."[74] Ch'iao Kuan-hua's behavior at this meeting was so unusual that one participant offered the following observation: "I got the impression that there was a strong *personal* animosity between Malik and Ch'iao, although I do not know for sure whether there was any basis for this. Ch'iao was so upset during the debate that he stood up—which one never does during the Security Council debate—and shook his fingers at Malik sitting across the table."

That the Soviet-American draft resolutions had the unanimous support of all the members of the Council was beside the point, as far as Ch'iao Kuan-hua was concerned. The Chinese are not opposed to consultative-consensual practice as such, but oppose the consultative process in which the two superpowers play a dominant role. The Chinese conceptualization of consensual decision making follows closely "participatory democracy," in which all the members of the Council are involved on an equal footing. It must also be noted here that China, despite her vehement objection to the substance and manner, opted for nonparticipation, thus allowing the Soviet-American draft resolutions to be adopted "unanimously" as Security Council Resolutions 338 and 339 (1973). (See Appendix H.)

It must be emphasized here that there is a clear distinction between China's *nonparticipation* in the vote, such as on the above-mentioned resolutions and her *participation* in the behind-the-scenes consultative process prior to public debate. There are two ways of working out a

[73] UN Doc. S/PV.1747 (21 October 1973), p. 67; emphasis added.
[74] UN Doc. S/PV.1748 (23 October 1973), p. 13; emphasis added. As if to further aggravate the situation, there were constant interruptions to the Chinese speeches by the Soviet representative.

draft consensual resolution behind the scenes. The first method is to invite all the members for informal consultation; the second is a series of bilateral consultations. It is up to the discretionary judgment of the president of the Council. What infuriated the Chinese in the above incident was the fact that the Soviet-American draft resolutions were worked out secretly between Henry Kissinger and Andrei Gromyko, thus deviating from normal consultative practice. The United States and the Soviet Union took China's "support" or "nonparticipation" for granted in presenting their draft resolutions as a *fait accompli*. Such behavior is bound to trigger off Chinese retaliation; if repeated, it might even invite a Chinese veto.

What is the *modus operandi* of Chinese consultative behavior in the Security Council? Participants who have had firsthand experience on this matter offer the following observations:

> It [the PRC's consultative behavior] is one that is strongly influenced by a sense of autonomy. China, being an entity of its own, would stress its own point of view. The Chinese delegates would seldom say that they agreed or disagreed with the viewpoints expressed by the previous speakers. They would always make it clear that the Chinese position is a separate one, and that China does not belong to a group or a bloc, and that nobody can speak for China except China herself. This pattern of behavior deviates from the behavior of many other member states, who follow an ideological or geographical bloc voting line. Of course, China would normally support the position of the Third World.

> Chinese consultative behavior is unique insofar as there is very little of it. On numerous occasions when I sought in advance what the Chinese were thinking about the subject that was due to come up in the Council, my colleagues and I could find very little in the way of clues. The Chinese tactics as practiced by Ambassador Huang Hua and his chief deputy is to listen and to ask questions—sometimes many questions—but seldom answer any questions put to them that would indicate in the slightest in which way they were even leaning. So it became very frustrating.

> Of course, they [the PRC delegates] would be invited and they would come and listen. They would state their own position, whether it was germane or not, and that would be all. We consulted the Chinese in several informal consultations that we initiated without any hope of receiving specific commitments.

> As a rule, most member states of the Security Council would approach China in as correct a manner as possible during the consultative process.

A word of caution is in order here. None of the participants quoted above came from the Third World. Hence, their observations should be accepted in that limited perspective. Whether the Chinese would adopt the same evasive and noncommittal posture when approached by Third World Member States in the Security Council, I have been unable to ascertain. What is clear is that the Chinese do *participate* in the consultative process even on those issues to which they are opposed as a matter of principle (UN peace-keeping), and that they maintain a posture of independence without fully consenting or dissenting in the formulation of consensual draft resolutions. In effect, such a participation amounts to Chinese "consent by acquiescence" in the decision-making process.

One major qualification needs to be made about Chinese consultative behavior in the Security Council. China has refused—and would probably continue to refuse—to participate in behind-the-scenes consultations among the Big Five, as revealed in Huang Hua's public statement at the 1751st meeting of the Council: "Mr. Malik accused China of refusing to take part in his proposed five-Power consultations. That is indeed true. China refuses and will refuse to take part in the so-called five-Power consultations. The reasons are very simple: we have all along been opposed to a big Power striking political deals behind the backs of the Palestinians and other Arab peoples."[75] Thus, one thing seems quite clear. To avoid a public confrontation such as the one previously referred to, the two superpowers—or for that matter, the Big Five—must take into account not only the substance but also the manner and style of their "consultative cooperation" in the Council's decision-making process. It can also be argued that the frequent use of nonparticipation by the Chinese has actually expedited the decision-making process in the Council, by generating some politically inspired incentive for Soviet cooperation in its competition with China to curry favor with the Third World Member States in the Council. However, if the Soviet Union overplays its cooperative role in an overt attempt to put China on the spot, or if the Soviet Union projects its cooperation with the United States as a gesture of détente, China could very easily be disruptive.

On the whole, then, the impact of Chinese participation upon the decision-making process in the Security Council has been more positive than negative. It must be recalled in this connection that the ROC's representation of China in the Council during the PRC's exclusion period brought about absurd situations from time to time. When it was China's month to preside in the Council, for example, "The normal

---

[75] UN Doc. S/PV.1751 (26 October 1973), pp. 78-80.

arrangements for informal consultations under the auspices of the President could not be relied on, and members of the Council would solemnly thank the representative of China the following month for his consideration in not calling any [consultative] meetings."[76]

The General Assembly went much further by conspicuously excluding the ROC, a permanent member of the Security Council, from the 33-nation Special Committee on Peace-keeping Operations established at the end of the 19th Session, with a mandate to review the whole question of United Nations peace-keeping operations. Viewed in this light, the PRC's participation in the Council has also legitimized its decision-making process. But this should not lead us to underestimate the disruptive potential of China.

Impact on Peace-keeping and Enforcement Activities

During the preentry period as a whole, China generally showed a negative attitude toward UN peace-keeping activities. Both ideology and experience dictated this attitude, to be sure, but her approach was more political than legal. On this question she seemed to be wanting to have her cake and eat it too. As a result, some ambiguities and contradictions crept into the development of her position. The Chinese publicists repeatedly insisted that the United Nations, in exercising its role in the maintenance of international peace and security, should not intervene in the internal affairs of states in violation of Article 2(7) of the Charter. The Uniting for Peace Resolution was attacked on the ground that it undermined the unanimity principle and impaired the functions of the Security Council.[77] Moreover, China specifically condemned the UN "interventions" in Korea, Hungary, the Congo (ONUC), Cyprus (UNFICYP), Vietnam, Tibet, Hong Kong, and Macao as contraventions of the Charter principles.[78]

However, China argued forcefully in support of the UN interventions and sanctions in the Suez Crisis of 1956,[79] and in colonial and apartheid questions involving Portugal, Southern Rhodesia, and South Africa, as noted in Chapter 3. It should be recalled here that the UN role in bringing about a cessation of hostilities in the 1956 Suez Crisis was made possible by invoking the Uniting for Peace procedure in the General Assembly, following the British and French vetoes in the Security Council (see Table 4.1). But the Assembly action in establishing UNEF I is, a Chinese publicist argued, *ultra vires*, because only

[76] Bailey, *The Procedure of the UN Security Council*, pp. 166-67.
[77] Kuo Ch'ün, *Lien-ho-kuo*, pp. 103-104.
[78] *JMJP*, January 9, 1965, p. 3.
[79] *SCMP*, No. 1412 (November 16, 1956), 22, and No. 1421 (November 30, 1956), 32.

the Security Council is empowered to take actions for the maintenance of international peace and security and the suppression of aggression.[80] China's apparent double standard in judging UN peace-keeping and peace-making activities has already been explained and need not be repeated.

Since her entry into the United Nations, China has begun to take a somewhat more positive and flexible view of the UN role. Still, a political and opportunistic approach seems to dominate her behavior. For example, when the Council was immobilized in the matter of the Indo-Pakistani War by Soviet vetoes, China, along with the United States, voted for Security Council Resolution 303 (1971) without any reservations or qualifications. It should be noted that this resolution referred the deadlocked issue to the General Assembly for consideration, based specifically on the Uniting for Peace Resolution.[81] Likewise, China voted for the Assembly's Cease-Fire and Troops Withdrawal Resolution on the Indo-Pakistani War, without raising any objections to the citation of the Uniting for Peace Resolution as a legal basis for this Assembly action.[82]

Similarly, doctrinal purity or logical consistency on the part of China should have dictated her voting against peace-keeping instrumentalities of the Security Council. At the peak of her disenchantment with the United Nations in 1965, for example, China strongly attacked the Soviet-American negotiation in the Special Committee on Peace-keeping Operations as aiming at the establishment of "an imperialist-revisionist international gendarmerie." China also characterized all of UN peace-keeping operations up to 1965 as having "always protected the interests of imperialism and undermined the efforts of the peoples to win freedom and independence," and therefore held that they "have been and remain the docile special detachments of the international gendarmerie of US imperialism and reaction."[83]

Yet, after her entry into the United Nations, China's opposition to peace-keeping became more verbal than real. She cast no negative

[80] Sun Nan, "What is the United Nations Emergency Force?" *SCCS*, No. 24 (December 20, 1956), 22.

[81] The operative paragraph of Security Council Resolution 303 (1971) reads: "Decides to refer the question contained in document S/Agenda/1606 to the General Assembly at its twenty-sixth session, *as provided for in Assembly resolution 377 A (V) of 3 November 1950*." SCOR, 26th Year, *Resolutions and Decisions of the Security Council 1971*, p. 10; emphasis added.

[82] General Assembly Resolution 2793 (XXVI) of 7 December 1971, was adopted by a roll-call vote of 104 in favor, 11 against, with 10 abstentions. One of the preambular paragraphs of the resolution reads: "Mindful of the purposes and principles of the Charter and of the General Assembly's responsibilities under the relevant provisions of the Charter *and of Assembly resolution 377 A (V) of 3 November 1950*." (Emphasis added.)

[83] *PR*, No. 17 (April 23, 1965), 27-28.

vote on such instrumentalities of the Security Council as the United Nations Force in Cyprus (UNFICYP), the second United Nations Emergency Force in the Middle East (UNEF II) established after the 1973 October War, the United Nations Disengagement Observer Force (UNDOF), and the Rhodesian Sanctions Committee. As a result, the above-mentioned operations continued unhampered.

In less than a month after her arrival in the Security Council, China was presented with a first test of her position on UN peace-keeping when the Council had to renew the mandate of UNFICYP on December 13, 1971. Even though UNFICYP was specifically attacked in 1965 as US-manipulated international gendarmerie, and even though the United Kingdom continued to play a major role in UNFICYP operation despite her status as a permanent member of the Security Council, China took a low-keyed, reticent posture during the debate preceding the vote. Huang Hua was not even present, but his deputy Ch'en Ch'u made a brief remark to the effect that "the dispute should be settled in a reasonable way by the countries concerned through consultation on an equal footing."[84] "As for the question of the UN forces," Ch'en Ch'u continued, "the Chinese government has always had its own principled stand. This is well known to all the representatives. Therefore, we could not participate in the voting on this resolution."[85]

This reticent posture continued throughout the subsequent Council debates on UNFICYP, except for an occasional warning to be "vigilant against Soviet revisionist social-imperialism, which is trying to rob the owner while his house is on fire."[86] Interestingly, China voted for five resolutions and joined in two consensual resolutions on the Cyprus question, limiting her opposition to references to UNFICYP (see Appendix H). Thus, UNFICYP continues its operation with little opposition from China, and occasional "cooperation by acquiescence."

The function of UNFICYP has remained unchanged since its inception in 1964: to prevent a recurrence of fighting between the Greek Cypriot and Turkish Cypriot communities and to contribute to the maintenance and restoration of law and order and a return to normal conditions. However, owing to the continuing constraints imposed by the Turkish forces, UNFICYP has been limited in its ability to provide security to Greek Cypriots living in the north. While adapting its operations to the requirements of the changing situation, UNFICYP has also carried out some humanitarian tasks. At the peak of its operation, the strength of UNFICYP reached 7,000 personnel—from Austria,

---

[84] UN Doc. S/PV.1612 (13 December 1971), pp. 1-2.
[85] *Ibid.*
[86] "Beware of the Soviet Revisionists: They are Out to Rob the Owner While His House is on Fire," *PR*, No. 32 (August 9, 1974), 11-12.

Canada, Denmark, Finland, Ireland, Sweden, and the United Kingdom —but dropped to 2,798 by December 6, 1976.[87] Its mandate is being renewed once every six months (see Appendix H) without any foreseeable prospect of resolving the conflict and withdrawing from the island.

Given the universal sense of apprehension that the Middle East is indeed a tinderbox for global conflagration, coupled with the deep political and military involvements of the two superpowers, the establishment of UNEF II in the wake of the October War in 1973 presented an extremely delicate diplomatic challenge to the Security Council. As noted earlier, the two superpowers quickly and decisively took charge of crisis management in the Council by presenting two joint draft resolutions at short notice, taking Chinese nonparticipation in the vote for granted. For the Chinese, however, this was indeed a tailor-made case of the two superpowers both contending and colluding for global hegemony. The situation invited a confrontation between the two communist giants in the Council meetings of October 21 and October 23, 1973.

When the Council resumed its debate on October 24, 1973, on the establishment of UNEF II, Chinese outrage continued to run high. In the still inflamed atmosphere, the Sino-Soviet verbal duel continued, but naturally the Soviet Union outscored and outmaneuvered China by posing as a peace-keeper and labeling China as a warmonger in the Middle East. The Soviet Union reminded the public that the revised draft resolution (S/11046/Rev.1) before the Council was not submitted by the two superpowers, as China like to call the Soviet Union and the United States, but by eight nonaligned countries. China was thus forced to demonstrate her credibility as a supporter of the United Nations and a self-styled member of the Third World.

Challenged in this manner, Huang Hua repeated all the ideological arguments of the preentry period against peace-keeping operations: that the dispatch of the UN emergency force would bring "infinite evil consequences in its wake and pave the way for further international intervention in the Middle East with the superpowers as the behind-the-scenes bosses"; that if the superpowers were not able to send in their own forces directly, "they try by all means to squeeze in the forces which they can influence so as to exercise indirect control";

[87] The composition of UNFICYP as of December 6, 1976, was divided into two categories—military (2,730) and civilian police (68)—with the following distribution among the participating countries: Austria (312); Canada (515); Denmark (360); Finland (290); Ireland (5); Sweden (425); and the United Kingdom (823). In addition, Australia, Austria and Sweden had 16, 32, and 20 respectively in UNFICYP's civilian police force. See *Report of the Secretary-General on the United Nations Operation in Cyprus*, UN Doc. S/12253 (9 December 1976), p. 3.

and that the fierce contention between the superpowers on the question of the composition of UNEF II during the informal consultations supported the correctness of the Chinese judgment.[88] However, China stopped short of resorting to the veto, simply refusing to be "a party to the agreement on the composition of the so-called UN emergency force," and opted instead for the nonparticipation route. Ever since, the Chinese have dissociated themselves from all subsequent Council proceedings on UNEF II and its financing.

As if to confirm the Chinese projection of the social-imperialists constantly looking for international expeditionary adventures in troubled waters, the Soviet Union quickly seized the chance to fashion UN peace-keeping according to her own ideas. She demanded, as a price of her cooperation for the establishment of UNEF II, that the principle of equitable geographical distribution be applied in the composition of UNEF II with a proper balance among the Western, nonaligned, and socialist states, and that UNEF II operate under the immediate authority of the Council, meaning that "the Security Council itself takes decisions concerning all aspects of the establishment of United Nations armed forces and the discharge of the peace-keeping missions entrusted to it."[89]

Although Security Council Resolution 340 (1973) merely states that UNEF II is to be composed of personnel drawn from Member States other than the permanent members of the Security Council, the consensual statement issued by the president of the Council on November 2, 1973—from which China dissociated herself—instructs the Secretary-General to consult with Ghana (from the African regional group). Indonesia and Nepal (from the Asian regional group), Panama and Peru (from the Latin American regional group), Poland (from the East European regional group) and Canada (from the West European and other states regional group) so as to bring about a better geographical distribution of UNEF II personnel.[90] Table 4.4 lists the strength and composition of UNEF II.

UNEF II departs from the past peace-keeping operations in one important principle. By deciding to set up UNEF II "under its authority"[91] and by deciding also that the Force shall be established for an initial period of six months and that "it shall continue in operation thereafter, if required, provided the Security Council so decides,"[92] the Council has weakened the consent principle which had hitherto

[88] UN Doc. S/PV.1754 (2 November 1973), p. 7.

[89] UN Doc. S/PV.1750 (25 October 1973), pp. 28-30.

[90] SCOR, 28th Year, *Resolutions and Decisions of the Security Council 1973*, p. 12.

[91] Security Council Resolution 340 (1973), *ibid.*, p. 11.

[92] Security Council Resolution 341 (1973), *ibid.*

TABLE 4.4. Strength and Composition of UNEF II, 1974-76

Country	As of 1/27/74	As of 10/12/74	As of 4/12/75	As of 9/17/76
Austria	598	3		
Australia				44
Canada	1,096	862	842	871
Finland	615	468	506	640
Ghana	499	500	501	597
Indonesia	552	402	400	510
Ireland	271	1		
Panama	409	442		
Peru	497			
Poland	821	921	878	865
Senegal	396	410	402	
Sweden	620	482	500	647
Total	6,374	4,491	4,029	4,174

Source: SCOR, 29th Year, Supp. for Jan.-March 1974, p. 3; Supp. for Oct.-Dec. 1974, p. 29; SCOR, 30th Year, Supp. for Apr.-June 1975, p. 10; UN Doc. S/12212 (18 Oct. 1976), p. 2.

remained as one of the cardinal principles of all peace-keeping operations. It was made clear in this way that any withdrawal or termination of the Force could be decided only by the Council itself, an obvious move aimed at safeguarding against any recurrence of the 1967 Egyptian demand for the withdrawal of UNEF I. A wide and even geographical distribution in the composition of UNEF II made it possible to dilute the consent principle.

Nonetheless, the new guidelines for UNEF II stressed that the Force would act with "complete impartiality and would avoid any action that could prejudice the rights, claims or positions of the parties."[93] The functions of UNEF II have remained the same since its inception: "to man, patrol and control the zone of disengagement and to conduct weekly inspections of the Egyptian and Israeli limited forces areas and 30 kilometre zones."[94] The total strength of the Force is to be in the order of 7,000 personnel and its mandate is to be renewed by the Council once every six months.

In sharp contrast to UNEF II, the authorization process of the United Nations Disengagement Observer Force (UNDOF) by the

[93] Report of the Secretary-General on the Work of the Organization (16 June 1973-15 June 1974), GAOR, 29th Sess., Supp. No. 1 (A/9601), p. 7.
[94] SCOR, 30th Year, Supplement for April, May and June 1975 (S/11536/Add.1), p. 7.

Security Council generated no heated debate or Sino-Soviet confrontation. Following the Secretary-General's transmittal of the text of the Agreement on Disengagement between Israeli and Syrian Forces, Ambassador Scali of the United States requested an urgent Security Council meeting. The Protocol to the Agreement called for a 1,250-man UNDOF to maintain the cease-fire and to supervise the Agreement with regard to the areas of separation and limitation. At its 1774th meeting on May 31, 1974, the Council adopted unanimously a draft resolution, cosponsored by the United States and the Soviet Union, which "decides to set up immediately under its authority a United Nations Disengagement Observer Force, and requests the Secretary-General to take the necessary steps to this effect."[95]

Perhaps determined to avoid embarrassment or confrontation over another peace-keeping operation, Huang Hua was conspicuously absent, but his deputy Chuang Yen politely reminded the members of the Council that "China has always held her principled position on the dispatch of troops in the name of the UN under whatever form" and that "it is only out of consideration for the present attitude of the victim of aggression [Syria] that the Chinese delegation has decided not to participate" in the vote rather than to veto the draft resolution. Chuang Yen also made a specific request to the president of the Council "to place on official record China's position of dissociation from the matter."[96] UNDOF thus had an easy birth with China standing by as a disinterested observer. In effect, China's total dissociation from UNEF II and UNDOF means her total noninterference in the continuing authorizing process, as the mandates of UNEF II and UNDOF require periodic renewal by the Council.

The function of UNDOF is to maintain and supervise the cease-fire in the areas of separation and limitation between the Israeli and Syrian forces. UNDOF is to enjoy the freedom of movement and communication necessary for its mission. It carries out its function by means of static posts, which are manned 24 hours a day, and mobile patrols. The strength of the Force was set at 1,250, to be selected by the Secretary-General in consultation with the parties concerned, from Member States that were not permanent members of the Security Council. As of May 24, 1976, the strength of UNDOF stood at 1,194, with the following breakdown: Austria (515); Canada (126); Iran (391); Poland (84); and UN military observers (detailed from UNTSO, 78).[97]

[95] SCOR, 29th Year, *Resolutions and Decisions of the Security Council 1974*, p. 4.
[96] UN Doc. S/PV.1774 (31 May 1974), pp. 13-15.
[97] SCOR, 31st Year, Supplement for April, May, and June 1976, p. 32.

Besides those supervised by UNFICYP, UNEF II, and UNDOF, since China's entry four cases of territorial dispute deemed to threaten international peace and security have been brought to the attention of the Security Council in 1971-76. When the Iran-Iraq frontier incidents were brought to the Council's attention in February 1974, China took the position of supporting "a settlement of such questions through friendly consultations on an equal footing between the parties in dispute," disapproving any form of UN involvement in boundary disputes. China opted for nonparticipation in the vote that led to the adoption of Security Council Resolution 384 (1974).[98]

In October and November 1975 the Security Council was faced with the crisis in Western Sahara, a territory in Africa administered by Spain, which both Morocco and Mauritania claimed as being originally part of their own territories. The crisis was first brought to the Council's attention by Spain, which stated that the announced plan of King Hassan of Morocco to conduct a march of 350,000 people into Western Sahara—"the Great March"—created a situation threatening to international peace and security in the area. In the course of its proceedings, the Council adopted three consensual resolutions (see Appendix H), requesting the Secretary-General to enter into immediate consultations with the parties concerned, urging all parties to avoid any unilateral action which might further aggravate the situation, and calling upon Morocco immediately to withdraw from the territory of Western Sahara all the participants who had entered there through the Great March. In curious contrast to the Iran-Iraq frontier dispute, China joined in all three consensual resolutions, thus supporting the roles of the Council and the Secretary-General in the settlement of the territorial dispute. In a brief remark during the Council debate, Huang Hua's deputy, Lai Ya-li, urged particular vigilance "to prevent the super-Power from seizing the opportunity to meddle in the matter."[99]

China played a passively supportive role in the crisis involving East Timor. Following a complaint by Portugal that Indonesian troops had launched military aggression against the Portuguese Territory of East Timor on December 7, 1975, the Security Council held five meetings in December 1975 and eight meetings in April 1976, adopting two resolutions in the process. Both resolutions call upon Indonesia to withdraw all her forces from East Timor, and authorize the Secretary-General to appoint a special representative for the purpose of making an on-the-spot investigation of the situation and of establishing con-

[98] UN Docs. S/PV.1764 (28 February 1974), and S/PV.1770 (28 May 1974).
[99] UN Doc. S/PV.1852 (2 November 1975), p. 17.

tact with all parties in order to ensure the implementation of the Council's resolutions.

China voted in favor of both resolutions but expressed doubt about "the necessity and usefulness of sending a representative of the Secretary-General."[100] "In our view," Lai Ya-li observed, "the responsibility of the Secretary-General is none other than to supervise the Indonesian Government's immediate withdrawal of its forces from East Timor."[101] A Chinese publicist also observed in *Jen-min jih-pao* on December 9, 1975: "Both Indonesia and East Timor belong to the third world. The people of the two countries have suffered from imperialist colonial domination, and share a common historical fate. Indonesia, which has attained independence, ought to have shown understanding, sympathy and support for the East Timor people's aspiration and action for independence. . . . The social system of East Timor can only be chosen and decided by the East Timor people themselves and cannot be imposed by any other country."[102]

In August 1976 the Security Council met three times to consider a complaint by Greece against Turkey in the Aegean territorial dispute. Greece complained of repeated flagrant violations by Turkey of the sovereign rights of Greece on her continental shelf in the Aegean, thus creating a situation dangerous to international peace and security in the area. Turkey counter-argued that if there was tension in the Aegean, the reason was that Greece had, without any legal right, resorted to military harassment of a Turkish civilian vessel, *Sismik I*, conducting research outside Greek territorial waters. After an extensive debate, the Council adopted by consensus (see Appendix H) the draft resolution sponsored by France, Italy, the United Kingdom, and the United States. The resolution called on both parties "to resume direct negotiations" so as to arrive at mutually acceptable solutions, and invited both parties "to continue to take into account the contribution that appropriate judicial means, in particular the International Court of Justice, are qualified to make to the settlement of any remaining legal differences which they may identify in connection with their present dispute."[103]

Huang Hua supported the consensual resolution because "the essential spirit of the plan lies in the appeal to Greece and Turkey to resume direct negotiations."[104] What is most revealing in this case is

[100] UN Doc. S/PV.1869 (22 December 1975), p. 7. See also UN Doc. S/PV. 1915 (22 April 1976), pp. 23-25.
[101] UN Doc. S/PV.1869 (22 December 1975), p. 7.
[102] Trans. in *PR*, No. 50 (December 12, 1975), 16.
[103] UN Doc. S/RES/395 (25 August 1976), p. 2.
[104] UN Doc. S/PV.1953 (25 August 1976) (in French), p. 46. The provisional

that, while Pakistan and Turkey expressed strong reservations about the reference to the International Court of Justice in the fourth operative paragraph in the resolution cited above, Huang Hua made no such reservations or qualifications in his support for the resolution.

In contrast to consensual peace-keeping where her words and deeds are often fraught with ambiguities and contradictions, China has more vigorously, if not always consistently, supported sanctions and enforcement measures under Chapter VII of the Charter as applied to colonial and apartheid questions. China has often linked the principle of state sovereignty (Article 2(1) of the Charter) with the principle of domestic jurisdiction (Article 2(7)) in attacking those UN activities smacking of "interventionism," which she has judged unilaterally to be "unjust."

However, neither national sovereignty nor domestic jurisdiction can stand in the way of UN support for anticolonial, antiracial, and antiimperial (antihegemonic) movements. "We maintain," declared Huang Hua before the General Assembly, "that the UN is duty-bound to support the people of various countries in their struggle against colonialism and neo-colonialism."[105] In the Security Council meeting of January 31, 1972, which was held in Africa for the first time in UN history, Huang Hua forcefully advocated that the Council should *further strengthen and expand* the sanctions against Rhodesian, South African, and Portuguese "colonialists." He then pointed out the sins of commission and of omission chargeable to the United Nations in the past:

> According to the purposes and principles of its Charter, the United Nations should support the African people's just cause of opposing imperialism, colonialism and neo-colonialism. However, as a result of obstruction and disruption by imperialism, colonialism and neo-colonialism, the United Nations *in the past* failed to play the role it should, but instead did things detrimental to the desires and interests of the African people. It was under the flag of the United Nations that imperialist aggressors [ONUC] overthrew the legitimate government of the Congo in the early days of its independence, which was led by its national hero Lumumba. And Lumumba himself was murdered in cold blood. . . . The UN must not be allowed to do anything *again* to harm the interests of the African people.[106]

verbatim record of the 1953rd meeting of the Security Council is missing from the Dag Hammarskjöld Library in its English version. I have therefore used the French version for this particular meeting.

[105] *PR*, No. 44 (November 3, 1972), 22.

[106] SCOR, 27th Year, 1630th meeting (31 January 1972), p. 10; emphasis added.

It is easy to overstate the impact of Chinese participation on UN sanction measures. It should be noted here that several committees in the General Assembly acquired in the 1960s powers to review, investigate, and admonish in this area considered as "essentially within the domestic jurisdiction" of states in the 1950s. Moreover, the Security Council had already made a formal determination through Resolution 232 (1966), that the situation in Southern Rhodesia constituted a threat to international peace and security within the meaning of the Charter and ordered political and economic sanctions, including an embargo on oil and petroleum products, under Article 41 *before* China entered the Security Council.[107] However, the Council refused to take any *military* measures against Southern Rhodesia. Hence, much of the debate centered on the implementation of Resolution 232, especially in reference to US Congressional action in the form of the Byrd Amendment, which lifted the embargo on the importation into the United States of Rhodesian chrome, ferrochrome, and nickel.

The issue came to the fore on November 16, 1971, when the General Assembly adopted a resolution, condemning, in effect, the US Congress for having passed the Byrd Amendment,[108] which constituted "a serious violation" of the relevant Security Council resolutions, and reminding all Member States of their obligations under Article 25 of the Charter to carry out the Council's decisions imposing mandatory sanctions against the illegal regime in Southern Rhodesia. The occasion presented China with her first opportunity to exercise the right to vote in the Assembly. Huang Hua voted in favor of the resolution because it was "in line with the basic stand of the Chinese Government," but quickly added that "the Chinese Delegation's support for the present resolution did not imply that it supported the previous resolutions on the subject adopted before the arrival of the Chinese Delegation."[109]

As Appendix H shows, China voted in favor of all the resolutions on the Rhodesian question that the Council adopted in 1971-76. Resolution 388, which the Council adopted unanimously on April 6, 1976, reflected in part the repeated Chinese appeal that mandatory sanctions against Rhodesia should be further strengthened and expanded. The

[107] For a detailed legal analysis of this resolution, see Myres S. McDougal and W. Michael Reisman, "Rhodesia and the United Nations: The Lawfulness of International Concern," *AJIL* 62 (January 1968), 1-19.

[108] An attempt to reimpose the embargo against the importation of Rhodesian chrome and other ores failed in Congress in September 1975 when the House defeated a motion to repeal the Byrd Amendment. However, it seems unfair to blame Congress exclusively, given the recent revelation that Henry Kissinger "took a dim view of fulfilling United Nations directives to stop importing chrome and other minerals from Rhodesia." See *NYT*, April 16, 1976, p. 4. See also note 110 below.

[109] *PR*, No. 49 (December 3, 1971), 21.

resolution, which comes under Chapter VII of the Charter, expanded mandatory sanctions to include insurance, trade names, and franchises. It was based on a recommendation in a special report (December 15, 1975) from the Council's Sanctions Committee, which has the same membership as the Council's. While voting for the resolution, Huang Hua argued that the measures adopted by the resolution were still far from adequate; moreover, he held that the sanctions should be extended to South Africa. It was also necessary to ask the United States to "cease immediately its acts of importing chrome, nickel and other materials from Southern Rhodesia in violation of the resolution on sanctions."[110]

As late as March 24, 1977, the Chinese representative Lai Ya-li was arguing in a Council meeting that the Chinese government and people "have always firmly stood by the great people of Azania [South Africa], Namibia [South West Africa], Zimbabwe [Southern Rhodesia] and the rest of Africa and resolutely support their struggle against racism, imperialism and hegemonism," and urged that the Security Council should adopt resolutions strongly condemning the crimes of the South African authorities and applying "mandatory arms embargo and economic sanctions" against South Africa.[111] In short, China's complaint about mandatory sanctions has not been that the United Nations has gone too far, as in the case of nonmandatory and noncoercive peace-keeping operations, but that it has not gone far or fast enough.

Even on the question of United Nations support for anticolonial struggles, Chinese behavior has not always shown clarity or consistency. Political expediency, more than ideological purity, seems to dictate Chinese policy on this issue. If Article 2(7) of the Charter cannot stand in the way of mandatory enforcement measures as applied to anticolonial, antiimperial, and antiracial movements, should not the United Nations be used as a lever to force withdrawal of "imperialistic" American troops from Taiwan, which the PRC claims to be

[110] UN Doc. S/PV.1907 (6 April 1976), p. 53. This issue has since become moot. On March 14, 1977, the House of Representatives repealed the Byrd Amendment of 1971 by a vote of 250-146, and the next day, March 15, 1977, the Senate followed suit with a vote of 66-26, providing the Carter Administration with a significant foreign policy victory. For details, see *NYT*, March 15, 1977, pp. 1-2, and March 16, 1977, p. A6.

[111] "Soviet Aggression Against Zaire Denounced by Chinese Representative UN Security Council," NCNA-English, United Nations (March 24, 1977) in *SPRCP*, No. 6311 (March 31, 1977), 146. It should be noted in this connection that the draft resolution that would have imposed an embargo on arms shipments to South Africa in an effort to force the South African government to relinquish control of Namibia (South-West Africa) and accede to free elections in that territory was killed on October 19, 1976, by a triple veto (see Table 4.2). China joined the 10-member majority in supporting the embargo draft resolution. See UN Doc. S/PV.1963 (19 October 1976). See also note 146 to Chapter 8.

an inalienable part of Chinese territory? Far from discussing the issue, the only interest in Taiwan the PRC has shown is to have any reference to it completely deleted from all UN documents. Likewise, as we noted in Chapter 3, the Chinese delegation has succeeded in getting Hong Kong and Macao deleted from the list of "colonial territories." Significantly, this request was never published in the Chinese media.

Perhaps the most serious challenge to the credibility of China as a firm and consistent supporter of UN sanctions against colonialism was presented by the Angolan crisis. China's credibility suffered by the strange bedfellows she made both during and after some nine years of the Angolan national liberation struggle against Portugal. Although the Alvor Agreement signed between Portugal and the Angolan national liberation movements—the Popular Movement for the Liberation of Angola (MPLA) under Agostinho Neto, the National Front for the Liberation of Angola (FNLA) under Holden Roberto, and the National Union for the Total Independence of Angola (UNITA) under Jonas Savimbi—in January 1975 granted to Angola independence from Portugal, the actual accession to independence was scheduled to take place on November 11, 1975.

However, the Agreement served as a catalytic agent in bringing about a civil war among the national liberation movements, in which the three competing organizations were all seeking and receiving varying degrees of external assistance. When the promised date of accession to independence came in November 1975, Portugal simply departed, handing the power over to the people of Angola. Though China preferred UNITA, she, along with the United States, Belgium, West Germany, France, Zaire, *and South Africa*, was providing assistance to the pro-Western FNLA, while the stronger and more radical movement, MPLA, was getting military assistance from the Soviet Union, Cuba, Algeria, Mozambique, and Guinea-Bissau. In response to the OAU's call for neutrality among the three rival movements, however, the Chinese made the decision to withdraw their military instructors from the FNLA camps in Zaire in July 1975, and two months later they did in fact do so.[112]

After the MPLA won the civil war, China refused to extend diplomatic recognition to the Angolan government headed by Neto. But a more critical test came on March 31, 1976, when the Security Council had to vote on a draft resolution sponsored by Benin, Guyana, the Libyan Arab Republic, Panama, Romania, and the United Republic of Tanzania. "We absolutely cannot agree to it," declared Huang Hua, much to the surprise of the Third World members of the Coun-

[112] Colin Legum, "The Soviet Union, China and the West in Southern Africa," *Foreign Affairs* 54 (July 1976), 751.

cil.[113] Huang Hua stopped short of vetoing the draft resolution by not participating in the vote, while France, Japan, Italy, the United Kingdom, and the United States abstained. Thus, the draft resolution barely passed by a vote of 9:0:5 with one nonparticipation. If we accept five abstentions and China's nonparticipation as "hidden oppositions," however, the vote followed the North-South bipolarity in UN politics.

What is so revealing of Chinese diplomacy in this case is that Security Council Resolution 387 appears *prima facie* as if it were made in Peking to reflect China's oft-declared "principled stand." It condemns South Africa's aggression against Angola; it demands that South Africa desist from utilizing the international territory of Namibia to mount provocative acts against Angola; it calls upon South Africa to meet the just claims of Angola for full compensation for the damage and destruction inflicted on its territory, and for the restoration of the equipment and materials seized by the invading forces.

In short, this was clearly an anti-South African resolution or, as Peking would have it, a resolution that makes a distinction between the aggressor and the victim of aggression. China's rationale for opposition followed closely the arguments of the abstaining Western powers and Japan to the effect that condemnation should be extended to all foreign military forces in Angola—referring, of course, to the Soviet and Cuban troops.

In a similar vein, China repeated her "opposition" in the form of nonparticipation on the Angolan membership question on June 23, 1976, while the United States carried the burden of killing Angola's application for membership through her solo veto. When the question came up again late 1976, the United States abstained, while China opted for nonparticipation.[114] In an emotional speech before the Assem-

[113] UN Doc. S/PV.1906 (31 March 1976), p. 137.

[114] For example, the representative of Benin reacted to the Chinese position in the following manner: "My delegation sincerely regrets also the position adopted last June by the PRC. The Chinese people is a lucid and moderate people, and we hope that a closer analysis of the situation will make it possible for them better to analyze the situation, in a way more in keeping with the aspirations of the Angolan people and of all the peoples of the African continent." See UN Doc. S/PV.1974 (22 November 1976), p. 12.

However, the Fifth Conference of Heads of States or Governments of Non-Aligned Countries avoided condemning China in its resolution on Angola's UN membership; instead, the resolution "strongly condemns the anachronistic stand taken by the United States of America which flouts the fundamental principles of international law as reflected by the inadmissibility of interference in the internal affairs of the People's Republic of Angola." A partial text of the resolution is reprinted in *Alternatives* 3 (December 1977), 294. As for China, Chinese representative Lai Ya-li refused to repeat the argument advanced when the Angolan membership was first brought to the attention of the Council in June 1976, saying that the PRC's position was known to all. See UN Doc. S/PV.1974 (22 November 1976), pp. 3, 83.

bly's plenary on December 1, 1976, immediately following the adoption of a resolution admitting Angola into the United Nations, Foreign Minister Jose Eduardo dos Santos of Angola attacked both the United States and China for their positions. There had been an "unnatural alliance" of China, imperialism, and South Africa, charged the foreign minister, adding that mercenaries recruited by South Africa had been paid in American dollars and killed Angolans with weapons "made by the Chinese proletariat."[115]

It does not require ideological purity to detect some inconsistencies and contradictions in Chinese behavior on peace-keeping and enforcement questions in the Security Council. However, modern Machiavellians could easily accept the Chinese inconsistencies as evidence of realism and flexibility in the pursuit of national interests, while Maoists could probably justify the Chinese contradictions as a short-term tactical necessity in the protracted diplomatic struggle in the United Nations. Caught between principles and interests, Chinese action often seems to follow the latter, while Chinese rhetoric pays lip service to the former. China has often escaped the burden of taking a clear and consistent stand on peace-keeping operations by opting for nonparticipation.

The routine and habitual escape from the responsibility incumbent upon China as a permanent member of the Security Council means, in effect, that the impact of Chinese participation on peace-keeping, and to a lesser extent on sanction measures, is negligible except on the matter of financing. China has made neither a positive contribution nor offered negative obstruction to the development of peace-keeping activities, as the Council is allowed to move without her interference. Nonparticipation, which had remained an oddity in the development of the Council's decision-making process before the PRC's entry, has been transformed into an art in Chinese diplomacy, as it signifies at one and the same time both passive opposition and passive cooperation.

Impact on Financing of UN Peace-keeping Operations

Until the establishment of UNEF II and UNDOF, the methods of financing UN peace-keeping activities varied widely. Such observer peace-keeping missions as UNTSO, UNMOGIP, UNOGIL, and UNIPOM were financed out of the regular budget, while the costs of some observer groups (UNYOM and UNTEA) were divided among the parties concerned. However, it was the financing of the two peace-keeping operations involving military forces—UNEF I and ONUC—that generated a serious constitutional, political, and financial crisis in 1964-65.

---

[115] *NYT*, December 2, 1976, p. 8.

The crucial issue was this: Which political organ of the United Nations, the General Assembly or the Security Council, could constitutionally determine the nature and scope of peace-keeping operations, as well as determine the form and assessment of some $400 million incurred in UNEF I and ONUC operations? In the face of this crisis, which threatened to wreck the Organization, the General Assembly took the time-honored approach of establishing a committee—the Special Committee on Peace-keeping Operations—and instructing the Committee to undertake a comprehensive review of the whole question of peace-keeping operations in all their aspects, including ways of overcoming the financial difficulties of the Organization.[116]

The Article 19 showdown was averted when the United States retreated in the Special Committee in August 1965, enabling the Committee to formulate and issue the following consensus: "(a) That the General Assembly will carry on its work normally in accordance with its rules of procedure; (b) That the question of the applicability of Article 19 of the Charter will not be raised with regard to the United Nations Emergency Force (UNEF) and the United Nations Operation in the Congo (ONUC); (c) That the financial difficulties of the Organization should be solved through voluntary contributions by Member States, with the highly developed countries making substantial contributions."[117] Thus, the 20th General Assembly was able to achieve a breakthrough when all Member States agreed to a formula of voluntary contributions to overcome the insolvency of the Organization.

The 1964 Cyprus conflict flared up in the midst of the financial crisis. To avoid aggravating the situation, the Security Council decided to establish UNFICYP, but its costs were to be financed entirely through voluntary contributions. This decision solved the political problem, to be sure, but the Secretary-General has been complaining annually that voluntary contributions are unsatisfactory as a practical method of financing major peace-keeping operations. The accumulated deficit of the UNFICYP account—the costs ($249.6 million) less the voluntary contributions ($204.9 million)—stood at $44.7 million as of December 15, 1976.[118]

Although the authorizing resolution for UNEF II makes no reference to the method of financing, the Council, through a series of informal consultations (from which China dissociated herself), accepted the statement of the Secretary-General that "the costs of the Force shall be considered as expenses of the Organization to be borne by the Mem-

[116] General Assembly Resolution 2006 (XIX) of 18 February 1965.
[117] GAOR, 19th Sess., Annexes, UN Doc. A/5911/Add.1, Annex No. 21, p. 92.
[118] *Report of the Secretary-General on the United Nations Operation in Cyprus*, UN Doc. S/12253 (9 December 1976), p. 19.

bers in accordance with Article 17, paragraph 2, of the Charter."[119] The Soviet Union voted in favor of the resolution "by way of an exception and in this particular instance" out of respect for the nonaligned members of the Council and Egypt.[120]

However, the most extensive debate on the question of financing UNEF II took place in the Fifth Committee at its 1603rd to 1610th meetings during the period November 19-26, 1973. As will be noted below, the PRC's most comprehensive exposition on the question was given in the course of the Committee's debate. When the 37-power draft resolution (A/C.5/L.1130/Rev.1) was finally put to a recorded vote on November 23, 1973, China opted for nonparticipation in the vote. The draft resolution was approved by a vote of 105:2 (Albania, Libyan Arab Republic), with 4 abstentions, and was submitted to the Assembly for final action.[121] It is worth noting that the Fifth Committee, while accepting the principle of collective responsibility, affirmed that a "different procedure is required from that applied to meet expenditures of the regular budget of the United Nations." Likewise, ACABQ favored creating a special account rather than providing for the expenses within the regular budget.

On December 11, 1973, the General Assembly adopted by a vote of 108:3:23—with China again not participating—Resolution 3101 (XXVIII) to appropriate $30 million for the first six months of UNEF II. It is worth pointing out several important features of this resolution. First, the Assembly reaffirmed that "a different procedure is required from that applied to meet expenditures of the regular budget of the United Nations." Second, it accepted the Soviet position by deciding that this particular method of financing was to be construed "as an *ad hoc* arrangement, without prejudice to the positions of principle that may be taken by Member States in any consideration by the General Assembly of arrangements for the financing of peace-keeping operations." Third, the Assembly adopted a special scale for UNEF II (later applied also to UNDOF) by recognizing the heavy responsibilities of the permanent members of the Security Council, on the one hand, and by applying more rigorously the capacity-to-pay principle to other Member States, on the other. As a result, the Assembly established four categories of Member States for the purpose of apportioning UNEF II expenses: (1) 63.15 percent of the total—instead of 54.64 percent if the regular budget assessment rates were used—among the

---

[119] UN Doc. S/11052/Rev.1 (27 October 1973). Article 17(2) of the UN Charter reads: "The expenses of the Organization shall be borne by the Members as apportioned by the General Assembly."
[120] UN Doc. S/PV.1750 (25 October 1973), pp. 26-27, 48, 57.
[121] UN Doc. A/9428 (10 December 1973), pp. 1-15.

permanent members of the Security Council; (2) 34.78 percent among the economically developed Member States who are not permanent members of the Security Council; (3) 2.02 percent among the economically less developed Member States; and (4) 0.05 percent among the economically least developed Member States. Finally, the Assembly established a special account for UNEF II in order to emphasize the *ad hoc* nature of the Force.

Table 4.5 gives a detailed quantitative breakdown of UNEF II and UNDOF apportionments among the four categories of Member States from 1973 to 1976 and China's share. China's assessments for the period under review amount to over $16 million, representing 6.36 percent of the total. Yet, the PRC joined her predecessor ROC and the other withholders of UNEF I and ONUC special accounts by refusing to pay. The PRC's noncompliance differs from that of the ROC in one aspect, however. The PRC dissociated herself from every vote on, or discussion of, the authorizing resolutions in both the Security Council and the General Assembly on UNEF II and UNDOF, whereas the ROC refused to pay even after she had voted for the authorizing resolutions for UNEF I and ONUC in the General Assembly.[122]

China's refusal to pay has a logic and explanation of its own. Her financial noncompliance on peace-keeping highlights once again the old problem in the United Nations: whether or not it is legal, a major power may refuse to pay its share of the cost of UN military operations if it deems this to be detrimental to its interests and/or principles. What is China's rationale? Chinese representative Wang Wei-tsai presented an authoritative exposition of China's stand in the Fifth Committee on November 20, 1973, when the issue was first discussed. Ever since, the PRC has assumed a reticent posture, stating that China's stand on the issue had already been explained and that there was no need for repetition.

Reduced to their essence, the PRC's arguments and explanations are all based on the simple proposition that UNEF II runs counter to her conceptualization of world order. Basing his stand on this premise, Wang Wei-tsai advanced the following arguments in the Fifth Committee. First, the two superpowers had lost no time in imposing a "cease-fire in place" on the Security Council so as to put an end to the Arab people's just war against Israeli aggression. The so-called cease-fire was in fact an attempt to perpetuate a status quo of "no war, no peace" in the Middle East at the very moment when the Israeli Zionists had been isolated for the first time. Second, UNEF II was the product of "secret deals" between the two superpowers, designed to institu-

---

[122] See General Assembly Resolution 1001 (ES-I) of 7 November 1956; and General Assembly Resolution 1474 (ES-IV) of 20 September 1960.

tionalize superpower hegemonic contention and collusion in this strategic theater. Third, it was "only in consideration of the wish expressed by the victims" of aggression (Egypt) that China had decided not to participate in the vote rather than to veto the authorizing resolution.

Given these circumstances, the argument continued, to regard the costs of the Force as *expenses of the Organization* "was tantamount to requesting all Member States to pull the chestnuts out of the fire for the two super-Powers." The United Nations had already been given serious lessons on peace-keeping activities, which brought about "a harmful influence on the normal activities of the Organization." China had done her very best to participate in the regular expenses of the Organization by supporting "all justified expenses that were in accord with the aims and principles of the Charter." The Soviet argument that anyone who refused to participate in the financing of UNEF II would violate the Charter was a distortion, as Article I of the Charter "explicitly provided that one of the purposes of the United Nations was to suppress acts of aggression." There was an almost schizophrenic quality in Wang Wei-tsai's argumentation when he asserted that China's position "had won the sympathy and support of many countries."[123] In fact, only three countries—Albania, Libya, and Syria—supported China's position by voting against General Assembly Resolution 3101 (XXVIII). Curiously, China herself opted for nonparticipation rather than voting against the resolution.

What has been the impact of the PRC's refusal to participate in the financing of UNEF II and UNDOF? Table 4.6 gives the Secretary-General's report on the status of contributions as of October 31, 1976. It is apparent—thanks to the compliance of the overwhelming majority of Member States—that China's refusal could hardly have any crippling or even serious effect on the continuing operation of UNEF II and UNDOF. As of October 31, 1976, for example, $226.2 million (83.8 percent of the total apportioned) had been received. More importantly, only $17.3 million was apportioned to the Member States that have declared their intention not to pay, and over $16.7 million of this sum

---

[123] GAOR, 28th Sess., Fifth Committee, 1604th meeting (20 November 1973), paras. 60-66. For the Chinese press release on this meeting, see "Debate at UN General Assembly on Cost of UNEF to Middle East," NCNA-English, United Nations (November 24, 1973), in *SMCP*, No. 5509 (December 5, 1973), 154-55. For repetition of Wang Wei-tsai's explanation in the Fifth Committee in subsequent discussions, see the following: UN Doc. A/PV.2303 (29 November 1974), pp. 76-80; GAOR, 29th Sess., Fifth Committee, 1654th meeting (31 October 1974), para. 16; UN Doc. A/PV.2389 (30 October 1975), p. 16; UN Doc. A/C.5/SR.1725 (4 November 1975), p. 3; UN Doc. A/C.5/SR.1752 (3 December 1975), p. 12; UN Doc. A/31/PV.41 (26 October 1976), p. 6; UN Doc. A/C.5/31/SR.14 (22 October 1976), p. 13.

TABLE 4.5. Assessments for UNEF II and UNDOF, and the PRC's Share, 1973-76 ($)

Operation	Inclusive Dates	Authorizing Resolution	Sum Appropriated	Apportioning Formula		PRC's Share
UNEF II	Oct. 25, 1973-Apr. 24, 1974	GA Res. 3101 (XXVIII)	30,000,000	A	18,945,000	1,907,762.00
				B	10,434,000	
				C	606,000	
				D	15,000	
UNEF II, UNDOF	Apr. 25, 1974-Oct. 24, 1974	GA Res. 3211 B (XXIX)	30,000,000	A	18,945,000	1,907,762.00
				B	10,434,000	
				C	606,000	
				D	15,000	
UNEF II, UNDOF	Oct. 25, 1973-Oct. 24, 1974	GA Res. 3211 B (XXIX)	19,800,000	A	12,503,700	1,259,122.59
				B	6,886,440	
				C	399,960	
				D	9,900	
UNEF II, UNDOF	Oct. 25, 1974-Apr. 24, 1975	GA Res. 3211 B (XXIX)	40,000,000	A	25,260,000	2,543,682.00
				B	13,912,000	
				C	808,000	
				D	20,000	
UNEF II, UNDOF	Apr. 25, 1975-Oct. 24, 1975	GA Res. 3374 B (XXX)	40,000,000	A	25,260,000	2,543,683.00
				B	13,912,000	
				C	808,000	
				D	20,000	

Operation	Period	Resolution	Amount	Category	Value	Amount
UNEF II	Oct. 25, 1975-Oct. 24, 1976	GA Res. 3374 B (XXX)	94,275,000	A	59,638,365	6,005,583.36
				B	32,647,432	
				C	1,932,638	
				D	56,565	
UNDOF	Oct. 25, 1975-Nov. 11, 1975	GA Res. 3374 C (XXX)	1,600,000	A	1,012,160	101,924.51
				B	554,080	
				C	32,800	
				D	960	
UNDOF	Dec. 1, 1975-May 31, 1976	GA Res. 3374 C (XXX)	7,731,818	A	4,891,148	492,538.60
				B	2,677,529	
				C	158,502	
				D	4,639	
Total			263,406,818			16,762,057.06

A = Permanent members of the Security Council; B = Economically developed Member States who are not permanent members of the Security Council; C = Economically less developed Member States; and D = Economically least developed Member States.

TABLE 4.6. Status of Contributions for UNEF II and UNDOF
as of October 31, 1976 (in million $)

| | For year ended | | | |
	Oct. 24, 1974	Oct. 24, 1975	Oct. 24, 1976[a]	Total
Amounts Appropriated	79.8	80.0	103.6	263.4
Additional Commitment	–	–	6.4	6.4
Amounts Apportioned	79.8	80.0	110.0	269.8
Payments Received	74.4	73.7	78.1	226.2
Balance Due	5.4	6.3	31.9	43.6
Apportioned to Member States who have stated they do not intend to pay	5.1	5.1	7.1	17.3
Estimated Collectable Balance	0.3	1.2	24.8	26.3

[a] Through October 31, 1976 in the case of UNDOF.

Source: *Financing of the United Nations Emergency Force and of the United Nations Disengagement Observer Force,* Report of the Secretary-General, UN Doc. A/31/288 (19 November 1976), p. 3.

belongs to the Chinese assessment. Unlike UNEF I and ONUC, then, the financing of UNEF II and UNDOF has avoided serious difficulties.

Field interviews revealed a rather curious tendency, among national delegates and international civil servants alike, to underplay consciously and deliberately the negative effect of the PRC's refusal to pay. Almost every person interviewed, when asked, responded cautiously and evasively that the less said on the subject of the PRC's refusal to pay, the better for the successful continuation of UNEF II and UNDOF. There was a strong determination not to reopen the Pandora's box of Article 19. In fact, there was no consensus that Article 19 could indeed be invoked, given the ambiguous and somewhat contradictory principles and qualifications embodied in General Assembly Resolution 3101 (XXVIII).[124] There was also a fear that China might easily

[124] To cite just one illustrative example, the operative paragraph 1 of the resolution decides and apportions $30 million among the Member States, but the last paragraph "invites voluntary contributions to the United Nations Emergency Force both in cash and in the form of services and supplies acceptable to the Secretary-General." Likewise, the need for voluntary contributions is stressed in all the subsequent Assembly resolutions—3211 B (XXIX) of 29 November 1974; 3374 B (XXX) of 28 November 1975; 3374 C (XXX) of 2 December 1975; 31/5 C of 22 December 1976; and 31/5 D of 22 December 1976—on the financing of UNEF II and UNDOF. One may ask why it is necessary for the Assembly to stress again and again such voluntary contributions if its assessments are

resort to the veto when pushed on this issue. Both UNEF II and UNDOF are subject to periodic renewal by the Council. Likewise, the question of finance has been relegated to secondary importance in the Special Committee on Peace-keeping Operations, which continues its tenacious efforts to establish guidelines for UN peace-keeping.[125]

A final ominous note on the financing of peace-keeping needs to be added. In an official communication (dated December 30, 1976) sent to the Secretary-General, the Soviet Union stated that she would not pay her full assessments for UNEF II. She gave as her reason that the Soviet Union had been excluded from the making of the second Egyptian-Israeli agreement on troop disengagement in the Sinai Peninsula, the culmination of Henry Kissinger's shuttle diplomacy in 1975. As a result, the Soviet note stated, UNEF II was incurring additional expenses through the enlarged responsibilities involved in implementing the second disengagement agreement. "The Soviet Union had nothing to do with this agreement," the Soviet note stated, "concluded on a separate basis and actually circumventing the Geneva peace conference. The Soviet Union, therefore, cannot bear any responsibility for the implications of the said agreement, including the financing of additional expenses of the United Nations forces resulting from the agreement."[126] The new Soviet permanent representative Oleg A. Troyanovsky refused to elaborate on the official communication of his government, but it has certainly struck an ominous note for the prospects of peace-keeping.[127]

AN ASSESSMENT

The foregoing analysis of reciprocal interactions between China and the Security Council affords a basis for a few broad generalizations. First of all, what has been the impact of Chinese participation on the Security Council? Symbolically, both the image and the prestige of the Security Council in the global community have been made more

---

mandatory. It is beyond the purview of this chapter to pursue this legal question. But it may be noted that the United States made a voluntary contribution to UNEF II in kind of about $10 million. See *Financing of the United Nations Emergency Force and of the United Nations Disengagement Observer Force*, Report of the Secretary-General, UN Doc. A/31/288 (19 November 1976), p. 3.

[125] For a recent progress report of the Special Committee, see *Comprehensive Review of the Whole Question of Peace-keeping Operations in All Their Aspects*, Report of the Special Committee on Peace-keeping Operations, UN Doc. A/31/337 (23 November 1976).

[126] *NYT*, January 7, 1977, p. A3.

[127] For the State Department's quick reaction to the Soviet note, see *NYT*, January 8, 1977, p. 7.

legitimate, more representative, more realistic, more colorful, and more relevant. In practical terms, the Security Council's political effectiveness has also been enhanced to the extent that the presence of China has contributed to bridging the gap between authority claims and power capabilities in the Council. The decision-making process will continue to be helped by Chinese participation, provided the Soviet Union and the United States avoid dominating the Council's consultative-consensual process and avoid projecting their cooperation as evidence of working détente. In fact, the consensual decision-making process is of mutual benefit to China and the Council, as it expedites the work of the Council while minimizing the attention paid to the inconsistencies and contradictions inherent in China's pursuit of multiple interests in the United Nations.

The continuous operation of UNFICYP, UNEF II, and UNDOF shows that Chinese ideological opposition to peace-keeping expressed in the form of nonparticipation and dissociation translates into Chinese "cooperation" in the form of noninterference in the authorization and implementation processes. It may also be argued that Chinese behavior has influenced the Soviet Union to become more cooperative about peace-keeping. However, the Chinese refusal to pay assessments for UNEF II and UNDOF operations has introduced an additional burden into the perennial search to solve the financial crisis in the United Nations.

The Council's impact on Chinese diplomacy is difficult to assess, since we know little about the foreign policy-making process in Peking or about interactions between the Chinese permanent mission in New York and the Foreign Ministry at home. It is also difficult to separate the real from the rhetorical, as they often seem two integral parts in the dialectical process. Nonetheless, the behavioral characteristics of Chinese diplomacy suggest that the influence of the Security Council is rather subtle and indirect. That is, the Security Council as an institution seems to exert less influence on China than its other members, especially the Soviet Union and Third World Member States. It was the pressure exerted by the nonaligned Third World members of the Council that dissuaded China from casting her veto on the authorizing resolution for UNEF II.

At times, Chinese diplomacy in the Security Council has conveyed the impression of following an actor-oriented rather than an issue-oriented approach. In the course of Council debate on the Angolan membership question, the Cuban representative charged that China's policy was governed by the Chinese saying: "We must oppose everything the enemy defends and defend everything the enemy opposes."[128]

[128] UN Doc. S/PV.1932 (23 June 1976), p. 146.

238

This is an exaggeration, to be sure, but the Chinese sometimes showed more interest and concern about the *who* question than about the *what* question. Despite his vehement attack on the Soviet abuse of the veto, Huang Hua expressed only mild *pro forma* regrets when the other permanent members cast their veto. When the French representative cast his solo veto, blocking the admission of the Comoros on February 6, 1976, China was reticent. Apparently, the Security Council is valued more as a sword with which to fight against the revisionist social-imperialists than as a shield to protect the interests of the Third World.

Has the Security Council reradicalized or deradicalized Chinese diplomacy? Actually, Chinese policy in the Council reveals a striking discrepancy between verbal behavior and voting behavior. If one judges by voting behavior in the Council, for example, Maoist ideology seems to have played a marginal role. That China has been inconsistent on some issues illustrates her tendency, at least for the moment, to zig-zag carefully in following the changing dictates of political and strategic calculus in the Security Council, especially on African questions. The Palmerstonian dictum about perennial national interests seems to offer a better guide than quotations from Chairman Mao. Of course, it would be premature to say whether such an approach represents a basic change in strategy or merely a transient tactical posture.

However, the opportunistic pursuit of national interests is often concealed by verbal behavior that relies extensively on legitimizing ideological dialectics or selective invocation of the Charter principles and relevant resolutions of the General Assembly or the Security Council. China has often sweetened her verbal behavior in the Council with repeated references to those resolutions that she deems valid, just, or convenient, as we have seen in the elaborate legal defense of her veto on the Bangladesh membership question. Yet she has also been contemptuous of certain other resolutions that she regards as unjust or ineffective. During the heated debate on the Middle East question on October 23, 1973, Huang Hua characterized Security Council Resolution 339 (1973) as "a scrap of paper that could solve no problems."[129] Would it not make more sense to veto a scrap of paper than to attack it after it had already been adopted? Not necessarily, because China, unlike the superpowers, always shows consideration and respect for "the requests repeatedly made by the victims of aggression." This is indeed a "have your cake and eat it, too" posture that China has adopted in the Security Council. It is the Chinese way of reconciling principles and interests.

[129] UN Doc. S/PV.1750 (25 October 1973), p. 6.

Finally, one may ask: What is China's conceptualization of world order as expressed in her behavior in the Security Council? How compatible is this with the Council's conceptualization of world order? While the Council and China have helped each other through a mutual enhancement of symbolic capabilities, there remains some serious conceptual conflict between the two. The Council has moved away from the Charter system of collective security to consensual peace-keeping, while China still clings to the grandiose notion in the Charter system that purports to make a clear distinction between the aggressor and the victim of aggression. In fact, the tendency of the Council to attempt to bring about a settlement while studiously avoiding the determination of the guilty aggressor has been one of the main Chinese complaints.

Consensual peace-keeping has developed the pacifistic tendency to condemn any or all use of violence in international relations. But the Chinese have repeatedly stressed the Maoist distinction between just and unjust war, revolutionary and counter-revolutionary violence. The Soviet advocacy of the nonuse of force in international relations has been condemned by the Chinese as a reactionary doctrine. The critical question for the Council is to localize and neutralize any violence so as to arrest its escalation into a wider and larger conflict. The critical question for the Chinese, on the other hand, is: *Who* uses force against *whom* for *what* purposes?

Moreover, the Council is more concerned about negative peace, while China is more concerned about positive peace.[130] The Council is more concerned about direct physical violence in international relations, while China is more concerned about structural violence in the system of world dominance. The tendency of the Council to concern itself exclusively with violence works toward the consolidation of the status quo. China as a revisionist newcomer is committed to changing the international status quo. The Council disdains disorder; China welcomes it as a challenge and opportunity to bring about a systemic change. The Council welcomes Soviet-American détente as a *sine qua non* for its effective operation, while China warns of the perils of superpower hegemony and presents itself as a countervailing force to check the danger of superpower domination in the Council's decision-making process.

As a revolutionary actor, China's long-range world order task in the United Nations centers on the development of new rules and

---

[130] For a lucid and authoritative exposition on the concepts of negative peace, positive peace, physical violence, and structural violence, and their uses in peace research, see Johan Galtung, *Peace: Essays in Peace Research* (Copenhagen: Christian Ejlers, 1975), Vol. I, pp. 109-40. The PRC's position on this question will be discussed in Chapter 8.

institutions congenial to the promotion of political and economic change. This orientation is both experiential and conceptual. China still suffers from the trauma of the Korean War and the Organization's involvement in that war. She refuses to make a distinction between the police action in Korea and peace-keeping operations. The experiential legacy of the Korean War still influences the Chinese response to UN peace-keeping.

Conceptually, China believes that it is imperative to restructure the present international system in such a way as to make it more responsive to the welfare of the weak and the poor. Her active interest and participation in the UN global conferences on population, food, environment, the law of the sea, desertification, and the status of women reflect this orientation. As noted briefly in Chapter 3 and as will be further elaborated in Chapter 5, Chinese support of the establishment of a New International Economic Order has been firm and consistent. In short, China works in her own way toward building a new conceptual environment for world order.

So far the Council and China have maintained a posture of mutual respect and peaceful coexistence in spite of the conceptual conflict. Experience in the United Nations may have a positive or negative impact on any Member State, depending largely on its original hopes and expectations. That China has shown no sign of disinterest or disillusionment with the Security Council is a hopeful sign. The underlying conceptual conflict notwithstanding, China has given no evidence of wanting to use the Security Council as a forum to proselytize her revolutionary political culture. In view of the many disappointments she has experienced with revolutionary movements and also her sense of protracted historical process, China may yet be able to make use of her symbolic capabilities to broaden and update the Council's conceptualization of world order in the nuclear-ecological age. The Security Council without China can hardly hope to do this. But the Security Council with China in just might—at least we can now hope so.

THE NEW INTERNATIONAL
ECONOMIC ORDER, I:
THE INAUGURAL PROCESS

Since the epochal 6th Special Session of the General Assembly, a New International Economic Order (NIEO) has become increasingly prominent in the vocabulary of Chinese global politics. China has integrated NIEO with her own principled stand on development. Such an integration has a dual and mutually interactive effect. China's own conceptualization of world order has been legitimized to a large degree by NIEO, on the one hand, and NIEO has been blessed with Chinese support, on the other. Chinese policy pronouncements and their elaboration in the various organs, agencies, and committees of the United Nations system charged with developmental activities have followed the NIEO conceptual guideline in the mid-1970s. Likewise, NIEO has become a legitimized instrument with which to remold the rules, structures, and programs of UN development enterprise. Even *Jen-min jih-pao* has begun to report and analyze global economic issues in terms of NIEO (*Hsin kuo-chi ching-chi chih-hsü*).[1]

The Chinese role in the development of NIEO cannot—and should not—be studied in isolation from the larger political and economic forces that emerged on the world scene in the early 1970s. Clearly, NIEO is an ongoing and protracted process, and the term NIEO is used in this sense throughout this study. For analytical convenience, however, we may divide the process into three separate stages: the disintegrating process of the old economic order (Stage I); the inauguration process of a new economic order (Stage II); and the implementation process of that order (Stage III). This chapter is confined to the first two stages and the next chapter deals with the third stage.

THE DISARRAY OF THE POSTWAR ECONOMIC ORDER

The postwar economic order established at Bretton Woods and Havana[2] was designed mainly to deal with the economic problems

---

[1] *Jen-min jih-pao* usually devotes page 5 or 6 to regular reporting and analysis of issues or activities related to NIEO.

[2] Delegates from all 44 of the United and Associated Nations attended a conference called by President Franklin D. Roosevelt, held at Bretton Woods, New

facing Western capitalist countries. The Third World, as we call it today, did not yet exist, and UN membership stood at about one-third of today's total. In its first two and a half decades, the postwar economic order served the rich and powerful nations well, it is widely believed in the Third World, while providing only first-aid measures for the poor countries in the world economic system. Helped by abundant raw materials and oil, bought at exploitative prices from the less developed countries (LDCs), the West and Japan experienced unparalleled economic growth and prosperity.

The postwar economic order also worked to perpetuate the established pattern of development-underdevelopment, dominance-dependence, and center-periphery relations. In the period 1950-68, for example, per capita gross domestic product grew at an annual average of 2.5 percent in the LDCs, compared with 3.3 percent in the developed part of the world.[3] The development gap between northern affluence and southern poverty in the world economic system is shown in Table 5.1: 17.9 percent of the world population in the center had at its disposal 65.7 percent of the Gross Global Product (GGP), that is, approximately 70 percent of the world's population enjoyed only about 30 percent of the world's income.

However, Table 5.1 does not reveal the grim reality: the absolute number of the hungry and the malnourished in the world had been increasing. "Of the 2,600 million inhabitants of the developing world," the nonaligned countries declared at the 1973 Algiers Summit, "800 million are illiterate, almost 1,000 million are suffering from malnutrition or hunger, and 900 million have a daily income of less than 30 U.S. cents."[4] This was a warning of a coming "revolution" from the periphery against the center in the world economic system.

Because of high rates of population growth, averaging 2.4 percent in the period 1950-70, the per capita growth rate in food production in

---

Hampshire, from July 1 to July 22, 1944. The Bretton Woods Conference produced the constitutions, or Articles of Agreement, of two agencies conceived as sister institutions: IBRD (or World Bank) and IMF. IMF came into existence on December 27, 1945. On the same day IBRD also came into existence, when the Bank's constitution (Articles of Agreement) was signed in Washington, D.C., by the representatives of the 29 governments. The creation of GATT has a complicated history, but the Havana Charter, produced at a 56-nation conference in Havana (from November 21, 1947, to March 24, 1948), laid the groundwork for later completion of a General Agreement on Tariffs and Trade. GATT came into force on January 1, 1948, with 23 contracting parties.

[3] Anibal Pinto, "The Center-Periphery System Twenty Years After," in Norman Girvan, ed., *Dependence and Underdevelopment in the New World and the Old* (*Social and Economic Studies*, 22:1 [March 1973]), p. 41.

[4] Fourth Conference of Heads of State or Government of Non-Aligned Countries, Algiers, September 5-9, 1973, *Economic Declaration*, UN Doc. A/9330 (22 November 1973), p. 60.

TABLE 5.1. Balance Between GNP and Population Distribution
in the World, 1973 (percent)

	GNP	Population
North America	30.0	6.1
Europe (excluding the USSR)	31.8	13.2
USSR	10.7	6.5
Asia (including Middle East and excluding Japan)	10.2	52.7
Japan	8.3	2.8
Central and South America	5.2	7.9
Africa	2.4	10.2
Oceania	1.5	0.6
Total	100.0	100.0
Developed Market Economies[a]	65.7	17.9
Centrally Planned Economies[b]	20.2	32.0
Developing Countries	14.2	50.1
Total	100.0	100.0

[a] Australia, Austria, Belgium, Canada, Denmark, Finland, France, Fed. Rep. of Germany, Iceland, Ireland, Italy, Japan, Luxembourg, Netherlands, New Zealand, Norway, Portugal, Puerto Rico, South Africa, Sweden, Switzerland, United Kingdom, and United States.

[b] Albania, Bulgaria, PRC, Cuba, Czechoslovakia, Dem. Rep. of Germany, Hungary, Dem. Rep. of Korea, Poland, Romania, USSR, Dem. Rep. of Vietnam.

Source: Based on World Bank Atlas, 1975: Population, Per Capita Product, and Growth Rates (Washington, D.C.: World Bank Group, 1975).

the LDCs actually declined from 0.7 percent in the 1950s to 0.2 percent (which represents a per capita gain of only 400 grams) in the 1960s, while the gain in the industrialized northern countries during the same period was nearly thirty times greater and averaged 11,250 grams.[5] As Table 5.2 shows, all the developing regions of the world used to export cereals before World War II, but now found themselves at the mercy of the breadbasket in North America.

That political liberation of developing countries from their colonial bondage betrayed the reality of their economic dependence is shown in a number of important indicators in the international monetary and trade systems. First and foremost, the LDCs' share of world trade steadily declined from 31.9 percent in 1950 to 21.4 percent in 1960 and to 17.2 percent in 1970. As the trade gap between the developed and developing parts of the world has increased, the LDCs' role in

[5] Reshaping the International Order, A Report to the Club of Rome (New York: Dutton, 1976), pp. 28-29.

TABLE 5.2. International Trade in Cereals, 1934/38-75
Import/Export (million tons)

		1934/38		1975	
		Import	Export	Import	Export
From Surplus to Deficit	Latin America		9	3	
	Africa		1	10	
	Asia		2	47	
	USSR		5	25	
Remaining in Deficit	Western Europe	24		17	
Becoming Major Exporters	North America	5			94
	Australia/New Zealand	3			9

Source: Lester R. Brown, *The Politics and Responsibility of the North American Breadbasket*, Worldwatch Paper 2, October 1975.

the expanding international economy has become correspondingly weakened. The generalized trade gap is reflected in an asymmetrical growth between the demand for primary commodities and the demand for industrial goods. As Figure 5.1 illustrates, the demand for primary commodities has a built-in stability, while the demand for manufactured goods accelerates in proportion to the rising appetite of the affluent society in the center.

Second, the trade gap is closely linked to the progressive deterioration of the terms of trade for developing countries. The asymmetry between the demands of the two types of goods (primary and manufactured) results in an asymmetry between the relative values of the two types of goods. That is, the value of primary commodities has declined relative to the value of manufactured products in world trade. This steady and long-term deterioration in the terms of trade for the exchange of commodities for industrial products is of crucial importance to developing countries, since they are typically large exporters of primary commodities that constitute roughly 80 percent of their export earnings. The deterioration of the terms of trade for the LDCs has reduced the purchasing power of their exports. "The loss in purchasing power amounted annually to approximately 2.5 billion dollars," declared the Charter of Algiers adopted at the Ministerial Meeting of the Group of 77 on October 24, 1967, "which represents nearly half of the flow of external public financial resources to developing

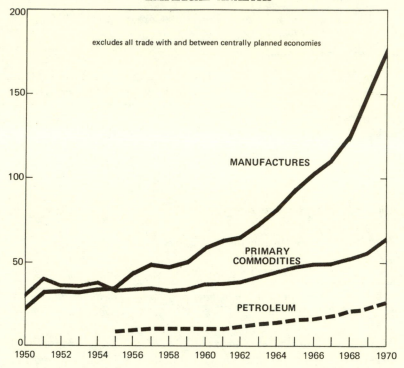

FIGURE 5.1. Trend in World Exports of Manufactures, Petroleum, and Primary Commodities, 1950-70 (US $ billion).

countries."[6] Figure 5.2 shows graphically the changing terms of trade for developed and developing countries in the period 1950-71.

Third, the LDCs have been subject to the discriminatory tariff structures of industrialized countries. While successive rounds of GATT negotiations have reduced the level of tariffs on manufactured and semimanufactured goods to about 10 percent, the goods that the LDCs could export—agricultural products, semiprocessed commodities, and labor-intensive consumer goods—have faced tariff barriers two to four times higher than those for manufactured goods.[7] Most tellingly of all, GATT negotiations practically ignored tariffs on primary commodities. It is little wonder, then, that Salvador Allende, responding to the proposals of the United States, Japan, and the EEC

[6] Charter of Algiers adopted at the Ministerial Meeting of the Group of 77 on October 24, 1967 (hereafter cited as the Charter of Algiers), *UNCTAD, Second Session*, New Delhi, Vol. I: Report and Annexes, p. 431.

[7] For a thorough discussion of obstacles to the LDCs' exports, see Harry Johnson, *Economic Policies Toward Less Developed Countries* (Washington, D.C.: The Brookings Institution, 1967), chap. 3.

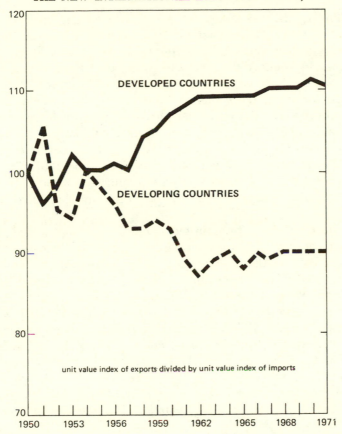

FIGURE 5.2. Changing Terms of Trade for Developed and Developing Countries, 1950-71 (1950 = 100).

to expand and liberalize international trade through GATT, declared in his inaugural address before the 3rd Session of UNCTAD (UNCTAD-III hereafter): "The General Agreement on Tariffs and Trade has always been essentially concerned with the interests of the powerful countries; it has no reliable linkage with the United Nations and is not obliged to adhere to its principles, and its membership is at odds with the concept of universal participation."[8]

Basically, then, the LDCs were obliged to sell their primary commodities and buy manufactured goods at prices determined by self-

[8] "Address Delivered by Mr. Salvador Allende Gossens, President of Chile at the Inaugural Ceremony on 13 April 1972," *Proceedings of UNCTAD, Third Session,* Santiago de Chile, 13 April to 21 May 1972, Vol. I: *Report and Annexes,* p. 354 (hereafter cited as The Allende Inaugural Address at UNCTAD-III).

propelling mechanisms designed to work to the advantage of the industrialized countries. What is notable in this connection is that "the final consumers in the industrialized countries pay over $200 billion for Third World commodities and the products derived directly from them," while "the poor nations receive only $30 billion."[9] Yet, primary production at the center yields relatively high incomes, while manufacturing activities at the periphery yield relatively low incomes, perpetuating the vicious process of unequal exchange.[10] "While the average prices for primary products exported from developing countries have decreased by 7 per cent since 1958," the 1967 Charter of Algiers pointed out, "those for primary products exported from developed countries increased by 10 per cent in the same period [1958-67]."[11]

Finally, another structural problem with developing countries in the world economic system is revealed in their service payments on external public debt. Outflows of financial resources from developing countries have two main components: (1) payments on account of amortization and interest on public debt; and (2) profits on private direct investments. According to a study prepared by the UNCTAD secretariat for UNCTAD-III, debt service payments of eighty developing countries increased from $3,416 million in 1965 to $4,968 million in 1969. Translated into the percentage terms of "gross public inflows" of foreign capital, this constituted 36.7 percent in 1965, 44.3 percent in 1966, 39.3 percent in 1967, 42.8 percent in 1968, and 48.8 percent in 1969 of the total inflow of foreign capital.[12] Likewise, the ratio of debt-

[9] *Reshaping the International Order*, p. 34.

[10] For exposition on the theory of unequal exchange, see Samir Amin, *L'échange inégal et la loi de la valeur* (Paris: Anthropos, 1973); and Arrighi Emmanuel, *Unequal Exchange: A Study of the Imperialism of Trade* (New York: Monthly Review Press, 1972).

[11] The Charter of Algiers, p. 432. Raúl Prebisch, the first secretary-general of UNCTAD, stated to the 1st Session of UNCTAD that developing countries must import by 1970 approximately $20,000 million over and above their export proceeds if they were to achieve the 5 percent minimum rate of annual income growth set for the First United Nations Development Decade. He characterized this $20,000 million trade gap as "a regressive redistribution of [world] income, representing a loss which can be offset only through the co-operation of the industrial countries." The net barter terms of trade of the LDCs, according to more recent UNCTAD estimates, declined by 12 percent between 1954 and 1970, and the losses resulting from such declines amounted to $10 billion for the LDCs in the period 1960-72. See statement by Mr. Raúl Prebisch, secretary-general of the United Nations Conference on Trade and Development (hereafter cited as The Prebisch Statement at UNCTAD-I), *Proceedings of UNCTAD*, Geneva, 23 March-16 June 1964, Vol. II: *Policy Statements*, pp. 76-77; "Long-Term Changes in the Terms of Trade 1954-71, Report by the UNCTAD Secretariat," *Proceedings of UNCTAD, Third Session*, Santiago de Chile, 13 April-21 May 1972, Vol. IV, p. 73.

[12] See "The Outflow of Financial Resources From Developing Countries,"

service payments to exports exceeded 20 percent for another twelve developing countries by 1972. For Chile, debt-service payments reached $408 million in 1972 out of her annual income of $1,200. "It is inconceivable," Salvador Allende noted, "that out of every $100 that flows into its coffers, a country should have to earmark $34 for the serving of its external debt."[13]

The structural inequities and disadvantages of developing countries reviewed above have not been sufficiently compensated for by the transfer of capital resources from the developed countries. In a resolution adopted in 1960, the General Assembly had recommended that the flow of international capital and assistance to developing countries should be about 1 percent of the combined national incomes of the economically developed countries. In the International Development Strategy for the Second United Nations Development Decade (the 1970s), the official development assistance target of 0.7 percent of GNP was set. Yet by 1974, only one country, Sweden, had achieved the transfer target.[14] The flow of official development assistance from the rich countries, as percent of GNP, has progressively declined from 0.87 percent in 1961, to 0.62 percent in 1966, and to 0.30 percent in 1975.

Even such a meager and steadily declining rate of capital inflow into developing countries papers over the reverse flow of capital—namely, interests and profits repatriated back to the metropolitan countries. That is, net transfer of financial resources—the difference between total gross inflows of capital and payments of interest, amortization, and profits—reveals a more accurate picture of the relationship between the center and the periphery in the world economic system. The copper-mining companies made a net initial investment of $30 million in Chile forty-two years ago, Salvador Allende pointed out

---

Proceedings of UNCTAD, Third Session, Santiago de Chile, 13 April-21 May 1972, Vol. II, p. 72. External public debt is defined by IBRD as "all debt (including private debt) that is repayable to external creditors in foreign currency with an original or extended maturity of more than one year, and that is a direct obligation of, or has repayment guaranteed by, the central or local government, a political subdivision or agency of either, or an autonomous public body, in the debtor country." See *ibid.*, p. 71.

[13] The Allende Inaugural Address at UNCTAD-III, p. 355.

[14] In addition, Sweden took the initiative among the developed countries in announcing on October 12, 1977, that she planned to cancel more than $200 million in debts owed by the governments of eight least developed countries (Bangladesh, Botswana, Ethiopia, India, Kenya, Pakistan, Sri Lanka, and Tanzania), representing almost 85 percent of Sweden's credits to developing countries. Canada soon followed suit by canceling $254 million in foreign debts owed to her. Both countries stated that they were planning to discontinue development loans and to make only outright grants. See Pranay Gupte, "Sweden Tells U.N. It Will Cancel $200 million Debt of Poor Nations," *NYT*, October 13, 1977, p. A5.

before UNCTAD-III in 1972, but "since then, without having subsequently brought in any fresh capital, have withdrawn the enormous sum of over $4,000 million—a sum almost the equivalent of our current external debt."[15] The reverse flow of capital should also take into account the often neglected aspect of the transfer of technology—the so-called brain drain—from developing to developed countries.[16]

How did the United Nations system respond to the widening gap between North and South? Its history in economic, social, and technical sectors until the 1970s was one of an uneven and haphazard search for a viable developmental strategy, accompanied by a lateral proliferation of new agencies and programs. The major thrust during the early postwar years was recovery, not development. The Expanded Program of Technical Assistance changed this somewhat by bringing together donors and recipients to generate a transfer of technology. But apart from the Bank Group, the focus was still on technical cooperation. With the establishment of the Special Fund in 1958, more funds began to be channeled into "preinvestment" projects of longer duration in order to improve the investment climate of recipient countries.

Following the membership explosion of the early 1960s brought about by the admission of forty-odd developing states, the main axis of UN politics began to shift southward. The powerful coalition of the poor countries in the United Nations has produced several important developments. First, the center of gravity in UN politics began to shift from an East-West to a North-South conflict. Second, the poor states, determined to exercise their political (voting) power, began to redefine and expand the concept of development, by progressively modifying and/or rejecting the rules, principles, and institutions of the UN developmental enterprise created by the industrialized Western nations.

Third, such a redefinition or expansion of the concept of development was soon reflected in the establishment of UNCTAD and UNIDO, as well as in the enlargement and modification of ECOSOC membership. The establishment of UNCTAD by the General Assembly on December 30, 1964, marked a conceptual turning point in the history of UN developmental enterprise. As will be seen later in the chapter, the Group of 77 bypassed ECOSOC and used UNCTAD as a springboard to gain political and strategic ascendency in NIEO politics.

Fourth, the Soviet bloc countries, which had boycotted many UN economic programs out of a conviction that they served Western

---

[15] The Allende Inaugural Address at UNCTAD-III, p. 351.
[16] For a graphic illustration of this point, see *Reshaping the International Order*, p. 36.

capitalist interests, joined the UN development activities, partly as an opportunity to influence UN development politics and partly to curry favor with the growing number of developing countries.[17]

Fifth and finally, the UN development system began to show a discrepancy between what it claims to do and what it actually accomplishes. This discrepancy resulted from the sharpening conflict between the political power of the South and the economic power of the North in global politics.

Gradually, the UN development system began to suffer from a credibility problem. Notwithstanding the conventional wisdom among students of international organization—which held that the peace-building functional approach, absorbing more than 85 percent of the total expenditures of the United Nations system in 1969 ($557.3 million), was doing well, while the high politics of peace-making and peace-keeping had fallen into relative desuetude—the gap between the need for effective developmental strategy and the capabilities of the Organization was growing.

Pressured by the phenomenon of intensified relative deprivation after absolute gains, the Third World was pushing for program after program, each of which seemed to require institutionalized care. By the end of the first Development Decade (the 1960s), the United Nations development system, according to the UNDP-sponsored Jackson Report, has "become the equivalent of principalities, free from any centralized control."[18] The report then noted:

> This "Machine" now has a marked identity of its own and its power is so great that the question must be asked "Who controls this 'Machine'?" So far, the evidence suggests that governments do not, and also that the machine is incapable of intelligently controlling itself. This is not because it lacks intelligent and capable officials, but because it is so organized that managerial direction is impossible. In other words, the machine as a whole has become unmanageable in the strictest sense of the word. As a result, it is becoming slower and more unwieldy, like some prehistoric monster.[19]

[17] For the evolution of Soviet policies toward UN economic and social activities, see Harold K. Jacobson, *The USSR and the UN's Economic and Social Activities* (Notre Dame: University of Notre Dame Press, 1963); and Alvin Z. Rubinstein, *The Soviets in International Organizations: Changing Policy Toward Developing Countries, 1953-1963* (Princeton, N.J.: Princeton University Press, 1964).

[18] *A Study of the Capacity of the United Nations Development System* [The Jackson Report], UN Doc. DP/5 (1969), p. v.

[19] *Ibid.*, p. iii. For a thorough analysis of the structural and managerial problem of the United Nations system, see Martin Hill, *Toward Greater Order, Coherence and Co-ordination in the United Nations System*, UNITAR Research Report No. 20 (New York: UNITAR, 1974).

The birth of both the League of Nations and the United Nations suggests that the establishment of a new supranational order requires as a precondition a common enemy or a common disaster of global proportions. Usually a new order does not emerge as a happy product of evolutionary transition from the old order. The old order must destroy itself or be destroyed before a new order can be established. The efforts to establish NIEO seem to follow this familiar historical path. That is, what made the establishment of NIEO in conceptual terms possible was the disarray—even the collapse, according to some economists[20]—of the old economic order. What, then, caused the disarray of the Bretton Woods order? Certainly, it was not the structural expansion or modification of the United Nations development system.

The confluence of several economic crises of global significance accelerated the disintegration of the Bretton Woods order in the early 1970s. The dollar-based international monetary order functioned relatively well as long as there was a symmetrical growth between the US balance-of-payments deficits and the needs of world reserves in an expanding international economy. It may be recalled here that the dollar emerged as the key international currency because the postwar world did not have sufficient gold to take care of the desired level of economic transactions. In addition, the distribution of gold was uneven, as the United States alone held a disproportionately large percentage of the world's gold supply—73 percent in 1940, 63 percent in 1945, and 68 percent in 1950.

Because of such a concentration of gold in the United States, coupled with America's dominant political and economic position in the world, the dollar and gold became synonymous in international finance. However, the relative decline in America's economic and political position in the world transformed the dollar shortage of the early postwar years into a dollar glut in the 1960s and early 1970s. In the period 1970-72, for example, world reserves skyrocketed, increasing US liabilities to foreign central banks to nearly 69 percent of the total. The explosion of world reserves of gold-convertible US liabilities to almost five times the global US gold and other reserve assets set in motion massive speculation against the dollar. As pressure increased, the dollar was devalued twice in fifteen months (December 1971 and February 1973), drastically reducing the value of huge reserves of dollars held by other countries. Finally, the dollar's convertibility with gold was suspended, signaling a major change, if not the collapse, of the Bretton Woods monetary order.

The disarray of the dollar-based monetary order contributed to the acceleration of world-wide inflation, trade dislocations, and debt-

[20] See, for example, *Reshaping the International Order*, p. 12.

service payment difficulties. To compound this monetary crisis, a major global food crisis soon followed. Two major factors seem to have contributed to it. First, the inflationary pressure in the industrialized countries generated a sharp upward movement in the prices of fertilizers and agricultural equipment. Second, adverse weather conditions, which struck the Soviet Union, China, India, Southeast Asia, and parts of Africa, brought about a drastic reduction in world food production, depleting world reserve stocks of food grains to virtually nothing in 1972. As a result, the price of food nearly quadrupled during the first half of the 1970s.

It was under the gathering storms of the monetary crisis, the food crisis, the world-wide recession coupled with inflation (stagflation), America's diminished role as dramatized by her military reversal in Indochina and the socioeconomic unrest at home, and another round of war in the Middle East that the sudden and historically significant OPEC action was initiated in late 1973. The price of crude oil, which in real terms had actually declined in the period 1950-70, was quadrupled.[21] The consequences of the increase in the price of oil in the international energy market are far reaching; so is the impact on most industrialized nations of the world because of their high dependence on imported energy.[22]

For the Third World, the OPEC action, even though it seriously affected the poor, non-oil-producing states, represented a strategic opportunity for self-assertion. Greater economic disparities among Third World countries themselves strengthened their collective solidarity against the Northern mighty for a fundamental structural reform in the old economic order. In the final analysis, however, the postwar economic order faced the crisis of survival less because of the OPEC action than because of its own inadequacy. It had outlived its usefulness even for the major industrial powers. The multiple problems of monetary disarray, balance-of-payments disequilibria, and global stagflation brought about a search for a new economic order by the end of 1973.

THE INAUGURATION OF THE FOUNDATIONS OF A NEW INTERNATIONAL ECONOMIC ORDER

Although the General Assembly issued a clarion call as early as 1971 that "the United Nations should evolve a concept of collective eco-

[21] Posted price of oil per barrel increased from $2.591 on January 1, 1973, to $11.651 on January 1, 1974.

[22] For a graphic illustration of varying degrees of dependency of selected developed countries on imported energy, see Committee for Economic Development, Research and Policy Committee, *International Economic Consequences of High-Priced Energy* (New York: CED, September 1975), p. 77.

nomic security,"[23] it was not until the 6th Special Session that an unprecedented review was provided of the basic structural problems in the world economic system that confronted the world community with a crisis of global dimensions. To oversimplify the situation: the oil crisis and the food crisis "united" the rich North and the poor South in a new partnership of economic misery.

In the midst of this twin economic crisis, the United States proposed a collective oil diplomacy on the part of consuming countries as a means of forcing OPEC to reduce the oil price. France countered this American move in mid-January 1974 by proposing instead a UN conference on energy.[24] However, it was Algeria, chairman of the Non-aligned Countries for 1973-76, that stole the show. On January 31, 1974, President Houari Boumedienne requested a special session of the General Assembly to consider the question of all raw materials and relations between developed and developing countries. Within two weeks, some seventy nations endorsed Boumedienne's proposal.

The 6th Special Session of the General Assembly met from April 9 to May 2, 1974, and adopted two historic resolutions concerning international economic relations: a Declaration on the Establishment of a New International Economic Order (hereafter referred to as the *Declaration*) and a Programme of Action on the Establishment of a New International Economic Order (hereafter, the *Programme of Action*).[25] The *Declaration* and the *Programme of Action*, together with the Charter of Economic Rights and Duties of States (hereafter, the *Charter*) adopted by the 29th General Assembly,[26] have been characterized by UNCTAD-IV as having laid down "the foundations of the new international economic order" in a comprehensive seven-page resolution on an Integrated Programme for Commodities designed to implement NIEO.[27]

[23] General Assembly Resolution 2880 (XXVI) of 21 December 1971. As was the case with so many other resolutions during the 26th Session of the General Assembly, the PRC did not participate in the vote on this resolution.

[24] Branislav Gosovic and John G. Ruggie note that in the letter proposing a UN conference on energy in mid-January 1974, "the French avoided using language that would have required the Secretary-General of the UN or the President of ECOSOC to act under the rules of procedure on their request. It is, therefore, difficult to say how serious France was about such a conference. Informal consultations were held, exploring various procedures that were possible, but no formal action was taken in response to the letter." See "On the Creation of a New International Economic Order: Issue Linkage and the Seventh Special Session of the UN General Assembly," *IO* 30 (Spring 1976), 317.

[25] General Assembly Resolution 3201 (S-VI) of 1 May 1974 and General Assembly Resolution 3202 (S-VI) of 1 May 1974.

[26] General Assembly Resolution 3281 (XXIX) of 12 December 1974.

[27] UNCTAD Resolution 93 (IV) adopted without dissent at its 145th plenary meeting on 30 May 1976. See UN Doc. TD/217 (12 July 1976), pp. 2-8. The phrase quoted in the text is taken from the first preambular paragraph of the resolution.

What role, if any, did China play in the establishment of the foundations of NIEO? Conceptually and operationally, the PRC was outside the postwar economic order that we have previously discussed. While China welcomed its disarray, she contributed little to its deepening crisis, as the system was suffering from its own inadequacy. Recently, however, the PRC delegates have repeatedly referred to the trinity of the three resolutions as the definitive conceptual framework for implementing NIEO throughout the United Nations development system. As a point of departure for our analysis of the Chinese role in NIEO politics, we may offer as a working hypothesis the two following observations of participants who are neither pro- nor anti-Peking in their political orientation:

> In the 6th and 7th Special Sessions, where the question of NIEO was first fully aired and embodied, the PRC's participation was minimal. Of course, Teng Hsiao-p'ing was there, but the Chinese participation merely represented a mark of interest—almost a spectator's interest. The Chinese had very little to say in the concrete formulation of ideas. Now I would grant that the proposal of the Third World reflected some Chinese ideas—for example, the concept of self-reliance, the concept of cooperation among developing countries. But the Chinese did not come forward, saying that this or that Chinese principle should be taken seriously in the formulation of NIEO principles. But they knew their ideas were there for others to explore and embody.

> Whatever may have been the motive for asking China to join the Group of 77 in the beginning, the developing countries did not wish to bring China into the bargaining process in the creation of NIEO, for fear that Chinese participation might politicize the issue to the detriment of their own economic interests. Basically, though, the Chinese do not agree with the developing nations in their repeated requests for more and more aid from the developed nations. I do not believe that China is yet in a position to provide economic assistance.

These observations illuminate the perceptions of some Member States from the Second World, but considerably oversimplify the actual NIEO process and the role China played in the establishment of the NIEO resolutions. To get a wider perspective, we need to note at the outset the following differences: (1) the *Declaration* consists of the seven broad principles of a general and declaratory nature; (2) the *Programme of Action* concerns itself with the structural problems of the world economic system as they affect the developing countries, and also recommends some specific reforms to deal with the immediate world economic crisis; and (3) the *Charter* adds to the *Declaration* and the *Programme of Action* a set of codified norms for the behavior of states in their international economic relations. In addition, the inaugural processes leading to the adoption of the three resolutions are different; hence, they need to be analyzed separately.

The Declaration *and the* Programme of Action

On May 1, 1974, the 6th Special Session of the General Assembly adopted without vote both the *Declaration* and the *Programme of Action*. However, to concentrate solely on the 6th Special Session in the creation of these two historic documents is to oversimplify and distort the historical process considerably. Figure 5.3 places the in-

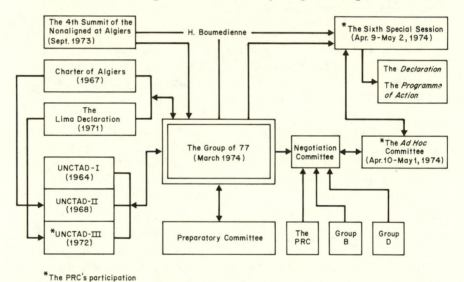

*The PRC's participation

FIGURE 5.3. Processes Leading to the Adoption of the *Declaration* and the *Programme of Action*.

augural process of the two resolutions in a larger historical and political framework. If the process leading to the establishment of the postwar economic order at Bretton Woods and Havana was completely dominated by the Western powers, the process leading to the adoption of the *Declaration* and the *Programme of Action* was almost completely dominated by the Group of 77, working through its sounding and springboard, UNCTAD. Hence, the Chinese role cannot be studied apart from its role in the Group of 77 and UNCTAD.

Immediately after her entry into the United Nations, China was invited to join the Group of 77. After long and due consideration, China declined on the official pretext that she could be more effective in helping the causes of the Third World by working outside rather than inside the Group. It may be recalled here that the Group derives its name from the number of developing countries that had signed the Joint Declaration of the Seventy-Seven Developing Countries Made at the Conclusion of the United Nations Conference on Trade and Development, held at Geneva in 1964.[28] The membership of the Group of 77 was brought to 110 at the Third Ministerial Conference of the Group of 77, held at Manila in February 1976, when Romania, the PLO, Surinam, and Malta were approved as full members.[29] The Group now represents developing countries of Africa, Asia, Latin America, and the Caribbean as well as Cyprus, Yugoslavia, and Romania (see Appendix K). As such, it is the most powerful and dominant pressure group on development questions in the UN political process. The PRC has repeatedly declared herself as a developing country belonging to the Third World; yet she stands conspicuously alone outside the Group of 77 by choice, in a curious contrast to the ROC, which had been excluded from the Group.

China's independence from the Group of 77 adds a curious dimension to her participation in UNCTAD's negotiation process between the developed and developing countries. When UNCTAD was first established as an organ of the General Assembly, the Assembly decided to group the Member States into the four categories: Group A, representing all countries of Asia except Japan, plus Yugoslavia, and all countries in Africa; Group B, representing the developed market-economy countries of Europe plus Australia, Canada, Japan, New Zealand, and the United States; Group C, representing the countries in Latin America and of the Caribbean; and Group D, representing the USSR and other socialist countries of Eastern Europe. At each quadrennial session of UNCTAD, new Member States have been placed in one of the four categories, and the number in each category has grown as follows:[30]

[28] See Joint Declaration of the Seventy-Seven Developing Countries Made at the Conclusion of the United Nations Conference on Trade and Development, UN Doc. E/CONF. 46/138 (1965). The 1st Session of UNCTAD was convened pursuant to ECOSOC Resolution 917 (XXXIV) and General Assembly Resolution 1985 (XVII). Thereafter, General Assembly Resolution 1995 (XIX) established the institutional framework of the Conference, providing for periodic meetings. Between quadrennial plenary conferences, the organization's purposes are pursued through its secretariat and the Trade and Development Board (TDB) located in Geneva. The Conference met twice before the PRC's entry: in 1964 at Geneva and in 1968 at New Delhi. For a history of UNCTAD, see Branislav Gosovic, *UNCTAD: Conflict and Compromise* (Leyden: Sijthoff, 1972).

[29] See "Unite To Smash the Old and Establish the New," *JMJP*, February 10, 1976, p. 6.

[30] For the quadrennial listing of the Member States in each of the four categories from UNCTAD-I to UNCTAD-IV, see the following: *Proceedings of UNCTAD* Geneva, 23 March-16 June 1964, Vol. I: *Final Act and Report* (1964),

	UNCTAD-I	UNCTAD-II	UNCTAD-III	UNCTAD-IV
Group A	61	70	79	87
Group B	29	30	30	30
Group C	22	24	24	27
Group D	9	9	9	10
Total	121	133	142	154

It should be noted in this connection that "China" was placed in Group A in 1964. Since the PRC's entry into the United Nations was one of representation rather than of admission, there was no attempt at UNCTAD-III in 1972 to change China's affiliation with Group A. Actually, China's *de jure* membership in Group A was largely moot, because the developing countries from Group A and Group C immediately organized themselves into a formidable working "Caucus of 75," establishing the original basis for the Group of 77. Within the Group of 77, the developing countries established regional caucuses, a coordinating group, a steering committee, an informal contact group, and a rotational system of leadership in order to formulate a common position and strategy vis-à-vis the developed nations, both East and West.

By the time China joined UNCTAD, the pattern of negotiations was already clearly established, with the Group of 77 and Group B occupying the opposite sides of the negotiation process, while Group D played a somewhat detached role. China formed an additional "group" of her own in UNCTAD, playing a passive but generally supportive role toward the Group of 77. Figure 5.4 shows the transformation of group politics in the UNCTAD negotiation process between the developed and developing countries.

A more detailed analysis of the Chinese behavior in UNCTAD will be presented in Chapter 6. Suffice it here to say that the parameters of the PRC's maneuverability in UNCTAD, apart from the question of the Chinese desire and willingness to play an active role, were severely limited by the established *modus operandi* of UNCTAD politics. For UNCTAD politics is an extreme example of group politics. Most UNCTAD meetings break up into groups that first solidify their respective group position and strategy and then negotiate through elected group spokesmen. In short, China has been boxed into a passive or

pp. 61-62; *UNCTAD, Second Session*, New Delhi, Vol. I: *Report and Annexes*, pp. 57-58; *Proceedings of UNCTAD, Third Session*, Santiago de Chile, 13 April to 21 May 1972, Vol. I: *Report and Annexes*, pp. 112-13; *Report of the UNCTAD On Its Fourth Session*, Nairobi, 5 to 31 May 1976, UN Doc. TD/217 (12 July 1976), pp. 82-83.

The Preentry Model   The Postentry Model

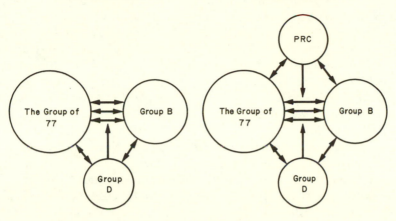

FIGURE 5.4. Transformation of Group Politics in UNCTAD Since the PRC's Entry.

reactive situation without a group basis. A national representative to UNCTAD, who had averaged from fifteen to twenty hours a week in observing Chinese behavior at various UNCTAD meetings at Geneva during the past few years, aptly noted: "The only way that the Chinese can be active in UNCTAD politics is to initiate something. But to do so you need a group basis. So realistically there is not much that the Chinese can do except to sit, watch, and give moral support to the well-established position of the Group of 77."

Although the 6th Special Session was convened in the midst of the oil crisis, the Group of 77 played a central role in steering it toward the establishment of new principles guiding relations between rich and poor countries in the age of global interdependence. Following a well-trodden path in the context of UNCTAD politics, the Group of 77 held a preparatory meeting in New York in March 1974. It soon established a preparatory committee, charged with the task of formulating a draft declaration and a draft programme of action on the establishment of NIEO. Even though convened on short notice, the task of the preparatory committee was relatively simple, for it relied extensively on the fifteen principles adopted at UNCTAD-I in 1964, and on the principles and programs adopted at the ministerial meetings of the Group of 77 in Algiers (Charter of Algiers) in 1967 and in Lima (the Lima Declaration) in 1971, which were held in preparation for UNCTAD-II and UNCTAD-III respectively.[31] In addition, the committee relied on the

[31] In his letter dated 30 January 1974, requesting the Secretary-General to initiate the appropriate procedure for the convening of the 6th Special Session of the General Assembly, President Boumedienne made specific reference to the

Economic Declaration adopted at the Fourth Summit of the Non-aligned Countries held at Algiers in September 1973.[32]

China did not play any direct role in the preparatory process leading to the convocation of the 6th Special Session, but she did display in public a spectacular show of support for it. The PRC delegation, headed by Teng Hsiao-p'ing, was given a warm send-off at the Peking airport by Chou En-lai and some 4,000 people.[33] Likewise, the return of the delegation was described as "triumphant" by the Chinese press and was also greeted by Chou En-lai and a similarly large crowd at the airport. Teng Hsiao-p'ing's major policy speech before the 2209th plenary meeting of the session on April 10, 1974, was perhaps one of the most important statements of the PRC's conceptualization of world order ever made at any international forum.[34] In addition to expounding on the establishment of a new economic order, Teng also pronounced to the world audience China's new three-world typology for the first time.[35]

Chinese participation in the establishment of the NIEO principles at the 6th Special Session took three forms. First, China participated in the general debate at the plenary, making four speeches or statements in the course of twenty-five plenary meetings between April 9 and May 2: Teng Hsiao-p'ing's major policy speech, already alluded to; Chuang Yen's statement on credential questions, involving Cambodia, South Africa, and Portugal; Huang Hua's summation of the *Declaration* and the *Programme of Action* after both were adopted; and Huang Hua's attack on the Soviet theory of the three D's: détente, disarmament, and development.[36]

Second, China participated in the *Ad Hoc* Committee of the session.

Charter of Algiers and the Lima Declaration as an illustration of the desire on the part of the developing countries "for co-operation with a view to instituting a just and lasting international balance" in economic relations between the rich North and the poor South. See GAOR, 6th Special Sess., Annexes, pp. 11-12. For the texts of the Charter of Algiers and the Lima Declaration, see the Charter of Algiers (note 6), pp. 431-41; and *Proceedings of UNCTAD, Third Session*, Santiago de Chile, 13 April-21 May 1972, Vol. I: *Report and Annexes*, annex VIII. F.

[32] For the text of the Economic Declaration, see UN Doc. A/9330 (22 November 1973), pp. 58-74.

[33] See "Chinese Delegation to UN Special Session Triumphantly Returns to Peking," NCNA-English, Peking, April 19, 1974, in *SPRCP*, No. 5604 (May 1, 1974), 142-44.

[34] For the full text of Teng Hsiao-p'ing's speech, see *PR*, No. 16 (April 19, 1974), 6-11; and GAOR, 6th Special Sess., 2209th plenary meeting (10 April 1974), paras. 15-19.

[35] See Chapter 2 on this point.

[36] GAOR, 6th Special Sess., 2209th plenary meeting (10 Apr. 1974), 2228th plenary meeting (30 April 1974), 2229th plenary meeting (1 May 1974), and 2231st plenary meeting (2 May 1974).

At its 2210th plenary meeting on April 11, the General Assembly decided to allocate to the Committee the consideration of agenda item 7, entitled "Study of the Problems of Raw Materials and Development." In effect, the crucial drama was played out in the *Ad Hoc* Committee, centering on the revisions of the draft declaration and program of action submitted by the Group of 77. China played a more active supportive role in the Committee than in the plenary, making ten statements in the course of twenty-one meetings held between April 10 and May 1.[37]

In the face of steady pressure from Group *B* and Group *D*, the Group of 77 set up a negotiating committee (see Figure 5.3) to make some alterations, without changing the basic spirit of their draft documents. In this process, the Group of 77 adopted the third drafts of the declaration and the program of action, keeping the second drafts in reserve. At the last meeting of the *Ad Hoc* Committee on May 1, Chairman of the Committee Fereydoun Hoveyda of Iran put before the Committee the third drafts of the Group of 77, recommending that they be adopted without a vote. The chairman warned that if the Committee rejected this procedure, the Group of 77 would submit the second drafts and put them to a vote at the plenary meeting. After some debate, the chairman declared the third drafts of the Group of 77 adopted without a vote. On the evening of the same day, the plenary adopted without a vote the third draft declaration and program of action of the Group of 77.

Third, China participated in the negotiation process between the regional groups (see Figure 5.3). In order to make its draft documents as acceptable as possible to the other regional groups, the Group of 77 quickly established an 18-nation negotiation committee (composed of Iran, Algeria, and sixteen Third World nations) to negotiate on its behalf. This negotiation process took the form of the two regional groups—Group *B* and Group *D*—expressing their respective views on the second drafts of the Group of 77. Inasmuch as China constituted a "group" of her own, she was invited to express her views before the negotiation committee. Huang Hua appeared before the negotiation committee on April 27 to point out that "the Soviet attempt to pack 'disarmament' into the Declaration ran counter to the desires already explicitly stated by many Third World countries." He argued that "the Soviet attempt was aimed at leading the conference astray, sabotaging

[37] For a comprehensive report on the work of the *Ad Hoc* Committee, see *Report of the Ad Hoc Committee of the Sixth Special Session*, UN Doc. A/9556, in GAOR, 6th Special Sess., Annexes, Agenda Item 7, pp. 13-37. For all the statements the PRC's delegates made in the *Ad Hoc* Committee, see GAOR, 6th Special Sess., *Ad Hoc* Committee, 1st meeting (10 April 1974)-21st meeting (1 May 1974).

it and provoking disputes, which the Chinese Delegation definitely could not agree to."[38] In short, China's participation in this negotiation process took the form of encouraging the Third World not to succumb to the Soviet pressure to add "political and ideological riders" to the second draft documents of the Group of 77.

To say that China made no contribution or played a marginal role in the making of NIEO at the 6th Special Session is to misjudge both the substance and the style of Chinese global politics. In reviewing the session, China characterized it as a "major victory of Third World's united struggle against hegemonism."[39] Indeed, China acted as if the 6th Special Session was a confirmation of her "trend-of-history" analysis of world politics and that the Third World was the motive force pushing forward the wheel of history in this irreversible historical process. In Chinese metaphorical terms, the Third World's persistence "in [the] struggle with a clear-cut stand and flexible tactics" in the *Ad Hoc* Committee reflected "the decline of the two superpowers." As the verse goes, "Flowers fall off, do what one may."[40] If this line of reasoning were correct, there would have been little need for China to play anything but a supportive role in this inexorable historical process.

Moreover, to play a leading role in multilateral diplomacy runs counter to the Chinese diplomatic style. As we have examined in some detail in Chapter 3, China's support for the Third World is generally that of a partisan spectator who cheers, moralizes, and votes, when necessary, rather than an active, not to say leading, player in the game of global politics. Viewed in this light, China's role in the formulation of the NIEO principles at the Sixth Special Session was more active and more supportive than might have been expected. As on most other questions in the General Assembly, China has shown little interest or inclination to intervene in such a way as to have her own views incorporated in the *Declaration* and the *Programme of Action*. Teng Hsiao-

[38] "Victory of Third World's Struggle in Unity—A review of the special session of U.N. General Assembly," *PR*, No. 19 (May 10, 1974), 12. This 3-page review article (pp. 11-13 in *ibid.*) is rather unusual in that it gives a blow-by-blow account of the behind-the-scenes consultative process in the *Ad Hoc* Committee. As such, it deviates from the unwritten norm that the statements and views expressed during the consultative process are not to be published.

[39] See *JMJP*, editorial, May 5, 1974, p. 1.

[40] "Two Superpowers Heavily Besieged on All Sides—Summary of first week's meetings of Ad Hoc Committee of special session of UN General Assembly," NCNA-English, United Nations, April 21, 1974, in *SPRCP*, No. 5606 (May 3, 1974), 222. This one represents another summary article (pp. 215-222 in *ibid.*), giving a detailed account of proceedings in the *Ad Hoc* Committee. Huang Hua used the same metaphorical expression in his summing-up speech of May 1, 1974, in the plenary, to drive home his point that it is indeed futile for the superpowers to try to stop an irreversible historical process. See GAOR, 6th Special Sess., 2229th plenary meeting (1 May 1974), para. 45.

p'ing made a major policy speech in the plenary, explaining where China stands, but China did not submit any explanatory memorandum, supporting documents, or proposals as many Member States did.

What can we make of the *Declaration* and the *Programme of Action*? Do they represent a global compact, embodying a universal consensus with some legal force? Perceptions and interpretations of the Member States differ on this crucial question. Speaking on behalf of the African group of states, the representative of Sierra Leone (Joka-Bangura) stated: "We realize that consensus does not necessarily mean unanimity. That has been amply proved by the reservations that were expressed both yesterday and this morning. . . . However, the adoption by consensus of the draft principles and *Programme of Action* before the General Assembly marks an important step—that of having been able to obtain substantial agreement on a set of guidelines for future action that would give the United Nations a central role in the continuing battle against inflation, poverty and economic inequilibrium."[41]

However, US representative John Scali differed sharply: "We are— I must confess—disappointed that it was not possible to emerge from our deliberations with unanimous agreement on how these problems can best be solved. . . . We seriously question what value there is in adopting statements on difficult and controversial questions that represent the views of only one faction."[42] Scali then expressed the American interpretation of the question of consensus:

> Some have referred to the procedure by which these documents have been formulated as that of 'consensus'. My delegation believes that the word 'consensus' cannot be applied in this case. The document which will be printed as the written product of this special General Assembly does not in fact—whatever it is called—represent a consensus in the accepted meaning of that term. My delegation did not choose to voice objection to the resolution presented to us this evening even though, at the last moment, it was presented without mention of the word 'consensus'.[43]

As for China, Huang Hua declared the support of his government for the *Declaration* and the *Programme of Action* "because these documents basically reflect the earnest demands and just propositions of the third world."[44] Characteristically, Huang Hua refused to get himself involved in a legal or procedural argument. However, Chinese representative Chang Tsien-hua made a rather startling declaration in

[41] GAOR, 6th Special Sess., 2231st plenary meeting (2 May 1974), para. 93.
[42] GAOR, 6th Special Sess., 2229th plenary meeting (1 May 1974), para. 77.
[43] *Ibid.*, para. 79.
[44] GAOR, 6th Special Sess., 2229th plenary meeting (1 May 1974), para. 46.

the *Ad Hoc* Committee even before the plenary adopted the two documents: "The Programme of Action *should be binding on States*."[45] Chang stopped short of elaborating on this declaration.

The PRC's participation in the 6th Special Session on Raw Materials and Development affords us a unique insight into the evolving Chinese image of a world economic order. Interestingly enough, China expressed her support for the two documents because they represented the just and legitimate demands of the Third World. Throughout the drafting and negotiating processes, China assumed an *amicus curiae* posture. She never stated directly if these two documents also reflected the interests or demands of China in the world economic system. One analytical problem here is the tendency of the Chinese to disguise their interest in terms of principles.

This diplomatic propensity has led one national delegate to ECOSOC to observe: "I have never encountered a single incident when China's own economic interests played a major role in any UN debate." As if to reinforce this kind of perception on the part of other Member States, Chinese representative Chang Tsien-hua argued in the *Ad Hoc* Committee, for example, that "it might be wiser to await agreement on the text of the Declaration before taking up the related points in the Programme."[46] Hence, a more logical approach here is to ask whether the *Declaration* and the *Programme of Action* in fact represented the Chinese conceptualization of a new international economic order, and, if so, to what degree and extent.

Approached in this manner, the two documents appear to reflect to a large degree China's own conceptualization of world economic order. We can cite a number of points that tend to support this hypothesis. First, the PRC's public display of support for the 6th Special Session was unprecedented both in terms of the press coverage and in terms of the power and prestige of the delegation it sent. Second, the PRC's desire to have the two draft documents submitted by the Group of 77 adopted was so strong that it took a "depoliticized approach" during the negotiation process. Chou Nan stated in the *Ad Hoc* Committee that "his delegation objected to the inclusion of references to controversial or political matters which were not directly related to the subject of the draft Declaration."[47] Third, the PRC's delegates, as will be seen later in the chapter, have made repeated references to the *Declaration*, the *Programme of Action*, and the *Charter* as the binding prin-

[45] GAOR, 6th Special Sess., *Ad Hoc* Committee, 13th meeting (22 April 1974), para. 27; emphasis added.

[46] GAOR, 6th Special Sess., *Ad Hoc* Committee, 11th meeting (19 April 1974), para. 27.

[47] GAOR, 6th Special Sess., *Ad Hoc* Committee, 9th meeting (18 April 1974), para. 46.

ciples for all the organs and agencies of the United Nations development system.

Actually, Huang Hua in his summing-up speech in the plenary chose his words carefully when he expressed China's disagreement with some of the provisions. He said that some formulations in the two documents were "deficient"; he then used the term "reservations" in referring to the formulations, not the two documents themselves.[48] There were, he said, two types of deficiencies—phraseological and terminological. First, some formulations suffered from ambiguity, repetition, and lack of clarity or forceful expression. Specifically, the question of "urgency" in economic relations between the rich and poor countries should have been made clearer in the preamble. Second, of all the concepts and principles embodied in the two documents, Huang Hua singled out two terms—"interdependence" and "international division of labor"—as being particularly susceptible to distortion by the superpowers. Using a vivid Chinese metaphor, he held that interdependence in the contemporary world economic system could easily turn into an interdependence "between a horseman and his mount."[49]

In short, the Chinese were warning that the concept of interdependence between rich and poor countries works ultimately to the advantage of the former against the latter. In addition, interdependence could easily become a license to compromise another cardinal principle that had been embodied in both the *Declaration* and the *Programme of Action*—the concept of the full permanent sovereignty of every state over its natural resources and all its economic activities.

Likewise, the term "international division of labour," which appears in the *Programme of Action*, was first criticized in the *Ad Hoc* Committee as a new label designed to perpetuate the old economic order, with its lopsided and abnormal development of national economies throughout the world.[50] Huang Hua also stated in the plenary that the term "might be used by the super-Powers to push under that name their self-seeking 'economic division of labour' and 'economic integration' and to maintain the most unjust and abnormal state of 'industrial Europe and North America, but Asia, Africa and Latin America with their agricultural and mineral produce' [sic]."[51] However, the PRC's "reservations," considered in the context of the whole of the two comprehensive documents, are few and insignificant.

---

[48] GAOR, 6th Special Sess., 2229th plenary meeting (1 May 1974), para. 47.
[49] GAOR, 6th Special Sess., *Ad Hoc* Committee, 10th meeting (18 April 1974), para. 15.
[50] GAOR, 6th Special Sess., *Ad Hoc* Committee, 17th meeting (24 April 1974), paras. 26-28.
[51] GAOR, 6th Special Sess., 2229th plenary meeting (1 May 1974), para. 47.

The Charter

The Charter (hereafter the *Charter*) of Economic Rights and Duties of States complements the *Declaration* and the *Programme of Action* by adding a set of codified behavioral norms for the states in their international economic relations with each other. As Figure 5.5 shows,

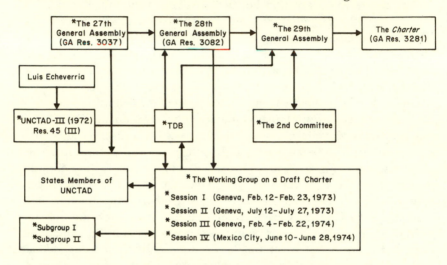

*The PRC's membership and/or participation

FIGURE 5.5. The Making of the Charter of Economic Rights and Duties of States.

UNCTAD played an even more important and direct role in the making of the *Charter* than it did in the establishment of the other two foundations of NIEO. The original idea came from President Luis Echeverria of Mexico. In his address before the 92nd plenary meeting of UNCTAD-III held at Santiago in 1972, President Echeverria suggested the desirability of drawing up a charter of economic rights and duties of states.[52] Following upon this initiative, UNCTAD-III adopted a resolution by a roll-call vote of 90 in favor to none against, with 19 abstentions—the PRC joined the majority—whereby it decided to establish a Working Group composed of government representatives of thirty-one Member States to draw up the text of a draft charter.[53]

The 27th General Assembly enlarged the composition of the Work-

[52] See the address in *Proceedings of UNCTAD, Third Session,* Vol. IA, Part one, p. 184.

[53] UNCTAD Resolution 45 (III) adopted at the 115th plenary meeting on May 18, 1972, in *Proceedings of UNCTAD, Third Session,* Vol. I: Report and Annexes, pp. 58-59.

ing Group to forty Member States.[54] The 29th General Assembly extended the mandate of the Working Group "in the light of the progress achieved" and urged it "to complete, as the first step in the codification and development of the matter, the elaboration of a final draft Charter of Economic Rights and Duties of States, to be considered and approved by the General Assembly at its twenty-ninth session."[55]

As Figure 5.5 shows, China participated in every phase of the preparatory process. China was designed as a member of the original 31-nation Working Group. Apparently, Chinese participation was made easier because the Working Group allowed a considerable degree of individual play and was less subject to the rigid UNCTAD structure of group politics. The issue at stake was not the critical economic question of how the pie should be sliced or whose hands should control the knife, but one of formulating a generally acceptable code of behavioral norms for all the states. In fact, the UNCTAD authorizing resolution specifically stated that "the draft prepared by the Working Group shall be sent to States members of UNCTAD in order that they can communicate their suggestions, it being understood that the Working Group shall reconvene to elaborate the draft charter further in the light of comments and suggestions to be received from Governments of member States."[56]

Such an instruction allowed continuous interactions between the Working Group and interested Member States. During the 2nd Session of the Working Group, for example, the Philippines submitted a complete draft text, while comments and suggestions were received from some thirty-two Member States.[57] To make its work more manageable, the Working Group decided to set up two subgroups. Subgroup I was to consider the preamble and chapter I of the draft, and subgroup II to consider chapters II-V of the draft with self-elected membership in each subgroup. China elected herself a member in both subgroups, thus showing a strong interest in the drafting process.

The 1st Session of the Working Group was confined largely to organizational matters and general exchange of viewpoints. The 2nd Session was most important and most critical, as the Group and its two subgroups got down to the business of drafting a charter based

[54] General Assembly Resolution 3037 (XXVII) of 19 December 1972. This resolution was adopted by a recorded vote of 124 in favor, none against, with no abstention.
[55] General Assembly Resolution 3082 (XXVIII) of 6 December 1973. This resolution was adopted without objection.
[56] The third operative paragraph of UNCTAD Resolution 45 (III), in *Proceedings of UNCTAD, Third Session,* Vol. I: Report and Annexes, p. 59.
[57] UN Doc. TD/B/AC.12/2 (8 August 1973), p. 2. The Philippine text was circulated as UN Doc. TD/B/AC.12/R.17.

largely on the Philippines text. China sent a large delegation of eight, headed by Pi Chi-lung from the Ministry of Foreign Affairs. In his opening speech, Pi Chi-lung put forward the PRC's position and propositions on the formulation of a draft charter in the Working Group. Two points of a methodological nature for the Working Group are worth mentioning. First, he argued that the draft charter "should not come out as an abstract document devoid of substance and, instead, it should contain specific guiding principles related to major economic issues."[58] Second, the Working Group, Pi Chi-lung also suggested, "should, first of all, bring together those commonly accepted rational principles in the spirit of consultation on an equal basis, then make efforts to iron out some of the differences and finally hammer out those principles in the form of a charter."[59]

China did not submit any advance written text, working paper, or document as some Member States did. But, uncharacteristically, she participated fully and actively, presenting no less than twenty-five separate proposals, amendments, or additions in the course of the Working Group's actual drafting process during its 2nd and 3rd Sessions. Appendix I gives a complete verbatim listing of all the proposals, amendments, or additions submitted by the Chinese delegates. Stripped to their essence, they represent the Chinese conceptualization of the Charter of Economic Rights and Duties of States.

The salient feature of the Chinese model of the behavioral norms of states in international economic relations is the notion that every country has—or should have—a permanent and inalienable sovereign right to manage and control its resources and economic activities in its own way without any kind of external interference. But this concept of resource sovereignty stops at the water's edge, as China has consistently advocated the principle of participatory democracy in the management of international political and economic affairs. It was in this vein that China proposed a specific text on the resources of the international seas to be included in Chapter III of the draft charter. It is worth juxtaposing here the proposed Chinese text and Article 29 in Chapter III of the finalized *Charter*:

The Chinese Text	*Chapter III, Article 29 of the Charter*
The international seas and the resources thereof, beyond the territorial waters and the domestic jurisdiction of	The sea-bed and ocean floor and the subsoil thereof, beyond the limits of national jurisdiction, as well as the resources of the area, are the common heritage of mankind. On

[58] "China's Position and Propositions on Drafting of 'Charter of Economic Rights and Duties of States' Expounded," NCNA-English, Geneva, July 28, 1973, in *SCMP*, No. 5431 (August 8, 1973), 137.

[59] *Ibid.*, p. 139.

The Chinese Text	*Chapter III, Article 29 of the Charter*
States, are the common heritage of mankind and belong to all peoples. The question of their exploitation and utilization should be settled jointly by all countries through consultation on an equal basis.	the basis of the principles adopted by the General Assembly in resolution 2749 (XXV) of 17 December 1970, all States shall ensure that the exploitation of the area and exploitation of its resources are carried out exclusively for peaceful purposes and that the benefits derived therefrom are shared equitably by all States, taking into account the particular interests and needs of developing countries; an international regime applying to the area and its resources and including appropriate international machinery to give effect to its provisions shall be established by an international treaty of a universal character, generally agreed upon.

The Working Group completed its work on the draft charter on June 28, 1974 in Mexico City, well in time for the 29th Session of the General Assembly. The plenary of the 29th General Assembly allocated to its Second Committee agenda item 48 on the draft charter. At its 1639th meeting on November 27, 1974, the representative of Mexico, Alfonso Garcia Robles, introduced the draft charter of the Working Group in the form of a draft resolution (A/C.2/L.1386) on behalf of ninety-nine Member States all belonging to the Group of 77. Thus, China was excluded from the long list of cosponsors.

Given the solidarity of the ninety-nine Member States in the Committee, it was clearly futile for the developed countries to delete or dilute any provisions in the draft charter before the Committee. Nonetheless, Australia, Belgium, Canada, Denmark, France, West Germany, Ireland, Italy, Japan, Luxembourg, the United Kingdom, and the United States all introduced amendments to delete and reword some provisions in the draft charter. Sensing the predictable outcome of these amendments, the representative of the United States "requested that all the votes taken under this item [item 48 on the draft charter] should be recorded."[60] In the ensuing recorded votes, all the amendments were defeated, clearing the path for the adoption of the draft charter. Yet the representative of the United States again intervened, asking "for a separate vote on each preambular paragraph, each subparagraph of chapter I and each article of the draft Charter of Economic Rights and Duties of States, as revised."[61] Table 5.3 shows how each of the Big Five voted on each separate item as well as on the

[60] GAOR, 29th Sess., Annexes, Agenda Item 48, para. 11.
[61] *Ibid.*, para. 19.

TABLE 5.3. Voting Record of the Big Five on the Charter of Economic Rights and Duties of States[a]

Item			PRC	USA	USSR	UK	FRANCE
Preamble, para.	1		y	y	y	y	y
	2		y	y	y	y	y
	3		y	y	y	y	y
	4		y	a	y	y	y
	5		y	y	y	y	y
	6		y	y	y	y	y
	7		y	n	y	a	a
	8		y	y	y	y	y
	9		y	y	y	y	y
	10		y	y	y	y	y
	11		y	y	y	y	y
	12		y	y	y	y	y
	13		y	y	y	y	y
I, Introduction			y	a	y	a	a
subpara.		(a)	y	y	y	y	y
		(b)	y	y	y	y	y
		(c)	y	y	y	y	y
		(d)	y	y	y	y	y
		(e)	y	y	y	y	y
		(f)	np	y	y	n	a
		(g)	y	y	y	y	y
		(h)	y	y	y	y	y
		(i)			No Vote Taken		
		(j)	y	y	y	y	y
		(k)	y	y	y	y	y
		(l)	y	y	y	y	y
		(m)	y	y	y	y	y
		(n)	y	y	y	y	y
		(o)	y	y	y	y	y
II, Art. 1			y	y	y	y	y
Art. 2, para.	1		y	n	y	n	n
	2	(a)	y	n	y	n	n
		(b)	y	n	y	n	a
		(c)	y	n	y	n	n
Art. 3			a	y	y	a	a

TABLE 5.3. (*cont'd*)

Item		PRC	USA	USSR	UK	FRANCE
II, Art.	4	y	a	y	n	n
	5			No Vote Taken		
	6	y	a	y	n	n
	7	y	y	y	y	y
	8	y	y	y	y	y
	9	y	y	y	y	y
	10	y	y	y	y	y
	11	y	y	y	y	y
	12	y	y	y	y	y
	13	y	y	y	y	y
	14	y	y	y	y	y
	15			No Vote Taken		
	16			No Vote Taken		
	17	y	y	y	y	y
	18	y	y	y	y	y
	19			No Vote Taken		
	20	np	y	y	y	y
	21	y	y	y	y	y
	22	y	y	y	y	y
	23	y	y	y	y	y
	24	y	y	y	y	y
	25	y	y	y	y	y
	26	np	n	y	n	n
	27	y	y	y	y	y
	28			No Vote Taken		
III, Art.	29	y	a	a	a	a
	30	y	a	y	a	a
IV, Art.	31	y	y	y	y	y
	32	y	a	y	a	a
	33	y	y	y	y	y
	34	y	a	y	a	a
Draft Charter as a whole[b]		y	n	y	n	a
Draft Charter as a whole[c]		y	n	y	n	a

y = Yes; n = No; a = Abstain; np = Not Participating.

[a] Except the last entry in the second column (c), the votes were taken in the Second Committee of the General Assembly.

[b] At its 1648th meeting, the Second Committee voted on the draft resolution (A/C.2/L.1386 and Corr. 6) as a whole.

[c] At its 2315th meeting the plenary voted on the draft resolution (Charter) as a whole.

draft charter as a whole, both in the Second Committee and in the plenary.

At its 2315th plenary meeting on December 12, 1974, the General Assembly adopted the draft charter by a roll-call vote of 120 in favor, 6 against, with 10 abstentions. Belgium, Denmark, Federal Republic of Germany, Luxembourg, the United Kingdom, and the United States all voted against the draft charter on the following grounds: that some provisions or statements—such as political or military statements on colonialism, apartheid, occupation of foreign lands, and disarmament —did not properly belong to the charter; the charter was unbalanced as between the rights and the duties of states, since it favored the economic rights of one group of states over another group of states; and the charter did not adequately protect the economic rights of private international investors and corporations in accordance with international law.

"It is a fundamental purpose of the present Charter," the preamble of the final *Charter* declared, "to promote the establishment of the new international economic order, based on equity, sovereignty equality, interdependence, common interest and co-operation among all States, irrespective of their economic and social systems." The *Charter* then specifies in Chapter I, fifteen "fundamentals of international economic relations":

(a) Sovereignty, territorial integrity and political independence of States

(b) Sovereign equality of all States

(c) Non-aggression

(d) Non-intervention

(e) Mutual and equitable benefit

(f) Peaceful coexistence

(g) Equal rights and self-determination of peoples

(h) Peaceful settlement of disputes

(i) Remedying of injustices which have been brought about by force and which deprive a nation of the natural means necessary for its normal development

(j) Fulfilment in good faith of international obligations

(k) Respect for human rights and fundamental freedoms

(l) No attempt to seek hegemony and spheres of influence

(m) Promotion of international social justice

(n) International co-operation for development

(o) Free access to and from the sea by land-locked countries within the framework of the above principles

How closely does the *Charter* reflect China's image of economic rights and duties of states? In the general debate just before the plenary vote on the draft charter, Chinese representative Chang Hsien-wu stated that "the drafting of the charter is a component part of the just struggle of the third world countries to safeguard their State sovereignty, control their national resources, and develop their national economies"; it also represents "a break in the old and inequitable international economic relations and the establishment of a new, just, and reasonable international economic order."[62] It was in this spirit that China voted in favor of most items in the draft resolution (charter), as well as of the draft charter as a whole, in both the Second Committee and the plenary.

However, China expressed regrets that the *Charter* contained a few "irrational and even harmful articles."[63] Predictably, most of the objectionable provisions in the *Charter* were Soviet-sponsored pet projects. China registered her strongest objection to the insertion of Article 15 on disarmament into the *Charter*. The Chinese press even distorted the actual event by reporting that Albania and China "voted against Article 15."[64] As Table 5.3 shows, there was no separate vote on Article 15, because an amendment submitted by Belgium, France, the Federal Republic of Germany, Greece, Italy, Luxembourg, the United Kingdom, and the United States (A/C.2/L.1410), which called for the deletion of Article 15, had already been rejected by 76 to 22, with 24 abstentions. China joined the Western powers in voting in favor of the amendment.[65]

China did not participate in the vote on Article 20, another Soviet-sponsored item, which states that developing countries should give due attention to the possibility of expanding their trade with socialist countries by granting them conditions not inferior to those granted normally to the developed market economy countries. China simply declared that she had a "different view" on this article. Besides, the article was superfluous, Chinese representative Chang Hsien-wu noted, because explicit reference was already made in Article 4 "to the right of every State to engage in international trade and other forms of economic co-operation irrespective of any differences in political, economic, and social systems."[66]

[62] UN Doc. A/PV.2315 (12 December 1974), pp. 18-20.

[63] GAOR, 29th Sess., Second Committee, 1647th meeting (6 December 1974), para. 30.

[64] See "UN Committee Adopts Draft Charter of Economic Rights and Duties," NCNA-English, United Nations, December 7, 1974, in *SPRCP*, No. 5757 (December 19, 1974), 172.

[65] GAOR, 29th Sess., Annexes, Agenda Item 48, p. 11.

[66] GAOR, 29th Sess., Second Committee, 1647th meeting (6 December 1974), para. 34.

Likewise, China opted for nonparticipation in the vote on Article 26, which embodied another Soviet-sponsored item on the granting of "most-favored-nation" treatment. The insertion of the most-favored-nation clause in the article was irrational, she argued, because "each State had the sovereign right to decide whether or not to grant most-favoured-nation treatment, which should be arranged, after consultations, through bilateral and multilateral agreements between the countries concerned."[67] China also engaged in nit-picking on another Soviet item in Chapter I, subparagraph (f) on peaceful coexistence, on the grounds that she had her own Five Principles of Peaceful Coexistence.[68]

As in the case of the *Declaration* and the *Programme of Action*, China again registered her displeasure at the insertion of the term "interdependence" in the *Charter*. The result of such an interdependence, Chinese representative Chang Hsien-wu argued in the Second Committee, "had been that the developing countries were exploited in trade and suffered an annual loss of some $10 thousand million, their external debts had reached the level of tens of thousands of millions of dollars, and the gap between rich and poor had widened further."[69] On Article 3, which states that "each State must co-operate on the basis of a system of information and prior consultations" in the exploitation of natural resources shared by two or more countries, China abstained because "some developing countries had different views on the question."[70] She stopped short of elaborating on this point. It is reasonable to assume that this is an area where China wants to retain maximum freedom of action, as her economic interest in enormous oil potential is now on a collision course with the interests of Vietnam, Taiwan, South Korea, and Japan, over conflicting claims to the continental shelves of the Yellow Sea and the East China Sea.[71]

The legal force of the *Charter* has not been made explicit. Yet, the rights and duties spelled out in the *Charter* were intended "to establish or improve norms of universal application for the development of international economic relations on a just and equitable basis."[72] Moreover, the title and some provisions in the *Charter* employ the peremptory

---

[67] *Ibid.*, para. 35.   [68] *Ibid.*, para. 36.   [69] *Ibid.*, para. 37.   [70] *Ibid.*, para. 38.

[71] For different analyses of this and related issues, see the following: Hungdah Chiu, "Chinese Attitude Toward Continental Shelf and Its Implications on Delimiting Seabed in Southeast Asia," *Occasional Papers/Reprints Series in Contemporary Asian Studies*, No. 1 (1977), 1-32; Hungdah Chiu and Choon-Ho Park, "Legal Status of the Paracel and Spratly Islands," *Ocean Development and International Law* 3 (1975), 1-28; Choon-Ho Park, "Oil Under Troubled Waters: The Northeast Asia Sea-Bed Controversy," *Harvard International Law Journal* 14 (Spring 1973), 212-60; "The Sino-Japanese-Korean Sea Resources Controversy and the Hypothesis of a 200-Mile Economic Zone," *Harvard International Law Journal* 16 (Winter 1975), 27-46; Selig S. Harrison, *China, Oil, and Asia: Conflict Ahead?* (New York: Columbia University Press, 1977).

[72] General Assembly Resolution 3082 (XXVIII) of 6 December 1973.

language of legal obligations. The Working Group was instructed to complete its work "as the first step in the codification and development of the matter." During the fourth and final session of the Working Group, an alternative draft employing the word "should" instead of "shall" was rejected.[73] As a result, the *Charter* enumerates in Chapter I with the fifteen fundamental principles which *shall* govern international economic relations.

Despite its normative character, however, the *Charter* was approved as a resolution of the General Assembly rather than as a multilateral convention. While an overwhelming majority voted in favor of it, all the major economic powers in the world—less the Soviet Union and China —either abstained or voted against it. Viewed in this light, the *Charter* amplifies the credibility problem of the United Nations earlier alluded to—the gap between the claims and the capabilities of the Organization as expressed in the dichotomy between the demands of the numerical majority and the defiance of the economically powerful minority.

There is a sense in which the adoption of the *Charter* in the form of a General Assembly resolution is a direct challenge to the legal opinion that the General Assembly cannot legislate. Regardless of the merit of legal objections, the *Charter* will undoubtedly be cited time and time again in subsequent resolutions of the General Assembly. In fact, Article 34 of the *Charter* specifically stipulated that "an item on the Charter of Economic Rights and Duties of States shall be included in the agenda of the General Assembly at its thirtieth session, and thereafter on the agenda of every fifth session," so as to have "a systematic and comprehensive consideration of the implementation of the Charter, covering both progress achieved and any improvements and additions which might become necessary."

Following this specific requirement, the 30th Session of the General Assembly adopted a resolution by a recorded vote of 114 in favor, 3 opposed (the Federal Republic of Germany, the United Kingdom, and the United States), and 11 abstentions, reaffirming the *Charter* and also entrusting ECOSOC with the task of reviewing its implementation.[74] Significantly, the opposition to the *Charter* dropped from 6 in the 29th Session to 3 in the 30th Session. As Judge Tanaka cogently stated in the *South West Africa* cases, such a practice of repeated reference to norms embodied in a General Assembly resolution constitutes evidence of customary law.[75] In short, in spite of the formalistic denial of a legal and

[73] UN Docs. TD/B/AC.12/3 (8 March 1974), p. 6; TD/B/AC.12/4 (1 August 1974), p. 6.
[74] General Assembly Resolution 3486 (XXX) of 12 December 1975.
[75] *I.C.J. Reports 1966*, p. 292. See also *A Memorandum by the Office of Legal Affairs*, UN Doc. E/CN.4/L.610 (1962).

legislative status of resolution by many traditional international lawyers, the *Charter* may very well contribute to the process of developing international law by custom and usage.

The Chinese Image of NIEO

All the principles and propositions advanced by the PRC delegates in the course of their participation in the inaugural process of NIEO provide a firm basis for drawing up the Chinese image of a new economic order. The dominant component in the Chinese image is the concept of independent and self-reliant development of the national economy. In the Chinese conceptualization, this is indeed the only way that developing countries can liberate their economic thinking from the exploitative center-generated concept of "interdependence"; this is the only way that developing countries can break away from the vicious process of exchanges of unequal values; this is the only way that developing countries can destroy the seemingly self-perpetuating structure of center-periphery and dominance-dependence relations. All other principles in the Chinese image are either variants on, or supplements to, this dominant principle.

To the Chinese, this is not the academic theory of neocolonialism or *dependencia* espoused by many radical intellectuals in the West.[76] In a rather circumlocutory way, the Chinese are trying to teach developing countries two historical lessons, ones which they themselves were forced to learn in a traumatic way. Old China was exploited and plundered by the Western imperialists, causing great damage to the Chinese economy and untold suffering for the Chinese people. New

[76] For a sample of writings of *dependencia* theorists, see the following: Susanne Bodenheimer, "Dependency and Imperialism: The Root of Latin American Underdevelopment," in K. T. Fann and D. C. Hodges, eds., *Readings in U.S. Imperialism* (Boston: Porter Sargent Publisher, 1971), pp. 155-82; Fernando Henrique Cardoso, "Associated-Dependent Development: Theoretical and Practical Implications," in Alfred Stepan, ed., *Authoritarian Brazil* (New Haven: Yale University Press, 1973), pp. 142-76; Johan Galtung, "A Structural Theory of Imperialism," *Journal of Peace Research* 8 (1971), 81-117; Andre Gunder-Frank, "Sociology of Development and Underdevelopment," in J. Cockcroft, A. G. Frank, and D. Johnson, *Dependence and Underdevelopment* (Garden City, N.Y.: Doubleday, 1972), pp. 321-98; David Horowitz, *The Free World Colossus* (New York: Hill and Wang, 1971); Gabriel Kolko, *The Limits of Power* (New York: Harper & Row, 1972); Harry Magdoff, *The Age of Imperialism* (New York: Monthly Review Press, 1969); Dieter Senghaas, "Peace Research and the Third World," *Bulletin of Peace Proposals*, No. 4 (1975), 158-72; William Appleton Williams, *The Tragedy of American Diplomacy* (New York: Dell, 1959). For a most sophisticated analysis of the concept of self-reliance against the conceptual framework of NIEO, which to a remarkable degree reflects the Chinese position, see Johan Galtung, "Implementing Self-Reliance," *Transnational Perspectives* 3 (1976), 18-24.

China, too, was short-changed by the "social-imperialists." The PRC's dependency on the Soviet Union in the 1950s, it may be recalled, came to a sudden halt in mid-1960, when the latter withdrew technical experts, managers, and industrial blueprints from China, thus inflicting maximum damage to the Chinese economy at a most vulnerable moment. It is only after China began to adhere, asserts a PRC publicist, "to the principle of building our country independently and through self-reliance" that a poor and backward nation transformed itself into "a socialist country with the beginnings of prosperity, having neither internal or external debts."[77]

Whether the principle of self-reliance was indeed the main factor contributing to economic progress is debatable.[78] What cannot be disputed is the tenacity with which the Chinese espoused the principle of self-reliance at international fora. Of course, China has never tried to impose this cherished principle on developing countries during the NIEO process, but it functioned as a model projection that developing countries could ignore only at their own economic peril. The moral of Peking's appeal for self-reliant and independent development of a national economy, whether this is perceived as such or not, is that eternal economic vigilance is indeed the price of political independence.

However, the Chinese principle of self-reliance does not imply autarky. Nor is this a declaration of abstention from bilateral and multilateral aid. The Chinese term, *tzu-li keng-sheng*, literally means "regeneration through one's own efforts"; it thus connotes a means, not an end. Put differently, it means simply that each country should rely *primarily* on her own efforts and resources. But it certainly does not exclude acceptance, as a *Jen-min jih-pao* editorial on the 6th Special Session emphasized, "of foreign aid based on equality and mutual benefit and in accordance with their [the developing countries'] actual needs as a *supplementary* means for developing their national economies."[79]

The principle of self-reliance seems to serve several functions for the Chinese. First, it symbolizes China's ability to stand on her own feet.

[77] Wang Yao-t'ing, "China's Foreign Trade," *PR*, No. 41 (October 11, 1974), 19. In a similar vein, Ch'iao Kuan-hua in his maiden policy speech before the 26th Session of the General Assembly declared: "Since the founding of the People's Republic of China, we, the Chinese people, defying the tight imperialist blockades and withstanding the terrific pressure from without, have built our country into a socialist state with initial prosperity by maintaining independence and keeping the initiative in our own hands and through self-reliance." *PR*, No. 47 (November 19, 1971), 6.
[78] See Alexander Eckstein, *China's Economic Revolution* (London and New York: Cambridge University Press, 1977), especially chap. 4.
[79] *JMJP*, editorial, April 9, 1974, p. 1; emphasis added.

(Note the decline of all external offers of assistance in the wake of the Tangshan earthquake in July 1976. Likewise, China absolutely refuses to receive any kind of UN assistance in any form.) Second, it serves as a diplomatic instrument with which to transform the "old exploitive international aid" into the one designed to accelerate independent and self-reliant development of the national economies of the developing countries. "Bilateral aid or multilateral aid through the United Nations should help recipient countries to progress towards independence and self-reliance," stated a Chinese delegate in the Second Commitee, "and should not reduce their economies to a subordinate position in the name of an 'international division of labour' ."[80] Third, self-reliance may serve Peking's strategy of making a virtue of necessity. New China did not start out with self-reliance; in fact, self-reliance, which Mao admitted was adopted in 1958, as we noted in Chapter 2, was in a way imposed upon China by the progressive deterioration of the Sino-Soviet relationship. In the political and economic circumstances in which China found herself in the late 1950s and early 1960s, there was no viable alternative to independent and self-reliant development of the national economy. Fourth and lastly, the principle of self-reliance may also serve the purpose of warning the developing countries not to expect too much from China, as well as rationalizing or justifying her modest role as a donor of foreign aid.[81]

Proceeding from the dominant concept of independence and self-reliance, China argued that NIEO "should be aimed above all at development of the developing countries."[82] In support of this basic objective, China advanced the following principles and propositions in the course of her participation in the making of the *Declaration*, the *Programme of Action*, and the *Charter*:

Permanent and inalienable resource sovereignty of each nation

Individual and collective self-reliance

Equality, mutual benefit, and mutual respect in international trade

Establishment of various organizations of raw-material-exporting countries for a united struggle against colonialism, imperialism, and hegemony

Economic aid without any political or military conditions (untied aid)

[80] GAOR, 27th Sess., Second Committee, 1455th meeting (5 October 1972), para. 49. For a cogent analysis by a *dependencia* theorist on this point, see Cardoso, "Associated-Dependent Development," pp. 142-76.

[81] See Wang Jun-sheng's speech before the 1824th plenary meeting of ECOSOC on this point. ECOSOR, 53rd Sess., 1824th plenary meeting (6 July 1972), para. 52.

[82] GAOR, 6th Special Sess., *Ad Hoc* Committee, 8th meeting (17 April 1974), para. 49.

Interest-free or low-interest loans to the developing countries

Consultative and participatory democracy in the management of world economic problems

Cancellation, moratorium on, or rescheduling of debt-service payments

Technology transfer to the developing countries to be practical, efficient, economical, and convenient for use

Aid personnel to pass on technical know-how to the people as well as respect and obey the laws and customs of host countries; they must not make special demands or ask for special amenities

All countries, particularly the industrialized countries, to fulfill their bounden duty to protect and improve the human environment

The indemnification principle for the victims of industrial pollution

Aid for the development of the developing countries to be provided by every country

Necessity to reform the Bank Group

No monopoly, discrimination, or dumping in the international market

Imperative of foreign enterprises (MNCs) to meet the needs for economic development as well as to respect and observe the laws of host countries

Economic cooperation among developing countries

Developing countries to help each other politically and economically

Principles of nonreciprocity and special and more favorable treatment of the developing countries, in order to improve their terms of trade

Necessity of emergency measures for helping those developing countries most severely affected by economic problems

Indexation of commodity prices with prices of manufactured goods

A close examination shows that the principles and propositions listed above represent an updated and expanded version of China's own Eight Principles of Foreign Aid.[83] Thus, Chinese participation in the NIEO process provided a historic opportunity for China to refine and broaden the nature and scope of her model of foreign economic relations, which had remained largely bilateral. In short, China's participation in the NIEO process had the effect of multilateralizing its operational principles and behavioral norms governing international economic relations. On the other hand, the *Declaration*, the *Programme*

[83] See "Eight Principles for China's Aid to Foreign Countries," *PR*, No. 17 (April 28, 1972), 15.

of Action, and the *Charter*, in varying degrees and expressions, reflected the essence of the Chinese image of world order. The principle of permanent and inalienable resource sovereignty is firmly embodied in the *Declaration* (operative para. 4(e)), the *Programme of Action* (VII, 1(b)), and the *Charter* (Art. 1). Even the Chinese antihegemony principle found its way into one of the fifteen fundamental principles of international economic relations in the *Charter*, in the following language: "No attempt to seek hegemony and spheres of influence" (Chap. 1(1)).

The Chinese principle of self-reliance has made its influence felt in various forms. The *Programme of Action* makes reference to "collective self-reliance" twice (I, 1, para.b; VII, 1). The *Charter* reiterates in its preambular paragraph 11 that "the responsibility for the development of every country rests primarily upon itself, but that concomitant and effective international co-operation is an essential factor for the full achievement of its own development goals." The *Charter* also makes reference to "the creation of indigenous technology" (Art. 13, 2).

The Chinese developmental model of self-reliance, which used to be pooh-poohed in the world economic community, has now become a serious and respected concept in many UN organs and agencies charged with development activities. In a statement made before the 120th plenary meeting of UNCTAD-IV held in Nairobi in May 1976, Secretary-General Kurt Waldheim summed up "certain significant changes in the current thinking about the content and the style of development": the optimistic assumptions of the 1950s and 1960s about the international developmental approach have been challenged not only in policies but also in philosophical premises. The "key expression" in this reconceptualizing process is "self-reliance." "The national self-reliant approach has its natural extension," continued the Secretary-General, "in the important concept of 'collective self-reliance' as an expression of solidarity within the Third World."[84]

Similarly, in the foreword to his 1975 Annual Report, Bradford Morse, UNDP administrator, stated: "The main emphasis of the [UNDP] programme, and the theme of this report, is the promotion of self-reliance in developing countries, a goal of profound significance for all peoples, regardless of their economic status, social organization or geographical location."[85] Likewise, in his 1976 Annual Report

[84] *Statement Made By the Secretary-General of the United Nations At the 120th Plenary Meeting on 5 May 1976*, UN Doc. TD/202 (5 May 1976), p. 4. See also "Secretary-General Welcomes Third World Collective Self-Reliance Movement," *UN Chronicle* 13 (October 1976), 26.

[85] UNDP, *1975 Annual Report: Building Self-Reliance in Developing Countries*, p. 2.

released in early May 1977, the administrator again noted: "All of these [UNDP] activities had but one purpose: to strengthen the self-reliance of the countries we are privileged to serve."[86] At its 4th Session held in Kinshasa, Zaire, from February 24 to March 3, 1977, the Conference of Ministers of the Economic Commission for Africa (ECA) adopted by consensus a record number of forty resolutions, all of which "reflected a greater awareness by the African States of the need for self-help."[87]

To be sure, there is nothing magical or even profound in the Chinese developmental model of self-reliance. There has been since the late 1960s a groping search for a conceptual alternative to the "international charity" which has had little effect in closing the gap between the rich and the poor in the world economic system, or in alleviating the economic misery of the developing countries on the periphery. There is a sense, then, in which the concept of self-reliance, as it began to be linked with the global search for a *new* economic order, has served as a powerful psychological weapon of self-assertion by the poor against the old economic order.

Viewing the matter in this light, the Chinese also profited from the process of establishing the NIEO principles. However, the most important conclusion to be drawn here is what may be called a "mutual legitimization" between China and NIEO. When all is said and done, the three historic documents of NIEO boil down to a proposition for a global redistribution of economic wealth and political influence on a more just and equitable basis. The principle of sovereignty over national resources, the demand for improved terms of trade for the raw-material-producing countries, and the request for increased transfer of real resources to the developing countries are all designed to carry out that central proposition.

Hence, the fundamentals of NIEO at the conceptual level are congenial to the populist-revisionist orientation in the Maoist image of world order that we have alluded to in Chapter 2. It is in this sense, then, that the three foundations of NIEO have gained a measure of legitimacy because of Chinese participation and approval, on the one hand, and that the Chinese conceptualization of world order has also been legitimized to a large degree by NIEO, on the other.

[86] UNDP, *Report of the Administrator for 1976* (DP/255), p. 4.
[87] "Conference of African Ministers Stresses Self-Help, Stronger ECA Role," *UN Chronicle* 14 (April 1977), 41. Likewise, in his opening address before a conference of the nonaligned nations held in New Delhi in April 1977, Morarji R. Desai, India's prime minister, declared: "[W]e must persist in solving our own problems, rather than depend on the charity and benevolence of others." See "India's Leader Stresses Self-Reliance for Third World," *NYT*, April 8, 1977, p. A4.

· 6 ·

THE NEW INTERNATIONAL
ECONOMIC ORDER, II:
THE IMPLEMENTATION PROCESS

To implement the new international economic order conceptualized in the three historic resolutions is indeed a Titanic task, for it would involve nothing less than restructuring the entire machinery of the world economy. In the wake of the North-South ideological confrontation at the 6th Special Session and the 29th Session of the General Assembly, such varied institutions as the World Bank, the Trilateral Commission, the Brookings Institution, and the Overseas Development Council all counseled for accommodation. But the forces of the neo-conservative school, as exemplified in the writings of Irving Kristol and Daniel P. Moynihan in *The Wall Street Journal* and *Commentary*, championed a major counter-offensive in "the New Cold War."[1] To the Chinese, who have developed a protracted sense of history, "our fighting tasks are arduous, and the road ahead is not smooth, but the future is bright."[2]

What actually happened following the establishment of the three conceptual foundations of NIEO was neither a new cold war nor a North-South confrontation, as many predicted or hoped, but a global negotiation explosion. Figure 6.1 below attempts to simplify the complex, ongoing, multi-channel negotiation processes involved in implementing a new international economic order. Clearly, the 7th Special Session of the General Assembly, devoted to the problems of development and international economic cooperation, played a trail-blazing role in defining broad policy guidelines and parameters of future negotiations.

THE 7TH SPECIAL SESSION

The original idea of the 7th Special Session can be traced to the 4th Summit of the Non-Aligned Countries held in Algiers in September

[1] See Irving Kristol, "The 'New Cold War'," *The Wall Street Journal*, July 17, 1975, p. 18; *The Wall Street Journal*, editorial ("A Word to the Third World"), p. 18; and Daniel P. Moynihan, "The United States in Opposition," *Commentary* 59 (March 1975), 31-44.

[2] This is how Huang Hua projected the future in his summing-up speech before the plenary of the 6th Special Session following the adoption of the *Declaration* and the *Programme of Action*. See GAOR, 6th Special Sess., 2229th plenary meeting (1 May 1974), para. 51.

1973. In its Action Programme for Economic Co-operation, the Summit extended an invitation to the Secretary-General "to convene a special session of the General Assembly at a high political level devoted exclusively to the problems of development."[3] Following the invitation from the Algiers Summit, the 28th Session of the General Assembly decided to hold a special session devoted to development and international cooperation just before its regular 30th Session in 1975, entrusting ECOSOC with all the necessary preparatory tasks.[4] However, two momentous developments occurred between the adoption of this resolution on December 17, 1973 and the convocation of the scheduled special session in the fall of 1975: the adoption of the *Declaration* and the *Programme of Action* by the 6th Special Session and the adoption of the *Charter* by the 29th Session of the General Assembly.

In the face of these developments, the 29th Session of the General Assembly still decided to hold the special session from September 1 to September 12, 1975, but requested ECOSOC, in discharging its overall responsibilities for the preparation of the special session, to convene the Preparatory Committee to work on the recommendations to be submitted to the special session. In addition, the Assembly requested the Secretary-General to collaborate with the heads of UNCTAD, UNIDO, UNDP, IBRD, and IMF so as to enable them to submit to the Preparatory Committee a comprehensive report on the state of international economic activities,

> . . . focusing on constraints of a general policy nature which face the *implementation* of the Programme of Action, as well as the International Development Strategy, with particular emphasis on an integrated approach in the field of commodities, agricultural and industrial development, the transfer of real resources to developing countries, technical assistance, the transfer and development of technologies, the developments in the monetary field and the role of transnational corporations in the development process, so as to enable the special session to contribute further to the appropriate changes in the over-all pattern of international economic relations.[5]

In short, the task of the 7th Special Session, which would have been devoted to the formulation of the conceptual framework for NIEO, was transformed into one of spelling out broad implementation guide-

[3] Fourth Conference of Heads of State or Government of Non-Aligned Countries, Algiers, September 5-9, 1973, *Action Programme for Economic Co-operation*, UN Doc. A/9330 (22 November 1973), p. 99.

[4] General Assembly Resolution 3172 (XXVIII) of 17 December 1973.

[5] General Assembly Resolution 3343 (XXIX) of 17 December 1974; emphasis added.

lines for all the appropriate organs and agencies of the United Nations development system.

In carrying out its preparatory mandate, ECOSOC recommended that the 7th Special Session should focus on the following areas of concern: international trade; transfer of real resources; international monetary reform; science and technology; industrialization; food and agriculture; and restructuring of the economic and social sectors of the system. ECOSOC's recommendation for the provisional agenda was accepted by the plenary of the 7th Special Session. In addition, the plenary decided on the first day, September 1, 1975, acting upon a recommendation made by ECOSOC, to establish an *Ad Hoc* Committee of the session and allocate to it agenda item 7, entitled "Development and International Economic Co-operation." Hence, the negotiation format followed that of the 6th Special Session by consigning to the *Ad Hoc* Committee the task of working out a comprehensive draft resolution by whatever methods it chose to adopt, while conducting the general debate in the plenary.

The *Ad Hoc* Committee, open to all Member States, held only three formal meetings between September 2 and September 16. In the face of a number of documents and position papers submitted by various groups, countries, and organizations, the Committee decided to use the position paper of the Group of 77 as a basis of discussion, "on the understanding this would not preclude the submission and discussion of other proposals."[6] From September 4 to September 15, the members of the *Ad Hoc* Committee held a series of informal meetings and consultations. At its third and final meeting on September 16, the chairman of the Committee (Jan Pronk of the Netherlands) presented a draft resolution (A/AC.176/L.3 and Add.7) formulated during the consultative process, which was unanimously adopted. On the same day the plenary of the 7th Special Session adopted the draft resolution recommended by the *Ad Hoc* Committee as General Assembly Resolution 3362 (S-VII).

The comprehensive omnibus resolution thus adopted specifically states, *inter alia*: (1) that the *Declaration*, the *Programme of Action* and the *Charter* had laid down "the foundations of the new international economic order"; (2) that the overall objective of the new international economic order is to increase the capacity of developing countries, individually and collectively, to pursue their development; and (3) that "to this end and in the context of the foregoing, to set in motion the following measures as the basis and framework for the

[6] GAOR, 7th Special Sess., Annexes, Agenda Item 7, p. 6. For the position paper submitted by the Group of 77, see *UN Chronicle* 12 (October 1975), 70-73, 76.

work of the competent bodies and organizations of the United Nations system."

In short, the resolution assumes that the conceptual foundations of NIEO have already been laid down by the three historic documents, and that what is now called for is a set of broad policy options and implementation guidelines for the United Nations development system. Proceeding from this premise, the resolution called for many measures, including the following:

International Trade: expansion and diversification of the developing countries' trade, improvement of their productive capacity, and the increase of their export earnings;

Transfer of Real Resources and International Monetary Reforms: confirmation of continued commitment of developed countries in respect of the targets relating to the transfer of resources, in particular the official development assistance target of 0.7 per cent of GNP, as agreed in the International Development Strategy for the Second United Nations Development Decade; establishment of a link between the special drawing rights and development assistance should form part of the consideration by IMF of the creation of new special drawing rights as and when they are created according to the needs of international liquidity; the resources of the development institutions of the United Nations system, in particular UNDP, should also be increased; the World Bank Group is invited to consider new ways of supplementing its financing with private management, skills, technology and capital;

Science and Technology: The establishment, strengthening and development of the scientific and technological infrastructure of developing countries; significant expansion of assistance for direct support to science and technology programmes of developing countries; establishment of an international code of conduct for the transfer of technology; an urgent need to formulate national and international policies to avoid the "brain drain" and to obviate its adverse effects;

Industrialization: Endorsement of the Lima Declaration and Plan of Action on Industrial Development Co-operation and a request to all governments to take individually and/or collectively the necessary measures and decisions required to implement effectively their undertakings in terms of the Lima Declaration and Plan of Action (see Figure 6.1);

Food and Agriculture: Developed countries and developing countries in a position to do so should pledge, on a voluntary basis, substantial contributions to the proposed International Fund for

Agricultural Development (IFAD) so as to enable it to come into being by the end of 1975, with initial resources of SDR $1,000 million;

Cooperation Among Developing Countries: Both developed countries and the United Nations system should provide support and assistance to developing countries in strengthening and enlarging their mutual cooperation at subregional, regional, and interregional levels;

Restructuring of Sectors of the United Nations System: To initiate the process of restructuring the United Nations system so as to make it more responsive to the requirements of the *Declaration*, the *Programme of Action*, and the *Charter*, an *Ad Hoc* Committee on the Restructuring of the Economic and Social Sectors of the United Nations System should be established to prepare detailed action proposals.

The above represents a small sampling of the voluminous measures and proposals contained in the resolution. Jahangir Amuzegar, one of the most articulate spokesmen for the Third World, characterized the resolution as "one of the most productive resolutions by the United Nations in recent years."[7] Even Daniel P. Moynihan, in his capacity as the chief US representative, remarked at the closing of the session: "Perhaps never before in the history of the United Nations has there been so intensive and so genuine a negotiation among so many nations on so profoundly important a range of issues. We have shown that we can negotiate in good faith and, in doing so, reach genuine accord. Not least, we have shown that this can be done in the unique and indispensable setting of the United Nations. The system works."[8]

There is a general agreement in both North and South that the spirit of conciliation, compromise, and consensus prevailed during the 7th Special Session, producing one of the most comprehensive resolutions in UN history. In the aftermath of the bitter ideological confrontation at the 6th Special Session, both sides engaged in some soul searching, and both sides approached the 7th Special Session in a spirit of compromise and conciliation. During the preparatory process, the moderate faction prevailed over the militant faction within the Group of 77; as a result, the position paper of the Group of 77 avoided some

[7] "The North-South Dialogue: From Conflict to Compromise," *Foreign Affairs* 54 (April 1976), 551-52.

[8] GAOR, 7th Special Sess., 2349th plenary meeting (16 September 1975), para. 63. This can hardly be accepted as Moynihan's *personal* view. For Moynihan's personal essay, which sharply differs in tone and substance from his closing remarks at the 7th Special Session, see Daniel P. Moynihan, "Abiotrophy in Turtle Bay: The United Nations in 1975," *Harvard International Law Journal* 17 (Summer 1976), 465-502.

of the most controversial questions.[9] Apparently in a spirit of conciliation, Garcia Robles of Mexico, speaking on behalf of the Group of 77,
nominated Jan Pronk of the Netherlands for the office of chairman of
the *Ad Hoc* Committee. Although the Committee decided to use the
position paper of the Group of 77 as a basis of discussion, the *modus
operandi* was consultation, not confrontation, striving toward a consensus.

While persisting in its substantive policy position, the United States,
too, adopted a moderate and accommodating posture toward the 7th
Special Session, as noted in Moynihan's closing remarks. The United
States was willing to negotiate each of the Third World demands on
its intrinsic merit, but refused to accept a sweeping or integrated approach. While the United States was willing to allow the *Ad Hoc*
Committee to adopt the chairman's submission of the draft resolution
unanimously, Ambassador Meyerson stated that the American position
on the *Declaration*, the *Programme of Action*, the *Charter* as well as
on the Lima Declaration and Plan of Action had not changed; that is,
the United States "could not and did not accept any implication that
the world was now embarked on the establishment of something called
the 'New International Economic Order'."[10]

Clearly, the 7th Special Session did not—and could not—implement
this in one stroke. But, in the spirit of constructive North-South dialogue, it did take the first crucial step in the implementation process
by setting in motion a series of global negotiations. Perhaps wisely,
ECOSOC reached an understanding during its preparatory process
that the session should concentrate on broad implementation guidelines, entrusting specialized and technical agencies of the United Nations development system with the task of negotiating specific agreements. "This negotiation is about change," remarked Secretary-General
Kurt Waldheim at the closing of the session, "it is not about a smoother
management of the *status quo*."[11] The complex negotiation (implementation) processes that have followed the 7th Special Session are
illustrated in a simplified form in Figure 6.1.

The PRC's participation in the 7th Special Session resumed a low-
keyed tone in giving support to the Third World. In sharp contrast to
the 6th Special Session, the 10-man delegation headed by Li Ch'iang,
minister of foreign trade, returned to Peking without much public ado;
the press coverage was also routine. In the course of twenty-five ple-

[9] Gosovic and Ruggie, "On the Creation of a New International Economic
Order," p. 321.

[10] GAOR, 7th Special Sess., *Ad Hoc* Committee, 3rd meeting (16 September
1975), paras. 10-11.

[11] GAOR, 7th Special Sess., 2349th plenary meeting (16 September 1975),
para. 93.

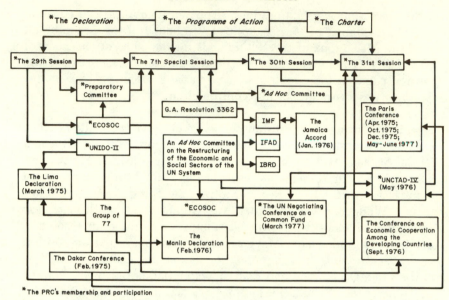

FIGURE 6.1. The Implementation Process of the New International Economic Order.

nary meetings of the session, the Chinese made only two speeches: Li Ch'iang's opening policy speech on September 2 and Huang Hua's closing remarks on September 16. In the *Ad Hoc* Committee, Chinese representative Chang Hsien-wu made one short statement, expressing China's support "for all the just demands and reasonable proposals contained in the position paper of the Group of 77, which should form the basis for continued negotiations between the interested parties at the seventh special session of the General Assembly."[12]

In his opening speech before the plenary, Li Ch'iang defined the 7th Special Session in the following terms: "The Declaration and the Programme of Action adopted by the U.N. General Assembly at its sixth special session have laid down a series of correct principles for the establishment of a new international economic order. Our task now is to continue to uphold and conscientiously implement these principles."[13] Proceeding from this premise, Li Ch'iang conceptualized the problem of development as one of "combating imperialist and particularly superpower control, plunder and exploitation, thoroughly destroying the old international economic relations built thereon, establishing

[12] GAOR, 7th Special Sess., *Ad Hoc* Committee, 2nd meeting (3 September 1975), para. 15.
[13] *PR*, No. 37 (September 12, 1975), 16.

288

a new international economic order and clearing away the numerous obstacles on the road to the independent development of their national economy."[14] Predictably, China gave her verbal support to the demands and propositions advanced at the Conference of Developing Countries on Raw Materials held in Dakar in February 1975 as well as those contained in the Lima Declaration and Plan of Action. Specifically, China supported: (1) establishment of various associations of raw material exporting countries for a united struggle; (2) the integrated programme for commodities; (3) indexation of commodity prices; (4) reform of the international monetary system through consultation on an equal footing; (5) removal of all unreasonable restrictions in the way of technology transfer; and (6) restructuring of the economic sectors of the United Nations system to meet the needs of establishing a new international economic order.

Perhaps the most interesting feature of Li Ch'iang's speech came in the form of a model projection about how China herself was handling the development problem. It was essential, Li Ch'iang argued, to handle correctly the relationship between agriculture, light industry, and heavy industry. He then stated:

> In the light of her own conditions, China has formulated a general policy of taking agriculture as the foundation and industry as the leading factor in developing the national economy and made her national economic plans according to this order of priorities: agriculture, light industry and heavy industry. . . . It must be stressed that if a country is not basically sufficient in foodgrain but has to rely on imports, it may be taken by the neck at any time and find itself in a very passive and dangerous position.[15]

At this and other international fora, the Chinese have repeatedly defined the NIEO process not in terms of a North-South problem but in terms of a united struggle of the Second and Third Worlds against the First World (the two superpowers). Yet in tone and in varying degrees of substance, the Chinese have been more trenchant in their attack on the Soviet social imperialists than on American imperialists. Throughout my field interviews with American officials in the organs and agencies of the United Nations development system, I have found that the Chinese are getting along well with Americans in their day-to-day functional activities. While applauding "the struggle of the second world countries against superpower control and exploitation and their tendency to establishing ties with third world countries," Li Ch'iang declared: "What calls for special attention is that this superpower

[14] *Ibid.*, p. 13.   [15] *Ibid.*, p. 14.

[the Soviet Union], taking advantage of its rival's decline and loss of initiative, is stepping up its aggression, infiltration and expansion in the third world and actively extending its social-imperialist system of exploitation."[16]

The Chinese anti-Soviet stand is in part a reaction to the position the Soviet Union has consistently taken throughout the NIEO process. While giving verbal support to the demands of the Third World as embodied in the *Declaration*, the *Programme of Action*, and the *Charter*, the Soviet Union has set herself apart from the mainstream of NIEO politics. Simply stated, the Soviet Union, whether speaking through her own representatives or through an appointed spokesman of Group *D*, has refused to see NIEO in terms of North-South or rich-poor problems; instead, it is conceptualized as a West-South conflict. Soviet spokesmen have repeatedly attempted to wrap the demands of the Third World in the package of the indemnification thesis. That is, the demands of the Third World represent a just and legitimate indemnity for Western colonial exploitation of the developing countries in the Southern hemisphere. Hence, the Soviet Union cannot be expected to share any responsibility in the compensation process. It was in this vein that the Soviet representative tried—without success and with vigorous Chinese opposition—to strike out the word "new" from "the new international economic order" at the 6th Special Session. Likewise, the representative of Czechoslovakia, speaking on behalf of the Soviet bloc Member States in the United Nations—Bulgaria, the Byelorussia SSR, the German Democratic Republic, Hungary, Mongolia, Poland, the Ukrainian SSR, the Soviet Union, and Czechoslovakia—issued the following statement of "reservation" in the *Ad Hoc* Committee of the 7th Special Session just before its unanimous adoption of the draft resolution: "While supporting the developing countries in their just demands, we maintain that there cannot be an equal responsibility of all for the unfavourable economic situation of the developing countries which was inherited from the colonial system and preserved and, in many cases, even made worse by neo-colonial policies. Our non-acceptance of such an untrue placing of responsibility [on all developed countries] will be relevant as regards some recommendations in the final document."[17]

The above statement, which sums up the Soviet position on the new international economic order, represents to the Chinese a confirmation of their belief that the Soviet leadership is indeed practicing socialism in words but imperialism in deeds. Yet, the Chinese assessment of the 7th Special Session was curiously guarded, lacking complete enthusi-

[16] *PR*, No. 37 (September 12, 1975), 14.
[17] GAOR, 7th Special Sess., Annexes, Agenda Item 7, p. 15.

asm. Even the radical spokesman of the Group of 77, Abdelaziz Bou-teflika, the foreign minister of Algeria who served as the president of both the 29th and 7th Special Sessions, held that the work of the 7th Special Session "would go down in history as a milestone of progressive ideas."[18] In his closing remarks at the session, Huang Hua cautiously observed: "Through a series of struggles, the session finally achieved *relatively* positive results. The Chinese delegation supports the resolution adopted by the current session. In our opinion, this document basically reflects some of the just propositions and reasonable demands of the developing countries in the fields of international economics and trade."[19] Huang Hua then concluded that the proceedings of the session clearly showed that the establishment of the new international economic order "is by no means all plain sailing and that the obstacle comes mainly from the two super-Powers."[20]

The PRC's Participation in the NIEO Implementation Process

As noted earlier, the 7th Special Session confined itself to providing broad implementation guidelines. Owing to the high degree of fragmentation and decentralization of the United Nations development system, the actual processes of implementing the new international economic order through global negotiations are inevitably diffused, with each particular organ or agency dealing with the particular demand of the Third World within its competence or jurisdiction. In fact, the resolution adopted by the 7th Special Session specifically decided in the last preambular paragraph "to set in motion the following measures as the basis and framework for the work of the competent bodies and organizations of the United Nations system."

Figure 6.1 and Figure 6.2 together give some idea of the competent bodies and organizations referred to in the resolution. The most important and most immediately related organs and agencies in the NIEO implementation processes include ECOSOC, IBRD, IMF, UNCTAD, UNIDO, UNDP, as well as such newly established organs or programs as the Special Fund, the *Ad Hoc* Committee on the Restructuring of the Economic and Social Sectors of the United Nations System, the International Fund for Agricultural Development (IFAD), and the World Food Council (WFC). It should be noted in this connection that the General Assembly has also linked the (Paris) International

[18] *UN Chronicle* 12 (October 1975), 6.
[19] GAOR, 7th Special Sess., 2349th plenary meeting (16 September 1975), para. 39; emphasis added.
[20] *Ibid.*, para. 43.

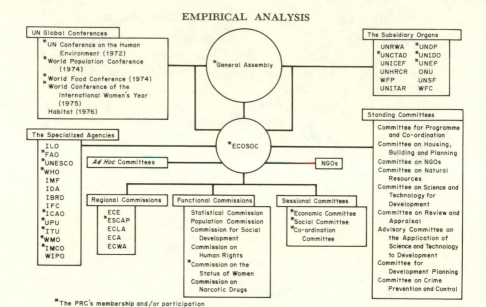

FIGURE 6.2. Structure of the United Nations System for Economic, Social, and Technical Activities (1976).

Economic Co-operation Conference—also known as North-South dialogue—to the NIEO implementation processes by (1) requesting the participating governments in the Conference to ensure that their deliberations and decisions take full account of the NIEO principles; (2) inviting the Conference to report on its conclusions to the General Assembly; and (3) requesting the Secretary-General of the United Nations to submit to the General Assembly through ECOSOC a report on his participation in the Conference.[21] It may be recalled here that the Paris Conference started on the original Western proposal for a producer-consumer forum on energy. The Third World thus succeeded, first, in expanding the scope of this North-South dialogue to all the NIEO issues dividing the rich from the poor and, second, in linking the Conference to the General Assembly, where it enjoys a greater political leverage.

For a number of reasons, Chinese participation in the implementation processes through the competent organs and agencies of the United Nations development system has been selective and passive.

[21] General Assembly Resolution 3515 (XXX) of 15 December 1975. In a follow-up resolution (31/14), the 31st General Assembly expressed its "growing concern that most of the developed countries participating in the Conference on International Economic Co-operation have yet to demonstrate the necessary political will to achieve concrete results" and urged all the countries participating "to make all the necessary efforts to ensure the success of the Conference."

Nonetheless, the Chinese have explicitly and repeatedly stated that "the essential task before the United Nations bodies concerned with development activities was to implement those two documents [the *Declaration* and the *Programme of Action*] and to readjust their work in the light of the principles and spirit of the Declaration."[22] Specifically, the Chinese argued that the policies and programs of the following bodies should now be reformulated or readjusted toward the implementation of the new international economic order: ECOSOC, UNCTAD, UNIDO, the Regional Economic Commissions, the World Food Conference, UNDP, and the specialized agencies.[23] Before elaborating on the reasons for the Chinese selective and passive participation, however, we need to mention the organs, agencies, and programs in which China opted not to participate.

It may be logically argued that greater participatory decision making in the United Nations development system has to precede the formulation of any new rules and the restructuring of the existing machinery. In fact, the Chinese have repeatedly stressed the need for this in order to implement NIEO principles. Yet, in a curious contradiction, the Chinese have shown little interest in, or enthusiasm for, participating in the restructuring process. They have opted not to participate in the *Ad Hoc* Committee on the Restructuring of the Economic and Social Sectors of the United Nations System. This Committee, open to the participation of all Member States, was created by the omnibus resolution adopted by the 7th Special Session with the specific task of restructuring the United Nations system in such a way as to make it more responsive to the requirements of the *Declaration*, the *Programme of Action*, and the *Charter*.

Between its establishment in September 1975 and April 1977, the Committee held five sessions. The mandate of the Committee, in the words of its chairman, Kenneth Dadzie of Ghana, differs from previous

[22] GAOR, 29th Sess., Second Committee, 1603rd meeting (9 October 1974), para. 32. See also UN Docs. E/AC.24/SR.522 (11 July 1974), p. 522; E/AC.24/SR.599 (28 July 1976), pp. 4-5.

[23] The Chinese statements to this effect were made in the Second Committee of the General Assembly, the ECOSOC plenary, and the ECOSOC's sessional committees. See the following: GAOR, 29th Sess., Second Committee, 1594th meeting (2 October 1974), para. 21; GAOR, 30th Sess., Second Committee, 1666th meeting (14 October 1975), para. 24; UN Doc. A/C.2/31/SR.13 (15 October 1976), p. 11; ECOSOR, 57th Sess., 1907th plenary meeting (9 July 1974), paras. 29, 37; ECOSOR, 57th Sess., 1916th plenary meeting (19 July 1974), para. 66; ECOSOR, 57th Sess., 1921st plenary meeting (2 August 1974), paras. 24-25; ECOSOR, 59th Sess., 1957th plenary meeting (4 July 1975), paras. 22-23; ECOSOR, 59th Sess., 1967th plenary meeting (14 July 1975), para. 44; UN Docs. E/AC.6/SR.691 (8 July 1974), p. 54; E/AC.6/SR.696 (11 July 1974), p. 108; E/AC.6/SR.702 (16 July 1974), p. 168; E/AC.6/SR.730 (23 April 1975), p. 87; E/AC.6/SR.735 (7 July 1975), p. 4; E/AC.24/SR.564 (15 July 1975), p. 89.

reform efforts in being "broader in scope, enormously complex, and governed by the unique conceptual framework of the new international economic order." The Committee has already identified eight "problem areas" and has reached some measure of agreement on the issues involved. The eight problem areas are: (1) the General Assembly; (2) ECOSOC; (3) other negotiating forums; (4) structures for regional and interregional cooperation; (5) operational activities; (6) planning programming, budgeting, and evaluation; (7) interagency coordination; and (8) Secretariat support services.[24] The 31st General Assembly extended the mandate of the Committee for another year so as to enable it to submit final recommendations to the 32nd General Assembly through ECOSOC.

Likewise, China declined to be elected a member of the *Ad Hoc* Committee on the Special Programme. This committee was created by the *Programme of Action* to make recommendations, *inter alia*, on the scope, machinery, and modes of operation of the Special Fund, which was created to provide emergency measures to mitigate the difficulties of those developing countries most seriously affected by economic crisis, particularly the least developed and landlocked countries. As such, it is conceptually congenial to China's repeated public support for special and emergency relief measures for the least developed countries. Yet, she excluded herself from this 36-member Committee.

China attended the World Food Conference held in Rome from November 5 to November 16, 1974, but decided not to participate in two of its offshoots: the World Food Council (WFC) and the International Fund for Agricultural Development (IFAD). Acting upon the recommendation of the World Food Conference,[25] the 29th Session of the General Assembly established a 36-member WFC as an organ of the United Nations, reporting to the General Assembly through ECOSOC.[26] It was designed "to serve as a co-ordinating mechanism to provide over-all, integrated and continuing attention for the successful co-ordination and follow-up of policies concerning food production, nutrition, food security, food trade and food aid, as well as other related matters, by all the agencies of the United Nations system."[27] China declined to be nominated as a member from the Asian Group for the Council membership.

IFAD, too, grew out of a resolution adopted at the World Food

[24] UN Press Release, GA/RES/41 (28 April 1977), pp. 1-4.
[25] Resolution XXII, in *Report of the World Food Conference, Rome, 5-16 November 1974*, UN Doc. E/CONF.65/20 (1975), pp. 18-19.
[26] General Assembly Resolution 3348 (XXIX) of 17 December 1974.
[27] Operative para. 1 of Resolution XXII adopted at the World Food Conference, in *Report of the World Food Conference, Rome, 5-16 November 1974*, UN Doc. E/CONF.65/20 (1975), p. 18.

Conference.[28] The omnibus resolution of the 7th Special Session makes special reference to the proposed IFAD, as we noted earlier. The UN Conference on the Establishment of an International Fund for Agricultural Development, convened by the Secretary-General in accordance with General Assembly Resolution 3503 (XXX), had taken place in Rome from June 10 to June 13, 1976. When the target of $1 billion in convertible currencies was achieved, the IFAD Agreement was to be opened for signature and thereafter, as soon as $750 million of pledges were ratified, IFAD would become operational.[29]

IFAD was thus designed to be a major new source of financial assistance to food production and agricultural development, particularly for the least developed countries. Following the 1976 Rome Conference, the WFC secretariat held a series of meetings involving the countries interested in participating in IFAD. As of mid-February 1977, some ninety-one countries pledged contributions totaling $1,022 million, thus exceeding the target. Of this, $567 million will be contributed by the developed countries, $435.5 million by the OPEC countries, and about $20 million by the developing countries. It was hopefully predicted at the WFC secretariat that the final ratification procedures would be completed by mid-1977, fulfilling the legal requirements to make IFAD operative.[30] China did not attend the 1976 Rome Conference, nor has she pledged any contributions to the Fund.

Of course, China could not—and would not—participate in any reforming or restructuring processes involving IBRD, IFC, and IMF. She has taken a step further by declaring that she would not participate in any activities sponsored by the World Bank Group even in the context of the NIEO implementation process. More significantly, China is not a member of the Group of 77 or of the nonaligned countries; as such, she does not participate in the numerous meetings, caucuses, and conferences sponsored by both groups. The importance and impact of these conferences in the global implementation processes of NIEO principles were illustrated in Figure 6.1. It may not be an exaggeration to say that the Group of 77 constitutes the strongest economic link and the nonaligned countries the strongest political link

---

[28] Resolution XIII in *ibid.*, pp. 12-13.

[29] *Report of the World Food Council*, UN Doc. WFC/29 (24 June 1976), p. 9.

[30] The data and figures used in this paragraph were obtained through my field interview at the WFC secretariat in Rome in February 1977 (see Interview Schedule). Since this chapter was completed, the following development took place. On October 27, 1977, Abdelmuhsin M. Al-Sudeary (Saudi Arabia), chairman of the Preparatory Commission of IFAD, announced at a press briefing at UN Headquarters that "the Fund would begin operations in December as a specialized agency." See *UN Chronicle* 24 (November 1977), 18. With the ratification of the Agreement by Finland, the fifty-second state to do so, IFAD became operational as a new UN specialized agency on December 1, 1977.

to the NIEO process. Yet, China has excluded herself from these linkage politics.

China could change her mind and ask for membership, following the Romanian example. She could send her observers to the periodic Non-Aligned Summit Conference and to the conferences sponsored by the Group of 77, as Sweden often does. China has done none of this, confining herself to editorial and moral support from a distant sideline.[31] As a result, she did not participate in the Dakar Conference (February 1975), the Lima Conference (March 1975), the Manila Conference (February 1976), or the Mexico City Conference (September 1976), all of which provided important inputs for NIEO implementation processes.

Thus, China's participation has been limited to the General Assembly, ECOSOC, UNCTAD, UNIDO, UNDP, and eight of the fourteen specialized agencies. China's participation and behavior in the Assembly need not be recapitulated here. Her behavior in the specialized agencies will be analyzed in Chapter 7. It is also beyond the purview of this chapter to give a detailed analysis of the Chinese participation in ECOSOC, UNCTAD, UNIDO, and UNDP. The present discussion is confined to highlighting some salient features of Chinese behavior in those four selected bodies, in order to show the institutional dimensions of the Chinese conceptualization of the new international economic order.

The Economic and Social Council (ECOSOC)

Chinese participation in ECOSOC tends to be more symbolic than substantive. As Figure 6.2 shows, China participates in only one functional commission—the Commission on the Status of Women—and, more significantly, in none of the nine standing committees. When asked to comment on the most salient characteristic of the Chinese behavior in ECOSOC, one European representative to ECOSOC responded with the phrase, "inward-looking and non-aggressive uniqueness." He then went on to say: "If I were to attempt to get a piece of a resolution passed by ECOSOC, I might approach the Soviet mission or African missions, but I won't bother the Chinese."

Yet, the PRC stands out symbolically in ECOSOC. What highlights her participation is the fact that the ROC was not only treated as a pariah in the United Nations' North-South politics, dominated by the Third World, but after the beginning of 1961 was also excluded from

---

[31] *Jen-min jih-pao* has been providing consistent editorial support to all the conferences sponsored by the nonaligned countries and the Group of 77.

ECOSOC membership, contrary to the well-established practice that the five permanent members of the Security Council are automatically reelected to membership. Between 1961 and 1971, the "China" seat in ECOSOC was conspicuously empty, showing that ECOSOC, too, was plagued by the question of Chinese representation. Immediately after the PRC's debut in the General Assembly in mid-November 1971, however, Thailand withdrew her candidacy for ECOSOC membership in deference to the greater importance of China. The PRC easily got herself elected after this Thai gesture, and was reelected in 1974 as a member of ECOSOC. By thus filling up the empty seat "reserved" for one of the Big Five since 1972, the PRC has cleared away the legitimacy problem of ECOSOC.

Irrespective of the scope and level of her participation, the representational and symbolic importance of China's presence in ECOSOC cannot be gainsaid. China's membership added a measure of legitimacy to ECOSOC's decision-making process. To a much greater extent than the Security Council, the decisions of ECOSOC are made through informal consultations. The established practice is that, after the secretary of ECOSOC has introduced the relevant documents, the members of the Council begin to hold informal consultative meetings to settle all major problems. Subsequently, it holds a formal debate to hear statements on substantive issues, but most decisions or resolutions are adopted without vote.[32] Between 1972 and 1976, for example, there were only 24 roll-call votes in the plenary and the three sessional committees combined.[33] Of these, China cast 22 positive votes, 1 negative vote, and 1 abstention.

Thus, the Chinese voting record in ECOSOC, though it centers on the controversial issues pressed to roll-call votes, shows a much higher "agreement score" with the organ's consensus than China's voting records in the Security Council and the General Assembly. One negative vote that China cast needs to be explained. In the course of debate in the Economic Committee of the Council centering on the Lebanese proposal to establish an Economic Commission for Western Asia, the United States submitted a draft resolution (E/AC.6/L.520) to solicit an advisory opinion of the International Court of Justice before acting on the Lebanese draft resolution. Chinese representative Wang Jung-

[32] For a reiteration of this past practice by the president of the 1976 Organizational Session of ECOSOC, see ECOSOR, Organizational Session for 1976, 1982nd plenary meeting (13 January 1976), paras. 22, 26. For consensual trend in the decision-making process within the United Nations, see also *Report of the Economic and Social Council on the Work of Its Fifty-Sixth and Fifty-Seventh Sessions*, GAOR, 29th Sess., Supp. No. 3 (A/9603), p. ix.

[33] This computation is based on UNDEX, Series B, Vol. III, No. 3 (March 1972)-Vol. VIII, No. 2 (February 1977).

sheng argued that ECOSOC, as the intergovernmental body in the United Nations responsible for economic and social affairs, "was fully authorized to decide on the establishment of an economic commission for Western Asia in accordance with the common desire of Arab countries of that region" and then voted against the US draft resolution.[34] The US draft resolution was rejected by 30 votes to 10, with 8 abstentions; the Committee then adopted the Lebanese draft resolution by a vote of 33 in favor to 8 opposed, with 9 abstentions, thus clearing the way for the establishment of an additional regional Economic Commission for Western Asia (ECWA).

What is the PRC's conceptualization of ECOSOC? The *Declaration* and the *Programme of Action* marked a turning point in the evolution of Chinese thinking on this question. Before the 6th Special Session, the Chinese held the view that ECOSOC was in a mess functionally and structurally and that its functions needed strengthening through streamlining. There was nothing unique in the Chinese view, which was almost universally shared in and out of the United Nations.[35] As Figure 6.2 shows, the Council has had an almost impossible multiple task to perform without sufficient power, prestige, or support. In spite of its expanding membership, ECOSOC was largely ignored by the Third World in the formulation of NIEO principles. As noted earlier, it was UNCTAD that served as a conceptual and strategic springboard in the Third World's concerted drive to establish the foundations of NIEO.

The Chinese advocated strengthening the functions of ECOSOC in accordance with the purposes and principles of the UN Charter. What kind of reform or strengthening? Here the Chinese merely repeated the well-known complaints about ECOSOC: the meetings of the Council and its related bodies had been too frequent and too ineffective; the agendas of these bodies were overloaded, lacking focus on important items; the documents were too abundant, too lengthy, and not made available in sufficient time to enable a delegation to study them thoroughly before each session; too many decisions were made too hastily, too often; there were too many organs and committees with overlapping functions. In sum, ECOSOC was overbureaucratized,

---

[34] UN Doc. E/AC.6/SR.658 (2 August 1973), p. 111.

[35] For the major problems and common criticisms of ECOSOC, see Robert W. Gregg, "UN Economic, Social, and Technical Activities," in Barros, *The United Nations*, pp. 240-43; Hill, *Towards Greater Order, Coherence and Coordination in the United Nations System*, chap. 9; Walter R. Sharp, *The United Nations Economic and Social Council* (New York: Columbia University Press, 1969). In addition, introductory remarks by the president of ECOSOC at the beginning of the annual *Report of the Economic and Social Council* (GAOR, Supp. No. 3) give a critical self-evaluation of the problems and challenges confronting ECOSOC.

lacking a clear sense of direction.[36] It was from this sense of dissatisfaction with the structure of ECOSOC that China decided not to participate in all the standing committees, but has participated fully in
the three sessional committees—the Economic Committee, the Social
Committee, and the Co-ordination Committee—as well as in the
plenary.

It was against this background that China seized the *Declaration* and
the *Programme of Action* as the principal criterion for redefining the
role of ECOSOC. After the 6th Special Session, references to the
principles and purposes of the UN Charter disappeared; ECOSOC
now had a new and clearly defined task. In less than two months after
the adoption of the *Declaration* and the *Programme of Action* by the
6th Special Session, Chinese representative Pu Ming declared at the
1907th plenary meeting of ECOSOC on July 9, 1974: "The Programme
of Action made the Council responsible for defining the policy framework and co-ordinating the activities of all organizations in the United
Nations systems [*sic*] implementing the Programme. The Council's
discussions on all the agenda items at the present session should therefore be guided by the purposes and principles embodied in the
Programme of Action and the Declaration. The Chinese delegation
would work with the other delegations in carrying out the task entrusted to the Council."[37] This point has been repeatedly stated by the
Chinese delegates in subsequent sessions. Likewise, the Chinese expressed pleasure in noting that some of the regional economic commissions had made references to the *Declaration* and the *Programme of
Action* in their annual reports to ECOSOC.[38] ECOSOC, whose task
had been made unfocused and unmanageable owing to its multiple
role,[39] received a new and coherent *raison d'être*. This has now become
the Chinese conceptualization of the central task confronting ECOSOC.

[36] See UN Docs. E/AC.24/SR.442 (12 July 1972), p. 121; E/AC.24/SR.469
(30 April 1973), pp. 101-02.
[37] ECOSOR, 57th Sess., 1907th plenary meeting (9 July 1974), para. 37. See
also UN Doc. E/AC.24/SR.545 (1 August 1974), p. 194. The *Programme of
Action* states in IX (3): "The Economic and Social Council shall define the
policy framework and co-ordinate the activities of all organizations, insttiutions
and subsidiary bodies within the United Nations system which shall be entrusted
with the task of implementing the present Programme of Action. . . ." Likewise,
the General Assembly decided in its Resolution 3486 (XXX) of 12 December
1975 "to entrust the Economic and Social Council with the task of reviewing
the implementation of the Charter of Economic Rights and Duties of States with
a view to preparing adequately its systematic and comprehensive consideration
by the General Assembly, as a separate item, as provided in article 34 of the
Charter, and to report on the progress achieved to the Assembly at its thirty-
second session."
[38] See ECOSOR, 59th Sess., 1967th plenary meeting (14 July 1975), para. 44;
and UN Doc. E/AC.6/SR.691 (8 July 1974), p. 54.
[39] See Sharp, *The United Nations Economic and Social Council*, chap. 1.

The United Nations Conference on Trade
and Development (UNCTAD)

Like so many of the UN committees and subsidiary bodies, UNCTAD has a somewhat misleading title. It represents a sort of semantic compromise between the objective of the developed countries, who did not want to give too much permanency and prestige to this offshoot, and that of the developing countries, who wanted an organization of a permanent nature. Despite its title, UNCTAD is more than *ad hoc* or periodic conference on trade and development.

Since its 4th Session in May 1976, the membership of UNCTAD has stood at 154, consisting of those states that are members of the United Nations or members of the specialized agencies or of IAEA. Besides the quadrennial session of the Conference, UNCTAD has its own secretariat (headed by its own secretary-general) in Geneva and a liaison office in New York. Its permanent executive body, the Trade and Development Board (TDB), which used to be a limited-membership organ, was made a committee of the whole open to all members of UNCTAD by the General Assembly at its 31st Session.[40]

TDB holds its annual session, as well as special sessions, as a permanent policy-recommending body for UNCTAD. The bulk of TDB's work is carried out in its seven main committees, each of which deals specifically and respectively with the following matters: (1) commodities; (2) manufactures; (3) invisibles and financing related to trade; (4) shipping; (5) preferences; (6) transfer of technology; and (7) economic cooperation among developing countries. In addition, UNCTAD has such subsidiary bodies as the working group on international shipping legislation, the committee on tungsten, and the permanent group on synthetics and substitutes.

There seems little doubt that UNCTAD served as one of the main conceptual architects in the establishment of the new international economic order. It was through Raúl Prebisch, the first secretary-general of UNCTAD, that the concept of development-oriented trade evolved to deal with the deepening crisis of deteriorating terms of trade for the developing countries.[41] It was through the Working

---

[40] See General Assembly Resolution 31/2 of 1 October 1976. Before this resolution was adopted, TDB had 68 members (the figure used to be 55, prior to UNCTAD-III), who were elected from the four groups of states at each quadrennial session of the Conference and served until the election of their successors at the next Conference. Here again, the PRC's election by UNCTAD-III in 1972 as a member of TDB from Group A stood out in a symbolic contrast to the exclusion of the ROC from TDB in previous years.

[41] See "Statement by Mr. Raúl Prebisch, Secretary-General of the United Nations Conference on Trade and Development," *Proceedings of UNCTAD*, Geneva, 23 March-16 June 1964, Vol. II: *Policy Statements*, pp. 76-77.

Group established by UNCTAD-III that the drafting of the *Charter* was successfully negotiated. And the *Declaration* and the *Programme of Action* represent a final product of the ideas and principles first debated and embodied in various UNCTAD resolutions prior to the 6th Special Session.

Since the enactment of the three historic documents and the omnibus resolution on implementation guidelines, UNCTAD has turned itself into one of the most active and important negotiational fora in the NIEO implementation politics. Likewise, the General Assembly affirmed and reaffirmed the important role of UNCTAD in the realization of the NIEO principles and objectives. In its Resolution 3459 (XXX) (1975), for example, the General Assembly affirmed "the importance of the fourth session of the United Nations Conference on Trade and Development in the negotiation and the implementation of concrete proposals, particularly on the question relating to trade in commodities and manufactures, monetary and financial issues and the transfer of technology emerging from the sixth and seventh special sessions of the General Assembly." The present discussion about Chinese participation in UNCTAD, therefore, centers on implementation politics in UNCTAD from the beginning of 1975 to early 1977.

Although her maneuverability is limited by the rigid structure of group politics, China as an "independent party" participated in a wide range of UNCTAD meetings. Based on the data obtained through my field interviews at the UNCTAD secretariat in Geneva, Table 6.1 is constructed to show the evolving pattern of Chinese participation. The table shows that China participated in UNCTAD-IV (as well as UNCTAD-III in 1972), in TDB, in four of the seven main committees, and even in two subsidiary bodies. At its third quadrennial session in 1972, the Conference instructed TDB to convert the main committees into committees open to the participation of all interested Member States of UNCTAD, on the understanding that those wishing to be a member of any or all of the main committees so notified their intention during the preceding regular session of TDB.

In short, membership in the main committees is both open-ended and self-appointed. Viewed in this light, China's nonparticipation in the Committee on Economic Co-operation Among Developing Countries, the newest main committee created by TDB at its 16th Session in 1976, is revealing. On the other hand, China participated more extensively and more actively in one of the subsidiary bodies—the Committee on Tungsten—tungsten having obvious interest or implications for the Chinese economy.

Chinese participation in UNCTAD meetings has generally taken the reactive and passive posture of supporting all the "just and legitimate"

TABLE 6.1. UNCTAD Meetings for Which Chinese Interpretation
Was Provided (January 1, 1975-April 2, 1977)

Dates	Meetings (Sessions)
1/27/75-2/7/75	Working Group on International Shipping Legislation (4th Sess.)
2/10/75-2/21/75	Committee on Commodities (8th Sess.)
3/10/75-3/21/75	Trade and Development Board (6th Special Sess.)
4/29/75	Trade and Development Board (2nd part of 14th Sess.)
6/23/75-7/4/75	Committee on Manufactures (7th Sess.)
7/7/75-7/18/75	Intergovernmental Group on Least Developed Countries
7/21/75-7/25/75	Committee on Commodities (2nd part of 8th Sess.)
7/28/75-8/1/75	Committee on Tungsten (9th Sess.)
8/5/75-8/16/75	Trade and Development Board (1st part of 15th Sess.)
9/30/75-10/20/75	Trade and Development Board (2nd part of 15th Sess.)
11/10/75-11/21/75	Committee on Shipping (7th Sess.)
11/24/75-12/5/75	Committee on Transfer of Technology (1st Sess.)
12/8/75-12/19/75	Committee on Commodities (3rd part of 8th Sess.)
1/5/76-1/16/76	International Working Group on Shipping Legislation (1st part of 5th Sess.)
1/19/76-1/23/76	Working Group on Tungsten (10th Sess.)
3/8/76-3/20/76	Trade and Development Board (7th Special Sess.)
5/3/76-5/4/76	Pre-Conference, UNCTAD IV
5/5/76-5/30/76	UNCTAD IV in Nairobi, Kenya
7/26/76-7/30/76	Working Group on International Shipping Legislation (2nd part of 5th Sess.)
10/5/76-10/23/76	Trade and Development Board (1st part of 16th Sess.)
11/15/76-11/19/76	Committee on Tungsten (10th Sess.)
11/24/76-11/26/76	Ad Hoc Intergovernmental Committee on the Integrated Programme for Commodities
11/29/76-12/4/76	Preparatory Meeting for the Negotiation of a Common Fund (1st Sess.)
1/24/77-1/28/77	Preparatory Meeting for the Negotiation of a Common Fund (2nd Sess.)
2/21/77-3/1/77	Preparatory Meeting for the Negotiation of a Common Fund (3rd Sess.)
3/7/77-4/2/77	The United Nations Negotiating Conference on a Common Fund under the Integrated Programme for Commodities

Source: UNCTAD secretariat.

demands of the Group of 77. China has never submitted any draft resolution or concrete proposal of her own. She has yet to submit any candidate for an UNCTAD secretariat post. Nor has China made herself available for any chairman posts, which rotate from group to group. And she has engaged in virtually no lobbying of any kind. "No, there is little lobbying on the part of the Chinese," responded one participant in UNCTAD politics, "but they are being sought after by the Group of 77. The Chinese do not lobby because they do not initiate anything; hence, there is really nothing to lobby for."

It may be mentioned in this connection that there is seldom any voting in UNCTAD. UNCTAD is an idea generator, moving on two separate tracks. One is to prod the Member States to accept and codify a certain idea in their national legislation; the other track is to formulate an idea as a basis for an international agreement, such as the current negotiations to establish a Common Fund for the Integrated Programme of Commodities. But when voting takes place, China invariably votes in support of the position taken by the Group of 77.

Although both Group D and China are somewhat excluded from the mainstream of North-South negotiations in UNCTAD, the two are not similar at the operational level. Group D, as a cohesive coalition of the Soviet-bloc countries with relatively developed and industrialized economies, has a more clearly delineated economic self-interest at stake. Although it would normally pay lip service to the demands of the Third World, its actual position changes rather rapidly and unpredictably from sector to sector, and from commodity to commodity, whereas China's position and behavior have remained stable and predictable. Moreover, the Group of 77 sometimes asks from Group D certain specific things, whereas it does not ask anything of China except the latter's moral and political support.

UNCTAD provides limited opportunities for anti-Soviet polemics because the line of adversary negotiation or confrontation is rather sharply drawn between the Group of 77 and Group B. However, the Chinese intervene reactively whenever the Soviet Union or any member of Group D injects the Soviet pet theory of the three Ds, linking development with détente and disarmament. Feeling left out of the main negotiating process in UNCTAD, the Soviet Union in this way attempts to impose her conceptualization of world economic order. Both China and Group B are firmly opposed to the Soviet theory of the three Ds, while the Group of 77, though it may theoretically accept the linkage between development and disarmament, finds it a practical hindrance.

In sum, then, Chinese behavior in UNCTAD politics is marked by the following characteristics: a relatively extensive participation in a wide variety of meetings; a passive and reactive support of the Group of 77; an occasional intervention to rebut and reject the Soviet linkage of development with disarmament; an uncharacteristically active participation in any debate relating to tungsten; and a generally modest, diligent, and self-effacing behavioral posture. In addition, there is a general agreement among the participants and Secretariat personnel that China is represented by a very competent team of two delegates, one of whom is described as speaking "absolutely flawless English" (Wu Chia-huang) and the other "absolutely flawless French" (Liu Hsien-ming). The behavior of these two delegates in UNCTAD activities has been summed up by one participant in the following words: "Exemplary! I find them very cooperative, helpful, extremely polite, and always correct. There are certain instances when the Chinese views are so strongly expressed that they might convey the impression to the outsider that the Chinese are somehow out of touch with the existing reality. However, this kind of behavior has noticeably decreased in recent years."

There is also a shared perception on the part of the UNCTAD secretariat personnel that the working relationship between them and the Chinese mission in Geneva is excellent. When China first joined UNCTAD, her delegation made it clear that it would like to rely extensively on the assistance of the UNCTAD secretariat in familiarizing itself with the working procedure of the organization. This kind of consultative relationship has continued unabated in the following years. "The PRC Mission to International Organizations at Geneva," observed one UNCTAD secretariat official, "is one of a few missions that I know of that invites the Secretariat personnel to dinner parties because it wants to maintain this good working relationship."

UNCTAD-IV, held in Nairobi from May 5 to May 31, 1976, provided the first major political test of the NIEO implementation process. Before discussing the Chinese role and position, however, several important and innovative characteristics of the Conference need to be mentioned. First, the Conference, following the NIEO principles, programs, and guidelines, concentrated on negotiations on specific measures, dispensing with general debates except in the plenary. To expedite the negotiating process, the UNCTAD secretariat produced a specific, succinct, and action-oriented documentation. In addition, a pre-Conference session of TDB was held (see Table 6.1) to clarify the negotiating positions of the major groups involved and to establish a more selective agenda. As a result, the Conference adopted only twelve resolutions, compared with forty-eight resolutions at UNCTAD-III.

Second, the Conference showed a keen awareness of its impact on other negotiating fora, especially on the North-South dialogue in Paris. Third, the Group of 77 demonstrated its increasing political influence and bargaining power by presenting a unified negotiating position on a number of specific issues, coupled with a willingness to commit its own resources to the achievement of certain major objectives. The united front of the Group of 77 had already been formulated at the 3rd Ministerial Conference of the Group of 77, held in Manila from February 2 to February 7, 1976, and embodied in the (Manila) Declaration and Programme of Action. On the other hand, Group B countries lacked a common counter-strategy as they were divided on many issues, particularly in relation to the integrated programme for commodities.

Fourth, the Conference failed, in spite of extensive behind-the-scenes negotiations, to provide remedial measures for the urgent external debt problem of developing countries. Since the adoption of the *Declaration* and the *Programme of Action*, the total indebtedness of developing countries continued to grow rapidly, resulting from a decline in their export earnings, an increase in their import costs, and insufficient concessional foreign aid. For example, the total external indebtedness of developing countries almost doubled during the period 1973-76, reaching some $170 billion by the end of 1976.[42] The Conference also failed on other key issues in the area of money and finance. On the crucial and long-range problem of restructuring international commodity markets, however, it adopted a compromise resolution "to convene a negotiating conference open to all members of UNCTAD on a common fund no later than March 1977."[43] Secretary of State Kissinger's proposal to establish an International Resources Bank was rejected on a roll-call vote of 31 in favor, 33 against (the PRC joining the opposition), with 44 abstentions and the rest absent during the voting.

China's role at UNCTAD-IV was largely limited to symbolic politics

[42] Helen Hughes, "The External Debt of Developing Countries," *Finance and Development* 13 (December 1977), 22. By the end of 1977 the external debt of developing countries reached some $200 billion. See General Assembly Resolution 32/187 of 19 December 1977 and "Debts of Developing Countries—Product of Imperialist Plunder," *PR*, No. 52 (December 26, 1977), 24-26.

[43] UNCTAD Resolution 93 (IV), in *Report of the United Nations Conference on Trade and Development on Its Fourth Session, held at the Kenyatta Conference Center, Nairobi, Kenya, from 5 to 31 May 1976*, UN Doc. TD/217 (12 July 1976), pp. 2-8. This comprehensive resolution on the integrated program for commodities was adopted on the last day of the Conference (May 30, 1976) as a compromise formula. Yet, the PRC characterized the resolution as "a new achievement of the third world countries in getting better prices for raw materials and in confirming their right to fix prices in the world market after the victories won by the Organization of Petroleum Exporting Countries and the various associations of raw materials producer nations." See "Third World Wins New Victories in Joint Struggle Against Hegemony," *PR*, No. 24 (June 11, 1976), 19.

during general debates in the plenary. Given the rigid structure of group politics in the informal negotiating process, there was little room for any active Chinese participation. In spite of the inconclusive outcome of the Conference, China adopted a positive and supportive posture because of the unity and solidarity demonstrated by the Third World. The NIEO implementation process, or the struggle of "smashing the old and establishing the new in international economic relations" as the Chinese put it, cannot possibly amount to much without the solidarity of the Third World. Though the struggle is protracted and arduous, the future is bright "as long as the third world countries and people close ranks, steadily increase their strength and carry on the fight indefatigably." Such a united front was shown in the adoption of the Manila Declaration and Programme of Action, because the fundamental interests of the Third World were identical.[44]

Proceeding from this line of reasoning, the Chinese maintained that "the Declaration and Programme of Action adopted recently at the Manila meeting of the Group of 77 embody the spirit of the Sixth and Seventh Special Sessions of the UN General Assembly, reflect the reasonable demands of the developing countries and should be taken as the basis for consideration at the current session of the conference."[45] Specifically, the Chinese endorsed such major measures envisaged in the integrated program for commodities as the establishment of international buffer stocks of various commodities, the establishment of a common fund for international stockpiles, and the indexing of commodity prices with prices of manufactured goods. In addition, the Chinese supported the reduction of external debt burdens of developing countries and the reform of the international monetary and financial system as being conducive to the implementation of the *Declaration* and the *Programme of Action*.[46]

The Chinese have conceptualized the integrated program for commodities as the key component in the struggle of the Third World to implement NIEO principles and programs. The US proposal for a case-by-case or commodity-by-commodity approach and the Soviet Union's "specific programme of action" and "medium- and long-term trade agreements" were lumped together as devices to perpetuate the old economic order, based on imperialism, colonialism, and hegemony. On the other hand, the integrated approach toward commodities advanced by the Group of 77 is conceptualized as a set of specific, action-

[44] "Unite to Smash the Old and Establish the New," *JMJP*, February 10, 1976, p. 6.
[45] "At 4th UNCTAD Session: Speech by Chou Hua-min, Head of the Chinese Delegation," *PR*, No. 21 (May 21, 1976), 19.
[46] UN Docs. A/C.2/31/SR.13 (15 October 1976), p. 13, and A/C.2/31/SR.52 (23 November 1976), p. 8.

oriented measures to stop the vicious exchange of unequal values, to improve the terms of trade, to stabilize and improve the prices of primary commodities, and thus to restructure international economic relations on a more just and equitable basis.

It was in this spirit that the Chinese participated in all the preparatory meetings for the negotiation of a common fund (see Table 6.1), as well as in the United Nations Negotiating Conference on a Common Fund under the Integrated Programme for Commodities, all of which were held in Geneva in accordance with the compromise resolution on the integrated programme for commodities (Resolution 93) adopted at UNCTAD-IV. Even though the United Nations Negotiating Conference on a Common Fund under the Integrated Programme for Commodities reached no substantive agreement "because of superpower obstruction," the Chinese still retained a positive and hopeful posture and supported a statement of the Group of 77, issued at the UN Negotiating Conference, expressing "the determination of the Group of 77 to strive for the establishment of a common fund to serve as the main instrument for attaining the objectives of the integrated programme for commodities."[47]

In sum, the Chinese played a symbolic role in UNCTAD politics, minimizing their own involvement in the negotiating process between the Group of 77 and Group *B*, or in the intragroup politics among Third World countries. The principal motive or rationale of the Chinese low-profiled approach seems both conceptual and strategic. Conceptually, the Chinese believe that the Third World is indeed playing "the main force role" in the struggle to establish the new world economic order.[48] If this is so, there is little need for active Chinese involvement.

Strategically, the Chinese have expressed an acute sense of concern about the unity and solidarity of the Third World in the face of all kinds of maneuvers and tricks by the two superpowers. If this is the case, Chinese symbolic support from a detached position is more likely to contribute to a united front of the Third World than Chinese entanglement or interference in the intragroup politics in the heterogenous Group of 77. Chinese nonparticipation in the work of the Committee on Economic Co-operation among Developing Countries should be viewed in this light. Given the marginal role and impact of NIEO on China's own economy or her foreign aid and trade, the Chinese symbolic politics in UNCTAD may very well be another manifestation of making a virtue of necessity.

[47] *JMJP*, April 12, 1977, p. 5.
[48] See "Commentary by Hsinhua Correspondent: New Victories in Anti-Hegemonic Struggle," NCNA-English, Nairobi, June 1, 1976, in *SPRCP*, No. 6114 (June 14, 1976), 54.

The United Nations Industrial Development Organization (UNIDO)

UNIDO was established by the General Assembly in 1966 as its subsidiary organ.[49] UNIDO has a modest secretariat of its own based in Vienna, with its executive director appointed by, and its activities accountable to, the Secretary-General of the United Nations. The principal policy-making organ of UNIDO is the Industrial Development Board (IDB), whose forty-five members are elected by the General Assembly for three-year terms. At its annual session the General Assembly revises the lists of states eligible for membership in IDB, following the UNCTAD typology of the four groups of states (Group A, Group B, Group C, and Group D).

At the time of the PRC's entry into the United Nations, China was already a member of UNIDO and was also included in Group A (Afro-Asian Group). But here again the ROC stood out as the only permanent member of the Security Council excluded from membership in IDB. However, the PRC was elected as a member of IDB by the 27th General Assembly and reelected by the 30th General Assembly; hence, China's membership in IDB began as of January 1, 1973, and her full participation began with the 7th (annual) Session of IDB in May 1973. Figure 6.3 shows the scope and extent of China's participation in UNIDO activities since the beginning of 1973.

UNIDO has the most ambitious objective of promoting industrialization in the developing countries with the slenderest of resources. Man must eat first before he can think of industry. On this premise, the United Nations has already set aside $1 billion for IFAD, as we noted earlier, but there is no such fund for industrial development. During the first decade of its undistinguished existence, UNIDO has nonetheless made some systematic effort to explore the problems of international cooperation in industrial development, through such methods as direct field assistance, studies, and investment promotional activities. Some of UNIDO's activities were aimed at generating cross-fertilization effects among the developing countries themselves as well as between the developed and developing countries.

Unlike UNCTAD, UNIDO played no role in the making of NIEO principles. However, the establishment of the foundations of NIEO has had a powerful and all-embracing effect on the activities of UNIDO since the 2nd General Conference of UNIDO (hereafter UNIDO-II), held in Lima, Peru, in March 1975. Figure 6.3 shows in what manner and to what extent UNIDO's activities became interlocked with the

---

[49] General Assembly Resolution 2152 (XXI) of 17 November 1966.

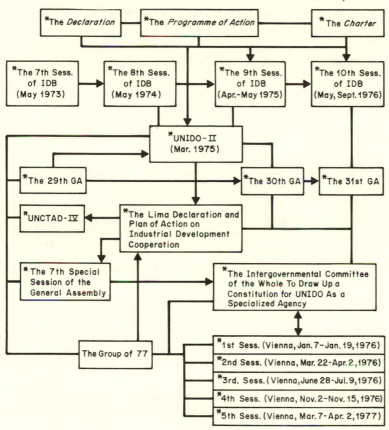

FIGURE 6.3. The PRC, UNIDO, and the New International Economic Order.

NIEO implementation process, as well as China's involvement in this linkage politics.

Even before such linkage politics began in the wake of the establishment of NIEO principles, however, China assumed a positive, cooperative, and contributory posture toward UNIDO. As Table 6.2 shows, UNIDO is one of a few UN organs or programs for which China has pledged and paid voluntary contributions. To be sure, the amounts pledged for the years 1973-77 are modest, but they represent a higher percentage of China's "share," if we use the assessment scales of the UN regular budget. They also stand out in symbolic contrast to the amounts pledged by the ROC for 1971.

TABLE 6.2. Chinese Voluntary Contributions to UNIDO, 1971-77 ($)

Year	Amount	% of Total	Total Pledged
1971[a]	10,000		
1972			
1973	200,000 (400,000 yüans)	7.2	2,848,350
1974	225,000 (450,000 yüans)	6.1	3,698,310
1975	263,158 (500,000 yüans)	6.5	4,040,378
1976	279,188 (550,000 yüans)	7.6	3,666,081
1977	279,188 (550,000 yüans)	7.4	3,752,491

[a] The ROC.
Source: GAOR, 28th Sess., Supp. No. 11 (A/9011), Annex II, p. 1; UN Docs. A/CONF.66/SR.1 (20 November 1974), p. 16; A/CONF.66/2 (18 July 1975), p. 5; A/CONF.66/2 (15 July 1976), p. 4; UNIDO Newsletter, No. 104 (December 1976), p. 1.

Apparently, UNIDO is congenial to China's conceptualization of an ideal UN agency for multilateral aid. It may be noted in this connection that China's voluntary contributions to UNIDO have been made as "special purpose contributions," which permits the determination and utilization of contributions through tripartite consultations among UNIDO, the donor, and the recipient countries. China is not alone in this respect, as Austria, the Federal Republic of Germany, Japan, and Switzerland have also pledged their contributions as special purpose contributions. In short, China as a donor country is allowed some say in the use of her money, whereas UNDP does not permit such control or flexibility. Viewed in this light, then, China's voluntary contributions to UNIDO represent a half-way adjustment between bilateral and multilateral aid.[50]

The Chinese have repeatedly argued that the system of UN multilateral assistance should reduce red tape to a minimum by doing away with all over-elaborate procedures. UNIDO as a UN agency for multilateral aid in the field of industry, the Chinese argued, "should lay stress on providing practical and effective aid to the developing countries."[51] Citing UNIDO officials who had argued that hundreds

[50] For example, the PRC's ambassador to Austria, Yu Pei-wen, and UNIDO's executive director, Abd-El Rahman Khane, signed an agreement on May 5, 1975, concerning the use of the voluntary contribution made to UNIDO by the PRC for 1976. Under the terms of the agreement, "China will arrange a study tour in cotton textile technology for approximately 15 participants from developing countries, to be jointly selected by the Government of China and UNIDO. The contribution will cover costs of travel and subsistence of the participants within the countries, as well as other related expenses to be agreed upon." UN Chronicle 13 (June 1976), 56.

[51] GAOR, 29th Sess., Second Committee, 1616th meeting (25 October 1974), para. 15.

of preinvestment survey reports had in fact led to no positive results, the Chinese argued that it might be necessary to give up the conventional practice of confining UN multilateral aid to preinvestment activities. In their view, the most practical and effective method of contributing to industrial advance in the developing countries, given the limited resources of UNIDO, lay in the building of small and medium-sized factories and the transfer of technical know-how.[52] The Chinese also supported IDB's Decision II (VII) concerning administrative autonomy for UNIDO as a means of enhancing its efficiency.[53]

The 2nd General Conference of UNIDO, held in Lima, Peru, in March 1975 represented an important historical transition from the first decade of exploratory measures to another of more ambitious objectives. The rising aspirations and frustrations of the poor countries were crystallized and embodied in the Lima Declaration and Plan of Action on Industrial Development Co-operation, which, *inter alia*, called for developing countries to increase their share of world industry to 25 percent by the end of the century. The ambitious nature of this target is suggested by the fact that the LDCs had only moved from 6.2 percent of world industrial output in the mid-1950s to less than 7 percent in the mid-1960s. If the target were reached by the end of the century, it is estimated, the volume of industrial production of the LDCs would equal the entire world production of 1976.

Furthermore, the linkage between UNIDO and NIEO was firmly established at UNIDO-II. In calling UNIDO-II, the General Assembly defined the role of the General Conference as one of implementing NIEO principles in the field of industrialization.[54] The Chinese strongly echoed this view. "It is the important task of this conference," declared Ch'en Mu-hua, head of the Chinese delegation, in her opening policy speech before the plenary on March 14, 1975, "to study the implementation of the resolutions of the Sixth Special Session of the U.N. General Assembly in order to contribute to the establishing of a new international economic order in the field of industrial development."[55] China's participation in the plenary took the form of reiterating her established line of arguments and principles, which need not be repeated here.

---

[52] GAOR, 28th Sess., Second Committee, 1538th meeting (24 October 1973), para. 42; UN Docs. E/AC.6/SR.712 (23 July 1974), pp. 264-65, and ID/B/144, para. 77.

[53] UN Doc. E/AC.6/SR.638 (12 July 1973), pp. 88-89.

[54] Operative paragraphs 2, 3, and 8 of General Assembly Resolution 3306 (XXIX) of 14 December 1974 adopted by a vote of 119:0:3 (the Federal Republic of Germany, the United Kingdom, and the United States).

[55] "Head of Chinese Delegation Chen Mu-hua's Speech at UNIDO Second General Conference," PR, No. 12 (March 21, 1975), 19.

In the face of Soviet attempts to introduce "sham détente" and "sham disarmament" in the First Committee of the Conference, however, the Chinese came forward with their own amendment to the draft declaration and plan of action on industrial development and cooperation submitted by the Group of 77. The Chinese "amendment" was actually proposed as a clause to be inserted in the draft, and it read: "Considering that the superpowers, in stepping up arms expansion and war preparations in their contention for world hegemony, in plundering, exploiting and bullying other countries, and in aggravating international tension, are gravely jeopardizing the process of industrialization of the developing countries."[56]

This was an extemporaneous device designed more to defeat Soviet attempts to squeeze détente and disarmament into the draft declaration and plan of action than to have China's own view incorporated in the final product. The Conference adopted, by a vote of 82 in favor, 1 against (the United States), and 7 abstentions (the United Kingdom, the Federal Republic of Germany, Japan, Israel, Belgium, Canada, and Italy), the Lima Declaration and Plan of Action based largely on the document drafted by the Group of 77. Even though their own amendment had not been incorporated in the final product, the Chinese characterized the Conference as having produced "gratifying achievements" and as having "reflected once again the mighty power of the third world countries fighting in unity against hegemonism."[57] In short, the Chinese judged UNIDO-II, as they do so many other international fora, not so much in terms of their own national interests as in terms of whether the Third World or the superpowers won.

In its omnibus resolution on development and international economic cooperation, the 7th Special Session of the General Assembly endorsed the Lima Declaration and Plan of Action on Industrial Development Co-operation. In addition, the session endorsed the recommendation of UNIDO-II to convert UNIDO into a specialized agency and decided "to establish an intergovernmental committee of the whole, including States which participated in the Second General Conference, to meet in Vienna to draw up a constitution for the United Nations Industrial Development Organization as a specialized agency, to be submitted to a conference of plenipotentiaries to be convened by the Secretary-General in the last quarter of 1976."[58] The Chinese also endorsed the recommendation of UNIDO-II as "a common aspiration of the developing

[56] "Chinese Delegation to UNIDO Proposes Condemnation of Superpower Hindrance to Industrialization," NCNA-English, Lima, March 17, 1975, in *SPRCP*, No. 5821 (March 31, 1975), 37.

[57] "Two Teachers by Negative Example at Lima Conference," *PR*, No. 14 (April 4, 1975), 20-21.

[58] General Assembly Resolution 3362 (S-VII) of 16 September 1975.

countries which believe that only by such a change can UNIDO be freed from superpower manipulation and control and embark on the road of independence."[59]

It was against this background that the Intergovernmental Committee of the Whole to Draw up a Constitution of UNIDO as a Specialized Agency was established. As Figure 6.3 shows, the Chinese participated in all five sessions of the Intergovernmental Committee. However, a procedural dispute erupted on March 23, 1976, when the chairman of the Committee announced that, following informal consultations, agreement had been reached on the composition of a Contact Group as follows: 18 from the Group of 77; 11 from Group B; 6 from Group D; and China. The chairman declared that the composition of the Contact Group was not to be regarded as a precedent for the composition of any other contact groups or bodies to be established in the future.[60]

The Soviet Union, supported by Czechoslovakia, quickly intervened and inquired as to the grounds on which one state had been appointed to the Contact Group on an individual basis, "in violation of established procedures for the election of the members of the Organization to various bodies and groups."[61] The granting of "special rights to one State," the representative of the Soviet Union argued, "created a serious precedent and was inconsistent with the spirit and letter of equitable [geographical] distribution."[62] Switzerland, speaking on behalf of Group B, stated that the various groups, particularly Group B and the Group of 77, were not represented equitably in the Contact Group, but in a spirit of cooperation had reluctantly agreed on this composition on the clear understanding that the said composition would not constitute a precedent for any other body.[63]

Algeria came forward to the defense of China. An undesirable precedent was being established, argued the representative of Algeria, by the public expression of opinions on the composition of the Contact Group, on which, in fact, agreement had already been reached through private consultations. He then rebutted the Soviet argument: "Contact groups had been used for some ten years within the United Nations system and the election to such unofficial groups had nothing to do with the rules and principles established for representation on official bodies. If any concern was to be voiced about inadequate representation on the Contact Group, it should have come from the Group of 77, which comprised 108 countries, but accounted for only one-half of the membership of the Contact Group."[64]

[59] "Two Teachers by Negative Example at Lima Conference," p. 21.
[60] *Working Résumé of the Second Session of the Intergovernmental Committee of the Whole to Draw Up a Constitution for UNIDO as a Specialized Agency,* Vienna, 22 March-2 April 1976, UN Doc. A/AC.180/6 (30 April 1976), p. 8.
[61] *Ibid.*   [62] *Ibid.*   [63] *Ibid.*   [64] *Ibid.*

Faced with this anomalous situation, China presented an equally anomalous argument. As a member of UNIDO, China was entitled to participate in all the organization's activities, which nobody questioned. *"As China did not belong to any geographical group,"* argued the representative of China, however, "it had to participate on an individual basis, as it had, in fact, already done during the sixth special session of the General Assembly and during the seventh special session of the Trade and Development Board (UNCTAD)."[65] Of course, China had acted throughout the United Nations system as if she did not belong to any group system, but now, for the first time, declared this publicly, no matter what anybody thought or what the laws said. Hence, what the chairman had done was both reasonable and logical. There could be no question, declared the representative of China, "of the present situation creating a precedent."[66] This was one of the few cases where China, instead of conforming to formalized rules, if not practice, actually imposed her own rules as the price of her participation in the process of creating another body of rules—a new constitution for UNIDO as a specialized agency.

Characteristically, China did not submit any draft constitution of her own, confining her role to that of an observer and commentator on the drafts submitted by other groups. Throughout the drafting process in the Intergovernmental Committee, China stressed that the transformation of UNIDO should not merely entail a change in its legal status and structure, but should be carried out in accordance with the NIEO principles and the provisions of the Lima Declaration and Plan of Action.

On the substantive provisions of various drafts, China did the following: (1) vigorously opposed the Soviet attempt "to insert their deceitful fallacies 'of peace, security and disarmament' into the Constitution of UNIDO"; (2) opposed a weighted voting formula with regard to the question of program and budget in the secretariat and the Group B drafts, characterizing it as "veto power or veto power in disguise"; (3) more firmly opposed the adoption of the "consensus" formula in the approval of the program and budget as proposed by Group D; (4) supported the position of the Group of 77 that the Conference of UNIDO should be the supreme organ of authority of the organization, having the power to examine and approve the program of work and the budget and to make any changes it deemed necessary; (5) argued that no dispute should be referred to the International Court of Justice "without prior consent of the parties concerned," thus supporting Article 20.1 in the Group of 77 draft; and (6) submitted an amendment to Article 3 on membership to give due account of General

[65] *Ibid;* emphasis added.   [66] *Ibid.*

Assembly Resolution 2758 (XXVI) on the restoration of the lawful rights of the PRC in the United Nations, and succeeded in having this amendment accepted by the Legal Drafting Group, to be included in the report of the Committee to the Plenipotentiary Conference.[67]

The Intergovernmental Committee failed to complete its work for the UN Secretary-General to convene the Plenipotentiary Conference "in the last quarter of 1976" as mandated by the Assembly resolution. The 31st General Assembly decided to extend the mandate of the Committee, requesting the Secretary-General to make the arrangements necessary for convening the Plenipotentiary Conference during the second half of 1977 at UN Headquarters.[68] Yet at the close of its 5th Session on April 2, 1977, the Committee decided to submit to the United Nations a report which includes the text already agreed upon, the existing differences, and the statements of various delegations,[69] thus throwing the question back to the General Assembly for further action. The question of UNIDO's transformation into another specialized agency is now in doubt.

To sum up, several factors account for the high respect UNIDO is accorded in the Chinese image of the United Nations development system. First, UNIDO's tripartite consultation ensures a measure of Chinese control over the use of its special purpose contributions. China will not contribute to any UN multilateral aid program unless she has a reasonable degree of assurance that her "scarce resources" are not used for what she regards as politically unjust causes or economically wasteful projects. As such, China's voluntary contributions to UNIDO represent more an extension of her bilateral aid than multilateral aid in its conventional sense. Second, UNIDO provides an ideal setting in which Peking can play its symbolic role in UN development politics; that is, China can easily contribute what she may consider her proper share —say, in the range of 5 to 7 percent of the total—without feeling too great a financial constraint. Finally, UNIDO is well suited to sponsoring a series of small-scale industrial projects as models to be emulated by developing countries seeking self-reliant national economies.

The United Nations Development Programme (UNDP)

UNDP was originally founded on July 1, 1950, as the Expanded Programme of Technical Assistance (EPTA) to finance technical assist-

[67] *Working Résumé of the Fourth Session of the Intergovernmental Committee of the Whole to Draw Up a Constitution for UNIDO As a Specialized Agency,* Vienna, 2-15 November 1976, UN Doc. A/AC.180/8 (30 November 1976), pp. 21, 23, 33-34.
[68] General Assembly Resolution 31/161 of 21 December 1976.
[69] See *JMJP*, April 8, 1977, p. 6.

ance programs through voluntary contributions. The General Assembly expanded the scope of UN technical assistance by establishing the Special Fund in 1958. The Fund, which began its operations in 1959, was designed as the United Nations' major channel for large-scale preinvestment surveys and feasibility studies on major national development projects that would lay the infrastructure for subsequent investment of capital. It also became a coordinating center for the work of various UN agencies. On November 22, 1965, the General Assembly unanimously voted to merge the two operations, effective as of January 1, 1966, into UNDP.[70] At the time of its formal inauguration, UNDP inherited from its two predecessors a combined commitment of some 2,000 projects, with a total cost of over $1.5 billion. UNDP has since remained the world's largest source of multilateral technical cooperation.

UNDP is headed by an administrator who is responsible to a 48-nation Governing Council. The members of the Governing Council are elected by ECOSOC for three-year terms from among Member States of the United Nations or members of the specialized agencies or the International Atomic Energy Agency. In increasing the membership of the Governing Council from 37 to 48, the General Assembly in 1971 laid down the following distributive formulae: (1) 27 seats should be filled by developing countries, allocating 11 for African countries, 9 for Asian countries and Yugoslavia, and 7 for Latin American countries; (2) 21 seats should be filled by economically more advanced countries, allocating 17 for Western European and other countries, and 4 for Eastern European countries; and (3) the composition of seats in each group should at all times give due expression to adequate subregional representation.[71]

The authority of the Governing Council of UNDP is defined as "the main policy-formulating body of the Programme" under the guidance of the General Assembly and the Economic and Social Council.[72] The administrator is supposed to receive all the necessary directives from the Governing Council for the general planning of the activities of the program. The Governing Council examines and approves all proposals for country programs; it makes its decisions through the consensual process, eschewing recorded voting.

UNDP cannot claim to have played any contributory role in the making of NIEO principles and objectives. As the largest source of UN multilateral aid, UNDP has preoccupied itself with the task of adminis-

[70] General Assembly Resolution 2029 (XX) of 22 November 1965.
[71] General Assembly Resolution 2813 (XXVI) of 14 December 1971, adopted by a recorded vote of 86 in favor, 2 against (Canada and the United States), with 25 abstentions. The PRC was either absent or did not participate in the vote.
[72] Operative para. 1 of General Assembly Resolution 2814 (XXVI) of 14 December 1971.

tering and monitoring its technical assistance projects throughout the world. It has paid little attention to the fundamental question of structural inequities in, or systemic transformation of, the world economic system. In fact, the new international economic order in a sense represents an ideological-conceptual challenge to the efficacy of UNDP's activities in bridging the gap between rich and poor. Moreover, its operations are confined to one phase of the development process—technical assistance and preinvestment.

Under the cumulative impact, however, of a number of major studies on the United Nations development system in the late 1960s—notably those of the Pearson Commission and Sir Robert Jackson—the Governing Council produced in 1970 a consensus (generally known as the 1970 Consensus) introducing some major organizational and procedural reforms. The pivotal change was to replace the former, *ad hoc*, first-come-first-served method with "country programming," a method of dividing up the bulk of UNDP's predictable resources over a five-year cycle (1972-76 and 1977-81) on a country-by-country basis, with smaller cycle allocations (about 15 percent of the total resources) for regional, interregional, and global programs.

The financing of UNDP-assisted projects is shared by both donors and recipients. The developing countries themselves bear at least 55 percent of the costs by paying the salaries of local personnel, by providing construction and maintenance of project buildings and facilities, and by purchasing locally available supplies and services. UNDP finances the remaining 45 percent by defraying the expenses of development experts, project equipment, and advanced technical services. UNDP's own resources come from voluntary contributions pledged at its annual pledging conference in New York. The funds thus raised are then allocated through five-year projections of "Indicative Planning Figures" (IPFs), which conform to five-year country programming cycles. Figure 6.4 shows the distribution of UNDP country programs by sector during the first IPF cycle (1972-76).

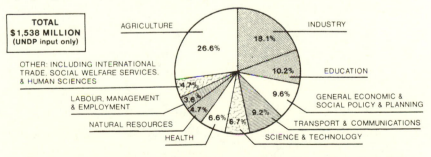

FIGURE 6.4. Distribution of UNDP Projects by Sector Based on 118 Country Programmes Approved During the First IPF Cycle (1972-76).

Against this background, China was rather slow in showing her interest in gaining a seat in the Governing Council during the first few years of her participation in the United Nations. By mid-1974, however, China allowed herself to be unanimously nominated by the Asian Group as a candidate for membership in the Council. At its 1897th plenary meeting, ECOSOC, filling the three seats available for the Asian States and Yugoslavia, elected China by acclamation and then proceeded to elect the remaining two states by secret ballot, all for a three-year term beginning January 1, 1975, and ending December 31, 1977.[73] As in TDB and IDB, there was a symbolic significance in China being represented for the first time in the policy-making body of the world's largest channel of multilateral technical assistance. China's participation in the Governing Council, which began with its 19th Session on January 13, 1975, also coincided with the process of linking UNDP with the NIEO implementation process throughout the United Nations development system.

Faced with the specific requirement of presenting to the forthcoming 7th Special Session of the General Assembly a comprehensive policy statement that outlined the approach of UNDP in providing for the changing needs of developing countries during the second half of the United Nations' Second Development Decade, the administrator prepared a comprehensive report, entitled "The Future Role of UNDP in World Development in the Context of the Preparations for the Seventh Special Session of the General Assembly."[74] At its 487th meeting on June 25, 1975, the Governing Council, basing its action on the administrator's report, adopted what came to be known as "New Dimensions in Technical Co-operation" as UNDP's response to the call for NIEO. The 30th Session of the General Assembly endorsed "New Dimensions" as a proper response, compatible with NIEO principles and objectives.[75]

"New Dimensions" defined UNDP's role in terms of self-reliance: "The basic purpose of technical co-operation should be the promotion of self-reliance in developing countries, by building up, *inter alia*, their productive capability and their indigenous resources—by increasing the availability of the managerial, technical, administrative and research capabilities required in the development process."[76] In addition, it projected UNDP's mandate in the following areas and terms:

An output- or result-oriented approach, as against the previous input-oriented approach in technical co-operation

[73] ECOSOR, 56th Sess., 1897th plenary meeting (16 May 1974), paras. 55-59.
[74] UN Doc. DP/114 (24 March 1975).
[75] General Assembly Resolution 3405 (XXX) of 28 November 1975.
[76] UNDP, *1975 Annual Report: Building Self-Reliance in Developing Countries*, p. 8.

A more liberal policy toward local cost-financing

A more diversified variety of sources of its supply, particularly including those from developing countries

An increased support to programs of technical cooperation among developing countries

A greater degree of responsibility on the part of recipient countries in executing UNDP-assisted projects

Technical cooperation at any level or stage of the development process, including assistance for project planning, pre-feasibility, feasibility, detailed engineering design and, where appropriate, construction and initial operations and management

Special attention to the requirements of the least developed among the developing countries.[77]

As far as UNDP is concerned, the overall objective of the New International Economic Order is conceptualized as increasing "the capacity of the developing countries, individually and collectively, to pursue their development."[78] Basing his approach on this premise, the administrator of UNDP translated the relevance of the omnibus resolution of the 7th Special Session into six specific references to the work of UNDP: (1) international trade; (2) transfer of real resources; (3) science and technology; (4) industrialization; (5) food and agriculture; and (6) cooperation among developing countries.[79]

In spite of such an accommodating posture on the part of UNDP to the NIEO call, China from the very beginning of her participation in the Governing Council assumed the posture of a revisionist challenger to the fundamental philosophical premise as well as to the operational procedure of UNDP. Repeatedly, China invoked the *Declaration* and the *Programme of Action* as the authority for some basic and fundamental reforms at UNDP. Table 6.3 sums up all the important statements Chinese representatives made in the Governing Council from its 19th Session (January 1975) to its 23rd Session (February 1977); as such, it represents a composite picture of the Chinese revisionist orientation toward the United Nations' multilateral aid program in general and UNDP operation in particular.

Rightly or not, UNDP has been perceived by China as serving neither her principles nor interests. When asked to describe the most salient characteristic of Chinese behavior in the Governing Council, a high-ranking UNDP secretariat official who regularly participated in the Council meetings responded with the phrase "an absolute respect for the sovereignty of other countries." In fact, most of the Chinese

[77] *Ibid.*, p. 14. [78] *Ibid.*, p. 10. [79] *Ibid.*, p. 11.

TABLE 6.3. The PRC's Conceptualization of UNDP as Expressed in
Her Statements in the Governing Council (19th to 23rd Sessions)

UNDP Should:	UNDP Should Not:
1. Request the World Bank Group to implement the Assembly resolution on the restoration of lawful rights of the PRC in the United Nations.	1. Provide any assistance to the Lon Nol clique, the Israeli Zionists, to the authorities in South Korea and South Vietnam.
2. Change the unreasonable allocation of seats in the Governing Council.	2. Limit its operations to preinvestment activities.
3. Provide emergency relief measures to disaster-stricken countries.	3. Regard itself as an alms giver, still less place itself above any sovereign state.
4. Leave the formulation of country programs and projects to the sovereignty of recipient countries.	4. Cling to obsolete rules and procedures.
5. Reform its organizational structures so as to reflect profound historical changes (NIEO).	5. Forge links with transnational corporations.
6. Carry out a fundamental reform and not to make some patchwork repairs to the old framework.	6. Ask the recipient governments to furnish details of their overall development plans and bilateral aid resources.
7. Do away with artificial and complicated bureaucratic procedures so as to make a better use of Chinese contributions in Renminbi.	7. Accept the idea that the largest contributor should have the greatest say in decision making as it runs counter to the spirit of NIEO.
8. Promote the individual and collective self-reliance of the developing countries and unity and mutual cooperation among them.	8. Separate the discussion of the guiding principles and policies of UNDP from developments in the world political and economic situation.
9. As far as possible, recruit experts and other technical personnel from developing countries.	9. Restrict itself to the terms of the 1970 Consensus in its consideration of the future of UNDP.
10. Not only recognize the fundamental principle of the sovereignty of the recipient countries in words but also actually implement it in all spheres of aid operations.	10. Accept the proposition that the UN organizations for multilateral assistance were "supra-international."
	11. Avoid the duty of opposing Soviet social imperialism.

Source: Based on the summary records of the Governing Council from its 443rd meeting (DP/SR.443, 15 January 1975) to its 566th meeting (DP/SR.566, 4 February 1977).

complaints stem from China's difficulties in accepting the unavoidable process of mutual interaction and accommodation between nationalism and supranationalism in UNDP's planning and programming process. The Chinese concept of national sovereignty seems so absolute and so rigid that to them almost every UNDP action, from the decision-making level in the Council down to the execution level of country programs in the field, smacks of an unprincipled exchange of aid for a piece of the sovereign rights of recipient countries.

Following this line of reasoning, the Chinese have insisted that UNDP should not regard itself as "an alms giver," still less place itself above any sovereign state. They have rejected the proposition that the UN agencies for multilateral assistance are "supra-international [sic]," because the external economic policies of the countries involved are bound to be reflected in their activities in these agencies. Likewise, the Chinese have argued that "the idea that the largest contributor should have the greatest say in decision-making was an outdated concept alien to the spirit of the new international economic order."[80] While they repeatedly invoke the NIEO principles as an overall guide for some fundamental reforms, the principle singled out most frequently is that of permanent and inalienable sovereignty over natural resources. It is also in this vein that the Chinese have called for a change in the "unreasonable allocation" of seats in the Governing Council.

Yet the Chinese respect for national sovereignty is neither immaculate in conception nor consistent in practice. It certainly does not extend to such bêtes noires as Israel, South Korea, Angola, or what used to be called the "Lon Nol clique" and South Vietnam, let alone the two superpowers. It is also difficult to reconcile China's insistence on absolute respect for the sovereignty of recipient countries, on the one hand, and her insistence that UNDP should provide practical and effective aid projects that would really strengthen the independent and self-reliant national economies of recipient countries, on the other. The primary responsibility of UNDP, the Chinese have argued, is to provide resources and technology, but "the formulation of country programmes and projects fell within the sovereignty of recipient countries."[81] Suppose a sovereign country asks for a boondoggling project. What should be the proper response of UNDP? In short, the Chinese approach to UNDP is fraught with both conceptual and operational difficulties.

[80] UN Doc. DP/SR. 487 (25 June 1975), p. 354.
[81] UN Doc. DP/SR.470 (13 June 1975), p. 81. For reiteration of the same theme, see also UN Docs. DP/SR.474 (17 June 1975), p. 160 and DP/SR.489 (26 June 1975), p. 391.

Another difficulty for the Chinese lies in the fact that the structure of power and influence in the Governing Council is not congenial to the pursuit of Chinese egalitarian norms and antihegemonic diplomacy. As the largest single contributor to the resources of UNDP, the United States retains a powerful influence in UNDP. As in the World Bank, an American has always occupied the position of administrator. Whether the Third World likes it or not, the "major stockholders run the bank." Whether the Chinese like it or not, UNDP has been, and continues to be, "an alms giver." No nation wants to give without retaining some say in the use of its money. And the largest contributor has categorically rejected the concept of the new international economic order. Despite some hopeful projections in the administrator's annual reports for 1975 and 1976—and the Chinese might well regard these as rhetorical embellishments—the possibility of transforming UNDP into an effective instrument of NIEO is problematic. In addition, the consensual decision-making process in the Governing Council neutralizes the slight numerical advantage of the developing countries. There is a sense in which Chinese influence was greatly restricted by the structure of power and influence in UNDP.

It was against this setting that one of the rare Sino-American confrontations in the United Nations system took place in the course of the Governing Council's deliberations on "New Dimensions." Clearly annoyed by what it considered to be improper and excessive politicization of the issues involved, the US delegation proposed that the following paragraph be inserted in the record:

> However, he [the representative of the United States] expressed concern at the efforts which had been made by one delegation to politicize the issue. He formally rejected the notion of the politicization of the Governing Council's work and hoped that the present occasion would be the last on which such irresponsible efforts would be made to introduce politics into the forum of the UNDP Governing Council, in which it was totally inappropriate.[82]

In the face of this highly unusual and politicized proposal, Chinese representative Wang Tzu-chuan quickly responded with a counter-proposal that the following paragraph be inserted in the record:

> One member State [China] pointed out that the super-Powers regarded the Declaration and the Programme of Action on the Establishment of a New International Economic Order as dreadful and monstrous concepts. They were extremely afraid of and strongly opposed to those texts and tried every means possible to prevent the

[82] UN Doc. DP/SR.493 (30 June 1975), p. 429.

realization of the just demands of the third world. At the current session of the Governing Council of UNDP, people had once again seen the vigorous obstruction and sabotage by the super-Powers against the draft decision tabled by developing countries.[83]

Revealingly enough, the Chinese have thus transformed the Sino-American confrontation into a valiant Chinese struggle against both superpowers. Clearly sensing an impasse and the futility of pursuing the matter, the United States decided to withdraw its amendment. This immediately induced the Chinese delegation to withdraw its own amendment with a protest against the US assertion that China had sought to introduce politics into the Council's work. "His delegation had merely said," Chinese representative Wang Tzu-chuan reminded the Council, "that all countries, rich and poor, should be placed on an equal footing and that no country should be privileged. All it had asked was that the new international economic order and the Declaration adopted by the General Assembly at its sixth special session should be put into effect."[84] It may be noted in this connection that the United States did not have to take a "politicized" approach to make its influence felt in the work of the Governing Council, while China, despite her curious protest, rejected both the desirability and the feasibility of the functional (nonpolitical) approach to development issues in the United Nations system.

Be that as it may, the Chinese transformation of the American provocation into anti-Soviet polemics was irrational. Like China, the Soviet Union pledges an extremely modest sum at the annual UNDP pledging conference, and that in nonconvertible rubles. Her influence, let alone domination, in the Governing Council is marginal. To argue, as the Chinese did, that "Members of the Council had the duty to oppose Soviet social imperialism—a monster which had added a new task to the anti-imperialist, anti-hegemonistic and anti-colonialist struggle in the economic and social sphere and a new item to the Council's agenda"[85] must be regarded as obsessive; as such, it compromises China's own integrity and credibility in her UN diplomacy. As in many other UN forums, the influence and prestige that China has methodically built up through her behavioral modesty and vigorous moral and political support for the causes of the poor face the continuing danger of being diminished by her excessive polemics against the Soviet Union in UNDP.

Are the limited resources of UNDP being utilized "properly" and "efficiently"? On this administrative-fiscal matter, China's posture of

[83] *Ibid.*
[84] *Ibid.*, p. 432.
[85] UN Doc. DP/SR.500 (20 January 1976), p. 19.

fiscal conservatism in the General Assembly has reasserted itself in UNDP. Descending from the political to the operational level, Ambassador Lai Ya-li summarized China's position as follows: "UNDP should adopt firm and effective measures to simplify its administrative structure, achieve economy, overcome red tape and significantly reduce administrative expenses, so as to make maximum use of the limited financial resources in actual assistance operations. Expenses for experts should be reasonable, so that the financial resources made available to recipient countries could be used to carry out as many projects as possible."[86]

The last sentence in Lai Ya-li's statement is a diplomatic euphemism. The Chinese are shocked by what they regard as "exorbitant" salaries of UN experts in the field. The Chinese are also disturbed by the percentage of UNDP expenditures for field experts. For example, $167 million, representing 58.8 percent of the 1974 UNDP project expenditures, went to the salaries of field experts.[87] This offends China's egalitarian norms and violates one of the Eight Principles for China's Aid to Foreign Countries—namely, the experts dispatched by China to help the recipient countries will have the same standard of living as the experts of the recipient country.[88] This principle stands as a serious obstacle in the way of direct Chinese participation in the administration of UNDP-sponsored projects through the specialized agencies. The 1976 FAO Fisheries (Aquaculture) Mission to China noted in its report: "The Chinese insistence on adopting the living standards of the localities in which they work, especially their insistence on doing so in their programmes of aid to others, make it difficult to fit individual Chinese experts into the usual FAO-managed projects . . ."[89]

The Chinese query, therefore, whether UNDP is really helping the poor countries or helping Western field experts. To add another difficulty, some $44.2 million (15.6 percent of the total project expenditures in 1974) are distributed through such executing agencies as the World Bank, ILO, and IAEA, of which Peking is not and refuses to be a member. In short, there is a conflict between what UNDP is actually doing and what China thinks UNDP ought to be doing in helping the developing countries. Specifically, this conflict is highlighted by the Chinese complaint that UNDP operations should not be limited to

[86] UN Doc. DP/SR.546 (19 January 1977), pp. 8-9.

[87] UNDP, *Report of the Administrator for 1974* (DP/111), p. 76.

[88] See "Eight Principles for China's Aid to Foreign Countries," *PR*, No. 17 (April 28, 1972), 15.

[89] *Freshwater Fisheries and Aquaculture in China*, A Report of the FAO Fisheries (Aquaculture) Mission to China, 21 April-12 May 1976, FAO Fisheries Technical Paper No. 168, FIR/T168 (Rome: FAO, June 1977), p. 72.

preinvestment activities. The developing countries should be helped instead "to build complete projects covering the whole process from survey to designing, equipment supply, construction and installation, guidance in trial production and transfer of technology."[90] Thus, the expansion of UNDP operations throughout the whole spectrum of the development process constitutes an important item for reform at UNDP. While advocating a fundamental reform, not just "some patchwork repairs to the old framework," however, China has also injected her "conservatism" by advising that "UNDP could not be reformed overnight."[91]

Viewed in the light of the above discussion, then, China's marginal financial contributions to UNDP are unavoidable. In a most comprehensive policy statement made in the Governing Council, Ambassador Lai Ya-li presented a detailed analysis of what UNDP should or should not do in order to conform to the profound historical change as already expressed in NIEO. He summarized China's role in the following terms:

China was a developing socialist country. In accordance with the eight principles guiding the provision of aid to other countries, it had been carrying on bilateral economic and technical co-operation with *friendly* countries within its capabilities. Bilateral programmes were the *principal* means for conducting China's economic and technical co-operation with other countries, but China was also participating in some United Nations multilateral aid operations. *That was, in fact, mutual economic and technical co-operation among developing countries, mutual support and assistance among poor friends.* China's purpose in offering contributions in its own currency to such multilateral aid organizations as UNDP, was to play its *modest part* in undertaking projects through the channels of multilateral co-operation to help other developing countries to develop their national economies independently and self-reliantly.[92]

In a word, China has decided to limit herself to a token or symbolic role in UN multilateral assistance. In this straightforward manner, she has made it clear to UNDP and other developing countries what they

[90] UN Doc. DP/SR.452 (21 January 1975), p. 122.
[91] UN Doc. DP/SR.500 (20 January 1976), p. 14.
[92] *Ibid.*, pp. 14-15; emphasis added. As summary records, the statements made by national representatives in the Governing Council are phrased in the past tense; hence, the quotation cited in the text should be read in this light. It may also be noted in this connection that Ambassador Wang Jun-sheng declared at the 1824th plenary meeting of ECOSOC on July 6, 1972: "At present that aid was mainly *political and moral*, but it would increase as China's socialist construction advanced." See ECOSOR, 53rd Sess., 1824th plenary meeting (6 July 1972), para. 54; emphasis added.

could realistically expect from her in the context of multilateral aid. Table 6.4, although pieced together from fragmentary and incomplete data from various sources, nonetheless highlights the contrast between bilateral and multilateral aid against the background of China's capability (GNP) during the first half of the 1970s.

TABLE 6.4. The PRC's Bilateral Aid, UNDP Contributions, and GNP, 1970-76 (million $)

Year	GNP	Bilateral Aid	UNDP Contributions	Total UNDP Voluntary Contributions
1970	157,000	728		
1971	178,000	562		
1972	193,000	558		268.4
1973	226,000	428	1.99	307.6
1974	259,000	272	2.2	337.5
1975	299,000	273	Suspended	406.5
1976	309,000	108	2.23	466.3

Source: Adapted from UN Docs. A/CONF.58/2 (17 October 1973), p. 2; A/CONF.59/2 (30 September 1974), p. 2; A/CONF.65/SR.1-2, pp. 25-26; A/CONF.69/SR.1-2, p. 23; UNDP, *Report of the Administrator for 1976* (DP/255), p. 11; U.S. Arms Control and Disarmament Agency, *World Military Expenditures and Arms Transfers 1966-1975* (December 1976), p. 25; CIA, *Communist Aid to the Less Developed Countries of the Free World, 1976*, ER 77-10296 (August 1977), p. 7; and the International Institute for Strategic Studies, *The Military Balance 1977-1978*, p. 54.

Even granting that China is a developing country, her contributions to UNDP, in which most Member States participate, are extremely modest, representing well under 1 percent of total voluntary contributions. In addition, China has joined Albania, Algeria, Bulgaria, Burma, Cuba, Czechoslovakia, the German Democratic Republic, Hungary, New Zealand, Poland, the Soviet Union, and Yugoslavia in contributing her own nonconvertible currency (Renminbi). In suspending her contributions for 1975 at the 1974 annual pledging conference, China argued that little progress had been made in arranging the projects that could utilize Chinese currency because of outmoded UNDP's restrictive regulations (Regulation 6.4 of the Financial Regulations and Rules of UNDP).[93] At the 1975 pledging conference, China pledged 4.4 million yüans for 1976 on the ground that "some progress" had been made in the utilization of Renminbi contributions.[94] At the

[93] UN Doc. A/CONF.65/SR.1-2 (8 December 1974), p. 25.
[94] The exchange rate between the US $ and the Chinese Renminbi (Jen-min pi,

1976 pledging conference, however, China again suspended her contributions for 1977 in the face of a glut in UNDP holdings of nonconvertible currencies, which had reached the value of $37,872,711 as of December 31, 1976.[95]

When asked to comment on the extremely modest Chinese contributions in Renminbi, UNDP secretariat officials reminded the author of three points. First, China is a developing country; hence, anything China can afford to contribute to UNDP is accepted with appreciation. Second, even such a developed country as the Soviet Union contributed (in nonconvertible rubles) only $3,829,787 for 1975 and $3,552,632 for 1976, less than 1 percent of total contributions for those years. Finally, China, as a developing country with a low per capita GNP, refuses to be a recipient of any UNDP assistance. For comparison, Brazil contributed $1,500,000 for 1975 but received approved projects amounting to $15,266,000 for the same year. The size and magnitude of China's proper share for UNDP assistance can be extrapolated from Figure 6.5 below. In short, in the author's field interviews, little con-

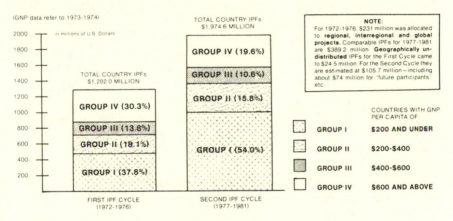

FIGURE 6.5. Allocation of Country IPFs Among Groups of Countries by GNP per Capita for the First and Second IPF Cycles.

cern or disappointment was expressed at the UNDP secretariat. What these officials stressed was the importance of China's symbolic participation in the annual pledging conference.

according to the Wade-Giles romanization system) in December 1976 was 1 : 1.97.

95 UN Doc. A/CONF.69/SR.1-2 (8 December 1975), p. 23. For the Administrator's analysis of UNDP holdings of accumulated nonconvertible currencies and the measures taken to deal with this problem, see UNDP, *Report of the Administrator for 1976* (DP/255), pp. 21-23.

Is it possible to follow the principle of untied aid in the real world of international politics? Is it possible to reconcile an absolute respect for the sovereignty of recipient countries with the practical requirements of "effective" aid? I doubt whether any donor countries, including China, can or want to fulfill such noble requirements. Judged by a more realistic and relative set of criteria, however, China's bilateral aid, according to a comprehensive recent study by Wolfgang Bartke, has "the character of a model."[96] Whatever political and symbolic interests may be disguised in Chinese bilateral aid—there seems to be a substantial amount of both in China's determination of amounts, recipients, and projects, as well as her behavioral style of execution in the field—the economic conditions and terms of Chinese aid stand out as being more unselfish than those granted by any other country in the world, capitalist or communist.[97]

In conclusion, Chinese participation in UNDP has remained more symbolic than substantive, more polemical than positive. There is a clash between China's conceptualization of the NIEO and the UNDP's practice. Given the dominant role of the largest contributors, the prospects for UNDP being transformed into Peking's image of an effective NIEO instrument are doubtful, and the Chinese know this. This further strengthens their skepticism about this sort of multilateral aid being an effective instrument for helping poor countries in the world. Under the circumstances, Chinese contributions to UNDP are likely to remain only token gestures.

On the other hand, China's bilateral aid allows a sufficient degree of control and flexibility for her to translate the Chinese image of world economic order into a number of model projects in a carefully selected number of countries. Note the completion of the 1,860 kilometer-long Zambia-Tanzania railway (the Tanzam Railway) a year ahead of schedule as China's showcase aid project in Africa.[98] What is important for both China and UNDP is the fact that the voice of China is being finally heard, if not always listened to, in the decision-making process of the Governing Council. Hence, the cumulative and long-term impact of mutual adjustment and mutual legitimization between the two should not be underestimated.

[96] Wolfgang Bartke, *China's Economic Aid* (London: Hurst, 1975), p. 9.

[97] For an elaboration of this thesis, see *ibid., passim.* See also CIA, *Communist Aid to the Less Developed Countries of the Free World, 1976,* ER 77-10296 (August 1977), p. 5.

[98] For details on the Tanzam Railway and the prestige China gained in Africa, see "Zambia-Tanzania Railway is Monument to Chinese Builders' Prestige," *NYT,* April 24, 1977, p. 55. See also "The Tanzam Railway," *PR,* No. 30 (July 23, 1976), 14-15; "Tanzam Railway in Its First Year," *PR,* No. 31 (July 29, 1977), 27-28.

CONCLUSION

Perhaps the most important conclusion to be drawn from the fore-going discussion is that the historic task of creating a new world order with justice has been made more legitimate through Chinese participation. It was fortuitous for both China and the global community that the PRC's entry into the United Nations system predated the in-augural process of establishing the foundations of NIEO. To design, let alone to execute, a global compact of this magnitude without the participation of one-fifth of humanity would have been self-contradic-tory and self-defeating. The Chinese support of the *Declaration*, the *Programme of Action*, and the *Charter* contributes to a process of mu-tual legitimization between China and NIEO, thus strengthening the prospects for the long and arduous journey ahead.

In spite of its somewhat restrictive title, NIEO for China—and for the Third World—is no less than a new world order. Even the compre-hensive report to the Club of Rome that was prepared and submitted by an international group of twenty-one specialists, giving a detailed prognosis of the provisions of NIEO, significantly omitted the word "economic" from its title, *Reshaping the International Order*. In the Chinese conceptualization of world order, there is no dividing line be-tween the political and the economic spheres. The highly politicized NIEO process has shattered the cherished assumption of the function-alists, and perhaps rightly so. In fact, what gives a measure of realism and challenge to NIEO is its politicized character. Conversely, what stands in the way of its implementation process is the political will of the developed countries. The NIEO struggle, in short, is largely a political process.

Viewed in this light, the politicized approach that the Chinese have taken in the inaugural and implementation processes of NIEO is neither unusual nor necessarily undesirable. The Chinese have differed in degree, not in kind, on this matter; they have been more candid and forthright than other Member States in stating their views without disguising the nature and scope of their support for a new world order. They have seldom allowed their obvious concern about popularity and image enhancement to stand in the way of expressing their deep convictions and cherished principles. Hence, Chinese participation in the NIEO process has afforded a reliable basis for assessing the Chi-nese image of world order in this and previous chapters.

What complicates the NIEO implementation process is that each of the major actors has redefined the new world order in its own image. For the Third World, it is basically a bread-and-butter struggle be-tween the rich and the poor in the global village. It is a new concept of global welfare, designed to do away with the structural inequities in the old economic order so as to redistribute the GGP on a more just and equitable basis. For the Soviet Union, NIEO is neither new in origin nor North-South in structure. It is basically a new manifestation of an old problem (Western colonialism), for which the Soviet Union cannot be expected to share any responsibility; it is, in short, a phenomenon of the West-South conflict. Hence, the Soviet Union has categorically rejected the 0.7 percent aid target.

As the creator of the old economic order and the most rich and powerful participant, the United States rejects the concept of a new order. While willing to accommodate on a case-by-case and country-by-country basis in regard to each specific economic problem of the Third World, the United States conceptualizes NIEO as an ideological overkill on the part of a tyrannical majority in the United Nations. The United States has taken a somewhat accommodating posture toward the omnibus resolution adopted at the 7th Special Session of the General Assembly, while retaining her opposition to the conceptual foundations of NIEO. Given the slightly more sympathetic attitude of the Carter Administration toward the Third World, an American contribution to the NIEO implementation process, whose principles and objectives she has hitherto vigorously opposed, is now somewhat more likely but no less problematic.

China, too, has redefined NIEO in her own image. At the highest level of conceptualization, NIEO is seen as part of an inexorable historical process in which the poor and the weak are finally rising in a united struggle against the rich and the powerful. It is the Third World that is playing the dominant role in destroying the old and creating the new international economic relations; it is the superpowers who are defending the old economic order, persisting in colonialism, imperialism, and hegemony. However, at the behavioral level, NIEO has been operationalized into an antihegemonic model, as illustrated in Figure 6.6.

This model is uniquely Chinese. It certainly has no logic in terms of classical Marxism. In fact, observing Chinese behavior in the NIEO process, the uninitiated could hardly guess that China was a socialist or a communist nation. This model also modifies the Maoist three-world typology by first setting China apart from the Third World and then by drawing a behavioral distinction between Soviet social-imperialism and American imperialism. In addition, the model poses an analytical problem, because it crystallizes the pervasive Chinese tendency to blur deliberately the conceptual distinction between descriptive and prescriptive definitions of the international situation.

Although Chinese participation in NIEO politics has been more

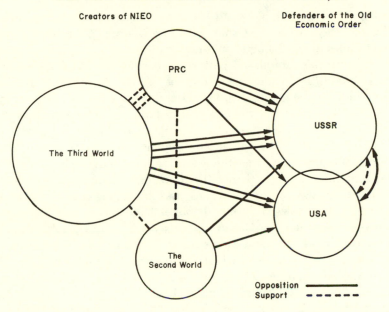

Creators of NIEO

Defenders of the Old
Economic Order

FIGURE 6.6. The PRC's Operationalization of the NIEO Implementation Process.

symbolic than substantive on most occasions, nonetheless there has been a discernible difference between the inaugural and the implementation processes. China has shown more interest, more enthusiasm, and greater participation in the formulation of NIEO principles than in their implementation. Her most active participation in the drafting process of the *Charter*—as well as in the drafting process of the Stockholm Declaration on the Human Environment—showed that three preconditions had to be met in order to activate her full participation: (1) that she be allowed to participate on an individual basis, without a rigid structure of group politics; (2) that the institutional framework of negotiations did not predate the PRC's entry into the United Nations; and (3) that the issues at stake should be in the nature of broad declaratory principles or normative rules to guide the future of international politics.

There are numerous reasons for China's generally selective, passive, and symbolic participation in the NIEO implementation process. First, the Maoist notion that human or national behavior is a reflection of its world view is translated into Chinese global politics: a greater interest and participation is shown in general debate on grandiose principles in the plenary than in detailed deliberations in committees and subsidiary bodies of the General Assembly. Second, there is a strategic problem. The structure of the NIEO implementation process has been well established, with the Group of 77 and Group *B* occupying the opposite sides in the dialogue or confrontation.

Faced with this established pattern of negotiations, China has had three options: (1) to join the Group of 77; (2) to establish herself as an additional negotiating group, complicating the united front of the Group of 77; and (3) to keep at a distance from the actual negotiating process, confining herself to the role of a symbolic supporter of the Group of 77. She has opted for the third course of action, and close examination shows that this was a rational move. The Group of 77, as a coalition of more than 110 nations, has maintained a remarkable degree of unity and cohesiveness in establishing a common position and strategy toward Group *B*, but it is no secret that the intragroup politics within the Group of 77 is marked by fluid leadership and factional and geographical quarrels on many specific questions. It is difficult to imagine what China could possibly gain in the midst of such intragroup fighting without complicating her bilateral relations with one faction as against another. Under the circumstances, the Chinese posture of giving moral and political support to the broad principles and large demands of the Group of 77 without getting herself entangled in intramural infighting makes sense. Her somewhat surprising nonparticipation in UNCTAD's Committee on Economic Co-operation among Developing Countries should be viewed in this light.

Third, the Chinese concept of self-reliance, especially if interpreted by the more radical Maoists, acts as a hindrance to a more active participation in the NIEO implementation process. Most NIEO negotiations involve a struggle between the rich and the poor over the division of the global pie. Yet the Chinese are profoundly skeptical about the "welfare mentality" shown by many developing countries, who become more and more dependent as they ask for more and more. The Chinese attack on the concept of "interdependence" is addressed to the Third World, but the developing countries, out of self-respect as well as for strategic reasons, need to present demands to the rich countries in terms of global interdependency.

Fourth, given her policy of self-reliance and the marginal involvement of Chinese economic interests in the global negotiations to implement NIEO principles, China feels no imperative to be actively involved. Simply put, she has little to gain and little to give. This was most clearly highlighted by her participation in the Governing Council of UNDP. The striking contrast between her negligible contributions to UNDP resources and her substantial bilateral aid is a case in point.

Finally, the antihegemonic model expresses itself in behavioral terms in the Chinese respect for the sovereignty of developing countries and in the high degree of sensitivity the Chinese have shown about playing a "proper role" in UN politics. "If one day China should change her colour and turn into a superpower, if she too should play the tyrant in the world, and everywhere subject others to her bullying, aggression and exploitation," declared Teng Hsiao-p'ing before the 6th Special Session, "the people of the world should identify her as social-imperialism [sic], expose it, oppose it and work together with the Chinese people to overthrow it."[99] The passive and supportive posture that China has adopted in the NIEO implementation process is consistent with the pledge that China will never seek to be or act like a superpower in international politics.

[99] "At Special Session of U.N. General Assembly: Chairman of Chinese Delegation Teng Hsiao-ping's Speech," PR, No. 16 (April 19, 1974), 11. In the most comprehensive foreign policy posture statement issued since the death of Mao Tse-tung, this point was reaffirmed. See "Chairman Mao's Theory of the Differentiation of the Three Worlds Is a Major Contribution to Marxism-Leninism," JMJP, November 1, 1977, p. 4.

· 7 ·

CHINA, FUNCTIONALISM, AND THE
SPECIALIZED AGENCIES

> The task that is facing us is how to build up the reality of
> a common interest in peace. . . . Not a peace that would
> keep the nations quietly apart, but a peace that would bring
> them actively together; not the old static and strategic view
> of peace, but a social view of it. . . . We must put our faith
> not in a protected but in a working peace; it would indeed
> be nothing more nor less than the idea and aspiration of
> social security taken in its widest range.
>
> David Mitrany, 1943

The objective and scope of this chapter are eclectic. The objective is
confined to delineating another behavioral dimension in the evolving
Chinese strategy of world order; the scope is limited to a cross-sample
of four of the eight specialized agencies in the UN family—FAO,
ICAO, IMCO, ITU, UNESCO, UPU, WHO, and WMO—in which
China participates. Even within these limits, no attempt is made to
provide any detailed description or analysis of the function, structure,
and historical evolution of each specialized agency under review, or to
provide a chronological, blow-by-blow account of Chinese participation in it. To do so would not only blur the focus, but constitute another
book-length project.

The specialized agencies, as functional intergovernmental organizations (IGOs) with highly specific tasks, are generally short on political documents. Except for the records of a conference or assembly held
once every two, three, or four years, the profuse documents and materials of a highly technical nature generated by the activities of various
subsidiary organs within each specialized agency say little about the
behavior of participating Member States. Hence, this chapter relies
mainly on documents of a general and political nature, such as the
annual report of the secretary-general (or director-general) of each
specialized agency on the work of his organization, and the plenary
records of a conference or assembly. For behavioral insights, however,
this chapter relies extensively on "live" sources—mainly secretariat
officials and national delegates—consulted during field interviews in
the cities where the headquarters of the specialized agencies under
review are located.[1]

[1] Of the 110 field interviews, 73 relate to the specialized agencies, distributed

The PRC's entry into each of the eight specialized agencies has had an immediate dual effect. On the one hand, it has changed, with varying degrees of significance, the political environment in which each specialized agency operates. On the other, it has broadened the operational base of Chinese global politics. The present analysis focuses on impacts and reciprocal interactions between China and the specialized agencies. As previously noted, the United Nations system embodies a pluralistic approach to world order. The specialized agencies provide a vital testing ground for functionalism, or a peace-building approach to world order. An analysis of Chinese behavior in the welfare-oriented specialized agencies may serve to shed some light on the evolving Chinese conceptualization of the functional approach to world order. To place our inquiry in the analytical framework of functionalism, however, we need to review very briefly functionalism in theory and practice.

FUNCTIONALISM IN THEORY AND PRACTICE

The term "functional" or "functionalism" in the literature of international relations admits of no neat and fixed definition.[2] It has a variety of referents and ùses. In the institutional sense, the "functional" sector in the international system refers to that part of the UN family engaged in social, economic, cultural, humanitarian, and technical matters. In the operational sense, the term has also been used as a synonym for "nonpolitical," or even "noncontroversial," however misleading such a usage might be in terms of diachronic change in the functional sector of the United Nations system. To some, the term suggests a task-oriented bureaucratic process or an institutional practice; to others, it conveys a pragmatic, as opposed to an ideological or dogmatic, intellectual temperament.

Despite such varied usage, the theory of functionalism as stated by its leading exponent, David Mitrany, in A Working Peace System, is

---

as follows: 16 for FAO; 15 for UNESCO; 10 for WHO; 10 for ICAO; 5 for ITU; 5 for WMO; 4 for IMCO; 2 for UPU; 2 for IBRD; 2 for IMF; 1 for WIPO; 1 for ILO; and 1 for GATT. The total comes to 74 because one interviewee represents his country at both ITU and UPU. The interviews at those specialized agencies in which the PRC does not participate were usually conducted with the head of the external relations department. GATT is a de facto specialized agency of the United Nations system and is treated as such in this book. For a detailed breakdown, see Interview Schedule.

2 For a lucid exegetical analysis of the semantics of functionalism, see Ernst B. Haas, Beyond the Nation-State: Functionalism and International Organization, (Stanford, Calif.: Stanford University Press, 1964), pp. 3-8. A comprehensive bibliography on functionalism is contained in A.J.R. Groom and Paul Taylor, eds., Functionalism: Theory and Practice in International Relations (London: University of London Press, 1975), pp. 284-338.

basically a prescriptive proposition for a welfare-oriented approach to world order. "Peace will not be secured," argued Mitrany, "if we organize the world by what divides it. But in the measure in which such peace-building activities develop and succeed, one might hope that the mere prevention of conflict, crucial as that may be, would in time fall to a subordinate place in the scheme of international things, while we would turn to what are the real tasks of our common society—the conquest of poverty and of disease and of ignorance."[3] As such, functionalism, while committed to world peace as an ideal end, suggests an incremental means for mankind to work its way toward the end. In Mitrany's terms, "the functional arrangements might indeed be regarded as organic elements of a federalism by installments."[4] In short, both the end and the means are embodied in functionalism; alternatively, it is an approach that has been characterized as "peace by pieces."[5]

Functionalism represents a most serious challenge to the realistic school of thought in international relations. It certainly rejects the Hobbesian image of human nature implicit in Realpolitik. Its central concern with the functional process of building a world community through an expansion of horizontal networks of transnational activities is based on the assumption that man's basic nature is good and malleable. It is also based on the assumption that man's national loyalty (nationalism) is transformable and transferable from functional to political sectors, and from national to international spheres. Functionalism is more interested in the low politics of cooperative endeavors than in the high politics of conflict management. In fact, the functionalists argue that the overemphasis on negative peace diverts our attention away from positive peace. The functionalists have reformulated the "swords into plowshares" approach into the "plowshares into peace" approach. Viewed in this light, the functionalists have not only offered an alternative approach to world order but also redefined the basic problem of world order.

To be sure, the welfare-oriented approach has a logic and rationality of its own, but to the functionalists this approach has a positive contributory value in building a working peace system in a manner suggestive of William James' "moral equivalent of war." The concept of national sovereignty is assumed to lose its relevance when experts and technicians get together at international forums to deal with the problems or opportunities created by such scientific developments as aviation, wireless communication, atomic energy, satellites, and space

[3] David Mitrany, *A Working Peace System* (Chicago: Quadrangle Books, 1966 [originally published in 1943 as a pamphlet]), p. 96.
[4] *Ibid.*, p. 83.
[5] Lyman C. White, "Peace by Pieces," *Free World* 11 (January 1946), 66-68.

exploration. At the social, cultural, and economic level, the welfare-oriented approach is also assumed to be capable of removing one of the major causes of the discontents that lead to international violence. As Mitrany wrote in 1944: "Give people a moderate sufficiency of what they need and ought to have and they will keep the peace; this has been proved time and time again nationally, but it has not yet been tried internationally."[6]

On the other hand, the functionalists, in keeping with their "pragmatic" temperament, are skeptical of any grand schemes or legal-institutional blueprints for the brave new world commonly envisioned in the idealistic school of thought in international relations. To design a structure at the outset is to rigidify the functional process of community building, and the functionalists assume that forms and structures will vary according to their functions in the course of the community-building process. Hence, functionalism represents a middle way between what is desirable (idealism) and what is feasible (realism) in international relations. Functionalism cherishes a radical vision tempered by a gradualist means.

Functionalism has been criticized and challenged for a variety of reasons. The realists predictably reject the assumption that the supremacy of national sovereignty can ever be tamed, given the wide disparity between the capacity of the nation-state and the capacity of the IGOs to satisfy the welfare and emotional needs of the citizen. "What the national government does or does not do is much more important for the satisfaction of individual wants," asserts Hans J. Morgenthau, a leading spokesman of the realist school, "than what an international functional agency does or does not do."[7]

Even such scholars as Inis Claude, Jr., Ernst B. Haas, and James P. Sewell, who are hardly committed to the realist tradition, challenge the central assumption that the functional and the political can indeed be separated or that the former can be given priority to transform the latter.[8] In an eloquent argument, Claude rejects the assumption that functional activities can be expanded or transferred without political support. "Does not this assumption [of separability-priority] fly in the face of the evidence," asks Claude, "that a trend toward the politicization of all issues is operative in the twentieth century?"[9]

[6] David Mitrany, "The Road to Security," in Peace News Pamphlet, No. 29 (London: National Press Council, 1944), 14.

[7] Morgenthau, Politics Among Nations, p. 507.

[8] Haas, Beyond the Nation-State; Inis L. Claude, Jr., Swords into Plowshares (4th ed., New York: Random House, 1971), chap. 17; and James Patrick Sewell, Functionalism and World Politics: A Study Based on United Nations Programs Financing Economic Development (Princeton, N.J.: Princeton University Press, 1966).

[9] Claude, Swords into Plowshares, p. 388.

Based on an empirical inquiry into the practice of the ILO, Ernst Haas concludes that *"the spill-over process at the global welfare level is less pronounced than at the regional level of congruent pluralisms,"* thus scaling down the implication of the automaticity process in functionalism.[10] Likewise, Sewell's careful study of dynamics in the Bank Group (IBRD, IDA, and IFC) rebuts the assumption of technical self-determination in functionalism as being insufficient and misleading. Instead of finding an expanding atmosphere of noncontroversiality, Sewell found that "the very impetus behind the origin and growth of these programs [at the Bank Group] seems to be a pervasive, multilevel system of tensions which are sometimes—but only sometimes—ridden to their optimum point and then partially and temporarily capped or re-channeled by distinctly political activity."[11]

Despite its moral appeal, the "plowshares into peace" proposition has yet to acquire empirical and historical validity. None of the major empirical studies on war by Lewis Richardson, Quincy Wright, David Singer, and Melvin Small has established the existence of any direct correlation between a proneness to war and social and economic welfare.[12] However, despite the methodological difficulties involved in conducting a controlled test by completely isolating social and economic variables from political ones, the plowshares-into-peace proposition still remains a heuristically useful hypothesis, yet to be confirmed or denied.

Functionalism also begot neofunctionalism. The euphoria generated by the European integration process in the 1950s gave birth to neofunctionalist theory, not a vindication but a revision and reformulation of functionalism in a specific regional setting. Both the Eurocrats and some students of international organization foresaw that the tide of supranationalism would be irreversible. According to Ernst Haas, its chief exponent and theoretician, the theory of neofunctionalism was "one of the most promising modes of analysis" in international relations; he went on to cite the emerging United States of Europe as "a new center, whose institutions possess or demand jurisdiction over the pre-existing ones."[13] As late as 1964, Haas still believed the nation-state to be in "full retreat."[14] However, in the wake of the 1965 EEC

---

[10] Haas, *Beyond the Nation-State*, p. 456; emphasis in original.

[11] Sewell, *Functionalism and World Politics*, p. 295.

[12] Lewis Richardson, *Statistics of Deadly Quarrels* (Pittsburgh: The Boxwood Press, 1960); Quincy Wright, *A Study of War* (2nd ed., Chicago: University of Chicago Press, 1965); and J. David Singer and Melvin Small, *The Wages of War 1816-1965: A Statistical Handbook* (New York: Wiley, 1972).

[13] Ernst B. Haas, *The Uniting of Europe* (Stanford, Calif.: Stanford University Press, 1958), pp. 3-4, 16.

[14] Ernst B. Haas, "International Integration: The European and the Universal Process," in Dale J. Hekuis, Charles G. McClintock, and Arthur L. Burns, eds., *International Stability* (New York: Wiley, 1964), p. 229.

crisis and the challenge posed to supranationalism by de Gaulle's high politics, it was Haas who began to retreat from his "pre-theorizing."[15] At the moment, both neofunctionalism and the promised United States of Europe are in abeyance, if not dead.

It may well be asked at this point: To what extent has the practice of the specialized agencies validated the central assumptions of the functional approach to world order? Actually, the functional IGOs predated the functional theory; the latter emerged to describe, explain, and prescribe the process or practice of the former. It came as a startling revelation in the course of the author's field interviews that many practitioners of functionalism—the high-ranking secretariat international civil servants at the specialized agencies—candidly admitted their ignorance of the theory of functionalism. Even Mitrany, faced with a plethora of scientific theorizing and paradigm construction of all kinds, wrote in 1975: "[T]here is no evidence that it [theorizing] has had any effect on actual practitioners and policy, nor any instances of political action based on one or the other of these 'scientific' models."[16] Therefore, the real question is not whether the specialized agencies conform to the description and prescription of the theory of functionalism; rather, it is whether the theory has accurately described and explained the practice of the specialized agencies.

Unlike the League of Nations, the United Nations system in its original conception embodied a pluralism of several approaches to world order. This pluralism was expressed institutionally in the stipulation of different and presumably complementary functions for the six principal organs of the United Nations. In theory, ECOSOC was supposed to coordinate the functional activities of the specialized agencies. In practice, however, the specialized agencies have developed their own constitutions, their own budgets, and their own policies, maintaining only affiliational relationships with the United Nations through ECOSOC.

The UN Charter gave no clear guideline as to the kinds of relationships that should be formed between the United Nations and the specialized agencies; it merely allowed ECOSOC to enter into agreements with each specialized agency, and define the particular terms of each.[17] ILO's entry into a relationship with the United Nations "as partners," willing to make some sacrifices of its "sovereignty" but hav-

---

[15] See, for example, Ernst B. Haas, *The Uniting of Europe and the Uniting of Latin America*, Reprint No. 241 (Institute of International Studies, University of California, n.d.), p. 325, and *The Study of Regional Integration: Reflections on the Joy and Anguish of Pretheorizing*, International Integration Series, Reprint No. 363 (Institute of International Studies, University of California, n.d.), p. 610.
[16] David Mitrany, "A Political Theory for the New Society," in Groom and Taylor, *Functionalism*, p. 26.
[17] See Articles 57 and 63 of the UN Charter.

ing no intention of acting "in a subordinate capacity," set a pattern of decentralized and autonomous development for the specialized agencies.[18] It may also have marked the beginning of the self-righteous practice of lionizing individual institutional interests as ends in themselves rather than as means in the global integrative process.

The diversified and decentralized character of the specialized agencies makes it risky to advance any broad generalization. With this caveat in mind, we can still suggest that the specialized agencies as international subsystems are organically bound to be affected by any major systemic changes in global politics. The norms, structures, and processes of the global system have changed significantly since the inception of the United Nations in 1945. First, the ideological climate of world politics improved, moderating the representational style of the two superpowers in their multilateral diplomacy. Second, bipolarity was laid to rest, pluralizing world politics. Third, the entry of developing countries into the United Nations changed the axis of UN politics from an East-West to a North-South orientation. Finally, such global economic crises as the ones reviewed in Chapter 5 set in motion the monumental task of translating NIEO from rhetoric to reality. All of these systemic changes have affected the specialized agencies, with the result that the pattern of events predicted by the functionalists has been reversed. That is, instead of the functional subsystems working their way upward to transform the global political system, the latter has significantly affected the former.

Within the context of the United Nations system, the full-fledged and decentralized character of its functional activities is largely a result of American initiative and insistence, to which the Soviet Union in a spirit of concession has reluctantly acquiesced. During the formative years, the United States played a dominant role in adapting the specialized agencies to her own image of world order. Taking advantage of the absence or perfunctory participation of the Soviet Union and her own controlling power of the purse, the United States used the specialized agencies as a testing ground to merge and develop her own political and economic strategies of world order, and an unnatural and unhealthy relationship of dependence and dominance developed, with the agencies hardly able to survive without US financial support.

Having thus "politicized" the specialized agencies, the United States began to resist vigorously any attempt on the part of adversary Member States to "repoliticize" them. Curiously, the American "defense" of the specialized agencies was often made in the name of maintaining the functional (nonpolitical) autonomy and integrity of each agency

[18] UN Doc. E/NSA/13 (10 June 1946); cited in Claude, Swords into Plowshares, p. 396.

concerned. Take the extreme example of the World Bank. The Bank was supposed to have no politics, yet its ideology was "totally non-functionalist" and its policy discernibly pro-American.[19] Under the leadership of Eugene Black, an American financial wizard, the Bank reflected a measure of his world view, "divided into the camp of freedom and the camp of Communism."[20] The absence of the Soviet Union and the PRC, coupled with the weighted voting, made it easier for the United States to carry out her own conception of world order at the Bank. Nonetheless, the systemic changes of global politics have now influenced the Bank, or its President Robert McNamara, to such a degree that the rhetoric of the Bank has begun to reflect some NIEO concerns.

To be sure, the term "politicization," which is central to an analysis of the practice of the specialized agencies in terms of functionalist assumptions, is very general and ambiguous. It is used here as an overt attempt to assert the supremacy of national political interests through a variety of means, ranging from rhetorics to sanctions. If the term is defined in this broad scope, most Member States take the politicized approach, given opportunities and means to do so. However, there are differences in the form and style of politicization, just as there are institutional differences among the specialized agencies in the degree to which they are susceptible.

A few examples may suffice here. Given the importance of political symbolism and social justice in global politics, it is not surprising that UNESCO and ILO are among the most vulnerable. In recent years, when the United States was unable to combat the politicizing influence of the Third World in these two agencies, she resorted to the legally dubious practice for which she had once condemned the Soviet Union —namely, financial withholding. In the case of ILO, she went a step farther by actually withdrawing from the organization on November 1, 1977. On the other hand, such highly technical organizations as IMCO, ITU, UPU, and ICAO have enjoyed a degree of self-determination.

Do these latter examples validate the functionalist theory? Not necessarily, for functional autonomy has been allowed only within such narrow limits as to make its spillover virtually negligible. Because political issues gain and lose varying degrees of relevance and saliency, no specialized agency is completely politicized or completely depoliticized. Still, the functionalist assumption of the separability of the political and the functional has not been validated. More accurately, the

[19] Thomas Weiss and Jean Siotis, "Functionalism and International Secretariats: Ideology and Rhetoric in the UN Family," in Groom and Taylor, *Functionalism*, pp. 182-84.
[20] Quoted in *ibid.*, p. 183.

intervention of politics has made it difficult to test the functionalist theory.

The impact of politicization is clearly reflected in the nature of the specialized agencies. None of them has been allowed to become a truly supranational organization with inherent or independent power to override the sovereign prerogatives of the Member States, even within the specified limit of each agency's bailiwick. Brock Chisholm, first director-general of WHO and a committed functionalist, had to admit: "WHO is not a supra-national health administration. It cannot act in place of and for the national health authorities in any area of public health. Its only role is to use all possible means of international co-operation in order to provide certain essential elements which those authorities need to promote the health of their peoples. The rest is up to each individual nation itself."[21]

In spite of such political constraints, varying degrees of functionalist ideology have been reflected in the general goals of most specialized agencies. The opening sentence of both the 1919 and the 1972 Constitutions of ILO embodied the functionalist premise that "universal and lasting peace can be established only if it is based upon social justice." The concept of social justice has also influenced the shaping of general goals at FAO and WHO. Likewise, the "minds-of-men" approach to world order as expressed in the Preamble to the UNESCO Constitution is congenial to the assumption of the functionalists that man's basic nature is malleable and that his loyalty can be transformed to provide a psychological foundation for world order.

In practice, however, most specialized agencies have been too pre-occupied with the execution of modest subgoals to pay much attention to lofty general goals. The focus and direction of the subgoals pursued are diffuse, and lack any global coordination. Some of these agencies are responsible for regulating a large number of technical activities in the fields of communication and transportation, to the extent of actually prescribing international standards. Standard setting and regulation making have become matters of common endeavor at IMCO, ITU, UPU, ICAO, and IAEA. Because of the highly technical nature of the subgoals pursued by these agencies, politicization has been kept to a minimum, but a sudden change in the international climate would increase it.

Other agencies, such as FAO, WHO, UNESCO, and the Bank Group, are more service oriented. Their task expansion and task performance have been uneven. Within each agency, too, performance has been uneven across different sectoral programs. WHO, for example, has a dismal record in regard to the world population problem,

21 *United Nations Bulletin* (December 1, 1951), 446.

but has made an outstanding contribution to subgoals that are non-controversial, such as health services and disease control. The World Bank pursued development for development's sake on the basis of nonfunctional business—that is, profit-oriented—criteria. UNESCO's performance is almost impossible to assess, as the institution has transformed itself into a plural system in which "everyone has his own hobbyhorse."[22] The contribution of FAO to the world food problem seems marginal, though such a judgment may be somewhat unfair and arbitrary, given the immense disparity between the magnitude of the problem and the limited resources and authority at FAO's disposal. Nonetheless, the establishment of WFC as a separate, high-level, political body to deal with the question of world food security stands out as a harsh indictment of the perceived ineffectiveness of FAO in regard to the problems of food production and nutrition.

The establishment of WFC highlights the phenomenon of an undisciplined proliferation of agencies with overlapping substantive jurisdictions. This phenomenon has been accelerated by the rise of "developmental functionalism." "The emerging developmental functionalism of our time," observed Inis Claude, "in contrast to regulatory functionalism, is a state-building enterprise, not a state-undermining project. It is directed towards making national sovereignty meaningful, not reducing it to meaninglessness."[23]

Developmental functionalism has also contributed to the amplification of the inherent bureaucratic tendency toward empire building. The UNDP-authorized Jackson Report found, for example, " 'inter-Agency rivalry for projects,' each Agency insisting, almost as a matter of right, to get a slice of the country pie, regardless of the value and propriety of the project from the country's point of view, at its particular stage of development."[24] Given the heavy dependence of the specialized agencies on the treasury of UNDP for their major field programs, however, the United Nations has a weapon of central control and coordination. But it is widely doubted whether it has actually used its purse strings to impose a degree of central coherence on the functional activities of the United Nations system.

Have the specialized agencies succeeded or failed in the tasks they set out to do? The answer depends on the criteria one chooses to apply. "The actual achievements thus far are substantial and signifi-

---

[22] James P. Sewell, "UNESCO: Pluralism Rampant," in Robert W. Cox and Harold K. Jacobson, The Anatomy of Influence: Decision Making in International Organization (New Haven, Conn.: Yale University Press, 1974), p. 173.

[23] Inis L. Claude, Jr., "Economic Development Aid and International Political Stability," in Robert W. Cox, ed., The Politics of International Organizations (New York: Praeger, 1970), p. 57.

[24] A Study of the Capacity of the United Nations Development System, p. 76.

cant," in the judgment of Claude, "even though not spectacular, world-shaking, or world-saving."[25] In Haas's judgment, "all these agencies were too 'political' to remain unaffected by the attributes of the global system, but not autonomous enough to transcend it. All, though, were sufficiently 'technical' to survive."[26] In short, accomplishments are few and far between as far as general goals are concerned. It has been at the level of specific, limited, and technical subgoals that most of these agencies have succeeded and some have even flourished. Thus, the functionalist theory remains yet to be tested, but one of its central assumptions about the separability of the political and the functional has been invalidated by the actual experience of the specialized agencies.

The PRC and the Specialized Agencies

The PRC's entry into the eight specialized agencies in the wake of the 1971 General Assembly action has to be viewed against the background of her almost total isolation from the global community, made up of hundreds of intergovernmental organizations (IGOs) and thousands of nongovernmental organizations (NGOs). As of December 1966, for example, the PRC was a member of only 2 out of some 193 IGOs, aside from the United Nations and its specialized agencies.[27] With respect to the NGOs, it is estimated that the PRC's participation was limited to only 60 out of a total of 2,188 as of December 1968.[28]

To be sure, the United States' policy of containment was in part responsible for this isolation. Byron Weng argues, however, that Peking's own policy choices accounted for a great deal of this situation. He suggests that four conditions had to be met for Peking's participation in international organizations in the 1950s and 1960s: (1) the international organization in which the PRC participated as a member had to have a "correct" ideological orientation; (2) the ROC must be excluded; (3) a "favorable" political climate had to exist within the international organization; and (4) "institutional safeguards" were required to protect its interests.[29] These four conditions should be kept in mind as we review Peking's mode of entry, as well as her behavior in each of the specialized agencies concerned.

The PRC's participation in these agencies has generated a multitude

[25] Claude, *Swords into Plowshares*, p. 407.
[26] Haas, *Beyond the Nation-State*, p. 438.
[27] Byron S. J. Weng, "Some Conditions of Peking's Participation in International Organizations," in Jerome Alan Cohen, ed., *China's Practice of International Law: Some Case Studies* (Cambridge, Mass.: Harvard University Press, 1972), p. 322.
[28] *Ibid.*, p. 324.　　　　[29] *Ibid.*, pp. 325-38.

of diplomatic activities and interactions. For analytical purposes, they can be typologized into the following nine categories:

Mission diplomacy: official visits paid to China by high-ranking secretariat officials—usually at the level of the director-general or deputy director-general, combining the elements of the banquet diplomacy and the people-to-people diplomacy. These visits involve a specific issue or problem that China wishes to work out privately with the responsible secretariat officials of each specialized agency;

Conference diplomacy: participation in a periodic general conference, where the chief delegate pronounces China's principled stand on the issues related to each specialized agency;

Executive diplomacy: participation in a limited-membership executive body, if China is a member. This environment provides an opportunity for China to make inputs into decision making;

Consultative diplomacy: relationships between Chinese permanent delegates and secretariat officials on an on-going basis, in which the former consult the latter on a variety of procedural and programmatic matters within the agency;

Delegation diplomacy: this is a medium for diplomatic lobbying; it also provides an additional forum for Chinese delegates to cultivate good social and political relationships with other delegates so as to enhance China's bilateral diplomatic relations with other Member States within each specialized agency;

Special conference diplomacy: participation in a variety of special international conferences sponsored by each specialized agency;

Cultural diplomacy: a variety of "study tours" arranged trilaterally by UNDP, each specialized agency, and China, in which a small group of personnel from developing countries or from the secretariat of each specialized agency spend some time in China studying a specific aspect of Chinese functional activities for possible application or adaptation elsewhere; the PRC's Renminbi contributions to UNDP are being utilized in defraying the costs of such cultural diplomacy;

Regional conference diplomacy: participation in the regional conferences of some specialized agencies;

Committee diplomacy: participation in *ad hoc*, special, or standing committees within each specialized agency whose work focuses on highly technical subject matters.

From the very beginning of the China controversy in the history of the United Nations, it was the General Assembly that established a political guideline for other organs and agencies of the United Nations

345

system to follow. On October 26, 1971, Secretary-General U Thant transmitted to the executive heads of all the organs and agencies the text of General Assembly Resolution 2758 (XXVI), the operative paragraph of which stated: "Decides to restore all its rights to the People's Republic of China and to recognize the representatives of its Government as the only legitimate representatives of China to the United Nations, and to expel forthwith the representatives of Chiang Kai-shek from the place which they unlawfully occupy at the United Nations and *in all the organizations related to it* [emphasis added]."

The Secretary-General, in transmitting the above resolution, also drew the attention of the executive heads of all the organizations concerned to General Assembly Resolution 396 (V) of December 1950 on recognition by the United Nations of the representation of a Member State. The General Assembly, in rejecting the PRC's bid for representation, recommended in this resolution that the position taken by the General Assembly or its Interim Committee concerning any representation question should be taken into account in other organs of the United Nations and in the specialized agencies. The Secretary-General further requested that all the executive heads should keep him informed of any relevant action taken within their respective organizations.

For her part, China was not content with the General Assembly action. In a note of January 12, 1972, addressed to Secretary-General Kurt Waldheim, Huang Hua urged the UN Secretariat to take all necessary measures to ensure the following: (1) that the United Nations and all its related organizations immediately cease all contacts with "the Chiang Kai-shek clique"; (2) that all the assistance and contacts of UNDP and the Office of Technical Co-operation, as well as other related to "the Chiang Kai-shek clique," including ongoing projects and projects that had not yet begun, should also cease, so that the resolution of the General Assembly on China might be implemented in earnest; and (3) that the PRC Permanent Mission should be informed at the earliest possible date of the results of actions taken in regard to these matters.[30] The implications of this request for the specialized agencies are obvious.

Table 7.1 provides the essential data related to the actions taken by these agencies—plus the two *de facto* specialized agencies—of the United Nations system on the question of Chinese representation, fol-

[30] See "Huang Hua Urges UN and All Related Organizations to Cease Immediately All Contacts with Chiang Kai-shek Clique," NCNA-English, United Nations, January 13, 1972, in *SCMP*, No. 5062 (January 26, 1972), 127 and *PR*, No. 3 (January 21, 1972), 15. As a result of this request, all UNDP programs for the ROC were suspended and 26 field experts were withdrawn from Taiwan in June 1972.

TABLE 7.1. Actions Taken by the Specialized Agencies on the
Question of Chinese Representation

Agency	Date	Decision Made by:	Vote	Nature of Decision
UNESCO	10/29/71	Executive Board	25:2:5	The government of the PRC is the only legitimate representative of China.
FAO	11/2/71	Council	None	Decided to authorize the director-general to invite the PRC to seek formal membership in FAO.
ILO	11/16/71	Governing Body	36:3:8	Decided to recognize the government of the PRC as the representative government of China.
GATT[a]	11/16/71	Contracting Parties	None	The chairman's consensus statement that the ROC should no longer have observer status at sessions of the contracting parties.
ICAO	11/19/71	Council	None	Decided, for the matters within its competence, to recognize the representatives of the government of the PRC as the only legitimate representatives of China to ICAO.
IAEA[a]	12/9/71	Board of Governors	13:6:5	Recognized the PRC as the only government of China.
WMO	2/24/72	Member States[b]	70:21:8	Recognized the representatives of the PRC as the only legitimate representatives of China.
UPU	4/13/72	Member States[b]	66:11:5	The representatives of the government of the PRC are henceforth the only representatives of China in the UPU.
WHO	5/10/72	Assembly	76:15:27	Recognized the representatives of the government of the PRC as the only legitimate representatives of China.
IMCO	5/23/72	Council	None	Decided to recognize the government of the PRC as the only government having the right to represent China in IMCO.
ITU	5/28/72	Administrative Council	20:5:3	Recognized the representatives of the PRC as the only legitimate representatives of China at the ITU.

[a] Both GATT and IAEA are widely regarded as *de facto* specialized agencies.
[b] By a postal ballot.

lowing the transmission of the Secretary-General's message. It should be noted that IMF, IDA, IBRD, IFC, and WIPO failed to take any action on the question, leaving the initiative to the PRC. On the other hand, the PRC herself refused to follow up the action taken by ILO, IAEA, and GATT. Furthermore, the PRC's entry into some of the eight specialized agencies was not a simple matter of taking up the seat vacated by the expelled representative of the ROC, as it was in the case of the United Nations; it required the additional step of recognizing, acceding to, or ratifying the Convention of the agency concerned. In the case of FAO, the PRC's entry was further complicated by the fact that the government of the ROC had withdrawn from the organization in 1951.

To keep the present analysis within the manageable limits of a chapter, only four of the eight specialized agencies in which China participates have been chosen: UNESCO, FAO, ICAO, and WMO. However, to minimize repetition and to depict Chinese participation as broadly as possible, I have chosen the four that differ most widely. All four agencies are located in different cities, operating in different political environments. All four differ in the nature of their functions as well as in the degree of their politicization. Even the actual dates of the PRC's participation in them are varied: UNESCO as of October 29, 1971; WMO as of February 24, 1972; FAO as of April 1, 1973; and ICAO as of February 15, 1974. In addition, the negotiation processes leading to the PRC's entry into the four agencies ranged from the most prompt and simple (WMO) to the most protracted and complicated (ICAO). The following analysis follows the chronological order shown in Table 7.1.

The United Nations Educational, Scientific, and Cultural Organization (UNESCO)

"Since wars begin in the minds of men," declares the Preamble to the UNESCO Constitution, "it is in the minds of men that the defenses of peace must be constructed." Starting from this functionalist premise, UNESCO's high calling as the intellectual conscience of mankind "is to contribute to peace and security by promoting collaboration among the nations through education, science and culture in order to further universal respect for justice, for the rule of law and for the human rights and fundamental freedoms which are affirmed for the peoples of the world, without distinction of race, sex, language or religion, by the Charter of the United Nations." This is the purpose of UNESCO.

UNESCO's Constitution provides three organs: a General Conference; an Executive Board, and a secretariat. The General Conference, which meets biennially, determines the policies of the organization. The Executive Board, whose membership has increased from eighteen to forty, prepares the provisional agenda for the Conference, examines the director-general's proposed program and estimated budget, and executes the program adopted by the Conference.

To a much greater degree than any other specialized agency, UNESCO deals with "an unending series of issues whose theme is the collective legitimation of the world's doers of good or the delegitimation of its doers of evil."[31] At the core of its symbolic politics lies what may be broadly termed the "representational issue," whether it is expressed in granting membership, in legitimating or delegitimating the representation of a Member State, or in expelling a Member State. The director-general of UNESCO stated in 1967, for example, that the two major turning points in the history of UNESCO were the admission of the Soviet Union in 1954, and that of the first big wave of newly independent African states in 1960 and after.[32] Note a more recent development in UNESCO's symbolic politics: the delegitimation of Israel by the 18th Session of the General Conference in 1974, which prompted the United States to withhold her financial contributions, thus bringing UNESCO to the precipice of financial bankruptcy, and the "relegitimation" of Israel by the 19th Session of the General Conference in 1976, which led the United States to deliver a check for $43,115,039 to UNESCO in mid-1977.[33]

After the Czech motion to replace the "Kuomintang group" with representatives of the PRC was rejected by a vote of 30 to 4 with 13 abstentions in 1950, the question of Chinese representation remained as one of the central issues in UNESCO's symbolic politics of competitive legitimation. Ironically enough, the PRC's entrance into UNESCO has not completely settled the China question once and for all, as it has in most other specialized agencies, because the PRC, as if to enrich the UNESCO tradition, has made the "two Chinas" question in the context of the organization's consultative relationships with the NGOs a central theme of her symbolic diplomacy at UNESCO.

UNESCO, like other specialized agencies, refused to upset the status quo of the ROC's occupation of the China seat in the 1950s and 1960s on the ground that such a political question as the issue of Chinese representation should be settled first by the "political" UN organs in New York. Rebutting this argument during the 1950 debate on the

[31] Sewell, "UNESCO: Pluralism Rampant," p. 149.
[32] James P. Sewell, *UNESCO and World Politics* (Princeton, N.J.: Princeton University Press, 1975), p. 337.
[33] *NYT*, July 2, 1977, p. 5.

China question, Sir Sarvepalli Radhakrishnan of India protested: "When it suits us, we claim that we are the conscience of the United Nations. When it does not suit us, we hand over our conscience to the United Nations."[34] Be that as it may, just four days after the General Assembly made its historic decision, the UNESCO Executive Board decided, on October 29, 1971, by a vote of 25 to 2, with 5 abstentions, "that from today onward, the Government of the People's Republic of China is the only legal representative of China, and invites the Director-General to act accordingly."[35]

This decision by the Board was preceded by two days of heated debate, in the course of which the United States and Brazil—the two who voted against the decision—forcefully argued that only the 127-member General Conference, not the 34-member Board, was legally authorized to act on this matter. This legalistic position was upheld by the director-general, René Maheu of France, and the legal counsellor of the organization, Claude Lussier of Canada. However, immediately after the Executive Board made its decision, the director-general was asked when the resolution would take effect. He replied: "Execution immediate." As for the Chinese offices at UNESCO headquarters, "The tenant has changed," the director-general declared. Immediately thereafter, he cabled the decision to Peking. As far as UNESCO was concerned, China had remained a member since 1946, but her representation was changed as of October 29, 1971.

Characteristically, the Chinese were rather cautious and methodical in responding to the series of actions taken by the specialized agencies in the wake of the 1971 General Assembly decision. Actual developments between the Executive Board's decision in October 1971 and the PRC's first participation in the 17th Session of the General Conference in October 1972 have all the elements of secret diplomacy secretly arrived at; there is no documentary record available to the researcher. However, on the basis of data obtained from UNESCO secretariat officials—one of whom was a direct participant in the mission diplomacy that took place during the preparatory stage of the PRC's entry into UNESCO—the following scenario may be constructed.

At the invitation of Liu Hsi-yao, head of China's Scientific and Educational Group under the State Council, an official team of UNESCO delegates composed of the director-general (Maheu), the legal adviser (Lussier), and the director of the Bureau of Relations with Member States and International Organizations and Programmes (Manuel Jimenez of Mexico), arrived in Peking on August 29, 1972.

[34] Quoted in Sewell, *UNESCO and World Politics*, p. 145.
[35] For details, see Summary Records of the Executive Board, 88th Sess., 88 EX/SR.18 (29 October 1971), pp. 191-211.

This was the mission diplomacy *par excellence* earlier referred to, through which China probed the attitude of the specialized agency concerned before deciding to participate in its work. Perhaps it was a device to reassess Weng's four conditions critically through personal diplomacy, because the actual behind-the-scenes consultations or negotiations involved Chi P'eng-fei, the minister of foreign affairs, not Liu Hsi-yao. Even before the Board's action on the China question, Maheu, in establishing a firmer control over UNESCO's budgetary process, had already "tapped the compendium-like knowledge of a secretariat official of Chinese ancestry who had earlier trained in the U.S. Bureau of the Budget."[36] Tien-cheng Young, an old-timer who is currently director of the Bureau of the Budget, also helped to arrange Maheu's trip to Peking. The Chinese embassy in Paris served as a go-between for the UNESCO secretariat and the Ministry of Foreign Affairs in Peking.

The critical meeting between the UNESCO delegation and Chinese officials took place in the afternoon of September 2, 1972, at the office of Chi P'eng-fei, the Chinese minister of foreign affairs. In addition to Maheu and Chi P'eng-fei, there were on hand Lussier, Jimenez, and a half-dozen Chinese officials, including Hu Sha, who later became Chinese permanent representative to UNESCO. Much to his astonishment, Maheu was told at this meeting that China was interested in UNESCO but was not yet ready to participate. The Chinese presented two arguments in this connection. First, the diplomatic isolation in which China had been kept for a number of years made it difficult to respond quickly and simultaneously to so many requests for Chinese participation from so many countries and so many international organizations. Second, China was short of qualified diplomatic and technical personnel. The implication in the Chinese argument was clear: they did not wish to plunge into the activities of international organizations without having first undergone what they thought to be an adequate or proper amount of probing and preparation.

As a dedicated UNESCO official, who started his career in 1946 and rose rapidly to deputy director-general (1959-61) and then to director-general (1961-74), as the man who declared in 1967 that the Soviet and African entry into UNESCO were the two chief turning points in its history and who now saw another major one in the offing, Maheu refused to be dissuaded by the Chinese argument.[37] He presented a powerful and persuasive counter-argument in support of immediate participation. The impression gained by the UNESCO participants at

[36] Sewell, *UNESCO and World Politics*, p. 216.
[37] For Maheu's personality and imprint on the development of UNESCO, see *ibid., passim.*

this meeting was that the Chinese were more interested in probing the sincerity and integrity of Maheu than in the logic of his argument.

At the end of the meeting, there was a smile on the face of the foreign minister. He simply responded: "I will not say yes or no; I will think it over and consult my colleagues and will let you know the answer within a few days." The director-general explained that he had to return to Paris, to which the Chinese replied: "Just in case we decide to participate, we would like to know more about the General Conference. Could you therefore leave one of your colleagues behind? He will bring you our formal reply." As a result, Jimenez was left behind for another week. Within a day or so, the Chinese replied in the positive. However, it was the distinct impression of one of the participants that the decision was made on the spot rather than by taking it to a higher authority. In the ensuing week, Jimenez helped the Chinese with the urgent task of preparing for the 17th Session of the General Conference, which was scheduled to be convened in Paris the following month (October 1972).[38]

In spite of, or perhaps because of, her complaint about the shortage of trained diplomatic and technical personnel, in her debut at UNESCO the PRC's was one of the largest delegations at the session. There were five delegates, three alternatives and eleven advisers. The composition and titles and institutional affiliations given to each of the five delegates in the official record of the General Conference are revealing: H.E. Mr. Huang Chen, ambassador of the People's Republic of China to France (head of delegation); Professor Chang Wei, vice-chairman, Revolutionary Committee of Tsinghua University, Peking; Mr. Ling Ch'ing, deputy director, Department of International Organizations, Conferences, Treaties and Law, Ministry of Foreign Affairs; Mr. Hu Sha, leading member of the General Office of the Sciences and Education Group under the State Council; and Mr. Kuo Jui, deputy head, China Peking Opera Troupe.[39]

[38] The New China News Agency [Hsinhua] reported the arrival and departure of the UNESCO delegation, as well as the banquet given its honor on August 30, 1972, by Liu Hsi-yao. As for the September 2 meeting, the New China News Agency simply reported that Ch P'eng-fei "met" the director-general of UNESCO and identified Ling Ch'ing, Tien Chih-tung, Hu Sha, Tien Chin, and Hu Shou-hsin as the Chinese participants (excluding interpreters) at the meeting. See "UNESCO Director-General René Maheu Arrives in Peking," NCNA-English, Peking, August 29, 1972 in *SCMP*, No. 5213 (September 12, 1972), 92; "UNESCO Director General Feted in Peking," NCNA-English, Peking, August 30, 1972, in *SCMP*, No. 5213 (September 12, 1972), 93; "Chinese Foreign Minister Meets UNESCO Director General," NCNA-English, Peking, September 2, 1972, in *SCMP*, No. 5215 (September 14, 1972), 187; "UNESCO Director General Leaves Peking," NCNA-English, Peking, September 5, 1972, in *SCMP*, No. 5217 (September 18, 1972), 38-39.

[39] UNESCO, Records of the General Conference, 17th Sess., Vol. 3, *Proceedings*, p. 1448.

During the first year of their participation in UNESCO, the Chinese assumed the modest and low-profiled posture of "observer," acting more like sponges absorbing as much information and knowledge as they could than trying to make any inputs into the decision-making process. They used this initial period to explore the subjects or sectors of major concern or interest to them. They relied rather extensively on the secretariat officials in this exploratory process. "They came to me on numerous occasions to ask all kinds of questions about UNESCO policy or protocol," remarked one secretariat official, "but I soon discovered that they would also go to see my colleagues in other departments to ask the same questions." The PRC's permanent mission to UNESCO, which consists of four personnel, seems well fitted to the modest nature of her participation.

The evolving pattern of this participation in the work of UNESCO has taken a definite shape. Apparently, the Chinese came to the conclusion that UNESCO was most useful as a forum for "symbolic-political-representational" politics. "In the General Conference and the Executive Board," according to one participant, "I would say about 90 percent of their intervention is addressed to political matters." Among the three major programmatic sectors—science, culture, and education —the Chinese priority is high on science, low on education, and medium on culture. There is also a sharp contrast between their militant verbal behavior in public and their self-effacing operational behavior on the Board. They have taken a "radical" position on substantive political issues consistent with their principled stand, but they fully abide by, and conform to, the whole structure of rules and procedures of the organization. "Even when they got off the track inadvertently and were reminded that this was out of line with established practice," observed one participant, "they would immediately accept the criticism and withdraw without argument or resistance."

Is it possible for China to accept such a "nefarious" functionalist notion as that wars begin in the minds of men without betraying her own principled stand on war and peace? China has never posed any *direct* challenge to this premise, which is embodied in the UNESCO Constitution. Instead, Huang Chen, in his maiden policy speech before the plenary of the 17th Session of the General Conference in 1972, expressed China's gratification that UNESCO was the first among the specialized agencies to implement the General Assembly's resolution on the China question. He also struck a positive note about the actual development of UNESCO in its recent history. What he found "extremely encouraging" was the growing importance of the Third World in UNESCO politics.[40]

[40] *Ibid.*, 17 C/VR.14 (25 October 1972), para. 6.3; emphasis added. It should

China has clearly rejected the notion that knowledge can be and should be developed for its sake, and asks UNESCO instead: "*Who* possesses the scientific and cultural knowledge and *whom* should it serve?"[41] The answer is given in the form of a model projection: the superstructure needs to be transformed first in order to serve the masses —this is the Chinese way. Knowledge is conceptualized as "the crystallization of labor and wisdom of working masses."[42] Western civilization itself has been nurtured—this follows closely Franz Fanon's argument[43] —through the blood and sweat of the Asian, African, and Latin American peoples. The fruits of a new world civilization should never again be allowed to be monopolized by imperialists. Hence hegemony, both capitalist and socialist, violates the spirit of UNESCO's commitment to world peace and justice. On the whole, China's maiden policy speech before the 17th Session of the General Conference was conciliatory and positive, emphasizing that the ennobling spirit of education, science, and culture should be enlisted to serve the causes of justice, equality, and world peace.

However, a major challenge came during the 18th Session of the Conference in 1974. Tseng T'ao (the PRC's ambassador to France, who headed the Chinese delegation), declared in his major policy speech during the general debate that it is of primary importance to ascertain the source of war and the threat to peace. To oversimplify, his extended argument can be summarized as follows: Since war begins in the hegemonic practices of the superpowers, it is against the hegemony of the superpowers that the defenses of peace must be constructed. Does this require a constitutional change? Here comes another model projection, in the form of a somewhat irrelevant thrust of domestic politics. The Cultural Revolution and the anti-Lin Piao and anti-Confucius movement have been projected as a profound educational experiment designed to prevent Chinese socialism from degenerating and to serve forever the causes of the masses and the oppressed nations.[44]

---

be noted here that speeches made by Chinese delegates are translated sometimes into English and sometimes into French. UNESCO publishes a single set of multilingual records, in which English translations are not translated into French or *vice versa*. All English translations from French texts are my own.

[41] *Ibid.*, para. 6.10.   [42] *Ibid.*

[43] Fanon stated his argument in the following terms: "Confronting this world [of underdevelopment and poverty], the European nations sprawl, ostentatiously opulent. This European opulence is literally scandalous, for it has been founded on slavery, it has been nourished with the blood of slaves and it comes directly from the soil and from the subsoil of that underdeveloped world. The well-being and the progress of Europe have been built up with the sweat and the dead bodies of Negroes, Arabs, Indians, and the yellow races. We have decided not to overlook this any longer." Frantz Fanon, *The Wretched of the Earth*, trans. Constance Farrington (New York: Grove Press, 1968), p. 96.

[44] UNESCO, Records of the General Conference, 18th Sess., Vol. III, Part one, *Proceedings*, 18 C/VR.18 (28 October 1974), para. 4.19.

Yet, in somewhat of a non sequitur, Tseng T'ao concluded his speech by declaring that the Chinese delegation supports the suggestions of the Third World countries for a revision of the UNESCO constitution. The constitution has some serious drawbacks, because it has not adequately reflected great changes in the world since its adoption in the mid-1940s. It is therefore indispensable, Tseng T'ao concluded, that UNESCO respond to the suggestions of the numerous Member States, especially those of the Third World, with "un examen global" of the constitutional revision question.[45]

At the 19th Session of the Conference held in Nairobi in November 1976, Chinese participation again concentrated on symbolic issues. First, China attached great symbolic importance to the fact that the General Conference was being held in Africa for the first time in UNESCO's history. Second, she lauded UNESCO's efforts to make its share of contributions to the implementation of NIEO principles and objectives.[46] Third, China voted for the UNESCO plan to bridge the "information gap" between the Third World and the West through the establishment of a news pool of nonaligned developing countries. This was to be done by giving developing countries greater control over reporting in and from their respective regions. Originally endorsed at the Fifth Conference of Heads of States or Governments of Non-Aligned Countries held in Colombo, Sri Lanka, in August 1976, the plan calls for "a balanced and equitable distribution of news and information to the peoples of the world" so as to correct the negative image of the Third World projected by international news agencies dominated by the West.

Fourth, China exploited the symbolism generated by the death of Mao Tse-tung and the extraordinary tributes paid to the Helmsman at the 100th Session of the Executive Board and the General Conference by singling out for UNESCO's emulation Mao's "penetrating elucidation of the dialectical relationship between culture, politics and economics."

However, what came as a startling and unprecedented thrust of domestic politics into UNESCO forums was an attempt to legitimize the new leadership of Hua Kuo-feng by delegitimizing the "Gang of Four": "At the time when the Great Leader and Teacher Chairman Mao Tsetung was seriously ill and after he passed away, and at the time when the Chinese people were plunged into tremendous grief, the anti-party clique of Wang Hung-wen, Chang Chun-chiao, Chiang Ching

[45] *Ibid.*, para. 4.23.
[46] For UNESCO's resolutions on its contribution to the establishment of a new international economic order, see UNESCO, Records of the General Conference, 18th Sess., Vol. I, *Resolutions*, pp. 114-18; UNESCO Doc. *Approved Programme and Budget for 1977-1978* (19 C/5 Approved, February 1977), pp. xiii-xv.

and Yao Wen-yuan lost no time in coming in an attempt to usurp the top party and state leadership."[47]

What impact or influence has China exerted on UNESCO? Before answering this question, a few notes of caution are in order. Given the pluralism brought about by the membership explosion in the 1960s, not even a great power can marshal necessary and sufficient resources to make its influence felt in every question or program. The United States exerted a controlling influence in the festering China controversy in the 1950s and 1960s because this was the issue "on which the United States pulled out all the stops."[48] Hence, it is incumbent on any Member State to choose among the following targets for diplomatic influence: symbolic, representational, political, financial, programming, and operational. In addition, there are various means of exerting influence: (1) to get elected as a member of the Executive Board and of other limited-membership organs; (2) to place candidates of one's own nationality in key secretariat posts; (3) to play a leadership role in the regional group; (4) to initiate new ideas and translate them into draft resolutions; (5) to engage in bilateral and multilateral diplomatic lobbying; and (6) to furnish experts of one's own nationality for UNESCO's work.

Viewed in this light, China's impact is virtually nil as far as the making and execution of UNESCO's major sectoral programs are concerned. The director-general consults selected Member States before he puts out the biennial program and budget; he sends out questionnaires to certain governments asking for comments and criticisms. China has never responded to this inquiry. As of February 1977, to cite another example, there were no less than 100 UNESCO-sponsored educational projects in Asia, but not a single one of them operated inside China, nor was China involved except indirectly through her contributions to UNDP. The 1974 *Report of the Director-General on the Activities of the Organization* has, as Appendix E, "1973-1974 Participation Programme Allocations By Country and Sector"; China stands out as the only Member State who is not involved in any one of the five sectoral programs: education; natural sciences; social sciences; humanities and culture; communication; and national commissions and copyright.

China has exerted no impact, positive or negative, on the operational procedures of the various organs. There is a consensus among partici-

[47] "Speech by Head of Chinese Delegation at 19th Session of General Conference of UNESCO," NCNA-English, Nairobi, November 2, 1976, in *SPRCP*, No. 6219 (November 15, 1976), 63-64. See also Michael T. Kaufman, "Chinese, in Unusual Digression, Tells UNESCO of Leftist Purge," *NYT*, November 3, 1976, p. 3.

[48] Sewell, "UNESCO-Pluralism Rampant," p. 157.

pants that the Chinese practice of anti-Soviet polemics has been ritualized in such a manner as not to disrupt the proceedings of any UNESCO meetings. In fact, one of the most salient characteristics of Chinese behavior in UNESCO is the lack of any evident desire or willingness to play an active—not to say leading or dominant—role in its politics. The few exceptions where China has played an active role, as will be shown later, are confined to symbolic issues of special importance to her.

A few examples will suffice to indicate the cautious Chinese approach. In the Asian Group of UNESCO, the chairmanship rotates alphabetically, but China specifically asked to be excluded from this leadership role even under such an automatic system. In the author's field interviews, China was singled out as one of the few countries that do not lobby in regard to electoral politics for the Executive Board. China has not sponsored draft resolutions except on two issues: the gradual introduction of Chinese as a working language of the General Conference and the Executive Board, and the issue of the ROC representation in some NGOs with consultative or working relationships with UNESCO. Likewise, there has been virtually no diplomatic lobbying on the part of China, except on the two above-mentioned issues for which she introduced draft resolutions.

Most significantly, China has shown no interest or readiness to place any of her nationals in secretariat posts, in spite of repeated prodding. As of July 15, 1976, the desirable range for the Chinese quota in UNESCO secretariat posts that are subject to the principle of geographical distribution was from a minimum of twenty-eight to a maximum of forty-seven. Yet there were only three Chinese in such posts—one at D-1 and two at P-2—all of whom had joined UNESCO with ROC passports.[49] As in the United Nations, these personnel are respected as international civil servants of Chinese ancestry and nationality; they are welcome to spend their home furlough in mainland China any time they wish. Two of them have accepted this offer, while one declined without any political repercussions.

However, China's impact on political symbolism has been noticeable. It can be argued that she has been on both the giving and the receiving end of UNESCO's symbolic politics. Although her negative objective of opposing the Soviet Union often appears to overshadow her positive objective of supporting the Third World, most developing countries, particularly the least developed ones, seem to receive vicarious pleasure from the special status that China enjoys and her

[49] For details, see "Geographical Distribution of Staff: Report by the Director-General," UNESCO Doc. 19 C/60 (24 September 1976). This report was presented as item 54 of the provisional agenda for the 19th Session of the General Conference.

fearless attack on the superpowers' domination of world politics. One high-ranking secretariat official from a Third World country remarked: "I used to be a national delegate to UNESCO before I joined the secretariat; believe me, the PRC's championship of equal rights for all states, big or small, has provided an enormous morale-boosting in our fight against big-power domination of UNESCO affairs. You should not underestimate this symbolic and psychological contribution of Chinese participation." In playing this antihegemonic role, however, China has been extremely cautious about not giving the impression of interference or domination. This appears to be the main reason why Chinese antihegemonic politics at UNESCO, as elsewhere, is played at the symbolic level, not in the context of a decision-making process or intergroup or intragroup politics.

As in so many limited-membership organs in the United Nations system, the established practice of UNESCO's electoral politics is that the Big Five always find themselves named on secret ballots for the Executive Board. The United States, the United Kingdom, France, and the Soviet Union (since 1954, when it first joined the organization) have all served on the Board without interruption. The ROC, too, was represented on the Board by Professor Chen Yuan from 1946 to 1950, but has failed to get herself reelected since the 1950 credentials controversy. At its debut at the 17th Session in 1972, the PRC's candidate, Professor Chang Wei of Tsinghua University, was easily elected, thus restoring China's representation. At the 19th Session in 1976, the PRC's candidate, Mrs. Yang Yun-yu, was elected a member for another term.

During the first two years of their participation, the Chinese brought their own interpreters to UNESCO meetings on an *ad hoc* basis. Following the methodical approach applied at the United Nations, China introduced a draft resolution at the 18th Session of the Conference to introduce Chinese as a working language of the Conference and the Board on an incremental basis. The Conference adopted the Chinese draft resolution without much debate. As a result, Chinese was to be introduced as a working language into the Conference in three stages and into the Board in two stages. The Conference also increased the appropriations of the budget by $266,000 for this purpose.[50] To implement this resolution, China finally sent one linguistic expert—Tcheng Young-kuan, who is fluent in French and English—to work in the Bureau of Conferences, Languages and Documents; Tcheng Young-kuan (P-4) is currently playing an important role in the preparations for thirteen more PRC linguistic personnel, scheduled to

[50] UNESCO, *Records of the General Conference*, 18th Sess., Vol. I, *Resolutions*, p. 181.

358

join the bureau sometime in mid-1977. As of February 1977, the total Chinese diplomatic manpower at UNESCO was as follows:

Permanent Mission to UNESCO: Hu Sha, ambassador; Sheng Yu, first secretary; Chou Chi-chi, second secretary; and Li Chao-tung, third secretary

Secretariat staff personnel subject to geographical distribution: Tien-cheng Young, director of the Bureau of the Budget (D-1); Chiu Shu-hua, assistant field programme officer (P-2); and Maejeanne Koutung Chang, assistant programme specialist (P-2)

Linguistic staff personnel not subject to geographical distribution: Tcheng Young-kuan, technical advisor (P-4)

The PRC's impact on UNESCO's financing needs no lengthy discussion, since it reflects the UN situation already discussed in Chapter 3. What is unique to UNESCO is the fact that a majority of its members have progressively reduced the assessment percentage of the vestigial "Chinese" government from 7 percent in 1950 to 5 percent in 1958 and 2.5 percent in 1967. This has invited a selective withholding from the Soviet Union, the Byelorussian SSR, and the Ukrainian SSR; they refused to pay their self-calculated shares to make up the losses resulting from the reduction in the "Chinese" assessment. The China controversy in UNESCO has thus had a more serious financial spillover than it did in the United Nations.

In the face of the PRC's adamant refusal to pay the debts left behind by the ROC to the amount of $2,644,877 for the period up to October 29, 1971, the General Conference took a political shortcut by canceling out the Chinese debts. Apparently, this resolution was a package deal, for section II also canceled out the debts of the Soviet Union, Byelorussia, and Ukraine.[51] Unlike her practice in the United Nations, however, the PRC has not engaged in any selective withholding, paying its dues in full and in good time. China's assessment for 1975-76 stood at 5.46 percent of the total and is projected at the same percentage for 1977-78 compared to 5.61 percent for France, 11.24 percent for the Soviet Union, 4.40 percent for the United Kingdom, and 25 percent for the United States.[52] Thus, the PRC's impact on the financing of UNESCO has been threefold: it cleared away the multiple financial entanglements and debts caused by the controversy over the "bankrupt Chiang regime"; it established a model for full and prompt payment; and it

[51] UNESCO, Records of the General Conference, 17th Sess., Vol. I, *Resolutions and Recommendations*, pp. 119-20.
[52] UNESCO Doc. "Contributions of Member States and Scale of Assessment," 19 C/51 (30 October 1976), Annex, pp. 1-7.

appreciably helped UNESCO's finances by increasing China's assessment from 2.5 percent to 5.46 percent.

Tellingly, the PRC's impact on the most controversial symbolic-representational issue in the recent history of UNESCO—the exclusion of Israel from the European group—was minimal. The 18th Session of the Conference assigned Member States to regional groups for purposes of participation in regional activities. The key vote was on the Israeli amendment, which read: "To include Israel in the European region." The amendment was rejected by a vote of 33 in favor to 48 against, with 31 abstentions. This vote quickly generated a political-financial crisis because of the vehement reactions of West European countries in general and the United States in particular. China passively joined the opposition by voting against the amendment, but made no statement of any kind in the course of the debate on the subject matter.[53]

Instead, China played her own symbolic politics in a different direction, focusing on the following issues at the 1974 General Conference: the election of Amadou-Mahtar M'Bow of Senegal, the Third World candidate,[54] as the new director-general; the admission of the Democratic People's Republic of Korea (DPRK); the unilateral representation of "the Saigon regime"; the Soviet application for membership in the Asian and Oceanic Group; and the representation of "bodies or elements linked with the Chiang Kai-shek clique" in some NGOs with working or consultative relationships with UNESCO. Chinese delegates made predictable speeches or statements on each of the above issues. The last two issues deserve a closer examination, however.

At the 42nd plenary meeting on November 21, 1974, Chinese representative Yeh Cheng-pa completely ignored the Israeli amendment earlier referred to, firing his salvos instead at "the unreasonable demand of the USSR to work its way into the Asian and Oceanic group" so as to participate in its regional activities. "Viewed politically, economically and culturally," argued Yeh Cheng-pa, "whether in the past or at present, the USSR has always been a European State. It has never been an Asian State. Still less a State with the dual capacity of both a

[53] UNESCO, Records of the General Conference, 18th Sess., Vol. III, Part two, Proceedings, 18 C/VR.42 (21 November 1974), para. 51.1. The Chinese press was also reticent on this question. It may also be noted that the 1972 General Conference decided to increase the membership of the Executive Board from 34 to 42 and allocated the 40 seats as follows: 10 for Group I; 4 for Group II; 7 for Group III; 6 for Group IV; and 13 for Group V. See UNESCO, Records of the General Conference, 17th Sess., Vol. I, Resolutions and Recommendations, p. 113.

[54] The Fourth Conference of Non-Aligned Countries recommended all non-aligned countries to support the nomination of M'Bow as director-general of UNESCO. See Fourth Conference of Non-Aligned Countries, Meeting of the Bureau, Algiers, March 1974, NA4/BI/Doc.16/Rev.1, p. 17.

European State and an Asian State."[55] Despite UNESCO's practice of allowing Member States to join more than one regional group (nine countries belong to two regional groups), the Chinese argument was simple: no Member State should belong simultaneously to two regional groups.

To complicate the matter, the Soviet application for membership in the Asian and Oceanic Group was buried in a draft resolution that contained a long list of all Member States on the left and of regions on the right. Hence, the Chinese delegate submitted an amendment advocating the simple deletion of the words "Asia and Oceanic" from the left column entry next to the Soviet Union. The Chinese amendment was rejected by 48 to 3, with 45 abstentions, thus admitting the Soviet Union. It is difficult, however, to make coherent sense out of this vote, because of the possible spillover effect of the Israeli question. It should be noted that the Israeli and Chinese amendments were addressed to the same draft resolution during the same debate on the same day, and both were rejected.

The Chinese reticence on the Israeli amendment is understandable. The Chinese should have voted for Israel's membership in the European region, given its stand that every member should belong to only one region. But logical or not, this would have been an untenable political position for a symbolic champion of the Third World. The Chinese did manage to maintain a modicum of credibility on this question at the 1976 General Conference. Faced with a dual membership application from a mini-state, the Republic of Seychelles, a Chinese delegate approached a secretariat official to probe "the real reason" behind this application. When this official returned from his consultation with Seychelles with the argument that one-third of the population in Seychelles were ethnically Indians and that therefore Seychelles would like to join both the African and the Asian and Oceanic Groups, the Chinese retorted: "If this is so, China should belong to every region in the world." This Chinese argument settled the matter in the caucusing of the Asian Group. The chairman of the Asian Group was asked to convey the consensus to Seychelles; Seychelles then withdrew her application.

Why has Peking shown an intensity and tenacity in the pursuit of the vestigial "two Chinas" question in UNESCO that it has not elsewhere in the United Nations system? Why has Peking departed from its passive and low-profile participation by introducing, and then lobbying for, draft resolutions on the NGO issue? Is this not a pathological manifestation of self-inflicted wounds in its world view? Is this not an

[55] UNESCO, Records of the General Conference, 18th Sess., Vol. III, Part two, *Proceedings*, 18 C/VR.42 (21 November 1974), para. 32.2.

expression of Peking's political and diplomatic paranoia in the unfamiliar terrain of multilateral diplomacy? Not necessarily, because of the unique relationship that exists between UNESCO and the NGOs.

In the case of UNESCO, NGOs do not merely maintain *pro forma* consultative relationships. UNESCO's directives to NGOs invite consultation and cooperation so that UNESCO can secure documentation, advice, and technical cooperation. Many NGOs maintain their offices in Paris; they send their representatives to many UNESCO meetings; some of them are even authorized to submit statements to the director-general. In practice, therefore, some NGOs actually do participate in formulating and executing some of the programs. The International Council of Scientific Unions (ICSU), which is the most powerful NGO and has therefore become the most prominent example in the China-NGO controversy, executes, according to the rough estimate of one high-ranking secretariat official, more than 50 percent of UNESCO's scientific programs. As if to highlight the saliency of NGOs in the organization—and thus placing the PRC on the spot—there were more than 300 UNESCO-accredited NGOs in 1973.

It was against this background that China tabled a draft resolution at the 93rd Session of the Executive Board. The resolution "urges international non-governmental organizations which maintain relations with UNESCO and in which bodies or elements linked with Chiang Kai-shek participate, having illegally usurped the name of China, to take measures to exclude them immediately and to break off all relations with them." It further requests the director-general to notify the NGOs concerned of the resolution and to request them to inform him of any action they had taken to comply with the resolution. The Chinese draft resolution was adopted on October 8, 1973, without any change in language, by a vote of 17 to 1 (the United States), with 10 abstentions. Chinese representative Hu Sha argued that "the Chiang Kai-shek clique" often sent its men, under the signboard of "science having nothing to do with politics" and "academic freedom" into some international organizations. These people were included, declared Hu Sha, "in what we referred to as elements who have relations with Chiang Kai-shek."

The director-general reported to the Board at the end of his efforts that 233 NGOs replied they had no representation in Taiwan and 38 replied they had. Of the 38 NGOs, 4 replied they had already complied with the resolution and 16 had not reached a decision or had decided to take no action. Faced with this situation, the 94th Session of the Executive Board adopted a resolution to include the question of excluding "Chiang Kai-shek elements" from the NGOs concerned in the provisional agenda of the 1974 General Conference.

At the 1974 General Conference China tabled a draft resolution which was almost identical with the resolution adopted by the 93rd Session of the Executive Board. Hu Sha argued that the only correct solution to this problem was to expel "the bodies or elements under the administration of the Chiang Kai-shek clique." Any other expedients would be tantamount to creating "two Chinas" or "one China and one Taiwan," which was absolutely unacceptable to the Chinese government.[56] The Conference adopted the Chinese draft resolution without any change in language and without any debate, by a vote of 75 to 2, with 22 abstentions.

In January 1975 the director-general sent another communication to 27 NGOs who still retained their affiliates in Taiwan. By mid-September 1975 the response to the director-general's communication was as follows: 21 NGOs replied; of the 21, only 12 reported decisions; of the 12 who had made decisions, 2 discontinued the use of the name "China" and 10 refused to comply with the resolution. The ICSU's decision was most serious: it could not and would not take the position of expelling one member as a precondition for another's applying for membership. The ICSU's reply stated, however, that it would be proper "for ICSU or a Union to insist that a national member not pretend to represent scientists in geographical areas over which it has no control," and that ICSU had obtained "a formal statement from the Academy of Sciences in Taiwan subscribing to this principle."[57]

Despite the substantial progress toward the resolution of the issue, China again tabled an identical resolution at the 1976 General Conference in Nairobi. On November 22, 1976, the Conference again adopted the Chinese draft resolution by an overwhelming majority. Thus, the issue has been "resolved" through a ritualizing process, in which China tables a draft resolution at the biennial Conference and the Conference without debate approves the Chinese draft resolution by an overwhelming majority.

Despite her intense feelings, China has never pushed the issue to the point of actually asking UNESCO itself to sever its relationships with the NGOs retaining ties with Taiwan. The Chinese draft resolutions were phrased in the form of a UNESCO recommendation, urging the NGOs concerned to exclude or expel the affiliates linked to Taiwan. UNESCO, for its part, has done as much as it could to accommodate the PRC's symbolic diplomacy on the matter without damaging its functional relationships with the NGOs. In spite of the ICSU's refusal

[56] *Ibid.*, 18 C/VR.30 (15 November 1974), para. 27.5.
[57] For a detailed documentary study of politicization at UNESCO that includes the politicized China-NGO issue, see Daniel G. Partan, *Documentary Study of the Politicization of UNESCO* (Boston: American Academy of Arts and Sciences, 1975).

to comply fully with the UNESCO resolutions, the PRC, too, gained her symbolic legitimation on the vestigial "two Chinas" question at the UNESCO forum. This is a symbolic victory, and it is doubtful that she had really expected more.

In conclusion, it may be asked: What is the Chinese image of UNESCO? Judging by Chinese behavior during the first four years of participation in its work, it seems to be a dual one. In theory, UNESCO embodies the ideas, rules, and structure of Western liberal or "bourgeois" values, about which the Chinese have profound doubts; these are not congenial to the advancement of the Maoist image of world order. Yet, the Chinese have never assumed the role of a revolutionary challenger or even a progressive reformer. They have supported the suggestions of the Third World for a constitutional reform in public, but privately have behaved more like an apprentice busily learning a new trade.

The other part of the Chinese image focuses on UNESCO in practice. Here, the Chinese have assumed a positive and hopeful posture. At an ECOSOC meeting in 1973, for example, Chinese Ambassador Wang Jun-sheng expressed the positive feeling that China had gained from one year of participation in the following manner: "In the past year UNESCO has done valuable work in facilitating scientific and cultural exchanges, in combating colonialism and racism, in promoting equality of access to education, particularly for migrant workers and their children, and in protecting the rights of the inhabitants of occupied territories."[58] The ambassador went on to say, however, that UNESCO was engaged in too many activities. It should concentrate on the most urgent problems "by promoting the scienific and cultural progress of the developing countries and by pressing for international exchanges; it should also publicize the developing countries' achievements in science and education."[59]

UNESCO serves several important functions in the development of the Chinese strategy of world order. First, it is an important multilateral forum for symbolic diplomacy; it provides a world stage and audience for model projection and image enhancement. Second, it provides a useful educational forum in which to learn about the symbolic politics of other countries. China's participation in global political symbolism may have an "educational" value for the refinement of her own bilateral and multilateral cultural diplomacy. Finally, there is a consensus among secretariat officials and delegates about an upward trend in Chinese participation. Steadily, China has already begun expanding her participation laterally into functional sectors,

[58] UN Doc. E/AC.24/SR.483 (11 July 1973), p. 49.
[59] Ibid.

especially the science sector. The fact that the Chinese have been asking for and getting materials even on the social sciences, plus the fact that they have already agreed to send thirteen linguistic experts to join the secretariat in 1977, promises a more active participation in the functional sectors in the years to come. The prospects of mutual osmosis and legitimation between China and UNESCO at this point look good and hopeful.

The Food and Agricultural Organization (FAO)

As stated in the preamble to the Constitution, Member States of the Food and Agricultural Organization (FAO) are pledged to promote the common welfare through separate and collective action to: (1) raise levels of nutrition and standards of living; (2) secure improvements in the efficiency of the production and distribution of all goods and agricultural products; (3) better the condition of rural populations; and (4) thus contribute toward an expanding world economy and ensure humanity's freedom from hunger.[60] FAO is committed to recommend national and international action on a variety of matters related to "agriculture," the term that is defined in the Constitution as embracing fisheries, marine products, forestry, and primary forestry products.

There are three organs of FAO: a Conference, a Council, and a staff headed by a director-general. The Conference, which meets once in every two years in regular session, determines the policy, adopts the budget, and reviews the work of the organization. The Council is the executive organ, with a membership of forty-two representatives of Member States (as of the 17th Session of the Conference), under an independent chairman appointed by the Conference. The Council meets at least three times between the Conference's biennial sessions. The director-general, elected by the Conference for a term of six years (after which he is not eligible for reappointment), has "full power and authority to direct the work of the Organization," subject to the general supervision of the Conference and the Council; he also appoints the staff of the organization.

FAO came into existence on October 16, 1945, and was the first of the permanent UN specialized agencies to be launched. It has the largest staff of them all; in all parts of the world it totaled some 6,546 in late 1975. It is the largest single executing agency of UNDP funds. During

---

[60] For the latest (1976) edition of FAO's basic texts—the Constitution, Financial Regulations, and Rules of Procedure of constituent organs—see *Basic Texts of the Food and Agricultural Organization of the United Nations*, Vol. I and II (1976 ed., hereafter cited as *Basic Texts of FAO*).

the UNDP's first cycle (1972-76), for example, FAO disbursed $471.20 million, representing 28.5 percent of UNDP's first-cycle project expenditure. FAO's headquarters are located in four separate buildings in Rome, with the following regional and liaison offices: Regional Office for Africa in Accra; Regional Office for Asia and the Far East in Bangkok; Regional Office for Europe in Rome; Regional Office for Latin America in Santiago; Regional Office for North America in Washington, D.C.; Regional Office for the Near East in Cairo; Liaison Office with the United Nations in New York City; and Liaison Office with UN Economic Commission for Africa in Addis Ababa.

From the outset the question of the PRC's entry into FAO was enmeshed in the legal issue of the devolution of state succession stemming from the ROC's withdrawal from the organization in 1951. At the November 1971 session of the Council, the director-general (Addeke Hendrik Boerma of the Netherlands) stated that the question of Chinese representation in FAO presented itself in a different way from that in other specialized agencies of which China (ROC) was currently a member. He then sought the Council's guidance as to whether an approach should be made to ascertain the intention of the PRC in seeking membership in FAO. The Council decided on November 2, 1971, to authorize the director-general to invite the PRC to seek "formal membership" in the organization and, if it so requested, to attend the 16th Session of the Conference scheduled in the same month.

Immediately following this Council action, the director-general sent a cable to the government of the PRC, extending an invitation for formal membership in the organization and also, if she so wished, to attend the 16th Session of the Conference. In the reply received by the director-general on November 23, 1971, from the acting foreign minister of the PRC, there was no reference to seeking formal membership. There was reason to believe, the director-general noted, however, that China would be interested in *resuming* her place in the organization. The director-general added that he had been advised in the meantime that it would be legally possible for the PRC to resume the seat of China, since the notice of withdrawal given in 1951 emanated from a government whose right to represent China had at that time already been formally contested. Hence, this notice of withdrawal would not be applied against the government of the PRC, which had no part in it, and which had now been recognized by the United Nations as being the legitimate representative of China.

Under the circumstances, the government of the PRC should not, the director-general advised, be deprived of the possibility of availing itself of the rights devolving from the original (1946) membership in the organization. It would be legally permissible for the PRC to resume her place in FAO without any special formality. Translated simply, the director-general's new legal interpretation was as follows. China was— and still is—one of the original members of the organization. Between 1949 (when the PRC was established) and 1951, however, the ROC's representation of China in FAO was a legally contested issue; hence, the ROC's notice of withdrawal could not be interpreted as having affected the status of China's original membership. Therefore, the PRC could now resume her FAO seat, which the ROC had "illegitimately" occupied between 1949 and 1951 and from which she had "illegally" withdrawn in 1951.

In the light of this new legal interpretation from the director-general, the 17th Session of the Conference adopted by a vote of 68 to 0, with 3 abstentions, a resolution authorizing the director-general to take "appropriate measures" to bring into effect the resumption by China of her place in the organization. This resolution set in motion the rather slow process of working out another mission diplomacy similar (except in tempo) to the one we have already observed in the preparatory process leading to the PRC's entry into UNESCO. The FAO official mission composed of the director-general and three other FAO secretariat officials (D. L. Umali, J. C. Westoby, and S. Aziz) arrived in Peking on February 20, 1973, and spent a week arranging the final details of China's "resumption" of membership in FAO. As a result, the PRC notified them that she would like to "resume" her membership in the organization as of April 1, 1973.[61]

The PRC's participation in FAO began in the 60th Session of the Council in June 1973. Even though China was not yet a member, she decided to participate in the capacity of an observer. There was nothing unusual or illegal in this move, as FAO's "Statement of Principles Relating to the Granting of Observer Status to Nations" stipulates that "as a general practice, Member Nations of the Organization that are not members of the Council, or Associate Members, should be admitted to private meetings, unless the Council decides otherwise in cases of necessity."[62] Five months later, China made her debut at the 17th Session of the Conference. On the occasion of both debuts, representatives of various groups and countries expressed warm and friendly sentiments.

[61] Chinese representative Li Yung-kai, in his short debut statement at the 60th Session of the Council, stated: "After its talks with Mr. Boerma, the Director-General of FAO, during his visit to Peking last February, the Chinese Government formally notified FAO that China would take part in the Organization's activities as from 1 April. As this is only the beginning of our participation, we need to familiarize ourselves with much of its work, and there are many new things for us to learn." See FAO, Verbatim Records of Plenary Meetings of the Council, 60th Sess., CL 60/PV/1 (11 June 1973), p. 5.
[62] Basic Texts of FAO, p. 151.

What is the signifiance of the PRC's participation for FAO? In his opening remarks at the 60th Session of the Council, as well as at the 17th Session of the Conference, the director-general first made personal and official statements of welcome to the Chinese delegation. He then assessed the significance of Chinese participation in three ways. First, the fact that China as the most populous nation in the world was now participating in the activities of the organization was of special importance to FAO. Second, "the remarkable progress that China has made in recent years in developing its agriculture" also had a special meaning for FAO. Third, the greatest significance of the resumption by China of its place in FAO, Boerma declared, lay in the fact that "a vast step has been taken toward universality of membership which is vital if FAO is to work as effectively as possible as a world Organization." "Without China," Boerma observed, "we were missing a crucial element in our struggle for world agricultural development."[63] Boerma left little doubt that he was also appealing to the Soviet Union to follow the Chinese path.

As a honorific gesture, the 1973 Conference elected Hao Chung-shih, head of the Chinese delegation, as one of the three vice-chairmen of the Conference. China was also elected a member of the Council for a three-year term (November 1973-December 1976), and was re-elected at the 1975 Conference for another term (January 1977-November 1979). Chinese participation in the FAO or FAO-related activities between mid-1973 and the end of 1976 was as follows: the 17th (1973) and 18th (1975) Sessions of the Conference; the 1974 United Nations World Food Conference held in Rome; the Council meetings from its 60th (June 1973) to 70th (December 1976) Sessions; and the 13th Regional Conference for Asia and the Far East of the FAO held in Manila in August 1976.

The PRC joined FAO at a time when the world was faced with the worst food crisis since the end of World War II. The inflationary pressure in industrialized countries, coupled with particularly adverse weather conditions in many parts of the world, had depleted the critical surpluses of food grain in the North American breadbasket to virtually nothing by 1972. As a result, most food prices nearly quadrupled during the first half of the 1970s.

What principles and strategies did China offer in the face of this global food crisis? Major policy speeches delivered by the heads of the Chinese delegations to the 1973 and 1975 FAO Conferences, the 1974 UN World Food Conference, and the 13th FAO Regional Confer-

[63] FAO, Verbatim Records of Plenary Meetings of the Conference, 17th Sess., C 73/PV/1 (10 November 1973), p. 3. See also FAO, Verbatim Records of Plenary Meetings of the Council, 60th Sess., CL 60/PV/1 (11 June 1973), pp. 4-5.

ence for Asia and the Far East in 1976 expounded China's principled stand on the subject, giving a coherent picture of her conceptualization of, and strategies toward, the global food crisis. Several characteristics are notable in the Chinese principled stand: a structural analysis of the problem; a reassertion of strategic optimism, coupled with Maoist populism; stress on self-reliant and independent national development of agriculture and on rural development as an integral part of the struggle to establish the new international economic order; and projection of the Chinese model of rural development.

Repeatedly, the Chinese have argued that such factors as bad weather and natural disasters, rising prices of fertilizers, and so on, are only superficial, partial and temporary factors. The superpowers are accused of propagating the long-discredited Malthusian theory of population with ulterior motives. The global food crisis is indeed a manifestation of the structural violence inherent in the old international economic order. Colonialism and imperialism have exploited the Asian, African, and Latin American countries, forcing on them a lopsided single-product economy and the exchange of unequal values. As a result, these countries have remained poor and backward.[64]

Given the unequal bargaining strength of the developed and developing countries and the hegemonic motives of the superpowers, the Chinese are skeptical that structural violence can be done away with through a global strategy of cooperation and interdependence. At the 1975 Conference, for example, the Chinese severely criticized Kissinger's "global food strategy" as being a strategy of "using food as a weapon."[65] "In fact," declared Yang Li-kung, head of the Chinese delegation, "this so-called strategy is nothing but a new trick by which this superpower seeks stubbornly to preserve the old international economic order and continue its policy of intensifying control and exploitation of the third world people by means of food."[66] Instead, the food problem has to be linked with the NIEO struggle. The Chinese conceptualization of NIEO as applied to the food problem is simple: a struggle against imperialism, old and new, in the international sphere, and a self-reliant and independent development of national economies, including agriculture, at home.

Just as Mao Tse-tung fought against recurring pessimism among the cadres at home, so have Chinese delegates against "the pessimistic view spread by imperialism" at international agricultural fora. Repeatedly,

[64] FAO, Verbatim Records of Plenary Meetings of the Conference, 17th Sess., C 73/PV/9 (15 November 1973), p. 191; "At U.N. World Food Conference: China's Views on Solving World Food Problem," *PR*, No. 46 (November 15, 1974), 10.

[65] FAO Doc. C 75/PV/11 (14 November 1975), p. 7.

[66] *Ibid.*

the Chinese projected as a psychological and mobilizational precondition to self-reliance the Maoist populism and strategic optimism as expressed in *The Bankruptcy of the Idealist Conception of History:* "*Of all things in the world, people are the most precious. Under the leadership of the Communist Party, as long as there are people, every kind of miracle can be performed.*"[67] The Chinese took great pride in the fact that both the 13th FAO Regional Conference for Asia and the Far East held in Manila in August 1976, and the 9th FAO Regional Conference for Africa held in Freetown in November 1976, adopted declarations embodying the principle of self-reliant agricultural development.[68]

To be sure, China's participation has brought FAO closer to its objective of universality. But what really generated a sense of probing curiosity and a sense of exciting challenge ahead at FAO was China's own self-reliant approach to rural development. The startling fact is, observed Sartaj Aziz (who accompanied the director-general on the 1973 FAO official mission and who made a number of trips to China before and after the mission), "that China has within a short period of 24 years already abolished absolute poverty, unemployment and inflation—the three problems that most other developing countries of Asia, Africa, and Latin America have failed to solve so far and see no hope of solving in the foreseeable future."[69] Responding to this kind of shared interest and admiration, China's model projection at FAO was more extensive than that at any other specialized agency.

The Chinese model of rural development as projected at FAO fora represents a mixture of normative and pragmatic elements as epitomized in the Maoist slogan: "Revolution plus production could solve the food problem." At the normative level, the Chinese reject the concept of value-free development, or development for development's sake. The people's fundamental (food) and other basic needs must be met first before mobilizing surpluses to other purposes. "In planning our national economy," declared Hao Chung-shih, "our order of priority is agriculture, light industry and heavy industry, with agriculture put the first place."[70]

Has China really solved the food problem? Hao Chung-shih answered this question in the following manner at the 1973 Conference:

[67] Quoted in "How China Solved Its Food Problem," *PR*, No. 45 (November 9, 1973), 8; emphasis in original.

[68] See "U.N. Food and Agricultural Organization: Self-Reliance—Keynote at Regional Conference," *PR*, No. 35 (August 27, 1976), 21-22 for the Manila Conference. For the Freetown Conference, see *JMJP*, November 27, 1976, p. 6.

[69] Sartaj Aziz, "The Chinese Approach to Rural Development," *International Development Review* 15 (1973), 7.

[70] FAO, Verbatim Records of Plenary Meetings of the Conference, 17th Sess., C 73/PV/9 (15 November 1973), p. 190.

"Now, although the average amount of food grain per capita is not yet high, food supply is guaranteed in our country and food prices have remained stable. This is without precedent in Chinese history."[71] But does not China import a large amount of food to feed her population? The official explanation given at the 1974 World Food Conference in Rome on this question is revealing:

> China has also imported some foodgrains from the world market, but China does not rely on imports for feeding her population. The main purpose of our imports is to change some food varieties. In about three years from 1972 up to now, we have imported over two billion U.S. dollars' worth of grain, mainly wheat. In the same period, we have exported grain, mainly rice, valued at the same total amount. Therefore China's food imports and exports in the past three years strike a rough balance in value. We have never engaged in any speculation in food. Our rice exports are largely for supply and aid to Third World countries. Since international rice exports are limited in amount, the prices of rice would further rise, causing even greater difficulties to many rice consumer countries if China should stop exporting rice.[72]

China has also used FAO fora to reveal to the outside world some specific accomplishments, as well as some specific methods related to Chinese agriculture. The total output of food grain was claimed to have increased from 110 million tons in 1949 to 250 million tons in 1971, 240 million tons in 1972 ("in spite of serious natural calamities"), and 274.9 million tons in 1974, representing, over twenty-five years, an average annual growth of 4 percent compared to an average annual growth of 2 percent in population. In addition, the number of big or medium-sized reservoirs increased from 20 before liberation to over 1,700 by 1972, and the Yellow River, which used to breach twice every three years before liberation, has not breached seriously since.[73]

At the 1974 World Food Conference, China explained her agricultural policy in terms of the Eight-Point Charter for Agriculture: (1) soil improvement; (2) use of fertilizer; (3) irrigation; (4) better seed strains; (5) close planting; (6) plant protection; (7) better farm implements and field management; and (8) scientific farming methods in a big way.[74] On the system of grain reserves, Yang Li-kung made the following statement at the 1975 Conference: "On the basis of en-

---

[71] Ibid., p. 191.

[72] "At U.N. World Food Conference," p. 12.

[73] See FAO, Verbatim Records of Plenary Meetings of the Conference, 17th Sess., C 73/PV/9 (15 November 1973), p. 190; "How China Solved Its Food Problem," p. 8; FAO Doc. C 75/PV/11 (14 November 1975), p. 8.

[74] "At U.N. World Food Conference," pp. 11-12.

suring food and clothing for the 800 million Chinese people, we have, in accordance with the policy of 'store grain everywhere,' established a system of grain reserves at the three levels of the state, the collectives and individual commune members. Grain reserves are being laid up on the principle of some grain reserves every year, more in bumper and less in average years, thus ensuring an ever-increasing total from year to year."[75]

What can China contribute beyond model projection? Publicly and privately, she has made conscious attempts to scale down whatever undue expectations others may have of her contribution to a solution of the global food crisis. At the 1974 World Food Conference, Hao Chung-shih declared before a world audience: "China is a country with a large population, and what we have achieved now is only a preliminary solution of the problem of feeding the Chinese people. Our contribution to solving the world food problem is yet very small. It is our hope that, along with the development of our industry and agriculture, we shall be able gradually to change this state of affairs."[76] In spite of this caveat, the impact of Chinese participation upon the activities of FAO has been more than symbolic or political. In fact, China has made some notable financial and functional contributions. As Table 7.2 shows, China's assessed contributions to the FAO budget

TABLE 7.2. The PRC's Contributions to the FAO Budget, 1973-76

Year	Total Budget ($)	PRC's Assessment ($)	PRC's Assessment (% of total)	Arrears Outstanding as % of the Budget
1973	41,332,050.00	1,487,250.00[a]	4.80	4.52
1974	53,543,441.26	3,739,835.00	7.01	5.98
1975	53,596,324.62	3,739,835.00	7.01	2.28
1976	82,013,545.44	5,719,459.00	7.01	7.57

[a] Contribution due for three calendar quarters commencing April 1, 1973 to be treated as miscellaneous income.
Source: FAO secretariat.

went up from 4.8 percent in 1973 to 7.01 percent in subsequent years, reflecting the PRC's assessment increase for the UN budget. However, the difference between her 5.50 percent assessment for the UN and her 7.01 percent assessment for the FAO reflects the difference in membership of the two organizations. The absence of the Soviet Union

[75] FAO Doc. C 75/PV/11 (14 November 1975), p. 8.
[76] "At U.N. World Food Conference," p. 12.

has the effect of increasing every Member State's assessment. Conversely, the PRC's participation has the effect of decreasing every Member State's assessment by 7.01 percent of the total budget.

Given the absence of "China" from the organization for some twenty years, there were no Chinese debts to be canceled out, as in the case of UNESCO. Today, China is one of the largest contributors to the FAO budget. This has made China sensitive to any "unreasonable" budget increases. One participant recalled Chinese budgetary behavior in the Council: "When we had a long debate about the budget in the Council, the United States and European countries argued for a modest and limited increase. We suddenly found ourselves standing shoulder to shoulder with the Chinese. They made their own separate and independent argument which, in essence, coincided with the American argument. Their argument was that there was not enough precision and justification for the increases requested."

The stand China took in Commission II of the 1975 Conference on the Programme of Work and Budget for the next biennium highlights the dichotomy between her "fiscal conservatism" and her desire to support the Third World. A Chinese delegate observed: "As regards the budget level, we think that the increase in the budget for the next biennium is too .high. However, in view of the opinion of most of the developing countries we have refrained from further observations of this kind since the last session of the Council. The position of China is understandable, particularly to the developing countries, and since China is a developing country we shall respect the views of most of the Third World countries."[77] To resolve the dilemma inherent in this posture, the Chinese have taken the position that "the use of big increases in the budget" is not the only way to implement the resolutions of the World Food Conference. The Chinese argued instead that FAO should reduce those activities that are remote from the Third World and its current needs, while giving priority to those projects which directly benefit the development of agriculture, forestry, animal husbandry, and fishery in the developing countries, particularly food production, and carry this out in earnest. The Chinese also argued that special consideration should be given to the conscientious implementation of the spirit of the principles of the 6th and 7th Special Sessions of the General Assembly in formulating or revising FAO's Programme of Work and Budget.

While China maintained her principled (politicized) stand in her major policy speeches before the plenary of the Conference, her operational behavior in all other contexts, including the Council, has been passive and consciously devoid of political controversy. There is a

[77] FAO Doc. C 75/II/PV 5 (14 November 1975), p. 5.

consensus among participants that China behaves more like an observer than an active member in the Council. China has never raised the ROC-NGO issue, even though FAO maintains three types of relationships with the NGOs—consultative status, specialized consultative status, and liaison status. When a political-legal controversy arose over the conflicting recommendations of the Council and Commission III of the 17th Conference, on the question of increasing the Council's membership from 34 to 40 or 42, China steered clear of interregional political-legal dispute by remaining totally silent.

Even on the Bangladesh membership question, which was raised at the 1973 Conference, Chinese delegate Li Yung-kai confined himself to a short statement, echoing the position taken by Pakistan. Yet China took a curiously contradictory stand on the Korean question. It may be recalled here that she opposed the admission of two Koreas into the United Nations, while criticizing the "unreasonableness" of the unilateral representation of the ROK in UNESCO. China and the Soviet Union, by warmly welcoming the DPRK's admission into UNESCO have maintained a contradictory stand: "one Korea" policy in the United Nations and "two Koreas" policy in UNESCO. At FAO, China added another twist by stating that the DPRK "is the genuine representative of the interests of the Korean people and therefore it is inappropriate for the South Korean authorities to send a representative to participate in this [1975] Conference."[78] This invited a firm and effective rebuttal from the ROK representative, recalls a participant: "The ROK's reply is simply that FAO is not the place to raise such a question; we are here to talk about agriculture—this would end the matter."

The PRC's behavior in FAO comes very close to being a *de facto* and incremental functionalism. In the beginning China was skeptical or suspicious of one offshoot of the 1974 World Food Conference, an early-warning system to provide for sharing information on crops, supplies, and any major projected changes in demand. Either out of ignorance or ideology, she did not like the use of satellites for prediction of crops and other agricultural activities. However, there is a consensus now that China has been providing more and more information on a slow but incremental basis. In contrast to the publicized complaint by American agricultural scientists about Chinese indifference to exchanges of the seeds of major food plant varieties,[79] no such complaint was voiced during the author's field interviews at FAO headquarters. In fact, when asked to single out the area or sector that invited the

[78] FAO Doc. C 75/PV/3 (10 November 1975), p. 8.
[79] See Victor K. McElheny, "Scientists Find Chinese Cool to Farm Research and Seed Exchanges," *NYT*, February 7, 1977, p. 6.

greatest Chinese interest and cooperation, the exchange of seed samples was most frequently mentioned.

The Chinese incrementalism in FAO's functional activities is also reflected in a steady flow of FAO visitors to China. Table 7.3 sums up one aspect of functional relationships between China and FAO. A subtle but steady pressure is being exerted on China by the FAO secretariat to open up China to all kinds of FAO missions, as well as to fellowship programs and study tours to be sponsored by UNDP so that many can learn and share the Chinese approach to rural development. What attracts special interest at FAO is to find out through field missions or study tours how the Chinese system really works and to explore its applicability to other developing countries. Those FAO officials who "shared" the Chinese experience in varying degrees through field trips seem to concur with the main findings of their colleague, Sartaj Aziz. After a careful study abroad and some "living experience" inside China, Aziz concludes that the Chinese system works for the following reasons:[80]

Labour-Intensive Methods: The ability of a Chinese commune to mobilize the unemployed and underemployed labour force for improving the land, building dykes and dams, digging irrigation channels, constructing roads and simply cultivating the land more intensively.

Diversification of Activities: The ability of a commune to diversify its activities—first within the agricultural sector to forestry, fisheries, and animal husbandry and then to small industry, using agricultural raw materials or providing inputs for agriculture.

Capital Formation: The inherent capacity for capital formation, which is close to 25 per cent and may be even higher.

Welfare and Social Services: The role of a commune in promoting welfare and providing essential social services, particularly in the fields of education and health.

Planning: The role of the Chinese commune in the system of planning, which in China is described in a simple phrase: "From the bottom up and from the top down." The primary merit of the Chinese system of planning is its emphasis on maximum exploitation of local resources for meeting local needs.

The Ideological and Political System: The main objective of the Chinese society is not the most rapid material progress or the creation of a consumer society, but the evolution of a classless society in which social inequalities are reduced to the minimum and there is a

[80] Aziz, "The Chinese Approach to Rural Development," pp. 4-7.

TABLE 7.3. FAO Visitors to the PRC, 1973-mid 1977

Date of Visit	Type	Party
2/20-28/73	OV	A. H. Boerma (DG); D. L. Umali (ADG, Bangkok); S. Aziz (Dir., ESC); J. C. Westoby (FO)
5/12-22/73	OV	H. W. Mandefield (Dir., Publications Div.)
4/26-5/26/74	TM	W. Ross Cockrill (Dep. Dir., AGA)
9/10-15/74	OV	G. Bula Hoyos (Independent Chairman, FAO Council); E. M. West (ADG, Programme and Budget)
10/8-14/74	OV	Sayed Ahmed Marie (SG, WFC); S. Aziz (DSG, WFC)
5/1-3/75	OV	R. Jackson (DDG); E. M. West (ADG, Programme and Budget)
5/28-6/3/75	OV	L. Umali (ADG, Bangkok); P. Mengin (Information Officer)
7/14-17/75	OV	A. H. Boerma (DG); D. L. Umali (ADG, Bangkok); A. de Vajda; Sillari-Medina
4/1-9/24/75	F	12 Fellows from Sri Lanka, six months (Fisheries)
9/8-10/7/75	TM	D. L. Umali; M. Crowley; C. de Fonseka; H. A. Al-Jibouri; P. R. Mengin; C. P. Pillai; Thet Zin; and T. Lehti (Agricultural Productivity and Study of People's Communes)
4/21-5/12/76	TM	D. Tapiador (Team Leader); F. Henderson; M. Delmendo; H. Tsutsui (FAO Fisheries Mission to China)
9/9-10/10/76	TM	King (Team Leader); Chandrasekharan; Polycarpou; Prakoso; Swiderski; Turbang (FAO Forestry Mission to China)
4/28-5/24/77	ST	Hauck (Team Leader); Lausanandana; Sant-Anna; and others from Afghanistan, Bangladesh, Burma, Cameroon, Egypt, Ethiopia, Ghana, India, Nepal, Nigeria, Pakistan, Philippines, Sri Lanka, and Tanzania (Organic Recycling in Agriculture)
5/17-24/77	OV	E. Sauma (DG); B. R. Sen; and V. Shah

DG = Director-General; ADG = Assistant Director-General; ESC = Commodities and Trade Division; FO = Forestry Department; AGA = Agricultural Department; DSG = Deputy Secretary-General; WFC = World Food Conference; OV = Official Visit; TM = Technical Mission; ST = Study Tour; F = FAO Fellowship in China.
Source: FAO secretariat.

high level of political and ideological consciousness—*it is ideology plus organization* [emphasis added].

In a comprehensive 84-page report prepared by the 1976 FAO Fisheries Mission to China upon its return to FAO headquarters, the mission concluded that "the potential for production of fish by intensive culture is more fully developed in China than in any other country."[81] The mission's report then stated six main points in its conclusion: (1) full integration of fishery and fish culture with water conservation, agriculture, forestry, animal husbandry, sideline occupations and intensive use of land and water resources; (2) practice of fish polyculture within the same body of water; (3) effective management of lakes and reservoirs for all-round development; (4) the policy of "open-door" research, education, and training, which translates itself into productivity increases; (5) decentralization and popular participation in program planning, resulting in more effective implementation; and (6) unremitting efforts to sustain community consciousness and collective action.[82]

What is the Chinese response to the unending series of "functional" demands from FAO? The Chinese have repeatedly cautioned FAO officials that what may work in China may not work elsewhere. They hesitate to state explicitly that it is the absence of Aziz's final factor—the Chinese ideology plus organization—that makes it impractical to transplant the Chinese model elsewhere. While the Chinese practice of model projection at the symbolic level and in the public international fora has been pervasive, the Chinese have adopted a cautious and somewhat ambivalent posture on the transferability of the Chinese model at the functional or implementation level.[83]

In the face of steady pressure, however, the Chinese response has been: "Yes, but not so fast, not so many, and not so uncritically." Some FAO officials also believe that the Chinese are reluctant to admit too many missions because of fear of possible functionalist spillover on the political and ideological consciousness of the masses. In short, the Chinese may be aware that the model-diffusing process works both ways. Be that as it may, the Chinese have taken a step-by-step approach in permitting FAO missions and UNDP-sponsored study tours

[81] *Freshwater Fisheries and Aquaculture in China*, p. 71.

[82] *Ibid.*, pp. 71-72.

[83] For discussion among economists on the question, "Is the Chinese Development Diffusible?" see the following: Eckstein, *China's Economic Revolution*, chap. 8; John G. Gurley, *China's Economy and the Maoist Strategy* (New York: Monthly Review Press, 1976), chap. 8; Lloyd Reynolds, "China as a Less Developed Economy," *American Economic Review* 65 (June 1975), 418-28; and Robert F. Dernberger, "The Relevance of China's Development Experience for Other Developing Countries," *Items* 31 (September 1977), 25-34.

and fellowship programs in China. A typical UNDP-sponsored fellowship program involves about a dozen technicians from a developing country studying one particular aspect of the Chinese approach to rural development for about six months. On March 26, 1977, for example, the second freshwater fish training course was inaugurated in Kwangchow, sponsored by FAO and UNDP, involving twelve students from Sri Lanka. According to FAO secretariat sources, three UNDP-sponsored study tours were scheduled for 1977, and four for 1978, and four for 1979.

In contrast, Chinese participation in the functional activities at FAO headquarters has been generally passive. China does not maintain a separate permanent mission to FAO (neither does the United States), but four personnel in the Chinese embassy in Rome—Jen Chih, counsellor; Li Chong-huan, third secretary; Hwang Woi-kuan, attaché; and Wang Ping-chung, attaché—participate in the Council and other meetings. As of February 1977, China did not have a single Chinese in the secretariat staff personnel subject to the principle of geographical distribution. At FAO headquarters, there were no less than 898 staff personnel belonging to the above category as of August 1976.

However, China sent 4 linguistic personnel to join the secretariat in August 1974; this number was increased to 8 by August 1976. As of February 1977, the secretariat had 10 Chinese in the professional category (translators) and 5 in the general service category (typists and clerks), none of whom, of course, was subject to the quota system based on geographical distribution. Chinese is one of the five official languages of FAO, but English, French, and Spanish—and Arabic for limited purposes—are the working languages. Yet the officials in the Library and Documentation Systems Division characterized Chinese as a "*de facto* working language" of FAO.[84]

In conclusion, Chinese participation in the activities of FAO may be characterized as an incremental functionalism. Except in major policy speeches, Chinese behavior has been devoid of politicization. The relationship between China and FAO has the character of functional cooperation through the practice of mission and cultural diplomacy. Several reasons may be suggested for this modest functionalism. First, the

[84] In every organ of the United Nations system, the Chinese have shown more interest in setting up a Chinese translation system than in placing Chinese personnel in secretariat posts. The Chinese sensitivity to the precision and clarity of documentation seems to be one of the main reasons. One example from Commission 1 of the 1975 Conference will suffice here. Li Yung-kai observed: "In REP/4, the English and French versions are not exactly the same. The Chinese version was a translation based on the English version, so which one should we base our discussion on? Do we discuss the question on the basis of the English version or the French? Paragraphs 6 and 7 mainly are different in English and French versions." See FAO Doc. C 75/I/PV/21 (25 November 1975), p. 10.

absence of the Soviet Union has deprived the Chinese of their chief target when playing the antihegemonic role. Second, FAO stands low on the scale of politicization among the specialized agencies; it does not have a rigid structure of confrontation between developed and developing countries. The FAO environment is less politicized, because most Member States, rich or poor, are interested in the organization's stated commitment to ensure humanity's freedom from hunger. Finally, agriculture represents one area where China can legitimately claim to possess a functional model. It may also be argued that, if China does nothing else, feeding one-fifth of humanity is a major contribution to the FAO's commitment to a world free of hunger.

THE INTERNATIONAL CIVIL AVIATION ORGANIZATION (ICAO)

The International Civil Aviation Organization (ICAO) officially came into existence on April 4, 1947, on the entry into force of the Convention on International Civil Aviation, which had been signed on December 7, 1944, at the Chicago Conference. ICAO was established on the functionalist premise that "the future development of international civil aviation can greatly help to create and preserve friendship and understanding among the nations and peoples of the world, yet its abuse can become a threat to the general security." Its aims and objectives, as stated in the 96-article Chicago Convention,[85] are to secure several kinds of freedom of the air through a continuing series of multilateral agreements so as to ensure the safe, orderly, and economic development of international air transportation.

The Chicago Convention accepts and codifies customary principles of international civil aviation, the most important of which is the principle that "every State has complete and exclusive sovereignty over the airspace above its territory" (Art. 1). The Convention also provides that "no scheduled international air service may be operated over or into the territory of a contracting State" without its previous consent (Art. 6). ICAO serves as a multilateral forum through which its 135 contracting states (as of December 31, 1976) cooperate in the establishment of international standards, to assure safety for the air traveling public of the world and for agreement in the technical, economic, legal, and technical assistance fields of civil aviation.

ICAO is made up of an Assembly, a Council, and such other bodies as may be necessary. The Assembly is a sovereign body. It meets at least once in three years to review the work of the organization and to

[85] ICAO Doc. 7300/5, *Convention on International Civil Aviation* (5th ed., 1975).

give such guidance as may be necessary to the other bodies of ICAO for their future work. The Council is a permanent body, responsible to the Assembly and is composed of thirty contracting states elected by the Assembly for a three-year term.[86] One of the major activities of the Council centers on rule making: It adopts international standards and recommended practices and incorporates these as annexes to the Chicago Convention. The Council may also act as an arbiter between Member States on matters concerning aviation and implementation of the Convention. The secretariat prepares the documentation for the work of the other organs and undertakes administrative and advisory tasks in regard to technical assistance.

On November 19, 1971, the Council convened to discuss ICAO's response to General Assembly Resolution 2758 (XXVI). After a brief debate, the United States first advanced a draft resolution (C-WP/5481), by which the Council would authorize the secretary-general of ICAO to ascertain the intentions of the government of the PRC with respect to participation in ICAO and adherence to the Chicago Convention. It was a device to postpone the Council decision until Peking's intentions had been clarified. The American draft resolution was defeated by 14 votes to 8, with 3 abstentions. The Council then adopted by a vote of 20 to 2 (Nicaragua and the United States), with 5 abstentions, the proposal of the People's Republic of the Congo. The resolution decided, "for the matters within its competence, to recognize the representatives of the Government of the People's Republic of China as the only legitimate representatives of China" to ICAO, and requested the secretary-general to communicate this decision immediately to all contracting states.[87]

The resolution had the immediate effect of barring the ROC from ICAO. The secretary-general (Assad Kotaite of Egypt) then communicated the Council resolution to Peking, together with the documents of the Chicago Convention and an account of the Chinese assessment for 1972 (see Table 7.7 below). The PRC's response, according to secretariat sources, was rather vague, saying in effect that the documents ICAO had sent were being carefully studied. The reply furthermore implied that the PRC considered herself neither a party to the Chicago Convention nor a member of ICAO at the moment, yet retained her legitimate right to represent China at ICAO. In short, it was

---

[86] The original number of Council members was 21; this was increased to 27 in 1962 and to 30 in 1973. The 21st Session of the Assembly adopted another amendment to Article 50(a) of the Convention, increasing the number of Council members from 30 to 33. This amendment will enter into force when ratified by 86 contracting states. As of December 31, 1976, 47 states have ratified the amendment.

[87] ICAO Doc. 8987-C/10004, *Action of the Council*, 74th Sess., pp. 47-49.

a response of noncommitment, confusing the actual legal status of the PRC vis-à-vis ICAO.

That the PRC was undergoing either a slow or a difficult appraisal of whether or not to join ICAO was indicated by the long delay in her initiation of mission diplomacy. It was not until November 23, 1973, more than two years after the Council action, that the official ICAO mission, headed by Walter Binaghi, president of the ICAO Council, and John Hutchison, chief of the External Relations Department of the ICAO secretariat, arrived in Peking to pave the way for China's entry into ICAO. The Binaghi mission was initiated at the invitation of Ma Jen-hui, director-general of the Civil Aviation Administration of China (CAAC), the PRC's airline. The Chinese officials who took active part in the discussions with the mission were Ma Jen-hui, Shen T'u, deputy director-general of CAAC, and Pi Chi-lung, deputy director of the Department of International Organizations and Conferences, Treaties and Laws in the Ministry of Foreign Affairs. Chinese Foreign Minister Chi P'eng-fei had a brief meeting with the mission on November 26, 1973, simply to legitimate the agreement reached between the Binaghi mission and other Chinese officials involved. Following the departure of the Binaghi mission, the Ministry of Foreign Affairs sent a letter dated February 15, 1974, declaring its intention to resume occupancy of China's seat, effective as of February 15, 1974.

While the Binaghi mission settled the question of the PRC's participation, it left a series of practical and legal questions unresolved. At the invitation of Ma Jen-hui, the second ICAO mission headed by Secretary-General Assad Kotaite (accompanied by Peter C. Armour, head of ICAO's Far East and Pacific Office) arrived in Peking on April 25, 1974. It was during the Kotaite mission that all the unresolved questions of China's obligations to ICAO were worked out to mutual satisfaction. Apparently, according to an informed source at the secretariat, it was not concern about the legal obligations spelled out in the Chicago Convention so much as the necessity to attend to more urgent problems in regard to other specialized agencies that delayed the PRC's initiation of mission diplomacy with ICAO. That is, ICAO occupied a low position in the PRC's priority list. However, in delaying more than two years, the PRC certainly complicated the nature of her legal obligations, especially the financial ones, toward ICAO.

Hence, the great bulk of the Kotaite mission centered on finding a mutually acceptable formula for the PRC's financial obligations. China's main concern was to maintain her principled stand—that she could not and would not pay any amount of the Chinese assessment accrued prior to the date of her actual representation in the organization, but at the same time this would not involve any financial burden on ICAO. Legal or not, Peking's formula was ingenious and practical: it would voluntarily increase its assessment to more than sufficiently offset the outstanding debts on the Chinese account. The decision of the 21st Session of the Assembly on the redetermination of the Chinese assessment was actually worked out during the Kotaite mission.

In the course of these discussions, the Chinese made a distinction between "continuity of state" and "continuity of representation." In a word, they held that the PRC's entry into ICAO should not be treated as a question of membership.[88] Rather, it should be regarded as a simple matter of resuming the interrupted representation of China in the organization. This position is of legal significance, because of the unique case of Chinese representation in ICAO. China was represented in ICAO by the ROC from its beginning through May 31, 1950, when the Taipeh government, in difficult and frustrating circumstances, renounced the Chicago Convention and withdrew from ICAO, effective as of May 31, 1951. However, the ROC reentered ICAO on January 1, 1954, having reratified the Convention on December 2, 1953. This anomalous situation invited several contracting states to reject the legal validity of either the ROC's withdrawal from or its reratification of the Convention.[89] However, the ROC continued to sign and ratify amendatory protocols to the Convention during the second period of her representation in ICAO, from 1954 to 1971, while the PRC showed little interest in the organization.

In a letter dated February 15, 1974, the PRC expressed her decision to resolve the legal issue of Chinese ratification or adherence of the Convention in her own way. The letter stated, for example, that "the Government of the People's Republic of China has decided to recognize the Convention on International Civil Aviation, which the then Government of China signed in Chicago on 9 December 1944 and of which an instrument of ratification was deposited by it on 20 February 1946."[90] In short, the PRC decided to ignore the ROC's second ratification of the Convention, while recognizing the first ratification. This action is consistent with the PRC's long-held and officially proclaimed

[88] During the preentry period the PRC writers had consistently argued that the China issue in the United Nations was a procedural (representational) issue, not a substantive (membership) question. See, for example, Chou Keng-sheng, "China's Legitimate Rights in the United Nations Must Be Restored," *JMJP*, December 5, 1961, p. 5; and Hsü Tun-chang, "The Question of Restoring the Legitimate Rights and Position of the People's Republic of China in the United Nations," *CFYC*, No. 5 (October 1956), 11-18.

[89] ICAO Doc. No. 7367, A7-P/1, p. 50.

[90] This excerpt from the PRC's letter is included in an explanatory footnote to Appendix 1 "States Parties to the Chicago Acts as of 31 December 1975," in ICAO Doc. 9166, *Annual Report of the Council—1975*, p. 116.

position of declaring null and void all the signatures, ratifications, or accessions by "the Chiang Kai-shek clique."

The PRC's curious legal position of adhering to the principle of state succession while declaring null and void all the ratifications by the rival government, coupled with the anomaly of both Chinas using the same title for the state, China, explains the discrepancies in ICAO official documents in the date of the Chinese ratification of the Chicago Convention. The documents prior to the PRC's entry give December 2, 1953 as the date of Chinese ratification, while the documents after the PRC's entry give the date of February 20, 1946. To further confuse the matter, the ICAO documents even after the PRC's entry list China as a signatory to both the Hague and Montreal Conventions, with the following notation buried in a multitude of footnotes: "The Government of the People's Republic of China has informed ICAO that it is not a party to The Hague (1970) and Montreal (1971) Conventions and that the inclusion of China in the list of States parties to them is a misrepresentation and therefore invalid."[91]

A number of articles in the Chicago Convention stand out as contrary to the PRC's principle or practice. "Each contracting State agrees," states Article 5, for example, "that all aircraft of the other contracting States, being aircraft not engaged in scheduled international air services, shall have the right, subject to the observance of the terms of this Convention, to make flights into or in transit non-stop across its territory and to make stops for non-traffic purposes *without the necessity of obtaining prior permission* [emphasis added]." This challenges Peking's rigid stand on national sovereignty. Article 67 requires each contracting state to file with the Council "traffic reports, cost statistics and financial statements showing among other things all receipts and the sources thereof." Yet the PRC has not published any civil aviation statistics since 1958. Is she likely to change this practice—or nonpractice—merely to conform to the Convention?

More seriously, Chapter XVIII (Art. 84-88) stipulates an elaborate set of arbitration procedures in the settlement of disputes between two or more contracting states relating to the interpretation or application of the Convention and its annexes. Yet, the PRC, like the Soviet Union, has opposed any reference of disputes arising from treaties, with the

---

[91] ICAO Doc. 9127, *Annual Report of the Council—1974*, p. 112. In the 1975 Annual Report of the Council, the explanatory footnote further states: "Its [PRC] Government has informed ICAO that 'since the founding of the People's Republic of China on 1 October 1949, the signing or ratification of any international treaty and convention by the Chiang Kai-shek clique, usurping the name of the Government of China is illegal, null and void.'" See ICAO Doc. 9166, *Annual Report of the Council—1975*, p. 122.

exceptions of trade agreements and a few other cases, to adjudication or third-party settlement.[92]

In spite of the problems posed by the above-mentioned articles in the Convention, a 1973 study of the PRC's aviation practice concluded: "With minor exceptions, then, PRC practice does not diverge from Chicago Convention principles. In many ways the PRC duplicates generally accepted international rules in its bilateral agreements. The deviations are not unusual, and the PRC's objection to unregulated fifth freedom traffic parallels the position of many other states which have signed the Chicago Convention."[93] In a letter dated February 15, 1974, for example, the PRC, in recognizing the signature and ratification of the Chicago Convention by the then government of China, did not attach any reservations. Instead, the PRC expressed a hope in the letter that Chapter XVIII would apply with due respect to Chinese sovereignty. Table 7.4 gives a full picture of the PRC's adherence to the Chicago Convention and its amendatory protocols as of December 31, 1976.

The PRC's decision to join ICAO raises the inevitable question: Why? ICAO is one of the most technical specialized agencies in the UN family; as such Peking could make little political use out of Chinese participation. In fact, as briefly noted above, this may impose some constraint on Peking's principled stand. The answer may be deduced from Table 7.5. What is most striking is the fact that China's international civil aviation has lagged far behind rapidly proliferating Chinese diplomatic and commercial activities in the world community. In 1975, for example, the PRC ranked 65th in total international operations in passengers, freight, and mail; 60th in international passenger operations; and 52nd in international freight tonne-kilometres. Yet the same year China showed percentage increases of 225, 230, and 233, respectively, in each category from the previous year. This suggests that the primary reason for Peking's decision to participate in ICAO is practical, and is related to expanding China's international civil aviation.[94]

This contention is sustained by the pattern of the PRC's participation in ICAO meetings during the first two and a half years. As Table 7.6 shows, China made her debut at the 1974 (triennial) Assembly, but more significantly has also participated in some highly technical and

[92] Hungdah Chiu, *The People's Republic of China and the Law of Treaties* (Cambridge, Mass.: Harvard University Press, 1972), p. 82.

[93] John R. King and Susan C. Roosevelt, "Civil Aviation Agreements of the People's Republic of China," *Harvard International Law Journal* 14 (Spring 1973), 322.

[94] See "More Modern Airports Built in China," NCNA-English, Peking, September 21, 1977, in SPRCP, No. 6433 (September 29, 1977), 279-81.

TABLE 7.4. The PRC's Adherence to or Recognition of the Chicago Convention and Related Protocols as of December 31, 1976

Subject	Date of Signature	Date of Entry into Force	No. of Ratifica- tions	PRC's Adher- ence or Recognition
Chicago Convention	12/7/44	4/4/47	135	2/20/46
Protocol Relating to an Amendment to the Convention				
Article 93 bis	5/27/47	3/20/61	72	3/24/48
Article 45	6/14/54	5/16/58	100	2/28/74
Articles 48(a), 49(e), and 61	6/14/54	12/12/56	103	2/28/74
Article 50(a)	6/21/61	7/17/62	104	2/28/74
Article 48(a)	9/15/62	9/11/75	68	2/28/74
Article 50(a)	3/12/71	1/16/73	95	2/28/74
Article 56	7/7/71	12/19/74	88	2/28/74
Article 50(a)	10/16/74	Not yet[a]	47	7/21/75
Protocol on the Authentic Trilingual Text of the Convention	9/24/68	10/24/68	81	2/28/74
International Air Services Transit Agreement	12/7/44	1/30/45	92	–
International Air Transport Agreement	12/7/44	2/8/45	12	–

[a] Will enter into force when ratified by 86 states.

Source: ICAO Doc. 9181, *Aeronautical Agreements and Arrangements*, and a draft copy of the Annual Report of the Council for 1976.

legal conferences. China's participation in the ICAO Council has more than political or symbolic significance, too. Unlike the executive bodies of some other specialized agencies, the Council enjoys a considerable degree of quasi-legislative, quasi-administrative, and quasi-judicial powers on matters relating to international civil aviation.

Characteristically, China made her debut at the 21st Session of the Assembly with a delegation that was large by ICAO standards. The PRC delegation was composed of Chief Delegate Shen T'u, Alternate Chief Delegate Wang Chu-liang, three delegates, one alternate, and three advisers. The most immediate problem was to settle the question of China's financial obligations to ICAO. There was little debate on

TABLE 7.5. Select Statistics on the PRC's Aviation Performance, 1975-76[a]

	1975	1976
TONNE-KILOMETRES PERFORMED (millions)		
(Passengers, Freight, and Mail)		
Rank Number in Intl & Domestic Operations	40	40
Estimate in Intl & Domestic Operations	170	180
Increase in Intl & Domestic Operations (%)	+55	+6
Rank Number in Intl Operations	65	64
Estimate in Intl Operations	39	41
Increase in Intl Operations (%)	+225	+5
PASSENGER-KILOMETRES PERFORMED (millions)		
Rank Number in Intl & Domestic Operations	42	42
Estimate in Intl & Domestic Operations	1,350	1,410
Increase in Intl & Domestic Operations (%)	+55	+4
Rank Number in Intl Operations	60	64
Estimate in Intl Operations	300	300
Increase in Intl Operations (%)	+230	–
FREIGHT TONNE-KILOMETRES PERFORMED		
(millions)		
Rank Number in Intl & Domestic Operations	36	37
Estimate in Intl & Domestic Operations	40	53
Increase in Intl & Domestic Operations (%)	+48	+15
Rank Number in Intl Operations	52	55
Estimate in Intl Operations	10	13
Increase in Intl Operations (%)	+233	+18

[a] Not including the Taiwan Province.
Source: Adapted from ICAO, Annual Report of the Council—1975, Doc. 9166, pp. 5-6. The 1976 data were taken from a draft copy of the Annual Report of the Council for 1976, which the author obtained from the ICAO secretariat during his field interviews in Montreal in May 1977.

this matter either in the Administrative Commission or in the Assembly, as both bodies accepted the recommendation of the Council. The Council itself had already agreed to the formula worked out during the Kotaite mission. The Administrative Commission in its Resolution 32/1 recommended for adoption by the Assembly a supplementary budget for 1974. However, what was included in the recommended resolution was an item that reads: "[T]he voluntary increase in the contribution of China results in an additional amount of $194,306 in 1974."[95]

Table 7.7 provides an explanation of this unusual move by China and ICAO. What is the computational basis for claiming an additional

[95] ICAO Doc. 9117, A21-AD, Report of the Administrative Commission, Assembly—21st Sess., p. 5.

TABLE 7.6. The PRC's Participation in Main ICAO Meetings, February 15, 1974-June 30, 1977

Date	Meeting	Represented by
9/24-10/15/74	21st Session of the Assembly	Shen T'u
10/3-22/74	21st Session of Legal Committee	Chu Liang-waing
10/21-12/20/74	83rd Session of the Council	Ho Feng-yuan[a]
2/4-3/27/75	84th Session of the Council	Ho Feng-yuan
6/2-27/75	85th Session of the Council	Ho Feng-yuan
9/3-25/75	International Conference on Air Law	?
9/30-12/19/75	86th Session of the Council	Ho Feng-yuan
3/15-4/15/76	87th Session of the Council	Ho Feng-yuan
4/21-5/14/76	The 9th Air Navigation Conference	Han Hsin-hua
6/7-30/76	88th Session of the Council	Ho Feng-yuan
9/8-24/76	Communications Divisional Meeting	Wang Yao-lin
9/28-12/15/76	89th Session of the Council	Liu Fu
2/2-4/7/77	90th Session of the Council	Liu Fu
4/13-26/77	Special Air Transport Conference	N. T. Wang
5/10-6/30/77	91st Session of the Council	Liu Fu

[a] As of December 12, 1974.

TABLE 7.7. Chinese Contributions to the ICAO Budget, 1971-77 ($)

Year	Total Net Budget	Chinese Assessment	(%)	Actual Payments by ROC	Actual Payments by PRC
1971	7,021,000.00	47,041.00	(0.67)	47,041	–
1972		59,328.00	(0.67)[a]	–	–
1973		67,194.00	(0.67)[a]	–	–
1974	9,778,000.00	65,512.60	(0.67)[a]	–	–
1974	9,778,000.00	384,153.00	(4.49)[b]	–	384,153.00[d]
1975	13,187,000.00	626,382.50	(4.75)[c]	–	626,382.50
1976	14,074,000.00	657,255.80	(4.67)[c]	–	657,255.80
1977	14,923,000.00	692,427.20	(4.64)[c]	–	692,427.20[e]

[a] Resolution A18-26.
[b] Resolution A21-38.
[c] Resolution A21-34.
[d] For the period February 15-December 31.
[e] Not paid as of May 6, 1977.

increase of $194,306 in 1974 for ICAO's treasury? It should be noted here that the 18th Session of the Assembly, which met in Vienna from June 15 to July 7, 1971, had already determined China's assessment at 0.67 percent for 1972, 1973, and 1974; it should also be noted that the ROC had already paid its assessed contributions in the amount of $47,041 for 1971. By voluntarily suggesting that its assessment for 1974 be increased from 0.67 percent to 4.49 percent, however, the PRC with a single payment of $384,153 for the period February 15-December 31, 1974, disposed of China's assessments for 1972, 1973, and 1974 and still produced a surplus of $194,306 for the year.

In effect, the PRC paid China's assessments for the period of its non-representation in ICAO without saying so. The Assembly resolution was also deliberately ambiguous in recommending that "the assessment percentage of China for 1974 be adjusted to 4.49%, effective 15 February 1974, and that the resulting payment be deemed to cover China's obligations with respect to the Organization's present General Fund appropriations through 31 December 1974."[96] At any rate, the impact of Chinese participation on ICAO's financing can be inferred from Table 7.7. What is unusual is that China, who ranks in the 60s in various performance categories of international civil aviation, decided to join the ranks of the top seven contributors—the Big Five, plus Japan and the Federal Republic of Germany—to the ICAO budget. In its Resolution A21-32, the Assembly also determined assessments of all contracting states for 1975, 1976, and 1977. Chinese assessments were determined at 4.75 percent for 1975, 4.67 percent for 1976 and 4.64 percent for 1977 on the basis of the newly adjusted 1974 assessment. So far China has paid her contributions without defaulting and without any selective withholding.

In addition to ICAO's financing, the PRC's participation has settled the old China problem. The organization is now free of this political controversy; it has also come closer to being universal. A vivid reminder of the representation of New China in the organization is the gift from the PRC, a lovely tapestry, entitled "This Land So Rich in Beauty," which hangs in the front of the conference hall in the new ICAO building in Montreal, Canada. In spite of her poor standing in international civil aviation, the PRC was elected as a member of the Council for a term of three years at the 21st Session of the Assembly. As in the other specialized agencies, the ROC was excluded from the ICAO Council.

The PRC's participation in the 21st Session of the Assembly afforded

[96] ICAO Doc. 9118, A21-RES, *Resolutions Adopted By the Assembly and Index to Documentation*, Assembly—21st Sess., p. 96.

her the first opportunity to state her principled stand on matters relating to international civil aviation. China took part in the Executive Committee, the Legal Committee, the Administrative Commission, and the Technical Commission of the Assembly, as well as in the plenary meetings. Yet her contributions to the discussions were extremely sparing. In most meetings, Chinese delegates acted more like invited observers than full-fledged members. In the meetings of the Legal Committee from October 3 to October 22, 1974, for example, no less than seven Chinese participated—only Canada exceeded China in the number of participants—but none of them made a single intervention or statement.[97]

The position the PRC took at the 1974 Assembly can be briefly summarized. On political questions, China voted with the Third World on such matters as the suspension of South Africa's voting right, the invitation of the PLO to take part in ICAO's work, and the Iraqi-Jordanian proposal appealing to all contracting states to refrain from giving permission to any airline to operate any air service to or from Jerusalem airport without prior permission. China also voted in favor of perhaps the most important resolution at the session—an amendment to Article 50(a) of the Chicago Convention to increase the Council membership from 30 to 33. China ratified this amendatory protocol on July 21, 1975, thus becoming the 22nd contracting state to do so. The protocol will enter into force when ratified by the 86 contracting states. As of December 31, 1976, 47 of them had ratified the protocol.

On issues of representation, China made predictable statements on "the Lon Nol clique," the "inappropriateness" of permitting the Saigon regime alone to attend the Assembly, and the "unreasonableness" of allowing only the South Korean authorities to be represented at ICAO. Shen T'u's major policy speech before the Assembly plenary was curiously devoid of any attack on the superpowers. Instead, he made a positive appeal:

> We believe that ICAO's work must be based primarily on the situation in the majority of the Member States, namely the third-world countries, and not merely on the situation in a minority of countries. Thus, in planning, it is necessary to weigh the practical usefulness of a project to that majority of Member States, consider their needs, and programme the work of ICAO accordingly. This alone will truly contribute to the general development of interna-

[97] For a list of delegates, observers, and advisers who attended the 21st Session of the Legal Committee, see ICAO Doc. 9131-LC/173-2, Vol. II: *Documents*, pp. 6-13. For the statements and interventions made by the delegates during the session, see ICAO Doc. 9131-LC/173-1, Vol. I: *Minutes*.

tional civil aviation, help change the present unreasonable state of affairs, and establish an equitable, fair and reasonable new order.[98]

The Chinese further argued that the most salient feature of international civil aviation at the present was its "inequitable development." While aeronautical technology had greatly advanced, a great many developing countries were still "in the juvenile stage of development." Since international civil aviation was world-wide, its uneven development called for greater attention from ICAO. The development of new types of aircraft, while providing new orders for the manufacturing states, presented problems to the developing countries, forcing them to go into reequipment before the life span of their present aircraft was over, as well as raising the problem of acquiring spare parts for the maintenance of their aircraft. The Chinese were quick to point out that they were by no means opposed to speedy advancement in aeronautical technology. On the contrary, they argued, the development of new types of aircraft was a welcome advance in international civil aviation. What the Chinese were appealing for was a more balanced approach on the part of ICAO in programming its future work.[99]

On technical issues the Chinese were reticent. However, they did intervene in the Technical Commission on the question of establishing the boundaries of Air Traffic Services (ATS) airspaces. On this matter, the Chinese argued, a contracting state should be asked as far as possible to take into account technical and operational requirements "only on the basis of full respect for its sovereign rights." The Chinese further argued that the delineation of an ATS airspace over a region of the high seas should be agreed upon by consultation among states whose territorial waters bordered on such region. "Failing agreement," declared the Chinese delegate, "the Council's responsibility, with the concurrence of such States, was to mediate and bring about a final agreement."[100] This is the Chinese interpretation of Chapter XVIII of the Chicago Convention to which we alluded earlier.

The impact of the PRC's participation in the activities of the organization has been virtually zero so far. According to a fellow national delegate, the Chinese representative made a politicized speech during his debut at the Council, which immediately brought "stunned silence and stares" from the other members of the Council. This ended Chinese politicization in the Council. Since then the Chinese have assumed the

---

[98] ICAO Doc. 9119, A21-Min. P/1-12, *Minutes of the Plenary Meetings*, Assembly—21st Sess., p. 65.

[99] *Ibid.*, p. 107.

[100] ICAO Doc. A21-Min. TE/1-13, *Minutes of the Technical Commission*, Assembly—21st Sess., p. 33.

posture of a functional novice eager to learn the technical intricacies of international civil aviation.

As of the end of 1976, there was not a single Chinese among the 257 secretariat staff personnel subject to geographical distribution.[101] When prodded by the secretariat, the Chinese response has always been the same: "We will put forward our candidates for secretariat posts when we are ready." However, the Chinese have quietly brought in eight linguistic "students"—two for English and six for French—for "on-the-spot training" on an *ad hoc* basis. Some secretariat officials anticipate that the Chinese will table a draft resolution at the forthcoming session of the Assembly in late 1977 to introduce Chinese as a "working language" of the Assembly and the Council. ICAO does not use the terms "official languages" and "working languages." Both Rule 56 of the Rules of Procedure for the Council and Rule 65 of the Standing Rules of Procedure of the Assembly merely stipulate that the English, French, and Spanish languages shall be used in the deliberations of both bodies. So far, this has presented no problem as far as the Council is concerned, because the three Chinese at the PRC permanent mission to ICAO in Montreal speak either French or English.[102]

Like the Soviet Union, the PRC does not fully comply with the requirement of Article 67 on her civil aviation statistics. The statistics section of the secretariat issues an "Air Transport Reporting Form," which needs to be filled out by each contracting state on a monthly basis in the case of international scheduled services and on an annual basis in the case of domestic scheduled services. China has ignored the form, submitting instead an annual report in which selected statistics are provided. She has also failed to provide statistics in three major categories: Nonscheduled flights; all-freight services only; and domestic operations.

However, China has provided statistics in the five subjects that fall in the category of scheduled flights: (1) international passenger-kilometres; (2) international tonne-kilometres performed in freight and mail; (3) international tonne-kilometres available; (4) total operations in domestic and international tonne-kilometres performed in passengers, freight, and mail; and (5) total operations in domestic and

[101] There were two Chinese—one at P-4 and the other at P-3—at the time of the Council action in 1971. In 1974, one resigned or retired and in 1975 the other also resigned or retired. There is no evidence that the PRC's entry had any direct bearing on this.

[102] At its 22nd Session held from September 13 to October 4, 1977, in Montreal, the Assembly of ICAO "endorsed the Council's recommendation that Chinese be adopted and introduced progressively as a working language of ICAO." See *UN Chronicle* 24 (November 1977), 15.

international tonne-kilometres. Hence, Table 7.5 should be read with caution. The statistics section of the secretariat practices the method of estimation and extrapolation to fill the gaps in the compilation of numerous statistical tables. Not surprisingly, China has declined to participate in the annual meeting of the Statistical Panel.

Article 83 of the Chicago Convention and *Rules for Registration With ICAO of Aeronautical Agreements and Arrangements* require each contracting state to register with ICAO all its bilateral aeronautical agreements currently in force. Has China met this requirement? Table 7.8 lists all the bilateral agreements the PRC registered with

TABLE 7.8. The PRC's Bilateral Aeronautical Agreements Registered with ICAO During the Year 1974

Party	Subject	Date of Signature	Date of Entry into Force
Canada	Civil Air Transport	6/11/73	6/11/73
Denmark	Civil Air Transport	5/18/73	5/18/73
Iraq	Air Transport	11/7/69	2/15/70
Pakistan	Air Transport	8/29/63	8/29/63
Sweden	Civil Air Transport	6/1/73	6/1/73

Source: ICAO Doc. 9181-LGB/319, *Aeronautical Agreements and Arrangements* (ICAO, 1977), p. 20.

ICAO during the year 1974. With one exception (Pakistan), none of the twenty-one bilateral aeronautical agreements or protocols found in *Agreements of the People's Republic of China 1949-1967: A Calendar,* by Douglas M. Johnston and Hungdah Chiu has been registered with ICAO. A cross-checking of the registration of each of the 131 contracting states of ICAO as published in ICAO's *Aeronautical Agreements and Arrangements* shows no discrepancy between China's registration and those of the other parties involved. However, it cannot be ascertained whether all the remaining twenty agreements are no longer in effect or whether the PRC has just not registered them.

It may be said in conclusion that the primary reason for Peking's decision to join ICAO was more practical than political. ICAO is uniquely unsuitable for Peking's symbolic politics or model projection. In fact, China has no model to project at ICAO. Recognizing the highly technical nature of the work of ICAO and also her own low ranking in international civil aviation, China has been diffident to advance any input into the rule-making and standard-setting process in the Council. Her entry into ICAO is a first step in the gradual process of expanding her modest international civil aviation. The relationship between China and ICAO has been cordial and professional, but how much one can really help the other remains to be seen.

THE WORLD METEOROLOGICAL ORGANIZATION (WMO)

Is it possible that one of the keys to world order may lie in unlocking the mystery of world weather? Scientists at the World Meteorological Organization (WMO) work on the assumption that their research and experimental programs may indeed unlock some of the secrets of world food production, water resources, pollution, tropical cyclones, climate, and weather modification. That this is not just the visionary dream of a few meteorologists may explain why WMO has managed to escape the political tornados that have swept through some of its sister specialized agencies.

Organized international collaboration in meteorology dates from the first official congress of governmental delegates held in Vienna in 1873; this led to the founding of the International Meteorological Organization (IMO). Under the auspices of the IMO a conference of directors of national meteorological services met in Washington, D.C., in 1947 and adopted the World Meteorological Convention, establishing WMO as a specialized agency of the United Nations. On March 23, 1950, after thirty signatory states had ratified or acceded to the Convention, WMO came into existence.

WMO was established to achieve the following objectives: (1) to facilitate international cooperation in the establishment of networks of stations and centers to provide meteorological services and observations; (2) to promote the establishment and maintenance of systems for the rapid exchange of meteorological information; (3) to promote standardization of meteorological observations and ensure the uniform publication of observations and statistics; (4) to further the application of meteorology to aviation, shipping, water problems, agriculture, and other human activities; and (5) to encourage research and training in meteorology.[103]

The supreme body of WMO is the World Meteorological Congress. It meets once every four years to determine general policies of the organization. The Executive Committee is made up of twenty-four members serving in an individual capacity: the president and the three vice-presidents of WMO; the presidents of the six regional associations; and fourteen directors of meteorological services of its members, selected by the quadrennial Congress. The Committee meets at least

[103] These five objectives are always reprinted inside the front cover of *WMO Bulletin*.

once a year—usually in June—to execute the decisions of the Congress. The task of coordinating meteorological activities throughout the different regions of the world is assigned to six regional associations: Regional Association I (Africa); Regional Association II (Asia); Regional Association III (South America); Regional Association IV (North and Central America); Regional Association V (South-West Pacific); and Regional Association VI (Europe).

In addition, WMO has eight Technical Commissions, composed of experts designated by Member States; they are responsible for studying the special technical branches relating to meteorological observation, analysis, forecasting, research, and the application of meteorology. The secretariat, headed by a secretary-general (D. A. Davies of the United Kingdom since 1955), is located in Geneva; its 291-member staff (as of December 31, 1976) operates in the increasingly technical and electronic field of weather study; it prepares publications, arranges meetings of the various WMO bodies, and coordinates the meteorological services of the world. The activities of WMO fall into the following six main program areas: (1) World Weather Watch (WWW); (2) Research; (3) Interaction of Man and His Environment; (4) Technical Cooperation; (5) Education and Training; and (6) Hydrology and Water Resources Development.

WHO adopted an unusual procedure in settling the question of Chinese representation. On November 26, 1971, the secretary-general of WMO addressed a letter to the foreign ministers of the Member States, drawing their attention to General Assembly Resolutions 396 (V) of December 1950 and 2758 (XXVI) of October 1971. As a result of consultations with the president and members of the Executive Committee, it had been decided, he further stated, that the question should be settled by Member States through a postal ballot. The ballot was to be returned no later than February 24, 1972. The postal ballot was completed by the designated deadline with the following results: 70 Member States voted in favor of the PRC; 21 voted against; and 8 abstained. On the basis of the returned votes—which exceeded the required quorum (62), and the number of affirmative votes (70) being greater than two-thirds of the majority of the votes cast for and against—WMO recognized the representatives of the PRC as the only legitimate representatives of China in the organization as of February 24, 1972.

In spite of this unusual mode of implementing the General Assembly action, the PRC's entry into WMO was uncomplicated and prompt. Following the WMO decision, announced on February 25, 1972, the secretary-general received an invitation from the PRC to pay a visit to Peking. The secretary-general proceeded to Peking from Bangkok, where he was on an official mission when the invitation was received, and arrived in Peking via Hong Kong and Canton on March 20, 1972.

During his four-day sojourn in Peking, Secretary-General Davies had "prolonged discussions" with Meng Ping, director of the Central Bureau of Meteorology, and "a friendly conversation" with Foreign Minister Chi P'eng-fei. Also involved in discussions were Pi Chi-lung, Chang Nai-chao, deputy-director of the Central Bureau of Meteorology (who was to become China's permanent representative to the WMO Executive Committee) and Yeh Cheng-pa. "The discussions," noted *WMO Bulletin*, "which were very constructive and encouraging and which were conducted in a very friendly and co-operative atmosphere, enabled the Secretary-General to explain in detail the procedures and activities of the Organization and to answer many related questions."[104] WMO also took pride in the fact that its secretary-general was the first of any secretariat officials from the UN family to be invited by Peking in the wake of the General Assembly action.

In yet another unusual move, Peking sent to WMO a study group of meteorologists, led by Chang Nai-chao, in July 1972, the first such mission from the PRC to a specialized agency of the United Nations. During the visit, the group "studied in detail the steps to be taken for the participation of the People's Republic of China in the various programmes of the Organization, special attention being paid to the World Weather Watch." Detailed discussions were held with the secretary-general and senior secretariat officials. At the closing ceremony of this unusual visit, Davies expressed a hope that this first step on the part of the PRC would lead to her full and effective participation in the work of WMO. Chang Nai-chao expressed his "complete satisfaction" with the visit and stated that he would report in such terms to his government in Peking.[105]

Although the PRC decided to participate in WMO as of February 24, 1972, it is not clear—and the secretary-general imposed an embargo on the release of details of the negotiations—when and how Peking's decision was made and communicated to WMO. The PRC's prompt decision to join WMO—the circumstantial evidence seems to indicate that the decision was made and communicated to WMO prior to the sending of the PRC's meteorological study group in July 1972—is also interesting in that China could not participate in policy-making bodies of the organization because the Executive Committee meets only once

[104] *Ibid.* (July 1972), 190. See also "Chinese Foreign Minister Chi P'eng-fei Meets D. A. Davies," NCNA-English, Peking, March 23, 1972, in *SMCP*, No. 5107 (April 6, 1972), 138; "Secretary General of World Meteorological Organization Leaves Peking," NCNA-English, Peking, March 24, 1972, in *SMCP*, No. 5108 (April 7, 1972), 184.
[105] *WMO Bulletin* 21 (October 1972), 259.

a year (and neither the PRC nor the ROC was a member) and the next Congress was still three years away.

Given the circumstances, why such a rush? A somewhat self-serving answer was provided to the author by one of the Chinese international civil servants who had joined a specialized agency in Geneva in 1949 and who had maintained contacts with both the ROC Mission to International Organizations at Geneva and the PRC embassy in Switzerland during the preentry period. He said: "Immediately after the General Assembly action, the Chinese came to me to discuss what international organizations in Geneva they should join. I advised them to join right away in two organizations—WMO and ITU—because you simply cannot separate China from the scientific networks of these organizations. As for the other international organizations in Geneva, I told them that you can pretty much forget about them, because you just pay huge sums in dues in return for nothing." It is not clear what role, if any, this advice played in the Chinese decision to join WMO immediately.

The PRC's decision to participate in WMO was part and parcel of the larger process of establishing a permanent network for multilateral diplomacy in Geneva, where a "mini-United Nations," headed by V. Winspeare Guicciardi, under-secretary-general of the United Nations and director-general of the UN offices at Geneva, is located at the site of the League of Nations. The headquarters of WMO, WHO, ITU, WIPO, ILO, GATT, and UNCTAD are all situated at or near the Palais des Nations complex; in addition, UPU in Berne is only an hour and a half's train ride from Geneva.

In a communication dated July 31, 1972, Chinese Foreign Minister Chi P'eng-fei informed Director-General Guicciardi of the Chinese government's decision to set up "a Permanent Mission of the People's Republic of China to the United Nations Offices at Geneva as well as to other international organizations in Switzerland," and to appoint Consul-General Wang Chung-li as acting permanent representative at the new mission.[106] However, it was not until October 28, 1975, that Ambassador An Chih-yüan presented his credentials to Director-General Guicciardi as the first permanent representative of the PRC's mission in Geneva.[107] As of October 1976, the Chinese Permanent Mission had fourteen personnel including An Chih-yüan—smaller than the US mission but larger than the French—looking after matters of Chinese representation at WMO, WHO, ITU, UNCTAD, and UPU. (See Appendix J.) In short, the day-to-day operations of Chinese multilateral

[106] "China to Establish Permanent Mission to UN Office at Geneva," NCNA-English, Geneva, August 8, 1972, in *SCMP*, No. 5199 (August 21, 1972), 38.

[107] "Chinese Representative Presents Credentials to Director-General to UN Offices at Geneva," NCNA-English, Geneva, October 28, 1975, in *SPRCP*, No. 5972 (November 11, 1975), 89.

diplomacy at WMO, as well as at the remaining four organizations, are all handled by the PRC's permanent mission in Geneva, while the major conferences sponsored by these organizations are attended by delegations dispatched by the Ministry of Foreign Affairs.

Table 7.9 sums up the PRC's participation in WMO and WMO-sponsored meetings during the period 1972-76. What is striking is the fact that China departed from her normal *modus operandi* of symbolic politics in a specialized agency: that is, a formal "triumphant" entry into the supreme political body—Conference, Congress, or Assembly—where she would be elected as a member of an executive body, followed by a deliberately slow lateral expansion of participation in a few select technical bodies of the organization. It is also of interest that China allowed her permanent representative at WMO, Chang Nai-chao, to be elected as an acting member of the Executive Committee and to participate in its deliberation in this capacity during the

TABLE 7.9. The PRC's Participation in WMO or WMO-Sponsored Meetings, 1972-76

Date	Meeting	Represented by
7/30/73-8/4/73	Joint Technical Conference on the Observation and Measurement of Atmospheric Pollution (WMO/WHO, Helsinki, Finland)	Tsou Ching-meng
8/6/73-8/18/73	Commission for Instruments and Methods of Observation, 6th Sess. (Helsinki, Finland)	Tsou Ching-meng
9/4/73-9/7/73	IMO/WMO Centenary Celebrations (Vienna)	Tsou Ching-meng
9/12/73-9/28/73	Executive Committee, 25th Sess.	Chang Nai-chao[a]
11/19/73-11/30/73	Commission for Atmospheric Sciences, 6th Sess. (Versailles, France)	Wang Shih-ping
6/4/74-6/13/74	Executive Committee, 26th Sess.	Chang Nai-chao[a]
9/2/74-9/14/74	Intl Conference on the Results of the Intl Hydrological Decade and on Future Programmes in Hydrology (UNESCO/WMO, Paris)	Chang Jui-chin
4/28/75-5/23/75	Seventh World Meteorological Congress	Tsou Ching-meng
5/26/75-5/30/75	Executive Committee, 27th Sess.	Tsou Ching-meng
9/8/75-9/19/75	Regional Association II (Asia), 6th Sess. (Colombo, Sri Lanka)	Tsou Ching-meng
6/8/76-6/17/76	Executive Committee, 28th Sess.	Tsou Ching-meng[b]

[a] As an acting member.
[b] In lieu of Chang Nai-chao who was unable to attend due to health reasons.

25th Session in 1973, until the 7th Congress, when Chang Nai-chao was formally elected a member of the Executive Committee.

The PRC's behavior at WMO, according to a number of participants, has been generally passive in most program areas and, "on the whole, more technical and professional than political or ideological." Let us first examine the issues in WMO toward which China has taken a political or ideological approach. As with UNESCO, ICSU represents the most important political issue in the PRC's relationship with WMO. Since 1919, when this powerful NGO was first established, ICSU has maintained close collaborative research relationship with IMO. At present, ICSU's main relationship with WMO falls within the area of the latter's research program. In fact, one of the most exciting research programs in the history of meteorology is WMO's Global Atmospheric Research Programme (GARP). And GARP was launched jointly by WMO and ICSU.[108]

At the 25th Session of the Executive Committee, where he made his debut, Chang Nai-chao assumed a passive but positive posture toward the organization. However, on GARP he observed: "Truly, it is necessary for WMO to cooperate with other international organizations in its activities. However, it should be pointed out that in the International Council of the Scientific Union [sic], the associated organization with WMO in the Global Atmospheric Research Programme activities, there still remain representatives of the Chiang Kai-shek clique who up to now unlawfully take part in the activities of this organization in the name of Taiwan."[109] He then declared: "China will not participate in the activities of the Global Atmospheric Research Programme until ICSU has expelled the representatives of the Chiang Kai-shek clique from its membership and broken all its relations with the latter."[110]

China took the same stand on the ICSU issue at the 7th World Meteorological Congress held in 1975. Unlike its policy toward UNESCO, however, China has not pursued the matter beyond the point of stating her principled stand and intention not to participate in the activities of GARP. That is, China has not introduced any draft resolution on the ICSU question nor has she applied any pressure on the secretariat, as she has done at UNESCO.

Whether it was necessary or not, China appealed for prompt admission of the DPRK and the Democratic Republic of Vietnam into WMO

[108] For a succinct analysis of the development of a collaborative research relationship between WMO and ICSU, see Kaare Langlo, "Impact of IMO and WMO on Meteorological Research," *WMO Bulletin* 22 (January 1973), 3-6.

[109] "25th Session of Executive Committee of World Meteorological Organization Holds in Geneva," NCNA-English, Geneva, September 27, 1973, in *SPRCP*, No. 5472 (October 11, 1973), 129-30.

[110] *Ibid.*, p. 130.

at the 7th Congress, where both were admitted as new members. China's chief delegate, Tsou Ching-meng, also argued that "whether the international meteorological work can have a universal and healthy development or not is inseparable from the meteorological development of the Third World countries." "We hope," continued Tsou Ching-meng, "that WMO will act in line with the world trend, reflect the eager aspiration and demand of the people all over the world, those of the Third World in particular, and make contributions to the development of the international meteorological work, particularly that of the Third World."[111]

China used the forum of the Congress to engage in a modest amount of model projection, emphasizing the self-reliant accomplishments of Chinese meteorology. As a first-time participant in the Congress, China scored two victories: Chang Nai-chao was chosen to fill one of the fourteen elective seats on the Executive Committee, and Chinese was adopted as one of the official and working languages of the organization, on condition that its implementation was to be effected on a step-by-step basis.[112]

At the 6th Session of Regional Association II (Asia) held in Colombo, Sri Lanka, in September 1975, China as a first-time participant showed an active political interest in the election of regional president for the next four years. According to the account of one participant, China uncharacteristically lobbied among the delegates to defeat the candidacy of D. Tubdendorj (of Mongolia) who was sponsored by the Soviet Union. As in the group politics of the Asian Group in the General Assembly, China showed only a negative interest in defeating the Mongolian candidate. As a vice-president during the preceding four years and as acting president of the association during the conference, Tubdendorj was widely expected to succeed to the presidency. However, through the Chinese intervention, he was defeated and Charoen Charoen-rajpark of Thailand was elected as president instead. The most significant effect of this unexpected change in the outcome of the election was that the latter replaced the former as a nonelected member of the Executive Committee.

What is the impact of Chinese participation on the main program areas of WMO? China has made no impact of any kind on the research program as she refuses to participate in the research activities of GARP because of the ICSU issue. What makes her participation in WMO unique is that it has brought about an immediate operational

[111] WMO, *Proceedings of Seventh World Meteorological Congress*, Geneva, 28 April-23 May 1975, WMO Official Report No. 428, p. 27.
[112] WMO, *Annual Report of the World Meteorological Organization—1975* (WMO, No. 439), pp. 7, 88.

impact on perhaps the most important program area of the organization—the World Weather Watch (WWW). If one draws on the comments and observations of the secretariat officials involved, China's contributions to WWW may be stated in the following terms.

There is little doubt that China's priority in WMO is concentrated in WWW and its associated areas, such as telecommunication, observation, and data processing. She is characterized as having "a very strong working relationship" with the WWW Department at WMO. "China has one of the biggest, if not *the* biggest, network of stations in the world," observed the director of WWW. "I would say about one-sixth of our data collected from our global observational networks is contributed by China," he continued. Thus, the integration of China into the WWW system has filled a crucial gap in WMO's earthwatch.

Why has China given such a clear-cut priority to WWW? There are several explanations. First, WWW is practical and utilitarian; its agrometeorological value can be appreciated in its day-to-day operation. Second, the data China provides to WWW are of a nonsensitive nature. Third, there is an element of reciprocity; China not only gives but also receives a substantial amount of data from WWW. The Chinese principle of self-reliance does not stand in the way of such an exchange of data. Finally, China has assigned an important role to meteorology and hydrology in her own development process. All of these factors have contributed to the development of a close functional relationship between China and WWW that we seldom find in any programmatic sector in the specialized agencies.

China's participation in the other program areas has shown a more slow and methodical expansion. There is a shared consensus at the secretariat that China is gradually broadening the scope of her participation by attending more and more meetings of technical commissions. In addition, the Chinese do their homework on technical questions. "They [the Chinese participants] must have read all WMO books, regulations, and references," remarked one secretariat official. While China has consistently refused to be the recipient of any assistance program from WMO—ninety-five countries received assistance under one program or another in 1975—she has gone along with the Technical Cooperation Department of WMO in working out UNDP-sponsored study tours in China. To cite a recent example, a group of ten meteorologists from Southeast Asia, accompanied by the director of WMO's Technical Cooperation Department, spent one month in 1976 in a meteorological study tour in China, utilizing Chinese Renminbi contributions to UNDP.

The impact of Chinese participation on the finances of WMO cannot be determined precisely. Unlike the other specialized agencies,

WMO does not provide any data on assessments and contributions of the Member States; they are made available only to governments upon request. We may surmise, however, that the impact of Chinese participation upon the financing of WMO is no less positive than that on the other specialized agencies we have reviewed in this chapter.

The cultural diplomacy between China and WMO is carried out on the shared assumption that Chinese experience is of particular interest for the WMO operational hydrology program, which was designed primarily to help developing countries to establish and strengthen their hydrological services. On the other hand, the Chinese specialists, according to J. Nemec, chief of the Hydrology and Water Resources Department at WMO who visited China in July 1975, "welcomed international exchanges of experience, since many techniques used in the rest of the world, such as those recommended by WMO in its guidance material, may be usefully adopted by the Chinese Hydrological Service, within the framework of the above-mentioned principle of self-reliance."[113]

Is Chinese experience in operational hydrology adaptable to the needs of developing countries? J. Nemec sums up his field trip to China by listing the three main principles that guide Chinese hydrologists at all regional and functional levels and that may be of particular relevance to a number of developing countries:[114]

(1) to enable hydrology to be of immediate use for production purposes, particularly in the agricultural field, following the frequently mentioned principle of the government that science is to serve the people;

(2) to be self-reliant. This principle of the government is not only followed at the national level, as witnessed by the Chinese-made hydrological instruments, but also at the provincial and district level. Indeed, self-reliance appears to be the only feasible way to operate the immense network; and

(3) the implication of large masses of the population in hydrological activities. The practice of technicians stationed in the People's Communes servicing the irrigation and drainage intakes and acquainting the peasants with simple techniques, as well as with the importance of hydrological operations, is another way in which the Chinese Hydrological Service performs its vast duties. Indeed, faced with the multitude of small hydraulic

[113] "Operational Hydrology in the People's Republic of China," *WMO Bulletin* 24 (October 1975), 252.
[114] *Ibid.*, pp. 250-52. See also "Chief of WMO Hydrology and Water Resources Department Leaves Peking for Southern China," NCNA-English, Peking, July 10, 1975, in *SPRCP*, No. 5899 (July 22, 1975), 90.

structures, all in need of hydrological design data, as well as operational hydrometry and forecasting, the professional Chinese hydrologists could never satisfy these needs without the active assistance and participation of volunteer observers and particularly of the rural population as a whole.

It may be said in conclusion that Chinese participation in the activities of WMO has an element of selective functionalism. To be sure, China takes a political approach to ICSU and other political-representational issues at the quadrennial Congress. But this political approach has not stood in the way of developing a close functional relationship with WWW and its slowly expanding participation in hydrology and water resources development. While it is premature to apply the concept of transferability—that is, a functional spillover into politics—China has proved herself quite capable of excluding politics from select programs or activities where she recognizes the need and mutual benefit of functional cooperation.

Conclusion

Chinese participation in the above four selected specialized agencies of the United Nations system provides an empirical basis for some broad generalizations and assessments. The most immediate impact of the PRC's entry into the specialized agencies was more symbolic than substantive, more political than functional. The vestigial China controversy was finally settled, disposing of at least one political problem standing in the way of more effective functional work. That China's entry has also changed the political-psychological environment of the specialized agencies concerned was suggested by the observation of one secretariat official: "It is refreshing to get new blood, new ideology, and new faces for the Organization."

China's entry also had an immediate impact on the financing of each of the specialized agencies. The voluntary increase in China's assessment, coupled with prompt and full payment without any selective withholding, has considerably strengthened their finances. However, China's impact on the program areas of the specialized agencies concerned, with the exception of WWW at WMO, has been virtually negligible. This is a corollary of a deliberately low-keyed, passive, selective, and only incrementally expanding participation in a few select functional programs or activities.

The low level of Chinese participation in the functional activities of the specialized agencies has generated a number of puzzling questions among fellow participants. Why does such a major contributor to the budget play so minor a role in the policy-making process? Why has not China assumed a more active leadership role for the Third World? Why send so large a delegation to the conferences sponsored by the specialized agencies only to make one or two politicized speeches but do virtually no diplomatic lobbying? Why does it take so long for the Chinese to "study and review" a situation? Why has China been so indifferent to the prodding of the secretariat to nominate candidates for top secretariat posts? Why has China been so fond of model projection at public forums but so lukewarm to the adaptation of its model to developing countries through the functional activities of the specialized agencies? Why has China taken so radical an approach in public but behaved so modestly and self-effacingly in private?

It is hazardous to provide one answer to all of these questions. Instead, a number of factors may be suggested to explain the low level of Chinese participation. First, there was—and still is, to a diminishing degree—a genuine desire on the part of the Chinese to master first the complexities and intricacies of the scientific and technical programs of the specialized agencies. The Chinese educational system, which is more practice oriented than theory oriented, ill prepares even Chinese technocrats to play an effective role in the highly specialized functions of the agencies involved. In addition, the Maoist axiom about being bold in strategy but cautious in tactics has greatly influenced Chinese diplomatic behavior.

Second, the Chinese learning process in the field has been made difficult by the linguistic problem. Even among the Chinese linguistic personnel, it is rare to find someone who is multilingual; they either speak English or French but seldom both. It is rarer still to find a Chinese technocrat who is at the same time multilingual. The chief Chinese delegate at the major conferences sponsored by the specialized agencies is always conspicuous not only because of his dress but also because of the entourage of interpreters who follow him around, owing to his inability to speak either English or French, the lingua franca of multilateral diplomacy. The linguistic handicap thus makes it difficult for the Chinese to assume a leadership role in many of the organs in the specialized agencies, even if they so desired. It is little wonder, then, that China has shown rare initiative toward making Chinese a working language of each specialized agency.

Third, the Chinese world view is hardly congenial to the assumptions, logic, and approaches of functionalism. It would be foolhardy to deny that the primary reason for the PRC's decision to participate in the specialized agencies was largely political and symbolic; that is, to restore the "legitimate" representation of China in international

403

organizations. The principle of self-reliance has also eliminated the possibility of using the specialized agencies as a source of technical assistance for China's own development process. China does not suffer from a credibility problem resulting from a discrepancy between what she says and what she does in any of the specialized agencies, because she does not say or promise anything she cannot deliver. In a word, China has orchestrated a level of participation commensurate with her own conceptualization of the specialized agencies. It can no longer be argued in 1977 that her low level of participation is a matter of necessity imposed by inexperience; it is by now a matter of a deliberate policy choice made in Peking.

This is not to suggest that China's approach to the specialized agencies has been exclusively political or that her low level of participation has been static. Although it is still premature to forecast any functional impact of Chinese participation in the specialized agencies on the evolution of Chinese global policy, we have noted in a few cases of *de facto*, selective, and incremental functionalism. Reading politicized policy speeches made at the plenary session of a specialized agency gives little clue to China's actual behavior, because she has developed a distinctive style of stating her principled stand in public while pursuing functional cooperation on those programs or activities where she finds a need or rationale. In spite of her conceptual difficulties with some of the policies, structures, and functionalist assumptions of the specialized agencies, China has yet to behave like a revolutionary challenger or even a progressive reformer.

There is, then, a contrast between the radical vision projected at public fora, on the one hand, and the modest behavior in a few select and slowly expanding areas of functional activities, on the other. In every one of the four specialized agencies reviewed in this chapter, there is a shared perception and a cautious optimism that China is expanding her participation into more and more functional sectors at her own slow but methodical pace. Even in such a politicized organization as UNESCO, the Chinese have blended political and functional approaches. This blending process fluctuates and varies, depending on the political situation at home, the political or functional saliency of the issues or programs involved, and the nature of each specialized agency. That an almost universal expression of hope among secretariat officials and national delegates centers on fuller Chinese participation suggests their shared belief that China will come to play a positive role, once she has decided to participate more fully in the functional activities of the specialized agencies.

· 8 ·

CHINA AND INTERNATIONAL
LEGAL ORDER

The entry of China into the world community has renewed an old question in a new global setting: Is China a help or a hindrance to international law and order? What impact, if any, has China made upon the evolution of international legal order? Conversely, what impact, if any, has international legal order had on the Chinese conception and practice of international law? China's participation in the United Nations, the specialized agencies, and UN-sponsored conferences, many of which are engaged in the law-developing and law-clarifying process, now makes it possible to subject the above questions to a disciplined empirical analysis.

China's participation in a multitude of UN meetings has added a multilateral dimension to her legal concepts and practice, which had remained largely bilateral in nature and application. Suddenly, China is now faced with a challenge from which she can hardly escape: the need to pronounce her *opinio juris* on a myriad of international legal issues before the Organization; and then to have her state practice subjected to continuing scrutiny during the conduct of her multilateral diplomacy. Even a refusal by China to participate in a committee or conference of legal import or her failure to state her position in the face of a challenge or opportunity runs the risk of being evaluated by other Member States as evidence of her legal behavior.

THE EVOLVING CHINESE ATTITUDE TOWARD THE
CHARTER CONCEPTION OF INTERNATIONAL
LEGAL ORDER

One of the salient characteristics of Chinese diplomats in the conduct of their multilateral diplomacy is their habit of repeatedly declaring that they always mean what they say and that they adhere to their principled stand. As already noted in Chapter 4, Chinese nonparticipation in the vote on UN peace-keeping questions has been little elaborated upon; it is merely justified as maintaining consistency with the principled stand of the past. Before examining China's contemporary theory and practice, therefore, it is necessary to review briefly the position she took during the preentry period on the Charter conception of international legal order.[1]

[1] The term "international legal order" lacks a universally operationalized defini-

However, an objective and thorough study does present serious conceptual and methodological difficulties. First, there were very few official policy pronouncements and commentaries on international legal issues. China showed—and still does to a lesser extent—a pronounced tendency to shy away from any elaboration of her official position on most legal issues. When such pronouncements were made, they were in reaction to external events or incidents, and took the form of accusations to other countries of their alleged violations of international law or of the UN Charter.

Second, there were gaps and discontinuities in both the coverage and the sources of China's theory and practice of international law. In constructing a calendar of some 2,000 agreements concluded by China between 1949 and 1967, for example, Johnston and Chiu had to rely on over eighty different sources in a dozen languages.[2] Such leading journals on international law and politics as *Cheng-fa yen-chiu* [Research on Politics and Law], *Kuo-chi wen-t'i yen-chiu* [Research on International Problems], *Fa-hsüeh* [Jurisprudence], and *Shih-chieh chih-shih* [World Knowledge] were all swept away by the Cultural Revolution in mid-1966 and have not resumed publication. Hence, the researcher is tempted to plug a gap in one period with available "evidence" from another period, thus running the risk of blurring the diachronic perspective in the process.

Third, the party-controlled press, coupled with the intense ideological ferment, makes it difficult to distinguish the real from the rhetorical in available written materials. Fourth, the problem of probing the discrepancy between words and deeds in Peking's legal position was made difficult, if not impossible, by China's exclusion from the activities of most international organizations and by the secrecy surrounding her actual state practice in bilateral treaty relations with other countries. In a word, there was an imbalance in the sources between verbal and behavioral referents.

Finally, the Moscow connection greatly complicates any analysis of Chinese conception and practice of international law. We can

---

tion. Richard A. Falk defines the international legal order "as an aggregate conception embodying those structures and processes by which authority is created, applied, and transformed in international society." I accept this definition. However, the term is used in a more restrictive sense in this chapter in order to focus on Chinese participation in the international legal processes within the institutional framework of the United Nations system. Hence, no reference is made to China's bilateral treaty practice. See Richard A. Falk, "The Interplay of Westphalia and Charter Conception of International Legal Order," in Falk and Black, *Trends and Patterns*, p. 33.

[2] Douglas M. Johnston and Hungdah Chiu, *Agreements of the People's Republic of China 1949-1967: A Calendar* (Cambridge, Mass.: Harvard University Press, 1968), p. xi.

hardly deny that Soviet jurists exerted a strong influence upon the development of Chinese jurisprudence in the 1950s, yet the deepening Sino-Soviet conflict in the late 1950s and 1960s also brought about a sharp attack on Soviet "revisionist" thinking.[3] Is it possible that the Sino-Soviet conflict may have imposed a heavy conceptual and ideological constraint upon Chinese jurisprudence in the 1960s and that the virtual demise of Chinese scholarly discussions of international law from the mid-1960s on cannot be attributed solely to the Cultural Revolution? Perhaps the problem of maintaining a measure of consistency in the Chinese principled stand was resolved by default— that is, by silence.

With these caveats in mind, we can suggest some salient characteristics of the evolving Chinese attitude toward the Charter conception of international legal order. The PRC's writers have rejected the feasibility and desirability of separating law from politics. In their view, law as "the superstructure of a particular economic base" is an instrument at the command of politics in both bourgeois and socialist states.[4] This is certainly a defensible proposition in terms of actual state practice, but it has presented two conceptual problems to Chinese writers. On the one hand, it injected an element of extreme caution and timidity into their writings as they struggled to expound the "correct" line. On the other hand, it led them to equate uncritically the interpretations of selected American legal scholars with the policy of the US government.[5]

The highly politicized nature of jurisprudence in China has led Chinese publicists to take a political approach to the UN Charter. Alternatively, this approach may be characterized as "selective legal-

[3] A trenchant critique of the Soviet concept on the role of international law was made by Wu Te-feng in his capacity as president of the Chinese Political Science and Law Association at its fourth general meeting on October 8, 1964. See "The Chinese Political Science and Law Association Held Its Fourth General Meeting," *CFYC*, No. 4 (November 1964), 28.

[4] See Chiang Yang, "The Reactionary Thought of 'Universalism' in American Jurisprudence," *JMJP*, December 17, 1963, p. 5; Chou Hsin-min, "Law is a Sharp Weapon of Class Struggle," *JMJP*, October 28, 1964, p. 5. To cite another example, Ch'en T'i-ch'iang, one of the most prominent Chinese scholars on international law, who headed the Division of International Law of the Institute of International Relations of the Chinese Academy of Sciences before he was purged in 1958, was attacked for having failed to grasp the fundamental fact that international law was a legal instrument in the service of Chinese foreign policy.

[5] Interestingly, the *American Journal of International Law, A Modern Law of Nations* by Philip Jessup, and the Hague Academy's *Recueil des Cours* are three widely used sources (not a single reference is made to the *State Department Bulletin*) in the "famous" book, *Hsien-tai ying-mei kuo-chi-fa te ssu-hsiang tung-hsiang* [Trends in Modern Anglo-American Thought on International Law] (Peking: Shih-chieh chih-shih ch'u-pan she, 1963), by Chou Keng-sheng, who may be regarded as the dean of Chinese jurists in the 1950s and 1960s.

ism." Within the framework of selective legalism, however, the Chinese conception of the Charter-based international legal order has evolved through three discernible stages during the preentry period: the first stage (1945-58) was marked by a strong interest in the United Nations and firm support of the Charter; the second stage (1958-64) witnessed a gradual "hardening" of the Chinese conceptualization of international legal order; and the third stage (1965-69) set in motion a process of negative polemics against the United Nations followed by a total lack of interest.

During the first stage, the PRC's support of the principles of the Charter was firm and strong. It also adopted a "soft" interpretation of the Charter-based international legal order. On the tenth anniversary of the United Nations, Tung Pi-wu, who was the CCP representative on the Chinese delegation to the San Francisco Conference and who later became president of the Supreme People's Court and afterward acting chairman of the PRC, declared the official policy: "The peace policy of the People's Republic of China is fixed and firm. Our support for the purposes and principles of the Charter of the United Nations is consistent. On this occasion, when the tenth anniversary of the adoption of the Charter is being commemorated, we state once again that the United Nations should become an effective international organization and play its proper part in maintaining international peace and security."[6] This official stand was also echoed in the writings of Chinese jurists during the first stage. "The Charter itself is beyond criticism," declared Ch'en T'i-ch'iang, a leading Chinese authority on international law.[7] Likewise, Wan Chia-chün argued in a book published in 1957 that the Charter itself contained many "democratic principles, reflecting the will of the people of the world."[8] Another jurist went so far as to say that the enactment of the UN Charter "symbolized the inception of modern international law."[9]

More revealingly, an anthology of documentary reference materials on public international law edited by the Institute of Diplomacy in

[6] Tung Pi-wu, "The Tenth Anniversary of the United Nations," PC, No. 14 (July 16, 1955), in Cohen and Chiu, People's China and International Law, Vol. II, p. 1294.

[7] "Uphold the United Nations Charter, Says Jurist," NCNA-English, Peking, December 2, 1955, in SCMP, No. 1183 (December 7, 1955), 6.

[8] Wan Chia-chün, Shen-ma shih lien-ho-kuo [What is the United Nations?] (Peking: T'ung-su tu-wu ch'u-pan she, 1957), p. 42.

[9] Chou Fu-lun, "On the Nature of Modern International Law—A Rejoinder to Comrade Lin Hsin," Chiao-hsüeh yü yen-chiu [Teaching and Research], No. 3 (March, 1958), 52-56; trans. in Chinese Law and Government 3 (Spring 1970), 12. Likewise, Ch'iu Jih-chin of Fu-tan University regarded the United Nations Charter as the foundation of general international law. See "Further Discussion on the System of International Law at the Present Stage," Fa-hsüeh (Legal Studies), No. 3 (March 1958), 41.

Peking in 1958 listed under the heading of sources of international law the following: (1) Article 38 of the Statute of the International Court of Justice (ICJ); (2) General Assembly Resolution on Progressive Development of International Law and Its Codification of 11 December 1946; and (3) General Assembly Resolution on Affirmation of the Principles of International Law Recognized by the Charter of the Nuremberg Tribunal of 11 December 1946.[10] In addition, reference to the Charter was repeatedly made in the PRC's bilateral treaties in the 1950s.

The PRC assumed the posture of a "strict constructionist" toward the Charter during the first stage, branding any proposals for Charter revision as imperialist plots to turn the United Nations into an instrument of aggression. China echoed the Soviet position by vigorously defending the principle of unanimity in the Security Council as a legal shield that protects not only the interests of big powers but also the sovereignty and interests of all other states as well.[11] Understandably, China's reaction was vehement against the Uniting for Peace Resolution, for it "legitimized" the UN police action in Korea. Moreover, it provided a procedural basis for the Assembly to adopt Resolution 498 (V) of 1 February 1951, which branded the PRC as having "itself engaged in aggression in Korea."

However, China did not reject General Assembly resolutions *in toto*. Her approach to the resolutions was highly selective, accepting certain resolutions as having evidentiary value for certain unspecified norms in international relations. General Assembly Resolution 626 (VII) of 16 December 1952, for example, dealing with permanent sovereignty over natural resources, had been invoked in support of the argument that a state enjoys the right under international law to nationalize its natural resources without incurring a legal obligation to compensate foreign investors.[12] In addition, several resolutions by the General Assembly during the 1956 Suez Crisis were characterized as exerting a profound and positive influence on the maintenance of international peace and security.[13] While China undoubtedly used political criteria in accepting or rejecting General Assembly resolutions,

[10] Hungdah Chiu, "Communist China's Attitude Toward International Law," *AJIL* 60 (April 1966), 259, n.55; Hsiung, *Law and Policy in China's Foreign Relations*, p. 22.

[11] Kuo Ch'ün, *Lien-ho-kuo*, p. 101.

[12] Li Hao-p'ei, "Nationalization and International Law," *CFYC*, No. 2 (April 1958), 14.

[13] Wan Chia-chün, *Shen-ma shih lien-ho-kuo*, p. 41. Likewise, *Jen-min jih-pao* gave editorial support by declaring that "this is the first time that the United Nations had adopted resolutions against aggression in conformity with the Charter." See *SCMP*, No. 1412 (November 16, 1956), 22.

the Charter and international law were invoked as the authoritative references for legitimizing her legal arguments.

Possibly as a result of the crushed hopes and rising frustrations that attended her soft-line approach to gaining a seat and legitimacy in the world organization, the Chinese image of the Charter-based international legal order hardened during the second stage. The Chinese began to take a "conservative" position, emphasizing what Richard A. Falk has called "the Westphalia conception of international legal order." This stressed the positivist notion of vesting national sovereignty with the highest authority in matters of international law, and held that the state could be legally bound only to the extent it had given its consent.[14] The Charter as a product of compromise between the realistic politicians and the visionary statesmen at the San Francisco Conference both reflects and transcends the Westphalia conception of international legal order. The principles of national equality and national sovereignty are the salient examples of dualism in the Charter.

Indeed, the thread that conceptually and analytically tied together virtually all Chinese writings on the Charter-based international legal order was the traditional positivist notion of sovereignty. For centuries, Chou Keng-sheng argued in 1963, sovereignty (chu-ch'üan) had always been and still was the most basic principle of international law and the most valuable characteristic of the state. There could not be any power superior to the sovereign state. Any attempts to subvert, dilute, or transform sovereignty through such devices as "world law" (shih-chieh-fa) or "transnational law" (ch'ao-kuo-chia-fa) were contrary to international law. The problem of modern states, Chou further argued, was how to maintain, not to relinquish or diminish, sovereignty.[15]

Other Chinese publicists all echoed Chou Keng-sheng's thesis during the second stage by declaring that the "universalism" theory in American jurisprudence was nothing less than a conspiratorial scheme to transform international law and the UN Charter into a "world legal order," "world government" or "world state" under the domination of the United States.[16] In addition, Chinese publicists denied a legal personality to the United Nations by attacking the notion that international organizations—the United Nations and its specialized agencies —could also become subjects of international law. Likewise, the

[14] Falk, "The Interplay of Westphalia and Charter Conceptions of International Legal Order," p. 43.

[15] Chou Keng-sheng, Hsin-tai ying-mei, pp. 65-66.

[16] See Chiang Yang, "The Reactionary Thought . . ."; Lu Shih-lin, "The Modern School of Natural Law Serves Imperialism," JMJP, June 29, 1963, p. 5; K'ung Meng, "A Criticism of the Theories of Bourgeois International Law Concerning the Subjects of International Law and Recognition of States," Kuo-chi wen-t'i yen-chiu [Research on International Problems], No. 2 (February 1960); trans. in Cohen and Chiu, People's China and International Law, Vol. I, pp. 88-99.

Chinese rejected the theory that individuals, too, could become subjects of international law. All of these theories were accused of having the effect of denying or devaluating the supremacy of state sovereignty. Any attempts to expand the functions of certain organs, such as the ICJ, were also branded as a plot to transform the United Nations into a *de facto* supranational organization above sovereign states.[17]

This was indeed a bizarre argument born of scholarly ignorance and ideological zeal. Actually, the logical target of their attack would have been Grenville Clark and Louis B. Sohn, the first edition of whose book, *World Peace Through World Law*, was already available in 1958. Yet none of the PRC publicists, including Chou Keng-sheng, made a single reference to the book or its authors,[18] while they erroneously characterized American jurisprudence and government as being dominated by this "reactionary" idea of "universalism." However, one point emerged with crystal clarity: the distinction between *international* legal order and *world* legal order. The former was based on the Charter principles of national sovereignty and equality, while the latter was an imperialist conspiracy to remake the Charter into an instrument of a world state under American domination.

In short, the Chinese image of the Charter-based international legal order denied any supranational character to the United Nations. Instead, the United Nations was conceptualized as one form of international organization among sovereign states, not a "world government" (*shih-chieh cheng-fu*) above them. Consistent with this image, China singled out for criticism the authorizing resolution for UNEF I, while applauding the remaining resolutions adopted by the emergency session of the General Assembly during the 1956 Suez Crisis. The UNEF resolution was *ultra vires*, an act in violation of the Charter because Article 24 of the Charter assigned to the Security Council the primary responsibility for the maintenance of international peace and security.[19]

In a similar vein, the PRC commentators have time and again insisted that the United Nations, in exercising its role in the maintenance of international peace and security, should not intervene in the internal affairs of states in violation of Article 2, paragraph 7 of the Charter. Specifically, the PRC has condemned the UN "interventions" in Korea, Hungary, the Congo (ONUC), Cyprus (UNFICYP), Vietnam, Tibet, Hong Kong, and Macao as contraventions of Charter principles.

[17] *Ibid.*, p. 95.
[18] In the preface to his book, Chou Keng-sheng makes the revealing admission that he did not have the complete works of the Anglo-American jurists in their original Western-language texts, and that some of the materials had been taken only from book reviews in professional journals.
[19] Sun Nan, "What is the United Nations Emergency Force?" *SCCS*, No. 24 (December 20, 1956), 22.

The Chinese view on the legal force of UN resolutions also sharpened during the second stage. These resolutions—with the exception of the decisions of the Security Council to maintain international peace and security, taken under Chapter VII of the Charter—are in the nature of recommendations and hence cannot bind the Member States. The United Nations was thus denied the possession of any legislative power; even legal drafts prepared by the International Law Commission and adopted by the General Assembly had to go through the treaty-making process before they could acquire legally binding force.[20] Perhaps reflecting this hard-line approach to the Charter-based international legal order, references to the Charter began to disappear also from the PRC's bilateral agreements in the 1960s.

In order to change the legal character of the United Nations as an international organization among sovereign states, the Chinese argued, the Charter would first have to be drastically revised. But the possibility of a revision along these lines was slim because of the veto obstacle (presumably referring to the Soviet veto). Hence, the American imperialists were busily engaged in the illegal process of transforming the United Nations into a supranational organization through interpretation. Yet Peking's own position on the Charter revision question, even on an issue it wholeheartedly supported, was curiously ambiguous. In rebutting the Soviet claim that the Charter could not be revised to accommodate the increasing pressure of Afro-Asian members for a more equitable distribution of seats in UN organs—the Security Council and ECOSOC, in particular—until the restoration of China's legitimate representation in the Organization, the Ministry of Foreign Affairs stated in 1963:

> There may be two ways to increase the seats for the Asian-African countries in the principal organs of the United Nations. One is to revise the related articles of the UN Charter, but this method involves very complicated questions and procedures. Another is to leave the Charter as it is for the time being, that is, while not altering the total number of seats as stipulated in the Charter, to make reasonable readjustment in the distribution of seats after consultation among the various parties concerned, so that at least half of the seats may go to Asian-African countries. This method is simpler and easier to carry out in the present circumstances.[21]

Consistent with the sovereignty-centered image of the international legal order, the ICJ was criticized in the *Corfu Channel* and *Anglo-*

---

[20] Chou Keng-sheng, *Hsien-tai ying-mei*, p. 67.
[21] "China Favors Increased Afro-Asian Representation in Principal UN Organs," *PR*, No. 51 (December 20, 1963), 21.

Iranian Oil Co. cases for having served the interests of the imperialists.[22] In addition, the Chinese were hypercritical of any suggestions smacking of an expansion or even a liberal interpretation of the functions of the ICJ. Since it was impossible now to impose compulsory jurisdiction by revising the Statute of the ICJ, wrote Chou Keng-sheng in 1963, the dominant theme in Anglo-American thought about international law was the maximization of the optional clause so as to promote wide acceptance of "voluntary compulsory jurisdiction." However, the principal aim was no less than the establishment of a so-called "world rule of law."[23] Likewise, K'ung Meng characterized any attempt to expand the function of the ICJ as a conspiracy to transform the United Nations into a supranational organization.[24]

In line with this image, China opposed any reference of her disputes with other countries to adjudication or third-party settlement. During the 1962 Sino-Indian border conflict, for example, China categorically rejected Nehru's suggestions of referring the dispute to an international tribunal. In a note to India, the Chinese Ministry of Foreign Affairs stated, *inter alia*:

> It goes without saying that this issue can be settled only through direct negotiations between the two parties, and absolutely not through any form of international arbitration. . . . The Indian government was clearly aware that the Chinese government could not agree to referring the Sino-Indian boundary question to international arbitration and that the International Court of Justice at the Hague is an organ of the United Nations, among whose judges there is an element of the Chiang Kai-shek clique; nonetheless it continues to propose to refer the Sino-Indian boundary dispute to the International Court or other organs of international arbitration.[25]

The Indonesian withdrawal from the United Nations on January 7, 1965, ushered in the third stage in the evolution of the Chinese image of the Charter-based international legal order. As already reviewed in Chapter 3, China launched negative polemics against the United Nations, presenting a comprehensive bill of complaints and new demands. Clearly, her cherished hopes for, and abiding interest in, the United Nations virtually disappeared during this stage, as revealed in Foreign

[22] Hsiung, *Law and Policy in China's Foreign Relations,* p. 310.
[23] Chou Keng-sheng, *Hsien-tai ying-mei,* p. 53.
[24] K'ung Meng, "A Criticism of the Theories of Bourgeois International Law Concerning the Subjects of International Law and Recognition of States," p. 95.
[25] "Text of Chinese Foreign Ministry Note to India" (October 9, 1963), NCNA-English, Peking (October 12, 1963), in *SCMP,* No. 3081 (October 16, 1963), in Cohen and Chiu, *People's China and International Law,* Vol. II, pp. 1441-42.

Minister Ch'en Yi's statement made at the September 29, 1965, press conference: "During the U.S. war of aggression against Korea, the United Nations adopted a resolution naming China as an aggressor. How can China be expected to take part in an international organization which calls her an aggressor? Calling China an aggressor and then asking the aggressor to join would not the United Nations be slapping its own face?"[26]

The foregoing review of the evolving Chinese image affords a few generalizations. In the first stage it was prematurely optimistic, naive, and underdeveloped. By the third stage it had swung to the other extreme, becoming no more than a polemical exercise. As Table 3.1 showed, Chinese commentaries on the United Nations system gradually ceased during this stage. It is the second stage that probably represents the most settled view of the Charter-based international legal order. There was no more of the 1957-58 theoretical debate as to how many systems of public international law really existed in the international system. By 1962, Chinese jurists seemed to have accepted the notion of a general international law that "stood over and above, as well as distinct from, the bourgeois body of law and contained more 'progressive' elements."[27]

The most salient feature of the Chinese image is the concept of state sovereignty and equality. There is no evidence that the traditional Chinese image of world order as expressed in the tribute system exerted any discernible influence in the development of the PRC's image of international legal order. However, historical grievances against the hierarchical order of Western and Japanese imperialism as institutionalized in unequal treaties seem to have exerted a powerful influence. The "protective" thinking enveloped in the Chinese obsession with sovereignty reflects a measure of the immense weight of past grievances.[28]

Just as Maoist nationalism lacked chauvinism, however, the Chinese concept of state sovereignty was devoid of an absolute or expansionist imperative. Sovereignty became for the Chinese a legal shield to protect themselves—and other underdogs as well—from actual or imaginary imperialists. Viewed in this perspective, sovereignty was defen-

[26] PR, No. 41 (October 8, 1965), 11-12.
[27] James C. Hsiung, review of People's China and International Law: A Documentary Study, by Jerome A. Cohen and Hungdah Chiu, in Harvard International Law Journal 16 (Winter 1975), 178. Chou Keng-sheng's book tends to substantiate Hsiung's interpretation.
[28] For a sensitive analysis of Nationalist and Communist Chinese views of unequal treaties, see Hungdah Chiu, "Comparison of the Nationalist and Communist Chinese Views of Unequal Treaties," in Cohen, China's Practice of International Law, pp. 239-67.

sive rather than offensive, and a protective rather than an imperialist instrument in the service of Chinese national interests.

The Chinese image of international legal order during the preentry period rejected the two extremes of the principle of state sovereignty—the theory of limited sovereignty and the theory of absolute sovereignty. As the Chinese saw it, one was the logical corollary of the other. That is, an exercise of absolute sovereignty by one nation was bound to undermine the sovereignty of another nation. The Soviet invasion of Czechoslovakia was a case in point, as the exercise of absolute sovereignty by the former inevitably resulted in limiting the sovereignty of the latter.[29] Hence, China advocated the principle of mutual respect for national sovereignty as the only correct interpretation of the sovereignty issue in modern international law.[30] In short, her advocacy was both self-serving and self-limiting.

THE NATURE AND SCOPE OF CHINESE LEGAL PRACTICE

The Chinese conception of the Charter-based international legal order which evolved during the period of exclusion was largely hypothetical. China was denied an opportunity to make her views known. Although the impact of this exclusion is difficult to quantify, it would be foolhardy to deny or to minimize its conceptual and psychological effects.[31] Once she was in the world community, would she confirm, revise, or repudiate her conception of the Charter-based international legal order? In order to give an analytical focus to this question, we may first describe the nature and scope of the PRC's "legal resources," then define the types of legal organs and activities in which China has refused to participate, and finally analyze Chinese legal practice in those subjects and organs in which she has participated.

[29] See Chi Hsiang-yang, "Smash the New Tsars' Theory of 'Limited Sovereignty'," HC, No. 5 (1969), 87-90.

[30] For an elaboration of this theme, see Yang Hsin and Ch'en Chien, "Expose and Criticize the Fallacious Reasoning of Imperialists on National Sovereignty Questions," CFYC, No. 4 (November 1964), 6-11. James C. Hsiung concludes in his well-documented and carefully reasoned study on the PRC's practice of international law: "[I]nternational law does seem to have exercised a *restraining* effect on the Chinese Communist decision-makers in foreign policy. Although she charged invasions of her sovereignty by Indian reconnaissance planes which flew well into Chinese airspace, the CPR [People's Republic of China] is not known to have sent reconnaissance planes over the territory of any other country, not even during her disputes with India." *Law and Policy in China's Foreign Relations*, pp. 317-38; emphasis in original.

[31] In part, the PRC's exclusion from the international legal community was self-imposed. In 1960 the Chinese Political Science and Law Association withdrew itself from the International Law Association in protest against the admission of the ROC. See PR, No. 32 (August 9, 1960), 24-25.

Quite tellingly, there is no evidence that the PRC's participation in the United Nations system has rejuvenated the study of international law in China or restored it to the position that it enjoyed in the 1950s. Chou Keng-sheng is now dead; Ch'en T'i-ch'iang remains purged, to the best of the author's knowledge; none of the semischolarly journals earlier referred to has resumed publication. The Chinese privately admitted to an official in the Office of Legal Affairs of the UN Secretariat that they did not have a single legal expert in their Permanent Mission to the United Nations in New York City.

Furthermore, the Ministry of Foreign Affairs in Peking does not have a functional department devoted exclusively to legal affairs. Strangely, two departments in the ministry were merged in 1972 into a single department with the ponderous title, "Department of International Organizations, Conferences, Treaties and Laws" or "Department of International Organizations, Law and Treaty."[32] Since An Chih-yüan was transferred to head the PRC Permanent Mission in Geneva on October 28, 1975, the department has been headed by two deputy-directors, Chi Chao-chu and Pi Chi-lung, as the government failed to appoint a new director.[33]

Pi Chi-lung has been the most active "legal worker" in Chinese multilateral diplomacy. He was a member of the Chinese delegation to the 27th and 30th Sessions of the General Assembly, taking part on each occasion in the deliberations of the Sixth Committee. He headed the Chinese delegation to the 1st Session (1974) of the Diplomatic Conference on the Reaffirmation and Development of International Humanitarian Law Applicable in Armed Conflicts. He headed the Chinese delegation to the 3rd Session of the Third United Nations Conference on the Law of the Sea in 1975. It may also be recalled that he headed the 8-member delegation to the Working Group on a Draft

[32] There is a confusing array of titles for this department. Donald Klein uses the term, "International Organizations and Conferences and Treaty and Law Department," while Wolfgang Bartke speaks of "International Organizations and Conferences, Treaties and Laws." The Chinese themselves have been inconsistent in identification (or translation) of the term for this department. In all the English translations of the list of delegates to the General Assembly or other international conferences, the department has been identified as "Department of International Organizations, Law and Treaty" or "Department of International Organizations, Law and Treaties," but in the French translation the department is referred to as "Département des organisations internationales et des traités et lois internationaux." See the following: Klein, "The Chinese Foreign Ministry," p. 174; Wolfgang Bartke, *The Diplomatic Service of the People's Republic of China as of January 1976 (including Biographies)* (Hamburg: Institut für Asienkunde, 1976), p. 7; UN Docs. A/CONF.62/INF.3/Rev.2 (16 January 1975), p. 12; A/CONF. 62/INF.4/Rev.1 (17 September 1975), p. 12; *Delegations to the General Assembly* 27th Sess. (November 1972), UN Doc. ST/SG/SER.B/26/Rev.1, pp. 39-42.

[33] For an analysis of geographical and functional departments in the Chinese Ministry of Foreign Affairs, see Klein, "The Chinese Foreign Ministry," chap. 4.

Charter of Economic Rights and Duties of States in Geneva, as well as taking an active part in the behind-the-scenes negotiations with the official missions of the specialized agencies we reviewed in Chapter 7.

One of the salient characteristics of Chinese participation in the United Nations system is a self-conscious avoidance of, and nonparticipation in, any organs and activities of a purely legal character. Although most issues in the United Nations have varying degrees of legal implications, international law issues defined in a traditional sense have not attracted Chinese interest or involvement. Of all the Main Committees of the General Assembly, for example, Chinese participation has been the lowest in the Sixth Committee, as shown in Table 3.3. The only subjects that invited a Chinese response in the Sixth Committee have been such highly politicized legal issues as the definition of aggression, the question of Charter review, and international terrorism.

China's indifference toward the international judicial process was highlighted by her posture toward the ICJ, the principal judicial organ of the United Nations. The ICJ was one of the few limited-membership organs in the entire United Nations system where the ROC managed to keep her nationals during most of her UN tenure. Hsu Mo (1946-57) and V. K. Wellington Koo (1957-69) represented "China" on the Court. Since her entry into the United Nations, the PRC has been presented with two opportunities to come forward with a candidate (in 1972 and 1975), when the General Assembly and the Security Council had to elect five judges for a nine-year term. On each occasion, China failed to advance a candidate, even though her nominee would easily have won, given the well-established practice of electing nationals of the Big Five to the Court. In the face of repeatedly friendly inquiries from the Office of Legal Affairs of the UN Secretariat on the submission of candidates for the World Court and the International Law Commission, the Chinese have been polite but deliberately ambiguous and noncommittal in their reply: "We are not ready yet."

In view of the absence of international law as an independent academic discipline in China today, it is doubtful that China can be, or even wants to be, ready for membership in the ICJ in the foreseeable future. It may not be an exaggeration to say that international law constitutes one of the most primitive academic disciplines in Chinese higher education.[34] Even if China should decide to claim her "legitimate" privilege to have a national on the Court, she might not wish to place herself in the embarrassing situation of having her candidate

[34] For discussions of the status and development of international law in China, see Chiu "Communist China's Attitude Toward International Law," pp. 263-66; and Suzanne Ogden, "China and International Law: Implications for Foreign Policy," *Pacific Affairs* 49 (Spring 1976), 28-31.

unfavorably evaluated against the candidates of other countries—let alone against such a prominent jurist as V. K. Wellington Koo of the ROC—for the highest position in the international legal profession. As already seen in Chapter 3, it is not the Chinese diplomatic style to advance a Trojan Horse on a disruptive political or ideological mission.

Unwillingly or not, China as a member of the United Nations *ipso facto* became a party to the Statute of the ICJ, but had the option, according to Article 36, paragraph 2, of the Statute, of accepting or rejecting its compulsory jurisdiction. Not surprisingly, the PRC made it known in a letter to the ICJ dated September 5, 1972, that she "does not recognize the statement made by the defunct Chinese Government on 26 October 1946 . . . concerning the acceptance of the compulsory jurisdiction of the Court."[35] As will be discussed later in the chapter, China also opposed the inclusion of provisions concerning the compulsory jurisdiction of an international judicial organ in a prospective international convention on the law of the sea at the Third United Nations Conference on the Law of the Sea.

It must be added that China is not alone in her indifference toward the ICJ or in her rejection of its compulsory jurisdiction. The extent to which its work has languished may be seen in the brevity of its annual reports. The 1971-72 annual report amounted to only four and a half printed pages. For the period August 1, 1974-July 31, 1976, it had so few activities to report that it combined two years' work into one "biennial" report that was no more than three printed pages long. While the 144 Member States of the United Nations, together with Liechtenstein, San Marino, and Switzerland, were parties to the Statute as of July 31, 1976, only 45 of them recognized—many of them with serious reservations—the jurisdiction of the ICJ as compulsory. More significantly, however, the following Member States terminated, abrogated, or refused to renew their former declarations of acceptance of the compulsory jurisdiction during the period August 1, 1971-July 31, 1976: the Philippines (January 18, 1972); Turkey (May 23, 1972); France (January 2, 1974); India (September 18, 1974); and Australia (March 17, 1975).[36]

Likewise, China has shown no interest in having a national on the 25-member International Law Commission or the 36-member UN Commission on International Trade Law.[37] On numerous occasions, Chinese

---

[35] *Report of the International Court of Justice, 1 August 1972-31 July 1973*, GAOR, 28th Sess., Supp. No. 5 (A/9005), p. 1.

[36] See the following: *Report of the International Court of Justice 1 August 1971-31 July 1972*, GAOR, 27th Sess., Supp. No. 5 (A/8705), p. 1; *Report of the International Court of Justice 1 August 1973-31 July 1974*, GAOR, 29th Sess., Supp. No. 5 (A/9605), p. 2; and *Report of the International Court of Justice 1 August 1974-31 July 1976*, GAOR, 31st Sess., Supp. No. 5 (A/31/5), p. 1.

[37] The UN Secretariat announced on November 9, 1971, that Chi P'eng-fei,

delegates stated privately and publicly that they were newcomers and had to acquaint themselves with the background of each legal issue under discussion before they could take a firm stand or an active part in its discussion. Chinese representative Ch'en Ch'u stated at the October 20, 1972, meeting of the First Committee of the General Assembly, for example: "The People's Republic of China did not participate in the Committee on the Peaceful Uses of Outer Space, and it still has to acquaint itself with and study the information and issues relevant to the peaceful uses of outer space. The Chinese Government reserves its right to make comments, and take action on related matters in the future."[38] Four years later, this still represented the Chinese approach to the question of outer space, as well as to most other legal issues— neither outright support nor opposition but a carefully designed diplomatic posture calculated to underplay indifference to, even possibly contempt for, many purely legal issues in the United Nations.

Given this lack of interest and of qualified legal personnel, it is not surprising that China failed to attend many of the UN meetings and conferences on questions of international law. The five major UN conferences on international law to which China did not send a delegation are worth listing:

The United Nations Conference on Prescription (Limitation) in the international Sale of Goods (UN headquarters, May 20, 1974-June 14, 1974)

The United Nations Conference on the Representation of States in Their Relations with International Organizations (Vienna, February 4, 1975-March 14, 1975)

The United Nations Conference of Plenipotentiaries on Territorial Asylum (Geneva, January 10, 1977-February 4, 1977)

The United Nations Conference on Succession of States in Respect of Treaties (Vienna, April 4, 1977-May 6, 1977)

The Diplomatic Conference on the Reaffirmation and Development of International Humanitarian Law Applicable in Armed Conflicts (Geneva, the 2nd Session, February 3-April 18, 1975; the 3rd Session, April 21-June 11, 1976; and the 4th [Concluding] Session, March 17-June 10, 1977)[39]

China's acting foreign minister, had informed Secretary-General U Thant by cablegram that China would not nominate candidates for membership in the International Law Commission at the present session of the General Assembly. See *NYT*, November 10, 1971, p. 16.

[38] GAOR, 27th Sess., First Committee, 1871st meeting (20 October 1972), para. 14.

[39] It is worth noting here that China sent her delegation to the 1st Session (1974) of the Diplomatic Conference on the Reaffirmation and Development of

China's practice in the acceptance of UN multilateral treaties is highly eclectic and deliberately ambiguous. As of December 31, 1976, there were 197 multilateral treaties conceived under UN auspices, yet China ratified or acceded to only 7, as shown in Table 8.1. The table may beg more questions than it answers, because it includes the UN Charter, the Statute of the ICJ (which is an integral part of the Charter), and the amendments to the UN Charter. China as a member of the United Nations is *ipso facto* bound by any amendments that have come into force.[40] However, a problem arises because of a discrepancy between China's declaration on UN multilateral treaties and the UN practice that has developed regarding the succession of states in relation to multilateral treaties in respect of which the Secretary-General performs depositary functions.

According to established UN practice, "States which recognize that they continue to be bound by a treaty made applicable to their territory by their predecessors address a formal notification to that effect to the Secretary-General, who, in the exercise of his depositary functions, informs all interested States accordingly."[41] In addition, a state making such a notification is deemed to become a party in its own right to the treaty in question from the date of its independence. Since the PRC has consistently claimed that the issue of China in the United Nations was one of procedure, not of substance—which, translated, means that the issue was one of representation, not of admission—we may assume that all the rights and obligations of the predecessor government devolved upon the government of the PRC based on the theory of state continuity. However, in a communication received by the Secretary-General on September 29, 1972, the PRC's minister of foreign affairs stated:

1. With regard to the multilateral treaties signed, ratified or acceded to by the defunct Chinese government before the establish-

---

International Humanitarian Law Applicable in Armed Conflicts but failed to do so for the three succeeding sessions. Apparently, China also sent an official explanation or pretext for her failure to attend the 2nd through the 4th (final) sessions, for the UN document of the 2nd Session of the Diplomatic Conference noted in a footnote: "The Government of China did not attend the second session of the Diplomatic Conference and had stated that it regretted having to take that decision, *the reason for which was the volume of the other internation conferences.*" UN Doc. A/10195 (5 September 1975), p. 10; emphasis added. See also UN Docs. A/9669 (12 September 1974); A/9669/Add.1 (19 November 1974); A/31/163 (18 August 1976); A/31/163/Add.1 (24 September 1976); A/32/144 (15 August 1977); and A/32/144/Add.1 (26 September 1977).

[40] Article 108 of the UN Charter.

[41] *Multilateral Treaties in Respect of Which the Secretary-General Performs Depositary Functions: List of Signatures, Ratifications, Accessions, etc. as at 31 December 1976,* UN Doc. ST/LEG/SER.D/10 (Sales No. E.77, V.7) (New York: United Nations, 1977, hereafter cited as *Multilateral Treaties*), p. xviii.

TABLE 8.1. The PRC's Recognition, Accession to, or Ratification of United Nations Multilateral Treaties in Respect of Which the Secretary-General Performs Depositary Functions (as of December 31, 1976)[a]

Subject	Date of Signature	Date of Entry into Force	Date of PRC's Action
Charter of the United Nations	6/26/45	10/24/45	9/28/45[b]
Statute of the International Court of Justice	6/26/45	10/24/45	9/28/45[b]
Amendments to Articles 23, 27 and 61 of the UN Charter	12/17/63	8/31/65	8/2/65[c]
Amendment to Article 109 of the UN Charter	12/20/65	6/12/68	7/8/66[c]
Amendment to Article 61 of the the UN Charter	12/20/71	9/24/73	9/15/72[d]
Vienna Convention on Diplomatic Relations	4/18/61	4/24/64	11/25/75[d]
Amendments to Articles 24 and 25 of the WHO Constitution	5/23/67	5/21/75	1/14/74[d]
Amendments to Articles 34 and 35 of the WHO Constitution	5/22/73	Not Yet	3/5/76[d]
IMCO Convention	3/6/48	3/17/58	3/1/73[d]
Amendments to Articles 10, 16, 17, 18, 20, 28, 31, and 32 of the IMCO Convention	10/17/74	Not Yet	4/28/75[d]
Constitution of the Asia-Pacific Telecommunity	3/27/76	Not Yet	10/25/76[d]

[a] This table covers only those multilateral treaties which have been concluded under the auspices of the United Nations or its specialized agencies and the originals of which have been deposited with the Secretary-General. It does not therefore include the conventions of such specialized agencies as ICAO, UPU, ITU, etc.
[b] Presumably recognized but without public or official declaration to that effect.
[c] Presumably acceded to but without public or official declaration to that effect.
[d] Ratified or acceded to.
Source: Adapted from Multilateral Treaties in Respect of Which the Secretary-General Performs Depositary Functions: List of Signatures, Ratifications, Accessions, etc. as at 31 December 1976, ST/LEG/SER. D/10 (Sales No. E77.V.7), (New York: United Nations, 1977).

ment of the Government of the People's Republic of China, my Government will examine their contents before making a decision in the light of the circumstances as to whether or not they should be *recognized*.

2. As from October 1, 1949, the day of the founding of the People's Republic of China, the Chiang Kai-shek clique has no right at all to

represent China. Its signature and ratification of, or accession to, any multilateral treaties by usurping the name of "China" are all illegal and null and void. My Government will study these multilateral treaties before making a decision in the light of the circumstances as to whether or not they should be *acceded* to.[42]

The United Nations has simply decided to quote the PRC's declaratory statement in an explanatory preface, "Note concerning signatures, ratifications, accessions, etc., on behalf of China," along with General Assembly Resolution 2758 (XXVI) of 25 October 1971, in its annual publication, *Multilateral Treaties in Respect of Which the Secretary-General Performs Depositary Functions*, while at the same time recording all entries in respect of China throughout the publication in terms of "actions taken by the authorities representing China in the United Nations at the time of those actions." In other words, all the signatures, ratifications, or accessions by the ROC during the period October 1, 1949-October 25, 1971, except those which have been superseded by the PRC's accessions or ratifications, have been recorded in the annual *Multilateral Treaties* publication.

The PRC's own practice in carrying out her declaratory statement is also ambiguous. How should we interpret her reticence or lack of notification to the Secretary-General? We may safely assume that the PRC did not send official notifications of recognition or accession regarding the Charter, the Statute, and the amendments to the Charter because it was superfluous to do so, in spite of the implication in the communication of the foreign minister that nothing should be taken for granted without a specific decision by his government. What about all other UN multilateral treaties which the ROC had signed or ratified and which are still being recorded in the annual treaty publication? As of now, the PRC has not lodged any protest to the Office of Legal Affairs over such UN practice. Apparently, she is content with the explanatory preface and all the footnotes throughout the publication referring to that preface.

The PRC's position on the question of the succession of states in respect of treaties has remained a mystery, as she has said virtually nothing on this subject. The only Chinese words on the matter that the author was able to locate through perusal of the official records of all the UN organs and agencies was a brief statement by a Chinese delegate in the Sixth Committee of the General Assembly on October 9, 1972: "The question of succession of States in respect of treaties was complicated and required serious study. [The] Government should be given sufficient time to study it."[43] Surely, China had had sufficient

[42] *Ibid.*, pp. iii-iv; emphasis added.
[43] GAOR, 27th Sess., Sixth Committee, 1327th meeting (9 October 1972), para. 42.

time to study this question by April 1977, when the United Nations Conference on Succession of States in Respect of Treaties was convened in Vienna. Yet China failed to send a delegation to this important conference, which would have given her an opportunity to clarify her position on international law.[44]

Although Table 8.1 does not include the conventions, protocols, and constitutions of most of the specialized agencies and such other important multilateral conventions as the Geneva Protocol of 1925 for the Prohibition of the Use in War of Asphyxiating, Poisonous or Other Gases, and of Bacteriological Methods of Warfare and the Geneva Conventions of 1949 for the Protection of War Victims (consisting of four treaties relative to the Wounded and Sick, the Wounded, Sick and Shipwrecked at Sea, Prisoners of War, and Civilians), it does signify China's reluctance to be a party to multilateral agreements. Table 8.2, which is presented for the possible light it may shed on the diachronic change in the Chinese attitude toward multilateral treaties, shows that China's acceptance of 49 multilateral agreements in the table represents only 2.45 percent of some 2,000 agreements that she concluded between 1949 and 1967. Likewise, the 11 UN multilateral treaties in Table 8.1 represent only 5.6 percent of the 197 listed in the 1976 annual *Multilateral Treaties* publication. Both tables reveal China's minimal involvement.

The fact that the ROC had already signed and ratified many of the UN multilateral treaties, "usurping the name of China," seems to have been a hindering factor too. The PRC thus far has failed to decide whether she should accede to any of the ones that the ROC had already signed and ratified, with one important exception, the Vienna Convention on Diplomatic Relations of 1961, which the ROC had signed and ratified on April 18, 1961, and ratified on December 19, 1969, respectively, and which the PRC, to the surprise of many observers in the UN community, also accepted, depositing its instrument of accession on November 25, 1975. It is not clear whether the pressure of the General Assembly debate at its 30th Session and the ensuing resolution reaffirming the need for strict implementation by states of the provisions of the Vienna Convention exerted any influence on Peking's decision.[45] In acceding to it, however, the PRC attached reser-

[44] It should be noted in this connection that the International Law Commission at its 29th Session held in Geneva (from May 9 to July 29, 1977) adopted further draft articles and commentaries on three priority topics: (1) the responsibility of states for internationally wrongful acts; (2) succession of states in respect of matters other than treaties; and (3) treaties between states and international organizations or between two or more such organizations.

[45] General Assembly Resolution 3501 (XXX) of 15 December 1975, adopted without a vote. In its resolution 31/76 of 13 December 1976, the General Assembly noted that "since the adoption by the General Assembly of its resolution

TABLE 8.2. Multilateral Agreements (Four or More Parties)
Which the PRC Agreed to, Signed, Accepted,
or Recognized, 1949-67

12/5/50	"Acceptance" of 1947 Universal Postal Convention
7/13/52	"Recognition" of 1925 Protocol for Prohibition of Use in War of Asphyxiating, Poisonous, or Other Gases and of Bacteriological Methods of Warfare
7/13/52	"Recognition" of 1949 Convention for Amelioration of Condition of Wounded and Sick in Armed Forces in Field
7/13/52	"Recognition" of 1949 Convention for Amelioration of Condition of Wounded, Sick, and Shipwrecked Members of Armed Forces at Sea
7/13/52	"Recognition" of 1949 Convention relative to treatment of prisoners of war
7/13/52	"Recognition" of 1949 Convention relative to Protection of Civilian Persons in Time of War
7/31/53	Agreement: Railway (freight)
7/31/53	Agreement: Railway (passenger)
8/3/53	Agreement: Red Cross teams in Korea
10/2/53	Communiqué: Radio cooperation
1/1/54	Agreement: Railway
7/24/54	Final Declaration: Indo-China
4/24/55	Final Communiqué: Bandung Conference
3/26/56	Agreement: Nuclear research
6/12/56	Agreement: Fishery research, etc.
6/28/56	Regulations: Railway
9/23/56	Statute: Nuclear research
10/5/56	Agreement: Cooperation between institutes of agricultural research
10/31/56	Minutes: Conference on postal services, telecommunications, hydrography, and meteorology
6/7/57	Regulations: Railway
10/23/57	"Acceptance" of 1930 International Load Line Convention for Shipping
12/16/57	Agreement: Postal services and telecommunications
12/23/57	"Acceptance" of 1948 International Regulations for Preventing Collisions at Sea

TABLE 8.2. (*cont'd*)

3/24/58	Agreement: Scientific cooperation (specific project)
6/5/58	"Adherence" to 1929 Warsaw Convention for Unification of Certain Rules relating to International Carriage by Air
12/9/58	Protocol: Railway
1/21/59	Protocol: Nuclear research
4/28/59	Communiqué: Forthcoming summit conference on Germany and West Berlin
12/5/59	Protocols: Railway
12/11/59	Agreement: Currency (banking)
8/26/60	Protocol: Railway
11/28/60	Press Communiqué: Fisheries
4/27/62(?)	Protocol: Railway
6/22/62	(Miscellaneous): Railway
7/23/62	Declaration: Neutrality of Laos
7/23/62	Protocol: Military withdrawal from Laos
2/8/63	Agreement: Payments (noncommercial)
1/24/64	Protocol: Railway
4/15/64	Final Communiqué: Preparatory meeting of Second Afro-Asian Conference
9/10/64	Protocol: Railway
10/27/64	Protocol: Railway (passenger)
10/27/64	Protocol: Postal services and telecommunications
11/6/64	Protocol: Railway (freight)
11/27/64	Protocol: Postal services and telecommunications
2/21/65	Protocol: Railway
3/29/65	Minutes: Railway talks
6/30/65	Press Communiqué: Talks (top level)
7/15/65(?)	Protocol: Postal services and telecommunications
9/23/65	Communiqué: Games of Newly Emerging Forces (GANEFO)

Source: Douglas M. Johnston and Hungdah Chiu, *Agreements of the People's Republic of China, 1949-1967: A Calendar* (Cambridge, Mass.: Harvard University Press, 1968), pp. 275-76. Reprinted by permission of the publisher.

vations to "the provisions about nuncios and the representative of the Holy See in articles 14 and 16 and on the provisions of paragraphs 2, 3 and 4 of Article 37."[46]

The PRC's infrequent participation in multilateral treaties does not necessarily mean that she is opposed to the substance of each treaty she has failed to ratify.[47] Instead, it seems to reflect an ambivalence in the contemporary Chinese image of international legal order. This may be attributed to the contradictory demands and pressures in Chinese legal thinking. The fact that China has resorted on so many occasions and on so many legal issues to a combination of abstention and nonparticipation seems to suggest that she has not formulated a principled stand that is applicable to every legal issue arising in the conduct of her multilateral diplomacy.

What are the conflicting demands and pressures contributing to this ambiguous legal posture? The Chinese image of international legal order has been powerfully influenced by the Marxist notion that law, domestic and international, has always been used as a legitimizing instrument by the exploiting class or nation. Viewed in this light, law is seen more as an effective weapon for legitimizing an unjust status quo than as a revolutionary weapon for establishing a new order. In addition, the basic rules of UN multilateral treaties still follow closely the traditional international law formulated by Western bourgeois nations. Hence, the Chinese may doubt that they can ever "win" at this game.

The Chinese may also be skeptical of the assumption that a multilateral treaty can really control the recalcitrant behavior of sovereign states. That the Chinese do not see much political or practical utility in a UN multilateral treaty was reflected in the statement of a Chinese delegate in the Sixth Committee that "the protection of diplomatic agents and other internationally protected persons had already been provided for in international law and the internal laws of various countries" and that "Governments had the duty to adopt practical and effective measures to guarantee the safety of those persons."[48] Charac-

---

3501 (XXX) of 15 December 1975 the number of States parties to the Vienna Convention on Diplomatic Relations of 1961 has increased." This latter resolution was adopted by a recorded vote of 92:0:25, with China not participating.

[46] *Multilateral Treaties*, p. 55. For the text of the Vienna Convention, see United Nations, *Treaty Series*, Vol. 500, No. 7310, p. 95.

[47] Two examples can be cited here: The International Convention on the Suppression and Punishment of the Crime of Apartheid and the International Convention on the Elimination of All Forms of Racial Discrimination. See *Multilateral Treaties*, pp. 84, 110; GAOR, 29th Sess., Third Committee, 2061st meeting (10 October 1974), paras. 6-8; GAOR, 29th Sess., Special Political Committee, 940th meeting (28 November 1974), paras. 2-4; GAOR, 30th Sess., Third Committee, 2122nd meeting (6 October 1975), para. 30.

[48] GAOR, 27th Sess., Sixth Committee, 1327th meeting (9 October 1972), para. 37.

teristically, the Chinese delegate stopped short of elaborating this interesting proposition. In this spirit, however, China has refused to ratify the Convention on the Privileges and Immunities of the United Nations and the Convention on the Prevention and Punishment of Crimes against Internationally Protected Persons, including Diplomatic Agents.[49]

At the same time, the Chinese do realize that UN politics is no longer dominated by the superpowers, as of yore. If the Third World is indeed the motive force pushing forward the wheel of history, does it logically follow that the treaty-making process must also reflect this "irresistible historical trend"? Not necessarily. With a few exceptions, the Chinese do not believe that UN multilateral treaties can serve as a useful weapon in the united struggle of the Third World against the hegemonic power politics of the superpowers. With the exception of the Charter itself, none of the 197 UN multilateral treaties has ever been invoked by Chinese delegates in support of their arguments in UN diplomacy. Tellingly, however, Chinese delegates on numerous occasions have invoked the authority of the Geneva Conventions of 1949 for the Protection of War Victims, which they had recognized (see Table 8.2).[50]

True to her advocacy of international egalitarianism and participatory democracy in the management of world affairs, China has been prompt in ratifying one type of UN multilateral treaty: the amendatory protocols to the conventions or the constitutions of the specialized agencies and the amendment to Article 61 of the UN Charter, all of which were designed to increase the number of seats so as to broaden representation in the limited-membership organs throughout the United Nations system. The Chinese support and practice have been firm and unequivocal on this issue.

Toward a New International Legal Order?

Their highly politicized legalism and lack of qualified "legal workers" have led the Chinese to concentrate on the nebulous domain of a new international legal order. The pattern of Chinese participation through-

[49] See *Multilateral Treaties*, pp. 35, 73 and UN Doc. A/PV.2202 (14 December 1973), p. 103.

[50] Chinese delegates repeatedly invoked the Geneva Conventions of 1949 in support of their position on the Bangladesh and Middle East questions. Even *Jen-min jih-pao* cited the Geneva Conventions in legitimizing the Chinese position. For the references to the Geneva Conventions, see the following: *PR*, No. 33 (August 18, 1972), 12-13; *PR*, No. 35 (September 1, 1972), 7; *PR*, No. 49 (December 8, 1972), 9; *JMJP*, editorial, August 28, 1972, p. 1; GAOR, 27th Sess., Special Political Committee, 853rd meeting (6 December 1972), para. 53; GAOR, 27th Sess., 2105th plenary meeting (8 December 1972), para. 82; GAOR, 30th Sess., Special Political Committee, 988th meeting (2 December 1975), para. 37.

out the United Nations system and UN-sponsored international conferences reveals that they are indeed interested and involved in what Schachter has called "the evolving international law of development."[51] Given the Chinese conception of world order delineated throughout this study, this is neither surprising nor illogical. To start with a bird's-eye view, the nature and scope of Chinese participation in this evolving law may be summarized as follows:

The norm-defining and law-declaring resolutions of the General Assembly, which were formulated in juridical language, or the obligations and rights of the Member States (1971-76)

The laying of the three foundations of NIEO—the *Declaration*, the *Programme of Action*, and the *Charter*—especially participation in the UNCTAD Working Group on a Draft Charter (from the 1st Session in February 1973 to the 4th Session in June 1974)

The Sixth Committee of the General Assembly (1972-76), concentrating on the definition of aggression, international terrorism and the question of Charter review

The *Ad Hoc* Committee on the Charter of the United Nations (July-August 1975) and the Special Committee on the Charter of the United Nations and on the Strengthening of the Role of the Organization (from the 1st Session in February-March 1976 to the 2nd Session in February-March 1977)

The Committee on the Peaceful Uses of the Sea-bed and the Ocean Floor Beyond the Limits of National Jurisdiction (1972-73) and the Third United Nations Conference on the Law of the Sea (from the 1st Session in December 1973 to the 6th Session in May-July 1977)

The Intergovernmental Committee of the Whole to Draw Up a Constitution for UNIDO As a Specialized Agency (from the 1st Session in January 1976 to the 5th Session in March-April 1977)

The United Nations Conference on the Human Environment held in Stockholm (June 5 to June 16, 1972), especially in the drafting of the Stockholm Declaration containing a set of "common principles to inspire and guide the peoples of the world in the preservation and enhancement of the human environment"

The 1st Session of the Diplomatic Conference on the Reaffirmation and Development of International Humanitarian Law Applicable in Armed Conflicts (held in Geneva in February-March 1974), the main purpose of which was to draw up two draft protocols additional to the Geneva Conventions of 1949 for the Protection of War Victims.

[51] Oscar Schachter, "The Evolving International Law of Development," *Columbia Journal of Transnational Law* 15 (1976), 1-16.

The common conceptual theme running through the above list of Chinese involvements is the development of new rules, new values, and new norms of international legal order. Even though the Chinese have yet to use the term, "new international legal order" (*Hsin kuo-chi fa-lü chih-hsü*), China's theory and practice, as made manifest in the nature, type, and scope of her participation clearly suggest a movement in the direction of seeking revision in the structure of international legal order as part of an overall struggle of the Third World for "redistributive justice." To retain a sharp analytical focus and to keep the present discussion within a manageable scope and length, only four substantive areas—the legal force of General Assembly resolutions, the Charter review question, the Third United Nations Conference on the Law of the Sea, and the definition of aggression—are selected in this chapter to highlight the evolving Chinese concept and practice of a new international legal order.

The Legal Force of General Assembly Resolutions

For a number of years, many states and many international lawyers have rigidly adhered to the positivist assumption that international legal obligations of the state are coterminous with the extent to which it has actually given its consent. Moreover, they have denied—and many of them still do—any legislative status to General Assembly resolutions, except on internal decisions on budgetary matters under Articles 17 and 19 of the Charter. Thus Judge *Ad Hoc* van Wyk stated in the *South West Africa* cases that "applicants' contention involved the novel proposition that the organs of the United Nations possessed some sort of legislative competence whereby they could bind a dissenting minority." "It is clear from the provisions of the Charter," he went on to say, "that no such competence exists, and in my view it would be entirely wrong to import it under the guise of a novel and untenable interpretation of Article 38(1)(b) of the Statute of this Court."[52]

In recent years, however, an increasing number of legal scholars have challenged such a formalistic interpretation of the processes of law creation in international society.[53] They have rejected the artifi-

[52] *I.C.J. Reports 1966*, p. 170. It may also be noted in this connection that a proposal by the Philippine delegation at the United Nations Conference on International Organization to give legislative power to the General Assembly was overwhelmingly defeated.

[53] See Obed Y. Asamoah, *The Legal Significance of the Declaration of the General Assembly of the United Nations* (The Hague: Nijhoff, 1966); Bleicher, "The Legal Significance of Re-Citation of General Assembly Resolutions," pp. 444-78; Jorge Castañeda, *Legal Effects of United Nations Resolutions*, trans. Alba Amoia (New York: Columbia University Press, 1969); Hungdah Chiu, *The Capacity of International Organizations to Conclude Treaties, and the Special Legal Aspects of the Treaties So Concluded* (The Hague: Nijhoff, 1966); Ingrid Detter, *Law*

cially rigid demarcation line between binding and nonbinding norms, between treaty and custom, and between law-making and law-declaring activities in international organizations. They have also called our attention to the discernible trend from consent to consensus in the mode of the decision-making process in international organizations.

Hence, General Assembly resolutions have been characterized as having the status of "quasi-legislative force," or of being "soft laws," "*normes sauvages*," or "legal custom," if they meet the following conditions: (1) they were formulated as behavioral norms for the Member States or they employed the peremptory language of legal rights and obligations; (2) they were repeated with sufficient frequency and regularity;[54] and (3) they enjoyed consensus, if not unanimity. In short, norm-creating, value-realizing, and law-declaring activities of the General Assembly expressed through its resolutions have the characteristic of *opinio juris* and contribute to the development of customary international law. In this connection, Judge Tanaka's dissenting opinion in the *South West Africa* cases is worth quoting for the light it sheds on the Assembly's law-developing function, as well as on the position in which China finds herself:

> A State, instead of pronouncing its view to a few States directly concerned, has the opportunity, through the medium of an [international] organization, to declare its position to all members of the organization and to know immediately their reaction on the same matter. . . . In the contemporary age of highly developed techniques of communication and information, the formation of a custom through the medium of international organizations is greatly facili-

---

Making by International Organizations (Stockholm: Norstedt, 1965); Lino Di Qual, *Les effets des résolutions des Nations-Unis* (Paris: Pichon et Durand-Auzias, 1967); Richard A. Falk, "On the Quasi-Legislative Competence of the General Assembly," *AJIL* 60 (October 1966), 782-91; Rosalyn Higgins, *The Development of International Law Through the Political Organs of the United Nations* (London: Oxford University Press, 1963); "The United Nations and Lawmaking: The Political Organs," *Proceedings of the American Society of International Law at its Sixty-Fourth Annual Meeting* 64 (September 1970), 37-48; *A Memorandum by the Office of Legal Affairs*, UN Doc. E/CN.4/L.610 (1962); Schachter, "The Evolving International Law of Development," pp. 1-16; and Edward Yemin, *Legislative Powers in the United Nations and Specialized Agencies* (Leyden: A. W. Wijthoff, 1969).

[54] For an excellent analysis of the lawmaking significance of continually re-cited General Assembly resolutions, see Bleicher, "The Legal Significance of Re-Citation of General Assembly Resolutions," pp. 444-78. General Assembly Resolution 1514 (XV) of 14 December 1960, the Declaration on the Granting of Independence to Colonial Territories and Peoples, was re-cited 95 times in subsequent resolutions between the 15th (1960) and 21st (1966) Sessions; likewise, General Assembly Resolution 217 (III) of 10 December 1948, the Universal Declaration of Human Rights, was re-cited 75 times in subsequent resolutions until the 21st (1966) Session. See *ibid.*, pp. 456, 458-65, 470-75.

tated and accelerated; the establishment of such a custom would require no more than one generation or even far less than that. . . .[55]

During the period of exclusion from the United Nations, Chinese publicists specifically denied that General Assembly resolutions possessed any legislative or legally binding force. In addition, they had often invoked the principle of *pacta tertiis nec nocent nec prosunt* (treaties create rights and duties only for the parties to them but have no effect on third parties) in maintaining that the PRC could not be legally bound by a number of international conventions.[56] China had also invoked this principle whenever she rejected certain resolutions or decisions made by the United Nations. Wu Hsiu-ch'üan, the PRC's special representative, declared in the Security Council in November 1950, for example, that "without the participation of the lawful representatives of the People's Republic of China, the people of China have no reason to recognize any resolutions or decisions of the United Nations."[57]

At the peak of its disenchantment with the Organization in 1965, Peking's new demands included, *inter alia*, the cancellation of the UN resolutions against the PRC and the DPRK.[58] Therefore, the question was inevitably raised in the UN community on the eve of the PRC's entry as to whether she would stage an open confrontation in an attempt to undo the "unjust" resolutions of the past, especially General Assembly 377A (V) of 3 November 1950 (the Uniting for Peace Resolution) and General Assembly Resolution 498 (V) of 1 February 1951 (which condemned the PRC for having committed aggression in Korea).

On November 16, 1971, the day after her debut in the General Assembly, China was presented with her first opportunity to vote on a draft resolution and to clarify her position on the question of past resolutions. The draft resolution condemned the US Congress for having passed the Byrd Amendment, which would constitute a "serious violation" of the relevant Security Council resolutions imposing sanctions against the "illegal regime in Southern Rhodesia."[59] Huang Hua

[55] *I.C.J. Reports 1966*, p. 291. An argument along the same lines has also been advanced by a prominent international lawyer regarding the establishment of international environmental law. See Louis Sohn, "The Stockholm Declaration on the Human Environment," *Harvard International Law Journal* 14 (Summer 1973), 514.

[56] See Cohen and Chiu, *People's China and International Law*, Vol. II, pp. 1230-1238.

[57] SCOR, 5th Yr., 527th meeting (28 November 1950), p. 4.

[58] These new demands were spelled out by Foreign Minister Ch'en Yi in his press conference of September 29, 1965, in Peking. See *PR*, No. 41 (October 8, 1965), 11-12.

[59] General Assembly Resolution 2765 (XXVI) of 16 November 1971.

voted in favor of the resolution but stopped short of fully elaborating China's position on the question in everyone's mind: "[W]e wish to state that that [the support for the resolution on hand] does not mean that the Chinese Government is in favour of previous resolutions referred to therein."[60]

Although, contrary to some predictions,[61] China thus avoided an open confrontation on the question of past resolutions, Huang Hua's explanatory statement begged more questions. Did he really mean that the PRC would not be in favor of any past resolutions adopted during her exclusion? Surely, the Chinese government could not have any problem in supporting all the "previous resolutions referred to therein" since they had all dealt with the sanctions against the Smith regime in Southern Rhodesia. Faced with more questions, Chinese delegates replied in private that they would judge past resolutions on their intrinsic merits, challenging some and accepting others. This appears to contradict Huang Hua's explanatory statement. There was a great deal of confusion among Chinese delegates to the 26th Session of the General Assembly on this question. It was apparent that they did not have a clear instruction on this matter, probably because the Ministry of Foreign Affairs did not expect its delegation to be so persistently pressed on the question.

Be that as it may, the promised challenge to the past resolutions judged to be bad or unjust never came. Peking apparently made a decision not to drag these skeletons out of the UN closet. China has followed the practice of repeatedly invoking certain resolutions—all of which, with two exceptions, were adopted since her entry—in support of her multilateral diplomacy. Instead of attacking in public those resolutions which she judged to be ineffective, unjust, or in violation of the spirit of the Charter, China has decided simply to ignore them, with one exception to be noted later. When politically or tactically convenient, China has shown no hesitancy in invoking a resolution as an authoritative source of support in legitimizing her position or in attacking the policy and practice of others.

Does this mean that General Assembly resolutions have become legally binding? Characteristically, China has shied away from elaborating on such a legal question. Judging by China's state practice, however, it may be argued that resolutions that are regarded as being "just" or "in conformity with the spirit of the Charter" are held to be binding, while those that do not meet such subjective criteria are not

[60] GAOR, 26th Sess., 1984th plenary meeting (16 November 1972), para. 92. See also UN Doc. S/PV.1825 (3 June 1975), pp. 38-40; GAOR, 30th Sess., Fourth Committee, 2159th meeting (3 November 1975), para. 9.
[61] See NYT, November 17, 1971, p. 14.

binding. A few selected examples will illustrate this practice of selective legalism in Chinese multilateral diplomacy.

The PRC's practice of invoking UN resolutions as authoritative support for her position has centered on five issues: (1) the restoration of the lawful rights of the PRC in the United Nations; (2) the Bangladesh membership question; (3) colonial and apartheid questions related to Southern Rhodesia, South Africa, Portugal (before 1975), and Namibia; (4) NIEO; and (5) the law of the sea. As already noted in the preceding chapters, China has acted as if General Assembly Resolution 2758 (XXVI) of 25 October 1971 has somehow become a universally binding law, applicable to all the specialized agencies and all the NGOs, and has attacked IBRD, IMF, IFC, and ICSU for their failure to implement this historical resolution.

China has also invoked the relevant General Assembly resolutions in justification of her veto blocking Bangladesh's membership in the United Nations. Similarly, China voted in favor of Bangladesh's membership in 1974 on the grounds that all the relevant resolutions had been implemented. Based on the various resolutions of the General Assembly and the Security Council, China declared that the United Nations is indeed "the Administering Authority for Namibia" and that "it is the unshirkable duty of every Member State of the United Nations to fulfill and implement these resolutions."[62] Likewise, China argued that "concrete and effective measures were urgently required to give effect to the many United Nations conventions and resolutions on racism and *apartheid* which had been adopted in the past."[63] It was in this vein that China made one of her rare and specific attacks against the United States for the latter's failure to comply with Security Council resolutions on sanctions against Southern Rhodesia.

As elaborated in some detail in Chapter 6, China's invocation of the three NIEO resolutions—the *Declaration*, the *Programme of Action*, and the *Charter*—has been pervasive throughout the United Nations system. Either by design or accident, Chinese representative Chang Tsien-hua went so far as to say in the *Ad Hoc* Committee of the 6th Special Session of the General Assembly that "the Programme of Action should be binding on States."[64] Since the 29th Session of the General Assembly, the three NIEO resolutions have virtually replaced the UN Charter as the legitimizing source of China's position on devel-

[62] SCOR, 27th Yr., 1656th meeting (31 July 1972), para. 92. See also UN Doc. S/PV.1825 (3 June 1975), pp. 38-40; GAOR, 30th Sess., Fourth Committee, 2159th meeting (3 November 1975), para. 9.
[63] GAOR, 28th Sess., Third Committee, 2007th meeting (26 October 1973), para. 35; emphasis in original.
[64] GAOR, 6th Special Sess., *Ad Hoc* Committee, 13th meeting (22 April 1974), para. 27.

opment issues. In spite of this state practice, however, none of the Chinese delegates has ever made a single legal exposition as to why the three NIEO resolutions (two of which were adopted even without a vote) should be binding, or why the specialized agencies with their own constitutions, or even the NGOs should implement them.

At the 2nd Session of the Third United Nations Conference on the Law of the Sea held in Caracas in the summer of 1974, Chinese delegate Ko Tsai-shuo invoked "the relevant General Assembly resolutions on the international sea-bed regime" as the authoritative reference for the Conference to proceed on the issue. "Since the relevant General Assembly resolutions stated," continued Ko Tsai-shuo, "that the international sea-bed area should be used for peaceful purposes, military operations, the emplacement of nuclear and other weapons and activities of nuclear submarines in that area should be forbidden." However, what is most surprising is the invocation of General Assembly Resolution 2574D (XXIV) of 15 December 1968, which was adopted by a roll-call vote of 62:28:28 during the exclusion period. "The principle clearly stated in General Assembly resolution 2574D (XXIV)," argued Ko Tsai-shuo, "that, pending the establishment of the international regime, States and persons should refrain from the commercial exploitation of the international area, must be respected."[65]

As will be noted later in the chapter, Chinese representative Hsia Pu invoked General Assembly Resolution 2749 (XXV) of 17 December 1970 on the Declaration of Principles Governing the Seabed and the Ocean Floor and the Subsoil Thereof Beyond the Limits of National Jurisdiction in support of his argument for the establishment of an international seabed regime. The resolution was also cited approvingly in a "For Your Reference" commentary in the *Peking Review*, entitled "Struggle over Exploitation of International Seabed."[66]

Two additional cases of Chinese selective reliance on law may be mentioned. When the Security Council was immobilized by Soviet vetoes during the 1971 Indo-Pakistani War, China, without any reservations or qualifications, voted in favor of Security Council Resolution 303 (1971), which referred the deadlocked issue to the General Assembly for consideration based specifically on the Uniting for Peace Resolution. Likewise, China voted for the Assembly's Cease-Fire and Troops Withdrawal Resolution on the Indo-Pakistani War without raising any objections to the citation of the Uniting for Peace Resolution as a legal basis for this Assembly action.[67] When the United States

[65] Third United Nations Conference on the Law of the Sea, *Official Records*, Vol. II (1975), p. 37.

[66] "Struggle Over Exploitation of International Seabed," *PR*, No. 28 (July 8, 1977), 24.

[67] For the text of Security Council Resolution 303 (1971), in which a reference

threatened to unilaterally reduce its assessment if the Fifth Committee would not approve her proposal of a reduction from 31.52 percent to 25.00 percent, to cite another case, the Chinese representative Hsing Sung-yi quickly intervened: "China held that once the General Assembly had adopted the scale of assessments, it was incumbent upon every Member State to bear its share in accordance with the assessment [resolution]."[68]

What happened to China's principled stand on the Uniting for Peace Resolution? China has never made her position clear on this resolution, as she has never attacked the resolution since her entry into the United Nations. While she has never publicly attacked any General Assembly resolutions, she did attack once, and for the first time in open confrontation with the superpowers, Security Council Resolution 339 (1973) as a "scrap of paper," in the course of Council debate on the establishment of UNEF II on October 25, 1973. The details of this open showdown with the superpowers have already been discussed in Chapter 4 and need not be repeated here.

What is revealing about Huang Hua's polemics during the debate is the fact that he attacked the resolution on political rather than on legal grounds. To the Chinese, the ghost of the Korean police action returned to the Security Council as it groped to work out a formula for UNEF II that would receive the blessing of the superpowers. "Through their prolonged struggle against foreign aggression over the past century and more," Huang Hua argued passionately, "the Chinese people have come to realize that a scrap of paper cannot drive away the aggressors."[69] He then asked: "What 'United Nations emergency peace-keeping force'? To put it bluntly, this is an attempt to occupy Arab territories. Is not South Korea a living example?"[70]

From a legal point of view, Chinese practice here makes little sense. China had the Charter-given right to veto the authorizing resolution for UNEF II, yet declined to do so on political grounds. Having allowed the resolution to pass, she then attacked it as a "scrap of paper" and, as shown in Chapter 4, refused to assume any of the financial

---

to General Assembly Resolution 377 A (V) of 3 November 1950 is made, see SCOR, 26th Year, *Resolutions and Decisions of the Security Council 1971*, p. 10. The Assembly resolution referred to in the text is General Assembly Resolution 2793 (XXVI) of 7 December 1971, adopted by a roll-call vote of 104 in favor, 11 against, with 10 abstentions. One of the preambular paragraphs of the resolution reads: "Mindful of the purposes and principles of the Charter and of the General Assembly's responsibilities under the relevant provisions of the Charter and of Assembly resolution 377 A (V) of 3 November 1950."

[68] GAOR, 27th Sess., Fifth Committee, 1536th meeting (27 November 1972), para. 50.

[69] UN Doc. S/PV.1750 (25 October 1973), p. 6.

[70] *Ibid.*, pp. 7-10.

obligations incurred by UNEF-UNDOF operations. However, what makes little sense from a purely legal standpoint makes sense from the standpoint of China's evolving global strategy.

Does China herself practice what she criticizes others for not doing in regard to General Assembly resolutions? This is a difficult and, in a sense, a misleading question, because most General Assembly resolutions are of a hortatory and recommendatory nature. Besides, China is seldom the target of specific resolutions urging specific actions on her part. However, the budgetary question is an exception. We need not repeat our discussions in Chapters 3 and 4 on this matter, except to say that China's adamant refusal to assume the financial obligations incurred by the preceding regime, her selective withholding on the regular budget items that she unilaterally judges to be contrary to the spirit of the Charter, and her refusal to pay the assessed amounts for UNEF-UNDOF operations all provide contradictory evidence of Chinese legal practice.

China acted as if her nonparticipation in the vote made the Assembly resolutions on the financing of UNEF II and UNDOF not legally binding upon herself, and hence was not obliged to pay. To regard the costs of UNEF II and UNDOF as expenses of the Organization, Chinese representative Wang Wei-tsai argued in the Fifth Committee, "was tantamount to requesting all Member States to pull the chestnuts out of the fire for the two super-Powers."[71] However, the Chinese have never challenged the purse power of the General Assembly as provided for in Article 17 of the Charter. Instead, their challenge is directed to the meaning or interpretation of "expenses of the Organization," following the precedent set by the Soviet Union and France on the ONUC financing.

The fact that China has voluntarily increased her own assessment in her own "practical" fashion or that the amounts she has withheld are relatively small cannot erase this flaw in the Chinese record of compliance with the legally binding Assembly resolutions (*interna corporis*) on budgetary matters. Despite this problematic record of budgetary compliance, China has somehow managed to establish a reputation throughout the United Nations system for a high degree of credibility, as noted in Chapters 3 and 4. There is an almost universally shared assumption among the participants that such great powers as the United States (UNESCO, ILO), the Soviet Union (UNEF I and ONUC), and China (UNEF II and UNDOF) cannot be expected to pay for the programs or items that are perceived as being contrary to their national interests. This is a matter of perception, not of law,

[71] GAOR, 28th Sess., Fifth Committee, 1604th meeting (20 November 1973), para. 66.

which does not need to be debated here. However, the legal hazards and ambiguities in Chinese budgetary practice are self-consciously left unclarified by both China and other Member States. The desire not to reopen the Pandora's box of Article 19 seems to be universal.

Of course, China cannot escape from the right and responsibility of voting on issues of a purely legal nature. However, not many draft resolutions relating to legal (Sixth Committee) matters are pressed to a roll-call or recorded vote. Table 8.3 summarizes all the resolutions adopted by the plenary of the General Assembly upon the recommendation of the Sixth Committee between 1972 and 1976, with the exception of the resolution on the peaceful settlement of international disputes. Although the table is admittedly limited in the number of legal issues covered—the draft definition of aggression was adopted without vote, for example—it does nonetheless illustrate China's selective, pragmatic, and opportunistic posture on legal issues.

Despite the resort to a legally sweetening argument from time to time, the underlying basis of Chinese multilateral diplomacy is political. However, China has learned the art of legitimizing her multilateral diplomacy in terms of resolutions that she believes to be conceptually appealing to the Third World. The change of her vote from nonparticipation or absence to "yes" on the resolution regarding "respect for human rights in armed conflict" also suggests that the Chinese legal posture is amenable to "progressive" change and adaptation under the pressure of the Organization. The cumulative impact of China's practice of invoking resolutions in support of her multilateral diplomacy augurs well, too, since such a practice on the part of the Member States helps the General Assembly's law-developing and norm-creating process.

The Charter Review Question

The General Assembly first considered the Charter review question in 1955 in compliance with Article 109(3) of the Charter, and adopted a resolution deciding in principle that a conference to review the Charter should be held "at an appropriate time." The Assembly disposed of the issue by establishing a committee of the whole to keep the matter under review. The question was raised again at the 25th Session of the General Assembly, which then decided to request the Secretary-General to invite Member States to submit their views on the need to review the Charter and to report to the 27th Session of the General Assembly, which adopted a similar resolution with respect to the 29th Session of the General Assembly. Following heated debates in the General Committee and the Sixth Committee, the plenary of the 29th Session of the General Assembly finally adopted a resolution (see

TABLE 8.3. The PRC's Voting Record on Select Legal Resolutions
Adopted by the Plenary of the General Assembly, 1972-76

Subject	Resolution	Date	Vote	PRC's Vote
Report of the International Law Commission	2926 (XXVII)	11/28/72	93:0:26	NP or Ab
Respect for human rights in armed conflict	3032 (XXVII)	12/18/72	103:0:25	NP or Ab
Measures to prevent international terrorism, etc.	3034 (XXVII)	12/18/72	76:35:17	Yes
Respect for human rights in armed conflict	3102 (XXVIII)	12/12/73	107:0:6	Yes
Basic principles of the legal status of the combatants struggling against colonial and alien domination and racist regimes	3103 (XXVIII)	12/12/73	83:13:19	Yes
Peaceful settlement of international disputes	3283 (XXIX)	12/12/74	68:10:35	Yes
Need to consider suggestions regarding the review of the Charter	3349 (XXIX)	12/17/74	82:15:36	Yes
Implementation by states of the provisions of the Vienna Convention on Diplomatic Relations of 1961	31/76	12/13/76	92:0:25	NP or Ab

NP = Nonparticipation.
Ab = Absence.

Table 8.3) establishing a 42-member *Ad Hoc* Committee on the Charter of the United Nations, with a mandate to discuss and consider suggestions and observations from Member States on the need and desirability of the Charter review question.

Of the Big Five, China has clearly distinguished herself from the outset as the only revisionist supporter on this question. However, the nature of Chinese support is more symbolic than substantive, more generalized than specific. This may be a function of her diplomatic style rather than a tactical move to disguise her true intentions. For the demands of the Charter review and revision as advanced by many developing countries and Japan are congenial to the Chinese image of a new world order. Moreover, China's state practice is consistent with her advocacy of international egalitarianism, which is central to the question of Charter review.

The recorded vote of 82:15:36 on General Assembly Resolution 3349 (XXIX) of 17 December 1974 clearly showed a sharp and fundamental divergence of opinion among Member States on the need even to discuss the Charter review question. The 83 positive votes came from developing countries, plus Australia, China, Italy, Japan, New Zealand, and Spain, while the 15 opposing votes were cast by the United States, the United Kingdom, France, the Soviet Union, its "bloc member states," Saudi Arabia and Democratic Yemen. The 36 abstainers represented a mixture of some West European and developing countries. Thus, China stood out as the only permanent member of the Security Council supporting Charter review and revision.

Before examining the Chinese position on the Charter review question, it may be helpful to define the scope of Chinese participation. Even before the establishment of the *Ad Hoc* Committee, the Charter review question was one of the few legal issues that invited Chinese response in the Sixth Committee. Following the establishment of the *Ad Hoc* Committee, China immediately showed her interest in serving on it. The *Ad Hoc* Committee met from July 28, 1975 to August 22, 1975 in New York. At the 30th Session of the General Assembly, the *Ad Hoc* Committee was converted into a 47-member Special Committee on the Charter of the United Nations and on the Strengthening of the Role of the Organization. China as a member of the Special Committee participated in both its 1st Session (February 17, 1976, to March 12, 1976) and its 2nd Session (February 14, 1977, to March 11, 1977). While China has been characteristically modest, passive, and reactive in the *Ad Hoc* and Special Committees, she has, unlike her activities in so many other *ad hoc* or special committees of the General Assembly, participated in every phase of the deliberations on the question of Charter review. In addition, the Chinese review question has received extensive coverage in the Chinese press.

From the beginning, the Chinese have seen the question of Charter review as a political struggle between the defenders of the status quo, who tenaciously adhere to their privileged status (the veto), and the revisionist underdogs, who wish to review and revise the Charter so as to make it reflect a new or more equitable order in UN politics. Although simplistic, such a conceptualization has an element of truth. When all the legal arguments for and against the Charter review question are stripped to their essence, one of the core issues centers on the who, how, and what aspects of the veto. In short, the issue is more political than legal.[72]

To put the Chinese stand in a comparative frame of reference, the positions of the remaining four permanent members of the Security Council may be summarized. From the outset, the Soviet Union assumed an unyielding posture of opposition to even discussing the matter. When her proposal in the General Committee to delete the item from the provisional agenda for the 29th Session of the General Assembly was rejected by a vote of 19 against, 3 in favor, with 2 abstentions, the Soviet Union became more militant in the *Ad Hoc* and Special Committees, presenting her view in absolute and categorical terms. In the Soviet image, the United Nations is a unique international organization because it protects—thanks to the principle of unanimity, which is claimed to be the keystone of the Charter—the equality of different social systems. It is not only Utopian but also dangerous to imagine that the Organization can ever be transformed into some sort of supranational machinery, since this creates the possibility of subjecting states to a single social system. *Any* revision of the Charter, in particular any change in the principle of unanimity, may well shake the foundations of the United Nations and call into question its very existence. The Charter is such a coherent and integral whole in the Soviet view that *any* amendment made to one part "would have a self-defeating effect and would destroy the entire structure of international law."[73]

---

[72] For example, a resolution adopted at the Fifth Conference of Heads of States or Governments of Non-Aligned Countries held in Colombo, Sri Lanka, in August 1976, reads on this matter: "3. Calls upon all United Nations Member States to direct all their efforts towards the reconsideration of the United Nations Charter, particularly as regards the right of veto, enjoyed by the permanent members of the Security Council. 4. Requests all Non-Aligned Member Countries to strive for the amendment of the United Nations Charter with a view to safeguarding their interests and attaining their aspirations, and in order to implement the principle of equality among all United Nations Member States." Reprinted in *Alternatives* 3 (December 1977), 294.

[73] UN Doc. A/C.6/31/SR.47 (18 November 1976), p. 9. The Soviet position

The French position, though not as absolute or categorical as the Soviet Union's, is firmly opposed to any Charter review and revision. The Charter has proved to be flexible and adaptable, standing the test of time. "It is because the Charter gave the power of decision," the French position paper states, "in matters relating to international peace, to the organ governed by the principle of unanimity among the Powers bearing the heaviest responsibilities in this field, that this result, however inadequate it may still seem, has been achieved." What is required is "not a review of the Charter but the strict application of its provisions and full utilization of the possibilities that it affords." "In order to cope with future difficulties," the French conclude, "the potential of the Charter must therefore be kept intact."[74]

The British and American positions are strikingly similar in style and substance. While opposed to any general or comprehensive Charter review, both expressed willingness to consider specific amendment proposals on a case-by-case basis, provided they were well founded and had wide support among all sectors of UN membership. But to initiate the process of a general Charter review at this time in the absence of an overwhelming consensus (only forty-three Member States submitted position papers during a five-year period) is more likely to weaken than to strengthen the United Nations. In view of this conviction, the British and American position papers stopped short of elaborating their respective views on the principle of unanimity.[75]

In contrast, China's support of Charter review and revision predated the establishment of the *Ad Hoc* Committee by two years. In his annual major policy speech before the plenary of the General Assembly on October 3, 1972, Ch'iao Kuan-hua for the first time made known the Chinese position on the question of Charter review in the following terms: "We maintain that on the basis of upholding the purposes and principles of the U.N. Charter, careful consideration should be given to the views of various countries for necessary revisions of the Charter so as to effect truly the principle that all member states, big or small, are equal. Of course, we likewise consider that the revision of the Charter is a serious and important question, and we are ready to join you all in serious explorations."[76] Uncharacteristically, China has also sub-

summarized in the text is based on the following: *Report of the Ad Hoc Committee on the Charter of the United Nations*, GAOR, 30th Sess., Supp. No. 33 (A/10033), pp. 88-95 (hereafter cited as *Report of the Ad Hoc Committee*); UN Docs. A/AC.182/SR.11 (2 March 1976), pp. 2-5, and A/C.6/31/SR.47 (18 November 1976), pp. 7-11.

[74] *Report of the Ad Hoc Committee*, pp. 27-30; and UN Doc. A/AC.182/SR.8 (27 February 1976), pp. 3-6.

[75] *Report of the Ad Hoc Committee*, pp. 96-101.

[76] "Chairman of Chinese Delegation Chiao Kuan-hua's Speech," PR, No. 41 (October 13, 1972), 10.

mitted a position paper on this matter in response to the invitation of the Secretary-General.[77] Both Ch'iao Kuan-hua's statement quoted above and the position paper provided a basic diplomatic guideline for Chinese delegates to expound their position in the Sixth, *Ad Hoc*, and Special Committees.

How does China envisage the matter? In spite of her vague and often too generalized statements, one point emerges clearly: for China, the Charter review question is neither a legal issue nor an isolated political question. It is part of the larger struggle for "the establishment of a new international relations based on equality."[78] Rebutting the Soviet argument that the principle of unanimity (the veto) is "the keystone of the Charter," Ho Li-liang declared in the Sixth Committee that "the cornerstone upon which the Organization rested was the principle of equal rights for all countries."[79] China has also linked the Charter review question, the new international economic order, and "a new law of the sea" as the three separate but mutually complementary dimensions of the struggle of the developing countries to establish a new world order.[80]

Beyond the generalized guideline that "the Charter should be modified on the basis of the principle of the equality of all States,"[81] however, the Chinese position on specifics seems deliberately ambiguous. For example, on the central question of the veto, China has stopped short of advocating its abolition or modification. Instead, Chinese support is expressed in the form of an *amicus curiae* argument:

> Many countries had advanced views in principle on the revision of certain Charter provisions, such as expanding the power of the General Assembly, restricting the power of the Security Council, changing the composition of the Security Council, limiting or abolishing the veto rights of the States which were permanent members of the Council. Those views deserved serious consideration. He was convinced that, if consultations and discussions were held on

[77] Operative para. 1 of General Assembly Resolution 2968 (XXVII) of 14 December 1972 "requests the Secretary-General to invite Member States that have not already done so to submit to him, before 1 July 1974, their views on the desirability of a review of the Charter of the United Nations and their actual suggestions in this respect." For the Chinese position paper submitted in response to the invitation of the Secretary-General, see UN Doc. A/9739 (4 October 1974), pp. 3-4.

[78] GAOR, 29th Sess., Sixth Committee, 1513th meeting (3 December 1974), para. 37.

[79] GAOR, 30th Sess., Sixth Committee, 1569th meeting (19 November 1975), para. 32.

[80] UN Doc. A/PV.2440 (15 December 1975), p. 77.

[81] GAOR, 29th Sess., Sixth Committee, 1462nd meeting (24 September 1974), para. 31.

the basis of the principle of equality of all countries, it would be possible to find a rational solution acceptable to all.[82]

Such vague and generalized support for Charter revision has invited trenchant Soviet attack: "The Chinese delegation had attacked the right of veto but a three years previously [sic], when the representative of the USSR had asked the Chinese delegation whether it was going to forgo the rights it enjoyed as a member of the Security Council, it had received no answer. The Chinese delegation was using that issue for demagogic ends, in order to seek prestige in the eyes of the third world countries."[83] The Soviet Union thus exposes the Chinese position, which is fraught with legal ambiguities and logical inconsistencies.

China declares that she upholds the principles and purposes of the Charter; it is the structure of power in the Organization that needs to be reviewed and revised so as to reflect the "irreversible trend" of a new egalitarian order. If this is so, the veto is symbolically and practically the most logical target for reform. China should have, but has not, gone beyond the "serious consideration" proposal in attacking the veto as incompatible in theory and practice with the principle of the equality of all Member States, large or small, in the management of UN affairs. Indeed, there is little risk in taking this approach, since the veto cannot be abolished or modified without the unanimous consent of the Big Five. The great powers had already built into the Charter the mechanism for perpetuating their privileged status by making it impossible to amend any article in the Charter without their unanimous consent.[84]

Instead of attacking the veto in theory, however, China has attacked the veto in practice. Not a single statement has been made *directly* challenging the veto *per se* as being contrary to the principle of the sovereign equality of states; instead, Chinese salvos have been directed at the abusive practice of the superpowers. The Soviet Union is accused of "wilfully abusing the veto right to practice big-power hegemonism and to cover up its social-imperialist features."[85] The 1968 Czechoslovakian and the 1971 Indo-Pakistani issues have been singled out as illustrative examples (see Table 4.1).[86] The United States is less mildly criticized for having abused

[82] GAOR, 30th Sess., Sixth Committee, 1565th meeting (14 November 1975), para. 28. See also UN Doc. A/C.6/31/SR.47 (18 November 1976), p. 4; and *Report of the Ad Hoc Committee*, pp. 10-11.
[83] UN Doc. A/C.6/31/SR.47 (18 November 1976), p. 11.
[84] Article 108 of the UN Charter.
[85] "A Just Demand of the Third World Countries," *JMJP*, March 24, 1977, p. 6.
[86] See GAOR, 30th Sess., Sixth Committee, 1569th meeting (19 November 1975), para. 36 and UN Doc. A/C.6/31/SR.47 (18 November 1976), p. 3.

the veto in connection with draft resolutions on the Vietnam membership and South African questions.[87] Curiously, abuse of the veto on the part of the United Kingdom and France is either forgotten or forgiven, while China's own two vetoes were justified as a legitimate exercise, upholding the principles of the Charter and relevant UN resolutions.

Despite the ambiguities inherent in China's general support of Charter review, the question has brought in sharper focus the symbolic, normative, and behavioral dimensions of Chinese multilateral diplomacy. China has succeeded in symbolically projecting herself as the only permanent member of the Security Council willing to give moral and political support to the demands of the underdogs for a more egalitarian order and justice, even at the possible risk of forgoing her own privileged status in the United Nations. It may also be added here that the vehement Soviet opposition to Charter review has had the effect of "strengthening" the Chinese supportive position on the issue. However, the prospects of the Charter revision are now in serious doubt. When the things were not moving in his direction toward the end of the 2nd Session of the Special Committee in March 1977, Soviet representative Kolesnik threatened that "the subsequent participation of the Soviet delegation in the work of the Special Committee would have to be reconsidered."[88]

A New Law of the Sea?

China has a coastline of approximately 11,000 kilometers and another 10,000 kilometers surrounding its 3,416 islands,[89] yet the PRC paid little attention to the law of the sea (LOS) issues during her preentry period. She did not even specify the scope of her own territorial sea until September 4, 1958, when in the wake of the Quemoy-Matsu crisis she declared a 12-mile territorial sea for China,

[87] UN Doc. A/C.6/31/SR.47 (18 November 1976), p. 3. Since June 1977, when the United States changed its stand on the Vietnam membership question, the issue has become moot.

[88] UN Doc. A/AC.182/SR.20 (11 March 1977), p. 15. What infuriated the Soviet representative was that the Committee—through a roll-call vote of 30 (including China) to 8 against (the Soviet Union, the United Kingdom, the United States, Belgium, Czechoslovakia, France, German Democratic Republic, and Poland), with 5 abstentions—annexed to the committee report two papers containing suggestions for revising the Charter and strengthening the Organization's role. One paper (A/AC.182/L.12/Rev.1) was submitted by 16 countries and the other (A/AC.182/L.15) by Italy and Spain. For details, see UN Doc. A/AC.182/SR.20 (11 March 1977), pp. 1-17. For the Chinese reaction, see "A Just Demand of the Third World Countries," *JMJP*, March 24, 1977, p. 6.

[89] Park, "Oil Under Troubled Waters," p. 229.

embracing all ROC-held offshore islands within her jurisdiction.[90] The declaration adopted a straight base-line principle in defining the breadth of the territorial sea. Except for the promulgation by the State Council on June 5, 1964, of *Regulations Governing Foreign Nonmilitary Vessels Passing Through the Chiungchow Strait*,[91] the PRC's interest in and coverage of LOS issues apparently ceased in the 1960s.

The PRC's silence was broken on December 4, 1970, when *Jen-min jih-pao* published a "declaratory article," denouncing the proposed ROC-ROK-Japan joint development of the seabed in the vicinity of Taiwan and the Tiao-yü-t'ai (or, in Japanese, Senkaku) Islets.[92] (See Figure 8.1.) This was a protest, not an exposition of China's position on the continental shelf. In fact, the term, "continental shelf" (*ta-lu chia*) was not even used in the article. A month later, the PRC presented a proxy argument by publishing excerpts from an article by John Gittings, "Scramble for Oil in East China Sea," which was originally published in the British newspaper, *The Guardian*, on December 18, 1970.[93] It was not until the PRC's entry into the United Nations and her participation in the UN Committee on the Peaceful Uses of the Sea-bed and the Ocean Floor Beyond the Limits of National Jurisdiction (hereafter the Seabed Committee) in 1972-73 and the Third United Nations Conference on the Law of the Sea (1974—) that China's position on LOS issues began to take shape.

The Third United Nations Conference on the Law of the Sea has been important and unique in several respects.[94] First, it has at-

[90] For the text of the government's declaration on territorial waters, see *JMJP*, September 5, 1958, p. 1. See also Chou Keng-sheng, "The Great Significance of Our Government's Declaration Concerning Territorial Sea," *SCCS*, No. 18 (September 20, 1958), 16-17 and Kuo Chi, "Important Steps for Safeguarding the Sovereignty of the Country," *CFYC*, No. 5 (October 1958), 8-10.

[91] For the text of the Regulations, see *JMJP*, June 28, 1964, p. 2; English trans. in Cohen and Chiu, *People's China and International Law*, Vol. I, pp. 535-38.

[92] "U.S. and Japanese Reactionaries Out to Plunder Chinese and Korean Sea-Bed Resources," *JMJP*, December 4, 1970, p. 5.

[93] In the article excerpted, Gittings argued for the sovereign rights of the coastal state over the continental shelf, citing the Geneva Agreement of 1958 on the Continental Shelf, "to a depth of 200 metres or beyond the limit to where the depth of the waters admits of the exploitation of natural resources." See "China Possesses Sovereign Rights Over Continental Shelf in East China Sea—Article by the British paper 'Guardian'," *PR*, No. 2 (January 8, 1971), 15; see also *ibid.*, No. 1 (January 1, 1971), 22.

[94] After almost ten years of preparatory work by the International Law Commission, the First United Nations Conference on the Law of the Sea (1958) produced four basic conventions. The Second United Nations Conference on the Law of the Sea (1960) failed. However, neither Conference reached agreement on major issues.

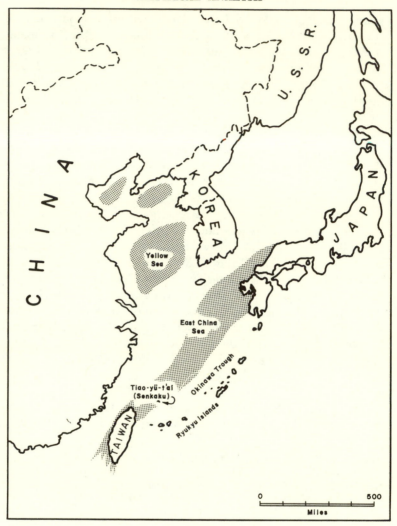

FIGURE 8.1. Sea-Floor Provinces Beneath the Yellow Sea and East China Sea for Future Discoveries of Oil and Gas Fields.

tempted to reach agreement on nothing less than a single comprehensive treaty of over 300 articles concerning the uses of the oceans and their resources. The economic and political stakes are extremely high, as the management or control of some $3 trillion worth of minerals under the sea is involved. Hence, political, economic, scientific, and legal issues are intertwined in the negotiation process at the Conference. Second, it is one of the largest UN-spon-

446

sored conferences ever held. There were no less than 5,000 delegates attending the 2nd (the first substantive) Session held at Caracas in the summer of 1974.

Third, it promises to be the longest conference in UN history. The Seabed Committee spent several years in its preparatory work for the Conference. The first six sessions of the Conference—held respectively during the period December 3-15, 1973, June 20-August 29, 1974, March 17-May 9, 1975, March 15-May 7, 1976, August 2-September 17, 1976, and May 23-July 15, 1977—all ended inconclusively. The 7th Session is scheduled to be convened on March 28, 1978, to make another try at the "Informal Composite Negotiating Text" which was drafted by Conference President Hamilton Shirley Amerasinghe of Sri Lanka, along with five other officials.[95]

Finally, the North-South dichotomy is less sharply drawn at the Conference. In addition to the United Nations' regular regional groups and the Group of 77, such special interest groups as the Evensen Group, the Group of Five, the Territorialist Group, the Coastal States Group, and the Landlocked and Geographically Disadvantaged Group have emerged at the Conference.[96]

Despite the complexity of the issues and the multiplicity of overlapping groups involved, China has conceptualized the Conference as another arena for the antihegemonic struggle and as another forum for the establishment of a new world order. "The central issue of the Conference was," declared Ch'ai Shu-fan, head of the Chinese delegation, in the opening policy speech at the 2nd Session on July 2, 1974, "whether or not super-Power control and monopoly of the seas should be ended and the sovereignty and interests of small and medium-sized countries defended."[97] As the Chinese saw it, the Conference had a simple choice between the outdated legal regime of the sea based on hegemony and "a fair and reasonable new law of the sea" as an important part of the establishment of a new international economic order.[98] Based on this conceptual premise, the Chinese argued that the Conference "should first focus on major questions of principle" before dealing with details.[99]

[95] For details, see *UN Chronicle* 14 (August/September 1977), 24-28.

[96] For a comprehensive and up-to-date analysis of the various aspects of the Third United Nations Conference on the Law of the Sea, see a special issue entitled "Restructuring Ocean Regimes: Implications of the Third United Nations Conference on the Law of the Sea," *IO* 31 (Spring 1977).

[97] Third United Nations Conference on the Law of the Sea, *Official Records*, Vol. I (1975), p. 80.

[98] *Ibid.*, Vol. IV (1975), p. 20, and Vol. V (1976), p. 60.

[99] *Ibid.*, Vol. IV (1975), p. 21, Vol. V (1976), p. 6, and Vol. VI (1977), p. 74.

What emerges from the three working papers submitted to the Seabed Committee[100] and numerous statements made at the Conference is a reaffirmation of the NIEO principle of permanent and inalienable resource sovereignty as applied to the LOS issues. During the heated procedural debate, China strongly attacked the "consensus" approach as a conspiratorial device of the superpowers to exercise a "*de facto* veto" at the Conference. The rules of procedure finally adopted by the Conference by consensus on June 27, 1974, following a series of informal consultations in which China took an active part, may be characterized as a qualified consensus method. There is to be a delay in a vote on a substantive matter in plenary and committees for a specified period, after which it will be determined that all efforts at consensus have been exhausted and that voting should take place. Yet China hailed this compromise as a triumph of the Third World. Interestingly enough, she singled out Rule 39, paragraph 1, as an example: "Decisions of the conference on all matters of substance, including the adoption of the text of the convention on the law of the sea as a whole, shall be taken by a two-thirds majority of the representatives present and voting, provided that such a majority shall include at least a majority of states participating in that session of the conference."[101]

China has also strongly reasserted the principle of equality in the decision-making process at the Conference. She argued that "a proliferation of working groups should be avoided so as to enable developing countries with small delegations to play their full part."[102] While accepting the method of candidate selection by the regional groups for the officials of the Conference as in the General Assembly, however, China argued that regional candidates, once elected, should serve the Conference as a whole rather than their respective regions, because there was no such a thing as "regional sovereignty."[103]

In a similar vein, China criticized an overrepresentation of the Soviet Union in the committees of the Conference, provoking Soviet

[100] UN Docs. A/AC.138/SC.II/L.34 (16 July 1973); A/AC.138/SC.III/L.42 (19 July 1973); and A/AC.138/SC.II/L.45 (6 August 1973).
[101] See "U.N. Conference on Law of the Sea: Entire Procedural Rules Approved," *PR*, No. 27 (July 5, 1974), 9-10; UN Doc. A/C.1/PV.1932 (22 October 1973), pp. 22-23; Third United Nations Conference on the Law of the Sea, *Official Records*, Vol. I (1975), pp. 27, 32, 58, Vol. II (1975), p. 37. What Peking ignored to publicize is Rule 37, para. 1, which stipulates: "Before a matter of substance is put to the vote, a determination that all efforts at reaching general agreement [consensus] have been exhausted shall be made by the majority specified in paragraph 1 of rule 39." See *Rules of Procedure*, Third United Nations Conference on the Law of the Sea, A/CONF.62/30/Rev.2 (1976), p. 8.
[102] Third United Nations Conference on the Law of the Sea, *Official Records*, Vol. IV (1975), p. 20.
[103] *Ibid.*, Vol. I (1975), p. 12.

representative Kolesnik to respond: "China, France, the USSR, the United Kingdom and the United States of America, as permanent members of the Security Council, bore primary responsibility for the maintenance of peace and security. That special responsibility carried with it certain rights, which were recognized both in the United Nations Charter and in international practice. Thus, in all international conferences affecting international security, including the codification of international law, the permanent members of the Security Council were given key offices."[104]

Figure 8.1 shows that the LOS issues touch not only Chinese principles but also Chinese interests. Yet China acted as if few of her own direct interests were at stake at the Conference. Instead, she formulated and projected her own principles in identical terms with the demands of the Third World countries for the establishment of a new legal order for the seas. However, the geographical and geological differences among the developing countries created a serious rift between the landlocked and littoral states, while uniting them more or less on the issue of deep-sea mining. It is little wonder, then, that China has refused to respond to the invitation of the Group of Landlocked and Geographically Disadvantaged States to join its ranks so as to provide its cause with the sponsorship of a major power.

However, a close examination of the Chinese press shows a strong Latin American connection. The issue of territorial waters is mentioned in virtually all Chinese discussions of Latin America. The expansive claims of Latin American countries on the questions of territorial seas and exclusive economic zones have received strong Chinese support. But this is the issue where Chinese principles and interests seem mutually complementary. For analytical purposes, the Chinese position may be examined separately on each of the major LOS issues at the Conference.

THE TERRITORIAL SEA AND CONTIGUOUS ZONE.

The PRC's concept of the territorial sea and contiguous zone is ambiguous at best and anarchical at worst. In a speech delivered before Subcommittee II of the Seabed Committee on March 20, 1973, Chuang Yen, chief representative of the Chinese delegation, flatly declared that "it is the sovereign right of each country to determine the limits of its territorial sea and national jurisdiction." "To require uniformity and deny particularity on this matter will lead to a dead end." Many Latin American countries have already declared 200 nautical miles to be the extent of their territorial seas, argued Chuang

---

[104] *Ibid.*, p. 19.

Yen, and quite a few Asian and African countries have already defined the breadth of their respective territorial seas as "extending from 18 to 25, 30, 130 or 200 nautical miles." "We hold," stated Chuang Yen, "that this is a matter of their proper and legitimate rights and interests, which should be respected by other countries." The superpowers are attempting to confine the territorial seas of other countries within 12 nautical miles for the sole purpose of enabling their warships "to prowl recklessly everywhere and do whatever they please in the seas and oceans and their fishing fleets to carry out unbridled plunder of the offshore marine resources of other countries."[105]

Such an anarchical concept has been modified at the Conference. A coastal state was entitled, it is now argued, "to define the breadth and limits of its territorial sea according to its geographical features and its economic development and national security needs, with due regard to the legitimate interests of neighbouring States and to the convenience of international navigation." The question of fixing a maximum limit for territorial seas with general international applicability should be decided by all countries through consultations on the basis of equality.[106] Curiously, China refused to specify a guideline nor has she defined the scope of her own territorial sea at the Conference. Instead, she has assumed the position that the question of *who* shall determine the limits of the territorial sea and the limits of national jurisdiction is more important than the question of *what kind* of limits will be defined.[107] China may easily accept the 12-mile limit on the territorial sea, since there is now growing consensus among most countries, developed and developing, on this point.[108]

[105] "U.N. Sea-Bed Committee: The Struggle in Defence of Maritime Rights," *PR*, No. 13 (March 30, 1973), 9-10.

[106] Third United Nations Conference on the Law of the Sea, *Official Records*, Vol. I (1975), p. 80, Vol. IV (1975), pp. 77-78.

[107] China assumed such a posture at the Seabed Committee and continued it at the Conference. In the opening paragraph of Chuang Yen's speech above quoted, for example, he states: "A major question of principle is involved in the present international struggle over territorial sea rights. It is: Who shall determine the limits of the territorial sea and the limits of national jurisdiction of a state? Shall it be dictated by the one or two superpowers, or shall it be determined reasonably by each state according to its own specific conditions?" See "U.N. Sea-Bed Committee," p. 9.

[108] As of mid-1977, for example, some 57 countries have already proclaimed the 12-mile territorial water limits and some 102 countries have already given their support to this territorial concept. In an article published in the December 31, 1970, issue of *Jen-min jih-pao* along with the excerpts from John Gittings' article alluded to above, the PRC declared: "China's own limit for her territorial waters was set at 12 miles as long as 1958, and there is no suggestion that it will be extended now." English trans. in *PR*, No. 2 (January 8, 1971), 16.

STRAITS USED FOR INTERNATIONAL NAVIGATION.

The Chinese position on freedom of passage through straits used for international navigation is relatively explicit, reasonable, and balanced. On the one hand, China recognizes the right of the coastal states concerned to make necessary laws and regulations in accordance with their security and other interests. On the other hand, she also recognizes the needs of international navigation and the necessity for some reasonable international guarantees and standards. She makes a clear distinction, however, between nonmilitary merchant vessels and military warships. The former should enjoy innocent passage, provided they observe and respect the laws and relevant regulations of the coastal states.[109] The passage of foreign military warships through straits lying within a state's territorial sea should be subject to prior notification and authorization. Thus, the ambiguity lies not in the Chinese position on the freedom of passage through straits, but in the lack of China's clear definition of the breadth of the territorial sea and contiguous zone.[110]

THE ECONOMIC ZONE.

Reaffirming its support for the position taken by many Latin American, African, and Asian countries, China argues that a coastal state may reasonably define an exclusive economic zone beyond and adjacent to its territorial sea up to the maximum of 200 nautical miles, measured from the baseline of the territorial sea. As the natural corollary of its resource sovereignty, the coastal state should exercise full sovereignty over the living and nonliving resources in its economic zone. The coastal state should also be permitted to decide whether foreign fishermen are to be allowed to fish in the area under its jurisdiction, either through bilateral or regional agreements.

However, the normal navigation and overflight on the water surface of, and in the airspace above, the economic zone by ships and aircraft of all states shall not be prejudiced. As for the predicament of the landlocked developing countries, China adds an ambiguous and unrealistic suggestion: "The land-locked countries should enjoy reasonable rights to and benefits from the resources in the economic zones of their respective neighbouring coastal States. Specific arrangements could be made by means of full consultations between coastal and land-locked countries."[111]

[109] China has defined "innocent passage" as follows: "Passage is innocent when it is not prejudicial to the peace, security and good order of a coastal State." UN Doc. A/AC.138/SC.II/L.34 (16 July 1973), p. 2.
[110] Third United Nations Conference on the Law of the Sea, *Official Records*, Vol. I (1975), p. 81, Vol. II (1975), pp. 133, 141, 187, 210.
[111] *Ibid.* p. 187. For a full elaboration on the economic zone, see UN Doc.

THE CONTINENTAL SHELF.

The PRC's position on the continental shelf was a mystery until its participation in the Seabed Committee. In a working paper submitted to Subcommittee II of the Seabed Committee on July 16, 1973, China defined the continental shelf as "the natural prolongation of the continental territory" of a coastal state. China thus adheres to the "natural prolongation of land territory principle," which, according to the ICJ judgment in the *North Sea Continental Shelf* cases (1969), gives a nation a claim to that part of a continental shelf that constitutes "a natural prolongation of its land territory into and under the sea, without encroachment on the natural prolongation of the land territory of the other. . . ."[112]

While China placed a maximum limit of 200 nautical miles on the economic zone, there was no such limit to the continental shelf. The coastal state, states one of the Chinese working papers, "may reasonably define, according to its specific geographical conditions, the limits of the continental shelf under its exclusive jurisdiction *beyond* its territorial sea or economic zone" (emphasis added).[113] States adjacent to each other and having interconnected continental shelves should jointly work out the delimitation of the limits of jurisdiction of the continental shelves through consultation on an equal footing. Such other matters as exploitation and regulation relating to natural resources in their contiguous parts of the continental shelf should also be worked out through consultations based on the principle of equality. However, normal navigation and overflight on the superjacent waters of the continental shelf and its airspace by ships and aircrafts of all states "shall not be prejudiced."[114]

Curiously, China evaded the question of the continental shelf at the Conference. However, the ratification by the Japanese Diet of the Japan-ROK Agreement on Joint Development of the Continental Shelf provoked the PRC's Ministry of Foreign Affairs to issue an official statement on the matter on June 13, 1977. Invoking the principle of natural prolongation, the PRC declared her "inviolable sovereignty over the East China Sea continental shelf." The question of delimiting those parts of the East China Sea continental shelf which involve other countries should be decided through consulta-

---

A/AC.138/SC.II/L.34 (16 July 1973), pp. 2-3; Third United Nations Conference on the Law of the Sea, *Official Records*, Vol. I (1975), p. 80, Vol. II (1975), pp. 187, 228, Vol. IV (1975), p. 78, Vol. VI (1977), p. 26.

[112] *I.C.J. Reports 1969*, p. 53.
[113] UN Doc. A/AC.138/SC.II/L.34 (16 July 1973), p. 3.
[114] *Ibid.*

tions. The Japanese-ROK Agreement worked out behind China's back is "entirely illegal and null and void."[115]

An article by a commentator in *Jen-min jih-pao* has stated that the Japanese act of ratification in spite of repeated warnings by China has "damaged the friendly relations between the two countries." The article invoked the principle of natural prolongation in justification of China's position. Interestingly enough, it also characterized the Japanese act as "deliberately trampling on the norms of international law (*kuo-chi-fa chun-tse*)," presumably referring to the ICJ judgment in the *North Sea Continental Shelf* cases.[116] Be that as it may, the conflicting unilateral claims to certain portions of the continental shelf, coupled with the PRC's adamant refusal to accept the compulsory jurisdiction of the ICJ or a third-party arbitration augur ill for future stability in East Asia.[117]

THE INTERNATIONAL SEABED REGIME.

The most serious and persistent obstacle to the conclusion of a new ocean treaty is the disagreement between developed and developing countries over the nature and role of a new international regime to regulate deep seabed mining. China has given her firm and unequivocal support to the united position of the Group of 77 on this question. Even though the Declaration of Principles Governing the Sea-Bed and the Ocean Floor and the Subsoil Thereof Beyond the Limits of National Jurisdiction was adopted by the General Assembly in 1970 before her entry,[118] Chinese representative Hsia Pu declared in the Seabed Committee: "We hold that the foregoing provisions in the declaration of principles are basically in conformity with the interests of the peoples of all countries. Therefore, we agree in principle to establish an international regime governing the international sea-bed area on the basis of these provisions."[119]

[115] For the text of the statement issued by the Ministry of Foreign Affairs, see *JMJP*, June 14, 1977, p. 1.

[116] "Chinese Sovereignty Over the Continental Shelf Is Inviolable" (by Commentator), *JMJP*, June 14, 1977, p. 4. Apparently due to this pressure from Peking, Japan delayed in passing procedural legislation needed for implementation of the Korean-Japanese agreement on joint seabed exploration. This invited a strong editorial attack from the ROK. See the *Korean Herald* (Seoul), editorial, November 20, 1977.

[117] For analyses of the continental shelf controversy involving the PRC, the ROC, ROK, and Japan, see Chiu, "Chinese Attitude Toward Continental Shelf"; Park, "Oil Under Troubled Waters," and "The Sino-Japanese-Korean Sea Resources Controversy and the Hypothesis of a 200-Mile Economic Zone"; and Harrison, *China, Oil, and Asia.*

[118] General Assembly Resolution 2749 (XXV) of 17 December 1970.

[119] "U.N. Sea-Bed Committee Ends Session," *PR*, No. 34 (August 25, 1972), 11.

Consistent with the above position, China faithfully echoed the position of the Group of 77 at the Conference. The international seabed should be used for peaceful purposes only. In a most uncharacteristic fashion, China elaborated her view on the structure of the international seabed authority: (1) it should have an assembly, a council, and an enterprise; (2) the assembly, the supreme organ, should be composed of all states formulating policy on all important matters and giving instructions to the council and other subsidiary organs; (3) the council, as an executive organ, should operate according to the guidelines set by the assembly; (4) the enterprise, as a subordinate body to the assembly and the council, would be responsible for all operations related to exploration, exploitation, and scientific research; (5) the composition of the assembly and the council should reflect the principle of equality among states and of rational geographical representation; and (6) the international seabed authority should have broad powers, including the right of direct exploration and exploitation of seabed resources and the right to regulate all activities, such as scientific research, production, processing, and marketing.[120]

However, the Conference is seriously divided on this issue. The Group of 77 proposed that activities in the international seabed area should be conducted *exclusively* by the proposed international seabed authority. The Soviet Union proposed that activities of deep seabed mining should be conducted by both the state enterprises and directly by the authority, while the United States proposed a parallel or dual access system. Hence, the Soviet and American positions are reconcilable. China again gave her unequivocal support to the position of the Group of 77 on this critical issue. The Chinese position as expounded at the 6th Session of the Conference is as follows:

1. Only the international seabed authority can represent all mankind, and accordingly it should be stipulated in the convention that exploitation of the international seabed resources should be carried on exclusively by the authority, and not through the "parallel system of exploitation" advocated by the superpowers.

2. If the authority deems it necessary, activities of exploitation can be conducted, as determined by the authority, under its full and effective control, through a form of association with the state parties or their enterprises. . . .

3. The basic objectives and policies of the system of exploitation to be set forth in the convention should be explicitly for the

[120] Third United Nations Conference on the Law of the Sea, *Official Records*, Vol. I (1975), p. 81, Vol. II (1975), p. 37, Vol. IV (1975), pp. 68-69, Vol. V (1976), p. 24.

benefit of mankind, so that all countries of the world, particularly the developing countries, whether landlocked or coastal, can share the practical benefits; they should promote the comprehensive development of the economy of the developing countries, narrow the present gap between the rich and the poor, and contribute to the establishment of a new international economic order.[121]

MARINE SCIENTIFIC RESEARCH.

Close to half the oceanographic research throughout the world is conducted within the 200-mile economic zone. Such research now falls in the exclusive domain of the developed countries. Aware of this fact, China argues that marine research, like any other scientific research, serves the political and economic purposes of the state. Freedom of scientific research in the hands of the superpowers easily transforms itself into freedom to violate the sovereignty of other states and to monopolize marine research. On this basis, China has rejected the concept of unrestricted marine research in what she referred to as "the sea area within the national jurisdiction of another coastal State."

At the 2nd Session of the Conference, China spelled out the four basic principles that should govern marine research. First, any marine research in "the sea area" must obtain the prior consent of the coastal state involved. Second, a coastal state has the right to take part in any scientific marine research carried out by other countries in "the sea area" to obtain data and have access to the results thereof. In addition, such data and results cannot be published or transferred without the prior consent of the coastal state concerned. Third, marine research in "the international sea area" (the high seas?) should be subject to the proposed international seabed authority. Finally, all states should promote international cooperation in marine research and actively help the developing countries to enhance their capability to conduct marine research independently, on the basis of mutual respect for sovereignty and equality and mutual benefit.[122] It may be inferred that "the sea area within the national jurisdiction" is coterminous with that state's exclusive economic zone.

PRESERVATION OF THE MARINE ENVIRONMENT.

China enunciated four major principles on this question at the 2nd Session of the Conference. First, the coastal states have the right to

---

[121] "China's Stand on the Question of Exploitation of International Seabed," *PR*, No. 28 (July 8, 1977), 22-23; Third United Nations Conference on the Law of the Sea, *Official Records*, Vol. VI (1977), pp. 26, 74.

[122] *Ibid.*, Vol. II (1975), p. 344, Vol. VI (1977), p. 96. See also UN Doc. A/AC.138/SC.III/L.42 (19 July 1973).

formulate their own environmental policy and take all necessary measures to protect their marine environment and prevent pollution in "the sea areas" under their jurisdiction. Tellingly, China has quietly dropped from this principle "the right to demand compensation from states causing damage to their marine environment by pollution," which she had declared in Subcommittee III of the Seabed Committee on August 2, 1972.[123]

Second, all states, especially the industrially developed countries, have a duty to take all effective measures to solve their problems of discharge of harmful substances and to prevent pollution of "the sea areas" under their jurisdiction from spreading to the marine environment of "the sea areas" of other coastal states, or of "international sea areas." Third, international antipollution measures and standards should be adopted and appropriate and necessary international regulations should be enforced for the protection of the marine environment in "the international sea area." Finally, all states and international organizations should cooperate in the conduct of antipollution research and promote the exchange and utilization of antipollution technology and data.[124]

SETTLEMENT OF DISPUTES.

China took a strong stand in the course of the April 6, 1976, plenary debate on the dispute settlement procedures. In opposing the provisions in the "Informal Single Negotiating Text" concerning the compulsory jurisdiction of the law of the sea tribunal,[125] Chinese representative Lai Ya-li stated:

> The Chinese Government had consistently held that States should settle their disputes through negotiation and consultation on an equal footing and on the basis of mutual respect for sovereignty and territorial integrity. Of course, States were free to choose other peaceful means to settle their disputes. However, if a sovereign State were asked to accept unconditionally the compulsory jurisdiction of an international judicial organ, that would amount to placing that organ above the sovereign State, which was contrary to the principle of State sovereignty.[126]

[123] See "On Prevention and Control of Marine Pollution," PR, No. 34 (August 25, 1972), 12.
[124] Third United Nations Conference on the Law of the Sea, Official Records, Vol. II (1975), pp. 328-29. See also "Chinese Representative on Marine Pollution," PR, No. 30 (July 26, 1974), 7-8.
[125] See "Informal Single Negotiation Text, Part IV, Presented by the President of the Conference," UN Doc. A/CONF.62/WP.9 (21 July 1975).
[126] Third United Nations Conference on the Law of the Sea, Official Records, Vol. V (1976), p. 24.

Realizing that the compulsory jurisdiction has received a considerable amount of support from Third World countries, China suggested a compromise solution that the provisions of the compulsory jurisdiction on the settlement of disputes "should not be included in the convention itself but should form a separate protocol so that countries could decide for themselves whether to accept it or not."[127]

The Chinese position on the LOS issues as expressed at the Third United Nations Conference on the Law of the Sea has been long on hortatory principles and statements designed to maintain her political and ideological identification with the Third World. In terms of substantive legal issues, the Chinese contribution has been minimal. The use of such vague terms as "the international sea area" or "the sea area within the national jurisdiction of the coastal state" is a measure of the serious deficiency of legal scholarship in the Chinese foreign service. Or it may be a deliberate exercise in ambiguity, motivated by China's strong belief in state sovereignty, on the one hand, and its strategic desire to support the demands of the Third World, on the other. In the face of cross-pressures stemming from a variety of sources, China has played "safe" symbolic politics, concentrating on broad political principles while shying away from substantive legal details. In spite of its ambiguity, however, the Chinese position on the LOS issues can no longer be characterized as the mystery it used to be during the exclusion period.

The Definition of Aggression

On December 14, 1974, the General Assembly adopted by consensus Resolution 3314 (XXIX), by which it, *inter alia*, approved the Definition of Aggression (hereafter the Definition) annexed thereto and called upon all states to refrain from all acts of aggression and other uses of force contrary to the UN Charter and the Declaration on Principles of International Law concerning Friendly Relations and Co-operation among States in accordance with the Charter of the United Nations. The resolution also called the attention of the Security Council to the Definition and recommended that it should, as appropriate, take account of the Definition as guidance in determining, in accordance with the Charter, the existence of an act of aggression.

The Definition contains a preamble, reaffirming the fundamental principles upon which it is based, followed by eight operative articles. Articles 1 and 2 provide the general definition of aggression, emphasizing the two elements: the use of *armed force* and the *first use* of armed force. Article 3 enumerates seven acts that qualify as an

[127] *Ibid.*

act of aggression and Article 4 states that the list is not exhaustive. Article 5 mentions the legal consequences of aggression. Articles 6 and 7 assure the compatibility between the Definition and Charter provisions concerning self-defense and the right of peoples to self-determination. And Article 8 states that the interpretation and application of the provisions in the Definition should proceed on the basis of the interrelation of all articles.[128]

To examine China's position in a broad historical perspective, several "background factors" that may have influenced the Chinese attitude toward the Definition should be mentioned. First, the term "aggression" in the context of UN politics may easily have evoked a bitter and negative emotional response in the Chinese mind, given the fact that the PRC itself was condemned as an aggressor in General Assembly Resolution 498 (V) of 1 February 1951.

Second, the Definition is the product of seven years of work by the Special Committee on the Question of Defining Aggression established by the General Assembly in 1967. As such, much of the Committee work was already in progress when the PRC entered the United Nations. There is no evidence that China has since shown any interest in serving on the Special Committee. The final report of the Special Committee as presented to the Sixth Committee therefore had no Chinese input. Finally, the excessive zeal traditionally shown by the Soviet Union on the question of defining aggression, in spite of her own dubious record, may have made China cynical as well as hardened her position.[129]

Since the plenary adopted the resolution with the Definition annexed thereto by consensus, the actual debate on the Definition took place in the Sixth Committee. However, that debate was not extensive; it was designed largely to accept and approve the *fait accompli*, the report of the Special Committee, while giving an opportunity to those Member States who had not served on the Special Committee to express their views, reservations, or interpretations of the Definition. The Sixth Committee adopted the draft resolution (A/C.6/L.993) without a vote at its 1503rd meeting on November 21, 1974. Chinese representative Ho Li-liang expressed the Chinese

---

[128] For careful textual analyses of the Definition, see Vernon Cassin, *et al.*, "The Definition of Aggression," *Harvard International Law Journal* 16 (Summer 1975), 589-613; and Julius Stone, "Hopes and Loopholes in the 1974 Definition of Aggression," *AJIL* 71 (April 1977), 224-46.

[129] It may be recalled that the Soviet Union was the first state to propose a definition of aggression in 1933 and has been active ever since on this question in her multilateral diplomacy. For the text of the Soviet proposal on aggression submitted to the 1933 Conference for the Reduction and Limitation of Armaments, see the Report of the Secretary General, GAOR, 7th Sess., Annexes, Agenda Item No. 54 (A/2211), pp. 34-35.

position by stating that "if a vote had been taken on the draft resolution which had just been adopted, her delegation would not have taken part in it."[130] In short, China would have opted for non-participation in a roll-call or recorded vote as an expression of her serious reservations about, if not outright opposition to, the Definition.

The Chinese press has virtually ignored the question of the definition of aggression in the United Nations. The analysis which follows is, therefore, based largely on the statements made by An Chih-yüan, Ho Li-liang, and Ling Ch'ing in the course of the debate in the Sixth Committee during the 28th and 29th Sessions of the General Assembly.

Characteristically, China took a deductive approach to the question of defining aggression. That is, China first expounded at a high conceptual level her own views on the subject before making specific comments on specific provisions or articles contained in the draft definition submitted by the Special Committee. In the Chinese view, aggression is identified with unjust or imperialistic war.[131] In stressing the critical importance of identifying the source of aggression in contemporary international politics, for example, Ling Ch'ing stated that "the contention for world hegemony was the main content of imperialist foreign policy and that imperialism was the source of contemporary wars of aggression."[132] Thus, aggression and imperialism are synonymous in the Chinese view.

More significantly, the Chinese concept of aggression is oriented more toward what Inis Claude calls "a system of *selective* security, embodying the principle of some for some,"[133] than toward a system of collective security. In the former view, the identity of the aggressor must be predetermined, while the latter embodies the concept that an attack against one automatically becomes the attack against all. In the Chinese view, the identification of the aggressor is more important and more necessary than the definition of aggression, for

---

[130] GAOR, 29th Sess., Sixth Committee, 1503rd meeting (21 November 1974), para. 11. Following the adoption of the resolution and the definition annexed thereto by the plenary, An Chih-yüan again made China's position clear by stating that his delegation would not have participated in the vote, if the resolution had been pressed to a roll-call or recorded vote. See UN Doc. A/PV.2319 (14 December 1974), pp. 32-35.

[131] I have discussed this problem at length elsewhere focusing on the Lorenzian theory of aggression and war. See my "The Lorenzian Theory of Aggression and Peace Research: A Critique," *Journal of Peace Research* 13 (1976), 253-76.

[132] GAOR, 28th Sess., Sixth Committee, 1442nd meeting (20 November 1973), para. 73.

[133] Claude, *Swords into Plowshares*, p. 266; emphasis in original. For a more extensive discussion on the concept of collective security, see Inis L. Claude, Jr., *Power and International Relations* (New York: Random House, 1962).

the latter becomes the logical corollary of the former. Apparently, the Chinese believe that the United Nations has taken a wrong approach by reversing the process, as implied in the following statement: "What deserved attention was that the very country that had proposed the reopening of the discussions on the question of defining aggression, while discussing the question with eloquence, sent out large numbers of troops for armed invasion and occupation of one of its allies by surprise attack."[134]

As already discussed in Chapter 4, one of the main Chinese complaints in the United Nations has been addressed to the inability or unwillingness of the Security Council to make a clear distinction between the aggressor and the victim of aggression in the discharge of its peace-keeping functions. This complaint is also implicitly and explicitly evident in Chinese comments on the question of defining aggression. What criteria, if any, does China offer in making such a critical distinction? This is not a question of an "abstract legal concept," the Chinese argue, but a question of respecting "the objective facts." The superpowers were accused of attempting to use abstract legal concepts in order to justify their distortion of the objective facts.

The Chinese rejected categorically the idea of introducing "aggressive intent" into the definition of aggression. Aggressive intent is a subjective element, which can be determined only when it is manifested through concrete objective acts of aggression. Therefore, the objective facts must be taken as the basis for judging whether a state had harbored aggressive intent, definitely not the other way round. In other words, the determination of an act of aggression cannot, and should not, be made on the basis of whether a state had an aggressive intent.[135]

To distinguish between the aggressor and the victim of aggression at the international level is the normative process of making a judgment between "right and wrong," in the Chinese conceptualization. China again asserted her egalitarian principles on this matter. The UN determination of the objective facts on aggression should be made by all the Member States, big or small, not by the superpowers in the Security Council. Ling Ch'ing argued: "The super-Powers were arguing very hard for their idea that it was only up to the Security Council to decide whether a specific act constituted an act of aggression. Obviously, what they had in mind was invariably their veto power in the Security Council. In the event of their aggression against other countries, they could remain unpunished by casting a single negative veto. Consequently it might well be asked whether the whole

---

[134] GAOR, 28th Sess., Sixth Committee, 1442nd meeting (20 November 1973), para. 74.
[135] *Ibid.*, para. 76.

text of the definition of aggression would not become a mere scrap of paper."[136]

Just as it is necessary to distinguish the aggressor from the victim of aggression, so it is necessary to distinguish just from unjust wars. Specifically, the Chinese argued that "it is absolutely impermissible to mention in the same breath wars of aggression and wars against aggression, which were different in nature."[137] Having made this point clear, the Chinese then suggested the following definition, which, in substance, is an amalgamation of Articles 1 and 7 in the Definition: "[A]ny country which first used armed force to encroach upon the sovereignty, independence or territorial integrity of other countries had naturally committed a crime of aggression, that a crime of aggression should be subjected to severe international condemnation and sanctions and that peoples had the right to wage wars of national liberation and revolutionary wars of self-defence."[138]

Comments by Chinese delegates on specific provisions and articles in the Definition were few and far between. Article 7 was singled out as having reflected to some degree the just proposals of the Third World, while "serious deficiencies" in other articles were indicated. The deficiencies in the Definition, as the Chinese saw them, were basically three. First, the draft was too restrictive, as it confined aggression to acts of armed aggression, making no reference to "other forms of aggression, such as territorial annexation and expansion, political interference and subversion, and economic control and plunder."[139] Yet, these other forms of aggression constituted "the living reality of international life" as far as the numerous small and medium-sized countries were concerned.

Second, it was too vaguely phrased, creating many loopholes in interpretation. Specifically, Article 3(d)—"An attack by the armed forces of a State on the land, sea or air forces, marine and air fleets of another State"—was singled out as being too loosely worded insofar as an attack on marine fleets was concerned. "In its present ambiguous form," it was argued, "it might be used by the super-Powers to slander a coastal State acting in defence of its sovereignty by labelling its action as an act of aggression." "Coastal States had the right to take action against fleets illegally entering their national waters," argued An Chih-yüan, "in order to protect their national economic rights and interests and their marine resources."[140] It seems obvious here that

---

[136] *Ibid.*, para. 77.   [137] *Ibid.*, para. 75.   [138] *Ibid.*

[139] GAOR, 29th Sess., Sixth Committee, 1475th meeting (14 October 1974), para. 14; GAOR, 29th Sess., Sixth Committee, 1503rd meeting (21 November 1974), para. 9.

[140] GAOR, 29th Sess., Sixth Committee, 1475th meeting (14 October 1974), para. 15.

China was fortifying her legal position for possible future action in the troubled waters over the disputed continental shelf boundaries in the East China Sea.

Finally, the draft was criticized as being deficient because it gave too much freedom of action to the superpowers. "As it stood," argued An Chih-yüan, "the definition would enable the super-Powers to take advantage of their position as permanent members of the Security Council to justify their acts of aggression and, by abusing their veto power, to prevent the Security Council from adopting any resolution condemning the aggressor and supporting the victim." "Since an aggressor could veto any draft resolution of the Security Council stating that it had committed an act of aggression," continued An Chih-yüan, "it was difficult to see how the definition could have the effect of deterring a potential aggressor, simplifying the implementation of measures to suppress acts of aggression and protecting the rights and interests of the victim, as provided in the preamble of the draft definition."[141] Again, the Soviet invasion of Czechoslovakia in 1968 and the subsequent Soviet veto on the matter in the Security Council were cited as an example supporting the Chinese contention.

China's position on a separate but somewhat related item, "international terrorism," may be briefly noted here. When the issue was first raised in the 27th General Assembly, China first opposed the inclusion of the item in the provisional agenda. Having failed on this, China then argued in the Sixth Committee that "the question was complex and multi-faceted and would require careful study by all delegations" and that the Committee should not rush on the item. When a full-blown and heated debate followed, in the course of which the Arab countries vigorously opposed the issue based on their belief that anti-terrorism efforts were no more than anti-Arab sentiments in disguise, China was forced to state her own principled stand on the matter.[142] Chinese representative Pi Chi-lung spelled out the three main points at the 1368th meeting of the Sixth Committee on November 21, 1972: (1) China had always been opposed to assassination and the hijacking of aircraft as a means of waging political or revolutionary struggles because these terrorist acts were detrimental to the cause of national liberation and the people's revolution; (2) however, the imperialists, racists, and Zionists had always been eager to launch a "guilt by association" campaign in order to vilify the national liberation movements and revolutionary struggles on the basis of a handful of criminal terrorists; and (3) the repression of such criminal terrorists fell basically

[141] *Ibid.*, para. 16.
[142] GAOR, 27th Sess., Sixth Committee, 1310th meeting (25 September 1972), para. 13.

within the sovereign right of the country in which the incident occurred, and China "could not agree to the forcible imposition of measures detrimental to State sovereignty in the form of an international convention."[143]

The issue was stalled until the 31st General Assembly when a rare unity of Western nations, the Third World, and the Soviet bloc countries was achieved on the draft resolution sponsored by West Germany and thirty-seven other countries for an international convention against hostage taking. Both the Sixth Committee and the plenary adopted by consensus a resolution setting up a 35-member *Ad Hoc* Committee on the Drafting of an International Convention Against the Taking of Hostages.[144] As introduced by West Germany, the proposal had an "exclusively humanitarian and legal objective." In the face of such unity, Chinese representative An Chih-yüan reiterated the first two points in China's principled stand, while quietly substituting for the last point the vague supportive statement that "China was ready to join with all countries that upheld justice in a common endeavour to that end."[145]

In conclusion, it is premature to assess the historical significance of the Definition or the full impact of China's "nonparticipation" in its adoption. By citing Articles 39, 41, and 42 of the UN Charter in a preambular paragraph, the framers of the Definition had clearly intended to enhance the effectiveness of the Security Council under Chapter VII. Yet—except in the case of Southern Rhodesia—the United States, the United Kingdom, and France had, until recently, consistently refused to invoke Chapter VII as applied to South Africa.[146] There is no reason to believe that they will change their posi-

---

[143] GAOR, 27th Sess., Sixth Committee, 1368th meeting (21 November 1972), paras. 28-31.

[144] General Assembly Resolution 31/103 of 15 December 1976.

[145] UN Doc. A/C.6/31/SR.58 (30 November 1976), pp. 6-7. The *Ad Hoc* Committee on the Drafting of an International Convention against the Taking of Hostages concluded its first session in New York (from August 1 to August 19, 1977) by recommending that the Assembly invite it to *continue* its work in 1978.

[146] On November 4, 1977, the Security Council unanimously adopted Resolution 418, which imposes a mandatory arms embargo on South Africa under Chapter VII of the UN Charter. Secretary-General Kurt Waldheim said that "the adoption of resolution 418 (1977) was an historic event marking the first time in the 32-year United Nations history that action had been taken under Chapter VII against a Member State." However, the impact of the resolution appears to be more symbolic than substantive. On October 31, 1977, the Security Council failed to adopt three strong draft resolutions favored by African Member States—including one involving an economic embargo—in three separate votes of 10 in favor (Benin, China, India, Libyan Arab Jamahiriya, Mauritius, Panama, Romania, Soviet Union, Venezuela), 5 against (Canada, France, Germany, Federal Republic of Germany, the United Kingdom, the United States). In short, three strong and substantive draft resolutions failed due to triple vetoes by France,

tion on this matter; in fact, the highly restrictive definition of aggression reflects a measure of their continuing interest and influence in *selective* use of the Security Council in the discharge of its peace-keeping and peace-enforcing functions.

On the other hand, China has shown in theory and practice that she wants the Security Council to broaden and expand its taking of sanctions measures under Chapter VII as applied to colonial and apartheid questions. The Chinese record on this matter has been fairly consistent. China does not believe that aggression, defined as the first use of armed force by a state against the sovereignty, territorial integrity, or political independence of another state, is a meaningful, relevant, or practical notion. It is the structural violence embedded in "economic aggression" that is of critical importance to China.

She is not alone on this matter. "Economic aggression," states a working paper submitted by the Philippines for the Special Committee on the Charter of the United Nations and on the Strengthening of the Role of the Organization, "is as much a breach of the peace and in contravention of the Charter as any other form of aggression and it consequently calls for effective measures for its prevention and removal."[147] Be that as it may, a fundamental divergence of opinions among the permanent members of the Security Council on the nature, scope, and applicability of aggression call into question the practical value of the Definition. As far as the Security Council is concerned, it may well prove to be less epochal than many have prematurely claimed it to be.

The Chinese Contribution Toward a New International Legal Order

Let us now return to the question raised at the beginning of this chapter: What contribution, if any, has China made toward the evolving process of an international legal order? The foregoing analysis of Chinese legal practice in the context of UN multilateral diplomacy provides an empirical basis for answering this question and for making a few broad observations. We may safely conclude that *substantive* Chinese contribution to or impact on legal issues has been virtually nil.

What about the political and symbolic contribution? This appraisal

---

the United Kingdom, and the United States, and one symbolic resolution was adopted in their place. For details, see *UN Chronicle* 14 (December 1977), 5-14, 66-69, 77-78. For Peking's reaction to Resolution 418, see *JMJP*, November 6, 1977, p. 5, and December 12, 1977, p. 5.

[147] UN Doc. A/32/58/Add.1 (7 March 1977), p. 2.

must be confined to the evolving international law of development, in the making of which China has participated. In the domain of UN multilateral treaties or conventions, or of purely legal issues of a traditional nature, China has assumed a self-conscious posture of no comment and no participation, rather than engaging in ideological repudiation. Some may even read into the Chinese posture of noncommittal an implied acquiescence. Certainly, China has not been a hindrance in the domain of traditional international law.

However, it is extremely difficult to assess fairly and accurately the political and symbolic impact of China on the evolving process of a new international order. First, Chinese legal practice has shown a contradictory mixture of qualified acceptance of traditional international law, on the one hand, and a revisionist challenge to destroy the old legal order and to establish a new one, on the other. Second, the "new international legal order" is now in a state of normative confusion, as shown in the question of Charter review and the hitherto inconclusive global conference to codify a new law of the sea. Part of the confusion stems from the mutually competing and often conflicting claims of law (or order) and justice (or equality).

As a latecomer to the world community, the PRC has had no part in the making and development of traditional international law. As a professed Marxist-Leninist state, China would have been expected to make an ideological assault on "bourgeois" international law. Yet in a curiously opportunistic manner, China, without saying so, has embraced the sovereignty-centered system of the Westphalia legal order. A tendency to carry the logic of state sovereignty to an appealing but untenable extreme makes China somewhat anachronistic in the politics of establishing a new international legal order. Both conceptually and psychologically, China seems to be suffering from a siege mentality that goes back to the traumatic period of unequal treaties.

If the Westphalia legal order proved to be inadequate in the halcyon days of the past, there is no reason to believe that it can work any more effectively or justly in the nuclear-ecological age. It is difficult to argue that the traditional principles of state sovereignty and equality can somehow become the energizing force in the establishment of a viable and more just legal order. On the contrary, they may well legitimize the law of the jungle and the sovereign prerogative of pursuing parochial or hegemonic interests and claims. That the poor and the weak cannot possibly win at this game hardly needs to be explained. In short, an excessive claim of state sovereignty may have the opposite effect of strengthening the structural violence inherent in the asymmetrical distribution of dignity and wealth in the global community. In strategic terms, therefore, the sovereignty-centered image of international legal order may be incompatible with the normative commitment of China to a new international legal order.

On the positive side of our balance sheet, we may argue that China is indeed committed to the establishment of a new international legal order to the extent that it is perceived as being justice oriented. Always an elusive and almost impossible concept to define, justice in the Chinese normative disposition requires no abstract theorizing or philosophizing: Equality is justice, justice is equality. China has been so consistent in both theory and practice on this point as to make her claim highly credible.

What is unique about China's advocacy of international egalitarianism is its apparent incongruity with her own status in the international system. In international politics as in domestic politics, justice or equality is the ideological weapon of the underdog, while law or order is the ideological weapon of the topdog. Surely, China can no longer be characterized as an underdog in the global community of the 1970s. Yet she has pressed international egalitarianism to the point of conceptually undermining her own privileged status in the Security Council.

Furthermore, there is no evidence that China has sought any special or privileged position in the United Nations system on the grounds of her size, financial contribution, or population. Available evidence indicates the opposite. The refusal to play an active, let alone a leading, role in many of the committees or conferences may be accepted as a corollary of a strong belief in and practice of international egalitarianism. It may also be argued that the anachronistic conception of state sovereignty is an extension of the commitment to state equality. Viewed in this light, China's *symbolic* contribution to the process of establishing a new and more equitable legal order cannot be gainsaid.

In addition, China's legal practice of invoking certain General Assembly resolutions, in particular, the NIEO resolutions which fall neatly into the category of the evolving international law of development, as the authoritative reference for her UN multilateral diplomacy can only contribute to the process of redefining and relegitimizing the sources of international law. "In institutional terms, the International Court of Justice, for example," Richard A. Falk perceptively observed, "lies primarily within the domain of law, while the General Assembly falls within the domain of justice."[148] If a new international legal

[148] Richard A. Falk, "The Domains of Law and Justice," *International Affairs* 31 (Winter 1976), 2. In a similar vein, Inis Claude, Jr. has argued "that the function of legitimization in the international realm has tended in recent years to be increasingly conferred upon international political institutions" and that "it

order is ever to be established, it is not likely to come from the advisory opinions or contentious judgments of the ICJ or from a definitive or formalistic codification of a new multilateral convention. It is most likely to evolve and crystallize from the political process of collective legitimization in the domain of justice.

In short, repeated references to certain resolutions in state practice may well have the effect of transforming consensus into consent in the Assembly's norm-formulating, value-realizing, and law-declaring activities. If this analysis is correct, the well-established Chinese legal practice of invoking General Assembly resolutions would have the two legal consequences. First, it will make it increasingly difficult for China to defy Assembly resolutions without suffering a serious credibility problem in her multilateral diplomacy. Second, it will contribute to the process of broadening the scope of the Assembly's law-developing and law-legitimizing functions. In other words, the most significant "contribution" of China toward the establishment of a new international legal order may lie in its participation in the General Assembly's long-term amending process of international law.

---

is a fact of present-day international life that, for whatever reasons of whatever validity, statesmen exhibit a definite preference for a political rather than a legal process of legitimization." See Inis L. Claude, Jr., "Collective Legitimization as a Political Function of the United Nations," *IO* 20 (Summer 1966), 370-71.

PART III. CONCLUSION: CHINA AND WORLD ORDER

· 9 ·

THE CHINESE IMAGE AND STRATEGY
OF WORLD ORDER

> The view of the earth from the moon fascinated me—
> a small disk, 240,000 miles away. It was hard to think that
> that little thing held so many problems, so many frustra-
> tions. Raging nationalistic interests, famines, wars, pesti-
> lence don't show from that distance. I'm convinced that
> some wayward stranger in a spacecraft, coming from some
> other part of the heavens, could look at earth and never
> know that it was inhabited at all. But the same way-
> ward stranger would certainly know instinctively that if
> the earth were inhabited, then the destinies of all who
> lived on it must inevitably be interwoven and joined. We
> are one hunk of ground, water, air, clouds, floating around
> in space. From out there it really is "one world."
>
> Frank Borman, on seeing Earth from Apollo 8

Toward a Clarification of Planetary Values

This chapter examines critically the Chinese image and strategy of
world order and their implications for the creation of a new and just
world order. While relying on empirical data and behavioral referents
presented in Part II, this final appraisal is made within the normative
framework of a preferred future for mankind. For our analytical and
reference convenience, the WOMP values may be restated and simplified as four planetary values (PVs): (PV_1) the minimization of large-
scale collective violence; (PV_2) the maximization of social and economic well-being; (PV_3) the realization of fundamental human rights
and conditions of political justice; and (PV_4) the rehabilitation and
maintenance of environmental quality.[1]

The present international system has largely failed to come to grips
with the fundamental causes of human misery: war and violence, poverty and inequitable growth and distribution of the GGP, oppression
and injustice, and ecological decay and degradation. The prospects of
human survival are not bright as the world moves in the direction of
increasing perils and diminishing opportunities. That the world in
1977 should have spent on arms in just two days the equivalent of a
year's budget for the United Nations and its specialized agencies is a

---

[1] See Falk, *A Study of Future Worlds*, pp. 11-30.

political reality in stark contrast to the image of "one world" seen from Apollo 8.[2] That 30 percent of the world's population should be sick from too much food while 60 percent is sick from too little presents another image of global reality.[3]

To be sure, such a normative and globalist perspective in the study of world politics is fraught with methodological hazards, but its heuristic value for science, scholarship, and policy-making is gradually gaining acceptance.[4] The WOMP modeling process is not an esoteric intellectual exercise; it offers instead a normative map for policy science. For our present purposes, it provides a framework for disciplined normative analysis of global reform in general and the Chinese image and strategy of world order in particular.

It behooves us to place any critical appraisal of the Chinese image of world order in a comparative frame of reference. The question inevitably arises as to the nature, scope, and depth of the commitment on the part of the UN Member States to the above-mentioned planetary values. Perhaps with the possible exception of the Nordic countries, the world view of most Member States does not seem to be deeply imbued with globalism or planetary humanitarianism. It becomes immediately apparent that the disparities in status, capabilities, and interests among the Member States have produced divergent degrees of moral and political commitment to the realization of the four planetary values.

What cannot be disputed is that the traditional notion of defining world order exclusively in terms of negative peace (war prevention or avoidance) is no longer relevant. For example, when the World Law Fund—later renamed the Institute for World Order—launched in 1966 a global effort to recruit groups of scholars in various parts of the world to direct nationally or regionally based inquiries into the problem of war prevention, it had little success. It was only after the scope of the normative framework had been expanded to include the related values of economic well-being and social and political justice that a

[2] For comparative budget estimates between arms expenditures and the budgets of the UN system, see Ruth Leger Sivard, *World Military and Social Expenditures 1977* (Leesburg, Va.: WMSE Publications, 1977), p. 5. See also "Experts See $350 Billion a Year Arms Race Damaging World Development Prospects," *UN Chronicle* 14 (October 1977), 41-44.

[3] Ali A. Mazrui and others, "State of the Globe Report 1977," *Alternatives* 3 (December 1977), 164.

[4] See the following: Louis Rene Beres and Harry R. Targ, "Perspectives on World Order: A Review," *Alternatives* 2 (June 1976), 177-98; Harold D. Lasswell, "The Promise of the World Order Modelling Movement," *World Politics* 29 (April 1977), 425-37; David Wilkinson, "World Order Models Project: First Fruits," *Political Science Quarterly* 91 (Summer 1976), 329-35; and James P. Sewell, *World Order Studies: A Critical Examination*, Research Monograph No. 43, Center of International Studies, Princeton University (July 1974).

global reform-oriented research enterprise, WOMP, was successfully inaugurated.[5]

While the WOMP collaborators from seven territorial groups (West Germany, Latin America, Japan, India, North America, Africa, the Soviet Union) and a nonterritorial group showed such common attributes as globalism, reformism, and futurism, and accepted the collective challenge of thinking, feeling, and acting on world order modeling, they have also shown contrasting, and sometimes competing, images of value hierarchies in the course of establishing common WOMP goals. The four WOMP values therefore represent a delicate balance of consensual compromise rather than a closed system of value hierarchy. "These [four] values," enunciates "State of the Globe Report 1974" prepared by Richard A. Falk in collaboration with his WOMP colleagues, "rather than national, regional or ideological interests, orient our thinking. At present there are widespread disagreements on the relative importance of these values and on the choice of means for their promotion."[6] It may be noted in this connection that the World Law Fund had also extended an invitation to a group of scholars in the PRC, hoping to get some form of participation from the Chinese, but predictably this effort was of no avail.[7]

If the independent scholars who are committed to the common enterprise of establishing a global, futurist, normative modeling for world order show such a contrast in their clarification of common values, it seems safe to assume that the contrasts between the images of world order held by their governments will be even more sharply divergent. Whether or not a new world order is peacefully established may be determined ultimately by the Big Five, given their special rights and responsibilities in the management of global politics. To the extent that a new world order is conceptualized as a radical change of the status quo, embodying the four planetary values, the commitment and cooperation of the Big Five are in serious doubt. The opposition of four of the Big Five to the Charter review/revision question may

[5] For details, see Mendlovitz, *On the Creation of a Just World Order*, pp. vii-xvii; Ian Baldwin, Jr., "Thinking About a New World Order for the Decade 1990," *War/Peace Report* (January 1970), 3-8; Yoshikazu Sakamoto, "The Rationale of the World Order Models Project," *Proceedings of the 66th Annual Meeting of the American Society of International Law* 66 (September 1972), 245-52.

[6] Richard A. Falk *et al.*, "State of the Globe Report 1974," *Alternatives* 1 (June/September 1975), 163.

[7] Baldwin, "Thinking About a New World Order for the Decade 1990," p. 4. In the absence of direct PRC participation in WOMP, Paul T. K. Lin, director of the Center for East Asian Studies, McGill University, Montreal, Canada, contributed a chapter, entitled "Development Guided by Values: Comments on China's Road and Its Implications," in Mendlovitz, *On the Creation of a Just World Order*, pp. 259-96.

well bear out the axiom that those who have privileges will not give them up of their own volition.

Table 9.1 gives one measure of the commitment on the part of the Big Five to a new world order, as revealed by their voting record on twenty "vital" world-order issues in the General Assembly. The table is adapted from the annual report on the General Assembly by Donald F. Keys, UN representative of the World Federalists. Keys selected from each General Assembly session what he regarded as twenty vital world-order issues and then scored the voting behavior of each Member State according to a set of explicitly normative criteria: (1) world peace and just relations among nations; (2) economic equity; (3) human rights and social justice; (4) effective world organization; and (5) preservation of environment and ecological balance.[8]

Both the issues selected and criteria used in Table 9.1 represent a broad spectrum of institutional, normative, behavioral, political, and attitudinal problems related to the challenge of establishing a new world order. They call for a few observations. First, the commitment of the Big Five in the General Assembly falls far below that of top performing Member States, who have scored in the 90s in Keys' normative "U.N. Voting Box Score." Second, Table 9.1 does not agree with Table 4.4 (which showed the voting record of the Big Five on all nonprocedural questions in the Security Council from November 23, 1971 to December 31, 1976), highlighting a relative weakness in China's commitment to PV_1 in comparison with the other planetary values.

Third, Table 9.1 tends to agree with the general thrust of Table 3.6, which showed the voting record of the Big Five on all the resolutions adopted by the General Assembly (by a roll-call or recorded vote) from the 26th to the 31st Sessions. Different interests and commitments among the Big Five are reflected in their voting behavior. China's poor voting record on PV_1 is more than sufficiently offset by her strong voting record on PV_2, PV_4 and, to a lesser extent, on PV_3. On the whole, then, the Chinese voting record on world-order issues is a respectable one. If the above points were not taken into account, our critical appraisal of the Chinese image and strategy of world order would be unfair and unbalanced.

THE CHINESE IMAGE OF WORLD ORDER

The Chinese image of world order that is projected throughout the United Nations system defines the international system as a Manichean

---

[8] Donald F. Keys, *The 31st General Assembly of the United Nations* (New York: The Institute for World Order, Planetary Citizens, World Federalists, 1977), p. 51.

TABLE 9.1. Normative Rating of Voting Record of the Big Five on
20 Important World-Order Issues in the General Assembly, 1972-76 (percent)

	27th Sess.	28th Sess.	29th Sess.	30th Sess.	31st Sess.	Average for 1972-76
PRC	68	57	58	48	62	59
USA	15	20	45	45	45	34
USSR	60	55	43	60	75	59
UK	25	27	53	52	65	44
FRANCE	30	27	49	65	75	49
	n = 20	n = 20	n = 20	n = 20	n = 20	

Source: Adapted from Donald F. Keys, The 27th General Assembly of the United Nations (Washington, D.C.: World Federalist Education Fund, 1973), pp. 62-65; The 28th General Assembly of the United Nations (Washington, D.C.: World Federalist Education Fund, 1974), pp. i-vi; The 29th General Assembly of the United Nations (New York: World Federalist Education Fund, 1975), pp. 68-70; The 30th General Assembly of the United Nations (New York: World Federalist Association, 1976), pp. 6-8; and The 31st General Assembly of the United Nations (New York: The Institute for World Order, Planetary Citizens, World Federalists, 1977), pp. 52-54.

struggle between the status quo defenders and the revolutionary chal-
lengers. It is an image deeply imbued with "justice" rather than with
order, with change rather than with stability. The moral and strategic
imperative of the Chinese image is that the old and unjust order had
to be destroyed first, before a new and just world order could be
established.

Hence, a negative vision tends to dominate the positive vision in the
Chinese perception. To a remarkable degree, the Maoist image of
world order as discussed in Chapter 2 has been retained intact at the
conceptual level in Chinese multilateral diplomacy. The stress on
sovereignty and self-reliance, the twin pillars in the Chinese strategy
for building a new world order, reflects China's powerful sense of past
grievances. At the same time, it also reflects the Maoist moral and
political commitment to build a conceptual environment conducive
to a new egalitarian international order.

The legacy of the past that impinges on the Chinese image is the
hierarchical order of Western and Japanese imperialism, not the hierarchical order of the tribute system. In fact, the Chinese image of
world order is so antihierarchical that it is difficult for the Chinese to
accept the concept of the "interdependent global village" in the planetary politics of cosurvival. It may be argued that the Chinese image
of world order is still afflicted with the siege mentality of an underdog
struggling to survive in a hostile environment. Hence, in spite of its
moral and ideological endorsement of a new and just world order,
China still lacks any coherent and viable strategies of transition. In
short, the Chinese image is not so much a product of a disciplined
analysis of contemporary international politics in a period of transition
between great system changes as a projection of the Maoist normative
interpretation of contemporary Chinese experience.

China and the Minimization of Large-Scale Collective Violence (PV₁)

Like the other great powers, China is eclectic in her commitment to
the planetary values. PV_1, for example, is the least compelling in the
Chinese image of world order. The repeated rhetorical theme that
"great disorder under heaven [t'ien-hsia ta-luan] is a good thing"
sums up the contemporary Chinese definition of the international situation. Is China advocating anarchy and disorder in international
relations? Not necessarily, because in the Chinese view of the world,
great disorder is an objective fact, independent of man's will.

In the Chinese perception, all basic contradictions in the world are
sharpening, particularly the contradictions between the two superpowers on the one hand and the peoples of all countries on the other,

as well as the contradictions between the two superpowers themselves.[9] Herein lies the source of the great disorder under heaven. However, this great disorder is a good thing, the Chinese argue, because it can only hasten the demise of the old order, based on colonialism, imperialism, and hegemony. "In this turbulent world," the Chinese metaphorically state, "the people in their fight are, like sea gulls flying high in the sky, harbingers of a rising storm. In this great disorder they have nothing to lose but their chains; they have a new world to win!"[10]

Until the end of 1974, the Chinese definition of the international situation adhered to the Maoist formulation of May 20, 1970, that "[t]he danger of a new world war still exists and the people of all countries must get prepared. But revolution is the main trend in the world today." At the 1st Session of the Fourth National People's Congress of the PRC in January 1975, however, a major change occurred. In the report on the work of the government that he delivered at the Congress, Premier Chou En-lai stated: "Their [the superpowers'] fierce contention is bound to lead to world war some day."[11] It should be noted, however, that the central theme of Chou's report was that China had to concentrate internally upon building herself into a powerful socialist state, while at the same time preparing a state of readiness in the event of war, which was now believed to be more and more likely.

China's assessment of the international situation has since been stressing the growing danger of a new world war, stemming from increased contention and/or collusion between the superpowers. At times, China has advanced a proposition that cannot be proven false: if the superpowers cooperate, that proves that collusion exists; if they fall short on détente, as in the nuclear arms race, that proves the existence of contention. Close examination reveals, however, that superpower collusion, according to the Chinese image, is partial, transient, and relative, whereas superpower contention is all-embracing, long-term, and absolute. Indeed, this is an application of the Maoist theory of contradictions to the analysis of détente in the nuclear age.

Either because of conceptual confusion or because of the deliberate exercise of ambiguity, the Chinese definition of the international situa-

[9] See Jen Ku-p'ing, "Year of Turbulence, Year of Victory," *JMJP*, January 8, 1975, p. 5; Yang Chün, "Great Disorder Under Heaven Is a Good Thing," *JMJP*, January 24, 1975, p. 6.
[10] "World in Great Disorder, Excellent Situation," NCNA-English, Peking, January 8, 1974, in *SPRCP*, No. 5537 (January 18, 1974), 166.
[11] Chou En-lai, "Report on the Work of the Government," *PR*, No. 4 (January 24, 1975), 24.

tion has been a pervasive mixture of *descriptive* and *prescriptive* analysis of war and peace. It is not always clear, for example, whether China is opposed to "sham" détente in favor of "genuine" détente, or whether China is opposed to détente *per se*. Such confusion or ambiguity provides Soviet opponents with a basis for depicting China as a clear and present danger to international peace and stability. Note the self-created predicament revealed in Chinese representative Lai Ya-li's somewhat weak rebuttal: "What calls for attention is that for some time the Soviet representative [Malik] has been nastily propagating the idea that China wants to provoke a world war and that China wishes to see a direct confrontation between the United States and the Soviet Union in the Middle East, and so on and so forth. As is known to all, China is a developing country. Like other third world countries, we need a favourable international environment in which to build our country. But as the Chinese saying goes, 'The trees may prefer calm but the wind will not subside.' "[12]

The Chinese have expounded on several important problems in their diagnosis of the PV_1 problem. They have pointed out the widening gap between the rhetoric of peace and the escalation of the arms race between the two superpowers. The arms race, in spite of, or perhaps because of, the overselling of détente, seems to have acquired a life of its own, expanding vertically, horizontally, quantitatively and qualitatively. The Chinese have also addressed themselves to the fundamentals of disarmament rather than to the technicalities of arms control. The Chinese argued cogently that the arms control agreements, especially the 1963 partial nuclear test ban treaty, have had the effect of forcing a new and more sophisticated round of arms escalation by redefining the rules of the game, as the nuclear arms race between the superpowers shifts from a quantitative to a qualitative direction. Based on this type of analysis of the behavior of the two superpowers, not on what China herself will do, the theory of inevitability of war has been advanced as a Chinese forecasting of an undefined future.[13]

However, the Chinese prescriptive remedy may be worse than the disease. The Maoist notion that to oppose war with war is the only way to abolish war is a restatement of the *si vis pacem, para bellum* doctrine—"if you want peace, prepare for war." As such it seems anachronistic at best and dangerous at worst in the nuclear age. Can China really play the *para bellum* game of deterrence effectively and

[12] UN Doc. A/PV.2394 (5 November 1973), p. 101.
[13] Likewise, the Stockholm International Peace Research Institute predicted in its publication, *Armaments and Disarmament in the Nuclear Age*, that nuclear war will become inevitable. See *NYT*, October 8, 1976, p. A5.

credibly? It is doubtful. A credible, effective deterrence requires a constant demonstration of the deterrer's capability as well as of his intention to use force. Thus, deterrence has structural imperatives both for extensive war preparations to enhance credible capability and for frequent demonstration of reckless behavior to enhance credible intention. The pursuit of such a strategy of demonstrative violence may provide a minimum deterrence or incur the risk of a Soviet preventive or preemptive attack, depending on the perceptions of Soviet strategic decision makers.

The Chinese advocacy of *selective* armament and disarmament— that is, armament on the part of the prey and disarmament on the part of the predator—is also conceptually naive and strategically self-defeating. In effect, the Chinese are urging the Third World to participate in the war system. "Contrary to folk wisdom," Fouad Ajami wisely cautioned the Third World, "the turtle should never race the rabbit, for if it does, it is certainly destined to lose."[14] In sum, the Chinese prescriptive remedy of protracted struggle in the domain of the international war system, if taken seriously, may well serve as a recipe for self-defeat rather than a preventive vaccine for PV_1. The basic flaw in the Chinese image of war lies not so much in diagnosis as in prescription.

The Chinese image of PV_1 is also marred by an excessive preoccupation with the dominant actors and by an inadequate attention to the structural problems in the war system. To be sure, the superpowers are the most active players and promoters of the war system. But it must also be pointed out that the power elites in many Third World countries also participate in the war system, accepting the rules of the jungle, devoting scarce resources to armament purchases, and inviting the active participation of the great powers in local conflict beyond their control. The Chinese insensitivity to the ever-present danger of local disorder escalating into a global conflict cannot be condoned. The link between local disorder and world disorder should not be cavalierly dismissed.

The obsession with the Soviet Union is a poisonous element in the Chinese image of world order. There is no evidence that the new leadership of Hua Kuo-feng has moderated this Maoist obsession. In fact, it seems to have taken a turn for the worse. In the June 16, 1977, issue of the authoritative *Jen-min jih-pao*, an anonymous commentator characterized the Soviet Union as (1) the most dangerous source of world war in the present era; (2) the most vicious type of neo-

---

[14] Fouad Ajami, *The Global Populists: Third World Nations and World-Order Crises*, Research Monograph No. 41, Center of International Studies, Princeton University (May 1974), p. 19.

colonialism in the present era; and (3) the worst renegade of Marxism-Leninism in the present era.[15] Likewise, in the most comprehensive foreign policy posture statement issued since the death of Mao Tse-tung, the editorial department of *Jen-min jih-pao* proclaimed the canonization of Mao's theory of the three worlds as the strategic principle to guide China's global policy as well as the powerful ideological weapon for pushing forward world history.[16]

Yet, the post-Mao leadership has already reformulated Mao's "superiority of man over weapons" dictum by claiming that the decisive factor for victory in war is "man with weapons in hand." On the basis of such a reformulation, China has already begun launching the "four modernizations"—the modernizations of industry, agriculture, national defense, and science and technology—without establishing a firm hierarchy of priorities among them. We may characterize this new drive as a Chinese counterpart of the "bread-and-gun" approach. In an interview with French journalists on October 21, 1977, the newly restored Teng Hsiao-p'ing went so far, and for the first time so explicitly, as to include the United States among countries which should unite with China, Europe and Japan in the broadest international front against Soviet policy for global hegemony. This quickly provoked a sharp Soviet counterattack. *Pravda* on October 23, 1977, reported Teng's interview in detail and declared it to be the "archreactionary essence" of the post-Mao Chinese leadership.[17]

In spite of her intense political and ideological hostility toward the Soviet Union, China's arms expenditures as measured in constant dollars stayed at about $3 billion per annum during the period 1970-75, compared with a steady rise in Soviet arms expenditures as shown in Appendix L.[18] A recent CIA study reveals that China is about twenty years behind the Soviet Union in most types of weapons technology.[19] Hence, China's modernization drive for both conventional and nuclear weapons has its own rationale and justification. Nonetheless, should this set in motion a Sino-Soviet arms rivalry, its significance should not be underplayed or dismissed as a regional conflict with no bearing on PV_1. The onset of a Sino-Soviet arms race is bound to complicate

[15] "Watch How They Are Going to Act," *JMJP*, June 16, 1977, p. 1.

[16] *JMJP*, November 1, 1977, pp. 1-6, English trans. in *PR*, No. 45 (November 4, 1977), 10-41. See also Shih Wen, "Chairman Mao's Great Strategic Concept—About Differentiating the Three Worlds," *Kuang-min jih-pao*, August 18, 1977; English trans. in *SPRCP*, No. 6416 (September 6, 1977), 1-7.

[17] *Soviet World Outlook* 2 (November 15, 1977), 5.

[18] The purge of Lin Piao in 1971 may be in part responsible for the rather drastic decline in military expenditures in the period 1971-75.

[19] "CIA Study Reveals—China Now Building Rocket, ICBM Force," The *Korean Herald* (Seoul), August 17, 1977. See also Drew Middleton, "What the Chinese Forces Lack: Most Types of Modern Weapons," *NYT*, June 24, 1977, p. A3.

further the chronic problem of comparing apples with oranges in bilateral SALT negotiations between the United States and the Soviet Union. Finally, any UN attempt at disarmament cannot progress beyond a rhetorical battle in the face of Chinese nonparticipation, Soviet propaganda-inspired manipulation, and American contempt and opposition.

As noted in Part II, China is not opposed to every ACD issue as a matter of dogma. Rather, her multilateral diplomacy on this crucial issue follows the dictates of what she perceives to be China's national security interests. This has been made evident by the Chinese support of such measures as the establishment of nuclear-free zones around the globe, the complete and thorough destruction of chemical and biological warfare, and the banning of any military use of the international seabed. Most symbolically, China's repeated pledge to the no-first-use principle stands in striking contrast with the refusal of the nuclear superpowers at the 1975 NPT review conference to pledge no-first-use of nuclear weapons against nonnuclear powers, despite the Third World's efforts to secure such a pledge.

At the operational and behavioral level, China has presented no threat to international peace as she has carefully avoided unilateral military interventions in local conflict situations around the world in recent years. As Figure 9.1 shows, China has also been the least active of the Big Five as a "merchant of death." Notwithstanding Chinese militant rhetorics in international forums, the perception that China presents no problem or threat to world order has emerged as one of the main consensuses in the author's field interviews. In the final analysis, the basic weakness of China's commitment to PV_1 lies not so much in any threat she presents to world order, as in her refusal to

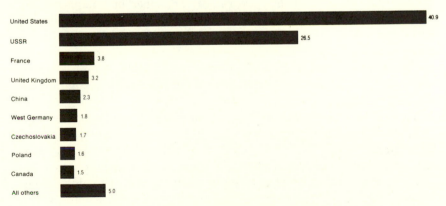

United States — 40.9
USSR — 26.5
France — 3.8
United Kingdom — 3.2
China — 2.3
West Germany — 1.8
Czechoslovakia — 1.7
Poland — 1.6
Canada — 1.5
All others — 5.0

FIGURE 9.1. The World's Major Arms Exporters, 1961-75
(US $ billion).

481

participate in the global search for a more viable and peaceful alternative to the present war system.

China and the Maximization of Social and Economic Well-Being (PV$_2$)

There is no need to repeat all the principles and propositions advanced by the PRC delegates in the courses of their participation in the inaugural process of NIEO. Suffice it here to say that China has already integrated NIEO in her own principled stand on development and that such an integration has produced mutually interactive and beneficial effects. China's own conceptualization of world order has been legitimized to a large degree by NIEO, on the one hand, and NIEO has been blessed with Chinese support, on the other. As already noted in Chapter 5, the dominant component in the Chinese image of a new world economic order is the concept of independent and self-reliant development of national economy.

It may also be noted in this connection that China's own development model at the conceptual level is congenial to PV$_2$. If development is still viewed in the traditional and purely quantitative way of measuring the growth of GNP, the Chinese model of self-reliance may seem somewhat inapplicable to some countries and anachronistic to others. However, PV$_2$ is in essence a value-realizing process. Hence, development needs to be viewed more in qualitative (distributive justice) than in quantitative (growth) terms, and more in terms of human welfare than in economic statistics.

Furthermore, development needs to be viewed within the framework of the existing structural inequities in the world economic system. That is, development should help developing countries to liberate themselves from the vicious process of exchanges of unequal value, the process which has helped dominant centers to penetrate deeply into dependent peripheries, with the latter becoming even more marginal in the world economic system.[20] Finally, development needs to be viewed in psychological terms, too—that is, as a means to enhance national dignity and self-respect, exorcising the pernicious influence of the "welfare mentality."

Viewed in such normative terms, the Chinese model of development is a major conceptual contribution to PV$_2$ as well as a potent prescription to deal with the problem of alienation among the poor and the weak in the global ghettoes. What is most striking about the Chinese image is the set of unorthodox assumptions and values it embodies: that development is both desirable and feasible only within

[20] The oil-rich Third World countries in the Middle East are exceptions to this generalization.

the closed system of populist feedbacks, mobilizing the creative power of the people only to serve the people; that the horizontal distribution cannot be decoupled from the vertical growth of the national pie; that equity is more important and desirable than efficiency; that an egalitarian social and economic order cannot be maintained without a continuing struggle to keep the superstructure pure and proletarian; and that development, in the final analysis, is possible only to those who help themselves (self-reliance), utilizing foreign aid as an auxiliary means. Even though the Chinese image of development does not agree with all the assumptions and principles of NIEO, the process of mutual legitimization between China and the New International Economic Order (which should be accepted as the most realistic expression of a global consensus on PV_2) has already begun.

China and the Realization of Fundamental Human Rights and Justice (PV_3)

Is China committed to PV_3? Defined in her own frame of reference, China's declared commitment has been strong, even though its application is not always consistent, following political calculus more than the universalized norms embodied in international human rights covenants. Although political and social justice is a complex and hazardous concept to operationalize because of its high susceptibility to selective reading and application, the concept within the WOMP framework addresses itself to such contemporary variants of "liberty, equality, and fraternity" as genocide, colonialism (old and new), racism and apartheid, torture and cruelty, as well as human equality and freedom of expression and self-realization. Put in the parlance of peace research, PV_3 purports to promote positive peace and eliminate structural violence in human existence.

While fundamental human rights have been codified in no less than nineteen multilateral treaties concluded under the auspices of the United Nations, their violation has been quite pervasive throughout the world. Two-thirds of the Member States of the United Nations violate the human rights they have vowed to uphold, according to the 1977 annual report of Amnesty International (the winner of the Nobel Peace Prize in 1977), and government-sanctioned torture is also widespread. The Universal Declaration of Human Rights, proclaimed by the General Assembly in 1948, is "violated in a majority of countries all over the world," the report further noted, adding: "All major regimes, all political or ideological blocs are involved."[21] This sad state of affairs calls our attention dramatically to the limitations of UN enforcement capability, on the one hand, and the gap between

---

[21] *NYT*, December 9, 1977, p. A2.

policy pronouncement and policy performance of the Member States on human rights, on the other.

Although China belongs to the category of two-thirds of the Member States where human rights are being violated, it is difficult to make a fair and disciplined inquiry into the actual conditions of human rights inside China for a number of reasons. First, the Chinese conceptualization of "human rights" follows a different normative direction from ours: it is more collective than individualistic; it is more instrumental than intrinsic; and it is more duties-oriented than rights-oriented. Second, the line between the formal and the informal processes in the Chinese legal system is indistinguishably blurred, although the informal part plays a greater role in the legal decision-making process. Third, the data available to outside analysts are extremely fragmentary; hence no empirical or systematic analysis is possible. Finally, there is some difficulty of striking a balance in our analysis between quantitative and qualitative aspects of the conditions of human rights in China, or for that matter, in any other country.

However, the year 1977 witnessed a steady stream of articles from *Jen-min jih-pao, Hung-ch'i* and other publications calling public attention to the importance of protecting life, liberty, and property against arbitrary harm. This can be safely interpreted to mean two things: that there have been widespread official and unofficial violations of human and property rights in the period 1966-76; and that the post-Mao leadership is determined to rectify the situation. In fact, the new CCP constitution adopted at the 11th Party Congress on August 18, 1977, declared flatly in Article 12 that "it is absolutely impermissible for anyone to suppress criticism or to retaliate. Those guilty of doing so should be investigated and punished."[22] Yet the irony is that the members of the "Gang of Four" are being denied their human rights, while at the same time being condemned for having violated the human rights of others.

Since her entry into the United Nations, China is caught up in the global politics of human rights. Significantly, she has refused to participate in the work of the Commission on Human Rights, while taking part in another ECOSOC functional commission, the Commission on the Status of Women (see Figure 6.2). Hence, most Chinese policy statements on human rights questions were made in the Social Committee of ECOSOC. It was in this committee that Chinese representative Wang Jun-sheng presented for the first time China's most comprehensive "principled stand" on human rights questions on May 30, 1972. Wang quickly defined human rights as the struggle for justice and then made specific linkage of this struggle to the peoples of

---

[22] *PR*, No. 36 (September 2, 1977), 21.

Azania [South Africa], Zimbabwe [Southern Rhodesia], Namibia [South West Africa], the Portuguese colonies, and the occupied Arab territories. In support of this struggle (human rights), the Chinese government, Wang declared, "had always refrained from having any diplomatic contacts with the South African and South Rhodesian white racist régimes, nor did it have any economic or trade relations with them, direct or indirect."[23] Having defined human rights in this way, Wang concluded: "The question of human rights was an important issue for the Economic and Social Council. China was ready to work together with all the countries and peoples who loved peace and upheld justice in supporting the struggles of the peoples of the world against imperialism, colonialism and racism and for the attainment and defence of national independence, national sovereignty and fundamental human rights in accordance with the spirit of the Charter."[24]

In this spirit, China has gone far beyond the minimalist conception of UN peace-keeping in her advocacy of stronger, broader, and all-embracing sanctions against Southern Rhodesia and South Africa under Chapter VII of the Charter. China has also voted in favor of General Assembly Resolution 3102 (XXVII) concerning respect for human rights in armed conflict, and joined in Assembly condemnation of the use of torture by governments. Yet China refused to join (nonparticipation in the vote) the three Assembly resolutions on "Protection of Human Rights in Chile."[25] "Only through the elimination of hegemonism, colonialism and imperialism," the Chinese representative explained in the Third Committee, "could human rights in Chile be restored."[26]

Furthermore, China has signed none of the nineteen multilateral treaties on human rights concluded under the auspices of the United Nations.[27] She has not openly criticized any of the human rights conventions but has adopted instead an evasive posture of noncommittal. In one of the rare statements on UN human rights conventions, Chinese representative Wang Tzu-chuan stated in the Social Committee of ECOSOC:

> . . . the Universal Declaration of Human Rights . . . , had been adopted at the third session of the General Assembly, prior to the founding of the People's Republic of China. It was therefore neces-

[23] UN Doc. E/AC.7/SR.699 (30 May 1972), p. 143.
[24] *Ibid.*, p. 145.
[25] General Assembly Resolution 3219 (XXIX) of 6 November 1974; General Assembly Resolution 3448 (XXX) of 9 December 1975; General Assembly Resolution 31/124 of 16 December 1976.
[26] UN Doc. A/C.3/31/SR.58 (23 November 1976), p. 7.
[27] See UN Doc. E/CN.4/907/Rev.13 (27 January 1977).

sary for his Government to examine and study its contents. The other document mentioned in the draft resolution, namely, the International Covenant on Economic, Social and Cultural Rights, had been adopted at a time when the People's Republic of China had been deprived of its lawful rights in the United Nations. It had been illegal for the Chiang Kai-shek clique to sign that Covenant in the name of China and the Chinese Government assumed no obligation thereunder. As in the case of the Universal Declaration of Human Rights, the Chinese Government had to examine and study the Covenant and reserved the right to comment on the two documents.[28]

In the Chinese image of world order, human rights represent an instrument in the global antihegemonic struggle against the superpowers. The Carter Administration's dispute with the Soviet Union over human rights has been characterized as a "hypocritical farce." Under the rule of the Western bourgeoisie capitalism, "the broad masses of the working people have only the right to lead an exploited and humiliated existence." Yet the United States is given credit for being candid in admitting culpability in some ways. "But, as the Soviet Union today has become a land of K.G.B. agents, bristling with prisons full of its citizens while many others have been exiled," ask the Chinese, "what 'human rights' can it talk about?" Thus, "the new tsars' model of utter violation of human rights" has been more harshly criticized than "Washington's F.B.I. shadowing."[29] China has also strongly criticized what she calls "the Russianization policy enforced by the Soviet revisionist ruling clique" against minority nationalities as well as against Soviet practice of torture against dissidents placed in the so-called psychiatric hospitals.[30]

At the same time, China declared that it was none of UN business to talk about Hong Kong, Macao, or Tibet. As noted in Chapter 3, one of the items in the regular UN budget targeted for Chinese withholding relates to the offices of UN High Commissioner for Refugees at Macao, New Delhi, and Katmandu. In short, China wants to have her cake and eat it too on the question of human rights. In practice, however, this has raised no serious operational problem either for Chinese multilateral diplomacy or for the world-order building process, because PV_3 in UN politics is concentrated largely on Africa.

[28] UN Doc. E/AC.7/SR.748 (13 May 1974), pp. 156-57.
[29] "Absurd Champion of 'Human Rights'," *PR*, No. 11 (March 11, 1977), 23-24.
[30] See "New Tsars Push a National Annexation Policy," *PR*, No. 10 (March 4, 1977), 20-21, and "Soviet 'Psychiatric Hospitals'—Prisons in Disguise," *Ibid.*, No. 11 (March 11, 1977), 20-22.

China and the Rehabilitation and Maintenance
of Environmental Quality (PV$_4$)

There is no consensus even among world-order specialists as to whether PV$_4$ should be included—and if so, with what priority—in the normative framework of WOMP. In a trenchant critique of *The Limits to Growth*, the celebrated study commissioned by the Club of Rome,[31] Johan Galtung has cogently argued that the ideology of "ecologism" is methodologically misleading—because of its "we are all in the same boat"—approach and normatively biased in favor of the status quo; as such, it runs counter to the welfare of the weak and the poor.[32] At the 1972 United Nations Conference on the Human Environment, a group of Third World scientists also made a sweeping attack on the limits-to-growth notion implied in the ecological movement prevalent in many rich, industrialized countries: "We strongly reject models of stagnation, proposed by certain alarmist Western ecologists, economists, industrialists, and computer-fans; and assert that holding economic growth per se responsible for environmental ills amounts to a diversion of attention from the real causes of the problem which lie in the profit-motivation of the systems of production in the capitalist world. . . ."[33]

The Chinese image of PV$_4$ was first projected at the United Nations Conference on the Human Environment. China declared her "active approval" and "strong support" of the Conference, sending a large delegation of thirty-one members. In this debut at a UN-sponsored global conference, China played an uncharacteristically active role. She first introduced a draft resolution to establish an *ad hoc* committee to review the draft declaration in its entirety so as to "give full expression to the views of various countries."[34] This was a euphemism for saying that China as a newcomer had had no part in the formulation of the draft and would now like to add her own inputs in the document's revision. Having made this unusual and unexpected move (accepting the Iranian amendment to change the title from an *ad hoc* committee to the Working Group on the Declaration on the Human Environment), China then succeeded in large measure in reformulating the preambular paragraphs 2, 4, 5, and 7 of the Declara-

---

[31] Donella Meadows *et al.*, *The Limits to Growth* (New York: Universe Books, 1972).

[32] Johan Galtung, " 'The Limits to Growth' and Class Politics," *Journal of Peace Research* 10 (1973), 101-114.

[33] Quoted in *ibid.*, p. 105.

[34] *Report of the United Nations Conference on the Human Environment*, Stockholm, 5-16 June 1972, UN Doc. A/CONF.48/14/Rev.1 (1973) (hereafter cited as *Report of the UNCHE*), p. 49.

tion in accordance with some of its own "Ten Cardinal Principles on Amending [the] 'Declaration on [the] Human Environment'."[35]

On June 16, 1972, the Conference adopted a Declaration on the Human Environment consisting of a preamble (7 paragraphs) and twenty-six principles. The Declaration purports to have embodied "the need for a common outlook and for common principles to inspire and guide the peoples of the world in the preservation and enhancement of the human environment."[36] Except for minor drafting changes, the Chinese text was accepted by the Conference as preambular paragraph 2, which reads: "The protection and improvement of the human environment is a major issue which affects the well-being of peoples and economic development throughout the world; it is the urgent desire of the peoples of the whole world and the duty of all Governments."[37]

Thus, the concept of environmental protection and improvement has been linked to: (1) the welfare of peoples; (2) economic development; and (3) the duty of all governments. Louis Sohn has observed in this connection: "The Chinese delegation was somehow able to persuade the other members of the Working Group not only to accept this [governmental] duty but also to put it most appropriately in the forefront of the Declaration. This was a striking accomplishment, though the language is more obscure than might have been desired, considering the importance of the principle involved."[38]

However, China suffered a major defeat on the question of nuclear tests at the Conference. The Conference adopted by 56 votes to 3 (China, France, and Gabon), with 29 abstentions, a draft resolution condemning nuclear tests aimed largely at China and France. Moreover, Principle 26 in the Declaration stipulates: "Man and his environment must be spared the effects of nuclear weapons and all other means of mass destruction. . . ."[39]

In spite of her strong objection to Principle 26, China's interest and participation in environmental issues have remained unaffected. At the 27th General Assembly, China was elected as a member of the Governing Council of the newly established United Nations Environment Programme (UNEP) and has remained a member, attending each of the Council's annual sessions. In an intense and emotional debate following the Stockholm Conference over the preferred site

[35] For analysis of Chinese participation in the Conference, see Sohn, "The Stockholm Declaration on the Human Environment," pp. 423-515; and Timmler, "Die Umwelt-Konferenz in Stockholm," pp. 618-23. For the text of "Ten Cardinal Principles on Amending 'Declaration on Human Environment'," see PR, No. 25 (June 23, 1972), 9-11.

[36] *Report of the UNCHE*, p. 3.   [37] *Ibid.*

[38] Sohn, "The Stockholm Declaration on the Human Environment," p. 440.

[39] *Report of the UNCHE*, p. 5.

of UNEP headquarters, China supported the pro-Nairobi group with the Third World, in spite of a UN Secretariat estimate that the annual cost of the UNEP secretariat in Nairobi would be $2.3 million compared with $1.4 million for a Geneva site. In 1973 China made a voluntary contribution of $131,628 (see Appendix G) to UNEP and in March 1976 appointed Chu Ko-ping as her first permanent representative to UNEP in Nairobi. On September 22, 1974, the New China News Agency announced the existence of an Office of Environmental Protection.

In the Chinese image, environmental pollution is a highly differentiated phenomenon from one country to another "due to the differences in their respective natural conditions, levels of economic development, social systems and positions held in the international political and economic fabric."[40] The primary responsibilities for and consequences of pollution should be borne by the major polluters—in short, China took the "polluters must pay" approach. As for the developing countries, however, the environmental problems stem primarily from underdevelopment. The domestic model China has projected at international forums is that development and environment should be viewed as having an interdependent relationship; the former increases the capability to protect the latter, while the latter promotes the former.[41] China also echoed the Third World position that population growth *per se* was not a cause of environmental degradation.

The Chinese approach to environment is defensible in several important areas and indefensible in one crucial one. China's differentiated analysis of pollution—that is, both overdevelopment (affluence and conspicuous consumption) and underdevelopment (poverty) contribute to pollutions of different sorts—places PV_4 in complementary rather than competing terms with the other planetary values. For herself and the Third World, China defines ecology in developmental terms. In the tug of war between extreme environmentalists and extreme developmentalists, China has taken a middle-of-the-road position, stressing mutual harmony between environment and development. The Chinese domestic strategy of rural industrialization, self-reliance, recycling, and resettlement of the urban population (*hsia-fang*) makes the Chinese claim credible.[42]

[40] "First Session of Governing Council of UN Environment Program Concludes General Debate," NCNA-English, Geneva, June 19, 1973, in *SCMP*, No. 5406 (July 2, 1973), 53.

[41] For an elaboration of this theme, see Chu Ko-ping, "Environment and Development," *PR*, No. 20 (May 14, 1976), 19-20.

[42] See Kieran Broadbent, "Agriculture, Environment and Current Policy in China," *Asian Survey* 16 (May 1976), 411-26.

When we take into account China's rhetorical posturing to the Third World, her chronic populist strategic optimism, and her actual population policy,[43] China may be more right than wrong in her approach to the relationship between population and pollution. Surely, the world's population cannot be treated as a single, global mass. An analysis of population's impact on environment must take into account its relationship to space, resources, and consumption power and habits. When measured in terms of the "true" rates of population explosion—that is, feeding into the calculation the differences in standards of living—the United States is estimated as growing ten times as fast as India.[44] China is right in linking environment to the welfare of the people. And she is right in stressing the concept of governmental duty and responsibility in regard to environmental protection. Profit-oriented private industries can hardly be expected to take self-sacrificing measures.

The most serious problem concerning the Chinese commitment to PV_4 is the continuation of atmospheric nuclear tests. To follow the logic of China's "polluters must pay" approach, the "victim" countries, including the United States, are now in a position to ask China to pay compensation for whatever damage is caused by Chinese nuclear fallouts.[45] What would be the Chinese response to such requests if they were made? Would she respond with a concept of "just" and "unjust" pollution? So long as China continues her atmospheric nuclear tests, irrespective of the merit of their justification for reasons of national security, her political-ideological argument that the major root cause of environmental pollution is the imperialistic policy of plunder, aggression, and war will be morally weak and unconvincing.

[43] The New China News Agency pronounced on February 27, 1977, that "China's rate of population growth has gone down year by year since 1965 because of the promotion of birth control." China's population policy, it is further claimed, is that "China's population should increase in relation to the development of its economy." However, "in areas inhabited by the minority nationalities," the Hsinhua further reported, "many of whom were once dying out, the policy is to encourage population increase." This strikes one as both sensible and humane. See "China's Achievement in Birth Control," NCNA-English, Peking, February 27, 1977, in *SPRCP*, No. 6294 (March 8, 1977), 72.

[44] See Wayne David, "Overpopulated America," *New Republic* (January 10, 1970), 13-15.

[45] Note the State of the Globe Report 1977 by the WOMP group on this matter: "On 26 September and 17 November [1976], China carried out atmospheric nuclear tests. The second and largest of these was estimated to be in the 4-megaton range. The fallout from these tests was detected as far away as the eastern United States, where it was observed that the radioactive iodine levels in milk were higher than normal. Rani samples collected eight to ten days after the first blast registered a 100% gross increase in radioactivity in the eastern United States. Dust on cars in Pennsylvania and New Jersey was 1000 to 3000 times more radioactive than usual. In Connecticut, radioactivity was up to 10000 times the normal level." Mazrui *et al.*, "State of the Globe Report 1977," pp. 173-74.

In summary, then, the Chinese image of PV_1 is fraught with some serious conceptual and normative problems. The Chinese prescriptive remedy for PV_1 seems worse than the disease. Even after her entry into the United Nations, China has refused to participate in the 31-nation international forum for disarmament in Geneva, the Conference of the Committee on Disarmament (CCD). To be sure, the permanent co-chairmanship shared by the two superpowers has discouraged both French and Chinese participation in the CCD. Still, China's commitment and contribution to the minimization of collective violence are problematic.

At the conceptual and symbolic level, China's pronounced commitment to PV_2, PV_3, and PV_4 has been strong, if not always consistent. It is in the domain of these planetary values that the Chinese image of world order accords well with Johan Galtung's formulation of "inequality as one of the major forms of structural violence" and imperialism as a special form of dominance relationship.[46] In the Chinese image, violence is more than somatic sufferance or incapacitation. Indeed, the Chinese define violence in behavioral, structural, and normative terms; it extends to the political, economic, social, scientific, and cultural spheres of contemporary international politics.

As noted earlier, a negative vision is dominant in the Chinese image of world order, but this is a function of the Chinese perception that the international system is pervaded with injustice. When all is said and done, the Chinese arguments and pronouncements throughout the United Nations system all come down to the proposition that justice is a function of equality. This becomes even more evident when we look closely at the normative structure of the Chinese image of world order, which can be summarized as containing eight identifiable value components: (1) antihegemony; (2) international egalitarianism; (3) populism; (4) antiracism; (5) nationalism (which is closer to Herder's cultural pluralism than to Hitler's romantic chauvinism); (6) struggle as the dialectical imperative in resolving all types of contradictions; (7) self-reliance; and (8) mutual respect for state sovereignty, equality, and territorial integrity.

THE CHINESE STRATEGY OF WORLD ORDER

The practical importance of China in the global search for a new world order lies not so much in the image projected as in the operationalization of that image in Chinese global politics. Let us therefore look closely at the salient strategies and tactics of Chinese global policy as expressed in the United Nations system.

[46] Galtung, "A Structural Theory of Imperialism," pp. 81-117.

The dominant structure of Chinese global strategy still embodies Mao's dialectical world outlook. The three-worlds typology is retained and even canonized as the great strategic legacy of Mao Tse-tung. In practice, however, it represents a uniquely Chinese variant of the selective security system alluded to in Chapter 8: a united struggle of all against one principal predator. The Soviet Union has now become the principal contradiction in Chinese global strategy. It may not be an exaggeration to say that Chinese strategy is an extension of the zero-sum game toward "Soviet social-imperialism."

At the operational level, even NIEO politics has been transformed into an antihegemonic model. China's anti-American posture has been moderate and muted; it is largely confined to predictable and perfunctory rhetoric in public. Out of the political limelight, the relationship between China and the United States cannot be characterized as adversary. On the other hand, China has greatly exaggerated the nature and scope of the Second World's contribution toward the establishment of a new international economic order. One would have to search in vain for Chinese attacks against Japan and West European countries in the conduct of Chinese multilateral diplomacy.

It is hazardous to dichotomize principles and interests in Chinese global policy. The antihegemonic strategy, for example, blends both Chinese principles and interests. Still, it is possible to discern an evolving pattern of interaction between principles and interests in the development of Chinese global strategy throughout the United Nations system. Chinese interests, more than principles, have dominated in issues concerning what may be called China's "regional security zone." Notable examples in this category include the two-Koreas issue, the question of Vietnam and Bangladesh membership, the issue of Cambodia's representation, the Indo-Pakistani conflict, and the continental shelf dispute in the East China Sea.

Except on ACD issues, Chinese principles, more than interests, have dominated in other global issues. China's obvious concern about popularity and image enhancement has seldom stood in the way of her stating any deep convictions and cherished principles. This may well represent a Chinese strategy of making a virtue out of necessity, for the Chinese strength lies in symbolic capability—ideological, political, and behavioral. Chinese multilateral diplomacy has concentrated more on the making of new rules, new norms, and new structures in the evolving process of a new world order than on commanding the capabilities that would assure implementation of a new order. As noted in Chapter 6, China's interest and participation in the implementation process of the New International Economic Order have been selective and passive.

There is, then, a discernible gap between Chinese symbolic and substantive contributions. She has shown no desire or willingness to assume a leadership role throughout the United Nations system. She has deliberately avoided occupying any leadership position. Except in the Security Council, where Huang Hua was automatically elevated to the presidency on four separate occasions through the rotational system, none of the PRC delegates has ever served as chairman of any committee or special body throughout the United Nations system. In terms of parliamentary politics, China has shown little interest in or readiness to intervene in such a way as to have her own views incorporated in the end-products of the decision-making process. It has been only in the domain of formulating *new* community norms of a prescriptive nature—the Stockholm Declaration on the Human Environment and the Charter of Economic Rights and Duties of States, to cite two notable examples—and in the advancement of justice claims by underdogs in the global political system that China has shown a high degree of interest and participation.

How do we account for such a pronounced discrepancy between symbolic activism and substantive passivism? How do we explain the curious contradiction between China's revisionist challenge to restructure the authority patterns of the Organization and her tenacious adherence to the Westphalia conception of international order, which impedes the development of the United Nations' supranational capability? A number of possible explanations can be suggested.

First, symbolic diplomacy is less costly and complicated in both political and economic terms; it is a diplomacy designed to please the greatest number of nations in the formation of the broadest possible united front against the most dangerous superpower in the contemporary international system—the Soviet Union—without seemingly compromising China's principles. In addition, it does not confine China in any tactical or strategic straitjacket.

Second, China's symbolic diplomacy may well be an expression of the Maoist epistemological principle that human or national behavior is a natural reflection of its world outlook. If this is so, the mobilization of China's symbolic capability in the service of her multilateral diplomacy becomes an extension of a "cultural revolution" into the international arena. This may also explain China's greater interest and participation in general debates on grandiose principles in the plenary of the General Assembly, in contrast to her passive posture in committees and subsidiary bodies.

Third, symbolic diplomacy may be a function of China's protracted sense of timing. It is a mistake to accept her conceptual challenges or recurring strategic optimism as definite blueprints for immediate action. What may appear to many observers as a Chinese waiting game—never committing too much, too soon, to any one area or issue —may be a function of the Chinese "protracted diplomatic struggle." On most issues, an immediate victory is not the goal. Repeatedly, the Chinese have applied a "trend-of-history" analysis in evaluating UN politics rather than counting the returns of votes on resolutions. Who controls the destiny of world history? This is the critical question for the Chinese.[47]

This protracted sense of timing may also explain another behavioral characteristic in Chinese multilateral diplomacy. China has self-consciously maintained an ideological rigidity or integrity (principled stand) at the level of policy pronouncements in public, while pursuing at the same time pragmatic, compromising, and somewhat contradictory tactics in private. Likewise, she has voted in favor of many resolutions on the basis of their overall merit, even if some of them contained objectionable parts.

Fourth, symbolic diplomacy may be a function of China's self-exclusion from the group-based influence structure of UN politics. As noted in Part II, China declined to join the Group of 77. Having thus excluded herself from the most dominant group of the Third World, she has lost a power basis for substantive influence. Given the fluid leadership and factional and geographical quarrels within the Group of 77, China's decision was a rational one. Yet to play too strong a role as an independent actor in UN politics would run counter to her repeated strategic plea for unity of the Third World against the superpowers. For China to play other than a symbolic and supportive role vis-à-vis the Third World might also complicate her delicate bilateral relationship with individual members of the Group of 77.

Fifth, symbolic diplomacy may be a behavioral corollary of China's ideological pledge never to be or act like a superpower. The line between playing an active and a domineering or bullying role may be treacherously thin and tangential. In view of the Chinese conceptual propensity to define a superpower in behavioral terms and the Chinese hypersensitivity about matching her words with her deeds, a modest and self-effacing behavior in private while playing an active symbolic role in public seems to be a rational strategic choice.

Finally, symbolic diplomacy may also be a function of the Chinese perception of the United Nations as more suited to being a legitimiz-

[47] Ch'iao Kuan-hua in his secret speech referred to earlier remarked: "It seems as if this [China's global policy of seeking an alliance with the capitalist Western Europe] is very contradictory; in fact there is nothing contradictory about this. It is only a matter of time. In talking about situations, the most important thing is not to depart from the concept of time." See "Ch'iao Kuan-hua's Secret Speech," p. 15.

ing dispenser of symbolic claims than a vehicle for promoting Chinese national interests. Chinese pride, embodied in the principle of self-reliance, is too strong to admit the possibility of China becoming a recipient of any UN assistance program in the foreseeable future. Even in NIEO politics, Chinese economic interests have not been directly or deeply involved. The contrast between China's bilateral and multi-lateral aid has been most revealing. The marginality of Chinese interests in UN politics or the unsuitability of the United Nations as a vehicle for Chinese national interests may also explain the unique Chinese representational style of expounding her principled stand on most issues—the ACD issues being the most notable exception—in support of the interests of the Third World rather than her own.

China and World Order: The Politics of Mutual Legitimization

Finally, one may ask: How has the mutual interaction between China and the United Nations influenced the evolving process of establishing a new and just world order? To recapitulate one of the main themes of this study, the most significant impact of Chinese participation upon the development of the United Nations system as the world organization has been symbolic. The United Nations system in general and the General Assembly in particular, as a forum to mobilize world political opinion on major issues of global concern (such as food, environment, population, disarmament, law of the sea, status of women, technology, water, and human habitat), have been symbolically strengthened and politically legitimized through China's participation —which means the participation of one-fifth of humanity.

Having jettisoned the old question of Chinese representation which had been plaguing almost every organ of the United Nations system, the Organization can now concentrate more effectively on the fundamental conditions of human existence in the nuclear-ecological age. In short, Chinese participation has made the United Nations more legitimate, more representative, and more relevant in responding to the challenge of establishing a new and just world order.

Another impact of Chinese participation has been psychological. For too long the viability of the Organization has been assessed too exclusively in terms of the attitudes of the great powers. This kind of analysis is still valid, but it must also be recognized that the future of the Organization depends on the extent to which the Third World (now representing an overwhelming majority of the membership) gains a sense of self-respect, capability, and relevance in the management of global affairs in the United Nations. For a major power such as China to participate, to champion the cause of international egalitarianism, and to counsel against the politics of despair and manifest a populist strategic optimism for the poor, the weak, and the despondent has had a morale-boosting effect. In short, China's participation, coupled with the casting of her lot with the Third World, makes a potent psychological impact on the rising frustration and alienation among the world's poor, weak, and helpless. To the extent that China succeeds in alleviating the alienation problem—evidence gathered from field interviews suggests this is so—the United Nations, too, becomes strengthened.

Beyond the symbolic and psychological realms of UN politics, China's commitment and contribution to the establishment of the NIEO principles—the *Declaration*, the *Programme of Action*, and the *Charter*—have been notable. By repeatedly invoking the authority of these principles in her multilateral diplomacy, China also helps the process of creating and developing new norms in areas previously ungoverned by any agreed rules. As far as China is concerned—and this also applies to the Third World—a new and just world order is no more or less than the New International Economic Order.

Even in the functional activities of the United Nations system, the impact of Chinese participation has been positive. While she has projected a radical vision in the open forum by attempting to arrest the tendency of UN global politics to move too narrowly in a technical direction that does not challenge basic normative assumptions, China has, in practice, settled for a compromise between her more radical requirements and existing functional needs. Among the participants of the specialized agencies that we reviewed in Chapter 7, there is a shared perception and a cautious optimism that China is expanding her participation in more and more functional sectors at a slow but methodical pace.

What about the disruptive impact of Chinese participation that was so widely predicted and feared during the exclusion period? Of course, this has not come to pass. The error in predictive analysis stemmed in part from an uncritical equation of Soviet and Chinese behavior and in part from an uncritical acceptance of China's long-range strategic goals as a short-term programmatic blueprint for action. China's opposition to issues and activities repugnant to her interests or principles has been expressed in the form of nonparticipation rather than of disruptive participation.

Even in the General Assembly and ECOSOC, where a negative vote would not cause a paralyzing veto effect, China has opted for nonparticipation in the vote rather than a negative vote on those resolutions to which she objects. There is now an almost universal hope among the secretariat officials and fellow delegates throughout the United Nations system of fuller and more active Chinese participation, and a belief that China will play a positive and constructive role once she has decided to participate in those sectors in which she does not presently take part.

The impact of the United Nations upon the development of Chinese global politics is more elusive. In symbolic and conceptual terms, the importance of the United Nations in Chinese global strategy is a function of the Chinese perception of the United Nations—in particular, as to whether UN politics reflects the dominant trend of world history. "If the United Nations is to play its due role," declared Huang Hua in the plenary of the General Assembly, "it must conform to the trend of the world, act strictly in accordance with the purposes and principles of the United Nations Charter, free itself from super-Power manipulation and control and truly reflect the just demands of the great number of its States Members and the people of the world."[48]

How, then, does China see the United Nations? As of the end of the 29th General Assembly, she perceived it as having gone through three stages of development. In the first stage—which is vaguely referred to as "in the past"—the United Nations served as a voting machine manipulated by the United States. In the second stage, referred to as "later," it became a tool of the Soviet-American condominium in their mutual contention and collusion for hegemony. But by 1974, in summing up the experience of Chinese participation in the first three years, the United Nations was described as looking "rather like an international court, with the United States and the Soviet Union in the dock as the Third World makes the charges and holds the trial."[49] Apparently, the 6th Special Session of the General Assembly, which opened the first chapter in the development of a new international economic order, was a milestone for Peking.

On October 7, 1974, China presented to the United Nations two gifts—a Great Wall tapestry (10 m. in length and 5 m. in height) and a Chengtu-Kunming Railway ivory carving (150 cm. in length and 110 cm. in height)[50]—that apparently symbolized the positive role the United Nations is playing in the Chinese image of world order. There

---

[48] UN Doc. A/PV.2314 (11 December 1974), p. 36.

[49] "Rise of Third World and Decline of Hegemonism," PR, No. 2 (January 10, 1975), 6. For Huang Hua's comprehensive assessment of the United Nations along the same lines, see UN Doc. A/PV.2314 (11 December 1974), p. 37. See also Jen Ku-p'ing, "Abundant Support for a Just Cause and Little Support for an Unjust Cause," JMJP, December 20, 1974, p. 6; and "Resolute Support for the Demands of the Third World," JMJP, editorial, April 9, 1974, p. 1.

[50] The Great Wall tapestry covers the wall of the delegates' lounge, which is undoubtedly the most important place outside the conference halls at UN Headquarters.

497

is no evidence that this positive perception has been modified since the death of Mao Tse-tung. In a meeting with Secretary-General Kurt Waldheim on August 6, 1977, in Peking, for example, Chairman Hua Kuo-feng is reported to have told Waldheim of "a need for strengthening of the world organization."[51] This accords well with the view of the Third World expressed at the Fifth Conference of Heads of States or Governments of Non-Aligned Countries.[52]

More specifically, the United Nations—or, more accurately, its most dominant group, the Group of 77—exerts a subtle but substantial influence on Chinese behavior. It may be appropriate to say that China, instead of manipulating the Third World, is actually being manipulated by it. It was the Third World that managed to "bend" China's principled stand on UN peace-keeping, converting the Chinese vote from a certain veto to nonparticipation. Other examples of the influence of the Third World on China in UN politics need not be repeated here. By casting her own fate with that of the Third World as a matter of cardinal strategic principle, China has in effect considerably restricted the boundaries of her own behavior in global politics. To depart too much from the position of the Third World on most issues—the ACD issues being the most notable exception[53] —would seriously undermine the ideological underpinnings of Chinese global strategy.

China's participation in the United Nations system may have slow but subtle effects on her cognitive map of international relations. Differing perceptions of reality are regarded in social psychology as one of the major causes of conflict. In his seminal work on the Chinese

[51] *UN Chronicle* 14 (August/September 1977), 23; *NYT*, August 7, 1977, p. 7. The August 7, 1977, issue of *Jen-min jih-pao* displayed on the front page two color photos showing Chairman Hua Kuo-feng and Secretary-General Kurt Waldheim.

[52] The resolution on the United Nations adopted at the Fifth Conference of Heads of States or Governments of Non-Aligned Countries reads in part: "1. *Express* their readiness to continue with their efforts to further the role and strengthen the effectiveness of the United Nations in world affairs . . . as the principal democratic instrument of equitable and peaceful co-operation among States . . . , 2. *Resolutely oppose* the organized campaigns and various forms of pressure and threats aimed at discrediting the whole system of the United Nations as well as tendencies and attempts to bypass or limit the participation of the United Nations in solving international problems of concern to all countries." Reprinted in *Alternatives* 3 (December 1977), 294; emphasis in original.

[53] Even on the ACD issues, China is susceptible to the pressure of the Third World, as evidenced in the Chinese positive vote for the establishment of a 35-member Special Committee on the World Disarmament Conference at the 27th Session of the General Assembly, by the Chinese ratification of Additional Protocol II to the Treaty of Tlatelolco (the Treaty for the Prohibition of Nuclear Weapons in Latin America), and by the Chinese support for the establishment of nuclear-free zones in Latin America, the Middle East, the Indian Ocean, Africa, and South Asia. See Chapter 3 for details.

decision to enter the Korean War, Allen S. Whiting also concluded that a breakdown in communications, a function of differing perceptions of reality, brought about an "entirely new war."[54] The United Nations system is a global communication network, and Chinese participation in it provides Peking's policy makers with a better means of communicating with the outside world.[55]

Since most Chinese diplomats who participate in the United Nations system eventually move on to other government posts, their learning experience in multilateral diplomacy may also have some feedback effect on Peking's definition of the international situation. In this connection, Alexander Dallin observed about Soviet UN officials: "While there are wide variations, one gains the impression that Soviet personnel stationed at the U.N.—be it with the U.S.S.R. mission or on the United Nations staff—tend to be more practical and pragmatic in outlook than those in the 'home office'; at times, they seem less concerned with doctrine than with success. And while it is easy to exaggerate such nuances, there are occasional suggestions of different perception of reality."[56] We do not have any behavioral referents to support a firm statement on this matter, but we may accept Huang Hua's promotion from his UN post to head the Ministry of Foreign Affairs in Peking as a hopeful sign.

The United Nations is more than the sum total of its Member States. It has developed its own political, administrative, and legal personality; it has its own bureaucracy capable of using information and knowledge as a source of power and influence; it has its own rules of procedures and body of binding internal administrative laws; it cultivates an allegiance of participating Member States to a set of cosmopolitan norms and values; and it builds up a certain momentum that works as peer-group pressure in the the behavior of Member States. All of these work toward the development of an organizational identity, and influences to varying degrees the rhetorical style of the participants toward UN norms. There may also be some functionalist spillover to the foreign policy establishment of each Member State.

Chinese behavior, too, is susceptible to these institutional pressures. In the PLA's secret documents, *Kung-tso t'ung-hsün*, two telling points were made about China and the United Nations in 1961. First, no major or minor international problems could be solved without Chinese participation, with the obvious implication that the United Nations was the real loser by excluding China. Second, China would

[54] Whiting, *China Crosses the Yalu*, pp. 171-72.

[55] Chadwick F. Alger, "United Nations Participation as a Learning Experience," *Public Opinion Quarterly* 27 (1963), 411-26.

[56] Alexander Dallin, *The Soviet Union at the United Nations* (New York: Praeger, 1962), p. 96.

lose its *freedom of action* if she were to participate in the United Nations.[57] Perhaps the latter point was made to make a virtue out of the forced exclusion. Nonetheless, it revealed Chinese awareness of reciprocal impacts and interactions between herself and the United Nations in the event of Chinese participation.

Once settled in the world organization, China has proved to be neither a revolutionary challenger attempting to impose her own conception of how the Organization should be operated, nor an institutional reformer. For most of the time, on most of the issues, she has been acting as a cautious and self-effacing newcomer, mastering her new trade and adjusting her ideological preconceptions to the rules and norms of the Organization. In short, China has played the diplomatic game by the established rules, rather than attempting to replace or repudiate them.

Finally, the United Nations, by first "admitting" and then bending some of its own rules to accommodate Peking's demands—the "cancellation" of the ROC's arrears and withdrawal of UNDP field experts from Taiwan, for example—has legitimized China's political status and strengthened her symbolic capability. The political prestige and symbolic influence that she enjoys in UN global politics and the extraordinary sensitivity of Member States to Chinese security interests—note their curious silence on China's detonation of her 22nd nuclear explosion on September 17, 1977, shortly before the 32nd General Assembly began, in contrast to their outcry against the French nuclear explosion in the Pacific two years previously—also tend to heal China's bruised national ego, to minimize her suspicion of international organizations, and to bring her into closer harmony with the rest of the world.

When all is said and done, the reciprocal interactions and impacts between China and the United Nations system have on the whole been positive. The relationship between the two during the first half of the 1970s may be characterized as a mutual adjustment, mutual legitimization, and mutual enhancement of each other's symbolic capability. What does this mean for the global pursuit of a new world order?

In spite of a conceptual conflict with PV_1, China is not a threat to world peace. In fact, the Chinese image and strategy of world order as expressed in the conduct of multilateral diplomacy are devoid of any military imperative for *Pax Sinica*. However, her contribution to PV_1 is problematic. China's preoccupation with what she considers to be the paralyzing psychological effect of excessive peace posturing

[57] "Several Important Problems Concerning the Current International Situation," *KTTH*, No. 17 (April 25, 1961), 19.

upon the revolutionary struggle of the global underdogs is a serious conceptual barrier in this regard. The bias in domestic politics against law and order has also been projected into the international arena; hence, the Chinese image of world order is more decisively oriented toward change than toward order. Though it is somewhat premature to forecast, a return to the more moderate and pragmatic policy officially inaugurated at the 11th Party Congress in August 1977 augers well for the establishment of a balance between order and change in the Chinese image and strategy of world order.

To the extent that one equates, as many do, a new world order with the New International Economic Order, China's contribution, though largely symbolic and psychological, has been important. A new world order is not yet a living reality; it is in the stage of global negotiations and consciousness raising. It could be misleading to appraise Chinese contributions too exclusively in terms of technical and substantive inputs to the global negotiation process. The value-oriented image of Chinese world order raises a necessary challenge to the tendency to conceive world order in technological terms.

It is often claimed that revolution devours its own children. What is the meaning of the mid-1977 restoration of Beethoven and Teng Hsiao-p'ing for domestic order? What would be the long-term implications for Chinese global strategy? Would China deviate from the value-oriented model of world order and move in the direction of a power-oriented one? Would this represent the camel's nose in the tent of an *embourgeoisement* process? This line of inquiry goes beyond the scope of the present study. Still, students of Chinese foreign policy and world order studies may do well to keep in mind Mao's poem as they study and project the shaping of Chinese global policy in the post-Mao era. In early 1975, when he was already well on his way to meet Marx, Mao Tse-tung wrote a poem for his ailing comrade Chou En-lai:

> Loyal parents who sacrificed so
>   much for the nation
> Never feared the ultimate fate.
> Now that the country has become
>   red, who will be its guardian?
> Our mission unfinished may take
>   a thousand years.
> The struggle tires us and our hair
>   is grey.
> You and I, old friends, can we just
>   watch our efforts be washed
>   away?

501

INTERVIEW SCHEDULE*

Ahrensdorf, Joachim. Chief, Far Eastern Division, IMF, IMF Hq., Washington, D.C., January 31, 1977.

Al-Jibouri, H. A.† Senior Officer, Plant Production and Protection Division, FAO, FAO Hq., Rome, February 22, 1977.

Allen, Robert. US Representative to UNCTAD, US Mission to International Organizations, Geneva, February 15, 1977.

Bari, Hassan.† Chief, Operational Division, WWW, WMO, WMO Hq., Geneva, February 15, 1977.

Bennett, W. Tapley, Jr. Ambassador Extraordinary and Plenipotentiary and Deputy Permanent US Representative to the United Nations, Permanent Mission of the United States to the United Nations, New York, February 3, 1977.

Binda, Jeffrey. International Health Attaché and a US Delegate to WHO, US Mission to International Organizations, Geneva, February 15, 1977.

Black, Clay. Shipping Attaché and US Representative to the IMCO Council; US Embassy, London, February 7, 1977.

Brochenin, Jean Claude. Counsellor, Permanent Mission of France to the United Nations, New York, March 8, 1977.

Burney, Mahmud. Deputy Special Representative, UN Organization, IBRD, IBRD Hq., Washington, D.C., January 31, 1977.

Burton, Robert. Chief, Conference Division, UNESCO, UNESCO Hq., Paris, February 11, 1977.

Casson, Peter. Deputy Director, External Relations, UN Offices at Geneva, Geneva, February 17, 1977.

Caulfield, Daniel W. Senior Legal Liaison Officer, Division for Conference Affairs and External Relations, UNCTAD, UNCTAD Hq., Geneva, February 17, 1977.

Cerra, Ronald. Political Officer, US Mission to International Organizations, Geneva, February 15, 1977.

Chang, Kuo-ho.‡ Chief of Staff Services, the UN Secretariat, UN Hq., New York, January 12, 1977.

Chang, Maejeanne Koutung. Assistant Programme Specialist, Fellowship Division, UNESCO, UNESCO Hq., Paris, February 11, 1977.

Chang, Min-kee. Chief of Asia and Oceania Division, Cooperation for Development and External Relations Sector, UNESCO, UNESCO Hq., Paris, February 10, 1977.

Chatenenay, L. Peter. External Relations Advisor, IBRD, IBRD Hq., Washington, D.C., January 31, 1977.

* Each entry shows the essential data in the following order: name, position (as of the date of each individual interview), place and date of interview.
† Visited the PRC on an official mission or an official invitation by the Chinese Government.
‡ Visited the PRC one or more times.

Chaubert, Leon. Legal Counsellor, UPU, UPU Hq., Berne, February 18, 1977.

Chen, Kwen.‡ Principal Officer, General Legal Division, Office of Legal Affairs, the UN Secretariat, UN Hq., New York, April 18, 1977.

Cheng, Yu-chien. Financial Officer, WHO, WHO Hq., Geneva, February 18, 1977.

Chiu, Shu-hua.‡ Assistant Field Programme Officer, Asia Section, Operational Programme Division, UNESCO, UNESCO Hq., Paris, February 10, 1977.

Collins, W. H. Chief, Finance Branch, ICAO, ICAO Hq., Montreal, May 6, 1977.

Croome, John. Director of External Relations and Information, GATT, GATT Hq., Geneva, February 17, 1977.

Delmendo, Medina N.† Fishery Resources Officer, Fisheries Department, FAO, FAO Hq., Rome, February 23, 1977.

Dewan, M. L.† Chief, Regional Bureau for Asia and the Far East, FAO, FAO Hq., Rome, February 22, 1977.

Dietrich, B. H.† Director, Division of Environmental Health, WHO, WHO Hq., Geneva, February 16, 1977.

Dillon, Betty C. US Representative to the ICAO Council, ICAO Hq., Montreal, May 6, 1977.

Dorsey, George. Chief, Press Branch, FAO, FAO Hq., Rome, February 21, 1977.

Dreyfus, Gerald. Deputy Chief, Asia and Oceania Division, Cooperation for Development and External Relations Sector, UNESCO, UNESCO Hq., Paris, February 10, 1977.

Fedele, M. C. Director, External Relations, WHO, WHO Hq., Geneva, February 16 1977.

Flache, S.† Director, Division of Coordination, WHO, WHO Hq., Geneva, February 16, 1977.

Fobes, John E. Deputy Director-General of UNESCO, UNESCO Hq., Paris, February 10, 1977.

Foote, Richard H.† Director, Technical Cooperation Department, WMO, WMO Hq., Geneva, February 15, 1977.

Friedland, Sydney. Telecommunications Attaché and US Delegate to ITU and UPU, US Mission to International Organizations, Geneva, February 15, 1977.

Gammacchio, Jean-Pierre. Acting Chief, External Relations Office, ICAO, ICAO Hq., Montreal, May 5, 1977.

Gazarian, Jean. Director of General Assembly Affairs, the UN Secretariat, UN Hq., New York, April 5, 1977.

Gloven, André. Chief, Administrative Services Branch, ICAO, ICAO Hq., Montreal, May 5, 1977.

Gomé-Jara, Carlos. Director of Legal Bureau, ICAO, ICAO Hq., Montreal, May 6, 1977.

Gratz, Norman.† Chief Officer, Vector Biological Control, WHO, WHO Hq., Geneva, February 16, 1977.

Guicciardi, V. Winspeare. Director-General of the UN Offices at Geneva, Geneva, February 17, 1977.

Hall, Donald. Chief, Conference and General Services Section, ICAO, ICAO Hq., Montreal, May 5, 1977.

Harden. Sheila. First Secretary, Permanent Mission of the United Kingdom to the United Nations, New York, November 19, 1976.

Hohler, Frederick. First Secretary, Permanent Mission of the United Kingdom to the United Nations, New York, December 14, 1977.

Hsueh, Tzu-ping.‡ Language Officer, Publications Division, FAO, FAO Hq., Rome, February 21, 1977.

Huang, Lin-sheng. Senior Engineer, ITU, ITU Hq., Geneva, February 18, 1977.

Ibnou-Zékri, M. Chief, External Relations Department, ITU, ITU Hq., Geneva, February 17, 1977.

Imanishi, Shojiro. First Secretary, Permanent Mission of Japan to the United Nations, New York, February 3, 1977.

Imbruglia, A. Chief of Budget, WHO, WHO Hq., Geneva, February 16, 1977.

Jackson, Roy I.† Deputy Director-General of FAO, FAO Hq., Rome, February 23, 1977.

Jankowitz, Peter. Ambassador Extraordinary and Plenipotentiary and Permanent Representative of Austria to the United Nations, Permanent Mission of Austria to the United Nations, New York, January 12, 1977.

Jimenez, M.† Inspector-General and former Director of Relations with Member States (November 1970-January 1975), UNESCO, UNESCO Hq., Paris, February 10, 1977.

Johnson, Nels. Director of International Affairs, National Oceanic and Atmospheric Administration (NOAA) and Advisor to US Representative to WMO, NOAA Hq., Washington, D.C., January 31, 1977.

Kemery, Raymond. Member of US Permanent Mission to UNESCO, UNESCO Hq., Paris, February 9, 1977.

Keys, Donald. UN Representative of the World Federalists, New York, May 4, 1977.

Kotaite, Assad.† The President of the ICAO Council and former Secretary-General of ICAO (1970-76), ICAO Hq., Montreal, May 6, 1977.

Lambert, Yves Maurice. Secretary-General of ICAO and former French Representative to the ICAO Council (1973-76), ICAO Hq., Montreal, May 6, 1977.

Landey, Marcel. Director of Administrative Division, IMCO, IMCO Hq., London, February 8, 1977.

Lawton, Paul.† Coordinator, Division of Coordination, WHO, WHO Hq., Geneva, February 16, 1977.

Lecompt, Jacques. Minister Plenipotentiary and Deputy Permanent Representative of France to the United Nations, Permanent Mission of France to the United Nations, New York, March 8, 1977.

Ledakis, G. A. Legal Counsel, WIPO, WIPO Hq., Geneva, February 16, 1977.

Lee, Roy Skwang. Economic Affairs Officer, Ocean Economics and Technology Office, the UN Secretariat, UN Hq., New York, February 3, 1977.

Lemoine, Jacques. Advisor for International Organization Affairs, ILO, ILO Hq., Geneva, February 14, 1977.

Liu, Fou-tchin.‡ Director, Office of the Under-Secretary-General for Special Political Affairs, the UN Secretariat, UN Hq., New York, December 13, 1976.

Loerbroks, I. R. Director, Agricultural Department, FAO, FAO Hq., Rome, February 23, 1977.

Mackenzie, Colin. Acting Director, Information Division, FAO, FAO Hq., Rome, February 21, 1977.

Mandefield, Harold.† Assistant Director-General, Department of General Affairs and Information, FAO, FAO Hq., Rome, February 21, 1977.

Mao, Yu-yueh.‡ Senior Counsellor, International Radio and Consultative Commission, ITU, ITU Hq., Geneva, February 14, 1977.

Mensah, Tom. Head of Legal Division, IMCO, IMCO Hq., London, February 8, 1977.

Morse, Bradford. UNDP Administrator and former Under-Secretary-General for Political and General Assembly Affairs (1972-75), UNDP Hq., New York, April 22, 1977.

Myerson, Jacob. Ambassador and US Representative to ECOSOC, Permanent Mission of the United States to the United Nations, New York, March 8, 1977.

Nhouyvanisvong, Khamliene. Programme Specialist, Asia and Oceania Division, Cooperation for Development and External Relations Sector, UNESCO, UNESCO Hq., Paris, February 10, 1977.

Norred, Christopher A., Jr. US Representative to FAO, US Embassy, Rome, February 24, 1977.

Nottidge, O. R. Chief, Planning and Information Section, Office of Personnel Services, the UN Secretariat, UN Hq., New York, December 13, 1976.

Polycarpou, A. Chief of Forestry Conservation Branch, Forestry Department, FAO, FAO Hq., Rome, February 23, 1977.

Prabhakar, E. Chief, Asia Section, Operational Programme Division, UNESCO, UNESCO Hq., Paris, February 10, 1977.

Rao, G. V. Deputy Assistant Director-General, Sector for Programme Support and Administration, UNESCO, UNESCO Hq., Paris, February 11, 1977.

Reid, Jay H. Director of Public Information, IMF, IMF Hq., Washington, D.C., January 31, 1977.

Rougé, M. Michel. Minister Plenipotentiary and Counsellor, Permanent Mission of France to the United Nations, New York, April 5, 1977.

Sacks, Michael. Former Deputy Director, Division of Coordination, WHO, UN Hq., New York, March 8, 1977.

St. Dumitrescue, Nicolae. Director, Library and Documentation Systems Division, FAO, FAO Hq., Rome, February 21, 1977.

Salathé, Noël. Chief, Personnel Branch, ICAO, ICAO Hq., Montreal, May 5, 1977.

Sandilya, Karti. Indian Representative to UNCTAD, Indian Mission to International Organizations, Geneva, February 17, 1977.

Savary, P. Director, Publications Division, FAO, FAO Hq., Rome, February 21, 1977.

Scali, John A. Former Ambassador Extraordinary and Plenipotentiary and US Permanent Representative to the United Nations (January 1973-July 1975), ABC Office, Washington, D.C., February 1, 1977.

Schaufele, William, Jr. Assistant Secretary of State for African Affairs and former Ambassador and Deputy US Representative to the Security Council, the Department of State, Washington, D.C., February 1, 1977.

Shigeta, Hiroshi. First Secretary, Permanent Mission of Japan to the United Nations, New York, February 3, 1977.

Shih, C. Chung-tse. Senior Advisor, UNCTAD, UNCTAD Hq., Geneva, February 17, 1977.

Sloan, F. Blaine. Director, General Legal Division, Office of Legal Affairs, the UN Secretariat, UN Hq., New York, April 18, 1977.

Srivastava, C. P.† Secretary-General of IMCO, IMCO Hq., London, February 8, 1977.

Stepanek, Vladimir. Secretary of General Conference and the Executive Board, UNESCO, UNESCO Hq., Paris, February 9, 1977.

Stretta, Etienne.† Chief, Latin American Section, Operational Unit, UNESCO, UNESCO Hq., Paris, February 10, 1977.

Suy, Erik. Under-Secretary-General and Legal Counsellor, Office of Legal Affairs, the UN Secretariat, UN Hq., New York, April 18, 1977.

Tcheng, Young-kuan.‡ Technical Advisor (Chinese Language), Bureau of Conferences, Languages and Documents, UNESCO, UNESCO Hq., Paris, February 11, 1977.

Tedesco, G. Officer-in-Charge, Conference, Council, and Protocol Affairs, FAO, FAO Hq., Rome, February 21, 1977.

Thomforde, Philip R. Senior Liaison Officer, Regional Bureau for Asia and the Far East, FAO, FAO Hq., Rome, February 22, 1977.

Tomiche, Fernand J. Director, Division of Public Information, WHO, WHO Hq., Geneva, February 16, 1977.

Tsien, Kia-kwei.‡ Chief, Division for West and South Asia, UNDP, UNDP Hq., New York, April 22, 1977.

Tsien, Patricia Koo. Chief, African Division, Department of Political Affairs, Trusteeship and Decolonization, the UN Secretariat, UN Hq., New York, January 4, 1977.

Tsui, Edward Kwok-wah. Assistant Secretary, Department of Economic and Social Affairs, the UN Secretariat, UN Hq., New York, January 4, 1977.

Tu, Nan.‡ Language Officer, Publications Division, FAO, FAO Hq., Rome, February 21, 1977.

Ungar, Harley. Chief, Statistics Section, ICAO, ICAO Hq., Montreal, May 5, 1977.

Urquhart, Brian.† Under-Secretary-General for Special Political Affairs, the UN Secretariat, UN Hq., New York, April 12, 1977.

Valderrama, Nicasio G. Minister, Permanent Mission of the Philippines to the United Nations, New York, May 5, 1977.

Walters, Harry E. Assistant Executive Director, World Food Council, Rome, February 23, 1977.

Wang, Nien-tzu.‡ Assistant Director, Financial Resources Development Branch, Central for Planning, Projections, and Policies, the UN Secretariat, UN Hq., New York, November 30, 1976.

Weiss, Godfrey.† Director of World Weather Watch, WMO, WMO Hq., Geneva, February 15, 1977.

White, Robert M. Administrator of NOAA and US Representative to the WMO Council, NOAA Hq., Washington, D.C., January 31, 1977.

Wilson, Ormes, Jr. Advisor, Political and Security Affairs, Permanent Mission of the United States to the United Nations, New York, February 3, 1977.

Yamada, Chusei. Minister, Permanent Mission of Japan to the United Nations, New York, February 3, 1977.

Young, Tien-cheng.‡ Director, Bureau of the Budget, UNESCO, UNESCO Hq., Paris, February 9, 1977.

APPENDIXES

APPENDIX A

Effective Date	Party	Effective Date	Party
10/3/49	USSR	12/17/60	Somalia
10/4/49	Bulgaria	2/10/61	Congo (Stanleyville)
10/5/49	Romania	7/19/61	Mauritania
10/6/49	Hungary	12/9/61	Tanzania
10/6/49	Czechoslovakia	7/3/62	Algeria
10/6/49	Korea (DPRK)	9/7/62	Laos
10/7/49	Poland	10/8/62	Uganda
10/16/49	Mongolia	12/11/63	Zanzibar[a]
10/27/49	Germany (Dem. Rep.)	12/14/63	Kenya
11/23/49	Albania	12/23/63	Burundi
1/18/50	Vietnam (Dem. Rep.)	1/11/64	Tunisia
4/1/50	India	1/27/64	France
5/9/50	Sweden	2/18/64	Congo (Brazzaville)
5/11/50	Denmark	9/29/64	Central African Rep.
6/8/50	Burma	10/29/64	Zambia
6/9/50	Indonesia	11/12/64	Dahomey (Benin)
9/14/50	Switzerland	3/22/65	PLO
10/28/50	Finland	9/19/65	Mauritania
5/21/51	Pakistan	2/2/68	Southern Yemen
6/17/54	United Kingdom	6/?/69	South Vietnam
10/5/54	Norway		(Liberation Front)
11/19/54	Netherlands	10/13/70	Canada
1/10/55	Yugoslavia	10/15/70	Equatorial Guinea
1/20/55	Afghanistan	11/6/70	Italy
8/1/55	Nepal	11/24/70	Ethiopia
6/30/56	Egypt	12/15/70	Chile
8/10/56	Syria	2/10/71	Nigeria
8/24/56	Yemen (North Yemen)	3/26/71	Cameroon
2/7/57	Ceylon (Sri Lanka)	3/29/71	Kuwait
7/23/58	Cambodia (Democratic Kampuchea)	5/6/71	San Marino[b]
		5/28/71	Austria
8/30/58	Iraq	7/29/71	Sierra Leone
11/1/58	Morocco	8/4/71	Turkey
12/1/58	Sudan	8/16/71	Iran
10/4/59	Guinea	10/10/71	Tunisia[c]
7/6/60	Ghana	10/13/71	Burundi[c]
9/28/60	Cuba	10/25/71	Belgium
10/27/60	Mali	10/25/71	United Nations

511

APPENDIX A (*cont'd*)

Effective Date	Party	Effective Date	Party
11/2/71	Peru	3/15/74	Guinea-Bissau
11/9/71	Lebanon	4/20/74	Gabon
11/12/71	Rwanda	5/31/74	Malaysia
12/7/71	Senegal	6/20/74	Trinidad and Tobago
12/8/71	Iceland	6/28/74	Venezuela
12/14/71	Cyprus	7/20/74	Niger
1/31/72	Malta	8/15/74	Brazil
2/14/72	Mexico	12/14/74	Gambia
2/19/72	Argentina	1/6/75	Botswana
2/29/72	Ghana[c]	6/9/75	Philippines
3/13/72	United Kingdom[d]	6/25/75	Mozambique
4/15/72	Mauritius	7/1/75	Thailand
5/18/72	Netherlands[d]	7/12/75	Sao Tome and Principe
6/5/72	Greece	9/16/75	European Economic Community
6/27/72	Guyana		
9/19/72	Togo	10/4/75	Bangladesh
9/29/72	Japan	11/5/75	Fiji
10/11/72	Germany (Fed. Rep.)	11/6/75	Western Samoa
10/14/72	Maldive Islands	11/13/75	Comoros
11/6/72	Malagasy	4/15/76[f]	India[d]
11/16/72	Luxembourg	4/25/76	Cape Verde
11/21/72	Jamaica	5/28/76	Surinam
11/24/72	Zaire[c]	6/30/76	Seychelles
11/28/72	Chad	8/20/76	Central African Empire[c]
12/21/72	Australia		
12/22/72	New Zealand	10/12/76	Papua New Guinea
12/29/72	Dahomey[c] (Benin)	2/17/77	Liberia
3/9/73[e]	Spain	4/7/77	Jordan
9/15/73	Upper Volta	5/30/77	Barbados

[a] United with Tanganyika in 1964.

[b] Diplomatic relations were established at the consular level.

[c] Suspended diplomatic relations were resumed

[d] Diplomatic relations were elevated to the ambassadorial level.

[e] It was announced on this date that diplomatic relations were to take effect within three months.

[f] It was announced by India on this date that she was sending her ambassador to Peking.

Source: Wolfgang Bartke, *The Diplomatic Service of the People's Republic of China as of January 1976 (including Biographies)* (Hamburg: Institut für Asienkunde, 1976); A. M. Halpern, ed., *Policies Toward China: Views from Six Continents* (New York: McGraw-Hill Book Co., 1965), pp. 496-99; changes and additions in recent years are drawn from *Peking Review* and *Jen-min jih-pao*.

APPENDIX B

Voting Record of the Question of Chinese Representation in the United Nations General Assembly, 1950-71

Year (Session)	Member-ship	Pro-PRC No. %	Anti-PRC No. %	Absten-tions	Sponsors and Doc. refs.
1950 (5th Sess.)	59	16 (27)	33 (56)	10	India (A/1365)
1951 (6th Sess.)	60	11 (18)	37 (62)	4	Moratorium[b]
1952 (7th Sess.)	60	7 (12)	42 (70)	11	"
1953 (8th Sess.)	60	10 (17)	44 (73)	2	"
1954 (9th Sess.)	60	11 (18)	43 (72)	6	"
1955 (10th Sess.)	60	12 (20)	42 (70)	6	"
1956 (11th Sess.)	79	24 (30)	47 (59)	8	"
1957 (12th Sess.)	82	27 (33)	48 (59)	6	"
1958 (13th Sess.)	81	28 (35)	44 (54)	9	"
1959 (14th Sess.)	82	29 (35)	44 (54)	9	"
1960 (15th Sess.)	98	34 (35)	42 (43)	22	"
1961 (16th Sess.)	104	36 (35)	48 (46)	20	USSR (A/L.360)
1962 (17th Sess.)	110	42 (38)	56 (51)	12	USSR (A/L.395)
1963 (18th Sess.)	111	41 (37)	57 (51)	12	Albania and Cambodia (A/L.427 and Add.1)
1964 (19th Sess.)[a]	114				
1965 (20th Sess.)	117	47 (40)	47 (40)	20	Albania plus 11 nations (A/L. 469)
1966 (21st Sess.)	121	46 (38)	57 (47)	17	Albania plus 10 nations (A/L. 496 and Add. 1)
1967 (22nd Sess.)	122	45 (37)	58 (48)	17	Albania plus 11 nations (A/L. 531 and Add.1)
1968 (23rd Sess.)	126	44 (35)	58 (46)	23	Albania plus 14 nations (A/L. 549 and Add.1)
1969 (24th Sess.)	126	48 (38)	56 (44)	21	Albania plus 16 nations (A/L. 569)
1970 (25th Sess.)	127	51 (40)	49 (39)	25	Albania plus 17 nations (A/L. 605)
1971 (26th Sess.)	131	76 (58)	35 (27)	17	Albania plus 22 nations (A/L. 630)[c]

[a] No vote was taken due to financial crisis.

[b] Votes from 1951 to 1960 inclusive were on a US motion to keep the question off the agenda. For uniformity, the numbers in the Pro-PRC column reflect the votes in favor of the PRC.

[c] Adopted as General Assembly Resolution 2758 (XXVI) of 25 October 1971.

Source: Based on *Yearbooks of the United Nations 1950-1971*.

The Composition of the PRC's Delegation to the General Assembly, 1971-76

	1971 (26th Sess.)	1972 (27th Sess.)	1973 (28th Sess.)	1974 (29th Sess.)	1975 (30th Sess.)	1976 (31st Sess.)
Size of Delegation (No. of Personnel)	39	49	40	45	43	40
Ch'iao Kuan-hua	C,VM	C,VM	C,VM	C,VM	C,MFA	C,MFA
Huang Hua[a]	VC,PR	VC,PR	VC,PR	VC,PR	VC,PR	VC,PR
Fu Hao	R,A					
Hsiung Hsiang-hui	R,A					
Ch'en Ch'u[a]	R,DPR	R,DPR				
T'ang Ming-chao	AR,A	USG	USG	USG	USG	USG
An Chih-yüan	AR,Cr			R		R,A,PRG
Wang Hai-jung[b]	AR,Cr					
Hsing Sung-yi	AR,Cr,P	AR,Cr,P	AR,Cr,P	AR,Cr,P	AR,Cr,P	AR,Cr,P
Chang Yung-kuan	AR,Cr,	AR,Cr,P	Cr,P			
Wang Jun-sheng[a]		R,DPR	R,DPR			
Pi Chi-lung		R			R	
Chuang Yen[a]		AR,DPR, Cr	R,DPR	R,DPR	R,DRP	
Chang Tsien-hua		AR				
Chang Hsien-wu		AR		AR,Cr,P	AR,Cr,P	
Ling Ch'ing			R			
Wang Ming-hsiu			AR			
Wang Wei-tsai			AR			
Chi Tsung-hua[b]			AR	AR		
Chang Han-chih[b]	SS		AR	AR	AR	
Chou Chüeh			R			
Wu Miao-fa	SS,P	SS,P	SS,P	AR,Cr,P	AR,Cr,P	AR,Cr,P
Lai Ya-li[a]					R,DPR	R,DPR
Lo Hsu[b]					AR	
Chi Chao-chu						R
Ho Li-liang[b]		Cr,P	Cr,P	Cr,P	Cr,P	AR,Cr,P
Wu Hsiao-ta						AR,Cr,P
Chou Nan	FS,P	FS,P	Cr,P	Cr,P	Cr,P	AR,Cr,P

C=Chairman of the delegation; VM=Vice Minister for Foreign Affairs; MFA=Minister for Foreign Affairs; VC=Vice-Chairman of the delegation; PR=Permanent Representative to the UN; R=Representative; A=Ambassador; DPR=Deputy Permanent Representative to the UN; AR=Alternative Representative; USG=Under-Secretary-General; Cr=Counsellor; P=Member of Permanent Mission to the UN; PRG=Permanent Representative to the UN Offices in Geneva and to Other International Organizations in Switzerland; FS=First Secretary; SS=Second Secretary.

[a] Ambassador Extraordinary and Plenipotentiary.   [b] Female.

APPENDIX D

DESIRABLE RANGE OF UN SECRETARAT STAFF; BY THE
NINE LARGEST CONTRIBUTORS TO THE UN BUDGET

Member State	Desirable Range		Actual No. of Staff		Spread in Range	
	1963	1973	6/30/72	6/30/73	1963	1973
Ukrainian Soviet Socialist Rep.	26-22	36-30	16	16	-4	-6
Canada	41-31	60-44	61	61	-10	-16
Italy	29-24	68-50	35	37	-5	-18
China	59-43	76-56	46	49	-16	-20
Japan	30-24	103-74	62	76	-6	-29
United Kingdom	98-69	113-79	124	124[b]	-29	-34
France	77-55	115-80	136	139	-22	-35
Soviet Union	193-131	270-183	123	135	-62	-87
United States	412-276	599-398	450	452	-136	-201
Total	965-675	1,440-994	1,053[a]	1,089[c]	-290	-466

[a] Represents 46.7% of all Secretariat personnel.

[b] Includes one staff member from Dominica, one from Hong Kong, and four from Southern Rhodesia.

[c] Represents 47.1% of all Secretariat personnel.

Source: Report of the Secretary-General: Personnel Questions: Composition of the Secretariat, UN Doc. A/9120 (21 September 1973), p. 14; Annex pp. 9-12.

APPENDIX E

Appointments of Chinese Personnel to Secretariat Posts Subject to Geographical Distribution
(September 1, 1970-June 30, 1976)

Rank	9/1/70 to 8/31/71	9/1/71 to 6/30/72	7/1/72 to 6/30/73	7/1/73 to 6/30/74	7/1/74 to 6/30/75	7/1/75 to 6/30/76
USG		1				
ASG						
D-2						
D-1			1			
P-5			1			
P-4						
P-3						
P-2	1		1		2	1
P-1						2
Total	1	1	3	0	2	3

Source: Adapted from the following: UN Docs. A/8831, Annex, p. 24; A/8483, Annex, p. 32; A/9120, Annex, p. 17; A/9724, Annex, p. 17; A/10184, Annex, p. 16; and A/31/154, Annex, p. 15.

APPENDIX F

Chinese Staff in Posts with Special Language Requirements
(August 31, 1971-June 30, 1976)

As of	P-1	P-2	P-3	P-4	P-5	Total
8/31/71	0	9	26	19	3	57
6/30/72	0	8	26	15	4	53
6/30/73	1	20	27	21	4	73
6/30/74	0	27	21	24	4	76
6/30/75	3	21	34	25	5	88
6/30/76	2	18(3)[a]	42(4)[a]	31(3)[a]	4	97(10)[a]

[a] Female staff.

Source: Adapted from UN Doc. A/8483, Annex, p. 49; UN Doc. A/8831, Annex, p. 39; UN Doc. A/9120, Annex, p. 29; UN Doc. A/9724, Annex, p. 30; UN Doc. A/10184, Annex, p. 27; and UN Doc. A/31/154, Annex, p. 27.

APPENDIX G

CASH PAYMENTS RECEIVED FROM CHINA IN RESPECT OF
VOLUNTARY CONTRIBUTIONS, 1971-74 (US $)

	1971	1972	1973	1974
UNDP	200,000		1,988,684	2,200,000
UNCDF				
UNFPA	10,000			
UNITAR				
UNIDO	10,000		200,000	225,000
UNICEF	10,200	60,000		
UNRWA	30,000			
UNHCR	10,000			
WHO				
IAEA	10,000			
Trust Funds	20,000		30,000	
UNFICYP				
World Food Program				
UNEP			131,628	
UNDP-Administrative Trust Funds			100,000	100,000
ILO				
FAO				
UNESCO				
UPU				
ITU				
WMO				
WIPO				
Total Per Year	300,200	60,000	2,450,312	2,525,000

Source: Adapted from Report of the Committee on Contributions, GAOR, 28th Sess., Supp. 11 (A/9011); GAOR, 30th Sess., Supp. 11 (A/10011).

APPENDIX H

Voting Record of the Big Five on Resolutions Adopted by the Security Council Since the PRC's Entry (November 14, 1971-December 31, 1976)

S/Res/No.	Date of Adoption	Vote (Yes:No:Abstain)	ITEM	PRC	USA	USSR	UK	FRANCE
302	11/24/71	14:0:1	Complaints by Senegal	Y	A	Y	Y	Y
303	12/6/71	11:0:4	India v. Pakistan	Y	Y	A	A	A
304	12/8/71	15:0:0	Admission of United Arab Emirates	Y	Y	Y	Y	Y
305[a]	12/13/71	14:0:0	Extension of UNFICYP	NP	Y	Y	Y	Y
306[a]	12/21/71		Appointment of the Secretary-General	Adopted unanimously				
307[a]	12/21/71	13:0:0	India v. Pakistan	Y	Y	A	Y	Y
308[a]	1/19/72	15:0:0	OAU Request for SC Meetings in an African Capital	Y	Y	Y	Y	Y
309[a]	2/4/72	14:0:0	The Namibian Question	NP	Y	Y	Y	Y
310[a]	2/4/72	13:0:2	Ditto	Y	Y	Y	A	A
311	2/4/72	14:0:0	Apartheid	Y	Y	Y	Y	A
312	2/4/72	9:0:6	Portuguese Colonialism	Y	A	Y	A	A
313	2/28/72	15:0:0	The Middle East Question	Y	Y	Y	Y	Y
314	2/28/72	13:0:2	Southern Rhodesia	Y	A	Y	A	Y
315[a]	6/15/72	14:0:1	Extension of UNFICYP	A	Y	Y	Y	Y
316	6/26/72	13:0:2	The Middle East Question	Y	A	Y	Y	Y
317	7/21/72	14:0:1	Ditto	Y	A	Y	Y	Y
318	7/28/72	14:0:1	Southern Rhodesia	Y	A	Y	Y	Y
319	8/1/72	14:0:0	Namibia	NP	Y	Y	Y	Y
320	9/29/72	13:0:2	Southern Rhodesia	Y	A	Y	A	Y
321[a]	10/23/72	12:0:3	Complaint by Senegal	Y	A	Y	A	Y
322	11/22/72	15:0:0	Portuguese Colonialism	Y	Y	Y	Y	Y

S/Res/No.	Date of Adoption	Vote (Yes:No:Abstain)	ITEM	PRC	USA	USSR	UK	FRANCE
323	12/6/72	13:0:1	Namibia	NP	Y	A	Y	Y
324a	12/12/72	14:0:1	Extension of UNFICYP	A	Y	Y	Y	Y
325a	1/26/73	15:0:0	Panama's Request for Holding SC Meetings in Panama City	Y	Y	Y	Y	Y
326	2/2/73	13:0:2	Complaint by Zambia	Y	A	Y	A	Y
327	2/2/73	14:0:1	Ditto	Y	Y	A	Y	Y
328	3/10/73	13:0:2	Ditto	Y	A	A	A	Y
329	3/10/73	15:0:0	Ditto	Y	Y	Y	Y	Y
330	3/21/73	12:0:3	Latin America	Y	A	Y	A	A
331	4/20/73		The Middle East Question	Adopted without a vote				
332	4/21/73	11:0:4	Ditto	A	A	A	Y	Y
333	5/22/73	12:0:3	Southern Rhodesia	Y	A	Y	A	A
334a	6/15/73	14:0:1	Extension of UNFICYP	A	Y	Y	Y	Y
335a	6/22/73		Admission of German Democratic Republic and Federal Republic of Germany	Adopted without a vote				
336	7/18/73	15:0:0	Admission of the Bahamas	Y	Y	Y	Y	Y
337	8/15/73	15:0:0	The Middle East Question	Y	Y	Y	Y	Y
338	10/21/73	14:0:0	Ditto	NP	Y	Y	Y	Y
339	10/23/73	14:0:0	Ditto	NP	Y	Y	Y	Y
340	10/25/73	14:0:0	Ditto (UNEF II)	NP	Y	Y	Y	Y
341	10/27/73	14:0:0	Ditto	NP	Y	Y	Y	Y
342a	12/11/73	15:0:0	Ditto	Y	Y	Y	Y	Y
343a	12/14/73	14:0:1	Extension of UNFICYP	A	Y	Y	Y	Y
344	12/15/73	10:0:4	The Middle East Question	NP	Y	Y	Y	Y
345a	1/17/74		Inclusion of Chinese Among the Working Languages of the Council	Adopted without a vote				
346a	4/8/74	13:0:0	The Middle East Question	NP	Y	Y	Y	Y

APPENDIX H (cont'd)

S/Res/No.	Date of Adoption	Vote (Yes:No:Abstain)	ITEM	PRC	USA	USSR	UK	FRANCE
347[a]	4/24/74	13:0:0	Ditto	NP	Y	Y	Y	Y
348[a]	5/28/74	14:0:0	Iraq v. Iran	NP	Y	Y	Y	Y
349[a]	5/29/74	14:0:1	Extension of UNFICYP	A	Y	Y	Y	Y
350	5/31/74	13:0:0	The Middle East Question (UNDOF)	NP	Y	Y	Y	Y
351[a]	6/10/74		Admission of Bangladesh	Adopted without a vote				
352	6/21/74	15:0:0	Admission of Grenada	Y	Y	Y	Y	Y
353[a]	7/20/74	15:0:0	Cyprus	Y	Y	Y	Y	Y
354[a]	7/23/74	15:0:0	Ditto	Y	Y	Y	Y	Y
355[a]	8/1/74	12:0:2	Cyprus and the S-G	NP	Y	A	Y	Y
356	8/12/74	15:0:0	Admission of Guinea-Bissau	Y	Y	Y	Y	Y
357[a]	8/14/74	15:0:0	Cyprus	Y	Y	Y	Y	Y
358[a]	8/15/74	15:0:0	Ditto	Y	Y	Y	Y	Y
359[a]	8/15/74	14:0:0	Status and safety of UNFICYP	NP	Y	Y	Y	Y
360	8/16/74	11:0:3	Cyprus	NP	Y	A	Y	Y
361	8/30/74	15:0:0	Ditto	Y	Y	Y	Y	Y
362[a]	10/23/74	13:0:0	Extension of UNEF II	NP	Y	Y	Y	Y
363	11/29/74	13:0:0	Extension of UNDOF	NP	Y	Y	Y	Y
364[a]	12/13/74	14:0:0	Extension of UNFICYP	NP	Y	Y	Y	Y
365[a]	12/13/74		Cyprus	Adopted by consensus				
366[a]	12/17/74	15:0:0	Namibia	Y	Y	Y	Y	Y
367[a]	3/12/75		Cyprus	Adopted without a vote				
368[a]	4/17/75	13:0:0	Extension of UNEF II	NP	Y	Y	Y	Y
369[a]	5/28/75	13:0:0	Extension of UNDOF	NP	Y	Y	Y	Y
370[a]	6/13/75	14:0:0	Extension of UNFICYP	NP	Y	Y	Y	Y
371[a]	7/24/75	13:0:0	Extension of UNEF II	NP	Y	Y	Y	Y
372	8/18/75	15:0:0	Admission of Cape Verde	Y	Y	Y	Y	Y
373	8/18/75	15:0:0	Admission of Sao Tome & Principe	Y	Y	Y	Y	Y

No.	Date	Subject	Vote					
374	8/18/75	Admission of Mozambique	15:0:0	Y	Y	Y	Y	Y
375	9/22/75	Admission of Papua New Guinea	15:0:0	Y	Y	Y	Y	Y
376	10/17/75	Admission of the Comoros	14:0:0	Y	Y	Y	Y	Y
377[a]	10/22/75	West Sahara	Adopted without a vote					
378[a]	10/23/75	Extension of UNEF II	13:0:0	NP	Y	Y	Y	Y
379[a]	11/2/75	West Sahara	Adopted without a vote					
380[a]	11/6/75	Ditto	Adopted by consensus					
381	11/30/75	Extension of UNDOF	13:0:0	NP	Y	Y	Y	Y
382	12/1/75	Admission of Surinam	15:0:0	Y	Y	Y	Y	Y
383[a]	12/13/75	Extension of UNFICYP	14:0:0	NP	Y	Y	Y	Y
384[a]	12/22/75	East Timor	15:0:0	Y	Y	Y	Y	Y
385	1/30/76	Namibia	15:0:0	Y	Y	Y	Y	Y
386	3/17/76	Mozambique v. South Africa	15:0:0	Y	Y	Y	Y	Y
387	3/31/76	Angola v. South Africa	9:0:5	NP	A	A	A	A
388[a]	4/6/76	Sanctions against S. Rhodesia	15:0:0	Y	Y	Y	Y	Y
389	4/22/76	East Timor	12:0:2	Y	A	A	A	Y
390[a]	5/28/76	Extension of UNDOF	13:0:0	NP	Y	Y	Y	Y
391[a]	6/15/76	Extension of UNFICYP	13:0:0	NP	Y	Y	Y	Y
392	6/19/76	South Africa	Adopted by consensus					
393	7/30/76	S. Africa	14:0:1	Y	A	A	Y	Y
394	8/16/76	Admission of Seychelles	15:0:0	Y	Y	Y	Y	Y
395[a]	8/25/76	Greece v. Turkey	Adopted without a vote					
396[a]	10/22/76	Extension of UNEF II	13:0:0	NP	Y	Y	Y	Y
397	11/22/76	Admission of Angola	13:0:1	NP	A	A	A	Y
398	11/30/76	Extension of UNDOF	12:0:0	NP	Y	Y	Y	Y
399	12/1/76	Admission of Western Samoa	15:0:0	Y	Y	Y	Y	Y
400	12/7/76	Appointment of the Secretary-General	15:0:0	Adopted unanimously				
401[a]	12/14/76	Extension of UNFICYP	13:0:0	NP	Y	Y	Y	Y
402[a]	12/22/76	Lesotho v. South Africa	Adopted by consensus					

[a] Consensual resolution.

Source: Adapted from UN Docs. S/PV.1601 (24 November 1971)-S/PV.1982 (22 December 1976).

APPENDIX I

PROPOSALS, ADDITIONS AND AMENDMENTS SUBMITTED BY THE
PRC DURING THE DRAFTING PROCESS IN THE WORKING GROUP
ON THE CHARTER OF ECONOMIC RIGHTS AND DUTIES OF STATES

1. In the Philippine proposal, after "maintenance of international peace and security" add "and opposition to aggression and intervention."

2. The main purposes and objectives of the present Charter are:—To promote the development of the independent national economies of all countries, in particular, those of the developing countries, to attain the higher living standard of peoples and to narrow the economic gap between poor countries and rich countries.

3. To establish international economic relations on the basis of equality, mutual benefit and mutual respect, to expand international economic exchanges, to promote the economic development of all countries and to enhance friendship among all peoples.

4. Paragraph 4 should read: "Non-intervention in internal affairs."

5. Each country has permanent and inalienable sovereignty over all its natural resources. No country should, on any pretext or in any form, seize, control, plunder or damage other countries' natural resources. Each country has the right to dispose of the national resources in its coastal waters and sea-bed, and sub-soil thereof, within the limits of its national jurisdiction.

6. The following text could be included in Chapter III: "The international seas and the resources thereof, beyond the territorial waters and the domestic jurisdiction of States, are the common heritage of mankind and belong to all peoples. The question of their exploitation and utilization should be settled jointly by all countries through consultation on an equal basis."

7. Replace both sub-paragraphs, i.e. paragraph 4(a) and (b) of the Philippine text by the following: "States have the right to engage in international trade and other forms of economic co-operation on the basis of equality and mutual benefit, without any kind of discrimination whatsoever. No State is allowed to establish its monopoly and to conduct dumping in the international market. In pursuit of international trade and other forms of economic co-operation, States may enter into bilateral or multilateral arrangements."

8. It is incumbent upon States to introduce reforms into the world economic structure in order for the world community to establish just and rational international economic relations.

9. Add to sub-paragraph 3 of the Mexican text, the following: "Foreign enterprises must observe the laws of host countries."

10. Every country has the duty to provide aid for the development of the developing countries. Any aid shall be provided on the basis of equality, mutual benefit and mutual respect. The sovereignty and the will of recipient countries shall be strictly respected. No conditions shall be attached and no privileges demanded.

11. All countries shall, irrespective of different economic and social systems, observe the five principles of mutual respect for sovereignty and territorial integrity, mutual non-aggression, non-interference in each other's internal affairs, equality and mutual benefit and peaceful co-existence in the conduct of their mutual relations, including economic and trade relations. No country or group of countries shall seek to establish hegemony and spheres of influence in any part of the world.

12. All countries, in particular the industrially developed countries, have the bounden duty to protect and improve the human environment. The policies and measures relating to the improvement of the human environment adopted by each country shall be designed to respect the sovereignty and economic interest of other countries, especially the immediate and long-range interest of the developing countries. The interests of developing countries shall not be impaired under any pretext of environmental protection. Victim countries have the right to apply sanctions against those countries polluting their environment and to demand compensation for the damage caused.

13. To be inserted after paragraph 19 or after paragraph 20 of the Philippine text: "Every country has equal rights to participate in cargo carriage in international maritime transport. The developing countries have the right to build up their own national merchant marines. No country or maritime organization shall monopolize the international shipping industry or engage in any discriminatory practice. The developing countries have the right to participate in various shipping conferences"; "All countries shall develop international re-insurance operations on the principle of equality and mutual benefit. The developing countries have the right to develop their own national insurance industry."

14. Replace both sub-paragraphs of the Philippine proposal by the following: "States have the right to engage in international trade and other forms of economic co-operation on the basis of equality and mutual benefit, without any kind of discrimination whatsoever. No State is allowed to establish its monopoly and to conduct dumping in the international market. In pursuit of international trade and other forms of economic co-operation States may enter into bilateral or multilateral arrangements."

15. The last sentence of the Philippine proposal should be amended to read: "World economic problems shall be solved by all countries through consultations on an equal basis"; A new sentence should be added at the end of the paragraph: "No country or group of countries shall make any decision detrimental to the interests of others behind the back of the majority of countries and manipulate or monopolize the international economic affairs."

16. Advances and developments in science and technologies shall serve the interests of all peoples. The right of every country to benefit therefrom shall not be curtailed. Access thereto and transfer hereof shall be facilitated. The industrially developed countries have the special duty to provide the developing countries with new technologies commensurate with the needs of their economic development. The fee charged in respect of transfer of technology must be low or gratuitous.

17. Every country has the right to achieve and safeguard its economic independence. Foreign investments must meet the needs of recipient countries and be conducive to their economic development. Foreign enterprises shall strictly respect the sovereignty of host countries, observe their laws and carry on normal economic activities. They shall not interfere in the internal affairs of host countries and damage their resources. The developing countries have the right, in keeping with the requirements of their national security and the interests of their national economic development, to define policies and adopt measures for regulation, restriction and nationalization of foreign enterprises, free from any kind of foreign interference.

18. Loans shall be made on a long term basis, free from interest or, at least, at low interest. If recipient countries are unable to repay at maturity, aid-giving countries shall allow for extension of the period of repayment and refrain from pressing them for debt-serving, still less make use of debt problems to exert political and economic pressure.

19. The developed countries and international community, including the international organizations concerned, have the duty to support the efforts of the developing countries to strengthen and expand their economic co-operation and trade exchanges and to promote the development of their national economy.

20. All countries shall, irrespective of different economic and social systems, observe the Five Principles of mutual respect for sovereignty and territorial integrity, mutual non-aggression, non-interference in each other's internal affairs, equality and mutual benefit and peaceful co-existence in the conduct of their mutual relations, including economic and trade relations. No country or group of countries shall seek to establish hegemony and spheres of influence in any part of the world.

21. Every country has equal rights to participate in cargo carriage in international maritime transport. The developing countries have the right to build up their own national merchant marines. No country or maritime organization shall monopolize the international shipping industry or engage in any discriminatory practice. The developing countries have the right to participate in various shipping conferences.

22. All countries shall develop international re-insurance operations on the principle of equality and mutual benefit. The developing countries have the right to develop their own national insurance industry.

23. Replace paragraph 2 of the Philippine proposal by the following: "All countries, in particular the industrially developed countries, have the bounden duty to protect and improve the human environment. The policies and measures relating to the improvement of the human environment adopted by each country shall be designed to respect the sovereignty and economic interest of other countries, especially the immediate and long-range interest of the developing countries. The interests of developing countries shall not be impaired under any pretext of environmental protection. Victim countries have the right to apply sanctions against those countries polluting their environment and to demand compensaion for the damage caused."

24. Every country has equal rights to participate in cargo carriage in international maritime transport. The developing countries have the right to build up their own national merchant marines. No country or maritime organization shall monopolize the international shipping industry or engage in any discriminatory practice. The developing countries have the right to participate in various shipping conferences.

25. All countries shall develop international re-insurance operations on the principle of equality and mutual benefit. The developing countries have the right to develop their own national insurance industry.

Source: Based on *Report of the Working Group on the Charter of the Economic Rights and Duties of States on Its Second Session, held at the Palais des Nations, Geneva, from 13 to 27 July 1973*, UN Doc. TD/B/AC.12/2 (8 August 1973); and *Report of the Working Group on the Charter of Economic Rights and Duties of States on Its Thrid Session, held at the Palais des Nations, Geneva, from 4 to 22 February 1974*, UN Doc. TD/B/AC.12/3 (8 March 1974).

APPENDIX J

PERMANENT MISSION OF THE PRC TO THE UN OFFICES AT GENEVA AND TO OTHER INTERNATIONAL ORGANIZATIONS (OCTOBER 1976)

An Chih-yüan
Ambassador
Permanent Representative

Yi Su-chih
Deputy Permanent Representative

Wang Chung-yuan
Counsellor
Deputy Permanent Representative

Jung Tsien
First Secretary

Kao Yen-ping
First Secretary

Liu Hsien-ming
Second Secretary

Yu Meng-chia
Second Secretary

Cheng Wen-to
Third Secretary

Wu Chia-huang
Third Secretary

Cheng Fu-hsing
Third Secretary

Chung Chia-mao
Attaché

Kao Yung-ming
Attaché

Sun Chih-shen
Attaché

Wang Shou-jen
Attaché

Source: Mission Permanentes auprès des nations unies à Genève et Organes Principaux des Nations Unies, No. 41 (ST/GENEVA/SER.A/Rev.2/October 1976).

APPENDIX K

The Membership of the Group of 77 as of December 31, 1977 (115)

Afghanistan
Algeria
Angola
Argentina
Bahamas
Bahrain
Bangladesh
Barbados
Benin
Bhutan
Bolivia
Botswana
Brazil
Burma
Burundi
Cape Verde
Central African
   Empire
Chad
Chile
Colombia
Comoros
Congo
Costa Rica
Cuba
Cyprus
Democratic
   Kampuchea
Democratic People's
   Republic of Korea
Democratic Yemen
Djibouti
Dominican Republic
Ecuador
Egypt
El Salvador
Equatorial Guinea
Ethiopia
Fiji
Gabon
Gambia
Ghana

Grenada
Guatemala
Guinea
Guinea-Bissau
Guyana
Haiti
Honduras
India
Indonesia
Iran
Iraq
Ivory Coast
Jamaica
Jordan
Kenya
Kuwait
Lao People's
   Democratic Republic
Lebanon
Lesotho
Liberia
Libyan Arab
   Jamahiriya
Madagascar
Malawi
Malaysia
Maldives
Mali
Malta
Mauritania
Mauritius
Mexico
Morocco
Mozambique
Nepal
Nicaragua
Niger
Nigeria
Oman
Pakistan
Palestine Liberation
   Organization

Panama
Papua New Guinea
Paraguay
Peru
Philippines
Qatar
Republic of Korea
Romania
Rwanda
Sao Tome and
   Principe
Saudi Arabia
Senegal
Seychelles
Sierra Leone
Singapore
Somalia
Sri Lanka
Sudan
Surinam
Swaziland
Syrian Arab Republic
Thailand
Togo
Trinidad and Tobago
Tunisia
Uganda
United Arab Emirates
United Republic of
   Cameroon
United Republic of
   Tanzania
Upper Volta
Uruguay
Venezuela
Viet Nam
Yemen
Yugoslavia
Zaire
Zambia

APPENDIX L

Select Data on Military Expenditures (MILEX), GNP, Population, and Armed Forces of the Big Five, 1966-75

Year	Military Expenditures (MILEX) Million $ Current	Constant	Gross National Product (GNP) Million $ Current	Constant	MILEX as % of GNP	People Million	MILEX per Capita Constant $	GNP per Capita Constant $	Armed Forces thous	MILEX Armed Forces Constant $	Armed Forces per 1,000 people
CHINA, PEOPLES REPUBLIC OF											
1966	15800	24000	107000	162000	14,80	766,900	31,20	212	2600	9231	3,39
1967	16300	24000	107000	158000	15,20	784,000	30,60	201	2710	8856	3,46
1968	17700	25000	112000	158000	15,80	802,000	31,10	197	2800	8929	3,49
1969	20100	27000	131000	176000	15,30	820,700	32,90	214	2830	9541	3,45
1970	23500	29900	157000	200000	15,00	840,100	35,60	238	2850	10491	3,39
1971	25600	31000	178000	216000	14,40	859,900	36,10	251	2970	10438	3,45
1972	25800	30000	193000	225000	13,40	879,500	34,10	255	3040	9868	3,46
1973	27300	30000	226000	249000	12,10	898,700	33,40	277	3250	9231	3,62
1974	30000	30000	259000	259000	11,60	917,300	32,70	282	4300	6977	4,69
1975	32800	30000	299000	274000	11,00	934,600	32,10	293	4300	6977	4,60
FRANCE											
1966	5740	8700	114000	173000	5,02	49,194	177,00	3520	580	15000	11,79
1967	6210	9150	124000	182000	5,03	49,569	185,00	3670	595	15378	12,00
1968	6510	9170	135000	191000	4,80	49,932	184,00	3820	570	16088	11,42
1969	6410	8600	153000	206000	4,18	50,350	171,00	4080	570	15088	11,32
1970	7130	9090	171000	218000	4,17	50,784	179,00	4290	570	15947	11,22
1971	7580	9190	189000	229000	4,01	51,283	179,00	4470	565	16265	11,02
1972	8170	9510	210000	245000	3,89	51,736	184,00	4730	560	16982	10,82
1973	8870	9760	233000	256000	3,81	52,173	187,00	4900	560	17429	10,73
1974	9920	9920	266000	266000	3,73	52,577	189,00	5060	580	17103	11,03
1975	11400	10400	284000	260000	4,00	52,876	197,00	4910	575	18087	10,87

SOVIET UNION

Year											
1966	54100	82000	361000	547000		233,533	351,00	2340	3800	21600	16,30
1967	57700	85000	395000	582000		235,994	360,00	2470	3900	21800	16,50
1968	63800	89900	423000	596000		238,317	377,00	2500	4100	21900	17,20
1969	69300	93000	458000	615000		240,554	387,00	2560	4200	22100	17,50
1970	74600	95100	519000	661000		242,757	392,00	2720	4300	22100	17,70
1971	80800	98000	565000	685000		245,083	400,00	2800	4400	22300	18,00
1972	85000	99000	599000	697000		247,459	400,00	2820	4400	22500	17,80
1973	94500	104000	679000	747000		249,747	416,00	2990	4500	23100	18,00
1974	106000	106000	779000	779000		252,064	421,00	3090	4500	23600	17,90
1975	119000	109000	870000	796000		254,300	428,00	3130	4600	23700	18,10

UNITED KINGDOM

Year											
1966	5810	8800	103000	156000	5,64	54,624	161,00	2860	425	20700	7,78
1967	6130	9030	109000	160000	5,65	54,900	165,00	2910	425	21300	7,74
1968	6280	8860	117000	165000	5,37	55,152	161,00	2990	410	21600	7,43
1969	6190	8310	125000	167000	4,96	55,379	150,00	3020	390	21300	7,04
1970	6430	8190	134000	171000	4,79	55,530	148,00	3080	373	21900	6,75
1971	7150	8660	144000	175000	4,95	55,712	156,00	3140	370	23400	6,64
1972	7970	9280	154000	180000	5,17	55,882	166,00	3210	370	25100	6,62
1973	8440	9290	174000	191000	4,86	56,021	166,00	3410	370	25100	6,60
1974	9730	9730	192000	192000	5,08	56,056	174,00	3420	350	27800	6,24
1975	10200	9310	205000	188000	4,96	56,075	166,00	3350	345	27000	6,15

APPENDIX L (cont'd)

Year	Military Expenditures (MILEX) $ Million		Gross National Product (GNP) $ Million		MILEX as % of GNP	People Million	MILEX per Capita Constant $	GNP per Capita Constant $	Armed Forces thous	MILEX Armed Forces Constant $	Armed Forces per 1,000 people
	Current	Constant	Current	Constant							
UNITED STATES											
1966	63600	96400	753000	1140000	8,44	196,560	490,00	5810	3090	31200	15,70
1967	75400	111000	796000	1170000	9,47	198,712	559,00	5900	3380	32900	17,00
1968	80700	114000	868000	1220000	9,30	200,706	567,00	6100	3550	32100	17,70
1969	81400	109000	935000	1260000	8,71	202,677	539,00	6200	3460	31600	17,10
1970	77900	99200	982000	1250000	7,92	204,878	484,00	6110	3070	32300	15,00
1971	74900	90800	1060000	1290000	7,04	207,053	438,00	6230	2720	33400	13,10
1972	77600	90400	1170000	1360000	6,63	208,846	433,00	6530	2320	39000	11,10
1973	78300	86200	1310000	1440000	5,99	210,410	409,00	6830	2250	38300	10,70
1974	85900	85900	1410000	1410000	6,08	211,894	405,00	6670	2170	39600	10,20
1975	91000	83300	1520000	1390000	6,00	213,631	390,00	6490	2130	39100	9,97

Source: Adapted from U.S. Arms Control and Disarmament Agency, World Military Expenditures and Arms Transfers 1966-1975 (Publication 90, December 1976).

BIBLIOGRAPHY

I. Primary Sources

A. *Field Interviews*

See Interview Schedule at pp. 503-508.

B. *United Nations Documents**

(1) THE GENERAL ASSEMBLY

Verbatim records of the plenary of the General Assembly: A/PV.1934 (21 September 1971)-A/31/PV.107 (22 December 1976).†

Verbatim records of the First Committee of the General Assembly: A/C.1/PV.1829 (16 November 1971)-A/C.1/31/PV.58 (10 December 1976).

Summary records of the Special Political Committee of the General Assembly: A/SPC/SR.780 (16 November 1971)-A/SPC/31/SR.36 (13 December 1976).

Summary records of the Second Committee of the General Assembly: A/C.2/SR.1455 (5 October 1972)-A/C.2/31/SR.69 (15 December 1976).

Summary records of the Third Committee of the General Assembly: A/C.3/SR.1878 (19 November 1971)-A/C.3/31/SR.77 (10 December 1976).

Summary records of the Fourth Committee of the General Assembly: A/C.4/SR. 1486 (16 December 1971)-A/C.5/31/SR.62 (22 December 1976).

Summary records of the Fifth Committee of the General Assembly: A/C.4/SR.1486 (16 December 1971)-A/C.5/31/SR.62 (22 December 1976).

Summary records of the Sixth Committee of the General Assembly: A/C.6/SR.1310 (25 September 1972)-A/C.6/31/SR.70 (10 December 1976).

Summary records of the General Committee of the General Assembly: A/BUR/SR.199 (20 September 1972)-A/BUR/31/SR.2 (4 October 1976).

Summary records of the *Ad Hoc* Committee of the 6th Special Ses-

---

* Throughout the notes of this study a proper distinction was made between official records (GAOR, SCOR, ESCOR) and provisional verbatim records (A/PV. and S/PV., etc.). Where official records were not yet available, provisional verbatim records have been consulted.

† Documentary symbols change with the 31st Session of the General Assembly.

sion: A/AC.166/SR.1 (10 April 1974)-A/AC.166/SR.21 (1 May 1974).

Summary records of the *Ad Hoc* Committee of the 7th Special Session: A/AC.176/SR.1 (2 September 1975)-A/AC.176/SR.3 (16 September 1975).

Summary records of the Special Committee on the Charter of the United Nations and on the Strengthening of the Role of the Organization: A/AC.182/SR.1 (17 February 1976)-A/AC.182/SR.20 (11 March 1977).

Delegations to the General Assembly (Annual): ST/SG/SER.B/26-ST/SG/SER.B/32.

Economic Co-operation Among Developing Countries, Report of the Secretary-General: A/31/304/Add.1 (11 November 1976).

Financial Report and Accounts (Annual): GAOR, 26th Sess., Supp. No. 7 (A/8407); GAOR, 27th Sess., Supp. No. 7 (A/8707); GAOR, 28th Sess., Supp. No. 7 (A/9007); GAOR, 29th Sess., Supp. No. 7 (A/9607); and GAOR, 31st Sess., Supp. No. 7 (A/31/7).

Permanent Missions to the United Nations: ST/SG/SER.A/229 (January 1972)-ST/SG/SER.A/240 (February 1977).

Personnel Questions: Composition of the Secretariat, Report of the Secretary-General (Annual): A/8831; A/9120; A/9724; A/10184; A/31/154.

Publications and Documentation of the United Nations, Report of the Secretary-General: A/C.5/1670 (27 June 1975).

Report of the Ad Hoc Committee on the Charter of the United Nations: GAOR, 30th Sess., Supp. No. 33 (A/10033).

Report of the Ad Hoc Committee of the Sixth Special Session, Doc. A/9556 in GAOR, 6th Special Sess., Annexes Agenda Item 7.

Report of the Committee on Contributions (Annual): GAOR, 26th Sess., Supp. No. 11 (A/8411); GAOR, 27th Sess., Supp. No. 11 (A/8711); GAOR, 28th Sess., Supp. No. 11 (A/9011); GAOR, 30th Sess., Supp. No. 11 (A/10011); GAOR, 31st Sess., Supp. No. 11 (A/31/11).

Report of the Secretary-General on the Work of the Organization (Annual): GAOR, 27th Sess., Supp. No. 1 (A/8701); 28th Sess., Supp. No. 1 (A/9001); 29th Sess., Supp. No. 1 (A/9601); 30th Sess., Supp. No. 1 (A/10001); 31st Sess., Supp. No. 1 (A/31/1).

Report of the Special Committee on the Charter of the United Nations and on the Strengthening of the Role of the Organization: GAOR, 31st Sess., Supp. No. 33 (A/31/33).

Report of the Special Committee on the Financial Situation of the United Nations, GAOR, 27th Sess., Supp. No. 29 (A/8729).

Reports of the Special Committee on the Question of Defining Aggression: GAOR, 27th Sess., Supp. No. 19 (A/8719); 28th Sess., Supp. No. 19 (A/9019); 29th Sess., Supp. No. 19 (A/9619).

Rules of Procedure of the General Assembly (embodying amendments and additions adopted by the General Assembly up to 31 December 1973), A/520/Rev.12 (1974).

Verbatim records of the Special Committee on Implementation of Declaration on Granting of Independence to Colonial Countries and Peoples [The Committee of 24]: A/AC.109/PV.833 (21 January 1972)-A/AC.109/PV.1068 (9 March 1977).

(2) UN-SPONSORED GLOBAL CONFERENCES

Informal Single Negotiating Text, Part IV, presented by the President of the Conference, A/CONF.62/WP.9 (21 July 1975).

Official Records of the Third United Nations Conference on the Law of the Sea, Vol. I (1975)-Vol. VI (1977).

Report of the Committee on the Peaceful Uses of the Sea-Bed and the Ocean Floor Beyond the Limits of National Jurisdiction, Vol. III, GAOR, 28th Sess., Supp. No. 21 (A/9021).

Report of the United Nations Conference on the Human Environment, Stockholm, 5-16 June 1972, A/CONF.48/14/Rev.1 (1973).

Report of the World Food Conference, Rome, 5-16 November 1974, E/CONF.65/20 (1975).

Rules of Procedure, Third United Nations Conference on the Law of the Sea (adopted at its 20th meeting on 27 June 1974 and amended at its 40th and 52nd meetings on 12 July 1974 and 17 March 1975 respectively), A/CONF.62/30/Rev.2 (1976).

United Nations Conference on the Establishment of an International Fund for Agricultural Development, *Agreement Establishing the International Fund for Agricultural Development, as adopted by the Conference on 13 June 1976*, A/CONF.73/15 (4 August 1976).

United Nations Conference on the Establishment of an International Fund for Agricultural Development, *Reports on the Sessions of the Meetings of Interested Countries on the Establishment of an International Fund for Agricultural Development*, A/CONF.73/INF.2 (10 May 1976).

(3) UNITED NATIONS DEVELOPMENT PROGRAMME

Annual report of the Administrator for 1973 and report to the Economic and Social Council for its comprehensive policy review of operational activities throughout the United Nations system, DP/49 (5 April 1974).

A Study of the Capacity of the United Nations Development System [The Jackson Report], DP/5 (1969).

Budgetary, Administrative and Financial Matters: Financial outlook for 1977-1981, with comprehensive report on financial activities during 1976 and other related matters, DP/266 (6 May 1977).

Contributions Pledged to the United Nations Development Programme and the United Nations Capital Development Fund: Memorandum by the Secretary-General (Annual): A/CONF.58/2 (17 October 1973); A/CONF.59/2 (30 September 1974); A/CONF.65/2 (7 July 1975); A/CONF.69/2 (29 July 1976).

General Review of Programmes and Policies of UNDP: The Future Role of UNDP in World Development in the Context of the Preparations for the Seventh Special Session of the General Assembly, DP/144 (24 March 1975).

Report of the Administrator for 1974 (DP/111).

Report of the Administrator for 1975 (DP/184).

Report of the Administrator for 1976 (DP/255).

Rules of Procedure of the Governing Council of the United Nations Development Programme (August 1976, DP/1/Rev.1).

Summary records of the annual United Nations Pledging Conference on the United Nations Development Programme and the United Nations Capital Development Fund: A/CONF.58/SR.1-2 (23 November 1972)-A/CONF.76/SR.2 (5 November 1976).

Summary records of the meetings of the Governing Council: DP/SR.443 (15 January 1975)-DP/SR.566 (4 February 1977).

(4) UNITED NATIONS INDUSTRIAL DEVELOPMENT ORGANIZATION

Contributions pledged or Paid to the United Nations Industrial Development Organization (Annual): A/CONF.66/2 (8 July 1975)-A/CONF.68/2 (15 July 1976).

Report of the Intergovernmental Committee of the Whole to Draw Up a Constitution for UNIDO As a Specialized Agency, A/AC.180/9 (17 November 1976).

Summary records of the annual United Nations Pledging Conference on the United Nations Industrial Development Organization: A/CONF.66/SR.1 (20 November 1974)-A/CONF.75/SR.1 (29 October 1976).

Working Résumé of the Intergovernmental Committee of the Whole to Draw Up a Constitution for UNIDO As a Specialized Agency: 2nd Sess. (A/AC.180/6)-4th Sess. (A/AC.180/8).

(5) THE UNITED NATIONS CONFERENCE ON TRADE AND DEVELOPMENT

Proceedings of UNCTAD, Geneva, 23 March-16 June 1964, Vol. I: *Final Act and Report* (1964); Vol. II: *Policy Statement* (1964).

UNCTAD; *Scond Session*, New Delhi, Vol. I: *Report and Annexes*.

Proceedings of UNCTAD, Third Session, Santiago de Chile, 13 April-21 May 1972, Vol. I: *Report and Annexes*; Vol. II: *Merchandise Trade*.

Report of the United Nations Conference on Trade and Development on Its Fourth Session, held at the Kenyatta Conference Center, Nairobi, Kenya, from 5 to 31 May 1976, TD/217 (12 July 1976).

Report of the Working Group on the Charter of the Economic Rights and Duties of States on Its First Session, held at the Palais des Nations, Geneva, from 12 to 23 February 1973, TD/B/AC.12/1 (6 March 1973).

Report of the Working Group on the Charter of the Economic Rights and Duties of States on Its Second Session, held at the Palais des Nations, Geneva, from 13 to 27 July 1973, TD/B/AC.12/2 (8 August 1973).

Report of the Working Group on the Charter of the Economic Rights and Duties of States on its Third Session, held at the Palais des Nations, Geneva, from 4 to 22 February 1974, TD/B/AC.12/3 (8 March 1974).

(6) THE WORLD FOOD COUNCIL

Report of the World Food Council on Its First Session, Note by the Secretary-General, WFC/13 (1 July 1975).

Report of the World Food Council, Note by the Executive Director, WFC/29 (24 June 1976).

(7) THE SECURITY COUNCIL

Comprehensive Review of the Whole Question of Peace-keeping Operations in All Their Aspects, Report of the Special Committee on Peace-keeping Operations, UN Doc. A/31/337 (23 November 1976).

Documents of the United Nations Conference on International Organization San Francisco, 1945, Vol. XI: Commission III (Security Council), (New York, 1945).

Financing of the United Nations Emergency Force Established Pursuant to Security Council Resolution 340 (1973), Report of the Fifth Committee, A/9428 (10 December 1973).

Financing of the United Nations Emergency Force and of the United Nations Disengagement Observer Force, Report of the Fifth Committee (Part I), A/31/278 (22 October 1976).

Financing of the United Nations Emergency Force and of the United Nations Disengagement Observer Force, Report of the Fifth Committee (Part II) A/31/278/Add.1 (30 November 1976).

Financing of the United Nations Emergency Force and of the United

Nations Disengagement Observer Force, Report of the Fifth Committee (Part III), A/31/278/Add.2 (21 December 1976).

Financing of the United Nations Emergency Force and of the United Nations Disengagement Observer Force, Report of the Secretary-General, A/31/288 (19 November 1976).

Provisional Rules of Procedure of the Security Council, S/96/Rev.6 (January 1974).

Repertory of Practice of UN Organs, Supp. No. 3 (1973).

Report of the Security Council 16 June 1971-15 June 1972, GAOR, 27th Sess., Supp. No. 2 (A/8702).

Report of the Security Council 16 June 1972-15 June 1973, GAOR, 28th Sess., Supp. No. 2 (A/9002).

Report of the Security Council 16 June 1973-15 June 1974, GAOR, 29th Sess., Supp. No. 2 (A/9602).

Report of the Security Council 16 June 1974-15 June 1975, GAOR, 30th Sess., Supp. No. 2 (A/10002).

Report of the Security Council 16 June 1975-15 June 1976, GAOR, 31st Sess., Supp. No. 2 (A/31/2).

Resolutions and Decisions of the Security Council 1971, SCOR, 26th Yr.

Resolutions and Decisions of the Security Council 1972, SCOR, 27th Yr.

Resolutions and Decisions of the Security Council 1973, SCOR, 28th Yr.

Resolutions and Decisions of the Security Council 1974, SCOR, 29th Yr.

Supplements of SCOR: January 1972-December 1976.

Verbatim records of Security Council meetings: S/PV.1599 (23 November 1971)-S/PV.1982 (22 December 1976).

(8) THE ECONOMIC AND SOCIAL COUNCIL

Report of the Economic and Social Council on the Work of Its Fifty-Second and Fifty-Third Sessions, GAOR, 27th Sess., Supp. No. 3 (A/8703).

Report of the Economic and Social Council on the Work of Its Fifty-Fourth and Fifty-Fifth Sessions, GAOR, 28th Sess., Supp. No. 3 (A/9003).

Report of the Economic and Social Council on the Work of Its Fifty-Sixth and Fifty-Seventh Sessions, GAOR, 29th Sess., Supp. No. 3 (A/9603).

Report of the Economic and Social Council on the Work of Its Organizational Session for 1975 and of Its Fifty-Eighth and Fifty-Ninth Sessions, GAOR, 30th Sess., Supp. No. 3 (A/10003).

Report of the Economic and Social Council on the Work of Its Organizational Session for 1976 and of Its Sixtieth and Sixty-First Sessions, GAOR, 31st Sess., Supp. No. 3 (A/31/3).

Rules of Procedure of the Economic and Social Council, E/5715 (1975).

Summary records of the *Ad Hoc* Committee on Rationalization of ECOSOC: E/AC.60/SR.1 (6 May 1974)-E/AC.60/SR.9 (15 May 1974).

Summary records of the Coordination Committee of ECOSOC: E/AC.24/SR.434 (5 July 1972)-E/AC.24/SR.604 (2 August 1976).

Summary records of the Economic Committee of ECOSOC: E/AC.6/SR.540 (16 May 1972)-E/AC.6/SR.782 (4 August 1976).

Summary records of plenary meetings of ECOSOC: E/SR.1809 (5 January 1972)-E/SR.2037 (17 November 1976).

Summary records of the Preparatory Committee for the Special Session of the General Assembly Devoted to Development and International Economic Cooperation: E/AC.62/SR.1 (3 March 1975)-E/AC.62/SR.16 (27 March 1975).

Summary records of the Social Committee of ECOSOC: E/AC.7/SR.681 (15 May 1972)-E/AC.7/SR.787 (6 May 1976).

(9) THE INTERNATIONAL COURT OF JUSTICE AND LEGAL MATTERS

ICJ: Reports of Judgments, Advisory Opinions and Orders (Annual).

Materials on Succession of States, ST/LEG/SER.B/14 (1967).

Multilateral Treaties in Respect of Which the Secretary-General Performs Depositary Functions, List of Signatures, Ratifications, Accessions, etc. as at 31 December 1975, ST/LEG/SER.D/9 (1976).

Multilateral Treaties in Respect of Which the Secretary-General Performs Depositary Functions, List of Signatures, Ratifications, Accessions, etc. as at 31 December 1976, ST/LEG/SER.D/10 (1977).

Report of the International Court of Justice, 1 August 1971-31 July 1972, GAOR, 27th Sess., Supp. No. 5 (A/8705).

Report of the International Court of Justice, 1 August 1972-31 July 1973, GAOR, 28th Sess., Supp. No. 5 (A/9005).

Report of the International Court of Justice, 1 August 1973-31 July 1974, GAOR, 29th Sess., Supp. No. 5 (A/9605).

Report of the International Court of Justice, 1 August 1974-31 July 1976, GAOR, 31st Sess., Supp. No. 5 (A/31/5).

United Nations Juridical Yearbook, 1971-74.

C. *Documents Submitted by the PRC*

A/8470; A/8536; A/L.671/Rev.1; A/8654; A/8660; A/8663; A/8752/Add.1; A/AC.138/66; A/8752/Add.9; A/8775/Add.2; A/

9033; A/AC.138/66/Rev.1; A/AC.138/L.11/Rev.1; A/AC.138/SC. II/L.34; A/AC.138/SC.III/L.42; A/AC.138/SC.II/L.45; A/9033; E/AC.6/L.498/Rev.1; A/9091; A/9137; A/9091; A/9145; A/9171; A/9195; A/9196; A/9196/Add.1; A/L.702; A/9209; A/L.714; A/9344; A/9703; A/L.733; A/9742/Add.1; A/9703/Add.3; A/ 9718; A/9713; A/L.729; A/L.730; A/L.736; A/9739; A/9797; A/10061; A/10191; A/L.760; A/L.762; A/L764; A/L.761; A/L. 763; A/10033; A/10361; A/L.772; A/L.781/Rev.1; A/31/119; A/31/192; A/31/28; A/31/L.21; A/31/L.32.

D. *Documents of the Specialized Agencies*

(1) UNESCO

Approved Programme and Budget for 1977-1978 (19 C/5 Approved, February 1977).

Contributions of Member States, 30 October 1976 (19 C/51).

Election of Members of the Executive Board (19 C/NOM/9, 9 September 1976).

Geographical Distribution of Staff: Report by the Director-General (19 C/60, 24 September 1976).

Manual of the General Conference (1977 ed.).

Records of the General Conference, 17th Sess., Paris, 1972, Vol. I: *Resolutions, Recommendations* (1973).

Records of the General Conference, 17th Sess., Paris, 1972, Vol. II: *Reports, Programme Commissions, Administrative Commission, Legal Committee* (1974).

Records of the General Conference, 17th Sess., Paris, 1972, Vol. III: *Proceedings* (1974).

Records of the General Conference, 18th Sess., Paris, 1974, Vol. I: *Resolutions* (1975).

Records of the General Conference, 18th Sess., Paris, 1974, Vol. II: *Reports* (1976).

Records of the General Conference, 18th Sess., Paris, 1974, Vol. III: *Proceedings* (1976).

Records of the General Conference, 19th Sess., Nairobi, 26 October-30 November 1976, Vol. I: *Resolutions* (1977).

Records of the General Conference, 3rd Extraordinary Sess., Paris, 1973. *Resolutions and Proceedings* (1974).

Report of the Director-General on the Activities of the Organization in 1974, communicated to Member States and Executive Board in Accordance with Article VI.3.b of the Constitution (19 C/3).

Report of the External Auditor and Financial Report of the Director-General on the Accounts of UNESCO For the Two-Year Financial Period Ended 31 December 1974 (19 C/48, 1 July 1976).

Report on the International Hydrological Programme (IHP), (19 C/85, 6 August 1976).

Summary records of the Executive Board: 95th Sess. (95 EX/SR.1-23, 18 September-23 November 1974)-100th Sess. (100 EX/SR.1-20, 27 September-30 November 1976).

(2) FAO

Basic Texts of the Food and Agricultural Organization of the United Nations, Vols. I and II (1976).

Food and Agricultural Organization of the United Nations Contribution Statement: Position at 31 December 1973 (WA/E5777/c).

Food and Agricultural Organization of the United Nations Contribution Statement: Position at 30 November 1974 (WA/F4937/c).

Food and Agricultural Organization of the United Nations Contribution Statement: Position at 31 December 1975 (WA/H6300/c).

Food and Agricultural Organization of the United Nations Contribution Statement: Position at 31 December 1976 (W/K3647/c).

Geographical Distribution of Professional Staff on the Regular Programme—Monthly Situation 1973 (WA/E6564/c).

Geographical Distribution of Professional Staff on the Regular Programme—Monthly Situation 1974 (WA/F6921/c).

Geographical Distribution of Professional Staff on the Regular Programme—Monthly Situation 1975 (WA/H0827/c).

Geographical Distribution of Professional Staff on the Regular Programme—Monthly Situation 1976 (W/K1804/c).

Freshwater Fisheries and Aquaculture in China, FAO Fisheries Technical Paper No. 168, FIR/T 168 (FAO, Rome, June 1977).

Permanent Representatives Accredited to the Food and Agricultural Organizations of the United Nations (30 November 1975).

Report of the Conference of FAO, 16th Sess., Rome, 6-25 November 1971.

Report of the Conference of FAO, 17th Sess., Rome 10-29 November 1973.

Report of the Conference of FAO, 18th Sess., Rome 8-27 November 1975.

Verbatim records of plenary meetings of the Conference, 17th Plenary Sess., Rome, 10-29 November 1973 (C 73/PV.1-C 73/PV.24).

Verbatim records of plenary meetings of the Conference, 18th Plenary Sess., Rome, 8-27 November 1975 (C 75/PV.1-C 75/PV.23) [First Draft].

Verbatim records of Commission I of the Conference, 18th Sess., Rome, 12-25 November 1975 (C 75/I/PV.1-C 75/I/PV.21).

Verbatim records of Commission II of the Conference, 18th Sess., Rome, 12-26 November 1975 (C 75/II/PV.1-C 75/II/PV.22).

Verbatim records of Commission III of the Conference, 18th Sess., Rome, 20-26 November 1975 (C 75/III/PV.1-C 75/III/PV.6).

Verbatim records of plenary meetings of the Council, 60th Sess. (CL 60/PV)-70th Sess. (CL 70/PV).

(3) ICAO

Action of the Council, 74th Sess. (Doc. 8987-C/1004).
Action of the Council, 83rd Sess. (Doc. 9130-C/1023).
Action of the Council, 84th Sess. (Doc. 9136-C/1025).
Action of the Council, 85th Sess. (Doc. 9141-C/1027).
Action of the Council, 86th Sess. (Doc. 9163-C/1029).
Action of the Council, 87th Sess. (Doc. 9164-C/1030).
Action of the Council, 88th Sess. (Doc. 9171-C/1033).
Annual Report of the Council—1971 (Doc. 8982).
Annual Report of the Council—1972 (Doc. 9046).
Annual Report of the Council—1973 (Doc. 9085).
Annual Report of the Council—1974 (Doc. 9127).
Annual Report of the Council—1975 (Doc. 9166).
Annual Report of the Council—1976 [Draft Copy].
Aeronautical Agreements and Arrangements: Tables of Agreements and Arrangements Registered with the Organization, 1 January 1946-31 December 1974 (Doc. 9181-LGB/319).
Civil Aviation Statistics of the World 1975 (Doc. 9180).
Communications Divisional Meeting, Preparatory to the ITU World Administrative Radio Conference, Aeronautical Mobile (R) Service, Montreal, 8-24 September 1976, *Report* (Doc. 9187, COM/76).
Convention on International Civil Aviation (5th ed., 1975, Doc. 7300/5).
Financial Statements for the Year Ended 31 December 1975 and Reports of the External Auditor (14 May 1976).
ICAO Bulletin.
The ICAO Financial Regulations (6th ed., Doc. 7515/6, 1975).
International Conference on Air Law, Montreal, September 1975, Vol. II: *Documents* (Doc. 9154-LC/174-2).
Legal Committee, 21st Sess., Montreal, 3-22 October 1974, Vol. I: *Minutes* (Doc. 9131-LC/173-1).
Legal Committee, 21st Sess., Montreal, 3-22 October 1974, Vol. II: *Documents* (Doc. 9131-LC/173-2).
Minutes of the Plenary Meetings, Assembly—21st Sess. (Doc. 9119, A21-Min. P/1-12).
Minutes of the Technical Commission, Assembly—21st Sess. (A21-Min. TE/1-13).

Repertory-Guide to the Convention on International Civil Aviation (2nd ed., 1977, Doc. 8900/2).

Report of the Administrative Commission, Assembly—21st Sess. (Doc. 9117, A21-AD).

Report of the Executive Committee, Assembly—21st Sess. (Doc. 9113, A21-EX).

Resolutions Adopted by the Assembly and Index to Documentation, Assembly—21st Sess. (Doc. 9118, A21-Res.).

Report of the Ninth Air Navigation Conference, Montreal, 21 April-14 May 1976 (Doc. 9168, AN-CONF/9).

Rules of Procedure for the Council (Rev. 4, April 1970, Doc. 7559/4).

Standing Rules of Procedure of the Assembly of the International Civil Aviation Organization (2nd ed., 1963, Doc. 7600/2).

(4) WMO

Annual Report of the World Meteorological Organization 1970 (WMO, No. 287).

Annual Report of the World Meteorological Organization 1971 (WMO, No. 320).

Annual Report of the World Meteorological Organization 1972 (WMO, No. 348).

Annual Report of the World Meteorological Organization 1973 (WMO, No. 376).

Annual Report of the World Meteorological Organization 1974 (WMO, No. 412).

Annual Report of the World Meteorological Organization 1975 (WMO, No. 439).

Agreements and Working Arrangements with Other International Organizations (1973 ed., WMO, No. 60).

Annual Report of the World Meteorological Organization 1976 (WMO, No. 470).

Basic Documents (excluding the Technical Regulations) (1971 ed., WMO, No. 15).

Sixth World Meteorological Congress: *Abridged Report with Resolutions* (WMO, No. 292).

Sixth World Meteorological Congress: *Proceedings* (WMO, No. 297).

Seventh World Meteorological Congress: *Proceedings* (WMO, No. 428).

WMO Bulletin.

E. Chinese Sources

Break the Nuclear Monopoly, Eliminate Nuclear Weapons. Peking: Foreign Languages Press, 1965.

Chinese People's Institute of Foreign Affairs (ed.), *Oppose U.S. Occupation of Taiwan and "Two Chinas" Plot*. Peking: Foreign Languages Press, 1958.

Ch'ing-tai ch'ou-pan i-wu shih-mo [The complete account of the management of barbarian affairs under the Ch'ing dynasty], 80 *chüan* for the later Tao-kuang period, 1836-50; 80 *chüan* for the Hsien-feng period, 1851-61; and 100 *chüan* for the T'ung-chih period, 1862-74. Peiping: Palace Museum, 1930.

Confessions Concerning the Line of Soviet-U.S. Collaboration Pursued by the New Leaders of the CPSU. Peking: Foreign Languages Press, 1966.

Documents of the First Session of the Fourth National People's Congress of the People's Republic of China. Peking: Foreign Languages Press, 1975.

Jen-min jih-pao [People's Daily].

Jen-min shou-ts'e [People's Handbook].

Kuang-ming jih-pao [Enlightenment Daily].

Kung-tso t'ung-hsün [The Work Bulletin].

Mao Tse-tung. *On the Correct Handling of Contradictions Among the People*. Peking: Foreign Languages Press, 1966.

——— *Mao Tse-tung hsüan-chi* [Selected Works of Mao Tse-tung]. Peking: Jen-min ch'u-pan she, 1969.

——— *Mao Tse-tung ssu-hsiang wan-sui* [Long Live Mao Tse-tung's Thought]. N.p.: 1967.

——— *Mao Tse-tung ssu-hsiang wan-sui* [Long Live Mao Tse-tung's Thought]. N.p.: August 1969.

——— *Selected Works of Mao Tse-tung*, 4 vols. Peking: Foreign Languages Press, 1961, 1965.

——— *Talks At the Yenan Forum on Literature and Art*. Peking: Foreign Languages Press, 1967.

——— *Where Do Correct Ideas Come From?* (May 1963). Peking: Foreign Languages Press, 1966.

More on the Differences Between Comrade Togliatti and Us—Some Important Problems of Leninism in the Contemporary World. Peking: Foreign Languages Press, 1963.

New China News Agency [Hsinhua].

Oppose the New U.S. Plots To Create "Two Chinas." Peking: Foreign Languages Press, 1962.

Oppose U.S. Military Provocations in the Taiwan Straits Area: A Selection of Important Documents. Peking: Foreign Languages Press, 1958.

Peaceful Coexistence—Two Diametrically Opposed Policies. Peking: Foreign Languages Press, 1963.

Peking Review (in English).

People's China (in English).

People of the World, Unite, For the Complete, Thorough, Total and Resolute Prohibition and Destruction of Nuclear Weapons! Peking: Foreign Languages Press, 1963.

People of the World, Unite and Struggle for the Complete Prohibition and Thorough Destruction of Nuclear Weapons! Peking: Foreign Languages Press, 1971.

The Sino-Indian Boundary Question (enlarged ed.). Peking: Foreign Languages Press, 1962.

Speeches Welcoming the Delegation of the People's Republic of China By the U.N. General Assembly President and Representatives of Various Countries at the Plenary Meeting of the 26th Session of the U.N. General Assembly (November 15, 1971). Peking: Foreign Languages Press, 1971.

Survey of Mainland China Press.

Survey of the People's Republic of China Press.

Three Major Struggles on China's Philosophical Front (1949-64). Peking: Foreign Languages Press, 1973.

Two Different Lines on the Question of War and Peace. Peking: Foreign Languages Press, 1963.

Vice-Premier Chen Yi Answers Questions Put by Correspondents. Peking: Foreign Languages Press, 1966.

II. Miscellaneous Reference And Documentary Sources

Bartke, Wolfgang. *The Diplomatic Service of the People's Republic of China as of January 1976 (including Biographies).* Hamburg: Institut für Asienkunde, 1976.

CIA. *Communist Aid to the Less Developed Countries of the Free World, 1976.* ER 77-10296, August 1977.

———— China: *Energy Balance Projections.* A(ER) 75-76, November 1975.

———— *Foreign Trade in Machinery and Equipment Since 1952.* A(ER) 75-60. January 1975.

———— *People's Republic of China: Handbook of Economic Indicators.* A(ER)75-72, August 1975.

———— *People's Republic of China: International Trade Handbook.* A(ER) 74-63, September 1974.

The *Christian Science Monitor.*

The *Diplomatic World Bulletin* (Biweekly).

Ho, Paul, compiler, *The People's Republic of China and International Law: A Select Bibliography of Chinese Sources.* Washington, D.C.: Library of Congress, 1972.

Hsia, Tao-tai. *Guide to Selected Legal Sources of Mainland China.* Washington, D.C.: Library of Congress, 1967.

The International Institute for Strategic Studies. *The Military Balance* (Annual).

—— *Strategic Survey* (Annual).

Klein, Donald W., and Clark, Anne B. *Biographic Dictionary of Chinese Communism, 1921-1965.* 2 vols. Cambridge, Mass.: Harvard University Press, 1971.

Lieberthal, Kenneth. *A Research Guide to Central Party and Government Meetings in China, 1949-1975.* White Plains, N.Y.: International Arts and Sciences Press, 1976.

The *New York Times.*

Sivard, Ruth Leger. *World Military and Social Expenditures 1974.* New York: The Institute for World Order, 1974.

—— *World Military and Social Expenditures 1977.* Leesburg, Va.: WMSE Publications, 1977.

UN Chronicle (*UN Monthly Chronicle* until March 1975).

United Nations Documentation, ST/LIB/34. New York: United Nations, 1974.

United Nations Journal.

United Nations Yearbook.

U.S. Arms Control and Disarmament Agency. *World Military Expenditures and Arms Trade 1963-1973.* Publication 74. Washington, D.C.: Government Printing Office, 1975.

—— *World Military Expenditures and Arms Transfers 1965-1974.* Publication 84. Washington, D.C.: Government Printing Office, 1976.

—— *World Military Expenditures and Arms Transfers 1966-1975.* Publication 90. Washington, D.C.: Government Printing Office, 1976.

U.S. Congress. House. Committee on Foreign Affairs. *Expressions by the House of Representatives, the Senate, and the Committee on Foreign Affairs that the Chinese Communists are not entitled to and should not be recognized to represent China in the United Nations.* 84th Cong., 2nd Sess.

U.S. Congress. Joint Economic Committee. *Allocation of Resources in the Soviet Union and China—1975. Hearings* before the Subcommittee on Priorities and Economy in Government of the Joint Economic Committee. 94th Cong. 1st Sess. Washington, D.C.: Government Printing Office, 1975.

—— Joint Economic Committee. *China: A Reassessment of the Economy.* 94th Cong. 1st Sess. Washington, D.C.: Government Printing Office, 1975.

———— Joint Economic Committee. *China and the Chinese: A Compendium of Papers submitted to the Joint Economic Committee.* 94th Cong., 2nd Sess. Washington, D.C.: Government Printing Office, 1976.

———— Joint Economic Committee. *An Economic Profile of Mainland China*, Studies Prepared for the Joint Economic Committee. Vol. II. Washington, D.C.: Government Printing Office, 1967.

———— Joint Economic Committee. *Mainland China in the World Economy. Hearings* before the Joint Economic Committee. 90th Cong., 1st Sess. Washington, D.C.: Government Printing Office, 1967.

———— Joint Economic Committee. *People's Republic of China: An Economic Assessment.* 92nd Cong. 2nd Sess. Washington, D.C.: Government Printing Office, 1972.

U.S. Congress. Senate. Committee on Government Operations. *U.S. Participation in International Organizations.* Committee Reprint, 95th Cong., 1st Sess. Washington, D.C.: Government Printing Office, 1977.

U.S. Department of State. *The United States and the Third World.* Department of State Publication 8863. Washington, D.C.: Government Printing Office, 1976.

Who's Who in Communist China. 2 vols. Rev. ed. Hong Kong: Union Research Institute, 1969-1970.

Who's Who in the United Nations and Specialized Agencies. New York: Arno, 1975.

Wu, Yuan-li, ed. *China: A Handbook.* New York: Praeger, 1973.

III. SECONDARY SOURCES

A. Books and Monographs

Adams, Mervyn W. "Communist China and the United Nations: A Study of China's Developing Attitude Towards the UN Role in International Peace and Security." Unpublished M.A. thesis, Columbia University, 1964.

Adelman, Irma, and Morris, Cynthia. *Economic Growth and Social Equity in Developing Countries.* Stanford, Calif.: Stanford University Press, 1973.

Ajami, Fouad. *The Global Populists: Third World Nations and World-Order Crises.* Research Monograph No. 41, Center of International Studies, Princeton University, May 1974.

Alger, Chadwick F. "Personal Contact in Intergovernmental Organizations." *The United Nations System and Its Functions.* Ed.

Robert W. Gregg and Michael Barkun. Princeton, N.J.: Van Nostrand, 1968.

Alker, Hayward, and Russett, Bruce. *World Politics in the General Assembly*. New Haven, Conn.: Yale University Press, 1965.

Amin, Samir. *L'échange inégal et la loi de la valeur*. Paris: Anthropos, 1973.

Appleton, Sheldon. *The Eternal Triangle? Communist China, the United States and the United Nations*. East Lansing, Mich.: Michigan State University Press, 1961.

Asamoah, Obed Y. *The Legal Significance of the Declaration of the General Assembly of the United Nations*. The Hague: Nifhoff, 1966.

Bailey, Sydney B. *The General Assembly of the United Nations: A Study of Procedure and Practice*. Rev. ed. New York: Praeger, 1964.

———— *The Procedure of the UN Security Council*. London: Clarendon Press, 1975.

———— *Voting in the Security Council*. Bloomington, Ind.: Indiana University Press, 1969.

Banno, Masataka. *China and the West 1858-1861*. Cambridge, Mass.: Harvard University Press, 1964.

Bartke, Wolfgang. *China's Economic Aid*. Trans. Waldraut Jarke. London: Hurst, 1975.

Bodenheimer, Susanne. "Dependency and Imperialism: The Roots of Latin American Underdevelopment." *Readings in U.S. Imperialism*. Ed. K. T. Fann and Donald C. Hodges. Boston, Mass.: An Extending Horizons Book, 1971.

Boulding, Kenneth E. *The Image*. Ann Arbor, Mich.: University of Michigan Press, 1956.

———— "National Images and International Systems." *International Politics and Foreign Policy: A Reader in Research and Theory*. Ed. James N. Rosenau. Rev. ed. New York: Free Press, 1969.

Boyd, James M. *United Nations Peacekeeping Operations*. New York: Praeger, 1971.

Building Peace. Reports of the Commission to Study the Organization of Peace 1939-1972, 2 vols. Metuchen, N.J.: Scarecrow Press, 1973.

Cardoso, Fernando Henrique. "Associated-Dependent Development: Theoretical and Practical Implications." *Authoritarian Brazil*. Ed. Alfred Stepan. New Haven, Conn.: Yale University Press, 1973.

Castañeda, Jorge. *Legal Effects of United Nations Resolutions*. Trans. Alba Amoia. New York: Columbia University Press, 1969.

Chai, F. T. *Consultation and Consensus in the Security Council*. New York: United Nations Institute for Training and Research, 1971.

Ch'en, Jerome. *Mao and the Chinese Revolution.* New York: Oxford University Press, 1967.

———— ed. *Mao: Great Lives Observed.* Englewood Cliffs, N.J.: Prentice-Hall, 1969.

———— ed. *Mao Papers: Anthology and Bibliography.* New York: Oxford University Press, 1970.

Chen, Lung-chu, and Lasswell, Harold. *Formosa, China, and the United Nations: Formosa in the World Community.* New York: St. Martin's Press, 1967.

Chiang Kai-shek. *China's Destiny.* New York: Roy Publishers, 1974.

Chiu, Hungdah. *The Capacity of International Organizations to Conclude Treaties and the Special Legal Aspects of the Treaties So Concluded.* The Hague: Nijhoff, 1966.

———— "Comparison of the Nationalist and Communist Chinese Views of Unequal Treaties." *China's Practice of International Law: Some Case Studies.* Ed. Jerome A. Cohen. Cambridge, Mass.: Harvard University Press, 1972.

———— *The People's Republic of China and the Law of Treaties.* Cambridge, Mass.: Harvard University Press, 1972.

Chou Keng-sheng. *Hsien-tai ying-mei kuo-chi-fa te ssu-hsiang tung-hsiang* [Trends in Modern Anglo-American Thought on International Law]. Peking: Shih-chieh chih-shih ch'u-pan she, 1963.

Chun, Hae-jong. "Sino-Korean Tributary Relations in the Ch'ing Period." *The Chinese World Order.* Ed. John K. Fairbank. Cambridge, Mass.: Harvard University Press, 1968.

Clark, Grenville, and Sohn, Louis B. *World Peace Through World Law.* 3rd ed. enlarged. Cambridge, Mass.: Harvard University Press, 1966.

Claude, Inis L., Jr. "Economic Development and International Political Stability." *The Politics of International Organizations: Studies in Multilateral Social and Economic Agencies.* Ed. Robert W. Cox. New York: Praeger, 1970.

———— "The Peace-keeping Role of the United Nations." *The United Nations in Perspective.* Ed. E. Berkeley Tompkins. Stanford, Calif.: Hoover Institution Press, 1972.

———— *Power and International Relations.* New York: Random House, 1962.

———— "The Security Council." *The Evolution of International Organizations.* Ed. Evan Luard. New York: Praeger, 1966.

———— *Swords into Plowshares.* 4th ed. New York: Random House, 1971.

Cohen, Arthur A. *The Communism of Mao-Tse-tung.* Chicago: University of Chicago Press, 1964.

Cohen, Jerome A., ed. *China's Practice of International Law: Some Case Studies*. Cambridge, Mass.: Harvard University Press, 1972.

—— ed. *Contemporary Chinese Law: Research Problems and Perspectives*. Cambridge, Mass.: Harvard University Press, 1970.

—— and Chiu, Hungdah. *People's China and International Law*. 2 vols. Princeton, N.J.: Princeton University Press, 1974.

Cordier, Henri. *L'expédition de Chine de 1860: histoire diplomatique, notes et documents*. Paris: F. Alcan, 1906.

—— *Histoire des relations de la Chine avec les Puissances Occidentales, 1860-1900*. 3 vols. Paris: F. Alcan, 1901-02.

Cox, Robert W., and Jacobson, Harold K. *The Anatomy of Influence: Decision Making in International Organization*. New Haven, Conn.: Yale University Press, 1974.

Dallin, Alexander. *The Soviet Union at the United Nations*. New York: Praeger, 1962.

Detter, Ingrid. *Law Making by International Organizations*. Stockholm: Norstedt, 1965.

Di Qual, Lino. *Les effets des résolutions des Nations-Unis*. Paris: Pichon et Durand-Auzias, 1967.

Dial, Roger L., ed. *Advancing and Contending Approaches to the Study of Chinese Foreign Policy*. Halifax: Center for Foreign Policy Studies, Dalhousie University, 1974.

Doolin, Dennis J. *Territorial Claims in the Sino-Soviet Conflict: Documents and Analysis*. Stanford, Calif.: The Hoover Institution on War, Revolution, and Peace, 1965.

Eckstein, Alexander. *China's Economic Revolution*. London and New York: Cambridge University Press, 1977.

Emmanuel, Arrighi. *Unequal Exchange: A Study of the Imperialism of Trade*. New York: Monthly Review Press, 1972.

Fabian, Larry L. *Soldiers Without Enemies*. Washington, D.C.: The Brookings Institution, 1971.

Fairbank, John K. "Synarchy Under the Treaties." *Chinese Thought and Institution*. Ed. John K. Fairbank. Chicago: University of Chicago Press, 1957.

—— *Trade and Diplomacy on the China Coast: The Opening of the Treaty Ports, 1842-1854*. 2 vols. Cambridge, Mass.: Harvard University Press, 1954.

Falk, Richard A. *A Global Approach to National Policy*. Cambridge, Mass.: Harvard University Press, 1975.

—— "The Interplay of Westphalia and Charter Conception of International Legal Order." *The Future of the International Legal Order*, Vol. I: *Trends and Patterns*. Ed. Richard A. Falk and Cyril E. Black. Princeton, N.J.: Princeton University Press, 1969.

—— *Legal Order in a Violent World*. Princeton, N.J.: Princeton University Press, 1968.

—— *The Status of Law in International Society*. Princeton, N.J.: Princeton University Press, 1970.

—— *A Study of Future Worlds*. New York: Free Press, 1975.

—— *This Endangered Planet*. New York: Vintage Books, 1972.

Fanon, Frantz. *The Wretched of the Earth*. Trans. Constance Farrington. New York: Grove Press, 1968.

Feeney, William R. "The Participation of the PRC in the United Nations." *Sino-American Détente and Its Policy Implications*. Ed. Gene T. Hsia. New York: Praeger, 1974.

Ferencz, Benjamin B. *Defining International Aggression: The Search for World Peace*. 2 vols. Dobbs Ferry, N.Y.: Oceana Publications, 1975.

Fitzgerald, C. P. *The Chinese View of Their Place in the World*. London: Oxford University Press, 1967.

Franke, Wolfgang. *China and the West*. Trans. R. A. Wilson. New York: Harper Torchbooks, 1967.

Fu Chu. *Kuan-yü wo-kuo ti ling-hai wen-t'i* [Questions Concerning Our Country's Territorial Seas]. Peking: Shih-chieh chih-shih ch'u-pan she, 1959.

Galtung, Johan. *Methodology and Ideology: Essays in Methodology*, Vol. I. Copenhagen: Christian Ejlers, 1977.

—— *Peace: Research, Education, Action*. Vol. I. Copenhagen: Christian Ejlers, 1975.

—— *The True Worlds: A Transnational Perspective*. New York: Free Press, 1978.

Ginsburg, Norton. "On the Chinese Perception of a World Order." *China in Crisis*, Vol. II: *China's Policies in Asia and America's Alternatives*. Ed. Tang Tsou. Chicago: University of Chicago Press, 1968.

Gittings, John. *A Chinese View of China*. New York: Pantheon Books, 1973.

—— *Survey of the Sino-Soviet Dispute: A Commentary and Extracts from the Recent Polemics 1963-1967*. New York: Oxford University Press, 1968.

—— *The World and China, 1922-1972*. New York: Harper & Row, 1974.

Goodrich, Leland M. "The UN Security Council." *The United Nations*. Ed. James Barros. New York: Free Press, 1972.

Gordenker, Leon, ed. *The United Nations in International Politics*. Princeton, N.J.: Princeton University Press, 1971.

Gosovic, Branislav, *UNCTAD: Conflict and Compromise.* Leyden: Sijthoff, 1972.

Gregg, Robert W., and Barkun, Michael, eds. *The United Nations System and Its Functions.* Princeton, N.J.: Van Nostrand, 1968.

Griffith, William E. *The Sino-Soviet Rift.* Cambridge, Mass.: M.I.T. Press, 1964.

Groom, A.J.R., and Taylor, Paul, eds. *Functionalism: Theory and Practice in International Relations.* London: University of London Press, 1975.

Haas, Ernst B. *Beyond the Nation-State: Functionalism and International Organization.* Stanford, Calif.: Stanford University Press, 1964.

———— "Collective Security and the Future International System." *The Future of the International Legal Order*, Vol. I: *Trends and Patterns.* Ed. Richard A. Falk and Cyril E. Black. Princeton, N.J.: Princeton University Press, 1969.

———— "Dynamic Environment and Static System: Revolutionary Regimes in the United Nations." *Dynamics of World Politics: Studies in the Resolution of Conflict.* Ed. Linda B. Miller. Englewood Cliffs, N.J.: Prentice-Hall, 1968.

———— "International Integration: The European and the Universal Process." *International Stability.* Ed. Dale J. Hekuis, Charles G. McClintock, and Arthur L. Burns. New York: Wiley, 1964.

———— *The Uniting of Europe.* Stanford, Calif.: Stanford University Press, 1958.

Halperin, Morton H. and Perkins, Dwight H. *Communist China and Arms Control.* New York: Praeger, 1965.

Harrison, Selig S. *China, Oil, and Asia: Conflict Ahead?* New York: Columbia University Press, 1977.

Hermann, Charles F., ed. *International Crises: Insights from Behavioral Research.* New York: Free Press, 1972.

Higgins, Rosalyn. *The Development of International Law Through the Political Organs of the United Nations.* London: Oxford University Press, 1963.

Hill, Martin. *Towards Greater Order, Coherence and Co-ordination in the United Nations System.* New York: UNITAR Research Report No. 20, 1974.

Hinton, Harold C. "China and Vietnam." *China Today.* Ed. William Richardson. Maryknoll, N.Y.: Maryknoll Publications, 1969.

———— *Communist China in World Politics.* New York: Houghton Mifflin, 1966.

Hiscocks, Richard. *The Security Council: A Study in Adolescence.* New York: Free Press, 1973.

Hsiung, James C. "China's Foreign Policy: The Interplay of Ideology, Practical Interests, and Polemics." *China Today*. Ed. William Richardson. Maryknoll, N.Y.: Maryknoll Publications, 1969.

—— *Ideology and Practice: The Evolution of Chinese Communism*. New York: Praeger, 1970.

—— *Law and Policy in China's Foreign Relations*. New York: Columbia University Press, 1972.

Hsü, Immanuel C. Y. *China's Entrance into the Family of Nations*. Cambridge, Mass.: Harvard University Press, 1960.

Hu Sheng. *Ti-kuo chu-i yü chung-kuo cheng-chih* [Imperialism and Chinese Politics]. Peking: Jen-min ch'u-pan she, 1952.

Jacobson, Harold K. *The USSR and the UN's Economic and Social Activities*. Notre Dame: University of Notre Dame Press, 1963.

Jervis, Robert. *The Logic of Images in International Relations*. Princeton, N.J.: Princeton University Press, 1970.

—— *Perception and Misperception in International Politics*. Princeton, N.J.: Princeton University Press, 1976.

Johnson, Cecil. *Communist China and Latin America 1959-67*. New York: Columbia University Press, 1970.

Johnson, Harry. *Economic Policies Toward Less Developed Countries*. Washington, D.C.: The Brookings Institution, 1967.

Johnston, Douglas M., and Chiu, Hungdah. *Agreements of the People's Republic of China 1949-1967: A Calendar*. Cambridge, Mass.: Harvard University Press, 1968.

Kay, David A. "Instruments of Influence in the United Nations Political Process." *The United Nations Political System*. Ed. David A. Kay. New York: Wiley, 1967.

Kelman, Herbert C., ed. *International Behavior: A Social-Psychological Analysis*. New York: Holt, Rinehart and Winston, 1966.

Keohane, Robert O. "Political Influence in the General Assembly." *The United Nations System and Its Functions*. Ed. Robert W. Gregg and Michael Barkun. Princeton, N.J.: Van Nostrand, 1968.

Keys, Donald F. *The 27th General Assembly of the United Nations*. Washington, D.C.: World Federalist Education Fund, January 1973.

—— *The 28th General Assembly of the United Nations*. Washington, D.C.: World Federalist Education Fund, January 1974.

—— *The 29th General Assembly of the United Nations*. New York: World Federalist Education Fund, n.d.

—— *The 30th General Assembly of the United Nations*. New York: World Federalists Association, n.d.

—— *The 31st General Assembly of the United Nations*. New York: The Institute for World Order, Planetary Citizens, World Federalists, n.d.

Kim, Samuel S. "The Developmental Problems of Korean Nation-alism." *Korea: A Nation Divided.* Ed. Se-jin Kim and Chang-hyun Cho. Silver Spring, Md.: The Research Institute on Korean Affairs, 1976.

Klein, Donald. "The Chinese Foreign Ministry." Unpublished Ph.D. dissertation, Columbia University, 1974.

——— "The Management of Foreign Affairs in Communist China." *China: The Management of a Revolutionary Society.* Ed. John M. H. Lindbeck. Seattle, Washington: University of Washington Press, 1971.

——— "The Men and Institutions Behind China's Foreign Policy." *Sino-American Relations, 1949-71.* Ed. Roderick MacFarquhar. New York: Praeger, 1972.

Kothari, Rajini. *Footsteps into the Future: Diagnosis of the Present World and a Design for an Alternative.* New York: Free Press, 1974.

Kuo Ch'ün. *Lien-ho-kuo* [The United Nations]. Peking: Shih-chieh chih-shih she, 1956.

Lagos, Gustavo, and Godoy, Horacio H. *Revolution of Being.* New York: Free Press, 1977.

Larkin, Bruce D. *China and Africa 1949-1970.* Berkeley, Calif.: University of California Press, 1973.

Lee, Luke T. *China and International Agreements: A Study of Compliance.* Leyden: Sijthoff, 1969.

Legge, James. *The Chinese Classics.* Vol. I. London: Trubner, 1861.

——— *The Four Books: Confucian Analects, the Great Learning, the Doctrine of the Mean, and the Works of Mencius.* New York: Paragon Book Reprint Corp., 1966.

Leng, Shao-chuan, and Chiu, Hungdah, eds. *Law in Chinese Foreign Policy: Communist China and Selected Problems of International Law.* Dobbs Ferry, N.Y.: Oceana, 1972.

Levi, Werner. *Modern China's Foreign Policy.* Minneapolis, Minn.: University of Minnesota Press, 1953.

Lifton, Robert Jay. *Revolutionary Immortality: Mao Tse-tung and the Chinese Cultural Revolution.* New York: Vintage Books, 1968.

Lin, Paul T. K. "Development Guided by Values: Comments on China's Road and Its Implications." *On the Creation of a Just World Order.* Ed. Saul H. Mendlovitz. New York: Free Press, 1974.

Liu P'ei-hua, ed. *Chung-kuo chin-tai chien-shih* [A Short History of Contemporary China]. Peking: I ch'ang shu chü, 1954.

Lowenthal, Richard. "Soviet and Chinese Communist World Views." *Soviet and Chinese Communism: Similarities and Differences.* Ed.

Donald W. Treadgold. Seattle: University of Washington Press, 1967.

McDougal, Myres S. and Associates. *Studies in World Public Order.* New Haven, Conn.: Yale University Press, 1960.

Magdoff, Harry. *The Age of Imperialism.* New York: Monthly Review Press, 1969.

Malraux, André. *Anti-Memoirs.* Trans. Terence Kilmartin. New York: Holt, Rinehart and Winston, 1968.

Mancall, Mark. "The Ch'ing Tribute System: An Interpretative Essay." *The Chinese World Order.* Ed. John K. Fairbank. Cambridge, Mass.: Harvard University Press, 1968.

Manno, Catherine Senf. "Majority Decisions and Minority Responses in the UN General Assembly." *The United Nations System and Its Functions.* Ed. Robert W. Gregg and Michael Barkun. Princeton, N.J.: Van Nostrand, 1968.

———— "Problems and Trends in the Composition of Nonplenary UN Organs." *The United Nations System and Its Functions.* Ed. Robert W. Gregg and Michael Barkun. Princeton, N.J.: Van Nostrand, 1968.

Maxwell, Neville. *India's China War.* New York: Doubleday (Anchor Books), 1972.

Mayers, William F., ed. *Treaties between the Empire of China and Foreign Powers.* Shanghai: Kelley and Walsh, 1906.

Mazrui, Ali A. *A World Federation of Cultures: An African Perspective.* New York: Free Press, 1976.

Meadows, D. H., *et al. The Limits to Growth.* New York: Universe Books, 1972.

Mendlovitz, Saul H., ed. *On the Creation of a Just World Order.* New York: Free Press, 1975.

Merton, Robert K. *Social Theory and Social Structure: Toward the Codification of Theory and Research.* Glencoe, Ill.: Free Press, 1949.

Mitrany, David. *A Working Peace System.* Chicago: Quadrangle, 1966.

Morgenthau, Hans J. *Politics Among Nations.* 4th ed. New York: Knopf, 1967.

Newman, Robert P. *Recognition of Communist China? A Study in Argument.* New York: Macmillan, 1961.

Nicholson, [Sir] Harold. *Diplomacy.* 2nd ed. London: Oxford University Press, 1950.

Oksenberg, Michel. "Policy Making Under Mao, 1949-68: An Overview." *China: Management of a Revolutionary Society.* Ed. John M. Lindbeck. Seattle, Wash.: University of Washington Press, 1971.

Oksenberg, Michel. "Political Changes and Their Causes in China, 1949-1972." *China in Transition*. Ed. William A. Robson and Bernard Crick. Beverly Hills, Calif.: Sage, 1975.

———— "Sources and Methodological Problems in the Study of Contemporary China." *Chinese Communist Politics in Action*. Ed. A. Doak Barnett. Seattle and London: University of Washington Press, 1969.

Partan, Daniel G. *Documentary Study of the Politicization of UNESCO*. Boston: American Academy of Arts and Sciences, 1975.

Peng Kuang-hsi. *Why China Has No Inflation*. Peking: Foreign Languages Press, 1976.

Reshaping the International Order, A Report to the Club of Rome. New York: Dutton, 1976.

Rhodes, Robert I., ed. *Imperialism and Underdevelopment: A Reader*. New York: Monthly Review Press, 1970.

Richardson, Lewis. *Statistics of Deadly Quarrels*. Pittsburgh: Boxwood Press, 1960.

Robinson, Thomas W. "Peking's Revolutionary Strategy in the Developing World: The Failures of Success." Santa Monica, Calif.: RAND Corp., P-4169, August 1969.

Rubinstein, Alvin Z. *The Soviets in International Organizations*. Princeton, N.J.: Princeton University Press, 1964.

———— ed. *Soviet and Chinese Influence in the Third World*. New York: Praeger, 1975.

———— and Ginsburg, George, eds. *Soviet and American Policies in the United Nations*. New York: New York University Press, 1971.

Schachter, Oscar. *Toward Wider Acceptance of UN Treaties*. New York: Arno, 1971.

Schram, Stuart. *Mao Tse-tung*. Baltimore, Md.: Penguin Books, 1967.

———— *The Political Thought of Mao Tse-tung*. New York: Praeger, 1963.

———— ed. *Authority, Participation, and Cultural Change in China*. London: Cambridge University Press, 1973.

———— ed. *Chairman Mao Talks to the People: Talks and Letters 1956-1971*. New York: Pantheon Books, 1974.

Schurmann, Franz. *Ideology and Organization in Communist China*. 2nd ed. Berkeley, Calif.: University of California Press, 1968.

———— *The Logic of World Power*. New York: Pantheon Books, 1974.

Schwartz, Benjamin I. "The Chinese Perception of World Order, Past and Present." *The Chinese World Order*. Ed. John K. Fairbank. Cambridge, Mass.: Harvard University Press, 1968.

Schwebel, Stephen M., ed. *The Effectiveness of International Decisions*. Dobbs Ferry, N.Y.: Oceana, 1971.

Sewell, James P. *Functionalism and World Politics*. Princeton, N.J.: Princeton University Press, 1966.

———— *UNESCO and World Politics*. Princeton, N.J.: Princeton University Press, 1975.

———— "UNESCO: Pluralism Rampant." *The Anatomy of Influence*. In Robert W. Cox and Harold K. Jacobson. New Haven, Conn.: Yale University Press, 1974.

———— *World Order Studies: A Critical Examination*. Research Monograph No. 43, Center of International Studies, Princeton University, July 1974.

Sharp, Walter. *The United Nations Economic and Social Council*. New York: Columbia University Press, 1969.

Simmonds, John D. *China's World: The Foreign Policy of a Developing State*. New York: Columbia University Press, 1970.

Singer, J. David. "The Level-of-Analysis Problem in International Relations." *The International System: Theoretical Essays*. Ed. Klaus Knorr and Sidney Verba. Princeton, N.J.: Princeton University Press, 1961.

———— and Small, Melvin. *The Wages of War 1816-1965: A Statistical Handbook*. New York: Wiley, 1972.

Snow, Edgar. *The Long Revolution*. New York: Random House, 1972.

———— *Red China Today*. New York: Random House (Vintage Books), 1971.

———— *Red Star Over China*. New York: Grove Press, 1961.

Stoessinger, John G. "China and the United Nations." *Sino-American Détente and Its Policy Implications*. Ed. Gene T. Hsiao. New York: Praeger, 1974.

———— *Financing the United Nations System*. Washington, D.C.: The Brookings Institution, 1964.

———— *The United Nations and the Superpowers*. 3rd ed. New York: Random House, 1973.

Sun Yat-sen. *San Min Chu I: The Three Principles of the People*. Trans. Frank W. Price. Shanghai: Commercial Press, 1932.

Taylor, Jay. *China and Southeast Asia: Peking's Relations with Revolutionary Movements*. New York: Praeger, 1974.

Teng, Ssu-yü, and Fairbank, John K. *China's Response to the West: A Documentary Survey 1839-1923*. New York: Atheneum, 1963.

Tinbergen, Jan. *Towards a Better International Economic Order*. New York: UNITAR, 1971.

Van Ness, Peter. *Revolution and Chinese Foreign Policy*. Berkeley, Calif.: University of California Press, 1971.

Vernon, Raymond, ed. *The Oil Crisis*. New York: Norton, 1976.

Wainhouse, David W. *et al. International Peacekeeping at the Crossroads: National Support—Experience and Prospects*. Baltimore, Md.: Johns Hopkins University Press, 1973.

Wan Chia-chün. *Shen-ma shih lien-ho-kuo* [What is the United Nations?]. Peking: T'ung-su tu-wu ch'u-pan she, 1957.

Weiss, Thomas, and Siotis, Jean. "Functionalism and International Secretariats: Ideology and Rhetoric in the UN Family." *Functionalism*. Ed. A.J.R. Groom and Paul Taylor. London: University of London Press, 1975.

Weng, Byron S. J. *Peking's UN Policy: Continuity and Change*. New York: Praeger, 1972.

——— "Some Conditions of Peking's Participation in International Organizations." *China's Practice of International Law: Some Case Studies*. Ed. Jerome A. Cohen. Cambridge, Mass.: Harvard University Press, 1972.

Whiting, Allen S. *China Crosses the Yalu: The Decision to Enter the Korean War*. New York: Macmillan, 1960.

——— *The Chinese Calculus of Deterrence: India and Indochina*. Ann Arbor, Michigan: University of Michigan Press, 1975.

——— and Dernberger, Robert F. *China's Future: Foreign Policy and Economic Development in the Post-Mao Era*. New York: McGraw-Hill, 1977.

Wilkinson, David O. *Comparative Foreign Relations: Framework and Methods*. Belmont, Calif.: Dickenson Publishing Company, 1969.

Wolfers, Arnold. *Discord and Collaboration*. Baltimore, Md.: Johns Hopkins University Press, 1962.

Wright, Mary C. *The Last Stand of Chinese Conservatism: The T'ung-Chih Restoration, 1862-1874*. Stanford, Calif.: Stanford University Press, 1962.

Wright, Quincy. *A Study of War*. 2nd ed. Chicago: University of Chicago Press, 1965.

Xydis, Stephen G. "The General Assembly." *The United Nations*. Ed. James Barros. New York: Free Press, 1972.

Yahuda, Michael B. "Chinese Conceptions of Their Role in the World." *China in Transition*. Edited by William A. Robson and Bernard Crick. Beverly Hills, Calif.: Sage, 1975.

Yemin, Edward. *Legislative Powers in the United Nations and Specialized Agencies*. Leyden: Wifthoff, 1969.

Young, Kenneth T. *Negotiating with the Chinese Communists: The U.S. Experience*. New York: McGraw-Hill, 1966.

Young, Oran. "Trends in International Peacekeeping." *Dynamics of World Politics: Studies in the Resolution of Conflict.* Ed. Linda B. Miller. Englewood Cliffs, N.J.: Prentice-Hall, 1968.

———— "The United Nations and the International System." *The United Nations in International Politics.* Ed. Leon Gordenker. Princeton, N.J.: Princeton University Press, 1971.

Zagoria, Donald. *The Sino-Soviet Conflict 1956-1961.* Princeton, N.J.: Princeton University Press, 1962.

Articles

Alger, Chadwick F. "United Nations Participation as a Learning Experience." *Public Opinion Quarterly* 27 (1963), 411-26.

Alker, Hayward R. "Dimensions of Conflict in the General Assembly." *American Political Science Review* 58 (September 1964), 642-57.

———— "Supranationalism in the United Nations." *Peace Research Society (International) Papers* 3 (1965), 197-212.

Amin, Galal A. "Dependent Development." *Alternatives* 2 (December 1976), 379-403.

Ariz, Sartaj. "The Chinese Approach to Rural Development." *International Development Review* 15 (1973), 2-7.

Bailey, Sydney D. "Veto in the Security Council." *International Conciliation* No. 566 (January 1968), 5-66.

Baldwin, Ian, Jr. "Thinking About a New World Order for the Decade 1990." *War/Peace Report* (January 1970), 3-8.

Banno, Masataka. "Gaikō kōshō ni okeru Shinmatsu kanjin no kōdō yōshiki—1854-nen no jōyaku kaisei kōshō o chūshin to suru ichikōsatsu" [Behavior of Mandarins as diplomats in the late Ch'ing period—with special reference to the treaty revision negotiations of 1854]. *Kokusaihō Gaikō Zasshi* [Journal of International Law and Diplomacy] 48 (October 1949), 18-56; 48 (December 1949), 37-71.

Barber, Hollis W. "Decolonization: The Committee of Twenty-four." *World Affairs* 138 (Fall 1975), 128-51.

Beres, Louis Rene, and Targ, Harry R. "Perspectives on World Order: A Review." *Alternatives* 2 (June 1976), 177-98.

Berkowitz, Michael. "Bangladesh." *Harvard International Law Journal* 14 (Summer 1973), 563-73.

Bingham, Jonathan B. "The US, China and the UN." *Foreign Service Journal* (February 1972), 18-20.

Bissell, Richard E. "A Note on the Chinese View of United Nations Finances." *AJIL* 69 (July 1975), 628-33.

Blasius, Mark, and Fak, Richard A. "State of the Globe Report 1975." *Alternatives* 2 (September 1976), 223-78.

Bleicher, Samuel A. "The Legal Significance of Re-Citation of General Assembly Resolutions." *AJIL* 62 (July 1969), 444-78.

Bloomfield, Lincoln P. "China, the United States, and the United Nations." *International Organization* 20 (Autumn 1966), 653-76.

Boulding, Kenneth. "The Learning and Reality-Testing Process in the International System." *Journal of International Affairs* 21 (1967), 1-15.

Broadbent, Kieran. "Agriculture, Environment and Current Policy in China." *Asian Survey* 16 (May 1976), 411-26.

Burin, Frederic S. "The Communist Doctrine of the Inevitability of War." *American Political Science Review* 62 (June 1963), 334-54.

Cassin, Vernon *et al.* "The Definition of Aggression." *Harvard International Law Journal* 16 (Summer 1975), 589-613.

Chai, Winberg. "China and the United Nations: Problems of Representation Alternatives." *Asian Survey* 10 (May 1970), 397-409.

Ch'en Kang. " 'Territorial Waters' and 'internal waters.' " *SCCS* No. 3 (February 5, 1958), 31.

Ch'en T'i-ch'iang. "The Illegality of Atomic Weapons from the Viewpoint of International Law." *SCCS* No. 4 (February 20, 1955), 11-12.

———— "The So-Called 'Question of the Legal Status of Taiwan' Does Not Actually Exist." *CFYC* No. 3 (June 1955), 22-24.

Cheng Tao. "Communist China and the Law of the Sea." *AJIL* 63 (January 1969), 47-73.

Ch'i Hsiang-yang. "Smash the New Tsars' 'Theory of Limited Sovereignty,' " *HC* No. 5 (1969), 87-90.

"The Chinese Political Science and Law Association Held Its Fourth General Meeting." *CFYC* No. 4 (November 1964), 28-31.

Chiu, Hungdah. "Certain Legal Aspects of Communist China's Treaty Practice." *Proceedings of the American Society of International Law, Sixty-First Annual Meeting*, 117-26.

———— "Chinese Attitude Toward Continental Shelf and Its Implications on Delimiting Seabed in Southeast Asia." *Occasional Papers/Reprints Series in Contemporary Asian Studies* No. 1 (1977), 1-32.

———— "Communist China's Attitude toward International Law." *AJIL* 60 (April 1966), 245-67.

———— and Park, C. H. "Legal Status of the Paracel and Spratley Islands." *Ocean Development and International Law* 3 (1975), 1-28.

———— assisted by R. Randle Edwards. "Communist China's Attitude toward the United Nations: A Legal Analysis." *AJIL* 62 (January 1968), 20-50.

Chou Fu-lun. "On the Nature of Modern International Law." *Chiao-hsüeh yü yen-chiu* [Teaching and Research] No. 3 (March 1958), 52-56.

Chou Keng-sheng. "Don't Allow American and British Aggressors to Intervene in the Internal Affairs of Other States." *CFYC*, No. 4 (August 1958), 3-4.

—— "The Great Significance of Our Government's Declaration Concerning Territorial Seas." *SCCS* No. 18 (September 20 1958), 16-17.

—— "The Principles of Peaceful Coexistence from the Viewpoint of International Law." *CFYC* No. 6 (December 1955), 37-41.

—— "The United Nations' Intervention in the 'Question of Tibet' Is Illegal." *CFYC* No. 6 (December 1959), 8-11.

Chu Li-sun. "The Use of Atomic and Hydrogen Weapons Is the Most Serious Criminal Act in Violation of International Law." *CFYC* No. 4 (August 1955), 30-33.

Claude, Inis L. Jr. "The Central Challenge to the United Nations." *Harvard International Law Journal* 16 (Summer 1973), 517-29.

—— "Collective Legitimization as a Political Function of the United Nations." *International Organization* 20 (Summer 1966), 367-79.

—— "The Management of Power in the Changing United Nations." *International Organization* 15 (Spring 1961), 367-79.

—— "The UN and the Use of Force." *International Conciliation* No. 532 (March 1961), 325-84.

Cooper, Richard N. "A New International Economic Order for Mutual Gain." *Foreign Policy* No. 26 (Spring 1977), 66-120.

Crammer-Byng, John L. "The Chinese Perception of World Order." *International Journal* 24 (Winter 1968-69), 166-71.

—— "The Chinese View of Their Place in the World: An Historical Perspective." *CQ* No. 53 (January/March 1973), 67-79.

Dai, Poeliu. "Canada and the Two-China Formula at the United Nations." *Canadian Yearbook of International Law* 5 (1967), 217-28.

Dernberger, Robert F. "The Relevance of China's Development Experience for Other Developing Countries." *Items* 31 (September 1977), 25-34.

Dubitzky, Jonathan. "The General Assembly's International Economics." *Harvard International Law Journal* 16 (Summer 1975), 670-76.

Edwards, R. Randle. "The Attitude of the People's Republic of China Towards International Law and the United Nations." *Papers on China* 17 (December 1963), 235-71.

Fairbank, John K. "China's Foreign Policy in Historical Perspective." *Foreign Affairs* 47 (April 1969), 449-63.

────── and Teng, S. Y. "On the Ch'ing Tributary System." *The Harvard Journal of Asiatic Studies* 6 (1941-42), 135-246.

Falk, Richard A. "The American Attack on the United Nations: An Interpretation." *Harvard International Law Journal* 16 (Summer 1975), 566-75.

────── "Another Look at 'Development and the International Economic Order'." *International Development Review* 16 (1974), 19-20.

────── "The Domains of Law and Justice." *International Journal* 31 (Winter 1976), 1-13.

────── "The New States and International Legal Order." *Recueil des Cours* (1966), Part 2, 7-102.

────── "On the Quasi-Legislative Competence of the General Assembly." *AJIL* 60 (October 1966), 782-91.

────── *et al.* "State of the Globe Report 1974." *Alternatives* 1 (June/September 1975), 159-281.

Feuerwerker, Albert. "Chinese History and the Foreign Relations of Contemporary China." *The Annals of the American Academy of Political and Social Science* 402 (July 1972), 1-14.

Galtung, Johan. "Implementing Self-Reliance." *Transnational Perspectives* 3 (1976), 18-24.

────── "The Limits to Growth and Class Politics." *Journal of Peace Research* 10 (1973), 101-14.

────── "A Structural Theory of Imperialism." *Journal of Peace Research* 8 (1971), 81-117.

Gittings, John. "New Light on Mao: His Views of the World." *CQ* No. 60 (December 1974), 750-66.

Glaubitz, Joachim. "Anti-Hegemony Formulas in Chinese Foreign Policy." *Asian Survey* 16 (March 1976), 205-15.

Gosovic, Branislav, and Ruggie, John Gerard. "On the Creation of a New International Economic Order: Issue Linkage and the Seventh Special Session of the UN General Assembly." *International Organization* 30 (Spring 1976), 310-45.

Goulet, Denis. "Development and the International Economic Order." *International Development Review* 16 (1974), 10-16.

Greenfield, Meg. "The Lost Session at the U.N." *The Reporter* May 6, 1965, pp. 14-20.

Gross, Leo. "Voting in the Security Council: Abstention in the Post-1965 Amendment Phase and Its Impact on Article 25 of the Charter." *AJIL* 62 (April 1968), 315-34.

Gurtov, Melvin. "The Taiwan Strait Crisis Revisited: Politics and Foreign Policy in Chinese Motives." *Modern China* 2 (January 1976), 49-103.

Halperin, Ernest. "Peking and Latin American Countries." *CQ* No. 29 (July/September 1967), 111-54.

Halpern, A. M. "China, the United Nations, and Beyond." *CQ* No. 10 (April/June 1962), 72-77.

Higgins, Rosalyn. "The Place of International Law in the Settlement of Disputes by the Security Council." *AJIL* 64 (January 1970), 1-18.

———— "The United Nations and Lawmaking: The Political Organs." *Proceedings of the American Society of International Law at its Sixty-Fourth Annual Meeting* 64 (September 1970), 37-48.

Ho Hsü-shuang and Ma Chün. "A Criticism of the Reactionary Viewpoint of Ch'en T'i-ch'iang Concerning the Study of International Law." *CFYC* No. 6 (December 1957), 35-38.

Holsti, Ole. "The Belief System and National Images: A Case Study." *Journal of Conflict Resolution* 6 (1962), 244-52.

———— "Cognitive Dynamics and Images of the Enemy." *Journal of International Affairs* 21 (1967), 16-39.

Houn, Franklin W. "The Principles and Operational Code of Communist China's International Conduct." *Journal of Asian Studies* 27 (January 1968), 21-40.

Hsü Tun-chang. "The Question of Restoring the Legitimate Rights and Position of the People's Republic of China in the United Nations," *CFYC* No. 5 (October 1956), 11-18.

Hua Chih-hai. "Learn Some Geography." *HC* No. 11 (1972), 74-78.

Johnson, Chalmers. "The Two Chinese Revolutions." *CQ* No. 39 (July/September 1969), 12-29.

Johnston, Douglas M. "Treaty Analysis and Communist China: Preliminary Observations." *Proceedings of the American Society of International Law at its Sixty-First Annual Meeting*, 126-34.

Kim, Samuel S. "America's First Minister to China: Anson Burlingame and the Tsungli Yamen." *The Maryland Historian* 3 (Fall 1972), 87-104.

———— "Burlingame and the Inauguration of the Co-operative Policy." *Modern Asian Studies* 5 (October 1971), 337-54.

———— "Communist China's Nuclear Capability." *Military Review* 50 (October 1970), 35-46.

———— "The Influence of Personality in Sino-Western Relations." *Asian Profile* 3 (June 1975), 265-81.

———— "The Lorenzian Theory of Aggression and Peace Research: A Critique." *Journal of Peace Research* 13 (1976), 253-76.

Kim, Samuel S. *"Pax Atomica à la* Kissinger." *Bulletin of Peace Proposals* 7 (1976), 181-85.

———— "The People's Republic of China in the United Nations: A Preliminary Analysis." *World Politics* 26 (April 1974), 299-330.

———— "The Transitional Period of Chinese Diplomacy with the West: An Assessment." *The Ohio University Review* 12 (1970), 51-65.

King, John R., and Roosevelt, Susan C. "Civil Aviation Agreements of the People's Republic of China." *Harvard International Law Journal* 14 (September 1973), 316-44.

Kraus, Richard Curt. "The Limits of Maoist Egalitarianism." *Asian Survey* 16 (November 1976), 1081-96.

K'ung Meng. "A Criticism of the Theories of Bourgeois International Law on the Subjects of International Law and the Recognition of States." *Kuo-chi wen-t'i yen-chiu* [Research on International Problems] No. 2 (February 1960), 44-53.

Kuo Chi. "Important Steps for Safeguarding the Sovereignty of the Country." *CFYC* No. 5 (October 1958), 8-10.

Lang, Gordon. "UNESCO and Israel." *Harvard International Law Journal* 16 (Summer 1975), 676-82.

Lasswell, Harold D. "The Promise of the World Order Modelling Movement." *World Politics* 29 (April 1977), 425-37.

Lee, Rensselaer W. III. "The *Hsia Fang* System: Marxism and Modernization." *CQ* No. 28 (October/December 1966), 40-62.

Legum, Colin. "The Soviet Union, China and the West in Southern Africa." *Foreign Affairs* 54 (July 1976), 745-62.

Leifer, Michael. "Indonesia and the Incorporation of East Timor." *The World Today* 32 (September 1976), 347-54.

Lenefsky, David. "Note: The People's Republic of China and the Security Council—Deprived or Debatable?" *The Columbia Journal of Transnational Law* 9 (Spring 1970), 54-59.

Leng, Shao-chuan. "China and the International System." *World Affairs* 138 (Spring 1976), 267-87.

Levine, Steven I. "China and the Superpowers: Policies toward the United States and the Soviet Union." *Political Science Quarterly* 90 (Winter 1975-76), 637-58.

Li Hao-p'ei. "Nationalization and International Law." *CFYC* No. 2 (April 1958), 10-19.

Li, Victor H. "The Role of Law in Communist China." *CQ* No. 44 (October/December 1970), 66-111.

Lin Hsin. "On the System of International Law After the Second World War." *Chiao-hsüeh yü yen-chiu* [Teaching and Research], No. 1 (January 1958), 33-38.

McDougal, Myres S., and Goodman, Richard M. "Chinese Participation in the United Nations." *AJIL* 60 (October 1966), 671-727.

McDougal, Myres S., and Reisman, W. Michael. "Rhodesia and the United Nations: The Lawfulness of International Concern." *AJIL* 62 (January 1968), 1-19.

Mancall, Mark. "The Persistence of Tradition in Chinese Foreign Policy." *The Annals of the American Academy of Political and Social Science* 349 (September 1963), 14-26.

Mazrui, Ali A. *et al.* "State of the Globe Report 1977." *Alternatives* 3 (December 1977), 151-264.

Mei Ju-ao. "Denunciation of the Absurd Resolution of the United Nations." *CFYC* No. 1 (February 1955), 43-46.

—— "Struggle to Define Aggression." *CFYC* No. 2 (April 1956), 7-15.

Meisner, Maurice. "Utopian Goals and Ascetic Values in Chinese Communist Ideology." *Journal of Asian Studies* 28 (November 1968), 101-10.

Moynihan, Daniel P. "Abiotrophy in Turtle Bay: The United Nations in 1975." *Harvard International Law Journal* 17 (Summer 1976), 465-502.

—— "The United States in Opposition." *Commentary* 59 (March 1975), pp. 31-44.

Munro, Donald J. "The Malleability of Man in Chinese Marxism." *CQ* No. 48 (October/December 1971), 609-40.

Ogden, Suzanne. "China and International Law: Implications for Foreign Policy." *Pacific Affairs* 49 (Spring 1976), 28-48.

Oksenberg, Michel. "The Strategies of Peking." *Foreign Affairs* 49 (October 1971), 15-29.

Onate, Andres D. "The Conflict Interactions of the People's Republic of China, 1950-1970." *Journal of Conflict Resolution* 18 (December 1974), 578-94.

Onuf, N. G. "Professor Falk on the Quasi-Legislative Competence of the General Assembly." *AJIL* 64 (April 1970), 349-55.

Pao Sheng. "The Struggle of the Two Roads in the United Nations During the Past Ten Years." *SCCS* No. 12 (June 20, 1955), 11-13.

Park, Choon-Ho. "The Sino-Japanese-Korean Sea Resources Controversy and the Hypothesis of a 200-Mile Economic Zone." *Harvard International Law Journal* 16 (Winter 1975), 27-46.

"Penetrate Deeply into the Critique of the Bourgeois Theory of Human Nature." *HC* No. 4 (1974), 57-63.

"A Powerful Weapon To Unite the People and Defeat the Enemy." *HC* No. 9 (1971), 10-17.

563

Prybyla, Jan S. "Hsia-Fang: The Economics and Politics of Rustication in China." *Pacific Affairs* 48 (Summer 1975), 153-72.

Pumpelly, Raphael. "Western Policy in China." *The North American Review* 106 (April 1868), 592-612.

Pye, Lucian W. "Mao Tse-tung's Leadership Style." *Political Science Quarterly* 91 (Summer 1976), 219-35.

Rejai, Mostafa. "Communist China and the United Nations." *Orbis* 10 (Fall 1966), 823-38.

Reynolds, Lloyd. "China as a Less Developed Economy." *American Economic Review* 65, No. 3 (June 1975), 418-28.

Riggs, Robert E. "Overselling the UN Charter—Fact and Myth." *International Organization* 14 (Spring 1960), 277-90.

Sakamoto, Yoshikazu. "The Rationale of the World Order Models Project." *Proceedings of the Sixty-Sixth Annual Meeting of the American Society of International Law* (September 1972), 245-52.

Scalapino, Robert A. "China and the Balance of Power." *Foreign Affairs* 52 (January 1974), 349-85.

Schachter, Oscar. "The Evolving International Law of Development." *Columbia Journal of Transnational Law* 15 (1976), 1-16.

Schick, F. B. "The Question of China in the United Nations." *International and Comparative Law Quarterly* 12 (October 1963), 1232-50.

Schram, Stuart R. "Mao Tse-tung: A Self-Portrait." *CQ* No. 57 (January/March 1974), 156-65.

——— "Mao Tse-tung and the Theory of the Permanent Revolution." *CQ* No. 46 (April/June 1971), 221-44.

Schwartz, Benjamin I. "The Maoist Image of World Order." *Journal of International Affairs* 21 (1967), 92-102.

Schwarz, Henry G. "The Ts'an-k'ao Hsiao-hsi: How Well Informed Are Chinese Officials about the Outside World?" *CQ* No. 27 (July/September 1966), 54-83.

Senghaas, Dieter. "Conflict Formations in Contemporary International Society." *Journal of Peace Research* 10 (1973), 163-84.

——— "Multinational Corporations and the Third World: On the Problem of the Further Integration of Peripheries into the Given Structure of the International Economic System." *Journal of Peace Research* 12 (1975), 257-74.

——— "Peace Research and the Third World." *Bulletin of Peace Proposals* No. 4 (1975), 158-72.

Shao Chin-fu. "The Absurd Theory of 'Two Chinas' and Principles of International Law." *Kuo-chi wen-t'i yen-chiu* [Research on International Problems] No. 2 (February 1959), 7-17.

Shih Chün. "On Comprehending Some History of the National Liberation Movement." *HC* No. 11 (1972), 68-73.

Smith, Tony. "Changing Configurations of Power in North-South Relations Since 1945." *International Organization* 31 (Winter 1977), 1-27.

Snow, Edgar. "A Conversation with Mao Tse-tung." *Life* April 30, 1971, pp. 46-49.

———— "Chinese Communists and World Affairs: An Interview with Mao Tse-tung." *Amerasia* 1 (August 1937), 263-69.

———— "Interview with Mao." *The New Republic* February 27, 1965, pp. 17-23.

Sohn, Louis B. "The Stockholm Declaration on the Human Environment." *Harvard International Law Journal* 14 (Summer 1973), 423-515.

———— "United Nations Decision-Making: Confrontation or Consensus?" *Harvard International Law Journal* 15 (Summer 1974), 438-45.

Starvropoulos, Constantine A. "The Practice of Voluntary Abstentions by Permanent Members of the Security Council Under Article 27, Paragraph 3, of the Charter of the United Nations." *AJIL* 61 (July 1967), 737-52.

Steiner, H. Arthur. " 'On the Record' with Mao and His Regime." *Journal of Asian Studies* 7 (February 1958), 215-23.

Stepanov, V. "The Restructuring of International Economic Relations." *International Affairs* (Moscow) (August 1976), 27-31.

Stoessinger, John G. "Financing the United Nations." *International Conciliation* No. 535 (November 1961), 3-72.

Stone, Julius. "Hopes and Loopholes in the 1974 Definition of Aggression." *AJIL* 71 (April 1977), 224-46.

Strong, Anna Louise. "The Thought of Mao Tse-tung." *Amerasia* 11 (June 1947), 161-74.

———— "A World's Eye View from a Yenan Cave." *Amerasia* 11 (April 1947), 122-26.

Sun Nan. "What is the United Nations Emergency Force?" *SCCS* No. 24 (December 20, 1956), 22.

"A Symposium on the Criminal Acts by Britain and the United States Against International Law and the UN Charter." *CFYC* No. 4 (August 1958), 3-8.

Terrill, Ross. "China and the World: Self-Reliance or Interdependence?" *Foreign Affairs* 55 (January 1977), 295-305.

Timmler, Markus. "Die Umwelt-Konferenz in Stockholm." *Aussenpolitik* 23 (October 1972), 618-28.

Ting Liu. "The Question of Admission of New Members to the United Nations." *CFYC* No. 1 (February 1956), 32-35.

Tsien, Tche-hao. "Conception et pratique du droit international public en République populaire de Chine." *Journal du Droit International* No. 4 (1976), 863-97.

Tsou, Tang. "Mao Tse-tung and Peaceful Coexistence." *Orbis* 8 (Spring 1964), 36-51.

——— and Halperin, Morton H. "Mao Tse-tung's Revolutionary Strategy and Peking's International Behavior." *American Political Science Review* 59 (March 1965), 80-99.

Wei Wen-han. "Discussing the Question of the Width of the Territorial Sea." *Fa-hsüeh* [Legal Studies] No. 3 (1957), 23-26.

Weng, Byron S. J. "Communist China's Changing Attitudes Toward the United Nations." *International Organization* 20 (Autumn 1966), 677-704.

White, Lyman C. "Peace by Pieces." *Free World* 11 (January 1946), 66-68.

Whiting, Allen S. "Chinese Foreign Policy: A Workshop Report." *Items* 31 (March/June 1977), 1-3.

——— "New Light on Mao: Quemoy 1958: Mao's Miscalculations." *CQ* No. 62 (June 1975), 263-70.

——— "The Use of Force in Foreign Policy by the People's Republic of China." *The Annals of the American Academy of Political and Social Science* 402 (July 1972), 55-66.

Wilkinson, David. "World Order Models Project: First Fruits." *Political Science Quarterly* 91 (Summer 1976), 329-35.

Wilson, Dick. "China and the European Community." *CQ* No. 56 (October/December, 1973), 647-66.

Wright, Arthur F. "Struggle *v.* Harmony: Symbols of Competing Values in Modern China." *World Politics* 6 (October 1953), 31-44.

Yang Hsin and Ch'en Chien. "Expose and Criticize the Fallacious Reasoning of Imperialists on National Sovereignty Questions." *CFYC* No. 4 (November 1964), 6-11.

Ying T'ao. "A Criticism of Bourgeois International Law on the Question of National Sovereignty." *Kuo-chi wen-t'i yen-chiu* [Research on International Problems] No. 3 (March 1960), 47-52.

INDEX

abstention, 126, 186, 204, 209-10, 426
ACD (Arms Control and Disarmament), 126, 171-73, 261, 273, 303-04, 312, 478-79, 481, 492, 495. *See also* arms exports; CBW; CCD; no-first-use principle; NPT; nuclear-free zones; nuclear tests; Treaty of Tlatelolco
Adams, Mervyn W., 99n
Ad Hoc Committee on the Indian Ocean, 113
Ad Hoc Committee on the Restructuring of the Economic and Social Sectors of the United Nations System, 286, 291, 293-94
Aegean territorial dispute, 223
Afghanistan, 376, 511, 527
Africa, 72, 166, 253, 257, 354; African regional group, 219; Afro-Asian group, 173; OAU (Organization of African Unity), 200, 227, 518
aggression: definition of, 115, 417, 457-62; economic, 464; Special Committee on the Question of Defining Aggression, 458-59
Ajami, Fouad, 479
Albania, 231, 233, 273, 326, 511, 513
Alger, Chadwick F., 108n, 499n
Algeria, 166, 227, 254, 291, 313, 326, 511, 527
Ali, M. M., 78
Allende, Salvador, 246-47, 249-50
Al-Sudeary, Abdelmuhsin, 295n
Alvor Agreement, 227
Amerasinghe, Hamilton Shirley, 447
Amin, Samir, 248n
Amnesty International, 483
Amuzegar, Jahangir, 286
An Chih-yüan, 396, 416, 459, 461-63, 514, 526
Anglo-Iranian Oil Co. case, 412-13
Angola, 228, 238, 521, 527; civil war in, 166, 277; membership question of, 135, 228
Antihegemony, *see* superpower contention/collusion
apartheid, 125, 215, 224, 433, 464, 518
Arafat, Yasir, 165
Argentina, 188n, 512, 527
Armour, Peter C., 381
arms exporters, 481
Arrow War, 31, 35

Asamoah, Obed, 429n
Asian group, 131-32, 160, 219, 294, 318, 357, 361, 399
Australia, 257, 269, 418, 439, 512
Austria, 221, 310, 511
Azania, *see* South Africa
Aziz, Sartaj, 367, 370, 375-76

Bailey, Sydney D., 97n, 185n, 186n, 188n, 215n
Baldwin, Ian Jr., 473n
Bandung Conference, 75-76
Bangladesh, 249n, 376, 512, 520, 527; membership question of, 115, 167, 206-07, 239, 374, 433, 492
Banno, Masataka, 25n, 34n
Barbados, 512, 527
barbarians, Chinese concept of, 23-25, 27, 31-32, 40
Bartke, Wolfgang, 328, 416n, 512n
Beethoven, Ludwig von, 60, 60n, 501
Belgium, 166, 227, 269, 272-73, 312, 511
Benin, 227, 228n, 511-12, 527
Beres, Louis Rene, 472n
Berkowitz, Michael, 207n
Bethune, Norman, 89
Big Five (China, France, the Soviet Union, the United Kingdom, and the United States), 124, 178, 180, 190-91, 201, 205, 214, 216, 269, 272, 297, 358, 388, 417, 439, 443, 449, 473-75, 481; military expenditures, GNP, population, and armed forces, 528-29; scale of assessments of, 150; voting record, 124, 202-03, 210, 475, 518-21
Binaghi, Walter, 381
Bingham, Jonathan B., 104n
Bissell, Richard E., 3n, 151
Black, Eugene, 341
Bleicher, Samuel A., 173n, 429n, 430n
Bloomfield, Lincoln P., 99n, 105n, 106n, 179n
Board of Rites (*Li-pu*), 29, 45
Boardman, Robert, 13n
Bodenheimer, Susanne, 276n
Boerma, Addeke Hendrik, 366, 367n, 368, 376
Borman, Frank, 471
Botswana, 249n, 512, 527
Boulding, Kenneth E., 13n

567

Mauritius, 512, 527
Maxwell, Neville, 69n
Mayers, William F., 31n
Mazrui, Ali A., 5n, 472n, 490n
M'Bow, Amadou-Mahtar, 360
Meadows, Donella, 487n
Mencius, 25
Mendlovitz, Saul, 5n, 473n
Merton, Robert K., 13n
Mexico, 206, 266, 287, 512, 527
Mexico City Conference (1976), 296
Meyerson, Jacob, 287
Middle East question, 126, 164-66,
   208, 211, 218, 232, 253, 478, 518-20
military budgets, reduction of, 126, 172
mini-states, 108, 131, 361
Mitrany, David, 334-37, 339
Modern Law of Nations, 407n
Mongolia, 131-32, 399, 511; member-
   ship question of, 189
Monro, Ross H., 7n
Morgenthau, Hans J., 59n, 337
Morocco, 166, 222, 511, 527
Morse, Bradford, 280
Moynihan, Daniel P., 282, 286
Mozambique, 227, 512, 520-21, 527
MPLA (Popular Movement for the
   Liberation of Angola), 227

Namibia (South West Africa), 174,
   226, 228, 433, 485, 518-21
nationalism: Chinese theory and
   practice of, 24, 41-48, 77, 89-90,
   139, 321, 336, 414, 480
nationalization, 409n
NATO, 77, 164
Nehru, 413
Nepal, 219, 376, 511, 527
Netherlands, 284, 287, 366, 511-12
Neto, Agostinho, 227
New Zealand, 257, 326, 439, 512
NGOs (nongovernmental organiza-
   tions), 344, 349, 362, 374, 433
Nicaragua, 380, 527
Nicholson, Sir Harold, 120
NIEO (New International Economic
   Order), 14, 125, 153, 162, 169, 176,
   242, 250, 252, 254-55, 262, 289-90,
   314, 316, 318, 320, 325, 329-30,
   340, 355, 433, 448, 482-83, 492,
   495-96, 501; Chinese image of,
   276-81. *See also* Charter of Eco-
   nomic Rights and Duties of States;
   Declaration on the Establishment
   of a New International Economic
   Order; Programme of Action on the
   Establishment of a New International Economic Order
Niger, 512, 527

Nigeria, 376, 511, 527
no-first-use principle, 125, 171, 481
nonaligned countries, 218, 231, 243,
   254, 295-96; Fifth Conference of
   Heads of States or Governments of
   Non-Aligned Countries (1976),
   208n, 228n, 355, 440n; Fourth Conference of Heads of States or
   Government of Non-Aligned Countries (1973), 243, 282-83, 360n;
   Economic Declaration adopted at the
   Fourth Conference of Heads of
   States or Governments of Non-
   Aligned Countries, 260. *See also*
   Third World
nonparticipation, as voting option,
   127-28, 176-77, 187-89, 208-12, 214,
   218-19, 222, 228-29, 231, 233, 238,
   274, 426, 437, 459, 463, 485, 496
North Sea Continental Shelf cases,
   452-53
North-South politics, 126, 228, 250,
   282, 286, 289, 303, 447. *See also*
   International Economic Co-operation
   Conference
North Yemen, 511, 527
NPT (Non-Proliferation Treaty), 126,
   169, 172, 481
nuclear-free zones, 125, 172-73, 481
nuclear tests, 126, 488, 490, 500;
   test ban treaty, 77, 172, 478

Ogden, Suzanne, 417n
oil crisis, 253-54
Oksenberg, Michel, 7n, 50n, 52n
Onate, Andres D., 5n
OPEC, 253-54, 295
Opium War, 24, 30

Pacta tertiis nec nocent nec prosunt,
   431
Pakistan, 207, 209, 224, 249n, 374,
   376, 392, 511, 518, 527
Panama, 201, 219, 227, 519, 527
paper tiger thesis, 63, 67, 74, 84
Papua, New Guinea, 512, 521, 527
Park, Choon-Ho, 274n, 453n
Partan, Daniel G., 363n
Pax Sinica, 20, 500
peace: negative, 240, 336, 472;
   positive, 240, 336, 483; research on,
   240n, 483
peaceful coexistence, *see* state-to-state
   relations
Pearson Commission, 317
Peking Convention, 37
P'eng Chen, 79
People's Republic of Congo, 380, 527
Peru, 219, 512, 527

Books Written Under the Auspices of the
CENTER OF INTERNATIONAL STUDIES
Princeton University
1952-77

Gabriel A. Almond, *The Appeals of Communism* (Princeton University Press 1954)

William W. Kaufmann, ed., *Military Policy and National Security* (Princeton University Press 1956)

Klaus Knorr, *The War Potential of Nations* (Princeton University Press 1956)

Lucian W. Pye, *Guerrilla Communism in Malaya* (Princeton University Press 1956)

Charles De Visscher, *Theory and Reality in Public International Law*, trans. by P. E. Corbett (Princeton University Press 1957; rev. ed. 1968)

Bernard C. Cohen, *The Political Process and Foreign Policy: The Making of the Japanese Peace Settlement* (Princeton University Press 1957)

Myron Weiner, *Party Politics in India: The Development of a Multi-Party System* (Princeton University Press 1957)

Percy E. Corbett, *Law in Diplomacy* (Princeton University Press 1959)

Rolf Sannwald and Jacques Stohler, *Economic Integration: Theoretical Assumptions and Consequences of European Unification*, trans. by Herman Karreman (Princeton University Press 1959)

Klaus Knorr, ed., *NATO and American Security* (Princeton University Press 1959)

Gabriel A. Almond and James S. Coleman, eds., *The Politics of the Developing Areas* (Princeton University Press 1960)

Herman Kahn, *On Thermonuclear War* (Princeton University Press 1960)

Sidney Verba, *Small Groups and Political Behavior: A Study of Leadership* (Princeton University Press 1961)

Robert J. C. Butow, *Tojo and the Coming of the War* (Princeton University Press 1961)

Glenn H. Snyder, *Deterrence and Defense: Toward a Theory of National Security* (Princeton University Press 1961)

Klaus Knorr and Sidney Verba, eds., *The International System: Theoretical Essays* (Princeton University Press 1961)

Peter Paret and John W. Shy, *Guerrillas in the 1960's* (Praeger 1962)

George Modelski, *A Theory of Foreign Policy* (Praeger 1962)

Klaus Knorr and Thornton Read, eds., *Limited Strategic War* (Praeger 1963)

Frederick S. Dunn, *Peace-Making and the Settlement with Japan* (Princeton University Press 1963)

Arthur L. Burns and Nina Heathcote, *Peace-Keeping by United Nations Forces* (Praeger 1963)

Richard A. Falk, *Law, Morality, and War in the Contemporary World* (Praeger 1963)

James N. Rosenau, *National Leadership and Foreign Policy: A Case Study in the Mobilization of Public Support* (Princeton University Press 1963)

Gabriel A. Almond and Sidney Verba, *The Civic Culture: Political Attitudes and Democracy in Five Nations* (Princeton University Press 1963)

Bernard C. Cohen, *The Press and Foreign Policy* (Princeton University Press 1963)

Richard L. Sklar, *Nigerian Political Parties: Power in an Emergent African Nation* (Princeton University Press 1963)

Peter Paret, *French Revolutionary Warfare from Indochina to Algeria: The Analysis of a Political and Military Doctrine* (Praeger 1964)

Harry Eckstein, ed., *Internal War: Problems and Approaches* (Free Press 1964)

Cyril E. Black and Thomas P. Thornton, eds., *Communism and Revolution: The Strategic Uses of Political Violence* (Princeton University Press 1964)

Miriam Camps, *Britain and the European Community 1955-1963* (Princeton University Press 1964)

Thomas P. Thornton, ed., *The Third World in Soviet Perspective: Studies by Soviet Writers on the Developing Areas* (Princeton University Press 1964)

James N. Rosenau, ed., *International Aspects of Civil Strife* (Princeton University Press 1964)

Sidney I. Ploss, *Conflict and Decision-Making in Soviet Russia: A Case Study of Agricultural Policy, 1953-1963* (Princeton University Press 1965)

Richard A. Falk and Richard J. Barnet, eds., *Security in Disarmament* (Princeton University Press 1965)

Karl von Vorys, *Political Development in Pakistan* (Princeton University Press 1965)

Harold and Margaret Sprout, *The Ecological Perspective on Human Affairs, With Special Reference to International Politics* (Princeton University Press 1965)

Klaus Knorr, *On the Uses of Military Power in the Nuclear Age* (Princeton University Press 1966)

Harry Eckstein, *Division and Cohesion in Democracy: A Study of Norway* (Princeton University Press 1966)

Cyril E. Black, *The Dynamics of Modernization: A Study in Comparative History* (Harper and Row 1966)

Peter Kunstadter, ed., *Southeast Asian Tribes, Minorities, and Nations* (Princeton University Press 1967)

E. Victor Wolfenstein, *The Revolutionary Personality: Lenin, Trotsky, Gandhi* (Princeton University Press 1967)

Leon Gordenker, *The UN Secretary-General and the Maintenance of Peace* (Columbia University Press 1967)

Oran R. Young, *The Intermediaries: Third Parties in International Crises* (Princeton University Press 1967)

James N. Rosenau, ed., *Domestic Sources of Foreign Policy* (Free Press 1967)

Richard F. Hamilton, *Affluence and the French Worker in the Fourth Republic* (Princeton University Press 1967)

Linda B. Miller, *World Order and Local Disorder: The United Nations and Internal Conflicts* (Princeton University Press 1967)

Henry Bienen, *Tanzania: Party Transformation and Economic Development* (Princeton University Press 1967)

Wolfram F. Hanrieder, *West German Foreign Policy, 1949-1963: International Pressures and Domestic Response* (Stanford University Press 1967)

Richard H. Ullman, *Britain and the Russian Civil War: November 1918-February 1920* (Princeton University Press 1968)

Robert Gilpin, *France in the Age of the Scientific State* (Princeton University Press 1968)

William B. Bader, *The United States and the Spread of Nuclear Weapons* (Pegasus 1968)

Richard A. Falk, *Legal Order in a Violent World* (Princeton University Press 1968)

Cyril E. Black, Richard A. Falk, Klaus Knorr and Oran R. Young, *Neutralization and World Politics* (Princeton University Press 1968)

Oran R. Young, *The Politics of Force: Bargaining During International Crises* (Princeton University Press 1969)

Klaus Knorr and James N. Rosenau, eds., *Contending Approaches to International Politics* (Princeton University Press 1969)

James N. Rosenau, ed., *Linkage Politics: Essays on the Convergence of National and International Systems* (Free Press 1969)

John T. McAlister, Jr., *Viet Nam: The Origins of Revolution* (Knopf 1969)

Jean Edward Smith, *Germany Beyond the Wall: People, Politics and Prosperity* (Little, Brown 1969)

James Barros, *Betrayal from Within: Joseph Avenol, Secretary-General of the League of Nations, 1933-1940* (Yale University Press 1969)

Charles Hermann, *Crises in Foreign Policy: A Simulation Analysis* (Bobbs-Merrill 1969)

Robert C. Tucker, *The Marxian Revolutionary Idea: Essays on Marxist Thought and Its Impact on Radical Movements* (W. W. Norton 1969)

Harvey Waterman, *Political Change in Contemporary France: The Politics of an Industrial Democracy* (Charles E. Merrill 1969)

Cyril E. Black and Richard A. Falk, eds., *The Future of the International Legal Order*. Vol. I: *Trends and Patterns* (Princeton University Press 1969)

Ted Robert Gurr, *Why Men Rebel* (Princeton University Press 1969)

C. Sylvester Whitaker, *The Politics of Tradition: Continuity and Change in Northern Nigeria 1946-1966* (Princeton University Press 1970)

Richard A. Falk, *The Status of Law in International Society* (Princeton University Press 1970)

John T. McAlister, Jr. and Paul Mus, *The Vietnamese and Their Revolution* (Harper & Row 1970)

Klaus Knorr, *Military Power and Potential* (D. C. Heath 1970)

Cyril E. Black and Richard A. Falk, eds., *The Future of the International Legal Order*. Vol. II: *Wealth and Resources* (Princeton University Press 1970)

Leon Gordenker, ed., *The United Nations in International Politics* (Princeton University Press 1971)

Cyril E. Black and Richard A. Falk, eds., *The Future of the International Legal Order*. Vol. III: *Conflict Management* (Princeton University Press 1971)

Francine R. Frankel, *India's Green Revolution: Economic Gains and Political Costs* (Princeton University Press 1971)

Harold and Margaret Sprout, *Toward a Politics of the Planet Earth* (Van Nostrand Reinhold Co. 1971)

Cyril E. Black and Richard A. Falk, eds., *The Future of the International Legal Order*. Vol. IV: *The Structure of the International Environment* (Princeton University Press 1972)

Gerald Garvey, *Energy, Ecology, Economy* (W. W. Norton 1972)

Richard H. Ullman, *The Anglo-Soviet Accord* (Princeton University Press 1973)

Klaus Knorr, *Power and Wealth: The Political Economy of International Power* (Basic Books 1973)

Anton Bebler, *Military Rule in Africa: Dahomey, Ghana, Sierra Leone, and Mali* (Praeger Publishers 1973)

Robert C. Tucker, *Stalin as Revolutionary 1879-1929: A Study in History and Personality* (W. W. Norton 1973)

Edward L. Morse, *Foreign Policy and Interdependence in Gaullist France* (Princeton University Press 1973)

Henry Bienen, *Kenya: The Politics of Participation and Control* (Princeton University Press 1974)

Gregory J. Massell, *The Surrogate Proletariat: Moslem Women and Revolutionary Strategies in Soviet Central Asia, 1919-1929* (Princeton University Press 1974)

James N. Rosenau, *Citizenship Between Elections: An Inquiry Into The Mobilizable American* (Free Press 1974)

Ervin Laszlo, *A Strategy for the Future: The Systems Approach to World Order* (George Braziller 1974)

R. J. Vincent, *Nonintervention and International Order* (Princeton University Press 1974)

Jan H. Kalicki, *The Pattern of Sino-American Crises: Political-Military Interactions in the 1950s* (Cambridge Universiy Press 1975)

Klaus Knorr, *The Power of Nations: The Political Economy of International Relations* (Basic Books, Inc. 1975)

James P. Sewell, *UNESCO and World Politics: Engaging in International Relations* (Princeton University Press 1975)

Richard A. Falk, *A Global Approach to National Policy* (Harvard University Press 1975)

Harry Eckstein and Ted Robert Gurr, *Patterns of Authority: A Structural Basis for Political Inquiry* (John Wiley & Sons 1975)

Cyril E. Black, Marius B. Jansen, Herbert S. Levine, Marion J. Levy, Jr., Henry Rosovsky, Gilbert Rozman, Henry D. Smith, II, and S. Frederick Starr, *The Modernization of Japan and Russia* (Free Press 1975)

Leon Gordenker, *International Aid and National Decisions: Development Programs in Malawi, Tanzania, and Zambia* (Princeton University Press 1976)

Carl von Clausewitz, *On War*, edited and translated by Michael Howard and Peter Paret (Princeton University Press 1976)

Gerald Garvey and Lou Ann Garvey, *International Resource Flows* (D. C. Heath 1977)

Walter F. Murphy and Joseph Tanenhaus, *Comparative Constitutional Law: Cases and Commentaries* (St. Martin's Press 1977)

Gerald Garvey, *Nuclear Power and Social Planning: The City of the Second Sun* (D. C. Heath 1977)

Richard E. Bissell, *Apartheid and International Organizations* (Westview Press 1977)

David P. Forsythe, *Humanitarian Politics: The International Committee of the Red Cross* (Johns Hopkins University Press 1977)

Paul E. Sigmund, *The Overthrow of Allende and the Politics of Chile, 1964-1976* (University of Pittsburgh Press 1977)

Henry S. Bienen, *Armies and Parties in Africa* (Holmes and Meier 1978)

Harold and Margaret Sprout, *The Context of Environmental Politics: Unfinished Business for America's Third Century* (University Press of Kentucky 1978)

Library of Congress Cataloging in Publication Data

Kim, Samuel S.   1935-
   China, the United Nations, and world order.

   Bibliography: p.
   Includes index.
   1.   China—Foreign relations—1976-   2.   United
Nations—China.   3.   World politics—1975-1985.   I.   Title.
DS779.27.K55   327.51   78-51174
ISBN 0-691-07599-9
ISBN 0-691-10076-4 pbk.